1 MONTH OF
FREE
READING

at

www.ForgottenBooks.com

By purchasing this book you are eligible for one month membership to ForgottenBooks.com, giving you unlimited access to our entire collection of over 1,000,000 titles via our web site and mobile apps.

To claim your free month visit:

www.forgottenbooks.com/free19441

ISBN 978-1-5285-6792-3
PIBN 10019441

BIBLE MYTHS

AND THEIR

PARALLELS IN OTHER RELIGIONS

BEING A COMPARISON OF THE

Old and New Testament Myths and Miracles

WITH

THOSE OF HEATHEN NATIONS OF ANTIQUITY

CONSIDERING ALSO

THEIR ORIGIN AND MEANING

By T. W. DOANE

WITH NUMEROUS ILLUSTRATIONS

FOURTH EDITION

"He who knows only one religion knows none."—PROF. MAX MULLER.

"The same thing which is now called CHRISTIAN RELIGION existed among the Ancients. They have begun to call Christian the true religion which existed before."—ST. AUGUSTINE.

"Our love for what is old, our reverence for what our fathers used, makes us keep still in the church, and on the very altar cloths, symbols which would excite the smile of an *Oriental*, and lead him to wonder why we send missionaries to his land, while cherishing his faith in ours."—JAMES BONWICK.

NEW YORK

THE TRUTH SEEKER COMPANY

28 LAFAYETTE PLACE

Thomas A. Lempertz,

Hollywood, California,

March 3, 1950.

INTRODUCTION.

THE idea of publishing the work here presented did not suggest itself until a large portion of the material it contains had been accumulated for the private use and personal gratification of the author. In pursuing the study of the Bible Myths, facts pertaining thereto, in a condensed form, seemed to be greatly needed, and nowhere to be found. Widely scattered through hundreds of ancient and modern volumes, most of the contents of this book may indeed be found; but any previous attempt to trace exclusively the myths and legends of the Old and New Testament to their origin, published as a separate work, is not known to the writer of this. Many able writers have shown our so-called Sacred Scriptures to be unhistorical, and have pronounced them largely legendary, but have there left the matter, evidently aware of the great extent of the subject lying beyond. As Thomas Scott remarks, in his *English Life of Jesus: "How* these narratives (*i. e.*, the New Testament narratives), unhistorical as they have been shown to be, came into existence, *it is not our business to explain;* and once again, at the end of the task, as at the beginning and throughout, we must emphatically disclaim the obligation." To pursue the subject from the point at which it is abandoned by this and many other distinguished writers, has been the labor of the author of this volume for a number of years. The result of this labor is herewith submitted to the reader, but not without a painful consciousness of its many imperfections.

The work naturally begins with the Eden myth, and is followed by a consideration of the principal Old Testament legends, showing their universality, origin and meaning. Next will be found the account of the birth of Christ Jesus, with his history until the close of his life upon earth, showing, in connection therewith, the universality of the myth of the Virgin-born, Crucified and Resurrected Saviour.

Before showing the *origin* and *meaning* of the myth (which is done in Chapter **XXXIX.**), we have considered the *Miracles of Christ Jesus*, the *Eucharist, Baptism*, the *Worship of the Virgin, Christian Symbols*, the *Birthday of Christ Jesus*, the *Doctrine of the Trinity, Why Christianity Prospered*, and the *Antiquity of Pagan Religions*, besides making a comparison of the legendary histories of *Crishna and Jesus*, and *Buddha and Jesus*. The concluding chapter relates to the question, What do we really know about Jesus?

In the words of Prof. Max Müller (*The Science of Religion*, p. 11): "A comparison of all the religions of the world, in which none can claim a privileged position, will no doubt seem to many dangerous and reprehensible, because ignoring that peculiar reverence which everybody, down to the mere fetish worshiper, feels for his own religion, and for his own god. Let me say, then, at once, that I myself have shared these misgivings, but that I have tried to overcome them, because I would not and could not allow myself to surrender either what I hold to be the truth, or what I hold still dearer than truth, the right of testing truth. Nor do I regret it. I do not say that the *Science of Religion* is all gain. No, it entails losses, and losses of many things which we hold dear. But this I will say, that, as far as my humble judgment goes, it does not entail the loss of anything that is essential to *true religion*, and that, if we strike the balance honestly, *the gain is immeasurably greater than the loss.*"

INTRODUCTION.

" All truth is safe, and nothing else is safe ; and he who keeps back the truth, or withholds it from men, from motives of expediency, is either a coward or a criminal, or both."

But little beyond the arrangement of this work is claimed as original. Ideas, phrases, and even whole paragraphs have been taken from the writings of others, and in most, if not in all cases, acknowledged ; but with the thought in mind of the many hours of research this book may save the student in this particular line of study ; with the consciousness of having done for others that which I would have been thankful to have found done for myself ; and more than all, with the hope that it may in some way help to hasten the day when the mist of superstition shall be dispelled by the light of reason ; with all its defects, it is most cheerfully committed to its fate by the author.

BOSTON, MASS., *November,* 1882.

CONTENTS.

PART I.

CONTENTS.

PART II.

x CONTENTS.

LIST

OF

AUTHORS AND BOOKS QUOTED

IN THIS WORK.

ABBOTT (LYMAN)............A Dictionary of Religious Knowledge, for Popular and Professional Use; comprising full information on Biblical, Theological, and Ecclesiastical Subjects. Edited by Rev. Lyman Abbott, assisted by Rev. T. J. Conant, D. D.   New York: Harper & Bros., 1880.

ACOSTA (REV. JOSEPH DE)....The Natural and Moral History of the Indies, by Father Joseph De Acosta.   Translated by Edward Grimston. London: 1604.

ÆSCHYLUS.................The Poems of Æschylus.   Translated by the Rev. R. Potter, M. A.   New York: Harper & Bros., 1836.

ALLEN (REV. D. O.)..........India, Ancient and Modern, by David O. Allen, D. D., Missionary of the American Board for twenty-five years in India.   London: Trübner & Co., 1856.

AMBERLY (VISCOUNT).,,.....An Analysis of Religious Belief, by Viscount Amberly, from the late London Edition.   New York: D. M. Bennett, 1879.

ASIATIC RESEARCHES.........Asiatic Researches, or Transactions of the Society instituted in Bengal, for inquiring in the History and Antiquities, the Arts, Sciences, and Literature of Asia. London: J. Swain, 1801.

BARING-GOULD (REV. S.).....Curious Myths of the Middle Ages, by Rev. S. Baring-Gould, M. A.   Boston: Roberts Bros., 1880.

——— .....Legends of the Patriarchs and Prophets, and other Old Testament Characters, from various sources, by Rev. S. Baring-Gould, M. A.   New York: Holt & Williams, 1872.

——— .....The Origin and Development of Religious Belief, by S. Baring-Gould, M. A., in 2 vols.   New York: D. Appleton & Co., 1870.

BARNABAS.................The General Epistle of Barnabas, a companion and fellow-preacher with Paul.

BARNES (ALBERT)..........Notes, Explanatory and Practical, on the Gospels, by Rev. Albert Barnes, in 2 vols. New York: Harper & Bros., 1860.

BEAL (SAMUEL).............The Romantic Legend of Sâkya Buddha, from the Chinese Sanscrit (being a translation of the Fo-pen-hing), by Samuel Beal. London: Trübner & Co., 1875.

BELL (J.)..................Bell's New Pantheon, or Historical Dictionary of the Gods, Demi-Gods, Heroes, and Fabulous Personages of Antiquity ; also of the Images and Idols, adored in the Pagan World, together with their Temples, Priests, Altars, Oracles, Fasts, Festivals, &c., in 2 vols. London : J. Bell, 1790

BHAGAVAT-GEETA............The Bhagavat-Geeta, or Dialogues of Crishna and Arjoon, in 18 Lectures, with notes. Translated from the original Sanscrit by Charles Wilkes. London: C. Nourse, 1785.

BLAVATSKY (H. P.).........Isis Unveiled : A Master Key to the Mysteries of Ancient and Modern Science and Theology, by H. P. Blavatsky. in 2 vols. New York: J. W. Bouton, 1877.

BONWICK (JAMES)..........Egyptian Belief and Modern Thought, by James Bonwick, F. R. G. S. London: C. Kegan Paul & Co., 1878.

BRINTON (DANIEL)..........The Myths of the New World : A Treatise on the Symbolism and Mythology of the Red Race of America, by Daniel Brinton, A. M., M. D. New York : L. Holt & Co., 1868.

BRITANNICA (ENCYCLO.)......The Encyclopædia Britannica, Ninth Edition.

BUCKLEY (T. A.)............The Great Cities of the Ancient World, in their Glory and their Desolation, by Theodore A. Buckley, M. A. London : G. Routledge & Co., 1852.

BULFINCH (THOMAS)..........The Age of Fable, or Beauties of Mythology, by Thomas Bulfinch. Boston : J. E. Tilton & Co., 1870.

BUNCE (JOHN T.)...........Fairy Tales : Their Origin and Meaning, with some account of Dwellers in Fairy-land, by John Thackary Bunce. New York: D. Appleton & Co., 1878.

BUNSEN (ERNEST DE)........The Keys of St. Peter, or the House of Rechab, connected with the History of Symbolism and Idolatry, by Ernest de Bunsen. London: Longmans, Green & Co., 1867.

————   ....The Angel-Messiah of Buddhists, Essenes, and Christians, by Ernest de Bunsen. London : Longmans, Green & Co., 1880.

————   ....The Chronology of the Bible, connected with contemporaneous events in the history of Babylonians, Assyrians, and Egyptians, by Ernest de Bunsen. London : Longmans, Green & Co., 1874.

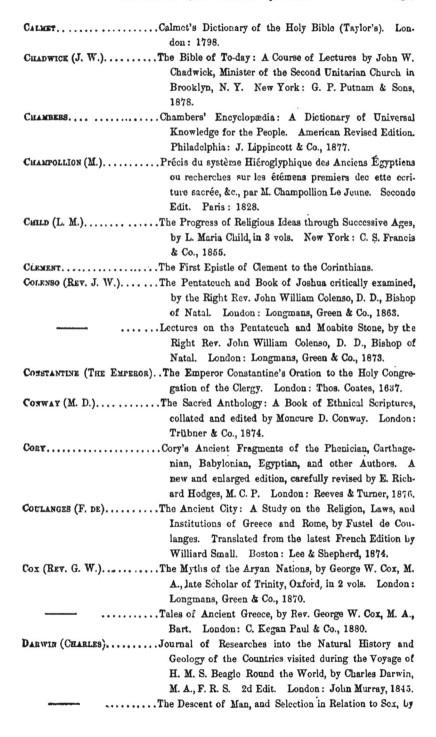

Charles Darwin, M. A. New York: D. Appleton & Co., 1876.

DAVIES (EDWARD)..........The Myths and Rites of the British Druids compared with Customs and Traditions of Heathen Nations, by Edward Davies, Rector of Brampton. London: J. Booth, 1809.

DAVIS (J. F.).............The Chinese: A General Description of the Empire of China and its Inhabitants, by John Francis Davis, Esq. F. R. S., in 2 vols. New York: Harper Bros., 1836.

DELITCH (F.)..............See Keil (C. F.).

DILLAWAY (C. K.).........Roman Antiquities and Ancient Mythology, by Charles K. Dillaway. Boston: Gould, Kendall & Lincoln, 1840.

DRAPER (J. W.)............History of the Conflict between Religion and Science, by John W. Draper, M. D. 8th Edit. New York: D. Appleton & Co., 1876.

DUNLAP (S. F.)............Vestiges of the Spirit History of Man, by S. F. Dunlap, Member of the American Oriental Soc., New Haven. New York: D. Appleton & Co., 1858.

————— ....The Mysteries of Adoni, by S. F. Dunlap. London: Williams & Northgate, 1861.

————— ....Söd, the Son of the Man, by S. F. Dunlap. London: Williams & Northgate, 1861.

DUPUIS....................The Origin of all Religious Worship, translated from the French of Mons. Dupuis. New Orleans: 1872.

EUSEBIUS..................The Life of Constantine, in Four Books, by Eusebius Pamphilius, Bishop of Cesarea. London: Thomas Coates, 1637.

————— ....The Ancient Ecclesiastical History of Eusebius Pamphilius, Bishop of Cesarea in Palestine, in Ten Books. London: George Miller, 1636.

FARRAR (F. W.)............The Life of Christ, by Frederick W. Farrar, D. D., F. R. S., late Fellow of Trinity College, Cambridge. Albany: Rufus Wendell, 1876.

FERGUSSON (JAMES).........Tree and Serpent Worship, or Illustrations of Mythology and Art in India, by James Fergusson. London: 1868.

FISKE (JOHN)..............Myths and Myth-Makers; Old Tales and Superstitions Interpreted by Comparative Mythology, by John Fiske, M. A., LL. B., Harvard University. Boston: J. R. Osgood & Co., 1877.

FROTHINGHAM (O. B.)........The Cradle of the Christ: A Study in Primitive Christianity, by Octavius Brooks Frothingham. New York: G. P. Putnam & Sons, 1877.

GAUGOOLY (J. C.)...........Life and Religion of the Hindoos, by Joguth Chunder Gaugooly. Boston: Crosby, Nichols & Co., 1860.

GEIKIE (C.)...............The Life and Words of Christ, by Cunningham Geikie, D. D., in 2 vols. New York: D. Appleton & Co, 1880.

GERBET (L'ABBÉ)...........The Lily of Israel, or the Life of the Blessed Virgin Mary, Mother of God. From the French of the Abbé Gerbet. New York : P. J. Kennedy, 1878.

GIBBON (EDWARD)...........The History of the Decline and Fall of the Roman Empire, by Edward Gibbon, Esq., in 6 vols. Philadelphia : Claxton, Remsen & Hoffelfinger, 1876.

GILES.....................Hebrew and Christian Records : An Historical Enquiry concerning the Age and Authorship of the Old and New Testaments, by the Rev. Dr. Giles, in 2 vols. London : Trübner & Co., 1877.

GINSBURGH (C. D.)..........The Essenes : Their History and Doctrines ; an Essay, by Charles D. Ginsburgh. London : Longman, Green, Roberts & Green, 1864.

GOLDZHIER (I.)............Mythology among the Hebrews, and its Historical Development, by Ignaz Goldzhier, Ph. D., Member of the Hungarian Academy of Sciences. Translated from the German by Russel Martineau. London : Longmans, Green & Co., 1877.

GORI.....................Etrurische Alterthümer. Nürnburg : G. Lichtensleger, 1770.

GREG (W. R.)..............The Creed of Christendom : Its Foundations contrasted with its Superstructure, by William Rathbone Greg. Detroit : Rose-Belford Pub. Co., 1878.

GROSS (J. B.).... ....The Heathen Religion in its Popular and Symbolical Development, by Rev. Joseph B. Gross. Boston : J. P. Jewett & Co., 1856.

GUTZLAFF.................The Journal of Two Voyages along the Coast of China (in 1831-2), and Remarks on the Policy, Religion, &c., of China, by the Rev. Mr. Gutzlaff. New York : John P. Haven, 1833.

HARDY (R. S.).............The Legends and Theories of the Buddhists compared with History and Science, with Introductory Notices of the Life of Gautama Buddha, by R. Spence Hardy, Hon. M. R. A. S. London : Williams & Northgate, 1866.

———— ....Eastern Monachism : An Account of the Origin, Laws, Discipline, &c., of the Order of Mendicants founded by Gautama Buddha, by R. Spence Hardy. London : Williams & Northgate, 1860.

———— ....A Manual of Buddhism in its Modern Development. Translated from the Singalese MSS. by R. S. Hardy. London : Williams & Northgate, 1860.

HERMAS..................The First Book of Hermas, Brother of Pius, Bishop of Rome, which is called his *Vision*.

HERODOTUS..............The History of Herodotus, the Greek Historian : A New and Literal Version, from the Text of Baehr, by Henry Cary, M. A. New York : Harper & Bros., 1871.

HIGGINS (GODFREY)..........The Celtic Druids, by Godfrey Higgins, Esq., F. R. A. S. London: Hunter & Co., 1827.

————— ....Anacalypsis: An Enquiry into the Origin of Languages, Nations, and Religions, by Godfrey Higgins, Esq., F. R. S., F. R. A. S., in 2 vols. London: Longman, Rees Orne, Brown & Longman.

HOOYKAAS (I.).............See Oort (H.).

HUC (L'ABBÉ).............Christianity in China, Tartary and Thibet, by M. L'Abbé Huc, formerly Missionary Apostolic in China, in 2 vols. London: Longman, Brown & Co., 1857.

HUMBOLDT (A. DE)..........Researches concerning the Institutions and Monuments of the Ancient Inhabitants of Mexico, by Alexander de Humboldt, in 2 vols. (Translated by Helen Maria Williams.) London: Longman, Rees & Co., 1814.

————— ....Political Essay on the Kingdom of New Spain, by Alexander de Humboldt, in 2 vols. (Translated by John Black.) London: Longman, Hurst & Co., 1822.

HUME (DAVID).............Essays and Treaties on Various Subjects, by David Hume (author of Hume's History of England). Boston: From the London Edit. J. P. Mendum.

HUXLEY (T. H.)............Evidence as to Man's Place in Nature, by Thomas H. Huxley, F. R. S., F. L. S. New York: D. Appleton & Co., 1873.

IGNATIUS................The Epistle of Ignatius, Bishop of Antioch in Syria, to the Ephesians.

————— ....The Epistle of Ignatius to the Magnesians.

————— ....The Epistle of Ignatius to the Trallians.

————— ....The Epistle of Ignatius to the Philadelphians.

INFANCY (APOC.)..........The Gospel of the Infancy of Jesus Christ (Apocryphal).

INMAN (THOMAS)..........Ancient Pagan and Modern Christian Symbolism Exposed and Explained, by Thomas Inman, M. D., Physician to the Royal Infirmary, &c. London: 1869.

————— ....Ancient Faiths Embodied in Ancient Names, or An Attempt to Trace the Religious Belief, Sacred Rites, and Holy Emblems of certain Nations, by Thomas Inman, M. D. London: Trübner & Co., 1872.

————— ....Ancient Faiths and Modern: A Dissertation upon Worship, Legends, and Divinities in Central and Western Asia, Europe, and Elsewhere, before the Christian Era, by Thomas Inman, M. D. London: Trübner & Co. 1876.

JAMESON................The History of Our Lord as Exemplified in Works of Art; commenced by the late Mrs. Jameson, continued and completed by Lady Eastlake, in 2 vols. London: Longmans, Green & Co., 1864.

JENNINGS (H.).............The Rosicrucians: Their Rites and Mysteries. Second

Edit. revised by Hargrave Jennings. London: Gatto & Windus, 1879.

JOHNSON (SAMUEL).........Oriental Religions, and their Relation to Universal Religion (India), by Samuel Johnson. Boston: J. R. Osgood, 1872.

JOSEPHUS (FLAVIUS).........Antiquities of the Jews, in Twenty Books, by Flavius Josephus, the learned and authentic Jewish Historian and celebrated Warrior. Translated by William Whiston, A. M. Baltimore: Armstrong & Berry, 1839.

——— ....The Wars of the Jews, or the History of the Destruction of Jerusalem, in Seven Books, by Flavius Josephus. Baltimore: 1839.

——— ....Flavius Josephus Against Apion, in Two Books. Baltimore: 1839.

KEIGHTLEY (T.)............The Mythology of Ancient Greece and Italy, by Thomas Keightley. New York: D. Appleton & Co., 1843.

KEIL (C. F.)...............Biblical Commentary on the Old Testament, by C. F. Keil, D. D., and F. Delitch, D. D., Professors in Theology, in 3 vols. Translated from the German by Rev. James Martin, B. A. Edinboro': T. & T. Clarke, 1872.

KENRICK (J.).............Ancient Egypt under the Pharaohs, by John Kenrick, M. A., in 2 vols. London: B. Fellows, 1850.

KING (C. W.).............The Gnostics and their Remains, Ancient and Mediæval, by C. W. King, M. A., Fellow of Trinity College, Cambridge. London: Bell & Dudley, 1864.

KINGSBOROUGH (LORD)........Antiquities of Mexico, comprising Fac-similes of Ancient Mexican Paintings and Hieroglyphics, preserved in the Royal Libraries of Paris, Berlin, and Dresden, in the Imperial Library of Vienna, &c., &c., together with the Monuments of New Spain, by Lord Kingsborough, in 7 vols. London: Robert Havill & Coyglen, Son & Co., 1831.

KNAPPERT (J.).............The Religion of Israel, a Manual: Translated from the Dutch of J. Knappert, pastor at Leiden, by Richard A. Armstrong, B. A. Boston: Roberts Bros., 1878.

KNIGHT (R. P.)............The Symbolical Language of Ancient Art and Mythology. An Enquiry, by Richard Payne Knight, author of "The Worship of Priapus," &c. A new Edit. with Introduction, Notes and Additions, by Alexander Wilder, M. D. New York: J. W. Bouton, 1876.

KORAN...................The Koran, commonly called the Al Coran of Mohammed; translated into English immediately from the original Arabic, by Geo. Sale, Gent.

KUNEN (A.)................See Oort (H.).

LARDNER (N.).............The Works of Nathaniel Lardner, D. D., with a Life, by Dr. Kipps, in 10 vols. London: Wm. Ball, 1838.

B

LELAND (CHAS. G.)............Fusang: or the Discovery of America by Buddhist Priests in the 5th Century, by Chas. G. Leland. London: Trübner & Co., 1875.

LILLIE (ARTHUR)............Buddha and Early Buddhism, by Arthur Lillie. London: Trubner & Co., 1881.

LUBBOCK (JOHN)............Pre-historic Times, as Illustrated by Ancient Remains, and the Manners and Customs of Modern Savages, by Sir John Lubbock, F. R. S. London: Williams & Northgate, 1865.

LUNDY (J. P.)............Monumental Christianity, or the Art and Symbolism of the Primitive Church as Witness and Teachers of the One Catholic Faith and Practice, by John P. Lundy, Presbyter. New York: J. W. Bouton, 1876.

MAHAFFY (J. P.)............Prolegomena to Ancient History, by John P. Mahaffy, A. M., M. R. I. A., Fellow and Tutor in Trinity College, and Lecturer in Ancient History in the University of Dublin. London: Longmans, Green & Co., 1871.

MALLET............Northern Antiquities; or an Historical Account of the Manners, Customs, Religion and Laws of the Ancient Scandinavians, by M. Mallet. Translated from the French by Bishop Percy. London: H. S. Bohn, 1847.

MARSH (HERBERT)............A Course of Lectures, containing a Description and Systematic Arrangement of the several Branches of Divinity by Herbert Marsh, D.D. Cambridge: W. Hillard, 1812.

MARY (APOC.)............The Gospel of the Birth of Mary, attributed to St. Matthew, Translated from the Works of St. Jerome.

MAURICE (THOMAS)............Indian Antiquities: or Dissertations on the Geographical Division, Theology, Laws, Government and Literature of Hindostan, compared with those of Persia, Egypt and Greece, by Thomas Maurice, in 6 vols. London: W. Richardson, 1794.

———............The History of Hindostan; Its Arts and its Sciences, as connected with the History of the other Great Empires of Asia, during the most Ancient Periods of the World, in 2 vols., by Thomas Maurice. London: Printed by H. L. Galabin, 1798.

MAURICE (F. D.)............The Religions of the World, and Their Relation to Christianity, by Frederick Denison Maurice, M. A., Professor of Divinity in Kings' College. London: J. W. Parker, 1847.

MIDDLETON (C.)............The Miscellaneous Works of Conyers Middleton, D. D., Principal Librarian of the University of Cambridge, in 4 vols. ("Free Enquiry" vol. I., "Letters from Rome" vol. III.). London: Richard Manby, 1752.

MONTFAUCON (B.)............L'Antiquité Expliqueé; par Dom Bernard de Montfaucon. Second edit. Paris: 1722.

MOOR (EDWARD).............Plates illustrating the Hindoo Pantheon, reprinted from the work of Major Edward Moor, F. R. S., edited by Rev. Allen Moor, M. A. London: Williams & Norgate, 1816.

MORTON (S. G.).............Types of Mankind: or Ethnological Researches based upon the Ancient Monuments, Paintings, Sculptures, and Crania of Races, by Samuel George Morton, M. D. Philadelphia: Lippincott, Grambo & Co., 1854.

MÜLLER (MAX).............A History of Ancient Sanscrit Literature, so far as it illustrates the Primitive Religion of the Brahmins, by Max Müller, M. A. London: Williams & Norgate, 1860.

——— ....Introduction to the Science of Religion: Four Lectures delivered at the Royal Institution, with Two Essays on False Analogies, and the Philosophy of Mythology, by (F.) Max Müller, M. A. London: Longmans, Green & Co., 1873.

——— ....Chips from a German Workshop; by Max Müller, M. A., in 3 vols. London: Longmans, Green & Co., 1876.

——— ....Lectures on the Origin and Growth of Religion, as Illustrated by the Religions of India. Delivered in the Chapel House, Westminster Abbey, by (F.) Max Müller, M. A. London: Longmans, Green & Co., 1878.

MURRAY (A. S.).............Manual of Mythology, by Alexander S. Murray, Department of Greek and Roman Antiquities, British Museum, 2d Edit. New York: Armstrong & Co., 1876.

NICODEMUS (APOC.)....... ...The Gospel of Nicodemus the Disciple, concerning the Sufferings and Resurrection of Our Master and Saviour Jesus Christ.

OORT (H.).......... ......The Bible for Learners, by Dr. H. Oort, Prof. of Oriental Languages, &c., at Amsterdam, and Dr. I. Hooykaas, pastor at Rotterdam, with the assistance of Dr. A. Kunen, Prof. of Theology at Leiden, in 3 vols. Translated from the Dutch by Philip A. Wicksteed, M. A. Boston: Roberts Bros., 1878.

ORTON (JAMES).............The Andes and the Amazon; or Across the Continent of South America, by James Orton, M. A., 8d Edit. New York: Harper & Bros., 1876.

OWEN (RICHARD)...........Man's Earliest History, an Address delivered before the International Congress of Orientalists, by Prof. Richard Owen. Tribune Extra, No. 23. New York Tribune Pub. Co., 1874.

PESCHEL (OSCAR) ....The Races of Man, and their Geographical Distribution from the German of Oscar Peschel. New York: D. Appleton & Co., 1876.

POLYCARP................The Epistle of Polycarp to the Philippians, translated by Archbishop Wake.

PORTER (SIR R. K.).........Travels in Georgia, Persia, Armenia, Ancient Babylonia, &c., by Sir Robert Kir Porter, in 2 vols. London: Longmans, Hurst, Rees, Orm & Brown, 1821.

PRESCOTT (WM. H.).........History of the Conquest of Mexico, with a preliminary view of the Ancient Mexican Civilization, and the life of the conqueror, Hernando Cortez, by Wm. H. Prescott, in 3 vols. Philadelphia: J. P. Lippincott & Co., 1873.

PRICHARD (J. C.)...........An Analysis of the Historical. Records of Ancient Egypt, by J. C. Prichard, M. D., F. R. S. London: Sherwood, Gilbert & Piper, 1838.

————   ....An Analysis of Egyptian Mythology, and the Philosophy of the Ancient Egyptians, compared with those of the Indians and others, by J. C. Prichard, M. D., F. R. S. London: Sherwood, Gilbert & Piper, 1838.

PRIESTLEY (JOSEPH).........A Comparison of the Institutions of Moses with those of the Hindoos and other Ancient Nations, by Joseph Priestley, LL. D., F. R. S. Northumberland: A. Kennedy, 1799.

PROTEVANGELION APOC........The Protevangelion, or, An Historical Account of the Birth of Christ, and the perpetual Virgin Mary, His Mother, by James the Lesser, Cousin and Brother to the Lord Jesus.

REBER (GEO.)...............The Christ of Paul, or the Enigmas of Christianity, by Geo. Reber. New York: C. P. Somerby, 1876.

RENAN (ERNEST)..............Lectures on the Influence of the Institutions, Thought and Culture of Rome on Christianity, and the Development of the Catholic Church, by Ernest Renan, of the French Academy. Translated by Charles Beard, B. A. London: Williams & Norgate, 1880.

RENOUF (P. LE PAGE).......Lectures on the Origin and Growth of Religion as Illustrated by the Religion of Ancient Egypt, by P. Le Page Renouf. London: Williams & Norgate, 1880.

REVILLE (ALBERT)...........History of the Dogma of the Deity of Jesus Christ, by Albert Reville. London: Williams & Norgate, 1870.

RHYS-DAVIDS (T. W.) ....Buddhism: Being a Sketch of the Life and Teachings of Gautama, the Buddha, by T. W. Rhys-Davids, of the Middle Temple, Barrister-at-Law, and late of the Ceylon Civil Service. London: Soc. for Promoting Christian Knowledge.

SCOTT (THOMAS).... ....The English Life of Jesus, by Thomas Scott. Published by the Author. London: 1872.

SEPTCHENES (M. LE CLERC DE)..The Religion of the Ancient Greeks, Illustrated by an Explanation of their Mythology. Translated from the French of M. Le Clerc de Septchenes. London: 1788.

SHARPE (SAMUEL)...........Egyptian Mythology and Egyptian Christianity, with their Influence on the Opinions of Modern Christendom, by Samuel Sharpe. London: J. R. Smith, 1863.

SHIH-KING (THE)...........The Shih-King, or Book of Poetry. Translated from the Chinese by James Legge. London: Macmillan & Co., 1879.

SHOBEIL (F.)..............Persia; containing a description of the Country, with an account of its Government, Laws, and Religion, by Frederick Shobeil. Philadelphia: John Grigg, 1828.

SMITH....................Smith's Comprehensive Dictionary of the Bible, with many important Additions and Improvements. Edited by Rev. Samuel Barnum. New York: D. Appleton & Co., 1879.

SMITH (GEORGE)...........Assyrian Discoveries: An account of Explorations and Discoveries on the Site of Nineveh during 1873 and 1874, by George Smith, of the Department of Oriental Antiquity, British Museum. New York: Scribner, Armstrong & Co., 1875.

——— ....The Chaldean Account of Genesis; containing the description of the Creation, the Fall of Man, the Deluge, the Tower of Babel, the Times of the Patriarchs and Nimrod; Babylonian Fables, and Legends of the Gods, from the Cuneiform Inscriptions, by George Smith, of the British Museum. New York: Scribner, Armstrong & Co., 1876.

SOCRATES.................The Ancient Ecclesiastical History of Socrates Scholasticus, of Constantinople, in Seven Books. Translated out of the Greek Tongue by Meredith Hanmer, D. D. London: George Miller, 1636.

SPENCER (HERBERT)........The Principles of Sociology, by Herbert Spencer, in 2 vols. New York: D. Appleton & Co., 1877.

SQUIRE (E. G.)...........The Serpent Symbol, and the Worship of the Reciprocal Principles of Nature in America, by E. G. Squire, A. M. New York: George P. Putnam, 1851.

STANLEY (A. P.)..........Lectures on the History of the Jewish Church, by Arthur P. Stanley, D. D., Dean of Westminster. New York: Charles Scribner, 1863.

——— ....In a Sermon preached in Westminster Abbey on February 28th, 1880, after the funeral of Sir Charles Lyell, entitled: "The Religious Aspect of Geology."

STEINTHAL (H.)...........The Legend of Samson: An Essay, by H. Steinthal, Professor of the University of Berlin. Appendix to Goldzhier's Hebrew Mythology.

SYNCHRONOLOGY............Synchronology of the Principal Events in Sacred and Profane History from the Creation to the Present Time. Boston: S. Hawes, 1870.

and C. S. Wake, with Appendix by Alexander Wilder, M. D. London: Trübner & Co., 1874.

WILLIAMS (MONIER).........Indian Wisdom; or Examples of the Religious, Philosoph. ical, and Ethnical Doctrines of the Hindoos, by Monier Williams, M. A., Prof. of Sanscrit in the University of Oxford. London: W. H. Allen, 1875.

————........Hinduism; by Monier Williams, M. A., D. C. L., Pub. lished under the Direction of the Committee of Gen. eral Literature and Education Appointed by the Society for Promoting Christian Knowledge. London: 1877.

WISDOM (APOC.)...........The Book of Wisdom, Attributed to Solomon, King of Israel.

WISE (ISAAC M.)...........The Martyrdom of Jesus of Nazareth. A Historic Treat. ise on the Last Chapters of the Gospel, by Dr. Isaac M. Wise. Cincinnati.

ADDITIONS TO THIRD EDITION.

Beausobres' *Histoire Critique de Manichée et du Manicheisme*, Amsterdam, 1734; Baronius' *Annales Ecclesiastici;* Hydes' *Historia Religionis Veterum Persarum;* Rawlinson's *Herodotus;* Lenormant's *The Beginnings of History;* Hardwick's *Christ and other Masters;* Daillé's *Treatise on the Right Use of the Fathers*, London, 1841; *Apollonius de Tyana, sa vie, ses voyages, et ses prodiges*, par Philostrate, Paris, 1862; Sir John Malcom's *History of Persia*, in 2 vols., London, 1815; Michaelis' *Introduction to the New Testament*, in 4 vols. edited by Dr. Herbert Marsh, London, 1828; Archbishop Wake's *Genuine Epistles of the Apostolical Fathers*, London, 1719; Jeremiah Jones' *Canon of the New Testament*, in 3 vols., Oxford, 1793; Milman's *History of Christianity;* Barrow's *Travels in China*, London, 1840; Deane's *Worship of the Serpent*, London, 1833; Baring-Gould's *Lost and Hostile Gospels*, London, 1874; B. F. Westcott's *Survey of the History of the Canon of the New Testament*, 4th Edit., London, 1875; Mosheim's *Ecclesiastical History*, in 6 vols., Amer. ed. 1810; J. W. Rosses' *Tacitus and Bracciolini*, London, 1878; and the writings of the Christian Fathers, Justin Martyr, St. Clement of Alexandria, Irenæus, Origen, Tertullian and Minucius Felix.

BIBLE MYTHS.

PART I.

THE OLD TESTAMENT.

CHAPTER I.

THE CREATION AND FALL OF MAN.

THE Old Testament commences with one of its most interesting myths, that of the Creation and Fall of Man. The story is to be found in the first *three* chapters of Genesis, the substance of which is as follows:

After God created the "Heavens" and the "Earth," he said: "Let there be light, and there was light," and after calling the light Day, and the darkness Night, the *first* day's work was ended.

God then made the "Firmament," which completed the *second* day's work.

Then God caused the dry land to appear, which he called "Earth," and the waters he called "Seas." After this the earth was made to bring forth grass, trees, &c., which completed the *third* day's work.

The next things God created were the "Sun,"[1] "Moon" and

---

[1] The idea that the sun, moon and stars were *set* in the firmament was entertained by most nations of antiquity, but, as strange as it may appear, Pythagoras, the Grecian philosopher, who flourished from 540 to 510 B. C.—as well as other Grecian philosophers—taught that the sun was placed in the centre of the universe, *with the planets roving round it in a cir-* cle, thus making day and night. (See Knight's Ancient Art and Mythology. p. 59. and note.) The Buddhists anciently taught that the universe is composed of limitless systems or worlds, called *sakwalas.*

They are scattered throughout space, and each sakwala has a sun and moon. (See Hardy: Buddhist Legends, pp. 80 and 87.)

"Stars," and after he had *set them in the Firmament*, the *fourth* day's work was ended.[1]

After these, God created great "whales," and other creatures which inhabit the water, also "winged fowls." This brought the *fifth* day to a close.

The work of creation was finally completed on the *sixth* day,[2] when God made "beasts" of every kind, "cattle," "creeping things," and lastly "man," whom he created "male and female," in his own image.[3]

"Thus the heavens and the earth were finished, and all the host of them. And on the *seventh* [4] day God ended his work which he had made: and he *rested* on the seventh day, from all his work which he had made. And God blessed the seventh day, and sanctified it, because that in it he had *rested* from all his work which God created and made."

After this information, which concludes at the *third* verse of Genesis ii., strange though it may appear, *another* account of the Creation commences, which is altogether different from the one we have just related. This account commences thus:

"These are the generations of the heavens and the earth when they were created, in the day (not days) that the Lord God made the earth and the heavens."

It then goes on to say that "the Lord God formed man of the dust of the ground,"[5] which appears to be the *first* thing he made. After planting a garden eastward in Eden,[6] the Lord God put the man therein, "and out of the ground made the Lord God to grow every tree that is pleasant to the sight, and good for food; the *Tree of Life*,[7] also in the midst of the garden, and the *Tree of*

---

[1] Origen, a Christian Father who flourished about A. D. 230, says: "What man of sense will agree with the statement that the first, second, and third days, in which the *evening* is named and the *morning*, were without sun, moon and stars?" (Quoted in Mysteries of Adoni, p. 176.)

[2] "The geologist reckons not by *days* or by *years*; the whole six thousand years, which were until lately looked on as the sum of the world's age, are to him but as a unit of measurement in the long succession of past ages." (Sir John Lubbock.)

"It is now certain that the vast epochs of time demanded by scientific observation are incompatible both with the six thousand years of the Mosaic chronology, and the six days of the Mosaic creation." (Dean Stanley.)

[3] "Let us make man in our own likeness," was said by Ormuzd, the Persian God of Gods, to his WORD. (See Bunsen's Angel Messiah, p. 104.)

[4] The number SEVEN was sacred among almost every nation of antiquity. (See ch. ii.)

[5] According to Grecian Mythology, the God Prometheus created men, in the image of the gods, *out of clay* (see Bulfinch: The Age of Fable, p. 25; and Goldzhier: Hebrew Myths, p. 373), and the God Hephaistos was commanded by Zeus to mold *of clay* the figure of a maiden, into which Athênê, the dawn-goddess, *breathed the breath of life*. This is Pandora—the gift of all the gods—who is presented to Epimetheus. (See Cox: Aryan Myths, vol. ii., p. 208.)

[6] "What man is found such an idiot as to suppose that God planted trees in Paradise, in Eden, like a husbandman." (Origen: quoted in Mysteries of Adoni, p. 176.) "There is no way of preserving the literal sense of the first chapter of Genesis, without impiety, and attributing things to God unworthy of him." (St. Augustine.)

[7] "The records about the ' *Tree of Life* ' are

Knowledge of good and evil. And a *river* went out of Eden to water the garden, and from thence it was parted, and became into *four* heads." These *four rivers* were called, first Pison, second Gihon, third Hiddekel, and the fourth Euphrates.[1]

After the "Lord God" had made the "Tree of Life," and the "Tree of Knowledge," he said unto the man:

"Of every tree of the garden thou mayest freely eat, but of the tree of the knowledge of good and evil, thou shalt not eat of it, *for in the day that thou eatest thereof thou shalt surely die.*" Then the Lord God, thinking that it would not be well for man to live alone, formed—out of the ground—"every beast of the field, and every fowl of the air; and brought them unto Adam to see what he would call them, and whatever Adam called every living creature, that was the name thereof."

After Adam had given names to "all cattle, and to the fowls of the air, and to every beast of the field," "the Lord God caused a deep sleep to fall upon Adam, and he slept, and he (the Lord God) took one of his (Adam's) ribs, and closed up the flesh instead thereof.

"And of the rib, which the Lord God had taken from man, made he a *woman*, and brought her unto Adam." "And they were both naked, the man and his wife, and they were not ashamed."

After this everything is supposed to have gone harmoniously, until a *serpent* appeared before the *woman*[2]—who was afterwards called Eve—and said to her:

"Hath God said, Ye shall not eat of every tree of the garden?"

The woman, answering the serpent, said:

"We may eat of the fruit of the trees of the garden: but of the fruit of the tree which is in the midst of the garden, God hath said, Ye shall not eat of it, *lest ye die.*"

Whereupon the serpent said to her:

---

the sublimest proofs of the unity and continuity of tradition, and of its Eastern origin. *The earliest records of the most ancient Oriental tradition refer to a 'Tree of Life,' which was guarded by spirits.* The juice of the fruit of this sacred tree, like the tree itself, was called *Sôma* in Sanscrit, and *Haôma* in Zend; it was revered as the life preserving essence." (Bunsen: Keys of St. Peter, p. 414)

[1] " According to the Persian account of Paradise, *four* great rivers came from Mount Alborj; two are in the North, and two go towards the South. The river Arduisir nourishes the *Tree of Immortality*, the Holy Hom." (Stiefelhagen: quoted in Mysteries of Adoni p. 149.) "According to the *Chinese* myth, the waters of

the Garden of Paradise issue from the fountain of immortality, which divides itself into *four rivers.*" (Ibid., p. 150, and Prog. Relig. Ideas, vol. i., p. 210.) The Hindoos call their Mount Meru the Paradise, out of which went *four* rivers. (Anacalypsis, vol. i., p. 357.)

[2] According to Persian legend, Arimanes, the Evil Spirit, *by eating a certain kind of fruit*, transformed himself into a *serpent*, and went gliding about on the earth to tempt human beings. His Devs entered the bodies of men and produced all manner of diseases. They entered into their minds, and incited them to sensuality, falsehood, slander and revenge. Into every department of the world they introduced discord and death.

"Ye shall *not* surely die" (which, according to the narrative, was the truth).

He then told her that, upon eating the fruit, their eyes would be opened, and that they would be as *gods*, knowing good from evil.

The woman then looked upon the tree, and as the fruit was tempting, "she took of the fruit, and did eat, and gave also unto her husband, and he did eat." The result was *not* death (as the Lord God had told them), but, as the serpent had said, "the eyes of both were opened, and they knew they were naked, and they *sewed* fig leaves together, and made themselves aprons."

Towards evening (*i. e.*, "in the cool of the day"), Adam and his wife "*heard* the voice of the Lord God *walking* in the garden," and being afraid, they hid themselves among the trees of the garden. The Lord God not finding Adam and his wife, said: "Where art thou?" Adam answering, said: "I heard thy voice in the garden, and I was afraid, because I was naked, and I hid myself."

The "Lord God" then told Adam that he had eaten of the tree which he had commanded him not to eat, whereupon Adam said: "The *woman* whom thou gavest to be with me, *she* gave me of the tree and I did eat."

When the "Lord God" spoke to the woman concerning her transgression, she blamed the *serpent*, which she said "beguiled" her. This sealed the serpent's fate, for the "Lord God" cursed him and said:

"Upon thy belly shalt thou go, and *dust* shalt thou eat all the days of thy life."[1]

Unto the woman the "Lord God" said:

"I will greatly multiply thy sorrow, and thy conception: in sorrow thou shalt bring forth children, and thy desire shall be to thy husband, *and he shall rule over thee.*"

Unto Adam he said:

"Because thou hast hearkened unto the voice of thy wife, and hast eaten of the tree, of which I commanded thee, saying, Thou shalt not eat of it: cursed is the ground for thy sake; in sorrow shalt thou eat of it all the days of thy life. Thorns also, and thistles shall it bring forth to thee; and thou shalt eat the herb of the field. In the sweat of thy face shalt thou eat bread, till thou return unto the ground, *for out of it wast thou taken: for dust thou art, and unto dust shalt thou return.*"

---

[1] Inasmuch as the physical construction of the serpent never could admit of its moving in any other way, and inasmuch as it *does not eat dust*, does not the narrator of this myth reflect unpleasantly upon the wisdom of such a God as Jehovah is claimed to be, as well as upon the ineffectualness of his first curse?

The " Lord God " then made coats of skin for Adam and his wife, with which he clothed them, after which he said:

" Behold, the man is become *as one of us*,[1] to know good and evil; and now, lest he put forth his hand, and take also of the tree of life, and eat, and live forever " (he must be sent forth from Eden).

" So he (the Lord God) drove out the man (and the woman); and he placed at the east of the garden of Eden, Cherubims, and a flaming sword which turned every way, to keep the way of the Tree of Life."

Thus ends the narrative.

Before proceeding to show from whence this legend, or legends, had their origin, we will notice a feature which is very prominent in the narrative, and which cannot escape the eye of an observing reader, *i. e.*, *the two different and contradictory accounts of the creation.*

The first of these commences at the first verse of chapter first, and ends at the third verse of chapter second. The second account commences at the fourth verse of chapter second, and continues to the end of the chapter.

In speaking of these contradictory accounts of the Creation, Dean Stanley says:

" It is now clear to diligent students of the Bible, that the first and second chapters of Genesis contain two narratives of the Creation, side by side, differing from each other in most every particular of time and place and order."[2]

Bishop Colenso, in his very learned work on the Pentateuch, speaking on this subject, says:

" The following are the most noticeable points of difference between the two cosmogonies:

" 1. In the first, the earth emerges from the waters and is, therefore, *saturated with moisture*.[3] In the second, the ' whole face of the ground ' *requires to be moistened*.[4]

---

[1] " Our writer unmistakably recognizes the existence of *many gods;* for he makes Yahweh say: ' See, the man has become as ONE OF US, knowing good and evil;' and so he evidently implies the existence of other similar beings, to whom he attributes immortality and insight into the difference between good and evil. Yahweh, then, was, in his eyes, the god of gods, indeed, but not the *only* god." (Bible for Learners, vol. i. p. 51.)

[2] In his memorial sermon, preached in Westminster Abbey, after the funeral of Sir Charles Lyell. He further said in this address:—

" It is well known that when the science of geology first arose, it was involved in endless schemes of *attempted* reconciliation with the letter of Scripture. There was, there are perhaps still, two modes of reconciliation of Scripture and science, which have been each in their day attempted, *and each have totally and deservedly failed.* One is the endeavor to wrest the words of the Bible from their natural meaning, and *force it to speak the language of science."* After speaking of the earliest known example, which was the interpolation of the word *"not"* in Leviticus xi. 6, he continues: " This is the earliest instance of *the falsification of Scripture to meet the demands of science;* and it has been followed in later times by the various efforts which have been made to twist the earlier chapters of the book of Genesis into *apparent* agreement with the last results of geology—representing days not to be days, morning and evening not to be morning and evening, the deluge not to be the deluge, and the ark not to be the ark."

[3] Gen. i. 9, 10.

[4] Gen. ii. 6.

"2. In the first, the birds and the beasts are created *before man.*[1] In the second, man is created *before the birds and the beasts.*[2]

"3. In the first, 'all fowls that fly' are made out of the *waters.*[3] In the second 'the fowls of the air' are made out of the *ground.*[4]

"4. In the first, man is created in the image of God.[5] In the second, man is made of the dust of the ground, and merely animated with the breath of life; and it is only after his eating the forbidden fruit that 'the Lord God said, Behold, the man has become *as one of us,* to know good and evil.'[6]

"5. In the first, man is made lord of the *whole earth.*[7] In the second, he is merely placed in the garden of Eden, 'to dress it and to keep it.'[8]

"6. In the first, the man and the woman are *created together,* as the closing and completing work of the whole creation,—created also, as is evidently implied, in the same kind of way, to be the complement of one another, and, thus created, they are blessed *together.*[9]

"In the second, the beasts and birds are created *between* the man and the woman. First, the man is made of the dust of the ground; he is placed by *himself* in the garden, charged with a solemn command, and threatened with a curse if he breaks it; *then the beasts and birds are made,* and the man gives names to them, and, lastly, after all this, *the woman is made out of one of his ribs,* but merely as a helpmate for the man.[10]

"The fact is, that the *second* account of the Creation,[11] together with the story of the Fall,[12] is manifestly composed by a *different writer* altogether from him who wrote the *first.*[13]

"This is suggested at once by the circumstance that, throughout the *first* narrative, the Creator is always spoken of by the name Elohim (God), whereas, throughout the *second* account, as well as the story of the Fall, he is always called Jehovah Elohim (Lord God), except when the writer seems to abstain, for some reason, from placing the name Jehovah in the mouth of the serpent.[14] This accounts naturally for the above contradictions. It would appear that, for some reason, the productions of two pens have been here united, without any reference to their inconsistencies."[15]

Dr. Kalisch, who does his utmost to maintain—as far as his knowledge of the truth will allow—the general historical veracity of this narrative, after speaking of the *first* account of the Creation, says :

"But now the narrative seems not only to pause, but to go backward. The grand and powerful climax seems at once broken off, and a languid repetition appears to follow. *Another cosmogony is introduced, which, to complete the perplexity, is, in many important features, in direct contradiction to the former.*

"*It would be dishonesty to conceal these difficulties. It would be weakmindedness and cowardice. It would be flight instead of combat. It would be an ignoble retreat, instead of victory. We confess there is an apparent dissonance.*"[16]

---

[1] Gen. i. 20, 24, 26.
[2] Gen. ii. 7, 9.
[3] Gen. i. 20.
[4] Gen. ii. 19.
[5] Gen. i. 27.
[6] Gen. ii. 7: iii. 22.
[7] Gen. i. 28.
[8] Gen. ii. 8, 15.
[9] Gen. i. 28.

[10] Gen. ii. 7, 8, 15, 22.
[11] Gen. ii. 4-25.
[12] Gen. iii.
[13] Gen. i. 1-ii. 3.
[14] Gen. iii. 1, 3, 5.
[15] The Pentateuch Examined vol. ii. pp. 171-173.
[16] Com. on Old Test. vol. i. p. 59.

Dr. Knappert says:[1]

"The account of the Creation from the hand of the *Priestly author* is utterly different from the *other narrative*, beginning at the fourth verse of Genesis ii. Here we are told that God created Heaven and Earth in six days, and rested on the *seventh* day, obviously with a view to bring out the holiness of the Sabbath in a strong light."

Now that we have seen there are two different and contradictory accounts of the Creation, to be found in the first two chapters of Genesis, we will endeavor to learn if there is sufficient reason to believe they are copies of *more ancient legends*.

We have seen that, according to the first account, God divided the work of creation into *six* days. This idea agrees with that of the ancient *Persians.*

The Zend-Avesta—the sacred writings of the Parsees—states that the Supreme being Ahuramazdâ (Ormuzd), created the universe and man in *six* successive periods of time, in the following order : First, the Heavens ; second, the Waters ; third, the Earth ; fourth, the Trees and Plants ; fifth, Animals ; and sixth, Man. After the Creator had finished his work, he rested.[2]

The Avesta account of the Creation is limited to this announcement, but we find a more detailed history of the origin of the human species in the book entitled *Bundehesh*, dedicated to the exposition of a complete cosmogony. This book states that Ahuramazdâ created the first man and women joined together at the back. After dividing them, he endowed them with motion and activity, placed within them an intelligent soul, and bade them " to be humble of heart ; to observe the law ; to be pure in their thoughts, pure in their speech, pure in their actions." Thus were born Mashya and Mashyâna, the pair from which all human beings are descended.[3]

The idea brought out in this story of the first human pair having originally formed a single androgynous being with two faces, separated later into two personalities by the Creator, is to be found in the Genesis account (v. 2). "Male and female created he them, and blessed them, and named their name Adam." Jewish tradition in the Targum and Talmud, as well as among learned rabbis, allege that Adam was created man and woman at the same time, having two faces turned in two opposite directions, and that the Creator separated the feminine half from him, in order to make of her a distinct person.[4]

---

[1] The Relig. of Israel, p. 186.
[2] Von Bohlen: Intro. to Gen. vol. ii. p. 4.
[3] Lenormant: Beginning of Hist. vol. i. p. 61.
[4] See Ibid. p. 64; and Legends of the Patriarchs, p. 31.

The ancient *Etruscan* legend, according to Delitzsch, is almost the same as the Persian. They relate that God created the world in *six* thousand years. In the first thousand he created the Heaven and Earth; in the second, the Firmament; in the third, the Waters of the Earth; in the fourth, the Sun, Moon and Stars; in the fifth, the Animals belonging to air, water and land; and in the sixth, Man alone.[1]

Dr. Delitzsch, who maintains to the utmost the historical truth of the Scripture story in Genesis, yet says:

"Whence comes the surprising agreement of the *Etruscan* and *Persian* legends with this section? How comes it that the *Babylonian* cosmogony in Berosus, and the *Phœnician* in Sanchoniathon, in spite of their fantastical oddity, come in contact with it in remarkable details?"

After showing some of the similarities in the legends of these different nations, he continues:

"These are only instances of that which they have in common. *For such an account outside of Israel, we must, however, conclude, that the author of Genesis i. has no vision before him, but a tradition.*"[2]

Von Bohlen tells us that the old *Chaldæan* cosmogony is also *the same.*[3]

To continue the *Persian* legend; we will now show that according to it, after the Creation man was tempted, and *fell.* Kalisch[4] and Bishop Colenso[5] tell us of the Persian legend that the first couple lived originally in purity and innocence. Perpetual happiness was promised them by the Creator if they persevered in their virtue. But an evil demon came to them in the form of a *serpent*, sent by Ahriman, the prince of devils, and gave them fruit of a wonderful *tree*, which imparted immortality. Evil inclinations then entered their hearts, and all their moral excellence was destroyed. Consequently they fell, and forfeited the eternal happiness for which they were destined. They killed beasts, and clothed themselves in their skins. The evil demon obtained still more perfect power over their minds, and called forth envy, hatred, discord, and rebellion, which raged in the bosom of the families.

Since the above was written, Mr. George Smith, of the British Museum, has discovered cuneiform inscriptions, which show conclusively that the Babylonians had this legend of the Creation and

---

[1] "The Etruscans believed in a creation of six thousand years, and in the successive production of different beings, the last of which was man." (Dunlap: Spirit Hist. p. 357.)

[2] Quoted by Bishop Colenso: The Pentateuch Examined, vol. iv. p. 115.

[3] Intro. to Genesis, vol. ii. p. 4.

[4] Com. on Old Test. vol. i. p. 63.

[5] The Pentateuch Examined, vol. iv. p. 152.

Fall of Man, some 1,500 years or more before the Hebrews heard of it.[1] The cuneiform inscriptions relating to the Babylonian legend of the Creation and Fall of Man, which have been discovered by English archæologists, are not, however, complete. The portions which relate to the *Tree* and *Serpent* have not been found, but Babylonian gem engravings show that these incidents were evidently a part of the original legend.[2] The *Tree of Life* in the Genesis account appears to correspond with the sacred grove of Anu, which was guarded by a sword turning to all the four points of the compass.[3] A representation of this Sacred Tree, with "*attendant cherubim,*" copied from an Assyrian cylinder, may be seen in Mr. George Smith's "Chaldean Account of Genesis."[4] Figure No. 1, which we have taken from the same work,[5] shows the tree of knowledge, fruit, and the serpent. Mr. Smith says of it :

FIG No. 1

"One striking and important specimen of early type in the British Museum collection, has two figures sitting one on each side of a *tree,* holding out their hands to the fruit, while at the back of one (the *woman*) is scratched a *serpent.* We know well that in these early sculptures none of these figures were chance devices, but all represented events, or supposed events, and figures in their legends; thus it is evident that a form of the story of the Fall, similar to that of Genesis, was known in early times in Babylonia."[5]

This illustration might be used to illustrate the narrative of *Genesis,* and as Friedrich Delitzsch has remarked (G. Smith's *Chaldäische Genesis*) is capable of no other explanation.

M. Renan does not hesitate to join forces with the ancient commentators, in seeking to recover a trace of the same tradition among the Phenicians in the fragments of Sanchoniathon, translated into Greek by Philo of Byblos. In fact, it is there said, in speaking of the first human pair, and of Æon, which seems to be the translation of *Havvâh* (in Phenician

---

[1] See Chapter xi.

[2] Mr. Smith says, "Whatever the primitive account may have been from which the earlier part of the Book of Genesis was copied, it is evident that the brief narration given in the Pentateuch omits a number of incidents and explanations—for instance, as to the origin of evil, the fall of the angels, the wickedness of the serpent, &c. Such points as these are included in the cuneiform narrative." (Smith: Chaldean Account of Genesis, pp. 13, 14.)

[3] Smith: Chaldean Account of Genesis, p. 88.

[4] Ibid. p. 89.

[5] Ibid. p. 91.

Havâth) and stands in her relation to the other members of the
pair, that this personage " has found out how to obtain nourishment
from the fruits of the tree."

The idea of the Edenic happiness of the first human beings
constitutes one of the universal traditions. Among the Egyptians,
the terrestial reign of the god Râ, who inaugurated the existence
of the world and of human life, was a golden age to which they
continually looked back with regret and envy. Its " like has never
been seen since."

The ancient Greeks boasted of their " Golden Age," when
sorrow and trouble were not known. Hesiod, an ancient Grecian
poet, describes it thus :

"Men lived like Gods, without vices or passions, vexation or toil. In
happy companionship with divine beings, they passed their days in tranquillity
and joy, living together in perfect equality, united by mutual confidence and
love. The earth was more beautiful than now, and spontaneously yielded an
abundant variety of fruits. Human beings and animals spoke the same
language and conversed with each other. Men were considered mere boys at a
hundred years old. They had none of the infirmities of age to trouble them,
and when they passed to regions of superior life, it was in a gentle slumber."

In the course of time, however, all the sorrows and troubles
came to man. They were caused by inquisitiveness. The story is
as follows : Epimetheus received a gift from Zeus (God), in the
form of a beautiful woman (Pandora).

" She brought with her a vase, the lid of which was (by the command of
God), to remain closed. The curiosity of her husband, however, tempted him
to open it, and suddenly there escaped from it troubles, weariness and illness
from which mankind was never afterwards free. All that remained was *hope.*" [1]

Among the *Thibetans,* the paradisiacal condition was more
complete and spiritual. The desire to eat of a certain sweet herb
deprived men of their spiritual life. There arose a sense of shame,
and the need to clothe themselves. Necessity compelled them to
agriculture ; the virtues disappeared, and murder, adultery and
other vices, stepped into their place.[2]

The idea that the Fall of the human race is connected with
agriculture is found to be also often represented in the legends of
the East African negroes, especially in the Calabar legend of the
Creation, which presents many interesting points of comparison
with the biblical story of the Fall. The first human pair are
called by a bell at meal-times to Abasi (the Calabar God), in heaven;
and in place of the forbidden tree of Genesis are put *agriculture*

[1] Murray's Mythology, p. 208.   [2] Kalisch's Com. vol. i. p. 64.

and *propagation*, which Abasi strictly denies to the first pair. The Fall is denoted by the transgression of both these commands, especially through the use of implements of tillage, to which the *woman* is tempted by a female friend who is given to her. From that moment man fell *and became mortal*, so that, as the Bible story has it, he can eat bread only in the sweat of his face. There agriculture is a curse, a fall from a more perfect stage to a lower and imperfect one.[1]

Dr. Kalisch, writing of the Garden of Eden, says:

"The *Paradise* is no exclusive feature of the early history of the Hebrews. *Most of the ancient nations have similar narratives about a happy abode, which care does not approach, and which re-echoes with the sounds of the purest bliss.*"[2]

The *Persians* supposed that a region of bliss and delight called *Heden*, more beautiful than all the rest of the world, *traversed by a mighty river*, was the original abode of the first men, before they were tempted by the evil spirit in the form of a *serpent*, to partake of the fruit of the forbidden tree *Hôm.*[3]

Dr. Delitzsch, writing of the *Persian* legend, observes:

"Innumerable attendants of the Holy One keep watch against the attempts of Ahriman, over the tree *Hôm*, which contains in itself the power of the resurrection.[4]

The ancient Greeks had a tradition concerning the "Islands of the Blessed," the "Elysium," on the borders of the earth, abounding in every charm of life, and the "Garden of the Hesperides," the Paradise, in which grew a *tree* bearing the golden apples of Immortality. It was guarded by three nymphs, and a Serpent, or Dragon, the ever-watchful Ladon. It was one of the labors of Hercules to gather some of these apples of life. When he arrived there he found the garden protected by a *Dragon*. Ancient medallions represent a tree with a serpent twined around it. Hercules has gathered an apple, and near him stand the three nymphs, called Hesperides.[5] This is simply a parallel of the Eden myth.

The Rev. Mr. Faber, speaking of *Hercules*, says:

"On the *Sphere* he is represented in the act of contending with the Serpent, the head of which is placed under his foot ; and this Serpent, we are told, is that which guarded the tree with golden fruit in the midst of the garden of the Hesperides. But the garden of the Hesperides *was none other than the garden of Paradise;* consequently the serpent of that garden, the head of which is crushed beneath the heel of Hercules, and which itself is described as encircling with its

1 Goldziher: Hebrew Mythology, p. 87.
2 Com. on the Old Test. vol. i. p. 70.
3 Ibid.
4 Ibid. "The fruit and sap of this 'Tree of Life' begat immortality." (Bonwick: Egyptian Belief, p. 240.)
5 See Montfaucon: L'Antiquité Expliquée, vol. i. p. 211, and Pl. cxxxiii.

folds the trunk of the mysterious tree, must necessarily be a transcript of that Serpent whose form was assumed by the tempter of our first parents. We may observe the same ancient tradition in the Phœnician fable representing Ophion or Ophioneus. "[1]

And Professor Fergusson says :

"*Hercules*' adventures in the garden of the Hesperides, is the Pagan form of the myth that most resembles the precious Serpent-guarded fruit of the Garden of Eden, though the moral of the fable is so widely different."[2]

The ancient *Egyptians* also had the legend of the "Tree of Life." It is mentioned in their sacred books that Osiris ordered the names of some souls to be written on this "Tree of Life," the fruit of which made those who ate it to become as gods.[3]

Among the most ancient traditions of the *Hindoos*, is that of the "Tree of Life"—called *Sôma* in Sanskrit—the juice of which imparted immortality. This most wonderful tree was guarded by spirits.[4]

Still more striking is the Hindoo legend of the "Elysium" or "Paradise," which is as follows :

"In the sacred mountain *Meru*, which is perpetually clothed in the golden rays of the Sun, and whose lofty summit reaches into heaven, no sinful man can exist. *It is guarded by a dreadful dragon.* It is adorned with many celestial plants and trees, and is watered by *four rivers*, which thence separate and flow to the four chief directions."[5]

The Hindoos, like the philosophers of the Ionic school (Thales, for instance), held *water* to be the first existing and all-pervading principle, at the same time allowing the co-operation and influence of an *immaterial* intelligence in the work of creation.[6] A Vedic poet, meditating on the Creation, uses the following expressions :

"Nothing that is was then, even what is not, did not exist then." "There was no space, no life, and lastly there was no time, no difference between day and night, no solar torch by which morning might have been told from evening." "Darkness there was, and all at first was veiled in gloom profound, as ocean without light."[7]

The Hindoo legend approaches very nearly to that preserved in the Hebrew Scriptures. Thus, it is said that Siva, as the Supreme Being, desired to tempt Brahmá (who had taken human form, and was called Swayámbhura—son of the self-existent), and for this object he dropped from heaven a blossom of the sacred *fig* tree.

[1] Faber: Origin Pagan Idolatry, vol. i. p. 443; in Anacalypsis, vol. i. p. 237.
[2] Tree and Serpent Worship, p. 13.
[3] Prog. Relig. Ideas, vol. i. p. 159.
[4] See Bunsen's Keys of St. Peter, p. 414.
[5] Colenso: The Pentateuch Examined, vol. iv. p. 153.
[6] Buckley: Cities of the Ancient World, p. 148.
[7] Müller: Hist. Sanskrit Literature, p. 559.

Swayambhura, instigated by his wife, Satarupa, endeavors to obtain this blossom, thinking its possession will render him immortal and divine; but when he has succeeded in doing so, he is cursed by Siva, and doomed to misery and degradation.[1] The sacred Indian *fig* is endowed by the Brahmins and the Buddhists with mysterious significance, as the " Tree of Knowledge " or "Intelligence."[2]

There is no Hindoo legend of the *Creation* similar to the Persian and Hebrew accounts, and Ceylon was never believed to have been the Paradise or home of our first parents, although such stories are in circulation.[3] The Hindoo religion states—as we have already seen—Mount Meru to be the Paradise, out of which went *four rivers.*

We have noticed that the " Gardens of Paradise " are said to have been guarded by *Dragons*, and that, according to the Genesis account, it was Cherubim that protected Eden. This apparent difference in the legends is owing to the fact that we have come in our modern times to speak of Cherub as though it were an other name for an Angel. But the Cherub of the writer of Genesis, the Cherub of Assyria, the Cherub of Babylon, the Cherub of the entire Orient, at the time the Eden story was written, was not at all an Angel, but an animal, and a mythological one at that. The Cherub had, in some cases, the body of a lion, with the head of an other animal, or a man, and the wings of a bird. In Ezekiel they have the body of a man, whose head, besides a human countenance, has also that of a *Lion*, an *Ox* and an *Eagle*. They are provided with four wings, and the whole body is spangled with innumerable eyes. In Assyria and Babylon they appear as winged bulls with human faces, and are placed at the gateways of palaces and temples as guardian genii who watch over the dwelling, as the Cherubim in Genesis watch the " Tree of Life."

Most Jewish writers and Christian Fathers conceived the Cherubim as Angels. Most theologians also considered them as Angels, until Michaelis showed them to be a mythological animal, a poetical creation.[4]

---

[1] See Wake: Phallism in Ancient Religions, pp. 46. 47; and Maurice: Hist. Hindostan, vol. i. p. 408.

[2] Hardwick : Christ and Other Masters, p. 215.

[3] See Jacolliot's "Bible in India," which John Fisk calls a " very discreditable performance," and "a disgraceful piece of charlatanry" (Myths, &c. p. 205). This writer also states that according to Hindoo legend, the first man and woman were called "Adima and Heva," which is certainly not the case. The

" bridge of Adima " which he speaks of as connecting the island of Ceylon with the mainland, is called "Rama's bridge ; " and the " Adam's footprints " are called "Buddha's footprints." The Portuguese, who called the mountain *Pico d'Adama* (Adam's Peak), evidently invented these other names. (See Maurice's Hist. Hindostan, vol. i. pp. 361, 362, and vol. ii. p. 242).

[4] See Smith's Bible Dic. Art. "Cherubim," and Lenormant's Beginning of History, ch. iii.

We see then, that our *Cherub* is simply a *Dragon*.

To continue our inquiry regarding the prevalence of the Eden-myth among nations of antiquity.

The *Chinese* have their Age of Virtue, when nature furnished abundant food, and man lived peacefully, surrounded by all the beasts. In their sacred books there is a story concerning a mysterious *garden*, where grew a *tree* bearing " apples of immortality," guarded by a winged serpent, called a Dragon. They describe a primitive age of the world, when the earth yielded abundance of delicious fruits without cultivation, and the seasons were untroubled by wind and storms. There was no calamity, sickness, or death. Men were then good without effort; for the human heart was in harmony with the peacefulness and beauty of nature.

The "Golden Age" of the past is much dwelt upon by their ancient commentators. One of them says :

"All places were then equally the native county of every man. Flocks wandered in the fields without any guide; birds filled the air with their melodious voices; and the fruits grew of their own accord. Men lived pleasantly with the animals, and all creatures were members of the same family. Ignorant of evil, man lived in simplicity and perfect innocence."

Another commentator says :

"In the first age of perfect purity, all was in harmony, and the passions did not occasion the slightest murmur. Man, united to sovereign reason within, conformed his outward actions to sovereign justice. Far from all duplicity and falsehood, his soul received marvelous felicity from heaven, and the purest delights from earth."

Another says :

" A delicious *garden* refreshed with zephyrs, and planted with odoriferous trees, was situated in the middle of a mountain, which was the avenue of heaven. The *waters* that moistened it flowed from a source called the ' *Fountain of Immortality.*' He who drinks of it never dies. Thence flowed *four rivers.* A Golden River, betwixt the South and East, a Red River, between the North and East, the River of the Lamb between the North and West."

The animal Kaiming guards the entrance.

Partly by an undue thirst for knowledge, and partly by increasing sensuality, and the seduction of *woman,* man fell. Then passion and lust ruled in the human mind, and war with the animals began. In one of the Chinese sacred volumes, called the Chi-King, it is said that :

"All was subject to man at first, *but a woman threw us into slavery.* The wise husband raised up a bulwark of walls, *but the woman, by an ambitious desire of knowledge, demolished them.* Our misery did not come from heaven, *but from a woman. She lost the human race.* Ah, unhappy *Poo See !* thou kindled the fire that consumes us, and which is every day augmenting. Our misery has lasted many ages. *The world is lost.* Vice overflows all things like a mortal poison."[1]

Thus we see that the Chinese are no strangers to the doctrine of original sin. It is their invariable belief that man is a fallen being; admitted by them from time immemorial.

The inhabitants of *Madagascar* had a legend similar to the Eden story, which is related as follows:

"The first man was created of the *dust of the earth,* and was placed in a *garden,* where he was subject to none of the ills which now affect mortality; he was also free from all bodily appetites, and though surrounded by delicious *fruit* and limpid *streams* yet felt no desire to taste of the fruit or to quaff the water The Creator, had, moreover, *strictly forbid him either to eat or to drink.* The great enemy, however, came to him, and painted to him, in glowing colors, the sweetness of the apple, and the lusciousness of the date, and the succulence of the orange."

After resisting the temptations for a while, he at last ate of the fruit, and consequently *fell.*[2]

A legend of the Creation, similar to the Hebrew, was found by Mr. Ellis among the *Tahitians,* and appeared in his "Polynesian Researches." It is as follows:

After Taarao had formed the world, he created man out of aræa, red earth, which was also the food of man until bread was made. Taarao one day called for the man by name. When he came, he caused him to fall asleep, and while he slept, he took out one of his *ivi,* or bones, and with it made a woman, whom he gave to the man as his wife, and they became the progenitors of mankind. The woman's name was *Ivi,* which signifies a bone.[3]

The prose Edda, of the ancient *Scandinavians,* speaks of the "Golden Age" when all was pure and harmonious. This age lasted until the arrival of *woman* out of Jotunheim—the region of the giants, a sort of "land of Nod"—who corrupted it.[4]

In the annals of the *Mexicans,* the first woman, whose name was translated by the old Spanish writers, "the woman of our flesh," is always represented as accompanied by a great male serpent, who seems to be talking to her. Some writers believe this to be the *tempter* speaking to the primeval mother, and others that it is intended to represent the *father* of the human race. This Mexican Eve is represented on their monuments as the mother of twins.[5]

[1] See Prog. Relig. Ideas, vol. i. pp. 206-210. The Pentateuch Examined, vol. iv. pp. 152, 153, and Legends of the Patriarchs, p. 38.
[2] Legends of the Patriarchs, p. 31.
[3] Quoted by Müller: The Science of Relig., p. 302.
[4] See Mallet's Northern Antiquities, p. 409.
[5] See Baring Gould's Legends of the Patriarchs; Squire's Serpent Symbol, p. 161, and Wake's Phallism in Ancient Religions, p. 41.

Mr. Franklin, in his "Buddhists and Jeynes," says:

"A striking instance is recorded by the very intelligent traveler (Wilson), regarding a representation of the Fall of our first parents, sculptured in the magnificent temple of Ipsambul, in Nubia. He says that a very exact representation of
Adam and Eve in the garden of Eden is to be seen in that cave, and that the
serpent climbing round the tree is especially delineated, and the whole subject of
the tempting of our first parents most accurately exhibited."[1]

Nearly the same thing was found by Colonel Coombs in the
South of India. Colonel Tod, in his "Hist. Rajapoutana," says:

"A drawing, brought by Colonel Coombs from a sculptured column in a cave-
temple in the South of India, represents the first pair at the foot of the ambro-
sial tree, and a *serpent* entwined among the heavily-laden boughs, presenting to
them some of the fruit from his mouth. The tempter appears to be at that part
of his discourse, when

'——— his words, replete with guile,
Into her heart too easy entrance won:
Fixed on the fruit she gazed.'

" *This is a curious subject to be engraved on an ancient Pagan temple.*"[2]

So the Colonel thought, no doubt, but it is not so very curious
after all. It is
the same myth
which we have
found—with but
such small vari-
ations only as
time and circum-
stances may be
expected to pro-
duce — among
different nations,
in both the Old
and New Worlds.

FIG. 2

work of Mont-
faucon,[3] repre-
sents one of
these ancient
Pagan sculp-
tures. Can any
one doubt that it
is allusive to the
myth of which
we have been
treating in this
chapter?

Fig. No. 2,
taken from the

That man
was originally
created a per-

fect being, and is now only a fallen and broken remnant
of what he once was, we have seen to be a piece of *mythology,* not only unfounded in fact, but, beyond intelligent question,
proved untrue. What, then, is the significance of the exposure
of this myth? What does its loss as a scientific fact, and as a portion of Christian dogma, imply? It implies that with it—although
many Christian divines who admit this to be a legend, do not,

---

[1] Quoted by Higgins: Anacalypsis, vol. i.   [2] Tod's Hist. Raj., p. 581, quoted by Hig-
p. 403.   gins: Anacalypsis, vol. i. p. 404.
          [3] L'Antiquité Expliquée, vol. i.

or do not *profess*, to see it—*must fall the whole Orthodox scheme, for upon this* MYTH *the theology of Christendom is built.* The doctrine of the *inspiration of the Scriptures*, the *Fall* of man, his *total depravity*, the *Incarnation*, the *Atonement*, the *devil*, *hell*, in fact, the entire theology of the Christian church, falls to pieces with the historical inaccuracy of this story, *for upon it is it built; 'tis the foundation of the whole structure.*[1]

According to Christian dogma, the Incarnation of Christ Jesus had become necessary, merely *because he had to redeem the evil introduced into the world by the Fall of man.* These two dogmas cannot be separated from each other. *If there was no Fall, there is no need of an atonement, and no Redeemer is required.* Those, then, who consent in recognizing in Christ Jesus a *God* and *Redeemer*, and who, notwithstanding, cannot resolve upon admitting the story of the Fall of man to be *historical*, should exculpate themselves from the reproach of *inconsistency*. There are a great number, however, in this position at the present day.

Although, as we have said, many Christian divines do not, or do not profess to, see the force of the above argument, there are many who do; and they, regardless of their scientific learning, cling to these old myths, professing to believe them, *well knowing what must follow with their fall.* The following, though written some years ago, will serve to illustrate this style of reasoning.

The Bishop of Manchester (England) writing in the " Manchester Examiner and Times," said :

" The very *foundation of our faith*, the very *basis of our hopes*, the very nearest and dearest of our consolations are taken from us, *when one line of that sacred volume, on which we base everything, is declared to be untruthful and untrust-worthy.*"

The " English Churchman," speaking of clergymen who have " *doubts*," said, that any who are not throughly persuaded " *that the Scriptures cannot in any particular be untrue*," should leave the Church.

The Rev. E. Garbett, M. A., in a sermon preached before the University of Oxford, speaking of the " *historical truth* " of the Bible, said:

---

[1] Sir William Jones, the first president of the Royal Asiatic Society, saw this when he said : " Either the first eleven chapters of Genesis, all due allowance being made for a figurative Eastern style, are *true*, or the whole fabric of our religion is false." (In Asiatic Researches, vol. i. p. 225.) And so also did the learned Thomas Maurice, for he says: " If the Mosaic History be indeed a fable, the whole fabric of the national religion is false, since the main pillar of Christianity rests upon that important original promise, that the seed of the woman should bruise the head of the serpent." (Hist. Hindostan, vol. i. p. 29.)

' It is the clear teaching of those doctrinal formularies, to which we of the Church of England have expressed our solemn assent, *and no honest interpretation of her language can get rid of it*

And that :

" In all consistent reason, *we must accept the whole of the inspired autographs, or reject the whole.*"

Dr. Baylee, Principal of a theological university—*St. Aiden's College*—at Birkenhead, England, and author of a " Manual," called Baylee's " *Verbal Inspiration*," written " *chiefly for the youths of St. Aiden's College*," makes use of the following words, in that work :

" *The whole Bible*, as a revelation, is a declaration of the mind of God towards his creatures on all the subjects of which the Bible treats."

" *The Bible is God's word*, in the same sense as if he had made use of no human agent, but had *Himself spoken it*."

" The Bible cannot be less than verbally inspired. *Every word, every syllable, every letter*, is just what it would be, had God spoken from heaven without any human intervention."

" Every scientific statement is infallibly correct, all its history and narrations' of every kind, *are without any inaccuracy.*"[1]

A whole volume might be filled with such quotations, not only from religious works and journals published in England, but from those published in the United States of America.[2]

---

[1] The above extracts are quoted by Bishop Colenso, in The Pentateuch Examined, vol. ii. pp. 10–12, from which we take them.

[2] " *Cosmogony* " is the title of a volume lately written by Prof. Thomas Mitchell, and published by the American News Co., in which the author attacks all the modern scientists in regard to the geological antiquity of the world, evolution, atheism, pantheism, &c. He believes—and rightly too—that, " *if the account of Creation in Genesis falls, Christ and the apostles follow : if the book of Genesis is erroneous, so also are the Gospels.*"

CHAPTER II.

THE DELUGE.[1]

AFTER "man's shameful fall," the earth began to be populated at a very rapid rate. "The sons of God saw the daughters of men that they were fair; and they took them wives of all which they chose. . . . . There were *giants* in the earth in those days,[2] and also . . . mighty men . . . men of renown."

But these "giants" and "mighty men" were very wicked, "and God saw the wickedness of man . . . *and it repented the Lord that he had made man upon the earth,*[3] and it grieved him at his heart. And the Lord said; I will destroy man whom I have created from the face of the earth, both man and beast, and the creeping thing, and the fowls of the air, for it repenteth me that I have made them. But Noah found grace in the eyes of the Lord (for) Noah was a just man . . . and walked with God. . . . And God said unto Noah, The end of all flesh is come before me, for the earth is filled with violence through them, and, behold, I will de-

---

[1] See "The Deluge in the Light of Modern Science," by Prof. Wm. Denton: J. P. Mendum, Boston.

[2] "There were *giants* in the earth in those days." It is a scientific fact that most races of men, in former ages, instead of being *larger*, were *smaller* than at the present time. There is hardly a suit of armor in the Tower of London, or in the old castles, that is large enough for the average Englishman of to-day to put on. Man has grown in stature as well as intellect, and there is no proof whatever—in fact, the opposite is certain—that there ever was a race of what might properly be called *giants*, inhabiting the earth. Fossil remains of large animals having been found by primitive man, *and a legend invented to account for them*, it would naturally be that: "There were giants in the earth in those days." As an illustration we may mention the story, recorded by the traveller James Orton, we believe (in "The Andes and the Amazon"), that, near Punin, in South America, was found the remains of an extinct species of the horse, the mastodon, and other large animals. This discovery was made, owing to the assurance of the natives that *giants* at one time had lived in that country, *and that they had seen their remains at this certain place.* Many legends have had a similar origin. But the originals of all the *Ogres* and *Giants* to be found in the mythology of almost all nations of antiquity, are the famous Hindoo demons, the *Rakshasas* of our Aryan ancestors. The *Rakshasas* were very terrible creatures indeed, and in the minds of many people, in India, are so still. Their natural form, so the stories say, is that of huge, unshapely *giants*, like *clouds*, with hair and beard of the color of the *red lightning*. This description explains their origin. *They are the dark, wicked and cruel clouds,* personified.

[3] "And it *repented* the Lord that he had made man." (Gen. iv.) "God is not a man that he should lie, neither the son of man that he should repent." (Numb. xxiii. 19.)

stroy them with the earth. Make thee an ark of gopher wood, rooms shalt thou make in the ark, (and) a window shalt thou make to the ark; . . . .   And behold I, even I, do bring a flood of waters upon the earth, to destroy all flesh, wherein is the breath of life, from under heaven, and every thing that is in the earth shall die. But with thee shall I establish my covenant; and thou shalt come into the ark, thou, and thy sons, and thy wife, and thy sons' wives, with thee. And of every living thing of all flesh, *two* of every sort shalt thou bring into the ark, to keep them alive with thee; they shall be male and female. Of fowls after their kind, and of cattle after their kind, of every creeping thing of the earth after his kind, *two* of every sort shall come in to thee, to keep them alive. And take thou unto thee of all food that is eaten, and thou shalt gather it to thee; and it shall be for food for thee and for them. *Thus did Noah, according to all that God commanded him.*"[1]

When the ark was finished, the Lord said unto Noah :

" Come thou and all thy house into the ark. . . .   Of every clean beast thou shalt take to thee by *sevens,* the male and his female; and of beasts that are not clean by two, the male and his female. Of fowls also of the air by *sevens,* the male and the female."[2]

Here, again, as in the Eden myth, there is a *contradiction.* We have seen that the Lord told Noah to bring into the ark " of every living thing, of all flesh, *two* of *every sort,*" and now that the ark is finished, we are told that he said to him: "Of every clean beast thou shalt take to thee by *sevens,*" and, " of fowls also of the air by *sevens.*" This is owing to the story having been written by *two different writers*—the Jehovistic, and the Elohistic—one of which took from, and added to the narrative of the other.[3] The account goes on to say, that:

" Noah went in, and his sons, and his wife, and his sons' wives with him, into the ark. . . .   Of *clean* beasts, and of beasts *that are not clean,* and of *fowls,* and of *every thing* that creepeth upon the earth, there went in *two and two,* unto Noah into the ark, the male and the female, *as God had commanded Noah.*"[4]

We see, then, that Noah took into the ark *of all kinds* of beasts, of *fowls,* and of every thing that creepeth, *two of every sort,* and that this was " *as God had commanded Noah.*" This clearly shows that the writer of these words knew nothing of the command

---

[1] Gen. iv.   [2] Gen. vi. 1–3.   Athyr (Nov. 13th), the very day and month on
[3] See chapter xi.   which Noah is said to have entered his ark.
[4] The image of Osiris of Egypt was by the   (See Bonwick's Egyptian Belief, p. 165, and
priests shut up in a sacred ark on the 17th of   Bunsen's Angel Messiah, p. 22.)

to take in *clean beasts*, and *fowls* of the air, by *sevens*. We are further assured, that, "*Noah did according to all that the Lord commanded him.*"

After Noah and his family, and every beast after his kind, and all the cattle after their kind, the fowls of the air, and every creeping thing, had entered the ark, the Lord shut them in. Then " were all the fountains of the great deep broken up, *and the windows of heaven were opened.* And the rain was upon the earth *forty days and forty nights. . . . .* And the waters prevailed exceedingly upon the earth ; and all the hills, that were under the whole heaven, were covered. Fifteen cubits upwards did the waters prevail ; and the mountains were covered. And all flesh died that moved upon the earth, both of fowl and of cattle, and of beast, and of every creeping thing that creepeth upon the earth, and every man. And Noah only remained alive, and they that were with him in the ark."[1] The object of the flood was now accomplished, "*all flesh died that moved upon the earth.*" The Lord, therefore, " made a wind to pass over the earth, and the waters assuaged. The fountains of the deep, and the windows of heaven, were stopped, and the rain from heaven was restrained. And the waters decreased continually. . . . . And it came to pass at the end of *forty days*, that Noah opened the window of the ark, which he had made. And he sent forth a raven, which went forth to and fro, until the waters were dried up from off the earth. He also sent forth a dove, . . . but the dove found no rest for the sole of her foot, and she returned unto him into the ark." . . .

At the end of *seven* days he again " sent forth the dove out of the ark, and the dove came in to him in the evening, and lo, in her mouth was an olive leaf, plucked off."

At the end of another *seven* days, he again "sent forth the dove, which returned not again to him any more."

And the ark rested in the *seventh* month, on the seventeenth day of the month, upon the mountains of Ararat. Then Noah and his wife, and his sons, and his sons' wives, and every living thing that was in the ark, went forth out of the ark. "And Noah builded an altar unto the Lord, . . . and offered burnt offerings on the altar. And the Lord smelled a sweet savour, and the Lord said in his heart, I will not again curse the ground any more for man's sake."[2]

---

[1] Gen. vi.   [2] Gen. viii.

We shall now see that there is scarcely any considerable race of men among whom there does not exist, in some form, the tradition of a great deluge, which destroyed all the human race, except *their own* progenitors.

The first of these which we shall notice, and the one with which the Hebrew agrees most closely, having been copied from it,[1] is the *Chaldean*, as given by Berosus, the Chaldean historian.[2] It is as follows:

"After the death of Ardates (the ninth king of the Chaldeans), his son *Xisuthrus* reigned eighteen sari. In his time happened a great *deluge*, the history of which is thus described: The deity Cronos appeared to him (Xisuthrus) in a vision, and warned him that upon the fifteenth day of the month Desius there would be a flood, by which mankind would be destroyed. He therefore enjoined him to write a history of the beginning, procedure, and conclusion of all things, and to bury it in the City of the Sun at Sippara; and to build a vessel, and take with him into it his friends and relations, and to convey on board everything necessary to sustain life, together with all the different animals, both birds and quadrupeds, and trust himself fearlessly to the deep. Having asked the deity whither he was to sail, he was answered: 'To the Gods;' upon which he offered up a prayer for the good of mankind. He then obeyed the divine admonition, and built a vessel five stadia in length, and two in breadth. Into this he put everything which he had prepared, and last of all conveyed into it his wife, his children, and his friends. After the flood had been upon the earth, and was in time abated, Xisuthrus sent out birds from the vessel; which not finding any food, nor any place whereupon they might rest their feet, returned to him again. After an interval of some days, he sent them forth a second time; and they now returned with their feet tinged with mud. He made a trial a third time with these birds; but they returned to him no more: from whence he judged that the surface of the earth had appeared above the waters. He therefore made an opening in the vessel, and upon looking out found that it was stranded upon the side of some mountain; upon which he immediately quitted it with his wife, his daughter, and the pilot. Xisuthrus then paid his adoration to the earth, and, having constructed an altar, offered sacrifices to the gods."[3]

This account, given by Berosus, which agrees in almost every particular with that found in Genesis, and with that found by George Smith of the British Museum on terra cotta tablets in Assyria, is nevertheless different in some respects. But, says Mr. Smith:

"When we consider the difference between the two countries of Palestine and Babylonia, these variations do not appear greater than we should expect. . . . It was only natural that, in relating the same stories, each nation should

[1] See chapter xi.
[2] Josephus, the Jewish historian, speaking of the flood of Noah (Antiq. bk. 1, ch. iii.), says: "All the writers of the Babylonian histories make mention of *this* flood and this ark."

[3] Quoted by George Smith: Chaldean Account of Genesis, pp. 42-44; see also, The Pentateuch Examined, vol. iv. p. 211; Dunlap's Spirit Hist. p. 138; Cory's Ancient Fragments, p. 61, et seq. for similar accounts.

color them in accordance with its own ideas, and stress would naturally in each case be laid upon points with which they were familiar. Thus we should expect beforehand that there would be differences in the narrative such as we actually find, and we may also notice that the cuneiform account does not always coincide even with the account of the same events given by Berosus from Chaldean sources."[1]

The most important points are the same however, *i. e.*, *in both cases* the virtuous man is informed by the Lord that a flood is about to take place, which would destroy mankind. *In both cases* they are commanded to build a vessel or ark, to enter it with their families, and to take in beasts, birds, and everything that creepeth, also to provide themselves with food. *In both cases* they send out a bird from the ark *three times*—the third time it failed to return. *In both cases* they land on a mountain, and upon leaving the ark they offer up a sacrifice to the gods. Xisuthrus was the tenth king,[2] and Noah the tenth patriarch.[3] Xisuthrus had three sons (Zerovanos, Titan and Japetosthes),[4] and Noah had three sons (Shem, Ham and Japhet).[5]

As Cory remarks in his "Ancient Fragments," "The history of the flood, as given by Berosus, so remarkably corresponds with the Biblical account of the Noachian Deluge, that no one can doubt that both proceeded from one source—they are evidently transcriptions, except the names, from some ancient document.[6]

This legend became known to the Jews from Chaldean sources,[7] it was not known in the country (Egypt) out of which they evidently came.[8] Egyptian history, it is said, had gone on un-

---

[1] Chaldean Account of Genesis, pp. 285, 286.

[2] Volney : New Researches, p. 119 ; Chaldean Acct. of Genesis, p. 290 ; Hist. Hindostan, vol. i. p. 417, and Dunlap's Spirit Hist. p. 277.

[3] Ibid.

[4] Legends of the Patriarchs, pp. 109, 110.

[5] Gen. vi. 8.

[6] The Hindoo ark-preserved Menu had *three* sons ; Sama, Cama, and Pra-Japati. (Faber: Orig. Pagan Idol.) The Bhattias, who live between Delli and the Panjab, insist that they are descended from a certain king called Salivahana, who had three sons, Bhat, Maha and Thamaz." (Col. Wilford, in vol. ix. Asiatic Researches.) The Iranian hero Thraetona had *three* sons. The Iranian Sethite Lamech had *three* sons, and Hellen, the son of Deucalion, during whose time the flood is said to have happened, had *three* sons. (Bunsen : The Angel-Messiah, pp. 70, 71.) All the ancient nations of Europe also describe their origin from the *three* sons of some king or patriarch. The Germans said that Mannus (son of the god Tuisco) had *three* sons, who were the original ancestors of the three principal nations of Germany. The Scythians said that Targytagus, the founder of their nation, had *three* sons, from whom they were descended. A tradition among the Romans was that the Cyclop Polyphemus had by Galatea *three* sons. Saturn had *three* sons, Jupiter, Neptune, and Pluto ; and Hesiod speaks of the *three* sons which sprung from the marriage of heaven and earth. (See Mallet's Northern Antiquities, p. 509.)

[7] See chap. xi.

[8] "It is of no slight moment that the Egyptians, with whom the Hebrews are represented as in earliest and closest intercourse, had no traditions of a flood, while the Babylonian and Hellenic tales bear a strong resemblance in many points to the narrative in Genesis." (Rev. George W. Cox : Tales of Ancient Greece, p. 340. See also Owen : Man's Earliest History, p. 28, and ch. xi. this work.)

interrupted for ten thousand years before the time assigned for the birth of Jesus.[1] And it is known as absolute fact that the land of Egypt was never visited by other than its annual beneficent overflow of the river Nile.[2] The Egyptian Bible, *which is by far the most ancient of all holy books,*[3] *knew nothing of the Deluge.*[4] The Phra (or Pharaoh) Khoufou-Cheops was building his pyramid, according to Egyptian chronicle, when the whole world was under the waters of a universal deluge, according to the Hebrew chronicle.[5] A number of other nations of antiquity are found destitute of any story of a flood,[6] which they certainly would have had if a universal deluge had ever happened. Whether this legend is of high antiquity in India has even been doubted by distinguished scholars.[7]

The *Hindoo* legend of the Deluge is as follows :

"Many ages after the creation of the world, Brahma resolved to destroy it with a deluge, on account of the wickedness of the people. There lived at that time a pious man named *Satyavrata*, and as the lord of the universe loved this pious man, and wished to preserve him from the sea of destruction which was to appear on account of the depravity of the age, he appeared before him in the form of *Vishnu* (the Preserver) and said: In *seven* days from the present time . . . the worlds will be plunged in an ocean of death, but in the midst of the destroying waves, a large vessel, sent by me for thy use, shall stand before thee. Then shalt thou take all medicinal herbs, all the variety of feeds, and, accompanied by *seven* saints, encircled by *pairs* of all brute animals, thou shalt enter the spacious ark, and continue in it, secure from the flood, on one immense ocean without light, except the radiance of thy holy companions. When the ship shall be agitated by an impetuous wind, thou shalt fasten it with a large sea-serpent on my horn; for I will be near thee (in the form of a fish), drawing the vessel, with thee and thy attendants. I will remain on the ocean, O chief of men, until a night of *Brahma* shall be completely ended. Thou shalt then

[1] See Taylor's Diegesis, p. 198, and Knight's Ancient Art and Mythology, p. 107. "Plato was told that Egypt had hymns dating back ten thousand years before his time." (Bonwick : Egyptian Belief, p. 185.) Plato lived 429 B. C. Herodotus relates that the priests of Egypt informed him that from the first king to the present priest of Vulcan who last reigned, were three hundred forty and one generations of men, and during these generations there were the same number of chief priests and kings. "Now (says he) three hundred generations are equal to ten thousand years, for three generations of men are one hundred years ; and the forty-one remaining generations that were over the three hundred, make one thousand three hundred and forty years," making *eleven thousand three hundred and forty years.* "Conducting me into the interior of an edifice that was spacious, and showing me wooden colossuses to the number I have mentioned, they reckoned them up ; for every high priest places an image of himself there during his life-time ; the priests, therefore, reckoning them and showing them to me, pointed out that each was the son of his own father ; going through them all, from the image of him who died last until they had pointed them all out." (Herodotus, book ii. Chs. 142, 143.) The discovery of mummies of royal and priestly personages, made at Deir-el-Bahari (Aug., 1881), near Thebes, in Egypt, would seem to confirm this statement made by Herodotus. Of the thirty-nine mummies discovered, one—that of King Raskenen — is about three thousand seven hundred years old. (See a Cairo [Aug. 8th,] Letter to the London Times.)

[2] Owen : Man's Earliest History, p. 28.
[3] Bonwick : Egyptian Belief, p. 185.
[4] Ibid. p. 411.
[5] Owen : Man's Earliest History, pp. 27, 28.
[6] Goldzhier : Hebrew Mytho. p. 319.
[7] Ibid. p. 320.

know my true greatness, rightly named the Supreme Godhead; by my favor, all thy questions shall be answered, and thy mind abundantly instructed."

Being thus directed, Satyavrata humbly waited for the time which the ruler of our senses had appointed. It was not long, however, before the sea, overwhelming its shores, began to deluge the whole earth, and it was soon perceived to be augmented by showers from immense clouds. He, still meditating on the commands of the Lord, saw a vessel advancing, and entered it with the saints, after having carried into effect the instructions which had been given him.

Vishnu then appeared before them, in the form of a fish, as he had said, and Satyavrata fastened a cable to his horn.

The deluge in time abated, and Satyavrata, instructed in all divine and human knowledge, was appointed, by the favor of *Vishnu*, the Seventh Menu. After coming forth from the ark he offers up a sacrifice to Brahma.[1]

The ancient temples of Hindostan contain representations of Vishnu sustaining the earth while overwhelmed by the waters of the deluge. *A rainbow is seen on the surface of the subsiding waters.*[2]

The *Chinese* believe the earth to have been at one time covered with water, which they described as flowing abundantly and then subsiding. This great flood divided the higher from the lower age of man. It happened during the reign of Yaou. This inundation, which is termed *hung-shwuy* (great water), almost ruined the country, and is spoken of by Chinese writers with sentiments of horror. The *Shoo-King*, one of their sacred books, describes the waters as reaching to the tops of some of the mountains, covering the hills, and expanding as wide as the vault of heaven.[3]

The *Parsees* say that by the temptation of the evil spirit men became wicked, and God destroyed them with a deluge, except a few, from whom the world was peopled anew.[4]

In the *Zend-Avesta*, the oldest sacred book of the Persians, of whom the Parsees are direct descendants, there are sixteen countries spoken of as having been given by Ormuzd, the Good Deity, for the Aryans to live in; and these countries are described as a land of delight, which was turned by Ahriman, the Evil Deity, into a

[1] Translated from the *Bhagavat* by Sir Wm. Jones, and published in the first volume of the "Asiatic Researches," p. 230, *et seq.* See also Maurice: Ind. Ant. ii. 277, *et seq.*, and Prof. Max Müller's Hist. Ancient Sanskrit Literature, p. 425, *et seq.*

[2] See Prog. Relig. Ideas, vol. i. p. 55.
[3] See Thornton's Hist. China, vol. i. p. 30. Prog. Relig. Ideas, vol. i. p. 205, and Priestley, p. 41.
[4] Priestley, p. 42.

land of death and cold, partly, it is said, by a great flood, which is described as being like Noah's flood recorded in the Book of Genesis.[1]

The ancient *Greeks* had records of a flood which destroyed nearly the whole human race.[2] The story is as follows:

"From his throne in the high Olympos, Zeus looked down on the children of men, and saw that everywhere they followed only their lusts, and cared nothing for right or for law. And ever, as their hearts waxed grosser in their wickedness, they devised for themselves new rites to appease the anger of the gods, till the whole earth was filled with blood. Far away in the hidden glens of the Arcadian hills the sons of Lykaon feasted and spake proud words against the majesty of Zeus, and Zeus himself came down from his throne to see their way and their doings. . . . Then Zeus returned to his home on Olympos, and he gave the word that a flood of waters should be let loose upon the earth, that the sons of men might die for their great wickedness. So the west wind rose in its might, and the dark rain-clouds veiled the whole heaven, for the winds of the north which drive away the mists and vapors were shut up in their prison house. On hill and valley burst the merciless rain, and the rivers, loosened from their courses, rushed over the whole plains and up the mountain-side. From his home on the highlands of Phthia, Deukalion looked forth on the angry sky, and, when he saw the waters swelling in the valleys beneath, he called Pyrrha, his wife, and said to her: 'The time has come of which my father, the wise Prometheus, forewarned me. Make ready, therefore, the ark which I have built, and place in it all that we may need for food while the flood of waters is out upon the earth.' . . . Then Pyrrha hastened to make all things ready, and they waited till the waters rose up to the highlands of Phthia and floated away the ark of Deukalion. The fishes swam amidst the old elm-groves, and twined amongst the gnarled boughs on the oaks, while on the face of the waters were tossed the bodies of men; and Deukalion looked on the dead faces of stalwart warriors, of maidens, and of babes, as they rose and fell upon the heavy waves."

When the flood began to abate, the ark rested on Mount Parnassus, and Deucalion, with his wife Pyrrha, stepped forth upon the desolate earth. They then immediately constructed an altar, and offered up thanks to Zeus, the mighty being who sent the flood and saved them from its waters.[3]

According to Ovid (a Grecian writer born 43 B. C.), Deucalion does not venture out of the ark until a dove which he sent out returns to him with an olive branch.[4]

[1] Bunce: Fairy Tales, Origin and Meaning, p. 18.

[2] The *oldest* Greek mythology, however, has no such idea; it cannot be proved to have been known to the Greeks earlier than the 6th century B. C. (See Goldzhier: Hebrew Mytho., p. 319.) This could not have been the case had there ever been a *universal* deluge.

[3] Tales of Ancient Greece, pp. 72–74. "Apollodorus—a Grecian mythologist, born 140 B.

c.,—having mentioned Deucalion consigned to the ark, takes notice, upon his quitting it, of his offering up an immediate sacrifice to God." (Chambers' Encyclo., art. *Deluge*.)

[4] In Lundy's Monumental Christianity (p. 299, Fig. 137) may be seen a representation of Deucalion and Pyrrha landing from the ark. *A dove and olive branch* are depicted in the scene.

It was at one time extensively believed, even by intelligent scholars, that the myth of Deucalion was a corrupted tradition of the Noachian deluge, *but this untenable opinion is now all but universally abandoned.*[1]

The legend was found in the West among the Kelts. They believed that a great deluge overwhelmed the world and drowned all men except Drayan and Droyvach, who escaped in a boat, and colonized Britain. This boat was supposed to have been built by the "Heavenly Lord," and it received into it a pair of every kind of beasts.[2]

The ancient *Scandinavians* had their legend of a deluge. The *Edda* describes this deluge, from which only one man escapes, with his family, by means of a bark.[3] It was also found among the ancient Mexicans. They believed that a man named Coxcox, and his wife, survived the deluge. Lord Kingsborough, speaking of this legend,[4] informs us that the person who answered to Noah entered the ark with six others; and that the story of sending birds out of the ark, &c., is the same in general character with that of the Bible.

Dr. Brinton also speaks of the *Mexican* tradition.[5] They had not only the story of sending out the *bird*, but related that the ark landed *on a mountain*. The tradition of a deluge was also found among the Brazilians, and among many Indian tribes.[6] The mountain upon which the ark is supposed to have rested, was pointed to by the residents in nearly every quarter of the globe. The mountain-chain of Ararat was considered to be — by the *Chaldeans* and *Hebrews*—the place where the ark landed. The *Greeks* pointed to Mount Parnassus; the *Hindoos* to the Himalayas; and in Armenia numberless heights were pointed out with becoming reverence, as those on which the few survivors of the dreadful scenes of the deluge were preserved. On the Red River (in America), near the village of the Caddoes, there was an eminence to which the Indian tribes for a great distance around paid devout homage. The Cerro Naztarny on the Rio Grande, the peak of Old Zuni in New Mexico, that of Colhuacan on the Pacific coast, Mount Apoala in Upper Mixteca, and Mount Neba in the province of Guaymi, are some of many elevations asserted by the neighbor-

1 Chambers' Encyclo., art. Deucalion.
2 Baring-Gould : Legends of the Patriarchs, p. 114. See also Myths of the British Druids, p. 95.
3 See Mallet's Northern Antiquities, p. 99.
4 Mex. Antiq. vol. viii.
5 Myths of the New World, pp. 203, 204.
6 See Squire : Serpent Symbol, pp. 189, 190.

ing nations to have been places of refuge for their ancestors when the fountains of the great deep broke forth.

The question now may naturally be asked, How could such a story have originated unless there was some foundation for it?

In answer to this question we will say that we do not think such a story could have originated without some foundation for it, and that most, if not all, legends, have a basis of truth underlying the fabulous, although not always discernible. This story may have an *astronomical* basis, as some suppose,[1] or it may not. At any rate, it would be very easy to transmit by memory the fact of the *sinking* of *an island*, or that of *an earthquake*, or a *great flood*, caused by overflows of rivers, &c., which, in the course of time, would be added to, and enlarged upon, and, in this way, made into quite a lengthy tale. According to one of the most ancient accounts of the deluge, we are told that at that time "the forest trees were dashed against each other;" "the mountains were involved with smoke and flame;" that there was "fire, and smoke, and wind, which ascended in thick clouds replete with lightning." "The roaring of the ocean, whilst violently agitated with the whirling of the mountains, was like the bellowing of a mighty cloud, &c."[2]

A violent earthquake, with eruptions from volcanic mountains, and the sinking of land into the sea, would evidently produce such a scene as this. We know that at one period in the earth's history, such scenes must have been of frequent occurrence. The science of geology demonstrates this fact to us. *Local deluges* were of frequent occurrence, and that some persons may have been saved on one, or perhaps many, such occasions, by means of a raft or boat, and that they may have sought refuge on an eminence, or mountain, does not seem at all improbable.

During the *Champlain* period in the history of the world—which came after the *Glacial* period—the climate became warmer, *the continents sank*, and there were, consequently, continued *local floods* which must have destroyed considerable animal life, including man. The foundation of the deluge myth may have been laid at this time.

---

[1] Count de Volney says : " The Deluge mentioned by Jews, Chaldeans, Greeks and Indians, as having destroyed the world, are one and the same *physico-astronomical event* which is still repeated every year," and that "all those personages that figure in the Deluge of Noah and Xisuthus, are still in the celestial sphere. It was a real picture of the calendar." (Researches in Ancient Hist., p. 124.) It was on the same day that Noah is said to have shut himself up in the ark. that the priests of Egypt shut up in their sacred coffer or ark the image of Osiris, a personification of the Sun. This was on the 17th of the month Athor, in which the Sun enters the Scorpion. (See Kenrick's Egypt, vol. i. p. 410.) The history of Noah also corresponds, in some respects, with that of Bacchus, another personification of the Sun.

[2] See Maurice's Indian Antiquities, vol. ii. p. 268.

Some may suppose that this is dating the history of man to far back, making his history too remote; but such is not the case. There is every reason to believe that man existed for ages *before the Glacial epoch.* It must not be supposed that we have yet found remains of the earliest human beings; there is evidence, however, that man existed during the *Pliocene*, if not during the *Miocene* periods, when hoofed quadrupeds, and Proboscidians abounded, human remains and implements having been found mingled with remains of these animals.[1]

Charles Darwin believed that the animal called man, might have been properly called by that name at an epoch as remote as the *Eocene* period.[2] Man had probably lost his hairy covering by that time, and had begun to look human.

Prof. Draper, speaking of the antiquity of man, says:

" So far as investigations have gone, they *indisputably* refer the existence of man to a date remote from us by many *hundreds of thousands of years*," and that, " it is difficult to assign a shorter date from the last glaciation of Europe than a quarter of a million of years, *and human existence antedates that.*"[3]

Again he says:

" Recent researches give reason to believe that, under low and base grades, the existence of man can be traced back into the *Tertiary* times. He was contemporary with the Southern Elephant, the Rhinoceros-leptorhinus, the great Hippopotamus, perhaps even in the *Miocene*, contemporary with the Mastodon."[4]

[1] " In America, along with the bones of the *Mastodon* imbedded in the alluvium of the Bourbense, were found arrow-heads and other traces of the savages who had killed this member of an order no longer represented in that part of the world." (Herbert Spencer: Principles of Sociology, vol. i. p. 17.)

[2] Darwin : Descent of Man, p. 156. We think it may not be out of place to insert here what might properly be called : " *The Drama of Life*," which is as follows :

Act i.   Azoic : Conflict of Inorganic Forces.
Act ii.   Paleozoic : Age of Invertebrates.
Primary —
  Scene i. Eozoic : Enter Protozoans and Protophytes.
  " ii. Silurian : Enter the Army of Invertebrates.
  " iii. Devonian : Enter Fishes.
  " iv. Carboniferous : (Age of Coal Plants) Enter First *Air* breathers.
Act iii.   Mesozoic : Enter Reptiles.
Secondary —
  Scene i. Triassic : Enter Batrachians.
  " ii. Jurassic : Enter huge Reptiles of Sea, Land and Air.
  " iii. Cretaceous : (Age of Chalk) Enter Ammonites.
Act iv.   Cenozoic : (Age of Mammals.)
Tertiary —
  Scene i. Eocene : Enter Marine Mammals, and probably *Man.*
  " ii. Miocene : Enter Hoofed Quadrupeds.
  " iii. Pliocene : Enter Proboscidians and Edentates.
Act v.   Post Tertiary : *Positive* Age of Man.
Post Tertiary —
  Scene i. Glacial : Ice and Drift Periods.
  " ii. Champlain : *Sinking Continents ;* Warmer; Tropical Animals go *North.*
  " iii. Terrace : Rising Continents ; Colder.
  " iv. Present : Enter Science, Iconoclasts, &c., &c.

[3] Draper : Religion and Science, p. 199.   [4] Ibid. pp. 195, 196.

Prof. Huxley closes his " Evidence as to Man's Place in Nature,"
by saying :

" Where must we look for primeval man? Was the oldest *Homo Sapiens*
Pliocene or Miocene, *or yet more ancient?* . . . If any form of the doctrine
of progressive development is correct, *we must extend by long epochs the most liberal estimate that has yet been made of the antiquity of man.*"[1]

Prof. Oscar Paschel, in his work on " Mankind," speaking of
the deposits of human remains which have been discovered in
caves, mingled with the bones of wild animals, says :

" The examination of one of these caves at Brixham, by a geologist as trustworthy as Dr. Falconer, convinced the specialists of Great Britain, as early as
1858, that man was a contemporary of the Mammoth, the Woolly Rhinoceros,
the Cave-lion, the Cave-hyena, the Cave-bear, *and therefore of the Mammalia of
the Geological period antecedent to our own.*"[2]

The positive evidence of man's existence during the *Tertiary*
period, are facts which must firmly convince every one—who is
willing to be convinced—of *the great antiquity of man.* We might
multiply our authorities, but deem it unnecessary.

The observation of shells, corals, and other remains of *aquatic
animals*, in places above the level of the sea, and even on high
mountains, may have given rise to legends of a great flood.

Fossils found imbedded in high ground have been appealed to,
both in ancient and modern times, both by savage and civilized
man, as evidence in support of their traditions of a flood ; and, moreover, the argument, apparently unconnected with any tradition, is
to be found, that because there are marine fossils in places away
from the sea, *therefore the sea must once have been there.*

It is only quite recently that the presence of fossil shells, &c.,
on high mountains, has been abandoned as evidence of the
Noachic flood.

Mr. Tylor tells us that in the ninth edition of " Horne's Introduction to the Scriptures," published in 1846, the evidence of fossils
is confidently held to prove the universality of the Deluge ; *but the
argument disappears from the next edition, published ten years
later.*[3]

Besides fossil remains of aquatic animals, *boats* have been found
on tops of mountains.[4] A discovery of this kind may have given
rise to the story of an *ark* having been made in which to preserve
the favored ones from the waters, and of its landing on a mountain.[5]

[1] Huxley : Man's Place in Nature, p. 184.
[2] Paschel : Races of Man, p. 36.
[3] Tylor : Early History of Mankind, p. 328.
[4] Ibid. pp. 329, 330

[5] We know that many legends have originated in this way. For example, Dr. Robinson,
in his " Travels in Palestine " (ii. 586), mentions a tradition that a city had once stood in a

Before closing this chapter, it may be well to notice a striking incident in the legend we have been treating, *i. e.*, the frequent occurrence of the number *seven* in the narrative. For instance: the Lord commands Noah to take into the ark clean beasts by *sevens*, and fowls also by *sevens*, and tells him that in *seven* days he will cause it to rain upon the earth. We are also told that the ark rested in the *seventh* month, and the *seventeenth* day of the month, upon the mountains of Ararat. After sending the dove out of the ark the first time, Noah waited *seven* days before sending it out again. After sending the dove out the second time, "he stayed yet another *seven* days" ere he again sent forth the dove.

This coincidence arises from the mystic power attached to the number seven, derived from its frequent occurrence in astrology.

We find that in *all religions* of antiquity the number *seven*—which applied to the *sun, moon* and the *five planets* known to the ancients—is a *sacred number*, represented in all kinds and sorts of forms;[1] for instance: The candlestick with *seven* branches in the temple of Jerusalem. The *seven* inclosures of the temple. The *seven* doors of the cave of Mithras. The *seven* stories of the tower of Babylon.[2] The *seven* gates of Thebes.[3] The flute of *seven* pipes generally put into the hand of the god Pan. The lyre of *seven* strings touched by Apollo. The book of "Fate," composed of *seven* books. The *seven* prophetic rings of the Brahmans.[4] The *seven* stones—consecrated to the *seven* planets—in Laconia.[5] The division into *seven* castes adopted by the Egyptians and Indians. The *seven* idols of the Bonzes. The *seven* altars of the monument of Mithras. The *seven* great spirits invoked by the Persians. The *seven* archangels of the Chaldeans. The *seven* archangels of the Jews.[6]

desert between Petra and Hebron, the people of which had perished for their vices, and been converted into stone. Mr. Seetzen, who went to the spot, found no traces of ruins, but a number of stony concretions, resembling in form and size the human head. *They had been ignorantly supposed to be petrified heads, and a legend framed to account for their owners suffering so terrible a fate.* Another illustration is as follows:—The Kamchadals believe that volcanic mountains are the abode of devils, who, after they have cooked their meals, fling the fire-brands out of the chimney. Being asked what these devils eat, they said "*whales.*" Here we see, *first*, a story invented to account for the volcanic eruptions from the mountains; and, *second*, a story invented to account for the *remains of whales found on the mountains.* The savages *knew* that this was true, "because their old people had said so, and believed it themselves." (Related by Mr. Tylor, in his "*Early History of Mankind,*" p. 326.)

[1] "Everything of importance was calculated by, and fitted into, this number (SEVEN) by the Aryan philosophers,—ideas as well as localities." (Isis Unveiled, vol. ii. p. 407.)

[2] Each one being consecrated to a *planet.* First, to Saturn; second, to Jupiter; third, to Mars; fourth, to the Sun; fifth, to Venus; sixth, to Mercury; seventh, to the Moon. (The Pentateuch Examined, vol. iv. p. 269. See also The Angel Messiah, p. 105.)

[3] Each of which had the name of a *planet.*

[4] On each of which the name of a *planet* was engraved.

[5] "There was to be seen in Laconia, *seven* columns erected in honor of the *seven planets.*" (Dupuis: Origin of Religious Belief, p. 34.)

[6] "The Jews believed that the Throne of Jehovah was surrounded by his *seven* high

The *seven* days in the week.[1]   The *seven* sacraments of the Christians.   The *seven* wicked spirits of the Babylonians.   The sprinkling of blood *seven* times upon the altars of the Egyptians.   The *seven* mortal sins of the Egyptians.   The hymn of *seven* vowels chanted by the Egyptian priests.[2]   The *seven* branches of the Assyrian "Tree of Life."   Agni, the the Hindoo god, is represented with *seven* arms.   Sura's[3] horse was represented with *seven* heads. *Seven* churches are spoken of in the Apocalypse.   Balaam builded *seven* altars, and offered *seven* bullocks and *seven* rams on each altar.   Pharaoh saw *seven* kine, &c., in his dream.   The " Priest of Midian " had *seven* daughters.   Jacob served *seven* years.   Before Jericho *seven* priests bare *seven* horns.   Samson was bound with *seven* green withes, and his marriage feast lasted *seven* days, &c., &c.   We might continue with as much more, but enough has been shown to verify the statement that, " in all religions of antiquity, the number SEVEN is a *sacred* number."

---

chiefs : Gabriel, Michael, Raphael, Uriel, &c."
(Bible for Learners, vol. iii. p. 46.)

[1] Each one being consecrated to a planet, and the Sun and Moon.   Sunday, " *Dies Solis*," sacred to the SUN.   Monday, " Dies Lunae," sacred to the MOON.   Tuesday, sacred to Tuiso or MARS.   Wednesday, sacred to Odin or Woden, and to MERCURY.   Thursday, sacred to Thor and others.   Friday, sacred to Freia and

VENUS.   Saturday, sacred to SATURN.   " The (ancient) Egyptians assigned a day of the week to the SUN, MOON, and five planets, and the number SEVEN was held there in great reverence."   (Kenrick : Egypt, i. 238.)

[2] " The Egyptian priests chanted the *seven* vowels as a hymn addressed to *Serapis*."   (The Rosicrucians, p. 143.)

[3] *Sura :* the Sun-god of the Hindoos.

CHAPTER III.

THE TOWER OF BABEL.

WE are informed that, at one time, "the whole earth was of one language, and of one speech. And it came to pass, as they (the inhabitants of the earth) journeyed from the East, that they found a plain in the land of Shinar, and they dwelt there.

"And they said one to another, Go to, let us make brick, and burn them thoroughly. And they had brick for stone, and slime had they for mortar.

"And they said, Go to, let us build us a city, and a tower, *whose top may reach unto heaven*, and let us make us a name, lest we be scattered abroad upon the face of the whole earth. *And the Lord came down to see the city and the tower*, which the children of men builded. And the Lord said, Behold, the people is one, and they have all one language ; and this they begin to do : and now nothing will be restrained from them, which they have imagined to do. Go to, *let us go down*, and there confound their language, that they may not understand one another's speech. So the Lord scattered them abroad from thence upon the face of all the earth : and they left off to build the city. Therefore is the name of it called *Babel*, because the Lord did there confound the language of all the earth ; and from thence did the Lord scatter them abroad upon the face of all the earth."[1]

Such is the "Scripture" account of the origin of languages, which differs somewhat from the ideas of Prof. Max Müller and other philologists.

Bishop Colenso tells us that :

"The story of the dispensation of tongues is connected by the Jehovistic writer with the famous unfinished temple of *Belus*, of which probably some wonderful reports had reached him. . . . The derivation of the name *Babel* from the Hebrew word *babal* (confound) which seems to be the connecting point between the story and the tower of Babel, *is altogether incorrect*."[2]

---

[1] Genesis xi. 1–9.　　　　[2] The Pentateuch Examined, vol. iv. p. 268.

The literal meaning of the word being *house*, or *court*, or *gate* of Bel, or gate of God.[1]

John Fiske confirms this statement by saying:

"The name '*Babel*' is really '*Bab-il*,' or '*The Gate of God ;*' but the Hebrew writer *erroneously* derives the word from the root '*babal*'—to confuse—and hence arises the *mystical explanation*, that Babel was a place where human speech became confused."[2]

The "wonderful reports" that reached the Jehovistic writer who inserted this tale into the Hebrew Scriptures, were from the Chaldean account of the confusion of tongues. It is related by *Berosus* as follows:

The first inhabitants of the earth, glorying in their strength and size,[3] and despising the gods, undertook to raise a tower whose top should reach the sky, in the place where Babylon now stands. But when it approached the heavens, the winds assisted the gods, and overthrew the work of the contrivers, and also introduced a diversity of tongues among men, who till that time had all spoken the same language. The ruins of this tower are said to be still in Babylon.[4]

Josephus, the Jewish historian, says that it was *Nimrod* who built the tower, that he was a very wicked man, and that the tower was built in case the Lord should have a mind to drown the world again. He continues his account by saying that when Nimrod proposed the building of this tower, the multitude were very ready to follow the proposition, as they could then avenge themselves on God for destroying their forefathers.

"And they built a tower, neither sparing any pains nor being in any degree negligent about the work. And by reason of the multitude of hands employed on it, it grew very high, sooner than any one could expect. . . . . It was built of burnt brick, cemented together, with mortar made of bitumen, that it might not be liable to admit water. When God saw that they had acted so madly, he did not resolve to destroy them utterly, *since they were not grown wiser by the destruction of the former sinners,* but he caused a tumult among them, by producing in them divers languages, and causing, that through the multitude of those languages they should not be able to understand one another. The place where they built the tower is now called Babylon."[5]

The tower in Babylonia, which seems to have been a foundation for the legend of the confusion of tongues to be built upon, was

[1] Ibid. p. 268. See also Bible for Learners, vol. i. p. 90.

[2] Myths and Myth-makers, p. 72. See also Encyclopædia Britannica, art. "Babel."

[3] "There were *giants* in the earth in those days." (Genesis vi. 4.)

[4] Quoted by Rev. S. Baring-Gould : Legends of the Patriarchs, p. 147. See also Smith : Chaldean Account of Genesis, p. 48, and Volney's Researches in Ancient History, pp. 130, 131.

[5] Jewish Antiquities, book 1, ch. iv. p. 30.

evidently originally built for *astronomical purposes.*[1] This is clearly seen from the fact that it was called the "Stages of the Seven Spheres,"[2] and that each one of these stages was consecrated to the Sun, Moon, Saturn, Jupiter, Mars, Venus, and Mercury.[3] Nebuchadnezzar says of it in his *cylinders :*

"The building named the 'Stages of the Seven Spheres,' which was the tower of Borsippa (Babel), had been built by a former king. He had completed forty-two cubits, but he did not finish its head. From the lapse of time, it had become ruined; they had not taken care of the exits of the waters, so the rain and wet had penetrated into the brick-work; the casing of burnt brick had bulged out, and the terraces of crude brick lay scattered in heaps. Merobach, my great Lord, inclined my heart to repair the building. I did not change its site, nor did I destroy its foundation, but, in a fortunate month, and upon an auspicious day, I undertook the rebuilding of the crude brick terraces and burnt brick casing, &c., &c."[4]

There is not a word said here in these cylinders about the confusion of tongues, nor anything pertaining to it. The ruins of this ancient tower being there in Babylonia, and a legend of how the gods confused the speech of mankind also being among them, it was very convenient to point to these ruins as evidence that the story was true, just as the ancient Mexicans pointed to the ruins of the tower of Cholula, as evidence of the truth of the similar story which they had among them, and just as many nations pointed to the remains of aquatic animals on the tops of mountains, as evidence of the truth of the deluge story.

The *Armenian* tradition of the "Confusion of Tongues" was to this effect :

The world was formerly inhabited by men "with strong bodies and huge size" (giants). These men being full of pride and envy, "they formed a godless resolve to build a high tower ; but whilst they were engaged on the undertaking, a fearful wind overthrew it, which the wrath of God had sent against it. *Unknown words were at the same time blown about among men,* wherefore arose strife and confusion."[5]

The *Hindoo* legend of the "Confusion of Tongues," is as follows : There grew in the centre of the earth, the wonderful " *World*

[1] "Diodorus states that the great tower of the temple of Belus was used by the Chaldeans as an *observatory.*" (Smith's Bible Dictionary, art. "Babel.")

[2] The Hindoos had a sacred *Mount Meru,* the abode of the gods. This mountain was supposed to consist of *seven stages,* increasing in sanctity as they ascended. Many of the Hindoo temples, or rather altars, were "studied transcripts of the sacred Mount Meru ;" that is, they were built, like the tower of Babel, in *seven stages.* Within the upper dwelt Brahm. (See Squire's Serpent Symbol, p. 107.) Herodotus tells us that the upper stage of the tower of Babel was the abode of the god Belus.

[3] The Pentateuch Examined, vol. iv. p. 269. See also Bunsen : The Angel Messiah, p. 106.

[4] Rawlinson's Herodotus, vol. ii. p. 484.

[5] Legends of the Patriarchs, pp. 148, 149.

Tree," or the "*Knowledge Tree.*" It was so tall that it reached almost to heaven. "It said in its heart: 'I shall hold my head in heaven, and spread my branches over all the earth, and gather all men together under my shadow, and protect them, and prevent them from separating.' But Brahma, to punish the pride of the tree, cut off its branches and cast them down on the earth, when they sprang up as *Wata trees, and made differences of belief, and speech, and customs*, to prevail on the earth, to disperse men over its surface."[1]

Traces of a somewhat similar story have also been met with among the *Mongolian Tharus* in the north of India, and, according to Dr. Livingston, among the Africans of Lake *Nganu*.[2] The ancient *Esthonians*[3] had a similar myth which they called "The Cooking of Languages;" so also had the ancient inhabitants of the continent of *Australia*.[4] The story was found among the ancient Mexicans, and was related as follows:

Those, with their descendants, who were saved from the deluge which destroyed all mankind, excepting the few saved in the ark, resolved to build a tower which would reach to the skies. The object of this was to see what was going on in Heaven, and also to have a place of refuge in case of another deluge.[5]

The job was superintended by one of the *seven* who were saved from the flood.[6] He was a *giant* called Xelhua, surnamed "the Architect."[7]

Xelhua ordered bricks to be made in the province of Tlamanalco, at the foot of the Sierra of Cocotl, and to be conveyed to *Cholula*, where the tower was to be built. For this purpose, he placed a file of men reaching from the Sierra to Cholula, who passed the bricks from hand to hand.[8] The gods beheld with wrath this edifice,— the top of which was nearing the clouds,—and were much irritated at the daring attempt of Xelhua. They therefore hurled fire from Heaven upon the pyramid, which threw it down, and killed many of the workmen. The work was then discontinued,[9] as each family interested in the building of the tower, *received a language of their own*,[10] and the builders could not understand each other.

[1] Ibid. p. 148. The ancient *Scandinavians* had a legend of a somewhat similar tree. "The Mundane Tree," called *Yggdrasill*, was in the centre of the earth; its branches covered over the surface of the earth, and its top reached to the highest heaven. (See Mallet's Northern Antiquities.)

[2] Encyclopædia Britannica, art. "Babel."

[3] *Esthonia* is one of the three Baltic, or so-called, provinces of Russia.

[4] Encyclopædia Britannica, art. "Babel."

[5] Higgins: Anacalypsis, vol. ii. p. 27.

[6] Brinton: Myths of the New World, p. 204.

[7] Humboldt: American Researches, vol. i. p. 96.

[8] Ibid.

[9] Ibid, and Brinton: Myths of the New World, p. 204.

[10] The Pentateuch Examined, vol. iv. p. 272.

Dr. Delitzsch must have been astonished upon coming across this legend; for he says :

" *Actually* the Mexicans had a legend of a *tower-building* as well as of a *flood.* Xelhua, one of the *seven giants* rescued from the flood, built the great pyramid of Cholula, in order to reach heaven, until the gods, angry at his audacity, threw fire upon the building and broke it down, whereupon every separate family received a language of its own."[1]

The ancient Mexicans pointed to the ruins of a tower at Cholula as evidence of the truth of their story. This tower was seen by Humboldt and Lord Kingsborough, and described by them.[2]

We may say then, with Dr. Kalisch, that :

" Most of the ancient nations possessed myths concerning impious giants who attempted to storm heaven, either to share it with the immortal gods, or to expel them from it. In some of these fables *the confusion of tongues* is represented as the punishment inflicted by the deities for such wickedness."[3]

---

[1] Quoted by Bishop Colenso: The Pentateuch Examined, vol. iv. p. 272.

[2] Humboldt: American Researches, vol. i. p. 97. Lord Kingsborough: Mexican Antiquities.

[3] Com. on Old Test. vol. i. p. 196.

CHAPTER IV.

THE TRIAL OF ABRAHAM'S FAITH.

THE story of the trial of Abraham's faith—when he is ordered by the Lord to sacrifice his only son Isaac—is to be found in Genesis xxii, 1-19, and is as follows:

"And it came to pass . . . that God did tempt Abraham, and said unto him: ' Abraham,' and he said: 'Behold, here I am.' And he (God) said: 'Take now thy son, thine only son, Isaac, whom thou lovest, and get thee into the land of Moriah, and offer him there for a burnt offering upon one of the mountains which I will tell thee of.'

"And Abraham rose up early in the morning, and saddled his ass, and took two of his young men with him, and Isaac his son, and clave the wood for the burnt offering, and rose up and went into the place which God had told him. . . . (When Abraham was near the appointed place) he said unto his young men: ' Abide ye here with the ass, and I and the lad will go yonder and worship, and come again to thee. And Abraham took the wood for the burnt offering, and laid it upon (the shoulders of) Isaac his son, and he took the fire in his hand, and a knife, and they went both of them together. And Isaac spake unto Abraham his father, and said: 'Behold the fire and the wood, but where is the lamb for the burnt offering?' And Abraham said: 'My son, God will provide himself a lamb for a burnt offering.' So they went both of them together, and they came to the place which God had told him of. And Abraham built an altar there, and laid the wood in order. and bound Isaac his son, and laid him on the altar upon the wood. And Abraham stretched forth his hand, and took the knife to slay his son. And the angel of the Lord called unto him out of heaven, and said: ' Abraham ! Abraham! lay not thine hand upon the lad, neither do thou anything unto him, for now I know that thou fearest God, seeing that thou hast not withheld thy son, thine only son from me.'

"And Abraham lifted up his eyes, and looked, and behold behind him a ram caught in a thicket by his horns, and Abraham went and took the ram, and offered him up for a burnt offering in the stead of his son. . . . And the angel of the Lord called unto Abraham, out of heaven, the second time, and said: ' By myself have I *sworn* saith the Lord, for because thou hast done this thing, and hast not withheld thy son. thine only son, . . . I will bless thee, and . . . I will multiply thy seed as the stars in the heaven, and as the sand which is upon the sea shore, and thy seed shall possess the gate of his enemies. And in thy seed shall all the nations of the earth be blest, because thou hast obeyed my voice.' So Abraham returned unto his young men, and they rose up and went together to Beer-sheba, and Abraham dwelt at Beer-sheba."

[38]

There is a Hindoo story related in the Sânkhâyana-sûtras, which, in substance, is as follows: King Hariscandra had no son ; he then prayed to Varuna, promising, that if a son were born to him, he would sacrifice the child to the god. Then a son was born to him, called Rohita. When Rohita was grown up his father one day told him of the vow he had made to Varuna, and bade him prepare to be sacrificed. The son objected to being killed and ran away from his father's house. For six years he wandered in the forest, and at last met a starving Brahman. Him he persuaded to sell one of his sons named Sunahsepha, for a hundred cows. This boy was bought by Rohita and taken to Hariscandra and about to be sacrificed to Varuna as a substitute for Rohita, when, on praying to the gods with verses from the Veda, he was released by them.'

There was an ancient *Phenician* story, written by Sanchoniathon, who wrote about 1300 years before our era, which is as follows:

"Saturn, whom the Phœnicians call *Israel*, had by a nymph of the country a *male* child whom he named Jeoud, that is, *one and only*. On the breaking out of a war, which brought the country into imminent danger, Saturn erected an altar, brought to it his son, clothed in royal garments, and sacrificed him."²

There is also a *Grecian* fable to the effect that one Agamemnon had a daughter whom he dearly loved, and she was deserving of his affection. He was commanded by God, through the Delphic Oracle, *to offer her up as a sacrifice.* Her father long resisted the demand, but finally succumbed. Before the fatal blow had been struck, however, the goddess Artemis or Ashtoreth interfered, and carried the maiden away, whilst in her place was substituted a stag.³

Another similar *Grecian* fable relates that:

"When the Greek army was detained at Aulis, by contrary winds, the augurs being consulted, declared that one of the kings had offended Diana, and she demanded the sacrifice of his daughter Iphigenia. It was like taking the father's life-blood, but he was persuaded that it was his duty to submit for the good of his country. The maiden was brought forth for sacrifice, in spite of her tears and supplications; but just as the priest was about to strike the fatal blow, Iphigenia suddenly disappeared, and a goat of uncommon beauty stood in her place."⁴

There is yet still another, which belongs to the same country, and is related thus:

"In *Sparta*, it being declared upon one occasion that the gods demanded a human victim, the choice was made by lot, and fell on a damsel named Helena.

¹ See Müller's Hist. Sanscrit Literature; and Williams' Indian Wisdom, p. 29.
² Quoted by Count de Volney: New Researches in Anc't Hist., p. 144.
³ See Inman's Ancient Faiths, vol. ii. p. 104.
⁴ Prog. Relig. Ideas, vol. i. p. 302,

But when all was in readiness, an eagle descended, carried away the priest's knife, and laid it on the head of a heifer, which was sacrificed in her stead."[1]

The story of Abraham and Isaac was written at a time when the Mosaic party in Israel was endeavoring to abolish idolatry among their people. They were offering up *human sacrifices* to their gods Moloch, Baal, and Chemosh, and the priestly author of this story was trying to make the people think that the Lord had abolished such offerings, as far back as the time of Abraham. The Grecian legends, which he had evidently heard, may have given him the idea.[2]

Human offerings to the gods were at one time almost universal. In the earliest ages the offerings were simple, and such as shepherds and rustics could present. They loaded the altars of the gods with the first fruits of their crops, and the choicest products of the earth. Afterwards they sacrificed animals. When they had once laid it down as a principle that the effusion of the blood of these animals appeased the anger of the gods, and that their justice turned aside upon the victims those strokes which were destined for men, their great care was for nothing more than to conciliate their favor by so easy a method. It is the nature of violent desires and excessive fear to know no bounds, and therefore, when they would ask for any favor which they ardently wished for, or would deprecate some public calamity which they feared, the blood of animals was not deemed a price sufficient, but they began to shed that of men. It is probable, as we have said, that this barbarous practice was formerly almost universal, and that it is of very remote antiquity. In time of war the captives were chosen for this purpose, but in time of peace they took the slaves. The choice was partly regulated by the opinion of the bystanders, and partly by lot. But they did not always sacrifice such mean persons. In great calamities, in a pressing famine, for example, if the people thought they had some pretext to impute the cause of it to their *king*, they even sacrificed him without hesitation, as the *highest price* with which they could purchase the Divine favor. In this manner, the first King of Vermaland (a province of Sweden) was burnt in honor of Odin, the Supreme God, to put an end to a great dearth; as we read in the history of Norway. The kings, in their turn, did not spare the blood of their subjects; and many of them even shed that of their children. Earl Hakon, of Norway, offered his son in sacrifice, to obtain of Odin the victory over the Jomsburg pirates. Aun, King of Sweden,

---

[1] Ibid.   [2] See chapter xi.

devoted to Odin the blood of his nine sons, to prevail on that god to prolong his life. Some of the kings of Israel offered up their first-born sons as a sacrifice to the god Baal or Moloch.

The altar of Moloch reeked with blood. Children were sacrificed and burned in the fire to him, while trumpets and flutes drowned their screams, and the mothers looked on, and were bound to restrain their tears.

The *Phenicians* offered to the gods, in times of war and drought, the fairest of their children. The books of Sanchoniathon and Byblian Philo are full of accounts of such sacrifices. In Byblos boys were immolated to Adonis; and, on the founding of a city or colony, a sacrifice of a vast number of children was solemnized, in the hopes of thereby averting misfortune from the new settlement. The Phenicians, according to Eusebius, yearly sacrificed their dearest, and even their only children, to Saturn. The bones of the victims were preserved in the temple of Moloch, in a golden ark, which was carried by the Phenicians with them to war.[1] Like the Fijians of the present day, those people considered their gods as beings like themselves. They loved and they hated; they were proud and revengeful, they were, in fact, savages like themselves.

If the eldest born of the family of Athamas entered the temple of the Laphystian Jupiter, at Alos, in Achaia, he was sacrificed, crowned with garlands, like an animal victim.[2]

The offering of human sacrifices to the Sun was extensively practiced in Mexico and Peru, before the establishment of Christianity.[3]

---

[1] Baring-Gould: Orig. Relig. Belief, vol. i. p. 368.

[2] Kenrick's Egypt, vol. i. p. 443.

[3] See Acosta: Hist. Indies, vol. ii.

CHAPTER V.

JACOB'S VISION OF THE LADDER.

In the 28th chapter of Genesis, we are told that Isaac, after blessing his son Jacob, sent him to Padan-aram, to take a daughter of Laban's (his mother's brother) to wife. Jacob, obeying his father, "went out from Beer-sheba (where he dwelt), and went towards Haran. And he lighted upon a certain place, and tarried there all night, because the sun was set. And he took of the stones of the place, and put them for his pillow, and lay down in that place to sleep. And he dreamed, and behold, a *ladder* set upon the earth, and the top of it reached to heaven. *And he beheld the angels of God ascending and descending on it.* And, behold, the Lord stood above it, and said : ' I am the Lord God of Abraham thy father, and the God of Isaac, the land whereon thou liest, to thee will I give it, and to thy seed.' . . . . And Jacob awoke out of his sleep, and he said : ' Surely the Lord is in this place, and I know it not.' And he was afraid, and said : ' How dreadful is this place, *this is none other than the house of God, and this is the gate of Heaven.'* And Jacob rose up early in the morning, *and took the stone that he had put for his pillow, and set it up for a pillar, and poured oil upon the top of it.* And he called the name of that place *Beth-el.*"

The doctrine of Metempsychosis has evidently something to do with this legend. It means, in the theological acceptation of the term, the supposed transition of the soul after death, into another substance or body than that which it occupied before. The belief in such a transition was common to the most civilized, and the most uncivilized, nations of the earth.[1]

It was believed in, and taught by, the *Brahminical Hindoos,*[2] the *Buddhists,*[3] the natives of *Egypt,*[4] several philosophers of

---

[1] See Chambers's Encyclo., art. "Transmigration."

[2] Chambers's Encyclo., art. "Transmigration." Prichard's Mythology, p. 213, and Prog. Relig. Ideas, vol. i. p. 59.

[3] Ibid. Ernest de Bunsen says : "The first traces of the doctrine of Transmigration of souls is to be found among the Brahmins and Buddhists." (The Angel Messiah, pp. 63, 64.)

[4] Prichard's Mythology, pp. 213, 214.

ancient *Greece*,[1] the ancient *Druids*,[2] the natives of *Madagascar*,[3] several tribes of *Africa*,[3] and *North America*,[3] the ancient *Mexi cans*,[3] and by some *Jewish* and *Christian* sects.[3]

[3] It deserves notice, that in both of these religions (*i. e.*, *Jewish* and *Christian*), it found adherents as well in ancient as in modern times. Among the *Jews*, the doctrine of transmigration—the Gilgul Neshamoth—was taught in the mystical system of the *Kabbala*."[5]

"All the souls," the spiritual code of this system says, "are subject to the trials of transmigration; and men do not know which are the ways of the Most High in their regard." "The principle, in short, of the *Kabbala*, is the same as that of *Brahmanism*."

"On the ground of this doctrine, which was shared in by Rabbis of the highest renown, it was held, for instance, that the soul of *Adam* migrated into *David*, and will come in the *Messiah ;* that the soul of *Japhet* is the same as that of *Simeon*, and the soul of *Terah*, migrated into *Job*."

"Of all these transmigrations, biblical instances are adduced according to their mode of interpretation—in the writings of Rabbi Manasse ben Israel, Rabbi Naphtali, Rabbi Meyer ben Gabbai, Rabbi Ruben, in the Jalkut Khadash, and other works of a similar character."[4]

The doctrine is thus described by Ovid, in the language of Dryden :

> " What feels the body when the soul expires,
> By time corrupted, or consumed by fires ?
> Nor dies the spirit, but new life repeats
> Into other forms, and only changes seats.
> Ev'n I, who these mysterious truths declare,
> Was once Euphorbus in the Trojan war ;
> My name and lineage I remember well,
> And how in fight by Spartan's King I fell.
> In Argive Juno's fane I late beheld
> My buckler hung on high, and own'd my former shield
> Then death, so called, is but old matter dressed
> In some new figure, and a varied vest.
> Thus all things are but alter'd, nothing dies,
> And here and there the unbodied spirit flies."

The Jews undoubtedly learned this doctrine after they had been subdued by, and become acquainted with other nations ; and the writer of this story, whoever he may have been, was evidently endeavoring to strengthen the belief in this doctrine—he being an advocate of it—by inventing this story, *and making Jacob a witness to the truth of it.* · Jacob would have been looked upon at the time the story was written (*i e.*, after the Babylonian captivity),

---

[1] Gross : The Heathen Religion. Also Chambers's Encyclo., art. "Transmigration."
[2] Ibid. Mallet's Northern Antiquities, p. 13; and Myths of the British Druids, p. 15
[3] Chambers's Encyclo.
[4] Ibid.

[5] Ibid. See also Bunsen : The Angel-Messiah, pp. 63, 64. Dupuis, p. 357. Josephus : Jewish Antiquities, book xviii. ch. 13. Dunlap : Son of the Man, p. 94 ; and Beal : Hist. Buddha.
[6] Chambers, art. "Transmigration."

as of great authority. We know that several writers of portions of the Old Testament have written for similar purposes. As an illustration, we may mention the book of *Esther*. This book was written for the purpose of explaining the origin of the festival of *Purim*, and *to encourage the Israelites to adopt it.* The writer, *who was an advocate of the feast,* lived long after the Babylonish captivity, and is quite unknown.[1]

The writer of the seventeenth chapter of Matthew has made Jesus a teacher of the doctrine of Transmigration.

The Lord had promised that he would send Elijah (Elias) the prophet, "before the coming of the great and dreadful day of the Lord,"[2] and Jesus is made to say that he had already come, or, *that his soul had transmigrated unto the body of John the Baptist,* and they knew it not.[3]

And in Mark (viii. 27) we are told that Jesus asked his disciples, saying unto them; "Whom do men say that *I* am?" whereupon they answer: "Some say Elias; and others, one of the prophets;" or, in other words, that the soul of Elias, or one of the prophets, had transmigrated into the body of Jesus. In John (ix. 1, 2), we are told that Jesus and his disciples seeing a man "*which was blind from his birth,*" the disciples asked him, saying; "Master, who did sin, *this man* (in some former state) or his parents." Being *born* blind, how else could he sin, *unless in some former state?* These passages result from the fact, which we have already noticed, that some of the Jewish and Christian sects believed in the doctrine of Metempsychosis.

According to some Jewish authors, *Adam* was re-produced in *Noah, Elijah,* and other Bible celebrities.[4]

The Rev. Mr. Faber says:

"Adam, and Enoch, and Noah, might in outward appearance be *different* men, but they were really the *self-same* divine persons who had been promised as the seed of the woman, successively animating various human bodies."[5]

We have stated as our belief that the vision which the writer of the twenty-eighth chapter of Genesis has made Jacob to witness, was intended to strengthen the belief in the doctrine of the Metempsychosis, that he was simply seeing the souls of men ascending and descending from heaven *on a ladder,* during their transmigrations.

We will now give our reasons for thinking so.

The learned Thomas Maurice tells us that:

---

[1] See The Religion of Israel, p. 18.
[2] Malachi iv. 5.
[3] Matthew xvii. 12, 13.
[4] See Bonwick: Egyptian Belief, p. 78.
[5] Faber: Orig. Pagan Idol, vol. iii. p. 612; in Anacalypsis, vol. i. p. 210.

The *Indians* had, in remote ages, in their system of theology, *the sidereal ladder of seven gates*, which described, in a symbolical manner, the *ascending and descending of the souls of men.*[1]

We are also informed by Origen that:

This descent (*i. e.*, the descent of souls from heaven to enter into some body), was described in a symbolical manner, *by a ladder which was represented as reaching from heaven to earth*, and divided into *seven* stages, at each of which was figured a gate; the eighth gate was at the top of the ladder, which belonged to the sphere of the celestial firmament.[2]

That souls dwell in the *Galaxy* was a thought familiar to the *Pythagoreans*, who gave it on their master's word, that the souls that crowd there, *descend and appear to men as dreams.*[3]

The fancy of the *Manicheans* also transferred pure souls to this column of light, *whence they could come down to earth and again return.*[4]

Paintings representing a scene of this kind may be seen in works of art illustrative of *Indian Mythology.*

Maurice speaks of one, in which he says:

" The souls of men are represented as ascending and descending (on a ladder). according to the received opinion of the sidereal Metempsychosis in Asia."[5]

Mons. Dupuis tells us that:

" Among the mysterious pictures of the *Initiation*, in the cave of the Persian God Mithras, there was exposed to the view *the descent of the souls to the earth, and their return to heaven*, through the seven planetary spheres."[6]

And Count de Volney says:

" In the cave of Mithra *was a ladder with seven steps*, representing the seven spheres of the planets by means of which *souls ascended and descended*. This is precisely the ladder of Jacob's vision. There is in the Royal Library (of France) a superb volume of pictures of the Indian gods, in which the ladder is represented with the souls of men ascending it."[7]

In several of the Egyptian sculptures also, the Transmigration of Souls is represented by the ascending and descending of souls from heaven to earth, *on a flight of steps*, and, as the souls of wicked men were supposed to enter pigs and other animals, therefore pigs, monkeys, &c., are to be seen on the steps, descending from heaven.[8]

" And he dreamed, *and behold a ladder set up on the earth, and the top of it reached to heaven ; and behold the angels of God ascending and descending on it.*"

[1] Indian Antiquities, vol. ii. p. 262.
[2] Contra Celsus, lib. vi. c. xxii.
[3] Tylor: Primitive Culture, vol. i. p. 824.
[4] Ibid.
[5] Indian Antiqities, vol. ii. p. 262.
[6] Dupuis: Origin of Religious Beliefs, p. 344.
[7] Volney's Ruins, p. 147, *note*.
[8] See Child's Prog Relig. Ideas, vol. I. pp. 160. 162.

These are the words of the sacred text.   Can anything be more convincing?   It continues thus:

> "And Jacob awoke out of his sleep . . .   and he was afraid, and said . . . this is none other but the house of God, *and this is the gate of heaven.*"

Here we have "the gate of heaven," mentioned by Origen in describing the *Metempsychosis.*

According to the ancients, the *top* of this ladder was supposed to reach *the throne* of *the most high God.*   This corresponds exactly with the vision of Jacob.   The ladder which he is made to see reached unto heaven, *and the Lord stood above it.*[1]

> "And Jacob rose up early in the morning, and took the *stone* that he had put for his pillow, *and set it up for a pillar, and poured oil upon the top of it.*"[2]

This concluding portion to the story has evidently an allusion to *Phallic*[3] worship.   There is scarcely a nation of antiquity which did not set up these stones (as emblems of the reproductive power of nature) and worship them.   Dr. Oort, speaking of this, says:

Few forms of worship were so universal in ancient times as the homage paid to sacred stones.   In the history of the religion of even the most civilized peoples, such as the Greeks, Romans, Hindoos, Arabs and Germans, we find traces of this form of worship.[4]   The ancient *Druids* of Britain also worshiped sacred stones, which were *set up on end.*[5]

Pausanias, an eminent Greek historian, says:

> "The *Hermiac* statue, which they venerate in Cyllenê above other *symbols,* is an erect *Phallus* on a pedestal."[6]

This was nothing more than a smooth, oblong *stone,* set erect on a flat one.[7]

The learned Dr. Ginsburg, in his "Life of Levita," alludes to the ancient mode of worship offered to the heathen deity Hermes, or Mercury.   A "Hermes" (*i. e.,* a *stone*) was frequently set up on the road-side, and each traveller, as he passed by, paid his homage to the deity by either throwing a stone on the heap (which was thus collected), or by *anointing* it.   This "Hermes" was the symbol of Phallus.[8]

---

[1] Genesis xxviii. 12, 13.
[2] Genesis xxviii. 18, 19.
[3] "Phallic," from "Phallus," a representation of the male generative organs. For further information on this subject, see the works of R. Payne Knight, and Dr. Thomas Inman.
[4] Bible for Learners, vol., i. pp. 175, 276. See, also, Knight: Ancient Art and Mythology; and Inman: Ancient Faiths, vol. i. and ii.
[5] See Myths of the British Druids, p. 300; and Higgins: Celtic Druids.
[6] Quoted by R. Payne Knight: Ancient Art and Mythology, p. 114, *note.*
[7] See Illustrations in Dr. Inman's Pagan and Christian Symbolism.
[8] See Inman: Ancient Faiths, vol. i. pp. 543, 544.

Now, when we find that *this form of worship was very prevalent among the Israelites*,[1] that these sacred stones which were "set up," were called (by the heathen), BÆTY-LI,[2] (which is not unlike BETH-EL), and that *they were anointed with oil*,[3] I think we have reasons for believing that the story of Jacob's *setting up* a stone, *pouring oil upon it*, and calling the place *Beth-el*, "has evidently an allusion to Phallic worship."[4]

The male and female powers of nature were denoted respectively by an upright and an oval emblem, and the conjunction of the two furnished at once the altar and the *Ashera*, or grove, against which the Hebrew prophets lifted up their voices in earnest protest. In the kingdoms, both of Judah and Israel, the rites connected with these emblems assumed their most corrupting form. Even in the temple itself, stood the *Ashera*, or the upright emblem, on the circular altar of Baal-Peor, the Priapos of the Jews, thus reproducing the *Linga* and *Yoni* of the Hindu.[5] For this symbol, the women wove hangings, as the Athenian maidens embroidered the sacred peplos for the ship presented to Athênê, at the great Dionysiac festival. This *Ashera*, which, in the authorized English version of the Old Testament is translated "*grove*," was, in fact, a pole, or stem of a tree. It is reproduced in our modern "Maypole," around which maidens dance, as maidens did of yore.[6]

---

[1] Bible for Learners, vol. 1. pp. 177, 178, 317, 321, 322,

[2] Indian Antiquities, vol. ii. p. 356.

[3] Ibid.

[4] We read in Bell's "Pantheon of the Gods and Demi-Gods of Antiquity," under the head of BAELYLION, BAELYLIA, or BAETYLOS, that they are "*Anointed Stones*, worshiped among the Greeks, Phrygians, and other nations of the East;" that "these Baetylia were greatly venerated by the ancient Heathen, many of their idols being no other;" and that, "in reality no sort of idol was more common in the East, than that of oblong stones *erected*, and hence termed by the Greeks *pillars*." The Rev. Geo. W. Cox, in his Aryan Mythology (vol. ii. p. 113), says: "The erection of these stone columns or pillars, the forms of which in most cases tell their own story, are common throughout the East, some of the most elaborate being found near Ghizni." And Mr. Wake (Phallism in Ancient Religions, p. 60), says: "Kiyun, or Kivan, the name of the deity said by Amos (v. 26), to have been worshiped in the wilderness by the Hebrews, signifies GOD OF THE PILLAR."

[5] We find that there was nothing gross or immoral in the worship of the male and female generative organs among the ancients, when the subject is properly understood. Being the most intimately connected with the reproduction of life on earth, the *Linga* became the symbol under which the *Sun*, invoked with a thousand names, has been worshiped throughout the world *as the restorer of the powers of nature* after the long sleep or death of winter. But if the *Linga* is the Sun-god in his majesty, the *Yoni* is the earth who yields her fruit under his fertilizing warmth.

The *Phallic tree* is introduced into the narrative of the book of Genesis: but it is here called a tree, not of life, but of the knowledge of good and evil, that knowledge which dawns in the mind with the first consciousness of difference between man and woman. In contrast with this tree of carnal indulgence, tending to death, is the tree of life, denoting the higher existence for which man was designed, and which would bring with it the happiness and the freedom of the children of God. In the brazen serpent of the Pentateuch, the two emblems of the *cross* and *serpent*, the quiescent and energising Phallos, are united. (See Cox : Aryan Mythology, vol. ii. pp. 113, 116, 118.)

[6] See Cox : Aryan Mytho., ii. 112, 113.

CHAPTER VI.

THE children of Israel, who were in bondage in Egypt, making bricks, and working in the field,[1] were looked upon with compassion by the Lord.[2] He heard their groaning, and remembered his covenant with Abraham,[3] with Isaac, and with Jacob. He, therefore, chose Moses (an Israelite, who had murdered an Egyptian,[4] and who, therefore, was obliged to flee from Egypt, as Pharaoh sought to punish him), as his servant, to carry out his plans.

Moses was at this time keeping the flock of Jeruth, his father-in-law, in the land of Midian. The angel of the Lord, or the Lord himself, appeared to him there, and said unto him:

"I am the God of thy Father, the God of Abraham, the God of Isaac, and the God of Jacob. . . . I have seen the affliction of *my people* which are in Egypt, and have heard their cry by reason of their tormentors; for I know their sorrows. And I am *come down* to deliver them out of the hands of the Egyptians, and to bring them up out of that land into a good land and a large, unto a land flowing with milk and honey. I will send thee unto Pharaoh, that thou mayest bring forth my people, the children of Israel, out of Egypt."

Then Moses said unto the Lord:

"Behold, when I come unto the children of Israel, and shall say unto them, the God of your fathers hath sent me unto you, and they shall say unto me: What is his name? What shall I say unto them?"

Then God said unto Moses:

"I AM THAT I AM."[5] "Thus shalt thou say unto the children of Israel, I AM hath sent me unto you."[6]

---

[1] Exodus i. 14.

[2] Exodus ii. 24, 25.

[3] See chapter x.

[4] Exodus ii. 12.

[5] The Egyptian name for God was "*Nuk-Pa-Nuk*," or "I AM THAT I AM." (Bonwick: Egyptian Belief, p. 395.) This name was found on a temple in Egypt. (Higgins · Anacalypsis, vol. ii. p. 17.) "'I AM' was a Divine name understood by all the initiated among the Egyptians." "The 'I AM' of the Hebrews, and the 'I AM' of the Egyptians are identical." (Bunsen: Keys of St. Peter, p. 38.) The name "*Jehovah*," which was adopted by the Hebrews, was a name esteemed sacred among the Egyptians. They called it Y-HA-HO, or Y-AH-

[6] Exodus iii. 1, 14.

And God said, moreover, unto Moses:

"Go and gather the Elders of Israel together, and say unto them: the Lord God of your fathers . . . appeared unto me, saying: 'I have surely visited you, and seen that which is done to you in Egypt. And I have said, I will bring you up out of the affliction of Egypt . . . unto a land flowing with milk and honey.' And they shall hearken to thy voice, and thou shalt come, thou and the Elders of Israel, unto the king of Egypt, and ye shall say unto him: ' the Lord God of the Hebrews hath met with us, and now let us go, we beseech thee, *three days journey in the wilderness*, that we may sacrifice to the Lord our God.'[1]

"*I am sure* that the king of Egypt will *not* let you go, no, not by a mighty hand. And I will stretch out my hand, and smite Egypt with all my wonders, which I will do in the midst thereof: *and after that he will let you go.* And I will give this people (the Hebrews) favor in the sight of the Egyptians, and it shall come to pass, that when ye go, *ye shall not go empty.* But every woman shall *borrow* of her neighbor, and of her that sojourneth in her house, jewels of silver and jewels of gold, and raiment. And ye shall put them upon your sons and upon your daughters, *and ye shall spoil the Egyptians.*"[2]

The Lord again appeared unto Moses, in Midian, and said:

" Go, return into Egypt, for all the men are dead which sought thy life. And Moses took his wife, and his son, and set them upon an ass, and he returned to the land of Egypt. And Moses took the *rod of God* (which the Lord had given him) in his hand."[3]

Upon arriving in Egypt, Moses tells his brother Aaron, " all the words of the Lord," and Aaron tells all the children of Israel. Moses, who was not eloquent, but had a slow speech,[4] uses Aaron as his spokesman.[5] They then appear unto Pharaoh, and falsify, " *according to the commands of the Lord,*" saying: " Let us go, we pray thee, *three days' journey in the desert*, and sacrifice unto the Lord our God."[6]

The Lord hardens Pharaoh's heart, so that he does not let the children of Israel go to sacrifice unto their God, in the desert.

WEH. (See the Religion of Israel, pp. 42, 43; and Anacalypsis, vol. i. p. 329, and vol. ii. p. 17.) "None dare to enter the temple of Serapis, who did not bear on his breast or forehead the name of JAO, or J-HA-HO, a name almost equivalent in sound to that of the Hebrew Jehovah, and probably of identical import ; and no name was uttered in Egypt with more reverence than this IAO." (Trans. from the Ger. of Schiller, in Monthly Repos., vol. xx.; and Voltaire: *Commentary on Exodus;* Higgins' Anac., vol. i. p. 329; vol. ii. p. 17.) " That this divine name was well-known to the *Heathen* there can be no doubt." (Parkhurst: Hebrew Lex. in Anac., i. 327.) So also with the name *El Shaddai.* "The extremely common Egyptian expression *Nutar Nutra* exactly corresponds in sense to the Hebrew *El Shaddai*, the

very title by which God tells Moses he was known to Abraham and Isaac and Jacob." (Prof. Renouf : Relig. of Anc't Egypt, p. 99.)

[1] Exodus iii. 15–18.
[2] Exodus iii. 19–22. Here is a command from the Lord to *deceive*, and lie, and *steal*, which, according to the narrative, was carried out to the letter (Ex. xii. 35, 36) ; and yet we are told that this *same Lord* said : " *Thou shalt not steal.*" (Ex. xx. 15.) Again he says : " *Thou shalt not defraud thy neighbor, neither rob him.*" (Leviticus xix. 13.) Surely this is inconsistency.
[3] Exodus iv. 19, 20.
[4] Exodus iv. 10.
[5] Exodus iv. 16.
[6] Exodus v. 3.

4

Moses and Aaron continue interceding with him, however, and, for the purpose of showing their miraculous powers, they change their rods into serpents, the river into blood, cause a plague of frogs and lice, and a swarm of flies, &c., &c., to appear. Most of these feats were imitated by the magicians of Egypt. Finally, the first-born of Egypt are slain, when Pharaoh, after having had his heart hardened, by the Lord, over and over again, consents to let Moses and the children of Israel go to serve their God, *as they had said*, that is, for *three* days.

The Lord·having given the people favor in the sight of the Egyptians, they borrowed of them jewels of silver, jewels of gold, and raiment, "*according to the commands of the Lord.*" And they journeyed toward Succoth, there being *six hundred thousand, besides children*.[1]

" And they took their journey from Succoth, and encamped in Etham, in the edge of the wilderness. And the Lord went before them by day, *in a pillar of a cloud*, to lead them the way; and by night *in a pillar of fire*, to give them light to go by day and night."[2]

" And it was told the king of Egypt, that the people fled. . . . And he made ready his chariot, and took his people with him. And he took six hundred chosen chariots, and all the chariots of Egypt, . . . and he pursued after the children of Israel, and overtook them encamping beside the sea. . . . And when Pharaoh drew nigh, the children of Israel . . . were sore afraid, and . . . (they) cried out unto the Lord. . . . And the Lord said unto Moses, . . . speak unto the children of Israel, that they go forward. But lift thou up thy rod, and stretch out thine hand over the Red Sea, and divide it, and the children of Israel shall go on dry ground through the midst of the sea. . . . And Moses stretched out his hand over the sea,[3] and the Lord caused the sea to go back by a strong east wind that night, and made the sea dry land, and the waters were divided. And the children of Israel went into the midst of the sea upon the dry ground; *and the waters were a wall unto them upon the right hand, and on their left*. And the Egyptians pursued, and went in after them to the midst of the sea, *even all Pharaoh's horses, and his chariots, and his horse-men.*"

After the children of Israel had landed on the other side of the sea, the Lord said unto Moses :

' Stretch out thine hand over the sea, that the waters may come again upon the Egyptians, upon their chariots, and upon their horse-men. And Moses stretched forth his hand over the sea, and the sea returned to his strength. . . . And the Lord overthrew the Egyptians in the midst of the sea. And the waters returned, and covered the chariots, and the horse-men, and all the host of Pharaoh

---

[1] Exodus vii. 35–37. Bishop Colenso shows, in his Pentateuch Examined, how ridiculous this statement is.

[2] Exodus xiii. 20, 21.

[3] " The sea over which Moses stretches out his hand with the staff, and which he divides, so that the waters stand up on either side like walls while he passes through, must surely have been originally the Sea of Clouds. . . . A German story presents a perfectly similar feature. The conception of the cloud as sea, rock and wall, recurs very frequently in mythology." (Prof. Steinthal : The Legend of Samson, p. 429.)

that came into the sea after them; there remained not so much as one of them. But the children of Israel walked upon dry land in the midst of the sea, and the waters were a wall unto them on their right hand, and on their left. . . . And Israel saw the great work which the Lord did upon the Egyptians, and the people feared the Lord, and believed the Lord and his servant Moses."[1]

The writer of this story, whoever he may have been, was evidently familiar with the legends related of the Sun-god, *Bacchus*, as he has given Moses the credit of performing some of the miracles which were attributed to that god.

Is is related in the hymns of Orpheus,[2] that Bacchus had a *rod* with which he performed miracles, and which he could change into a *serpent* at pleasure. *He passed the Red Sea, dry shod, at the head of his army.* He divided the waters of the rivers Orontes and Hydaspus, by the touch of his rod, and passed through them dry-shod.[3] *By the same mighty wand, he drew water from the rock,*[4] and wherever they marched, the land flowed with wine, milk and honey.[5]

Professor Steinthal, speaking of Dionysus (Bacchus), says:

Like Moses, he strikes fountains of wine and water out of the rock. Almost all the acts of Moses correspond to those of the Sun-gods.[6]

Mons. Dupuis says:

"Among the different miracles of Bacchus and his Bacchantes, there are prodigies very similar to those which are attributed to Moses; for instance, such as the sources of water which the *former* caused to sprout from the innermost of the rocks."[7]

In Bell's Pantheon of the Gods and Heroes of Antiquity,[8] an account of the prodigies attributed to Bacchus is given; among these, are mentioned his striking water from the rock, with his magic wand, his turning a twig of ivy into a snake, his passing thr ugh the Red Sea and the rivers Orontes and Hydaspus, and of his enjoying the light of the Sun (while marching with his army in India), when the day was spent, and it was dark to others. All these are parallels too striking to be accidental.

We might also mention the fact, that Bacchus, as well as Moses

---

[1] Exodus xiv. 5-13.

[2] Orpheus is said to have been the earliest poet of Greece, where he first introduced the rites of Bacchus, which he brought from Egypt. (See Roman Antiquities, p. 134.)

[3] The Hebrew fable writers not wishing to be outdone, have made the waters of the river Jordan to be divided to let Elijah and Elisha pass through (2 Kings ii. 8), and also the children of Israel. (Joshua iii. 15-17.)

[4] Moses, with his rod, drew water from the rock. (Exodus xvii. 6.)

[5] See Taylor's Diegesis, p. 191, and Higgins: Anacalypsis, vol. ii. p. 19.

[6] The Legend of Samson, p. 420.

[7] Dupuis: Origin of Religious Beliefs, p. 165.

[8] Vol. i. p. 122.

was called the "*Law-giver*," and that it was said of Bacchus, as
well as of Moses, that his laws were written on *two tables of
stone*.¹ Bacchus was represented *horned*, and so was Moses.²
Bacchus "was picked up in a box, that floated on the water,"³
and so was Moses.⁴ Bacchus had two mothers, one by nature, and
one by adoption,⁵ and so had Moses.⁶ And, as we have already
seen, Bacchus and his army enjoyed the light of the Sun, during
the night time, and Moses and his army enjoyed the light of "a
pillar of fire, by night."⁷

In regard to the children of Israel going out from the land of
Egypt, we have no doubt that such an occurrence took place,
although not in the manner, and not for such reasons, as is recorded
by the *sacred historian*. We find, from other sources, what is evidently nearer the truth.

It is related by the historian Choeremon, that, at one time, the
land of Egypt was infested with disease, and through the advice of
the sacred scribe Phritiphantes, the king caused the infected people
(who were none other than the brick-making slaves, known as the
children of Israel), to be collected, *and driven out of the country*.⁸

Lysimachus relates that:

" A filthy disease broke out in Egypt, and the Oracle of Ammon, being consulted on the occasion, commanded the king to purify the land *by driving out the
Jews* (who were infected with leprosy, &c.), a race of men who were hateful to
the Gods."⁹ *The whole multitude of the people were accordingly collected and driven
out into the wilderness.*"¹⁰

Diodorus Siculus, referring to this event, says:

"In ancient times Egypt was afflicted with a great plague, which was attributed to the anger of God, on account of the multitude of foreigners in Egypt:
by whom the rites of the native religion were neglected. *The Egyptians accordingly drove them out*. The most noble of them went under Cadmus and Danaus
to Greece, but the greater number followed *Moses*, a wise and valiant leader, to
Palestine."¹¹

---

¹ Bell's Pantheon, vol. i. p. 122; and Higgins: Anacalypsis, vol. ii. p. 19.
² Ibid. and Dupuis : Origin of Religious Belief, p. 174.
³ Taylor's Diegesis, p. 190 ; Bell's Pantheon,
vol. i. under "Bacchus ;" and Higgins: Anacalypsis ii. 19.
⁴ Exodus ii. 1-11.
⁵ Taylor's Diegesis, p. 191 ; Bell's Pantheon,
vol. i. under "Bacchus;" and Higgins : p. 19,
vol. ii.

⁶ Exodus ii. 1-11.
⁷ Exodus xiii. 20, 21.
⁸ See Prichard's Historical Records, p. 74 ;
also Dunlap's Spirit Hist., p. 40; and Cory's Ancient Fragments, pp. 80, 81, for similar accounts.
⁹ "All persons afflicted with leprosy were
considered displeasing in the sight of the Sun-
god, by the Egyptians." (Dunlap: Spirit Hist
p. 40.)
¹⁰ Prichard's Historical Records, p. 75.
¹¹ Ibid. p. 78.

After giving the different opinions concerning the origin of the Jewish nation, Tacitus, the Roman historian, says:

"In this clash of opinions, *one point seems to be universally admitted.* A pestilential disease, disfiguring the race of man, and making the body an object of loathsome deformity, spread all over Egypt. Bocchoris, at that time the reigning monarch, consulted the oracle of Jupiter Hammon, and received for answer, that the kingdom must be purified, by exterminating the infected multitude, as a race of men detested by the gods. After diligent search, the wretched sufferers were collected together, and in a wild and barren desert abandoned to their misery. In that distress, while the vulgar herd was sunk in deep despair, Moses, one of their number, reminded them, that, by the wisdom of his councils, they had been already rescued out of impending danger. Deserted as they were by men and gods, he told them, that if they did not repose their confidence in him, as their chief by divine commission, they had no resource left. His offer was accepted. Their march began, they knew not whither. Want of water was their chief distress. Worn out with fatigue, they lay stretched on the bare earth, heart broken, ready to expire, when a troop of wild asses, returning from pasture, went up the steep ascent of a rock covered with a grove of trees. The verdure of the herbage round the place suggested the idea of springs near at hand. Moses traced the steps of the animals, and discovered a plentiful vein of water. By this relief the fainting multitude was raised from despair. They pursued their journey for six days without intermission. On the seventh day they made halt, and, having expelled the natives, took possession of the country, where they built their city, and dedicated their temple."[1]

Other accounts, similar to these, might be added, among which may be mentioned that given by Manetho, an Egyptian priest, which is referred to by Josephus, the Jewish historian.

Although the accounts quoted above are not exactly alike, *yet the main points are the same,* which are to the effect that Egypt was infected with disease owing to the foreigners (among whom were those who were afterwards styled "the children of Israel") that were in the country, and who were an unclean people, and that they were accordingly driven out into the wilderness.

When we compare this statement with that recorded in Genesis, it does not take long to decide which of the two is nearest the truth.

Everything putrid, or that had a tendency to putridity, was carefully avoided by the ancient Egyptians, and so strict were the Egyptian priests on this point, that they wore no garments made of any animal substance, circumcised themselves, and shaved their whole bodies, even to their eyebrows, lest they should unknowingly harbor any filth, excrement or vermin, supposed to be bred from putrefaction.[2] We know from the laws set down in *Leviticus,* that the Hebrews were not a remarkably clean race.

[1] Tacitus : Hist. book v. ch. iii.
[2] Knight : Anc't Art and Mythology, p. 89, and Kenrick's Egypt, vol. i. p. 447. "The cleanliness of the Egyptian priests was extreme.

Jewish priests, *in making a history for their race,* have given us but a shadow of truth here and there; it is almost wholly mythical. The author of "The Religion of Israel," speaking on this subject, says:

"The history of the religion of Israel *must start from the sojourn* of *the Israelites in Egypt.* Formerly it was usual to take a much earlier starting-point, and to begin with a religious discussion of the religious ideas of the *Patriarchs.* And this was perfectly right, so long as the accounts of Abraham, Isaac and Jacob were considered *historical. But now that a strict investigation has shown us that all these stories are entirely unhistorical,* of course we have to begin the history later on."[1]

The author of "The Spirit History of Man," says:

"The Hebrews came out of Egypt and settled among the Canaanites. *They need not be traced beyond the Exodus. That is their historical beginning.* It was very easy to cover up this remote event by the recital of mythical traditions, and to prefix to it an account of their origin in which the gods (Patriarchs), should figure as their ancestors."[2]

Professor Goldzbier says:

"The residence of the Hebrews in Egypt, and their exodus thence under the guidance and training of an enthusiast for the freedom of his tribe, form a series of strictly historical facts, which find confirmation even in the documents of ancient Egypt (which we have just shown). But the traditional narratives of these events (were) *elaborated by the Hebrew people.*"[3]

Count de Volney also observes that:

"What Exodus says of their (the Israelites) servitude under the king of Heliopolis, and of the oppression of their hosts, the Egyptians, is extremely probable. *It is here their history begins. All that precedes* . . . *is nothing but mythology and cosmogony.*"[4]

In speaking of the sojourn of the Israelites in Egypt, Dr. Knappert says:

"According to the tradition preserved in Genesis, it was the promotion of Jacob's son, Joseph, to be viceroy of Egypt, that brought about the migration of the sons of Israel from Canaan to Goshen. The story goes that this Joseph was sold as a slave by his brothers, and after many changes of fortune received the vice-regal office at Pharaoh's hands through his skill in interpreting dreams. Famine drives his brothers—and afterwards his father—to him, and the Egyptian prince gives them the land of Goshen to live in. *It is by imagining all this that the*

They shaved their heads, and every three days shaved their whole bodies. They bathed two or three times a day, often in the night also. They wore garments of white linen, deeming it more cleanly than cloth made from the hair of animals. If they had occasion to wear a woolen cloth or mantle, they put it off before entering a temple; so scrupulous were they that nothing impure should come into the presence of the gods." (Prog. Relig. Ideas, i. 108.)

"Thinking it better to be clean than handsome, the (Egyptian) priests shave their whole body every third day, that neither lice nor any other impurity may be found upon them when engaged in the service of the gods." (Herodotus: book ii. ch. 37.)

[1] The Religion of Israel, p. 27.
[2] Dunlap: Spirit Hist. of Man, p. 266.
[3] Hebrew Mythology, p. 23.
[4] Researches in Ancient History, p. 149.

legend tries to account for the fact that Israel passed some time in Egypt. But we must look for the real explanation in a migration of certain tribes which could not establish or maintain themselves in Canaan, and were forced to move further on.

"We find a passage in Flavius Josephus, from which it appears that in Egypt, too, a recollection survived of the sojourn of some foreign tribes in the north-eastern district of the country. For this writer gives us two fragments out of a lost work by Manetho, a priest, who lived about 250 B. c. In one of these we have a statement that pretty nearly agrees with the Israelitish tradition about a sojourn in Goshen. *But the Israelites were looked down on by the Egyptians as foreigners, and they are represented as lepers and unclean.* Moses himself is mentioned by name, and we are told that he was a priest and joined himself to these *lepers* and gave them laws."[1]

To return now to the story of the Red Sea being divided to let Moses and his followers pass through—of which we have already seen one counterpart in the legend related of Bacchus and his army passing through the same sea dry-shod—there is another similar story concerning Alexander the Great.

The histories of Alexander relate that the Pamphylian Sea was divided to let him and his army pass through. Josephus, after speaking of the Red Sea being divided for the passage of the Israelites, says:

"For the sake of those who accompanied Alexander, king of Macedonia, who yet lived comparatively but a little while ago, the Pamphylian Sea retired and offered them a passage through itself, when they had no other way to go . . . *and this is confessed to be true by all who have written about the actions of Alexander.*"[2]

He seems to consider both legends of the same authority, quoting the latter to substantiate the former.

"Callisthenes, who himself accompanied Alexander in the expedition," "wrote, how the Pamphylian Sea did not only open a passage for Alexander, but, rising and elevating its waters, did pay him homage as its king."[3]

It is related in Egyptian mythology that Isis was at one time on a journey with the eldest child of the king of Byblos, when coming to the river Phœdrus, which was in a " rough air," and wishing to

[1] The Religion of Israel, pp. 31, 32.
[2] Jewish Antiq. bk. ii. ch. xvi.
[3] Ibid. *note.*
"It was said that the waters of the Pamphylian Sea miraculously opened a passage for the army of Alexander the Great. Admiral Beaufort, however, tells us that, ' though there are no tides in this part of the Mediterranean, considerable depression of the sea is caused by long-continued north winds; and Alexander, taking advantage of such a moment, may have dashed on without impediment ;' and we accept the explanation as a matter of course. But the waters of the Red Sea are said to have miraculously opened a passage for the children of Israel ; and we insist on the literal truth of *this* story, and reject natural explanations as monstrous." (Matthew Arnold.)

cross, she commanded the stream to be *dried up*. This being done she crossed without trouble.[1]

There is a *Hindoo* fable to the effect that when the infant Crishna was being sought by the reigning tyrant of Madura (King Kansa)[2] his foster-father took him and departed out of the country. Coming to the river Yumna, and wishing to cross, it was divided for them by the Lord, and they passed through.

The story is related by Thomas Maurice, in his "History of Hindostan," who has taken it from the *Bhagavat Pooraun*. It is as follows:

"Yasodha took the child Crishna, and carried him off (from where he was born), but, coming to the river Yumna, directly opposite to Gokul, Crishna's father perceiving the current to be very strong, it being in the midst of the rainy season, and not knowing which way to pass it, Crishna commanded the water to give way on both sides to his father, *who accordingly passed dry-footed, across the river*."[3]

This incident is illustrated in Plate 58 of Moore's "Hindu Pantheon."

There is another Hindoo legend, recorded in the *Rig Veda*, and quoted by Viscount Amberly, from whose work we take it,[4] to the effect that an Indian sage called Visvimati, having arrived at a river which he wished to cross, that holy man said to it: "Listen to the Bard who has come to you from afar with wagon and chariot. Sink down, become fordable, and reach not up to our chariot axles." The river answers: "I will bow down to thee like a woman with full breast (suckling her child), as a maid to a man, will I throw myself open to thee."

This is accordingly done, and the sage passes through.

We have also an Indian legend which relates that a courtesan named Bindumati, *turned back the streams of the river Ganges*.[5]

We see then, that the idea of seas and rivers being divided for the purpose of letting some chosen one of God pass through, is an old one peculiar to other peoples beside the Hebrews, and the probability is that many nations had legends of this kind.

That Pharaoh and his host should have been drowned in the Red Sea, and the fact not mentioned by any historian, is simply impossible, especially when they have, as we have seen, noticed the fact of the Israelites being driven out of Egypt.[6] Dr. Inman, speaking of this, says:

[1] See Prichard's Egyptian Mytho. p. 60.
[2] See ch. xviii.
[3] Hist. Hindostan, vol. ii. p. 312.
[4] Analysis Relig. Belief, p. 552.
[5] See Hardy: Buddhist Legenas, p. 140.
[6] In a cave discovered at Deir-el-Bahar.

"We seek in vain amongst the Egyptian hieroglyphs for scenes which recall such cruelties as those we read of in the Hebrew records; and in the writings which have hitherto been translated, we find nothing resembling the wholesale destructions described and applauded by the Jewish historians, as perpetrated by their own people."[1]

That Pharaoh should have pursued a tribe of diseased slaves, *whom he had driven out of his country*, is altogether improbable. In the words of Dr. Knappert, we may conclude, by saying that:

"*This story, which was not written until more than five hundred years after the exodus itself, can lay no claim to be considered historical.*"[2]

(Aug., 1881), near Thebes, in Egypt, was found *thirty-nine* mummies of royal and priestly personages. Among these was King Ramses II., the third king of the Nineteenth Dynasty, and the veritable Pharaoh of the Jewish captivity. It is very strange that he should be *here*, among a number of other kings, if he had been lost in the Red Sea. The mummy is wrapped in rose-colored and yellow linen of a texture finer than the finest Indian muslin, upon which lotus flowers are strewn. It is in a perfect state of preservation. (See a Cairo [Aug. 8th] letter to the *London Times*.)

[1] Ancient Faiths, vol. ii. p. 58.
[2] The Religion of Israel, p. 41.

CHAPTER VII.

THE receiving of the *Ten Commandments* by Moses, from the Lord, is recorded in the following manner:

"In the third month, when the children of Israel were gone forth out of the land of Egypt, the same day came they into the wilderness of Sinai, . . . and there Israel camped before the Mount. . . .

"And it came to pass on the third day that there were thunders and lightnings, and a thick cloud upon the Mount, and the voice of the tempest exceedingly loud, so that all the people that was in the camp trembled. . . .

"And Mount Sinai was altogether on a smoke, because the Lord descended upon it in fire, and the smoke thereof ascended as the smoke of a furnace, and the whole Mount quaked greatly. And when the voice of the tempest sounded long, and waxed louder and louder, Moses spake, and God answered him by a voice.

"*And the Lord came down upon the Mount,* and called Moses up to the top of the Mount, and Moses went up."[1]

The Lord there communed with him, and "he gave unto Moses .... two tables of testimony, tables of stone, *written with the finger of God.*"[2]

When Moses came down from off the Mount, he found the children of Israel dancing around a golden calf, which his brother Aaron had made, and, as his "anger waxed hot," he cast the tables of stone on the ground, and broke them.[3] Moses again saw the Lord on the Mount, however, and received two more tables of stone.[4] When he came down this time from off Mount Sinai, "the skin of his face did shine."[5]

---

[1] Exodus xix.
[2] Exodus xxxi. 18.
[3] Exodus xxii. 19.
[4] Exodus xxxiv.
[5] Ibid.

It was a common belief among ancient Pagan nations that the gods appeared and conversed with men. As an illustration we may cite the following, related by *Herodotus,* the Grecian historian, who, in speaking of Egypt and the Egyptians, says: "There is a large city called Chemmis, situated in the Thebaic district, near Neapolis, in which is a quadrangular temple dedicated to (the god) Perseus, son of (the Virgin) Danae; palm-trees grow round it, and the portico is of stone, very spacious, and over it are placed two large stone statues. In this inclosure is a temple, and in it is placed a statue of Perseus. The Chemmitæ (or inhabitants of Chemmis), *affirm that Perseus has frequently appeared to them on earth, and frequently within the temple.*" (Herodotus, bk. ii. ch. 91.)

These two tables of stone contained the *Ten Commandments*,[1] so it is said, which the Jews and Christians of the present day are supposed to take for their standard.

They are, in substance, as follows:

1—To have no other God but Jehovah.
2—To make no image for purpose of worship.
3—Not to take Jehovah's name in vain.
4—Not to work on the Sabbath-day.
5—To honor their parents.
6—Not to kill.
7—Not to commit adultery.
8—Not to steal.
9—Not to bear false witness against a neighbor.
10—Not to covet.[2]

We have already seen, in the last chapter, that Bacchus was called the "*Law-giver*," and that his laws were written on *two tables of stone*.[3] This feature in the Hebrew legend was evidently copied from that related of Bacchus, but, the idea of his (Moses) receiving the commandments from the Lord on a *mountain* was obviously taken from the *Persian* legend related of Zoroaster.

Prof. Max Müller says:

"What applies to the religion of Moses applies to that of Zoroaster. It is placed before us as a complete system from the first, *revealed by Ahuramazda* (Ormuzd), *proclaimed by Zoroaster*."[4]

The disciples of Zoroaster, in their profusion of legends of the master, relate that one day, as he prayed *on a high mountain*, in the midst of thunders and lightnings ("fire from heaven"), the Lord himself appeared before him, and delivered unto him the "Book of the Law." While the King of Persia and the people were assembled together, Zoroaster came down from the mountain unharmed, bringing with him the "Book of the Law," which had been revealed to him by Ormuzd. They call this book the *Zend-Avesta*, which signifies the *Living Word*.[5]

---

[1] *Buddha*, the founder of Buddhism, had TEN commandments. 1. Not to kill. 2. Not to steal. 3. To be chaste. 4. Not to bear false witness. 5. Not to lie. 6. Not to swear. 7. To avoid impure words. 8. To be disinterested. 9. Not to avenge one's-self. 10. Not to be superstitious. (See Huc's Travels, p. 328, vol. i.)

[2] Exodus xx. Dr. Oort says: "The original ten commandments probably ran as follows: I Yahwah am your God. Worship no other gods beside me. Make no image of a god. Commit no perjury. Remember to keep holy the Sabbath day. Honor your father and your mother. Commit no murder. Break not the marriage vow. Steal not. Bear no false witness. Covet not." (Bible for Learners, vol. i. p. 18.)

[3] Bell's Pantheon, vol. i. p. 122. Higgins, vol. ii. p. 19. Cox: Aryan Mytho. vol. ii. p. 295.

[4] Müller: Origin of Religion, p. 130.

[5] See Prog. Relig. Ideas, vol. i. pp. 257, 258. This book, the *Zend-Avesta*, is similar, in many respects, to the *Vedas* of the *Hindoos*.

According to the religion of the Cretans, Minos, their law-giver, ascended a *mountain* (Mount Dicta) and there received from the Supreme Lord (Zeus) the sacred laws which he brought down with him.[1]

Almost all nations of antiquity have legends of their holy men ascending a *mountain* to ask counsel of the gods, such places being invested with peculiar sanctity, and deemed nearer to the deities than other portions of the earth.[2]

According to Egyptian belief, it is Thoth, the Deity itself, that speaks and reveals to his elect among men the will of God and the arcana of divine things. Portions of them are expressly stated to have been written by the very finger of Thoth himself; to have been the work and composition of the great god.[3]

Diodorus, the Grecian historian, says:

The idea promulgated by the ancient Egyptians that their *laws* were received direct from the Most High God, *has been adopted with success by many other law-givers, who have thus insured respect for their institutions.*[4]

The Supreme God of the ancient Mexicans was *Tezcatlipoca.* He occupied a position corresponding to the Jehovah of the Jews, the Brahma of India, the Zeus of the Greeks, and the Odin of the Scandinavians. His name is compounded of Tezcatepec, the name of a *mountain* (*upon which he is said to have manifested himself to man*) *tlil*, dark, and *poca*, smoke. The explanation of this designation is given in the *Codex Vaticanus*, as follows:

This has led many to believe that Zoroaster was a Brahman; among these are Rawlinson (See Inman's Ancient Faiths, vol. ii. p. 831) and Thomas Maurice. (See Indian Antiquities, vol. ii. p. 219.)

The Persians themselves had a tradition that he came from some country to the East of them. That he was a foreigner is indicated by a passage in the *Zend-Avesta* which represents Ormuzd as saying to him: "Thou, O Zoroaster, by the promulgation of my law, shalt restore to me my former glory, which was pure light. Up! haste thee to the land of *Iran*, which thirsteth after the law, and say, thus said Ormuzd, &c." (See Prog. Relig. Ideas, vol. i. p. 263.)

[1] The Bible for Learners, vol. i. p. 301.

[2] "The deities of the Hindoo Pantheon dwell on the sacred Mount Meru; the gods of Persia ruled from Albordj; the Greek Jove thundered from Olympus; and the Scandinavian gods made Asgard awful with their presence. . . . Profane history is full of examples attesting the attachment to high places for purpose of sacrifice." (Squire: Serpent Symbols, p. 78.)

"The offerings of the Chinese to the deities were generally on the summits of high mountains, as they seemed to them to be nearer heaven, to the majesty of which they were to be offered." (Christmas's Mytho. p. 250, in Ibid.) "In the infancy of civilization, high places were chosen by the people to offer sacrifices to the gods. The first altars, the first temples, were erected on mountains." (Humboldt: American Researches.) The Himalayas are the "*Heavenly mountains.*" In Sanscrit *Himala*, corresponding to the M. Gothic, *Himins*; Alem., *Himil*; Ger., Swed., and Dan., *Himmel*; Old Norse, *Himin*; Dutch, *Hemel*; Ang.-Sax., *Heofon*; Eng., *Heaven*. (See Mallet's Northern Antiquities, p. 42.)

[3] Bunsen's Egypt, quoted in Isis Unveiled, vol. ii. p. 367. Mrs. Child says: "The *laws* of Egypt were handed down from the earliest times, and regarded with the utmost veneration as a portion of religion. Their first legislator represented them as dictated by the gods themselves, and framed expressly for the benefit of mankind by their secretary *Thoth*." (Prog. Relig. Ideas, vol. i. p. 173.)

[4] Quoted in Ibid.

Tezcatlipoca was one of their most potent deities; they say he once appeared on the top of a mountain. They paid him great reverence and adoration, and addressed him, in their prayers, as "Lord, whose servant we are." No man ever saw his face, for he appeared only "as a shade." Indeed, the Mexican idea of the godhead was similar to that of the Jews. Like Jehovah, Tezcatlipoca dwelt in the "midst of thick darkness." *When he descended upon the mount of Tezcatepec, darkness overshadowed the earth, while fire and water, in mingled streams, flowed from beneath his feet, from its summit.*[1]

Thus, we see that other nations, beside the Hebrews, believed that their laws were actually received from God, that they had legends to that effect, and that a *mountain* figures conspicuously in the stories.

Professor Oort, speaking on this subject, says:

"No one who has any knowledge of antiquity will be surprised at this, for similar beliefs were very common. All peoples who had issued from a life of barbarism and acquired regular political institutions, more or less elaborate laws, and established worship, and maxims of morality, attributed all this— their birth as a nation, so to speak—to one or more great men, all of whom, without exception, *were supposed to have received their knowledge from some deity.*

"Whence did Zoroaster, the prophet of the Persians, derive his religion? According to the beliefs of his followers, and the doctrines of their sacred writings, it was from Ahuramazda, the God of light. Why did the Egyptians represent the god Thoth with a writing tablet and a pencil in his hand, and honor him especially as the god of the priests? Because he was 'the Lord of the divine Word,' the foundation of all wisdom, from whose inspiration the priests, who were the scholars, the lawyers, and the religious teachers of the people, derived all their wisdom. Was not Minos, the law-giver of the Cretans, the friend of Zeus, the highest of the gods? Nay, was he not even his son, and did he not ascend to the sacred cave on Mount Dicte to bring down the laws which his god had placed there for him? From whom did the Spartan law-giver, Lycurgus, himself say that he had obtained his laws? From no other than the god Apollo. The Roman legend, too, in honoring Numa Pompilius as the people's instructor, at the same time ascribed all his wisdom to his intercourse with the nymph Egeria. It was the same elsewhere; and to make one more example,—this from later times— Mohammed not only believed himself to have been called immediately by God to be the prophet of the Arabs, but declared that he had received every page of the Koran from the hand of the angel Gabriel."[2]

[1] See Squire's Serpent Symbol, p. 175.　　　[2] Bible for Learners, vol. i. p. 301.

CHAPTER VIII.

SAMSON AND HIS EXPLOITS.

THIS Israelite hero is said to have been born at a time when the children of Israel were in the hands of the Philistines. His mother, who had been barren for a number of years, is entertained by an angel, who informs her that she shall conceive, and bear a son,[1] and that the child shall be a *Nazarite* unto God, from the womb, and he shall begin to deliver Israel out of the hands of the Philistines.

According to the prediction of the angel, "the woman bore a son, and called his name *Samson ;* and the child grew, and the Lord blessed him."

"And Samson (after he had grown to man's estate), went down to Timnath, and saw a woman in Timnath of the daughters of the Philistines. And he came up and told his father and his mother, and said, I have seen a woman in Timnath of the daughters of the Philistines; now therefore get her for me to wife."

---

[1] The idea of a woman conceiving, and bearing a son in her old age, seems to have been a Hebrew peculiarity, as a number of their remarkable personages were born, so it is said, of parents well advanced in years, or of a woman who was supposed to have been *barren.* As illustrations, we may mention this case of *Samson,* and that of *Joseph* being born of Rachel. The beautiful Rachel, who was so much beloved by Jacob, her husband, was barren, and she bore him no sons. This caused grief and discontent on her part, and anger on the part of her husband. In her old age, however, she bore the wonderful child Joseph. (See Genesis, xxx. 1-29.)

Isaac was born of a woman (Sarah) who had been barren many years. *An angel appeared to her* when her lord (Abraham) "was ninety years old and nine," and informed her that she would conceive and bear a son. (See Gen. xvi.)

Samuel, the " holy man," was also born of a woman (Hannah) who had been barren many years. In grief, she prayed to the Lord for a child, and was finally comforted by receiving her wish. (See 1 Samuel, i. 1-20.)

John the Baptist was also a miraculously conceived infant. His mother, Elizabeth, bore him *in her old age. An angel also informed her* and her husband Zachariah, that this event would take place. (See Luke, i. 1-25.)

Mary, the mother of *Jesus,* was born of a woman (Anna) who was " old and stricken in years," and who had been barren all her life. *An angel appeared to Anna and her husband* (Joachim), and told them what was about to take place. (See " The Gospel of Mary," Apoc.)

Thus we see, that the idea of a wonderful child being born of a woman who had passed the age which nature had destined for her to bear children, and who had been barren all her life, was a favorite one among the Hebrews. The idea that the ancestors of a race lived to a fabulous old age, is also a familiar one among the ancients.

Most ancient nations relate in their fables that their ancestors lived to be very old men. For instance ; the *Persian* patriarch Kaiomaras reigned 560 years ; Jemshid reigned 300 years ; Jahmurash reigned 700 years ; Dahûk reigned 1000 years ; Feridun reigned 120 years ; Manugeher reigned 500 years ; Kaikaus reigned 150 years ; and Bahaman reigned 112 years. (See Dunlap : Son of the Man, p. 155, *note.*)

Samson's father and mother preferred that he should take a woman among the daughters of their own tribe, but Samson wished for the maid of the Philistines, "for," said he, "she pleaseth me well."

The parents, after coming to the conclusion that it was the will of the Lord, that he should marry the maid of the Philistines, consented.

"Then went Samson down, and his father and his mother, to Timnath, and came to the vineyards of Timnath, and, behold, a young lion roared against him (Samson). And the spirit of the Lord came mightily upon him, and he rent him (the lion) as he would have rent a kid, and he had nothing in his hand."

This was Samson's *first* exploit, which he told not to any one, not even his father, or his mother.

He then continued on his way, and went down and talked with the woman, and she pleased him well.

And, after a time, he returned to take her, and he turned aside to see the carcass of the lion, and behold, "there was a swarm of bees, and honey, in the carcass of the lion."

Samson made a feast at his wedding, which lasted for *seven* days. At this feast, there were brought thirty companions to be with him, unto whom he said: "I will now put forth a riddle unto you, if ye can certainly declare it me, within the *seven* days of the feast, and find it out, then I will give you thirty sheets, and thirty changes of garments. But, if ye cannot declare it me, then shall ye give me thirty sheets, and thirty changes of garments." And they said unto him, "Put forth thy riddle, that we may hear it." And he answered them: "Out of the eater came forth meat, and out of the strong came forth sweetness."

This riddle the thirty companions could not solve.

"And it came to pass, on the *seventh* day, that they said unto Samson's wife: 'Entice thy husband, that he may declare unto us the riddle.'"

She accordingly went to Samson, and told him that he could not love her; if it were so, he would tell her the answer to the riddle. After she had wept and entreated of him, he finally told her, and she gave the answer to the children of her people. "And the men of the city said unto him, on the *seventh* day, before the sun went down, 'What is sweeter than honey, and what is stronger than a lion?'"

Samson, upon hearing this, suspected how they managed to find out the answer, whereupon he said unto them: "If ye had not ploughed with my heifer, ye had not found out my riddle"

Samson was then at a loss to know where to get the thirty sheets, and the thirty changes of garments; but, "the spirit of the Lord came upon him, and he went down to Ashkelon, *and slew thirty men of them,* and took their spoil, and gave change of garments unto them which expounded the riddle."

This was the hero's *second* exploit.

His anger being kindled, he went up to his father's house, instead of returning to his wife.[1] But it came to pass, that, after a while, Samson repented of his actions, and returned to his wife's house, and wished to go in to his wife in the chamber; but her father would not suffer him to go. And her father said: "I verily thought that thou hadst utterly hated her, therefore, I gave her to thy companion. Is not her younger sister fairer than she? Take her, I pray thee, instead of her."

This did not seem to please Samson, even though the younger was fairer than the older, for he "went and caught three hundred foxes, and took firebrands, and turned (the foxes) tail to tail, and put a firebrand in the midst between two tails. And when he had set the brands on fire, he let them go into the standing corn of the Philistines, and burned up both the shocks and also the standing corn, with the vineyards and olives."

This was Samson's *third* exploit.

When the Philistines found their corn, their vineyards, and their olives burned, they said: "Who hath done this?"

"And they answered, 'Samson, the son-in-law of the Timnite, because he had taken his wife, and given her to his companion.' And the Philistines came up, and burned her and her father with fire. And Samson said unto them: 'Though ye have done this, yet will I be avenged of you, and after that I will cease.' *And he smote them hip and thigh with a great slaughter,* and he went and dwelt in the top of the rock Etam."

This "great slaughter" was Samson's *fourth* exploit.

"Then the Philistines went up, and pitched in Judah, and spread themselves in Lehi. And the men of Judah said: 'Why are ye come up against us?' And they answered: 'To bind Samson are we come up, and to do to him as he hath done to us.' Then three thousand men of Judah went up to the top of the rock Etam, and said to Samson: 'Knowest thou not that the Philistines are rulers over us? What is this that thou hast done unto us?' And he said unto them: 'As they did unto me, so have I done unto them.' And they said unto him: 'We are come down to bind thee, that we may deliver thee into the hands of the Philistines.' And Samson said unto them: 'Swear unto me that ye will not fall upon me yourselves.' And they spake unto him, saying, 'No; but we will bind thee fast, and deliver thee into their hands: but surely we will not kill thee.' And they bound him with two new cords, and

[1] Judges, xiv.

brought him up from the rock. And when he came unto Lehi, the Philistines shouted against him; and the spirit of the Lord came mightily upon him, *and the cords that were upon his arms became as flax that was burned with fire, and his bands loosed from off his hands.* And he found a new jaw-bone of an ass, and put forth his hand and took it, *and slew a thousand men with it.*"

This was Samson's *fifth* exploit.

After slaying a thousand men he was "sore athirst," and called unto the Lord. And "God clave a hollow place that was in the jaw, and·there came water thereout, and when he had drunk, his spirit came again, and he revived."[1]

"Then went Samson to Gaza and saw there a harlot, and went in unto her. And it was told the Gazites, saying, 'Samson is come hither.' And they compassed him in, and laid wait for him all night in the gate of the city, and were quiet all the night, saying: 'In the morning, when it is day, we shall kill him.' And Samson lay (with the harlot) till midnight, and arose at midnight, and took the doors of the gate of the city, and the two posts, and went away with them, bar and all, and put them upon his shoulders, and carried them up to the top of a hill that is in Hebron."

This was Samson's *sixth* exploit.

"And it came to pass afterward, that he loved a woman in the valley of Soreck, whose name was Delilah. And the lords of the Philistines came up unto her, and said unto her: 'Entice him, and see wherein his great strength lieth, and by what means we may prevail against him.'"

Delilah then began to entice Samson to tell her wherein his strength lay.

"She pressed him daily with her words, and urged him, so that his soul was vexed unto death. Then he told her all his heart, and said unto her: 'There hath not come a razor upon mine head, for I have been a Nazarite unto God from my mother's womb. If I be shaven, then my strength will go from me, and I shall become weak, and be like any other man.' And when Delilah saw that he had told her all his heart, she went and called for the lords of the Philistines, saying: 'Come up this once, for he hath showed me all his heart.' Then the lords of the Philistines came up unto her, and brought money in their hands (for her).

"And she made him (Samson) sleep upon her knees; and she called for a man, and she caused him to shave off the *seven* locks of his head; and she began to afflict him, and his strength went from him."

The Philistines then took him, put out his eyes, and put him in prison. And being gathered together at a great sacrifice in honor of their God, Dagon, they said: "Call for Samson, that he may make us sport." And they called for Samson, and he made them sport.

"And Samson said unto the lad that held him by the hand, Suffer me that I may feel the pillars whereupon the house standeth, that I may lean upon them.

---

[1] Judges, xv.

"Now the house was full of men and women; and all the lords of the Philistines were there; and there were upon the roof about three thousand men and women, that beheld while Samson made sport.

"And Samson called unto the Lord, and said: 'O Lord God, remember me, I pray thee, and strengthen me, I pray thee, only this once, O God, that I may be at once avenged of the Philistines for my two eyes.'

"And Samson took hold of the two middle pillars upon which the house stood and on which it was borne up, of the one with his right hand, and of the other with his left. And Samson said: 'Let me die with the Philistines.' And he bowed himself with all his might; and (having regained his strength) the house fell upon the lords, and upon the people that were therein. So the dead which he slew at his death, were more than they which he slew in his life."[1]

Thus ended the career of the "strong man" of the Hebrews.

That this story is a copy of the legends related of Hercules, or that they have both been copied from similar legends existing among some other nations,[2] is too evident to be disputed. Many churchmen have noticed the similarity between the history of Samson and that of Hercules. In Chambers's Encylopædia, under "Samson," we read as follows:

'It has been matter of most contradictory speculations, how far his existence is to be taken as a reality, or, in other words, what substratum of historical truth there may be in this supposed circle of popular legends, artistically rounded off, in the four chapters of Judges which treat of him. . . .

"The miraculous deeds he performed have taxed the ingenuity of many commentators, and the text has been *twisted and turned in all directions*, to explain, *rationally*, his slaying those prodigious numbers single-handed; his carrying the gates of Gaza, in one night, a distance of about fifty miles, &c, &c."

That this is simply a *Solar* myth, no one will doubt, we believe, who will take the trouble to investigate it.

Prof. Goldziher, who has made "Comparative Mythology" a special study, says of this story:

"The most complete and rounded-off *Solar myth* extant in Hebrew, is that of Shimshôn (Samson), a cycle of mythical conceptions fully comparable with the Greek myth of Hercules."[3]

We shall now endeavor to ascertain if such is the case, by comparing the exploits of Samson with those of Hercules.

The first wonderful act performed by Samson was, as we have seen, *that of slaying a lion*. This is said to have happened when he was but a youth. So likewise was it with Hercules. At the age of eighteen, he slew an enormous lion.[4]

The valley of Nemea was infested by a terrible lion; Eurystheus ordered Hercules to bring him the skin of this monster. After

---

[1] Judges, xvi.
[2] Perhaps that of Izdubar. See chapter xi.
[3] Hebrew Mythology, p. 248.
[4] Manual of Mythology, p. 248. The Age of Fable, p. 200.

using in vain his club and arrows against the lion, Hercules strangled the animal with his hands. He returned, carrying the dead lion on his shoulders; but Eurystheus was so frightened at the sight of it, and at this proof of the prodigious strength of the hero, that he ordered him to deliver the accounts of his exploits in the future outside the town.[1]

To show the courage of Hercules, it is said that he entered the cave where the lion's lair was, closed the entrance behind him, and at once grappled with the monster.[2]

Samson is said to have torn asunder the *jaws* of the lion, and we find him generally represented slaying the beast in that manner. So likewise was this the manner in which Hercules disposed of the Nemean lion.[3]

The skin of the lion, Hercules tore off with his fingers, and knowing it to be impenetrable, resolved to wear it henceforth.[4] The statues and paintings of Hercules either represent him carrying the lion's skin over his arm, or wearing it hanging down his back, the skin of its head fitting to his crown like a cap, and the fore-legs knotted under his chin.[5]

Samson's second exploit was when he went down to Ashkelon and slew thirty men.

Hercules, when returning to Thebes from the lion-hunt, and wearing its skin hanging from his shoulders, as a sign of his success, met the heralds of the King of the Minyæ, coming from Orchomenos to claim the annual tribute of a hundred cattle, levied on Thebes. Hercules cut off the ears and noses of the heralds, bound their hands, and sent them home.[6]

Samson's third exploit was when he caught three hundred foxes, and took fire-brands, and turned them tail to tail, and put a fire-brand in the midst between two tails, and let them go into the standing corn of the Philistines.

There is no such feature as this in the legends of Hercules, the nearest to it in resemblance is when he encounters and kills the Learnean Hydra.[7] During this encounter a *fire-brand* figures conspicuously, and *the neighboring wood is set on fire.*[8]

[1] Bulfinch: The Age of Fable, p. 200.
[2] Murray: Manual of Mythology, p. 249.
[3] Roman Antiquities, p. 124; and Montfaucon, vol. i. plate cxxvi.
[4] Murray: Manual of Mythology, p. 249.
[5] See Ibid. Greek and Italian Mythology, p. 129, and Montfaucon, vol. i. plate cxxv. and cxxvi.
[6] Manual of Mythology, p. 247.
[7] "It has many heads, one being immortal, as the storm must constantly supply new clouds while the vapors are driven off by the *Sun* into space. Hence the story went that although Herakles could burn away its mortal heads, as the *Sun* burns up the clouds, still he can but hide away the mist or vapor itself, which at its appointed time must again darken the sky." (Cox: Aryan Mytho., vol. ii. p. 48.)
[8] See Manual of Mytho., p. 250.

We have, however, an explanation of this portion of the legend, in the following from Prof. Steinthal:

At the festival of Ceres, held at Rome, in the month of April, a fox-hunt through the circus was indulged in, *in which burning torches were bound to the foxes' tails.*

This was intended to be a symbolical reminder of the damage done to the fields by mildew, called the "*red fox,*" which was exorcised in various ways at this momentous season (the last third of April). It is the time of the *Dog-Star*, at which the mildew was most to be feared; if at that time great solar heat follows too close upon the hoar-frost or dew of the cold nights, this mischief rages like a burning fox through the corn-fields.[1]

He also says that:

"This is the sense of the story of the foxes, which Samson caught and sent into the Philistines' fields, with fire-brands fastened to their tails, to burn the crops. Like the lion, the fox is an animal that indicated the solar heat, being well suited for this both by its color and by its long-haired tail."[2]

Bouchart, in his "Hierozoicon," observes that:

"At this period (*i. e.*, the last third of April) they cut the corn in Palestine and Lower Egypt, and a few days after the setting of the Hyads arose the *Fox*, in whose train or tail comes the fires or torches of the dog-days, represented among the Egyptians by red marks painted on the backs of their animals."[3]

Count de Volney also tells us that:

"The inhabitants of Carseoles, an ancient city of Latium, every year, in a religious festival, burned a number of foxes *with torches tied to their tails.* They gave, as the reason for this whimsical ceremony, that their corn had been formerly burnt by a fox to whose tail a young man had fastened a bundle of lighted straw."[4]

He concludes his account of this peculiar "religious festival," by saying:

"This is exactly the story of Samson with the Philistines, but it is a Phenician tale. *Car-Seol* is a compound word in that tongue, signifying *town of foxes.* The Philistines, originally from Egypt, do not appear to have had any colonies. The Phenicians had a great many; and it can scarcely be admitted that they borrowed this story from the Hebrews, as obscure as the Druses are in our own times, or that a simple adventure gave rise to a religious ceremony; *it evidently can only be a mythological and allegorical narration.*"[4]

So much, then, for the foxes and fire-brands.

Samson's fourth exploit was when he smote the Philistines "hip and thigh," "with great slaughter."

---

[1] Steinthal: The Legend of Samson, p. 398. See, also, Higgins: Anacalypsis, vol. i. p. 240, and Volney: Researches in Anc't History, p. 42.

[2] Ibid.

[3] Quoted by Count de Volney: Researches in Ancient History, p. 42, *note.*

[4] Volney: Researches in Ancient History, p. 42.

It is related of Hercules that he had a combat with an *army* of Centaurs, who were armed with pine sticks, rocks, axes, &c. They flocked in wild confusion, and surrounded the *cave* of Pholos, where Hercules was, when a violent fight ensued. Hercules was obliged to contend against this large armed force single-handed, but he came off victorious, and slew a great number of them.[1] Hercules also encountered and fought against *an army of giants*, at the Phlegraean fields, near Cumae.[2]

Samson's next wonderful exploit was when "three thousand men of Judah" bound him with *cords* and brought him up into Lehi, when the Philistines were about to take his life. The cords with which he was bound immediately became as flax, and loosened from off his hands. He then, with the jaw-bone of an ass, slew one thousand Philistines.[3]

A very similar feature to this is found in the history of Hercules. He is made prisoner by the Egyptians, who wish to take his life, but while they are preparing to slay him, he breaks loose his bonds—having been tied with *cords*—and kills Buseris, the leader of the band, *and the whole retinue*.[4]

On another occasion, being refused shelter from a storm at Kos, he was enraged at the inhabitants, and accordingly *destroyed the whole town*.[5]

Samson, after he had slain a thousand Philistines, was "sore athirst," and called upon *Jehovah*, his father in heaven, to succor him, whereupon, water immediately gushed forth from "a hollow place that was in the jaw-bone."

Hercules, departing from the Indies (or rather Ethiopia), and conducting his army through the desert of Lybia, feels a burning thirst, and conjures *Ihou*, his father, to succor him in his danger.

---

[1] See Murray: Manual of Mythology, p. 251. "The slaughter of the Centaurs by Hercules is the conquest and dispersion of the vapors by the *Sun* as he rises in the heaven." (Cox: Aryan Mythology, vol. ii. p. 47.)

[2] Murray: Manual of Mythology, p. 257.

[3] Shamgar also slew six hundred Philistines with an ox-goad. (See Judges, iii. 31.)
"It is scarcely necessary to say that these weapons are the heritage of all the *Solar* heroes, that they are found in the hands of Phebus and Herakles, of Œdipus, Achilleus, Philoktetes, of Siguard, Rustem, Indra, Isfendujar, of Telephos, Meleagros, Theseus, Kadmos, Bellerophon, and all other slayers of noxious and fearful things." (Rev. Geo. Cox: Tales of Ancient Greece, p. xxvii.)

[4] See Volney: Researches in Ancient History, p. 41. Higgins: Anacalypsis, vol. i. p. 239; Montfaucon: L'Antiquité Expliquée, vol. i. p. 213, and Murray: Manual of Mythology, pp. 259-262.
It is evident that *Herodotus*, the Grecian historian, was somewhat of a skeptic, for he says: "The Grecians say that 'When Hercules arrived in Egypt, the Egyptians, having crowned him with a garland, led him in procession, as designing to sacrifice him to Jupiter, and that for some time he remained quiet, but when they began the preparatory ceremonies upon him at the altar, he set about defending himself and slew every one of them.' Now, since Hercules was but one, and, besides, a mere man, as they confess, how is it possible that he should slay many thousands?" (Herodotus, book ii. ch. 45).

[5] Murray: Manual of Mythology, p. 263.

Instantly the (celestial) Ram appears. Hercules follows him and arrives at a place where the Ram scrapes with his foot, *and there instantly comes forth a spring of water.*[1]

Samson's sixth exploit happened when he went to Gaza to visit a harlot. The Gazites, who wished to take his life, laid wait for him all night, but Samson left the town at midnight, and took with him the gates of the city, and the *two posts*, on his shoulders. He carried them to the top of a hill, some fifty miles away, and left them there.

This story very much resembles that of the "Pillars of Hercules," called the "*Gates of Cadiz.*"[2]

Count de Volney tells us that:

"Hercules was represented naked, carrying on his shoulders *two columns* called the Gates of Cadiz."[3]

"The *Pillars* of Hercules" was the name given by the ancients to the two rocks forming the entrance or *gate* to the Mediterranean at the Strait of Gibraltar.[4] Their erection was ascribed by the Greeks to Hercules, on the occasion of his journey to the kingdom of Geryon. According to one version of the story, they had been

FIG NO.3

united, but Hercules tore them asunder.[5]

Fig. No. 3 is a representation of Hercules with the two posts or pillars on his shoulders, as alluded to by Count de Volney. We have taken it from Montfaucon's "L'Antiquité Expliquée."[6]

J. P. Lundy says of this:

---

[1] Volney: Researches in Anc't History, pp. 41, 42.

In Bell's "Pantheon of the Gods and Demi-Gods of Antiquity," we read, under the head of *Ammon* or *Hammon* (the name of the Egyptian Jupiter, worshiped under the figure of a *Ram*), that: "*Bacchus* having subdued Asia, and passing with his army through the deserts of Africa, was in great want of water; but Jupiter, his father, assuming the shape of a *Ram*, led him to a fountain, where he refreshed himself and his army; in requital of which favor, Bacchus built there a

temple to Jupiter, under the title of *Ammon*."

[2] Cadiz (ancient Gades), being situated near the *mouth* of the Mediterranean. The first author who mentions the Pillars of Hercules is Pindar, and he places them there. (Chambers's Encyclo. "Hercules.")

[3] Volney's Researches, p. 41. See also Tylor: Primitive Culture, vol. i. p. 357.

[4] See Chambers's Encyclopædia, Art "Hercules." Cory's Ancient Fragments, p. 36, *note;* and Bulfinch: The Age of Fable, p. 201.

[5] Chambers's Encyclo., art. "Hercules."

[6] Vol. i. plate cxxvii.

"Hercules carrying his two columns to erect at the Straits of Gibraltar, may have some reference to the Hebrew story."[1]

We think there is no doubt of it. By changing the name Hercules into Samson, the legend is complete.

Sir William Drummond tells us, in his "Œdipus Judaicus," that:

"*Gaza* signifies a Goat, and was the type of the Sun in Capricorn. The *Gates of the Sun* were feigned by the ancient Astronomers to be in Capricorn and Cancer (that is, in *Gaza*), from which signs the tropics are named. Samson carried away the gates from Gaza to Hebron, the city of conjunction. Now, Count Gebelin tells us that at Cadiz, where Hercules was anciently worshiped, there was a representation of him, *with a gate on his shoulders*."[2]

The stories of the amours of Samson with Delilah and other females, are simply counterparts of those of Hercules with Omphale and Iole. Montfaucon, speaking of this, says:

"Nothing is better known in the fables (related of Hercules) than his amours with Omphale and Iole."[3]

Prof. Steinthal says:

"The circumstance that Samson is so addicted to sexual pleasure, has its origin in the remembrance that the *Solar god* is the god of fruitfulness and procreation. We have as examples, the amours of Hercules and Omphale; Ninyas, in Assyria, with Semiramis; Samson, in Philistia, with Delila, whilst among the Phenicians, Melkart pursues Dido-Anna."[4]

Samson is said to have had long hair. "There hath not come a razor upon my head," says he, "for I have been a Nazarite unto God from my mother's womb."

Now, strange as it may appear, Hercules is said to have had long hair also, and he was often represented that way. In Montfaucon's "L'Antiquité Expliquée"[5] may be seen a representation of Hercules *with hair reaching almost to his waist*. Almost all *Sun*-gods are represented thus.[6]

Prof. Goldzhier says:

"Long locks of hair and a long beard are mythological attributes of the Sun. The Sun's rays are compared with locks of hair on the face or head of the Sun.

[1] Monumental Christianity, p. 399.
[2] Œd. Jud. p. 360, in Anacalypsis, vol. i. p. 239.
[3] "Rien de plus connu dans la fable que ses amours avec Omphale et Iole."—L'Antiquité Expliquée, vol. i. p. 224.
[4] The Legend of Samson, p. 404.
[5] Vol. i. plate cxxvii.
[6] "Samson was remarkable for his long hair. The meaning of this trait in the original myth is easy to guess, and appears also from representations of the Sun-god amongst other peoples. *These long hairs are the rays of the Sun.*" (Bible for Learners, i. 416.)
"The beauty of the sun's rays is signified by the golden locks of Phoibos, *over which no razor has ever passed;* by the flowing hair which streams from the head of Kephalos, and falls over the shoulders of Perseus and Bellerophon." (Cox: Aryan Mytho., vol. I. p. 107.)

"When the sun sets and leaves his place to the darkness, or when the powerful Summer Sun is succeeded by the weak rays of the Winter Sun, then Samson's long locks, in which alone his strength lies, are cut off through the treachery of his deceitful concubine, Delilah, the 'languishing, languid,' according to the meaning of the name (Delilah).   The. Beaming Apollo, moreover, is called the *Unshaven;* and Minos cannot conquer the solar hero Nisos, *till the latter loses his golden hair.*"[1]

Through the influence of Delilah, Samson is at last made a prisoner.   He tells her the secret of his strength, the *seven* locks of hair are shaven off, and his strength leaves him.   The shearing of the locks of the Sun must be followed by darkness and ruin.

From the shoulders of Phoibos Lykêgenês flow the sacred locks, over which no razor might pass, and on the head of Nisos they become a palladium, invested with a mysterious power.[2] The long locks of hair which flow over his shoulders are taken from his head by Skylla, while he is asleep, and, like another Delilah, she thus delivers him and his people into the power of Minos.[3]

Prof. Steinthal says of Samson:

"His hair is a figure of increase and luxuriant fullness.   In Winter, when nature appears to have lost all strength, the god of growing young life has lost his hair.   In the Spring the hair grows again, and nature returns to life again. Of this original conception the Bible story still preserves a trace.   Samson's hair, after being cut off, grows again, and his strength comes back with it."[4]

Towards the end of his career, Samson's eyes are put out. Even here, the Hebrew writes with a singular fidelity to the old mythical speech.   The tender light of evening is blotted out by the dark vapors; the light of the *Sun* is quenched in gloom.   *Samson's eyes are put out.*

Œdipus, whose history resembles that of Samson and Hercules in many respects, tears out his eyes, towards the end of his career. In other words, the *Sun* has blinded himself.   Clouds and darkness have closed in about him, and the clear light is blotted out of the heaven.[5]

The final act, Samson's death, reminds us clearly and decisively of the Phenician Hercules, as Sun-god, who died at the Winter Solstice in the furthest West, where his *two pillars* are set up to mark the end of his wanderings.

Samson also died at the *two pillars,* but in his case they are not the Pillars of the World, but are only set up in the middle of a great banqueting-hall.   A feast was being held in honor of

[1] Hebrew Mytho., pp. 137, 138.   [4] The Legend of Samson, p. 408.
[2] Cox : Aryan Myths, vol. i. p. 84.   [5] Cox: Aryan Mytho., vol. ii. p. 72.
[3] Tales of Ancient Greece, p. xxix.

Dagon, the Fish-god; the Sun was in the sign of the Waterman, *Samson, the Sun-god, died.*[1]

The ethnology of the *name* of Samson, as well as his adventures, are very closely connected with the *Solar* Hercules. "*Samson*" *was the name of the Sun.*[2] In Arabic, "*Shams-on*" means the *Sun.*[3] Samson had *seven* locks of hair, the number of the planetary bodies.[4]

The author of "The Religion of Israel," speaking of Samson, says:

"The story of Samson and his deeds originated in a *Solar myth*, which was afterwards transformed by the narrator into a *saga* about a mighty hero and deliverer of Israel. The very *name* 'Samson,' is derived from the Hebrew word, and means 'Sun.' The hero's flowing locks were originally the *rays of the sun*, and other traces of the old myth have been preserved."[5]

Prof. Oort says:

"The story of Samson is simply a solar myth. In some of the features of the story the original meaning may be traced quite clearly, but in others the myth can no longer be recognized. The exploits of some Danite hero, such as Shamgar, who 'slew six hundred Philistines with an ox-goad' (Judges iii. 31), have been woven into it; the whole has been remodeled after the ideas of the prophets of later ages, and finally, it has been fitted into the framework of the period of the Judges, as conceived by the writer of the book called after them."[6]

Again he says:

"The myth that lies at the foundation of this story is a description of the sun's course during the six winter months. The god is gradually encompassed by his enemies, mist and darkness. At first he easily maintains his freedom, and gives glorious proofs of his strength; but the fetters grow stronger and stronger, until at last he is robbed of his crown of rays, and loses all his power and glory. *Such is the Sun in Winter.* But he has not lost his splendor forever. Gradually his strength returns, at last he reappears; and though he still seems to allow himself to be mocked, yet the power of avenging himself has returned, and in the end he triumphs over his enemies once more."[7]

Other nations beside the Hebrews and Greeks had their "mighty men" and lion-killers. The Hindoos had their Samson. His name was Bala-Rama, the "*Strong Rama.*" He was considered by some an incarnation of Vishnu.[8]

---

[1] The Legend of Samson, p. 406.
[2] See Higgins: Anacalypsis, vol. i. p. 237. Goldzhier: Hebrew Mythology, p. 22. The Religion of Israel, p. 61. The Bible for Learners, vol. i. p. 418. Volney's Ruins, p. 41, and Stanley: History of the Jewish Church, where he says: "His *name*, which Josephus interprets in the sense of 'strong,' was still more characteristic. He was 'the Sunny'— the bright and beaming, though wayward, likeness of the great luminary."
[3] Higgins: Anacalypsis, vol. i. p. 237, and Volney's Researches, p. 43, *note.*
[4] See chapter ii.
[5] The Religion of Israel, p. 61. "The yellow hair of Apollo was a symbol of the solar rays." (Inman: Ancient Faiths, vol. ii. p. 679.)
[6] Bible for Learners, vol. i. p. 414.
[7] Ibid, p. 422.
[8] Williams' Hinduism, pp. 108 and 167.

Captain Wilford says, in " Asiatic Researches : "

" The *Indian* Hercules, according to Cicero, was called *Belus*. He is the same as *Bala*, the brother of Crishna, and both are conjointly worshiped at Mutra; indeed, they are considered as one Avatar or Incarnation of Vishnou. *Bala* is represented as a stout man, *with a club in his hand*. He is also called *Bala-rama*."[1]

There is a Hindoo legend which relates that Sevah had an en-counter with a tiger, " whose mouth expanded like a cave, and whose voice resembled thunder." He slew the monster, and, like Hercules, covered himself with the skin.[2]

The Assyrians and Lydians, both Semitic nations, worshiped a Sun-god named Sandan or Sandon. He also was believed to be a *lion-killer*, and frequently figured struggling with the lion, or standing upon the slain lion.[3]

Ninevah, too, had her mighty hero and king, who slew a lion and other monsters. Layard, in his excavations, discovered a *bas-relief* representation of this hero triumphing over the lion and wild bull.[4]

The Ancient Babylonians had a hero lion-slayer, Izdubar by name. The destruction of the lion, and other monsters, by Izdubar, is often depicted on the cylinders and engraved gems belonging to the early Babylonian monarchy.[5]

Izdubar is represented as a great or mighty man, who, in the early days after the flood, destroyed wild animals, and conquered a number of petty kings.[6]

Izdubar resembles the Grecian hero, Hercules, in other respects than as a destroyer of wild animals, &c. We are told that he " wandered to the regions where gigantic composite monsters held and controlled the rising and setting sun, from these learned the road to *the region of the blessed*, and passing across *a great waste of land*, he arrived at a region where *splendid trees were laden with jewels*."[7]

He also resembles Hercules, Samson, and other solar-gods, in the particular of *long flowing locks of hair*. In the Babylonian and Assyrian sculptures he is always represented with a marked physiognomy, and always indicated as a man with *masses of curls over his head* and a large curly beard.[8]

---

[1] Vol. v. p. 270.

[2] Maurice: Indian Antiquities, vol. ii. p. 155.

[3] Steinthal : The Legend of Samson, p. 396.

[4] Buckley: Cities of the World, 41, 42.

[5] Smith: Assyrian Discoveries, p. 167, and Chaldean Account of Genesis, p. 174.

[6] Assyrian Discoveries, p. 205, and Chaldean Account of Genesis, p. 174.

[7] Chaldean Account of Genesis, p. 310.

[8] Ibid, pp. 193, 194, 174.

Here, evidently, is the Babylonian legend of Hercules. He too was a *wanderer*, going from the furthest East to the furthest West. He crossed "a great waste of land" (the desert of Lybia), visited "the region of the blessed," where there were "splendid trees laden with jewels" (golden apples).

The ancient Egyptians had their Hercules. According to Herodotus, he was known several thousand years before the Grecian hero of that name. This the Egyptians affirmed, and that he was *born* in their country.[1]

The story of Hercules was known in the Island of Thasos, by the Phenician colony settled there, five centuries before he was known in Greece.[2] Fig. No. 4 is from an ancient representation of Hercules in conflict with the lion, taken from Gorio.

Fig. 4

Another mighty hero was the Grecian Bellerophon. The minstrels sang of the beauty and the great deeds of Bellerophon throughout all the land of Argos. His arm was strong in battle; his feet were swift in the chase. None that were poor and weak and wretched feared the might of Bellerophon. To them the sight of his beautiful form brought only joy and gladness; but the proud and boastful, the slanderer and the robber, dreaded the glance of his keen eye. For a long time he fought the Solymi and the Amazons, until all his enemies shrank from the stroke of his mighty arm, and sought for mercy.[3]

The second of the principal gods of the Ancient *Scandinavians* was named Thor, and was no less known than Odin among the Teutonic nations. The Edda calls him expressly the most valiant of the sons of Odin. He was considered the "*defender*" and "*avenger*." He always carried a mallet, which, as often as he discharged it, returned to his hand of itself; he grasped it with gauntlets of iron, and was further possessed of a girdle which had the virtue of renewing his strength as often as was needful. It was with these formidable arms that he overthrew to the ground the monsters and giants, when he was sent by the gods to oppose their enemies. He was represented of gigantic size, and as the stoutest and strongest of the gods.[1] Thor was simply the Hercules of the Northern nations.   He was the Sun personified.[2]

Without enumerating them, we can safely say, that there was not a nation of antiquity, from the remotest East to the furthest West, that did not have its mighty hero, and counterpart of Hercules and Samson.[3]

---

[1] See Mallet's Northern Antiquities, pp. 94, 417, and 514.

[2] See Cox : Aryan Mythology.

[3] See vol. i. of Aryan Mythology, by Rev. G. W. Cox.

"Besides the fabulous Hercules, the son of Jupiter and Alcmena, there was, in ancient times, no warlike nation who did not boast of its own particular Hercules." (Arthur Murphy, Translator of Tacitus.)

CHAPTER IX.

In the book of Jonah, containing four chapters, we are told the word of the Lord came unto Jonah, saying: "Arise, go to Ninevah, that great city, and cry against it, for their wickedness is come up against me."

Instead of obeying this command Jonah sought to flee "from the presence of the Lord," by going to Tarshish. For this purpose he went to *Joppa*, and there took ship for Tarshish. But the Lord sent a great wind, and there was a mighty tempest, so that the ship was likely to be broken.

The mariners being afraid, they cried every one unto *his* God; and casting lots—that they might know which of them was the cause of the storm—the lot fell upon Jonah, showing him to be the guilty man.

The mariners then said unto him; "What shall we do unto thee?" Jonah in reply said, "Take me up and cast me forth into the sea, for I know that for my sake this great tempest is upon you." So they took up Jonah, and cast him into the sea, and the sea ceased raging.

And the Lord prepared a great fish to swallow up Jonah, *and Jonah was in the belly of the fish three days and three nights.* Then Jonah prayed unto the Lord out of the fish's belly. And the Lord spake unto the fish, and it vomited out Jonah upon the dry land.

The Lord again spake unto Jonah and said:

"Go unto Ninevah and preach unto it." So Jonah arose and went unto Ninevah, according to the command of the Lord, and preached unto it.

There is a *Hindoo* fable, very much resembling this, to be found in the *Somadeva Bhatta*, of a person by the name of *Saktideva* who was swallowed by a huge fish, and finally came out unhurt. The story is as follows:

"There was once a king's daughter who would marry no one

[77]

but the man who had seen the Golden City—of legendary fame—
and Saktideva was in love with her; so he went travelling about
the world seeking some one who could tell him where this Golden
City was. In the course of his journeys *he embarked on board a
ship* bound for the Island of Utsthala, where lived the King of the
Fishermen, who, Saktideva hoped, would set him on his way. On
the voyage *there arose a great storm* and the ship went to pieces,
and a great fish swallowed Saktideva whole. Then, driven by the
force of fate, the fish went to the Island of Utsthala, and there the
servants of the King of the Fishermen caught it, and the king,
wondering at its size, had it cut open, *and Saktideva came out
unhurt.*"[1]

In Grecian fable, Hercules is said to have been swallowed by a
whale, at a place called Joppa, *and to have lain three days in his
entrails.*

Bernard de Montfaucon, speaking of Jonah being swallowed by
a whale, and describing a piece of Grecian sculpture representing
Hercules standing by a huge sea monster, says :

"Some ancients relate to the effect that Hercules was also swallowed by
the whale that was watching Hesione, *that he remained three days in his belly,*
and that he came out bald-pated after his sojourn there."[2]

Bouchet, in his " Hist. d'Animal," tells us that :

" The great fish which swallowed up *Jonah,* although it be called a whale
(Matt. xii. 40), yet it was not a whale, properly so called, but a *Dog-fish,* called
Carcharias. Therefore in the Grecian fable *Hercules* is said to have been swal-
lowed up of a *Dag,* and to have lain three days in his entrails."[3]

Godfrey Higgins says, on this subject :

"The story of *Jonas* swallowed up by a whale, is nothing but part of the
fiction of *Hercules,* described in the Heracleid or Labors of Hercules, of whom
the same story was told, and who was swallowed up at the very same place,
Joppa, and for the same period of time, *three days.* Lycophron says that Hercules
was three nights in the belly of a fish."[4]

We have still another similar story in that of *"Arion the Musi-
cian,"* who, being thrown overboard, was caught on the back of a
Dolphin and landed safe on shore. The story is related in
" Tales of Ancient Greece," as follows :

Arion was a Corinthian harper who had travelled in Sicily and

---

[1] Tylor: Early Hist. Mankind, pp. 344, 345.

[2] " En effet, quelques anciens disent qu' Her-
cule fut aussi devorà par la beleine qui gardoit
Hesione, qu'il demeura trois jours dans son
ventre, et qu'il sortit chauve de ce sejour."
(L'Antiquité Expliqueé, vol. i. p. 204.)

[3] Bouchet: Hist. d'Animal, in Anac., vol. i.
p. 240.

[4] Anacalypsis, vol. i. p. 638. See also
Tylor . Primitive Culture, vol. i. p. 300, and
Chambers's Encyclo., art. " Jonah."

Italy, and had accumulated great wealth. Being desirous of again seeing his native city, he set sail from Taras for Corinth. The sailors in the ship, having seen the large boxes full of money which Arion had brought with him into the ship, made up their minds to kill him and take his gold and silver. So one day when he was sitting on the bow of the ship, and looking down on the dark blue sea, three or four of the sailors came to him and said they were going to kill him. Now Arion knew they said this because they wanted his money; so he promised to give them all he had if they would spare his life. But they would not. Then he asked them to let him jump into the sea. When they had given him leave to do this, Arion took one last look at the bright and sunny sky, and then leaped into the sea, and the sailors saw him no more. But Arion was not drowned in the sea, for a great fish called a dolphin was swimming by the ship when Arion leaped over; and it caught him on its back and swam away with him towards Corinth. So presently the fish came close to the shore and left Arion on the beach, and swam away again into the deep sea.[1]

There is also a Persian legend to the effect that Jemshid was devoured by a great monster waiting for him at the bottom of the sea, but afterwards rises again out of the sea, like Jonah in the Hebrew, and Hercules in the Phenician myth.[2] This legend was also found in the myths of the *New World.*[3]

It was urged, many years ago, by Rosenmüller—an eminent German divine and professor of theology—and other critics, that the miracle recorded in the book of Jonah is not to be regarded as an historical fact, "*but only as an allegory, founded on the Phenician myth of Hercules rescuing Hesione from the sea monster by leaping himself into its jaws, and for three days and three nights continuing to tear its entrails.*"[4]

That the story is an allegory, and that it, as well as that of Saktideva, Hercules and the rest, are simply different versions of the same myth, the significance of which is the alternate swallowing up and casting forth of *Day,* or the *Sun,* by *Night,* is now all but universally admitted by scholars. The *Day,* or the *Sun,* is swallowed up by *Night,* to be set free again at dawn, and from time to time suffers a like but shorter durance in the maw of the eclipse and the storm-cloud.[5]

Professor Goldzhier says:

---

[1] Tales of Ancient Greece, p. 296.
[2] See Hebrew Mythology, p. 203.
[3] See Tylor's Early Hist. Mankind, and Primitive Culture, vol. i.
[4] Chambers's Encyclo., art. Jonah.
[5] See Fiske : Myths and Myth Makers, p. 77, and *note* ; and Tylor : Primitive Culture, i. 302.

"The most prominent mythical characteristic of the story of Jonah is his celebrated abode in the sea in the belly of a whale. This trait is eminently *Solar.* . . . As on occasion of the storm the storm-dragon or the storm-serpent *swallows the Sun*, so when he sets, he (Jonah, as a personification of the Sun) is swallowed by a mighty fish, waiting for him at the bottom of the sea. Then, when he appears again on the horizon, he is *spit out on the shore* by the sea-monster."[1]

The *Sun* was called Jona, as appears from Gruter's inscriptions, and other sources.[2]

In the *Vedas*—the four sacred books of the Hindoos—when *Day* and *Night, Sun* and *Darkness,* are opposed to each other, the one is designated *Red,* the other *Black.*[3]

The *Red Sun* being swallowed up by the *Dark Earth* at *Night* —as it apparently is when it sets in the west—to be cast forth again at *Day,* is also illustrated in like manner. Jonah, Hercules and others personify the *Sun,* and a huge *Fish* represents the *Earth.*[4] *The Earth represented as a huge Fish is one of the most prominent ideas of the Polynesian mythology.*[5]

At other times, instead of a *Fish,* we have a great raving *Wolf,* who comes to devour its victim and extinguish the *Sun*-light.[6] The Wolf is particularly distinguished in ancient *Scandinavian* mythology, being employed as an emblem of the *Destroying Power,* which attempts to destroy the *Sun.*[7] This is illustrated in the story of Little *Red* Riding-Hood (the Sun)[8] who is devoured by the great *Black Wolf* (Night) and afterwards *comes out unhurt.*[9]

The story of Little Red Riding-Hood *is mutilated in the English version.* The original story was that the little maid, in her *shining Red Cloak,* was swallowed by the great *Black Wolf,* and that *she came out safe and sound* when the hunters cut open the sleeping beast.[10]

---

[1] Goldzhier: Hebrew Mythology, pp. 102, 103.

[2] This is seen from the following, taken from Pictet: "*Du Culte des Carabi,*" p. 104, and quoted by Higgins: *Anac.,* vol. i. p. 650: "Vallancy dit que *Ionn* étoit le même que Baal. En Gallois *Jon,* le Seigneur, Dieu, la cause première. En Basque *Jawna, Jon, Jona,* &c., Dieu, et Seigneur, Maître. Les Scandinaves appeloient le *Soleil* John. . . . Une des inscriptions de Gruter montre ques les Troyens adoroient *le même* astre sous le nom de *Jona.* En Persan le *Soleil* est appelé *Jawnah.*" Thus we see that the *Sun* was called *Jonah,* by different nations of antiquity.

[3] See Goldzhier: Hebrew Mythology, p. 146.

[4] See Tylor: Early History of Mankind, p. 345, and Goldzhier: Hebrew Mythology, pp. 102, 103.

[5] See Tylor: Early History of Mankind, p. 345.

[6] Fiske: Myths and Myth Makers, p. 77.

[7] See Knight: Ancient Art and Mythology, pp. 88, 89, and Mallet's Northern Antiquities.

[8] In ancient *Scandinavian* mythology, the *Sun* is personified in the form of a beautiful *maiden.* (See Mallet's Northern Antiquities, p. 458.)

[9] See Fiske: Myths and Myth Makers, p. 77. Bunce: Fairy Tales, 161.

[10] Tylor: Primitive Culture, vol. i. p. 307.
"The story of Little Red Riding-Hood, as we call her, or Little Red-Cap, came from the same (*i. e.,* the ancient Aryan) source, and refers to the *Sun* and the *Night.*"
"One of the fancies of the most ancient Aryan or Hindoo stories was that there was a

In regard to these heroes remaining *three days and three nights* in the bowels of the Fish, *they represent the Sun at the Winter Solstice.* From December 22d to the 25th—that is, *for three days and three nights*—the *Sun* remains in the *Lowest Regions,* in the bowels of the Earth, in the belly of the Fish; it is then cast forth and renews its career.

Thus, we see that the story of Jonah being swallowed by a big fish, meant originally the Sun swallowed up by Night, and that it is identical with the well-known nursery-tale. How such legends are transformed from intelligible into unintelligible myths, is very clearly illustrated by Prof. Max Müller, who, in speaking of "the comparison of the different forms of Aryan Religion and Mythology," in India, Persia, Greece, Italy and Germany, says:

"In each of these nations there was a tendency to change the original conception of divine powers; to misunderstand the many names given to these powers, and to misinterpret the praises addressed to them. In this manner some of the divine names were changed into half-divine, half-human heroes, *and at last the myths which were true and intelligible as told originally of the Sun, or the Dawn, or the Storms, were turned into legends or fables too marvellous to be believed of common mortals.* This process can be watched in *India,* in *Greece,* and in *Germany.* The same story, or nearly the same, is told of gods, of heroes, and of men. The *divine myth* became an *heroic legend,* and the *heroic legend* fades away into a *nursery tale.* Our nursery tales have well been called the modern *patois* of the ancient sacred mythology of the Aryan race."[1]

How striking are these words; how plainly they illustrate the process by which the story, that was true and intelligible as told originally of the *Day* being swallowed up by *Night,* or the *Sun* being swallowed up by the *Earth,* was transformed into a legend or fable, too marvellous to be believed by common mortals. How the "*divine myth*" became an "*heroic legend,*" and how the heroic legend faded away into a "*nursery tale.*"

In regard to Jonah's going to the city of Ninevah, and preaching unto the inhabitants, we believe that the old "Myth of Civiliza-

---

great dragon that was trying to devour the Sun, and to prevent him from shining upon the earth and filling it with brightness and life and beauty, and that Indra, the Sun-god, killed the dragon. Now, this is the meaning of Little Red Riding-Hood, as it is told in our nursery tales. Little Red Riding-Hood is the evening Sun, which is always described as red or golden; the old grandmother is the earth, to whom the rays of the Sun bring warmth and comfort. The wolf—which is a well-known figure for the clouds and darkness of night—is the dragon in another form. First he devours the grandmother; that is, he wraps the earth in thick clouds, which the evening Sun is not strong enough to pierce through. Then, with the darkness of night, he swallows up the evening Sun itself, and all is dark and desolate. Then, as in the German tale, the night-thunder and the storm-winds are represented by the loud snoring of the wolf; and then the huntsman, the morning Sun, comes in all his strength and majesty, and chases away the night-clouds and kills the wolf, and revives old Grandmother Earth, and brings Little Red Riding-Hood to life again." (Bunce, Fairy Tales, their Origin and Meaning, p. 161.)

[1] Müller's Chips, vol. ii. p. 260.

tion," so called,[1] is partly interwoven here, and that, in this respect, he is nothing more than the Indian *Fish Avatar of Vishnou*, or the Chaldean *Oannes*.   At his first Avatar, *Vishnou* is alleged to have appeared to humanity in form like a fish,[2] or half-man and half-fish, just as Oannes and Dagon were represented among the Chaldeans and other nations.   In the temple of *Rama*, in India, there is a representation of *Vishnou* which answers perfectly to that of *Dagon*.[3]   Mr. Maurice, in his "Hist. Hindostan," has proved the identity of the Syrian *Dagon* and the Indian Fish Avatar, and concludes by saying:

"From the foregoing and a variety of parallel circumstances, I am inclined to think that the Chaldean *Oannes*, the Phenician and Philistian *Dagon*, and the *Pisces* of the Syrian and Egyptian Zodiac, were the same deity with the Indian *Vishnu*."[4]

In the old mythological remains of the Chaldeans, compiled by Berosus, Abydenus, and Polyhistor, there is an account of one *Oannes*, a fish-god, who rendered great service to mankind.[5] This being is said to have *come out of* the Erythraean Sea.[6] This is evidently *the Sun rising out of the sea*, as it apparently does, in the East.[7]

Prof. Goldzhier, speaking of Oannes, says :

"That this founder of civilization has a *Solar character*, like similar heroes in all other nations, is shown . . . in the words of Berosus, who says: '*During the day-time* Oannes held intercourse with man, *but when the Sun set*, Oannes fell into the sea, where he used to pass the night.'   Here, evidently, only the *Sun* can be meant, who, in the evening, dips into the sea, and comes forth again in the morning, and passes the day on the dry land in the company of men."[8]

Dagon was sometimes represented as *a man emerging from a fish's mouth*, and sometimes as half-man and half-fish.[9] It was believed that he came *in a ship*, and taught the people. Ancient history abounds with such mythological personages.[10] There was also a *Durga*, a fish deity, among the *Hindoos*, represented as *a full grown man emerging from a fish's mouth*.[9] The Philistines wor-

---

[1] See Goldzhier's Hebrew Mythology, p. 198, et seq.

[2] See Maurice: Indian Antiquities, vol. ii. p. 277.

[3] See Isis Unveiled, vol. ii. p. 259. Also, Fig. No. 5, next page.

[4] Hist. Hindostan, vol. i. pp. 418–419.

[5] See Prichard's Egyptian Mythology, p. 190. Bible for Learners, vol. i. p. 87. Higgins: Anacalypsis, vol. i. p. 646. Cory's Ancient Fragments, p. 57.

[6] See Higgins: Anacalypsis, vol. i. p. 646. Smith: Chaldean Account of Genesis, p. 39, and Cory's Ancient Fragments, p. 57.

[7] Civilizing gods, who diffuse intelligence and instruct barbarians, are also *Solar Deities*. Among these *Oannes* takes his place, as the *Sun-god*, giving knowledge and civilization. (Rev. S. Baring-Gould: Curious Myths, p. 367.

[8] Goldzhier: Hebrew Mythology, pp. 214, 215.

[9] See Inman's Ancient Faiths, vol. i. p. 111.

[10] See Chamber's Encyclo., art "Dagon."

shiped Dagon, and in Babylonian Mythology *Odakon* is applied to a fish-like being, who *rose from the waters of the Red Sea* as one of the benefactors of men.[1]

On the coins of Ascalon, where she was held in great honor, the goddess Derceto or Atergatis is represented as a woman with her lower extremities like a fish. This is Semiramis, who appeared at *Joppa* as a mermaid. She is simply a personification of the *Moon*, who follows the course of the *Sun*. At times she manifests herself to the eyes of men, at others she seeks concealment in the Western flood.[2]

The Sun-god Phoibos traverses the sea in the form of a fish, and imparts lessons of wisdom and goodness when he has come forth from the green depths. All these powers or qualities are shared by Proteus in Hellenic story, as well as by the fish-god, Dagon or Oannes.[3]

In the Iliad and Odyssey, Atlas is brought into close connection with Helios, the bright god, the Latin Sol, and our Sun. In these poems he rises every morning from a beautiful lake by the deep-flowing stream of Ocean, and having accomplished his journey across the heavens, plunges again into the Western waters.[4]

The ancient Mexicans and Peruvians had likewise semi-fish gods.[5]

Jonah then, is like these other personages, in so far as they are all *personifications of the Sun ;* they all *come out of the sea ;* they are all represented as *a man emerging from a fish's mouth ;* and they are all *benefactors of mankind.* We believe, therefore, that it is one and the same myth, whether Oannes, Joannes, or Jonas,[6] differing to a certain extent among different nations, just

FIG. 5

as we find to be the case with other legends. This we have just seen illustrated in the story of " Little Red Riding-Hood," which is considerably mutilated in the English version.

---

[1] See Smith's Dictionary of the Bible, and Chambers's Encyclo., art. " Dagon " in both.
[2] See Baring-Gould's Curious Myths.
[3] See Cox : Aryan Mythology, vol. ii. p. 26.
[4] Ibid, p. 38.
[5] Curious Myths, p. 372.
[6] Since writing the above we find that Mr. Bryant, in his "*Analysis of Ancient Mythol-*ogy " (vol. ii. p. 291), speaking of the mystical nature of the name *John,* which is the same as *Jonah,* says : " The prophet who was sent upon an embassy to the Ninevites, is styled *Ionas :* a title probably bestowed upon him as a messenger of the Deity. The great Patriarch who preached righteousness to the Antediluvians, is styled *Oan* and *Oannes,* which is *the same as Jonah.*"

Fig. No. 5 is a representation of *Dagon*, intended to illustrate a creature half-man and half-fish; or, perhaps, a man emerging from a fish's mouth.   It is taken from Layard.   Fig. No. 6[1] is a repre-

sentation of the Indian Avatar of Vishnou, *coming forth from the fish.*[2]   It would answer just as well for a representation of Jonah, as it does for the Hindoo divinity.   It should be noticed that in both of these, the god has a crown on his head, surmounted with a *triple* ornament, both of which had evidently the same meaning, *i. e., an emblem of the trinity.*[3]   The Indian Avatar being represented with four arms, evidently means that he is god of the whole world, his *four* arms extending to the *four corners of the world.*   The *circle,* which is seen in one hand, is an emblem of eternal reward.   The *shell,* with its eight convolutions, is intended to show the place in the number of the cycles which he occupied. The *book* and *sword* are to show that he ruled both in the right of the book and of the sword.[4]

---

[1] From Maurice: Hist. Hindostan, vol. i. p. 495.

[2] Higgins: Anacalypsis, vol. i. p. 634.   See also, Calmet's Fragments, 2d Hundred, p. 78.

[3] See the chapter on "The Trinity," in part second.

[4] See Higgins: Anacalypsis, vol. i. p. 640.

CHAPTER X.

CIRCUMCISION.

In the words of the Rev. Dr. Giles:

"The rite of circumcision must not be passed over in any work that concerns the religion and literature of that (the Jewish) people."[1]

The first mention of Circumcision, in the Bible, occurs in Genesis,[2] where God is said to have commanded the Israelites to perform this rite, and thereby establish a covenant between him and his chosen people:

"This is my *covenant* (said the Lord), which ye shall keep, between me and you and thy seed after thee; every male child among you shall be circumcised."

"We *need not doubt*," says the Rev. Dr. Giles, "that a *Divine command* was given to Abraham that all his posterity should practice the rite of circumcision."[3]

Such may be the case. If we believe that the Lord of the Universe communes with man, we *need not doubt* this; yet, we are compelled to admit that nations other than the Hebrews practiced this rite. The origin of it, however, as practiced among other nations, has never been clearly ascertained. It has been maintained by some scholars that this rite drew its origin from considerations of health and cleanliness, which seems very probable, although doubted by many.[4] Whatever may have been its origin, it is certain that it was practiced by many of the ancient Eastern nations, who never came in contact with the Hebrews, in early times, and, therefore, could not have learned it from them.

The *Egyptians* practiced circumcision at a very early period,[5]

---

[1] Giles: Hebrew and Christian Records, vol. i. p. 249.

[2] Genesis, xvii. 10.

[3] Giles: Hebrew and Christian Records, vol. i. p. 251.

[4] Mr. Herbert Spencer shows (Principles of Sociology, pp. 290, 295) that the sacrificing of a part of the body as a religious offering to their deity, was, and is a common practice among savage tribes. Circumcision may have origin-ated in this way. And Mr. Wake, speaking of it, says: "The *origin* of this custom has not yet, so far as I am aware, been satisfactorily explained. The idea that, under certain climatic con-ditions, circumcision is necessary for cleanli-ness and comfort, does not appear to be well founded, as the custom is not universal even within the tropics." (Phallism in Ancient Religs., p. 36.)

[5] "Other men leave their private parts

at least as early as the *fourth* dynasty—pyramid one—and therefore, long before the time assigned for Joseph's entry into Egypt, from whom some writers have claimed the Egyptians learned it.[1]

In the decorative pictures of Egyptian tombs, one frequently meets with persons on whom the denudation of the prepuce is manifested.[2]

On a stone found at Thebes, there is a representation of the circumcision of Ramses II. A mother is seen holding her boy's arms back, while the operator kneels in front.[3] All Egyptian priests were obliged to be circumcised,[4] and Pythagoras had to submit to it before being admitted to the Egyptian sacerdotal mysteries.[5]

Herodotus, the Greek historian, says :

"As this practice can be traced both in Egypt and Ethiopia, to the remotest antiquity, it is not possible to say which first introduced it. The Phenicians and Syrians of Palestine acknowledge that they borrowed it from Egypt."[6]

It has been recognized among the *Kaffirs* and other tribes of *Africa*.[7] It was practiced among the *Fijians* and *Samoans of Polynesia*, and some races of *Australia*.[8] The *Suzees* and the *Mandingoes* circumcise their women.[9] The *Assyrians, Colchins, Phenicians*, and others, practiced it.[10] It has been from time immemorial a custom among the *Abyssinians*, though, at the present time, Christians.[11]

The antiquity of the custom may be assured from the fact of the *New Hollanders*, (never known to civilized nations until a few years ago) having practiced it.[12]

The *Troglodytes* on the shore of the Red Sea, the *Idumeans, Ammonites, Moabites* and *Ishmaelites*, had the practice of circumcision.[13]

The *ancient Mexicans* also practiced this rite.[13] It was also

---

as they are formed by nature, except those who have learned otherwise from them; but the Egyptians are *circumcised*. . . . They are circumcised for the sake of cleanliness, thinking it better to be clean than handsome." (Herodotus, Book ii. ch. 36.)

[1] We have it also on the authority of Sir J. G. Wilkinson, that: "this custom was established long before the arrival of Joseph in Egypt," and that "this is proved by the ancient monuments."

[2] Bonwick: Egyptian Belief, pp. 414, 415.

[3] Ibid. p. 415.

[4] Ibid. and Knight: Ancient Art and Mythology, p. 89.

[5] Bonwick's Egyptian Belief, p. 415.

[6] Herodotus: Book ii. ch. 36.

[7] See Bonwick's Egyptian Belief, p. 114. Amberly: Analysis Religious Belief, p. 67, and Higgins: Anacalypsis, vol. ii. p. 309.

[8] Bouwick's Egyptian Belief, p. 414, and Amberly's Analysis, pp. 63, 73.

[9] Amberly: Analysis of Relig. Belief, p. 73.

[10] Bonwick: Egyptian Belief. p. 414; Amberly's Analysis, p. 63; Prog. Relig. Ideas, vol. i. p. 163, and Inman: Ancient Faiths, vol. ii. pp. 18, 19.

[11] Bonwick : Egyptian Belief, p. 414.

[12] Kendrick's Egypt, quoted by Dunlap; Mysteries of Adoni, p. 146.

[13] Amberly's Analysis, p. 63, Higgins: Anacalypsis, vol. ii. p. 309, and Acosta, ii. 869.

found among the *Amazon* tribes of *South America.*¹ These Indians, as well as some African tribes, were in the habit of circumcising their women. Among the *Campas*, the women circumcised themselves, and a man would not marry a woman who was not circumcised.² They performed this singular rite upon arriving at the age of puberty.³

Jesus of Nazareth was circumcised,⁴ and had he been really the founder of the Christian religion, so-called, it would certainly be incumbent on all Christians to be circumcised as he was, and to observe that Jewish law which he observed, and which he was so far from abrogating, that he declared: "heaven and earth shall pass away" ere "one jot or one tittle" of that law should be dispensed with.⁵ But the Christians are not followers of the religion of Jesus.⁶ They are followers of the religion of the *Pagans.* This, we believe, we shall be able to show in Part Second of this work.

---

¹ Orton : The Andes and the Amazon, p. 322.

² This was done by cutting off the *clytoris.*

³ Ortou : The Andes and the Amazon, p. 322. Gibbon's Rome, vol. iv. p. 563, and Bible for Learners, vol. i. p. 319.

"At the time of the conquest, the Spaniards found circumcised nations in Central America, and on the Amazon, the Tecuna and Manaos tribes still observe this practice. In the South Seas it has been met with among three different races, but it is performed in a somewhat different manner. On the Australian continent, not all, but the majority of tribes, practiced circumcision. Among the Papuans, the inhabitants of New Caledonia and the New Hebrides adhere to this custom. In his third voyage, Captain Cook found it among the inhabitants of the Friendly Islands, in particular at Tongataboo, and the younger Pritchard bears witness to its practice in the Samoa or Fiji groups." (Oscar Peschel : The Races of Man, p. 22.)

⁴ Luke, ii. 21.

⁵ Matthew, v. 18.

⁶ In using the words "the religion of Jesus," we mean simply *the religion of Israel.* We believe that Jesus of Nazareth was a *Jew,* in every sense of the word, and that he did not establish a new religion, or preach a new doctrine, in any way, shape, or form. "The preacher from the Mount, the prophet of the Beatitudes, does but repeat with persuasive lips what the law-givers of his race proclaimed in mighty tones of command." (See chap. xl.)

CHAPTER XI.

THERE are many other legends recorded in the Old Testament which might be treated at length, but, as we have considered the principal and most important, and as we have so much to examine in Part Second, which treats of the New Testament, we shall take but a passing glance at a few others.

In Genesis xli. is to be found the story of

PHARAOH'S TWO DREAMS,

which is to the effect that Pharaoh dreamed that he stood by a river, and saw come up out of it *seven* fat kine, and *seven* lean kine, which devoured the fat ones. He then dreamed that he saw *seven* good ears of corn, on one stalk, spring up out of the ground. This was followed by *seven* poor ears, which sprang up after them, and devoured the good ears.

Pharaoh, upon awaking from his sleep, and recalling the dreams which he dreamed, was greatly troubled, "and he sent and called for all the magicians of Egypt, and all the wise men thereof, and Pharaoh told them his dreams, but there was none that could interpret them unto Pharaoh." Finally, his chief butler tells him of one Joseph, who was skilled in interpreting dreams, and Pharaoh orders him to be brought before his presence. He then repeats his dreams to Joseph, who immediately interprets them to the great satisfaction of the king.

A very similar story is related in the Buddhist *Fo-pen-hing*— one of their sacred books, which has been translated by Prof. Samuel Beal—which, in substance, is as follows:

Suddhôdana Raja dreamed *seven* different dreams in one night, when, "awaking from his sleep, and recalling the visions he had seen, was greatly troubled, so that the very hair on his body stood erect, and his limbs trembled." He forthwith summoned to his side, within his palace, all the great ministers of his council, and

[88]

exhorted them in these words: "Most honorable Sirs! be it known to you that during the present night I have seen in my dreams strange and potent visions—there were *seven* distinct dreams, which I will now recite (he recites the dreams). I pray you, honorable Sirs! let not these dreams escape your memories, but in the morning, when I am seated in my palace, and surrounded by my attendants, let them be brought to my mind (that they may be interpreted.)"

At morning light, the king, seated in the midst of his attendants, issued his commands to all the Brahmans, interpreters of dreams, within his kingdom, in these terms, "All ye men of wisdom, explain for me by interpretation the meaning of the dreams I have dreamed in my sleep."

Then all the wise Brahmans, interpreters of dreams, began to consider, each one in his own heart, what the meaning of these visions could be; till at last they addressed the king, and said: "Mahâ-raja! be it known to you that we never before have heard such dreams as these, *and we cannot interpret their meaning.*"

On hearing this, Suddhôdana was very troubled in his heart, and exceeding distressed. He thought within himself: "Who is there that can satisfy these doubts of mine?"

Finally a "holy one," called *T'so-Ping*, being present in the inner palace, and perceiving the sorrow and distress of the king, assumed the appearance of a Brahman, and under this form he stood at the gate of the king's palace, and cried out, saying: "I am able fully to interpret the dreams of Suddhôdana Râja, and with certainty to satisfy all the doubts."

The king ordered him to be brought before his presence, and then related to him his dreams. Upon hearing them, *T'so-Ping* immediately interpreted them, to the great satisfaction of the king.[1]

In the second chapter of Exodus we read of

MOSES THROWN INTO THE NILE,

which is done *by command of the king.*

There are many counterparts to this in ancient mythology; among them may be mentioned that of the infant Perseus, who was, *by command of the king* (Acrisius of Argos), shut up in a chest, and cast into the sea. He was found by one Dictys, who took great care of the child, and—as Pharoah's daughter did with the child Moses—educated him.[2]

---

[1] See Beal: Hist. Buddha, p. 111, *et seq.*   Ancient Art and Mytho., p. 178, and Bulfinch:
[2] Bell's Pantheon, under "Perseus;" Knight: Age of Fables, p. 161.

The infant Bacchus was confined in a chest, *by order of Cadmus, King of Thebes*, and thrown into the Nile.[1] He, like Moses, had two mothers, one by nature, the other by adoption.[2] He was also, like Moses, represented *horned*.[3]

Osiris was also confined in a chest, and thrown into the river Nile.[4]

When Osiris was shut into the coffer, and cast into the river, he floated to Phenicia, and was there received under the name of Adonis. Isis (his mother, or wife) wandered in quest of him, came to Byblos, and seated herself by a fountain in silence and tears. She was then taken by the servants of the royal palace, and made to attend on the young prince of the land. In like manner, Demeter, after Aidoneus had ravished her daughter, went in pursuit, reached Eleusis, seated herself by a well, conversed with the daughters of the queen, and became *nurse to her son*.[5] So likewise, when Moses was put into the ark made of bulrushes, and cast into the Nile, he was found by the daughters of Pharaoh, and his own mother became his nurse.[6] This is simply another version of the same myth.

In the second chapter of the second book of Kings, we read of

ELIJAH ASCENDING TO HEAVEN.

There are many counterparts to this, in heathen mythology.

Hindoo sacred writings relate many such stories—how some of their Holy Ones were taken up alive into heaven—and impressions on rocks are shown, said to be foot-prints, made when they ascended.[7]

According to Babylonian mythology, *Xisuthrus* was translated to heaven.[8]

The story of Elijah ascending to heaven in a chariot of fire may also be compared to the fiery, flame-red chariot of *Ushas*.[9] This idea of some Holy One ascending to heaven without dying was found in the ancient mythology of the *Chinese*.[10]

The story of

DAVID KILLING GOLIATH,

by throwing a stone and hitting him in the forehead,[11] may be com-

[1] Bell's Pantheon, vol. i. p. 118. Taylor's Diegesis, p. 190. Higgins: Anacalypsis, vol. ii. p. 19.   [2] Ibid.
[3] Bell's Pantheon, vol. i. p. 122. Dupuis: Origin of Religious Belief, p. 174. Goldziher: Hebrew Mythology, p. 179. Higgins: Anacalypsis, vol. ii. p. 19.
[4] Bell's Pantheon, art. "Osiris:" and Bulfinch: Age of Fable, p. 391.

[5] Baring-Gould: Orig. Relig. Belief, i. 159.
[6] Exodus, ii.
[7] See Child: Prog. Relig. Ideas, vol. i. p. 6, and most any work on Buddhism.
[8] See Smith: Chaldean Account of Genesis.
[9] See Goldziher: Hebrew Mythology, p. 128, *note*.
[10] See Prog. Relig. Ideas, vol. i. pp. 213, 214.
[11] I. Samuel, xvii.

pared to the story of *Thor*, the Scandinavian hero, throwing a hammer at Hrungnir, and striking him in the forehead.[1]

We read in Numbers[2] that

BALAAM'S ASS SPOKE

to his master, and reproved him.

In ancient fables or stories in which animals play prominent parts, each creature is endowed with the power of speech. This idea was common in the whole of Western Asia and Egypt. It is found in various Egyptian and Chaldean stories.[3] Homer has recorded that the *horse* of Achilles spoke to him.[4]

We have also a very wonderful story in that of

JOSHUA'S COMMAND TO THE SUN.

This story is related in the tenth chapter of the book of Joshua, and is to the effect that the Israelites, who were at battle with the Amorites, wished the day to be lengthened that they might continue their slaughter, whereupon Joshua said: "Sun, stand thou still upon Gibeon, and thou, Moon, in the valley of Ajalon. *And the sun stood still*, and the moon stayed, until the people had avenged themselves upon their enemies. . . . And there was no day like that before it or after it."

There are many stories similar to this, to be found among other nations of antiquity. We have, as an example, that which is related of Bacchus in the Orphic hymns, wherein it says that this god-man arrested the course of the sun and the moon.[5]

An Indian legend relates that the sun stood still to hear the pious ejaculations of Arjouan after the death of Crishna.[6]

A holy Buddhist by the name of Mâtanga prevented the sun, at his command, from rising, and bisected the moon.[7] Arresting the course of the sun was a common thing among the disciples of Buddha.[8]

The *Chinese* also, had a legend of the sun standing still,[9] and a legend was found among the *Ancient Mexicans* to the effect that one of their holy persons commanded the sun to stand still, which command was obeyed.[10]

[1] See Goldzhier: Hebrew Mythology, p. 430, and Bulfinch: Age of Fable, 440.
[2] Chapter xxii.
[3] See Smith's Chaldean Account of Genesis, p. 188, *et seq.*
[4] See Prog. Relig. Ideas, vol. i. p. 323.
[5] See Higgins: Anacalypsis, vol. ii. p. 19.
[6] Ibid, i. 191, and ii. 241; Franklin: Bud. & Jeynes, 174.
[7] Hardy: Buddhist Legends, pp. 50, 53, and 140.
[8] See Ibid.
[9] Higgins: Anacalypsis, vol. ii. p. 191.
[10] Ibid, p. 89.

We shall now endeavor to answer the question which must naturally arise in the minds of all who see, for the first time, the similarity in the legends of the Hebrews and those of other nations, namely: have the Hebrews copied from other nations, or, have other nations copied from the Hebrews? To answer this question we shall; *first*, give a brief account or history of the Pentateuch and other books of the Old Testament from which we have taken legends, and show about what time they were written; and, *second*, show that other nations were possessed of these legends long before that time, *and that the Jews copied from them.*

The Pentateuch is ascribed, in our *modern* translations, to *Moses*, and he is generally supposed to be the author. This is altogether erroneous, as Moses had *nothing whatever* to do with these five books. Bishop Colenso, speaking of this, says:

' The books of the Pentateuch *are never ascribed to Moses in the inscriptions of Hebrew manuscripts, or in printed copies of the Hebrew Bible.* Nor are they styled the ' *Books of Moses* ' in the Septuagint[1] or Vulgate,[2] *but only in our modern translations*, after the example of many eminent Fathers of the Church, who, with the exception of Jerome, and, perhaps, Origen, were, one and all of them, very little acquainted with the Hebrew language, and still less with its criticism.''[3]

The author of " The Religion of Israel," referring to this subject, says:

" The Jews who lived *after* the Babylonish Captivity, and the Christians following their examples, ascribed these books (the Pentateuch) to Moses; and for many centuries the *notion* was cherished that he had really written them. *But strict and impartial investigation has shown that this opinion must be given up ;* and that *nothing* in the whole Law really comes from Moses himself except the Ten Commandments. *And even these were not delivered by him in the same form as we find them now.* If we still call these books by his name, it is only because the Israelites always thought of him as their first and greatest law-giver, *and the actual authors grouped all their narratives and laws around his figure, and associated them with his name.*''[4]

As we cannot go into an extended account, and show *how this is known*, we will simply say that it is principally by *internal* evidence that these facts are ascertained.[5]

---

[1] "Septuagint."—The Old *Greek* version of the Old Testament.

[2] " Vulgate."—The *Latin* version of the Old Testament.

[3] The Pentateuch Examined, vol. ii. pp. 186, 187.

[4] The Religion of Israel, p. 9.

[5] Besides the many other facts which show that the Pentateuch was not composed until long after the time of Moses and Joshua, the following may be mentioned as examples:

Gilgal, mentioned in Deut. xi. 30, was not given as the name of that place till *after* the entrance into Canaan. *Dan*, mentioned in Genesis xiv. 14, was not so called till long *after* the time of Moses. In Gen. xxxvi. 31, the beginning of the reign of the kings over Israel is spoken of *historically*, an event which did not occur before the time of Samuel. (See, for further information, Bishop Colenso's Pentateuch Examined, vol. ii. ch. v. and vi.

Now that we have seen that Moses did not write the books of the Pentateuch, our next endeavor will be to ascertain *when* they were written, and *by whom*.

We can say that they were not written by any *one* person, nor were they written *at the same time*.

We can trace *three* principal redactions of the Pentateuch, that is to say, the material was *worked over*, and *re-edited*, with *modifications* and *additions*, by *different people*, at *three distinct epochs*.[1]

The two principal writers are generally known as the *Jehovistic* and the *Elohistic*. We have—in speaking of the "Eden Myth" and the legend of the "Deluge"—already alluded to this fact, and have illustrated how these writers' narratives conflict with each other.

The *Jehovistic* writer is supposed to have been a prophet, who, it would seem, was anxious to give Israel a history. He begins at Genesis, ii. 4, with a *short* account of the "*Creation*," and then he carries the story on regularly until the Israelites enter Canaan. It is to him that we are indebted for the *charming* pictures of the patriarchs. *He took these from other writings, or from the popular legends.*[2]

About 725 B. C. the Israelites were conquered by Salmanassar, King of Assyria, and many of them were carried away captives. *Their place was supplied by Assyrian colonists from Babylon, Persia, and other places.*[3] This fact is of the greatest importance, and should not be forgotten, as we find that the *first* of the three writers of the Pentateuch, spoken of above, *wrote about this time*, and the Israelites heard, *from the colonists from Babylon, Persia, and other places—for the first time—many of the legends which this writer wove into the fabulous history which he wrote, especially the accounts of the Creation and the Deluge.*

The Pentateuch remained in this, its *first* form, until the year 620 B. C. Then a certain *priest* of marked prophetic sympathies wrote a book of law which has come down to us in Deuteronomy, iv. 44, to xxvi., and xxviii. Here we find the demands which the *Mosaic* party at *that day* were making thrown into the form of laws. It was by King Josiah that this book was first introduced and proclaimed as authoritative.[4] It was soon afterwards *wove into* the work of the *first* Pentateuchian writer, and at the same time

[1] The Religion of Israel, p. 9
[2] Ibid. p. 10.
[3] Chambers's Encyclo., art. "Jews."
[4] The Religion of Israel, pp. 10, 11.

"*a few new passages*" were added, some of which related to
Joshua, the successor of Moses.[1]

At this period in Israel's history, Jehovah had become almost
forgotten, and "other gods" had taken his place.[2] The Mosaic
party, so called—who worshiped Jehovah exclusively—were in the
minority, but when King Amon—who was a worshiper of Moloch
—died, and was succeeded by his son Josiah, a change immediately took place. This young prince, who was only eight years
old at the death of his father, the Mosaic party succeeded in
winning over to their interests. In the year 621 B. C., Josiah,
now in the eighteenth year of his reign, began a thorough reformation which completely answered to the ideas of the Mosaic
party.[3]

It was during this time that the *second* Pentateuchian writer
wrote, and *he* makes *Moses* speak as the law-giver. This writer
was probably Hilkiah, *who claimed to have found a book, written
by Moses, in the temple,*[4] *although it had only just been drawn
up.*[5]

The principal objections which *were* brought against the claims
of Hilkiah, *but which are not needed in the present age of inquiry,*
was that Shaphan and Josiah read it off, not as if it were an *old*
book, *but as though it had been recently written,* when any person
who is acquainted, in the slightest degree, with language, must
know that a man could not read off, at once, *a book written eight
hundred years before.* The phraseology would necessarily be so
altered by time as to render it comparatively unintelligible.

We must now turn to the *third* Pentateuchian writer, *whose
writings were published* 444 B. C.

At that time Ezra (or Ezdras) *added* to the work of his two
predecessors a series of *laws* and *narratives* which had been drawn
up *by some of the priests in Babylon.*[6] This "series of laws and
narratives," which was written by "some of the (Israelitish) priests
in Babylon," was called "*The Book of Origins*" (probably containing the Babylonian account of the "*Origin of Things*," or the
"*Creation*"). Ezra brought the book from *Babylon* to Jerusalem.
He made some modifications in it and constituted it a code of
law for Israel, *dove-tailing it into those parts of the Pentateuch
which existed before.* A few *alterations* and *additions* were subse-

---

[1] The Religion of Israel, p. 11.
[2] See Ibid, pp. 120, 122.
[3] See Ibid, p. 122.
[4] The account of the *finding* of this book by

Hilkiah is to be found in II. Chronicles, ch.
xxxiv.
[5] See Religion of Israel, pp. 124, 125.
[6] Ibid, p. 11.

quently made, but these are of minor importance, and we may fairly say *that Ezra put the Pentateuch into the form in which we have it* (about 444 B. C.).

These priestly passages are partly occupied with historical matter, comprising a very free account of things from the creation of the world to the arrival of Israel in Canaan. Everything is here presented from the *priestly* point of view; some events, elsewhere recorded, are *touched up in the priestly spirit, and others are entirely invented.*[1]

It was the belief of the Jews, asserted by the *Pirke Aboth* (Sayings of the Fathers), one of the oldest books of the *Talmud,*[2] as well as other Jewish records, that Ezra, acting in accordance with a divine commission, re-wrote the Old Testament, the manuscripts of which were said to have been lost in the destruction of the first temple, when Nebuchadnezzar took Jerusalem.[3] This we *know* could not have been the case. The fact that Ezra wrote—adding to, and taking from the already existing books of the Pentateuch—was probably the foundation for this tradition. The account of it is to be found in the Apocryphal book of Esdras, a book deemed authentic by the Greek Church.

Dr. Knappert, speaking of this, says:

' For many centuries, both the Christians and the Jews supposed that Ezra had brought together the sacred writings of his people, united them in one whole, and introduced them as a book given by the Spirit of God—a Holy Scripture.

"The only authority for this supposition was a very modern and altogether untrustworthy *tradition*. The historical and critical studies of our times have been emancipated from the influence of this tradition, and the most ancient statements with regard to the subject have been hunted up and compared together. These statements are, indeed, scanty and incomplete, and many a detail is still obscure; but the main facts have been completely ascertained.

"*Before the Babylonish captivity, Israel had no sacred writings.* There were certain laws, prophetic writings, and a few historical books, but no one had ever thought of ascribing binding and divine authority to these documents.

"*Ezra brought the priestly law with him from Babylon, altering it and amalgamating it with the narratives and laws already in existence, and thus produced the Pentateuch in pretty much the same form* (though not quite, as we shall show) *as we still have it.* These books got the name of the 'Law of Moses,' or simply the 'Law.' Ezra introduced them into Israel (B. C. 444), and gave them binding authority, *and from that time forward they were considered divine.*"[4]

From the time of Ezra until the year 287 B. C., when the Pentateuch was translated into Greek by order of Ptolemy Phila-

---

1 The Religion of Israel, pp. 186, 187.
2 "*Talmud.*"—The books containing the Jewish traditions.
3 See Chambers's Encyclo., art. "Bible."
4 The Religion of Israel, pp. 240, 241.

delphus, King of Egypt, these books evidently underwent some changes. This the writer quoted above admits, in saying:

"Later still (viz., after the time of Ezra), *a few more changes and additions were made*, and so the Pentateuch grew into its present form."[1]

In answer to those who claim that the Pentateuch was written by *one* person, Bishop Colenso says:

"It is certainly inconceivable that, if the *Pentateuch* be the production of *one and the same hand throughout*, it should contain *such a number of glaring inconsistencies.* . . . No single author could have been guilty of such absurdities; but it is quite possible, and what was almost sure to happen in such a case, that, if the Pentateuch be the work of *different authors* in *different ages*, this fact should betray itself *by the existence of contradictions in the narrative*."[2]

Having ascertained the origin of the Pentateuch, or first five books of the Old Testament, it will be unnecessary to refer to the others *here*, as we have nothing to do with *them* in our investigations. Suffice it to say then, that: "In the earlier period after Ezra, *none of the other books* which already existed, enjoyed the same authority as the Pentateuch."[3]

It is probable[4] that Nehemiah made• a collection of historical and prophetic books, songs, *and letters from Persian kings*, not to form a second collection, but for the purpose of saving them from being lost. The scribes of Jerusalem, followers of Ezra, who were known as "the men of the Great Synagogue," *were the collectors of the second and third divisions of the Old Testament*. They collected together the historical and prophetic books, songs, &c., which were then in existence, *and after altering many of them*, they were added to the collection of *sacred* books. It must not be supposed that any fixed plan was pursued in this work, *or that the idea was entertained from the first, that these books would one day stand on the same level with the Pentateuch*.[5]

In the course of time, however, many of the Jews began to consider *some* of these books as *sacred*. The Alexandrian Jews adopted books into the canon which those of Jerusalem did not, *and this difference of opinion lasted for a long time, even till the second century after Christ. It was not until this time that all the books of the Old Testament acquired divine authority*.[6] It is not known, however, *just when* the canon of the Old Testament was closed. *The time and manner in which it was done is alto-*

---

[1] The Religion of Israel, p. 11.
[2] The Pentateuch Examined, vol. ii. p. 173.
[3] The Religion of Israel, p. 241.
[4] On the strength of II. Maccabees, ii. 13.
[5] The Religion of Israel, p. 242.
[6] Ibid, p. 243.

gether obscure.[1] Jewish tradition indicates that the full canonicity of several books was not free from doubt till the time of the famous Rabbi Akiba,[2] who flourished about the beginning of the second century after Christ.[3]

After giving a history of the books of the Old Testament, the author of "The Religion of Israel," whom we have followed in this investigation, says:

"The great majority of the writers of the Old Testament had no other source of information about the past history of Israel than simple *tradition*. Indeed, it could not have been otherwise, for in primitive times no one used to record anything in writing, and the only way of preserving a knowledge of the past was to hand it down by word of mouth. The father told the son what his elders had told him, and the son handed it on to the next generation.

"Not only did the historian of Israel draw from tradition with perfect free-dom, and write down without hesitation anything they heard and what was current in the mouths of the people, *but they did not shrink from modifying their representation of the past in any way that they thought would be good and useful.* It is difficult for us to look at things from this point of view, because our ideas of historical good faith are so utterly different. When we write history, we know that we ought to be guided solely by a desire to represent facts exactly as they really happened. All that we are concerned with is *reality ;* we want to make the old times live again, and we take all possible pains not to remodel the past from the point of view of to-day. All we want to know is what happened, and how men lived, thought, and worked in those days. The Israelites had a very different notion of the nature of historical composition. When a prophet or a priest related something about bygone times, his object was not to convey knowledge about those times; on the contrary, he used history merely as a vehicle for the conveyance of instruction and exhortation. Not only did he confine his narrative to such matters as he thought would serve his purpose but he never hesitated to modify what he knew of the past, *and he did not think twice about touching it up from his own imagination, simply that it might be more conducive to the end he had in view and chime in better with his opinions. All the past became colored through and through with the tinge of his own mind.* Our own notions of honor and good faith would never permit all this; but we must not measure ancient writers by our own standard; they considered that they were acting quite within their rights and in strict accordance with duty and con-science."[4]

It will be noticed that, in our investigations on the authority of the Pentateuch, we have followed, principally, Dr. Knappert's ideas as set forth in "The Religion of Israel."

This we have done because we could not go into an extended investigation, and because his words are very expressive, and just to the point. To those who may think that his ideas are not the same as those entertained by other Biblical scholars of the present

---

[1] Chambers's Encyclo., art. " Bible."
[2] Ibid.
[3] Chambers's Encyclo., art. "Akiba."
[4] The Religion of Israel, pp. 19, 23.

day, we subjoin, in a note below, a list of works to which they are referred.[1]

We shall now, after giving a brief history of the Pentateuch, refer to the legends of which we have been treating, and endeavor to show from whence the Hebrews borrowed them. The first of these is "*The Creation and Fall of Man.*"

Egypt, the country out of which the Israelites came, had no story of the Creation and Fall of Man, *such as we have found among the Hebrews*; they therefore could not have learned it from *them*. The *Chaldeans*, however, as we saw in our first chapter, had this legend, and it is from them that the Hebrews borrowed it.

The account which we have given of the Chaldean story of the Creation and Fall of Man, was taken, as we stated, from the writings of Berosus, the Chaldean historian, who lived in the time of Alexander the Great (356–325 B. C.), and as the Jews were acquainted with the story some centuries earlier than this, his works did not prove that these traditions were in Babylonia before the Jewish captivity, and could not afford testimony in favor of the statement that the Jews borrowed this legend from the Babylonians *at that time*. It was left for Mr. George Smith, of the British Museum, to establish, without a doubt, the fact that this legend was known to the Babylonians at least *two thousand years before the time assigned for the birth of Jesus*. The cuneiform inscriptions discovered by him, while on an expedition to Assyria, organized by the London "Daily Telegraph," was the means of doing this, and although by far the greatest number of these tablets belong to the age of Assurbanipal, who reigned over Assyria B. C. 670, it is "acknowledged on all hands that these tablets are not the originals, *but are only copies from earlier texts*." "The Assyrians acknowledge themselves that this literature was borrowed from Babylonian sources, and of course it is to Babylonia we have to look to ascertain the approximate dates of the original documents."[2] Mr. Smith then shows, from "fragments of the Cuneiform account of the Creation and Fall" which have been discovered, that, "*in the period from* B. C. 2000 *to*

[1] "What is the Bible," by J. T. Sunderland. "The Bible of To-day," by J. W. Chadwick. "Hebrew and Christian Records," by the Rev. Dr. Giles, 2. vols. Prof. W. R. Smith's article on "The Bible," in the last edition of the Encyclopædia Britannica. "Introduction to the Old Testament," by Davidson. "The Pentateuch and the Book of Joshua Examined," by Bishop Colenso. Prof. F. W. Newman's "Hebrew Monarchy." "The Bible for Learners" (vols. i. and ii.), by Prof. Oot and others. "The Old Testament in the Jewish Church," by Prof. Robertson Smith, and Kuenen's "Religion of Israel."

[2] Smith : Chaldean Account of Genesis, pp. 22, 29.

1500, *the Babylonians believed in a story similar to that in Genesis.*" It is probable, however, says Mr. Smith, that this legend existed as *traditions* in the country *long before it was committed to writing,* and some of these traditions exhibited great difference in details, *showing that they had passed through many changes.*[1]

Professor James Fergusson, in his celebrated work on "Tree and Serpent Worship," says :

" The two chapters which refer to this (*i. e.*, the Garden, the Tree, and the Serpent), as indeed the whole of the first eight of Genesis, are now generally admitted by scholars to be made up of fragments of earlier books or earlier traditions, belonging, properly speaking, to Mesopotamia rather than to Jewish history, the exact meaning of which the writers of the Pentateuch seem hardly to have appreciated when they transcribed them in the form in which they are now found."[2]

John Fiske says :

"The story of the Serpent in Eden is an Aryan story in every particular. The notion of Satan as the author of evil appears only in the later books, *composed after the Jews had come into close contact with Persian ideas.*"[3]

Prof. John W. Draper says :

"In the old legends of dualism, the evil spirit was said to have *sent a serpent to ruin Paradise.* These legends became known to the Jews *during their Babylonian captivity.*"[4]

Professor Goldziher also shows, in his " Mythology Among the Hebrews,"[5] that the story of the creation was borrowed by the Hebrews from the Babylonians. He also informs us that the notion of the *bôrê* and *yôsêr,* " Creator " (the term used in the cosmogony in Genesis) as an integral part of the idea of God, *are first brought into use by the prophets of the captivity.* " Thus also the story of the *Garden of Eden,* as a supplement to the history of the Creation, *was written down at Babylon.*"

Strange as it may appear, after the *Genesis* account, we may pass through the whole Pentateuch, and other books of the Old Testament, clear to the end, and will find that the story of the " *Garden of Eden* " and "*Fall of Man,*" is hardly alluded to, if at all. Lengkerke says : " One single *certain* trace of the employment of the story of Adam's fall is entirely wanting in the Hebrew Canon (after the Genesis account). Adam, Eve, the Serpent, the woman's

1 Ibid, pp. 29, 100. Also, Assyrian Discoveries, p. 397.
2 Tree and Serpent Worship, pp. 6, 7.
3 Myths and Myth-Makers, p. 112.
4 Draper: Religion and Science, p. 62.
5 Goldziher: Hebrew Mythology, p. 323, *et seq.*

seduction of her husband, &c., are all images, *to which the remain-ing words of the Israelites never again recur.*"[1]

This circumstance can only be explained by the fact that the first chapters of Genesis were not written until *after* the other portions had been written.

It is worthy of notice, that this story of the Fall of Man, upon which the whole orthodox scheme of a divine Saviour or Re-deemer is based, was *not* considered by the learned Israelites as *fact.* They simply looked upon it as a story which satisfied the ignorant, but which should be considered as *allegory* by the learned.[2]

Rabbi Maimonides (Moses Ben Maimon), one of the most cele-brated of the Rabbis, says on this subject:—

"We must not understand, or take in a literal sense, what is written in *the book* on the *Creation,* nor form of it the same ideas which are participated by the generality of mankind; *otherwise our ancient sages would not have so much recom-mended to us, to hide the real meaning of it, and not to lift the allegorical veil, which covers the truth contained therein.* When taken in its *literal sense,* the work gives the most absurd and most extravagant ideas of the Deity. 'Whosoever should divine its true meaning ought to take great care in not divulging it.' This is a maxim repeated to us by all our sages, principally concerning the understanding of the work of the six days."[3]

Philo, a Jewish writer contemporary with Jesus, held the same opinion of the character of the sacred books of the Hebrews. He has made two particular treatises, bearing the title of "*The Allegories,*" and he traces back to the *allegorical* sense the "Tree of Life," the "Rivers of Paradise," and the other fictions of the Genesis.[4]

Many of the early Christian Fathers declared that, in the story of the Creation and Fall of Man, there was but an *allegorical fiction.* Among these may be mentioned St. Augustine, who speaks of it in his "City of God," and also Origen, who says:

"'What man of sense will agree with the statement that the first, second, and third days, in which the *evening* is named and the *morning,* were without sun, moon and stars? What man is found such an idiot as to suppose that God planted trees in Paradise like an husbandman? *I believe that every man must hold these things for images under which a hidden sense is concealed.*"[5]

[1] Quoted by Bishop Colenso: The Penta-teuch Examined, iv. 285.

[2] "Much of the Old Testament which Chris-tian divines, in their ignorance of Jewish lore, have insisted on receiving and interpreting *literally,* the informed Rabbis never dreamed of regarding as anything but *allegorical.* The 'literalists' they called fools. The account of the Creation was one of the portions which the unlearned were specially forbidden to med-dle with." (Greg: The Creed of Christendom, p. 80.)

[3] Quoted by Dupuis: Origin of Religious Belief, p. 226.

[4] See Ibid. p. 227.

[5] Quoted by Dunlap: Mysteries of Adoni, p. 176. See also, Bunsen: Keys of St. Peter, p. 406.

Origen believed aright, as it is now almost universally admitted, that the stories of the "Garden of Eden," the "Elysian Fields," the "Garden of the Blessed," &c., which were the abode of the blessed, where grief and sorrow could not approach them, where plague and sickness could not touch them, were founded on *allegory*. These abodes of delight were far away in the *West*, where the sun goes down beyond the bounds of the earth. They were the "Golden Islands" sailing in a sea of blue—*the burnished clouds floating in the pure ether*. In a word, *the "Elysian Fields" are the clouds at eventide*. The picture was suggested by the images drawn from the phenomena of sunset and twilight.[1]

Eating of the forbidden fruit was simply a figurative mode of expressing the performance of the act necessary to the perpetuation of the human race. The "Tree of Knowledge" was a Phallic tree, and the fruit which grew upon it was Phallic fruit.[2]

In regard to the story of "*The Deluge*," we have already seen[3] that "Egyptian records tell nothing of a cataclysmal deluge," and that, "the land was *never* visited by other than its annual beneficent overflow of the river Nile." Also, that "the Pharaoh Khoufou-cheops was building his pyramid, according to Egyptian chronicle, when the whole world was under the waters of a universal deluge, according to the Hebrew chronicle." This is sufficient evidence that the Hebrews did not borrow the legend from the Egyptians.

We have also seen, in the chapter that treated of this legend, that it corresponded in all the principal features with the *Chaldean* account. We shall now show that it was taken from this.

Mr. Smith discovered, on the site of Ninevah, during the years 1873–4, cylinders belonging to the early Babylonian monarchy, (from 2500 to 1500 B. C.) which contained the legend of the flood,[4] and which we gave in Chapter II. *This was the foundation for the Hebrew legend, and they learned it at the time of the Captivity.*[5] The myth of Deucalion, the Grecian hero, was also taken from the same source. The Greeks learned it from the Chaldeans.

We read in Chambers's Encyclopædia, that:

"It was at one time extensively believed, even by intelligent scholars, that

---

[1] See Appendix, c.
[2] See Westopp & Wakes, "Phallic Worship."
[3] In chap. ii.
[4] See Assyrian Discoveries, pp. 167, 168, and Chaldean Account of Genesis.

[5] "Upon the carrying away of the Jews to Babylon, they were brought into contact with a flood of Iranian as well as Chaldean myths, *and adopted them without hesitation*." (S. Baring-Gould : Curious Myths, p. 316.)

the myth of Deucalion was a corrupted tradition of the *Noachian* deluge, but this *untenable* opinion is now all but universally abandoned."[1]

This idea was abandoned after it was found that the Deucalion myth was older than the Hebrew.

What was said in regard to the Eden story not being mentioned in other portions of the Old Testament save in Genesis, also applies to this story of the Deluge. *Nowhere* in the other books of the Old Testament is found any reference to this story, except in Isaiah, where "the waters of Noah" are mentioned, and in Ezekiel, where simply the *name* of Noah is mentioned.

We stated in Chapter II. that some persons saw in this story an *astronomical* myth. Although not generally admitted, yet there are very strong reasons for believing this to be the case.

According to the *Chaldean* account—which is the oldest one known—there were *seven* persons saved in the ark.[2] There were also *seven* persons saved, according to some of the *Hindoo* accounts.[3] That this referred to the sun, moon, and five planets looks very probable. We have also seen that Noah was the *tenth* patriarch, and Xisthrus (who is the Chaldean hero) was the *tenth* king.[4] Now, according to the Babylonian table, their *Zodiac* contained *ten* gods called the "*Ten Zodiac* gods."[5] They also believed that whenever all the *planets* met in the sign of Capricorn, *the whole earth was overwhelmed with a deluge of water.*[6] The *Hindoos* and other nations had a similar belief.[7]

It is well known that the Chaldeans were great astronomers. When Alexander the Great conquered the city of Babylon, the Chaldean priests boasted to the Greek philosophers, who followed his army, that they had continued their astronomical calculations through a period of more than forty thousand years.[8] Although this statement cannot be credited, yet the great antiquity of Chaldea cannot be doubted, and its immediate connection with Hindostan, or Egypt, is abundantly proved by the little that is known concerning its religion, and by the few fragments that remain of its former grandeur.

In regard to the story of "*The Tower of Babel*" little need be said. This, as well as the story of the Creation and Fall of Man, and the Deluge, was borrowed from the Babylonians.[9]

---

[1] Chambers's Encyclo., art. "Deucalion."
[2] See chapter ii.
[3] Prog. Relig. Ideas, vol. i. p. 185, and Maurice: Indian Antiquities, vol. ii. p. 277.
[4] Chapter ii.
[5] See Dunlap's Son of the Man, p. 153, *note.*
[6] See Prog. Relig. Ideas, vol. i. p. 254.
[7] See Ibid, p. 367.
[8] See Ibid, p. 252.
[9] Goldzhier: Hebrew Mythology, pp. 130-135, and Smith's Chaldean Account of Genesis.

"It seems," says George Smith, "from the indications in the (cuneiform) inscriptions, that there happened in the interval between 2000 and 1850 B. C. a general *collection* of the development of the various traditions of the Creation, Flood, Tower of Babel, and other similar legends." "These legends were, however, traditions before they were committed to writing, *and were common in some form to all the country.*"[1]

The Tower of Babel, or the confusion of tongues, is nowhere alluded to in the Old Testament outside of Genesis, where the story is related.

The next story in order is "*The Trial of Abraham's Faith.*"

In this connection we have shown similar legends taken from *Grecian* mythology, which legends may have given *the idea* to the writer of the Hebrew story.

It may appear strange that the *Hebrews* should have been acquainted with *Grecian* mythology, yet we know this was the case. The fact is accounted for in the following manner:

Many of the Jews taken captive at the Edomite sack of Jerusalem were sold to the *Grecians*,[2] who took them to their country. While there, they became acquainted with Grecian legends, and when they returned from "the Islands of the Sea"—as they called the Western countries—*they brought them to Jerusalem.*[3]

This legend, as we stated in the chapter which treated of it, was written at the time when the Mosaic party in Israel were endeavoring to abolish human sacrifices and other "abominations," and the author of the story invented it to make it appear that the Lord had abolished them in the time of Abraham. The earliest *Targum*[4] knows nothing about the legend, showing that the story was not in the Pentateuch at the time this Targum was written.

We have also seen that a story written by Sanchoniathon (about B. C. 1300) of one Saturn, whom the Phenicians called *Israel*, bore a resemblance to the Hebrew legend of Abraham. Now, Count de Volney tells us that "a similar tradition prevailed among the *Chaldeans*," and that they had the history of one *Zerban*—which means "rich-in-gold"[5]—that corresponded in many respects with the history of Abraham.[6] It may, then, have been from the Chaldean story that the Hebrew fable writer got his idea.

---

[1] Chaldean Account of Genesis, pp. 27, 28.
[2] See Note, p. 109.
[3] See Inman : Ancient Faiths, vol. ii. p. 685.
[4] "Targum."—The general term for the Aramaic versions of the Old Testament.

[5] In Genesis xxiii. 2, Abraham is called rich in gold and in silver.
[6] See Volney's Researches in Ancient History, pp. 144-147.

The next legend which we examined was that of "*Jacob's Vision of the Ladder.*" We claimed that it probably referred to the doctrine of the transmigration of souls from one body into another, and also gave the apparent reason for the invention of the story.

The next story was "*The Exodus from Egypt, and Passage through the Red Sea,*" in which we showed, from Egyptian history, that the Israelites were *turned out* of the country on account of their uncleanness, and that the wonderful exploits recorded of Moses were simply copies of legends related of the sun-god Bacchus. These legends came from "the Islands of the Sea," and came in very handy for the Hebrew fable writers; they saved them the trouble of *inventing*.

We now come to the story relating to "*The Receiving of the Ten Commandments*" by Moses from the Lord, on the top of a mountain, 'mid thunders and lightnings.

All that is likely to be historical in this account, is that Moses assembled, not, indeed, the whole of the people, but the heads of the tribes, and gave them the code which he had prepared.[1] The *marvellous* portion of the story was evidently copied from that related of the law-giver Zoroaster, by the *Persians*, and the idea that there were *two* tables of stone with the Law written thereon was evidently taken from the story of Bacchus, the Law-giver, who had *his* laws written on *two tables of stone.*[2]

The next legend treated was that of "*Samson and his Exploits.*"

Those who, *like the learned of the last century*, maintain that the Pagans copied from the Hebrews, may say that Samson was the model of all their similar stories, but now that our ideas concerning antiquity are enlarged, and when we know that Hercules is well known to have been the God *Sol*, whose *allegorical history* was spread among many nations long before the Hebrews were ever heard of, we are authorized to believe and to say that some Jewish *mythologist*—for what else are their so-called historians—composed the anecdote of Samson, by partly disfiguring the popular traditions of the Greeks, Phenicians and Chaldeans, and claiming that hero for his own nation.[3]

The Babylonian story of Izdubar, the lion-killer, who wandered

---

[1] The Religion of Israel, p. 49.
[2] Bell's Pantheon, vol. i. p. 122. Higgins: vol. ii. p. 19.
[3] In claiming the "mighty man" and "lion-killer" as one of their own race, the Jews were simply doing what other nations had done be-fore them. The Greeks claimed Hercules as *their* countryman; stated where he was born, and showed his tomb. The Egyptians affirmed that he was born in *their* country (see Tacitus, Annals, b. ii. ch. lix.), and so did many other nations.

to *the regions of the blessed* (the Grecian Elysium), who crossed *a great waste of land* (the desert of *Lybia*, according to the Grecian mythos), and arrived at a region *where splendid trees were laden with jewels* (the Grecian Garden of the Hesperides), is probably the foundation for the Hercules and other corresponding myths. This conclusion is drawn from the fact that, although the story of Hercules was known in the island of Thasus, by the *Phenician* colony settled there, *five centuries before he was known in Greece,*[1] yet *its antiquity among the Babylonians antedates that.*

The age of the legends of Izdubar among the Babylonians cannot be placed with certainty, yet, the cuneiform inscriptions relating to this hero, which have been found, may be placed at about 2000 years B. C.[2] "As these stories were *traditions*," says Mr. Smith, the discoverer of the cylinders, "before they were committed to writing, their antiquity as tradition is probably much greater than that."[3]

With these legends before them, the Jewish priests in Babylon had no difficulty in arranging the story of Samson, and adding it to their already fabulous history.

As the Rev. Dr. Isaac M. Wise remarks, in speaking of the ancient Hebrews: "They adopted forms, terms, ideas and myths of all nations with whom they came in contact, and, like the Greeks, in their way, *cast them all in a peculiar Jewish religious mold.*"

We have seen, in the chapter which treats of this legend, that it is recorded in the book of Judges. *This book was not written till after the first set of Israelites had been carried into captivity, and perhaps still later.*[4]

After this we have "*Jonah swallowed by a Big Fish,*" which is the last legend treated.

We saw that it was a *solar myth,* known to many nations of antiquity. The writer of the book—whoever he may have been—*lived in the fifth century before Christ*—after the Jews had become acquainted and had mixed with other nations. The writer of this wholly fictitious story, taking the prophet Jonah—who was evidently an historical personage—for his hero, was perhaps intending to show the loving-kindness of Jehovah.[5]

---

[1] See Knight: Ancient Art-and Mythology, pp. 92, 93.
[2] Chaldean Account of Genesis, pp. 168 and 174; and Assyrian Discoveries, p. 167.
[3] Chaldean Account of Genesis, p. 168.
[4] See The Religion of Israel, p. 12; and Chadwick's Bible of To-Day, p. 55.
[5] See The Religion of Israel, p. 41, and Chadwick's Bible of To-Day, p. 24.

We have now examined all the *principal* Old Testament legends, and, after what has been seen, we think that no *impartial* person can still consider them *historical facts*. That so great a number of educated persons still do so seems astonishing, in our way of thinking. They have repudiated Greek and Roman mythology with disdain ; why then admit with respect the mythology of the Jews ? Ought the miracles of Jehovah to impress us more than those of Jupiter ? We think not; they should all be looked upon as *relics of the past*.

That Christian writers are beginning to be aroused to the idea that another tack should be taken, differing from the old, is very evident. This is clearly seen by the words of Prof. Richard A. Armstrong, the translater of Dr. Knappert's " Religion of Israel " into English. In the *Preface* of this work, he says:

" It appears to me to be profoundly important that the youthful English mind should be faithfully and accurately informed of the results of modern research into the early development of the Israelitish religion. Deplorable and irreparable mischief will be done to the generation now passing into manhood and womanhood, if their educators leave them ignorant or loosely informed on these topics; for they will then be rudely awakened by the enemies of Christianity from a blind and unreasoning faith in the supernatural inspiration of the Scriptures; and being suddenly and bluntly made aware that Abraham, Moses, David, and the rest did not say, do, or write what has been ascribed to them, they will fling away all care for the venerable religion of Israel and all hope that it can nourish their own religious life. How much happier will those of our children and young people be who learn what is now known of the actual origin of the Pentateuch and the Writings, from the same lips which have taught them that the Prophets indeed prepared the way for Jesus, and that God is indeed our Heavenly Father. For these will, without difficulty, perceive that God's love is none the feebler and that the Bible is no less precious, because Moses knew nothing of the Levitical legislation, or because it was not the warrior monarch on his semi-barbaric throne, but some far later son of Israel, who breathed forth the immortal hymn of faith, 'The Lord is my Shepherd; I shall not want.' "

For the benefit of those who may think that the evidence of plagiarism on the part of the Hebrew writers has not been sufficiently substantiated, we will quote a few words from Prof. Max Müller, who is one of the best English authorities on this subject that can be produced. In speaking of this he says:

" The opinion that the *Pagan* religions were mere corruptions of the religion of the Old Testament, once supported by men of high authority and great learning, *is now as completely surrendered as the attempts of explaining Greek and Latin as the corruptions of Hebrew*."[1]

Again he says:

----

[1] The Science of Religion, p. 40.

'As soon as the ancient language and religion of India became known in Europe it was asserted that Sanskrit, *like all other languages*, was to be derived from Hebrew, and the ancient religion of the Brahmans from the Old Testament. There was at that time an enthusiasm among Oriental scholars, particularly at Calcutta, and an interest for Oriental antiquities in the public at large, of which we, in these days of apathy for Eastern literature, can hardly form an adequate idea. Everybody wished to be first in the field, and to bring to light some of the treasures which were supposed to be hidden in the sacred literature of the Brahmans. . . . No doubt the temptation was great. No one could look down for a moment into the rich mine of religious and mythological lore that was suddenly opened before the eyes of scholars and theologians, *without being struck by a host of similarities, not only in the languages, but also in the ancient traditions of the Hindoos,* the Greeks, and the Romans; and if at that time the Greeks and Romans were still *supposed* to have borrowed their language and their religion from Jewish quarters, *the same conclusion could hardly be avoided with regard to the language and the religion of the Brahmans of India.* . . .

''The student of Pagan religion as well as Christian missionaries were bent on discovering more striking and more startling coincidences, *in order to use them in confirmation of their favorite theory that some rays of a primeval revelation, or some reflection of the Jewish religion, had reached the uttermost ends of the world.*''[1]

The result of all this is summed up by Prof. Müller as follows :

''*It was the fate of all (these) pioneers, not only to be left behind in the assault which they had planned, but to find that many of their approaches were made in a false direction, and had to be abandoned.*''[2]

Before closing this chapter, we shall say a few words on the religion of Israel. It is supposed by many—in fact, we have heard it asserted by those who should know better—that the Israelites were always *monotheists*, that they worshiped One God only— *Jehovah*.[3] This is altogether erroneous; they were not different from their neighbors—the Heathen, so-called—in regard to their religion.

In the first place, we know that they revered and worshiped a *Bull*, called *Apis*,[4] just as the ancient Egyptians did. They

---

[1] They even claimed that one of the "lost tribes of Israel" had found their way to America, and had taught the natives *Hebrew*.

[2] The Science of Religion, pp. 285, 292.

[3] "It is an *assumption* of the popular theology, and an almost universal belief in the popular mind, that the Jewish nation was selected by the Almighty to preserve and carry down to later ages a knowledge of the *One* and true God—that the Patriarchs possessed this knowledge—that Moses delivered and enforced this doctrine as the fundamental tenet of the national creed ; and that it was, in fact, the received and distinctive dogma of the Hebrew people. This *alleged possession of the true*

faith by one only people, while all surrounding tribes were lost in Polytheism, or something worse, has been adduced by divines in general as a proof of the truth of the sacred history, and of the divine origin of the Mosaic dispensation." (Greg : The Creed of Christendom, p. 145.)

Even such authorities as Paley and Milman have written in this strain. (See quotations from Paley's "*Evidences of Christianity*," and Dean Milman's "*History of the Jews*," made by Mr. Greg in his "*Creed of Christendom*," p. 145.)

[4] See the Bible for Learners, vol. i. p. 321, vol. ii. p. 102; and Dunlap : Mysteries of Adoni, p. 108.

worshiped the *sun*,[1] the *moon*,[2] the *stars* and all the host of heaven.[3]

They worshiped *fire*, and kept it burning on an altar, just as the Persians and other nations.[4] They worshiped *stones*,[5] revered an *oak tree*,[6] and "bowed down" to *images*.[7] They worshiped a "Queen of Heaven" called the goddess *Astarte* or *Mylitta*, and "burned incense" to her.[8] They worshiped *Baal*,[9] Moloch,[10] and *Chemosh*,[11] *and offered up human sacrifices to them*,[12] after which in some instances, *they ate the victim*.[13]

It was during the Captivity that idolatry ceased among the Israelites.[14] The Babylonian Captivity is clearly referred to in the book of Deuteronomy, as the close of Israel's idolatry.[15]

There is reason to believe that the real genius of the people was first called into full exercise, and put on its career of development at this time; that Babylon was a *forcing nursery*, not a prison cell; *creating instead of stifling a nation*. The astonishing outburst of intellectual and moral energy that accompanied the return from the Babylonish Captivity, attests the spiritual activity of that "mysterious and momentous" time. As Prof. Goldziher says: "The intellect of *Babylon* and *Assyria* exerced a more than passing influence on that of the *Hebrews*, not merely touching it, but *entering deep into it*, and *leaving its own impression upon it*."[16]

---

[1] See the Bible for Learners, vol. i. pp. 317, 418; vol. ii. p. 301. Dunlap's Son of the Man, p. 3, and his Spirit Hist., pp. 68 and 182. Inman: Ancient Faiths, vol. ii. pp. 782, 783; and Goldziher: Hebrew Mythol., pp. 227, 240, 242.

[2] The Bible for Learners, vol. i. p. 317. Dunlap's Son of the Man, p. 3; and Spirit Hist., p. 68. Also, Goldziher: Hebrew Mythol., p.159.

[3] The Bible for Learners, vol. i. p. 26, and 317; vol. ii. p. 301 and 328. Dunlap's Son of the Man, p. 3. Dunlap's Spirit Hist., 68; Mysteries of Adoni, pp. xvii. and 108; and The Religion of Israel, p. 38.

[4] Bunsen: Keys of St. Peter, pp. 101, 102.

[5] The Bible for Learners, vol. i. pp. 175–178, 317, 322, 448.

[6] Ibid. 115.

[7] Ibid. i. 23, 321; ii. 102, 103, 109, 264, 274. Dunlap's Spirit Hist., p. 108. Inman: Ancient Faiths, vol. i. p. 438; vol. ii. p. 30.

[8] The Bible for Learners, vol. i. pp. 88, 318; vol. ii. pp. 102, 113, 300. Dunlap: Son of the Man, p. 3; and Mysteries of Adoni, p. xvii. Müller: The Science of Religion, p. 261.

[9] The Bible for Learners, vol. i. pp. 21–25, 105, 391; vol. ii. pp. 102, 136–138. Dunlap: Son of the Man, p. 3. Mysteries of Adoni, pp. 108, 177. Inman: Ancient Faiths, vol. ii. pp. 782, 783. Bunsen: The Keys of St. Peter, p. 91. Müller: The Science of Religion, p. 181. *Bal, Bel*, or *Belus* was an idol of the Chal-

deans and Phenicians or Canaanites. The word *Bal*, in the Punic language, signifies Lord or Master. The name *Bal* is often joined with some other, as *Bal*-berith, *Bal*-peor, *Bal*-zephon, &c. "The Israelites made him their god, and erected altars to him on which they offered human sacrifices," and "what is still more unnatural, they *ate* of the victims they offered." (Bell's Pantheon, vol. i. pp. 113, 114.)

[10] The Bible for Learners, vol. i. pp. 17, 26; vol. ii. pp. 102, 299, 300. Bunsen: Keys of St. Peter, p. 110. Müller: The Science of Religion, p. 285. *Moloch* was a god of the Ammonites, also worshiped among the Israelites. Solomon built a temple to him, on the Mount of Olives, *and human sacrifices were offered to him*. (Bell's Pantheon, vol. ii. pp. 84, 85.)

[11] The Bible for Learners, vol. i. p. 153; vol. ii. pp. 71, 83, 125. Smith's Bible Dictionary, art. "Chemosh."

[12] The Bible for Learners, vol. i. pp. 26, 147, 148, 319, 320; vol. ii. pp. 16, 17, 299, 300. Dunlap's Spirit Hist., pp. 108, 222. Inman: Ancient Faiths, vol. ii. pp. 100, 101. Müller: Science of Religion, p. 261. Bell's Pantheon, vol. i. 113, 114; vol. ii. 84, 85.

[13] See note 9 above.

[14] See Bunsen: Keys of St. Peter, 291.

[15] Ibid, p. 27.

[16] Goldziher: Hebrew Mythology, p. 319.

This impression we have already partly seen in the legends which they borrowed, and it may also be seen in the religious ideas which they imbibed.

The Assyrian colonies which came and occupied the land of the tribes of Israel filled the kingdom of Samaria with the dogma of the *Magi*, which very soon penetrated into the kingdom of Judah. Afterward, Jerusalem being subjugated, the defenseless country was entered by persons of different nationalities, who introduced their opinions, and in this way, the religion of Israel was doubly mutilated. Besides, the priests and great men, who were transported to Babylon, were educated in the sciences of the Chaldeans, and imbibed, during a residence of fifty years, nearly the whole of their theology. It was not until this time that the dogmas of the hostile genius (Satan), the angels Michael, Uriel, Yar, Nisan, &c., the rebel angels, the battle in heaven, the immortality of the soul, and the resurrection, were introduced and naturalized among the Jews.[1]

---

[1] The *Talmud* of Jerusalem expressly states that the names of the angels and the months, such as Gabriel, Michael, Yar, Nisan, &c., came from Babylon with the Jews. (Goldziher, p. 319.) "There is no trace of the doctrine of Angels in the Hebrew Scriptures composed or written before the exile." (Bunsen: The Angel Messiah, p. 285.) "The Jews adopted, during the Captivity, the idea of angels, Michael, Raphael, Uriel, Gabriel," &c. (Knight: Ancient Art and Mythology, p. 54.) See, for further information on this subject, Dr. Knappert's "Religion of Israel," or Prof. Kuenen's "Religion of Israel."

NOTE.—It is not generally known that the Jews were removed from their own land until the time of the Babylonian Nebuchadnezzar, but there is evidence that Jerusalem was plundered by the *Edomites* about 800 B. C., who sold some of the captive Jews to the Greeks (Joel. iii. 6). When the captives returned to their country from "the Islands which are beyond the sea" (Jer. xxv. 18, 22), they would naturally bring back with them much of the Hellenic lore of their conquerors. In Isaiah (xi. 11), we find a reference to this first captivity in the following words: "In that day the Lord shall set his hand again the *second time* to recover the remnant of his people, which shall be left, from Assyria, and from Egypt, and from Pathros, and from Cush, and from Elam, and from Shinar, and from Hamath, and from the *Islands of the sea*;" i. e., GREECE.

PART II.

THE NEW TESTAMENT.

CHAPTER XII.

THE MIRACULOUS BIRTH OF CHRIST JESUS.

ACCORDING to the dogma of the deity of Jesus, he who is said to have lived on earth some eighteen centuries ago, as *Jesus of Nazareth*, is second of the three persons in the Trinity, the Son, God as absolutely as the Father and the Holy Spirit, except as eternally deriving his existence from the Father. What, however, especially characterizes the Son, and distinguishes him from the two other persons united with him in the unity of the Deity, is this, that the Son, at a given moment of time, became incarnate, and that, without losing anything of his divine nature, he thus became possessed of a complete human nature; so that he is at the same time, without injury to the unity of his person, "*truly man and truly God.*"

The story of the miraculous birth of Jesus is told by the *Matthew* narrator as follows:[1]

"Now the birth of Jesus Christ was on this wise: When as his mother Mary was espoused to Joseph, before they came together, she was found with child of the Holy Ghost. Then Joseph, her husband, being a just man, and not willing to make her a public example, was minded to put her away privily. But while he thought on these things, behold, the angel of the Lord appeared unto him in a dream, saying, Joseph, thou son of David, fear not to take unto thee Mary thy wife: for that which is conceived in her is of the Holy Ghost. And she shall bring forth a son, and thou shalt call his name Jesus, for he shall save his people from their sins. Now all this was done, that it might be fulfilled which was spoken of the Lord by the prophet, saying: Behold, a virgin shall be with child, and shall bring forth a son, and they shall call his name Emmanuel, which being interpreted is, God with us."[2]

---

[1] Matthew, i. 18-25.

[2] The Luke narrator tells the story in a different manner. His account is more like that recorded in the KORAN, which says that Gabriel appeared unto Mary in the shape of a perfect man, that Mary, upon seeing him, and seeming

A Deliverer was hoped for, expected, prophesied, in the time of
Jewish misery[1] (and *Cyrus* was perhaps the first referred to); but
as no one appeared who did what the Messiah, according to prophecy, should do, they went on degrading each successive conqueror
and hero from the Messianic dignity, and are still expecting the
true Deliverer.   Hebrew and Christian divines both start from the
same assumed unproven premises, viz.: that a Messiah, having been
foretold, must appear; but there they diverge, and the Jews show
themselves to be the sounder logicians of the two: the Christians
assuming that Jesus was the Messiah *intended* (though not the one
expected), wrest the obvious meaning of the prophecies to show
that they were fufilled in him; while the Jews, assuming the ob
vious meaning of the prophecies to be their real meaning, argue
that they were not fulfilled in Christ Jesus, and therefore that the
Messiah is yet to come.

We shall now see, in the words of Bishop Hawes: "that God
should, in some extraordinary manner, visit and dwell with man, is
an idea which, as we read the writings of the *ancient Heathens*,
meets us in a thousand different forms."

Immaculate conceptions and celestial descents were so currently
received among the ancients, that whoever had greatly distinguished
himself in the affairs of men was thought to be of supernatural
lineage.   Gods descended from heaven and were made incarnate in
men, and men ascended from earth, and took their seat among the
gods, so that these incarnations and apotheosises were fast filling
Olympus with divinities.

In our inquiries on this subject we shall turn first to *Asia*,
where, as the learned Thomas Maurice remarks in his *Indian Antiquities*, "in every age, and in almost every region of the Asiatic
world, there seems uniformly to have flourished an immemorial
tradition that one god had, from all eternity, *begotten another
god*."

In India, there have been several *Avatars*, or incarnations of
Vishnu,[2] the most important of which is *Heri Crishna*,[4] or *Crishna
the Saviour*.

---

to understand his intentions, said: "If thou
fearest God, thou wilt not approach me."
Gabriel answering said: "Verily, I am the
messenger of the Lord, and am sent to give
thee a holy son." (Koran, ch. xix.)

[1] Instead, however, of the benevolent Jesus,
the "Prince of Peace"—as Christian writers
make him out to be—the Jews were expecting
a daring and irresistible warrior and conqueror,
who, armed with greater power than Cæsar,
was to come upon earth to rend the fetters in

which their hapless nation had so long groaned,
to avenge them upon their haughty oppressors,
and to re-establish the kingdom of Judah.

[2] Vol. v. p. 294.

[3] Moor, in his "*Pantheon*," tells us that a
learned Pandit once observed to him that the
English were a new people, and had only the
record of one Avatara, but the Hindoos were
an ancient people, and had accounts of a great
many.

[4] This name has been spelled in many dif-

In the *Maha-bharata*, an Indian epic poem, written about the sixth century B. C., Crishna is associated or identified with Vishnu the Preserving god or Saviour.[1]

Sir William Jones, first President of the Royal Asiatic Society, instituted in Bengal, says of him:

"Crishna continues to this hour the darling god of the Indian woman. The sect of Hindoos who adore him with enthusiastic, and almost exclusive devotion, have broached a doctrine, which they maintain with eagerness, and which seems general in these provinces, that he was distinct from all the *Avatars* (incarnations) who had only an *ansa*, or a portion, of his (*Vishnu's*) divinity, *while Crishna was the person of Vishnu himself in human form.*"[2]

The Rev. D. O. Allen, Missionary of the American Board, for twenty-five years in India, speaking of Crishna, says:

"He was greater than, and distinct from, all the *Avatars* which had only a portion of the divinity in them, while he was the very person of Vishnu himself in human form."[3]

Thomas Maurice, in speaking of *Mathura*, says:

"It is particularly celebrated for having been the birth-place of *Crishna*, who is esteemed in India, not so much an incarnation of the divine Vishnu, *as the deity himself in human form.*"[4]

Again, in his "*History of Hindostan*," he says:

"It appears to me that the Hindoos, idolizing some eminent character of antiquity, distinguished, in the early annals of their nation, by heroic fortitude and exalted piety, have applied to that character those ancient traditional accounts of an *incarnate God*, or, as they not improperly term it, an *Avatar*, which had been delivered down to them from their ancestors, the virtuous Noachidæ, to descend amidst the darkness and ignorance of succeeding ages, at once to reform and instruct mankind. We have the more solid reason to affirm this of the Avatar of Crishna, because it is allowed to be the most illustrious of them all; since we have learned, that, in the *seven* preceding Avatars, the deity brought only an *ansa*, or portion of his divinity; but, in the *eighth*, he descended in all the plentitude of the Godhead, *and was Vishnu himself in a human form.*"[5]

Crishna was born of a chaste virgin,[6] called *Devaki*, who, on account of her purity, was selected to become the "*mother of God.*"

According to the "BHAGAVAT POORAUN," *Vishnu* said:

"I will become incarnate at Mathura in the house of *Yadu*, and will issue

ferent ways, such as Krishna, Khrishna, Krishnu, Chrisna, Cristna, Christna, &c. We have followed Sir Wm. Jones's way of spelling it, and shall do so throughout.

[1] See Asiatic Researches, vol. i. pp. 259-275.
[2] Ibid. p. 260. We may say that, "In him dwelt the fulness of the Godhead bodily." (Colossians, ii. 9.)

[3] Allen's India, p. 397.
[4] Indian Antiquities, vol. iii. p. 45.
[5] Hist. Hindostan, vol. ii. p. 270.
[6] Like Mary, the mother of Jesus, Devaki is called the "Virgin Mother," although she, as well as Mary, is said to have had other children.

8

forth to mortal birth from the womb of Devaki. . . . It is time I should display my power, and relieve the oppressed earth from its load."[1]

Then a chorus of angels exclaimed :

"In the delivery of this favored woman, all nature shall have cause to exult."[2]

In the sacred book of the Hindoos, called " *Vishnu' Purana*," we read as follows :

"Eulogized by the gods, Devaki bore in her womb the lotus-eyed deity, the protector of the world. . . .

"No person could bear to gaze upon Devaki, from the light that invested her, and those who contemplated her radiance felt their minds disturbed. The gods, invisible to mortals, celebrated her praises continually from the time that *Vishnu* was contained in her person."[3]

Again we read :

"The divine *Vishnu himself*, the root of the vast universal tree, inscrutable by the understandings of all gods, demons, sages, and men, past, present, or to come, adored by Brahma and all the deities, he who is without beginning, middle, or end, being moved to relieve the earth of her load, descended into the womb of Devaki, and was born as her son, Vasudeva," *i. e., Crishna.*[4]

Again :

" Crishna is the very *Supreme Brahma*, though it be a *mystery*[5] how the Supreme *should assume the form of a man*."[6]

The Hindoo belief in a divine incarnation has at least, above many others, its logical side of conceiving that God manifests himself on earth whenever the weakness or the errors of humanity render his presence necessary. We find this idea expressed in one of their sacred books called the " *Bhágavat Geeta*," wherein it says:

"I (the Supreme One said), I am made evident by my own power, and as often as there is a decline of virtue, and an insurrection of vice and injustice in the world, I make myself evident, *and thus I appear from age to age*, for the preservation of the just, the destruction of the wicked, and the establishment of virtue."[7]

Crishna is recorded in the " *Bhágavat Geeta* " as saying to his beloved disciple Arjouna :

---

[1] Hist. Hindostan, vol. ii. p. 327.

[2] Ibid. p. 329.

[3] Vishnu Purana, p. 502.

[4] Ibid. p. 440.

[5] " Now to him that is of power to establish you according to my gospel, and the preaching of Jesus Christ, according to the revelation of the *mystery*, which was kept secret since the world began." (Romans, xvi. 15.) "And without controversy, great is the *mystery* of godliness : God was manifest in the flesh, justified in the spirit, seen of angels, preached unto the Gentiles, believed on in the world, received up into glory." (1 Timothy, iii. 16.)

[6] Vishnu Purana, p. 492, *note* 3.

[7] Geeta, ch. iv.

"He, O Arjoun, who, from conviction, acknowledgeth my *divine birth* (upon quitting his mortal form), entereth into me."[1]

Again, he says:

"The foolish, being *unacquainted with my supreme and divine nature, as Lord of all things,* despise me in this *human form,* trusting to the evil, diabolic, and deceitful principle within them. They are of vain hope, of vain endeavors, of vain wisdom, and void of reason; whilst men of great minds, trusting to their divine natures, *discover that I am before all things and incorruptible,* and serve me with their hearts undiverted by other gods."[2]

The next in importance among the *God-begotten* and *Virgin-born* Saviours of India, is *Buddha,*[3] who was born of the Virgin Maya or Mary. He in mercy left Paradise, and came down to earth because he was filled with compassion for the sins and miseries of mankind. He sought to lead them into better paths, and took their sufferings upon himself, that he might expiate their crimes, and mitigate the punishment they must otherwise inevitably undergo.[4]

According to the *Fo-pen-hing,*[5] when Buddha was about to descend from heaven, to be born into the world, the angels in heaven, calling to the inhabitants of the earth, said:

"Ye mortals! adorn your earth! for Bôdhisatwa, the great Mahâsatwa, not long hence shall descend from Tusita to be born amongst you! make ready and prepare! Buddha is about to descend and be born !"[6]

The womb that bears a Buddha is like a casket in which a relic is placed; no other being can be conceived in the same receptacle; the usual secretions are not formed; and from the time of conception, Maha-maya was free from passion, and lived in the strictest continence.[7]

The resemblance between this legend and the doctrine of the *perpetual virginity* of Mary the mother of Jesus, cannot but be remarked. The opinion that she had ever borne other children was called heresy by Epiphanius and Jerome, long before she had been exalted to the station of supremacy she now occupies.[8]

---

[1] Bhagavat Geeta, Lecture iv. p. 52.
[2] Ibid., Lecture iv. p. 79.
[3] It is said that there have been several Buddhas (see ch. xxix). We speak of *Gautama.* Buddha is variously pronounced and expressed Boudh, Bod, Bot, But, Bud, Badd, Buddou, Bouttu, Bota, Budso, Pot, Pout, Pota, Poti, and Pouti. The Siamese make the final *t* or *d* quiescent, and sound the word Po; whence the Chinese still further vary it to Pho or Fo. BUDDHA—which means *awakened* or *enlightened* (see Müller : Sci. of Relig., p. 308) —is the proper way in which to spell the name. We have adopted this throughout this work, regardless of the manner in which the writer from which we quote spells it.
[4] Prog. Relig. Ideas, vol. i. p. 86.
[5] FO-PEN-HING is the life of Gautama Buddha, translated from the Chinese Sanskrit by Prof. Samuel Beal.
[6] Beal : Hist. Buddha, p. 25.
[7] Hardy : Manual of Buddhism, p. 141.
[8] A Christian sect called Collyridians believed that Mary was born of a virgin, as Christ is related to have been born of her (See *note* to the "Gospel of the Birth of

M. l'Abbé Huc, a French Missionary, in speaking of Buddha, says :

'In the eyes of the Buddhists, this personage is sometimes a man and some-times a god, or rather both one and the other, *a divine incarnation, a man-god ;* who came into the world to enlighten men, to redeem them, and to indicate to them the way of safety.

"This idea of redemption by a *divine incarnation* is so general and popular among the Buddhists, that during our travels in Upper Asia, we everywhere found it expressed in a neat formula. If we addressed to a Mongol or a Thibetan the question, 'Who is Buddha?' he would immediately reply: '*The Saviour of Men.*'"[1]

He further says :

"The miraculous birth of Buddha, his life and instructions, contain a great number of the moral and dogmatic truths professed in Christianity."[2]

This Angel-Messiah was regarded as the divinely chosen and incarnate messenger, the vicar of God. He is addressed as "God of Gods," "Father of the World," "Almighty and All-knowing Ruler," and "Redeemer of All."[3] He is called also "The Holy One," "The Author of Happiness," "The Lord," "The Possessor of All," "He who is Omnipotent and Everlastingly to be Contem-plated," "The Supreme Being, the Eternal One," "The Divinity worthy to be Adored by the most praiseworthy of Mankind."[4] He is addressed by Amora—one of his followers—thus :

"Reverence be unto thee in the form of Buddha! Reverence be unto thee, the Lord of the Earth! Reverence be unto thee, an incarnation of the Deity! Of the Eternal One! Reverence be unto thee, O God, in the form of the God of Mercy; the dispeller of pain and trouble, the Lord of all things, the deity, the guardian of the universe, the emblem of mercy."[5]

The incarnation of Gautama Buddha is recorded to have been brought about by the descent of the divine power called The "*Holy Ghost*" upon the Virgin *Maya*.[6] This Holy Ghost, or

Mary " [Apocryphal]; also King : The Gnostics and their Remains, p. 91, and Gibbon's Hist. of Rome, vol. v. p. 108, *note*). This idea has been recently adopted by the Roman Catholic Church. They now claim that Mary was born as immaculate as her son. (See Inman's Ancient Faiths, vol. i. p. 75, and The Lily of Israel, pp. 6–15 ; also fig. 17, ch. xxxii.)

"The gradual *deification* of Mary, though slower in its progress, follows, in the Romish Church, a course analogous to that which the Church of the first centuries followed, in elab-orating the deity of Jesus. With almost all the Catholic writers of our day, Mary is the universal mediatrix ; *all power has been given* to her *in heaven and upon earth.* Indeed, more than one serious attempt has been al-ready made in the Ultramontane camp to unite Mary in some way to the *Trinity;* and if Mariolatry lasts much longer, this will prob-ably be accomplished in the end.". (Albert Ré-ville.)

[1] Huc's Travels, vol. i. pp. 326, 327.
[2] Ibid. p. 327.
[3] Oriental Religions, p. 604.
[4] See Bunsen's Angel-Messiah.
[5] Asiatic Researches, vol. ii. p. 309, and King's Gnostics, p. 167.
[6] See Bunsen's Angel-Messiah, pp. 10, 25 and 44.

Spirit, descended in the form of a *white elephant*. The *Tikas* explain this as indicating power and wisdom.[1]

The incarnation of the angel destined to become Buddha took place in a spiritual manner. The Elephant is the symbol of power and wisdom; and Buddha was considered the organ of divine power and wisdom, as he is called in the Tikas. For these reasons Buddha is described by Buddhistic legends as having descended from heaven in the form of an Elephant to the place where the Virgin Maya was. But according to Chinese Buddhistic writings, it was the Holy Ghost, or *Shing-Shin*, who descended on the Virgin Maya.[2]

The *Fo-pen-hing* says:

> " If a mother, in her dream, behold
> A white elephant enter her right side,
> That mother, when she bears a son,
> Shall bear one chief of all the world (Buddha);
> Able to profit all flesh;
> Equally poised between preference and dislike;
> Able to save and deliver the world and men
> From the deep sea of misery and grief."[3]

In Prof. Fergusson's "*Tree and Serpent Worship*" may be seen (Plate xxxiii.) a representation of Maya, the mother of Buddha, asleep, and dreaming that a white elephant appeared to her, and entered her womb.

This dream being interpreted by the Brahmans learned in the *Rig-Veda*, was considered as announcing the incarnation of him who was to be in future the deliverer of mankind from pain and sorrow. It is, in fact, the form which the Annunciation took in Buddhist legends.[4]

> " —— Awaked,
> Bliss beyond mortal mother's filled her breast,
> And over half the earth a lovely light
> Forewent the morn. The strong hills shook; the waves
> Sank lulled; all flowers that blow by day came forth
> As 'twere high noon; down to the farthest hells
> Passed the Queen's joy, as when warm sunshine thrills
> Wood-glooms to gold, and into all the deeps
> A tender whisper pierced. 'Oh ye,' it said,
> ' The dead that are to live, the live who die,
> Uprise, and hear, and hope! Buddha is come !'
> Whereat in Limbos numberless much peace
> Spread, and the world's heart throbbed, and a wind blew

[1] See Beal: Hist. Buddha, p. 36, *note*. Ganesa, the Indian God of Wisdom, is either represented as an elephant, or a man with an elephant's head. (See Moore's Hindu Pantheon, and vol. i. of Asiatic Researches.)
[2] Bunsen : The Angel-Messiah, p. 33.
[3] Beal: Hist. Buddha, pp. 38, 39.
[4] Tree and Serpent Worship, p. 131.

With unknown freshness over land and seas.
And when the morning dawned, and this was told,
The grey dream-readers said, ' The dream is good!
The Crab is in conjunction with the Sun;
The Queen shall bear a boy, a holy child
Of wondrous wisdom, profiting all flesh,
Who shall deliver men from ignorance,
Or rule the world, if he will deign to rule.'
In this wise was the holy Buddha born."

In Fig. 4, Plate xci., the same subject is also illustrated. Prof. Fergusson, referring to it, says :

"Fig. 4 is another edition of a legend more frequently repeated than almost any other in Buddhist Scriptures. It was, with their artists, as great a favorite as the Annunciation and Nativity were with Christian painters."[1]

When Buddha *avatar* descended from the regions of the souls, and entered the body of the Virgin Maya, her womb suddenly assumed the appearance of clear, transparent crystal, in which Buddha appeared, beautiful as a flower, kneeling and reclining on his hands.[2]

Buddha's representative on earth is the *Dalai Lama*, or *Grand Lama*, the High Priest of the Tartars. He is regarded as the vicegerent of God, with power to dispense divine blessings on whomsoever he will, and is considered among the Buddhists to be a sort of divine being. He is the Pope of Buddhism.[3]

The *Siamese* had a Virgin-born God and Saviour whom they called *Codom*. His mother, a beautiful young virgin, being inspired from heaven, quitted the society of men and wandered into the most unfrequented parts of a great forest, there to await the coming of a god which had long been announced to mankind. While she was one day prostrate in prayer, she was *impregnated by the sunbeams*. She thereupon retired to the borders of a lake, between Siam and Cambodia, where she was delivered of a " *heavenly boy*," which she placed within the folds of a *lotus*, that opened to receive him. When the boy grew up, he became a prodigy of wisdom, performed miracles, &c.[4]

The first Europeans who visited Cape Comorin, the most

---

[1] Tree and Serpent Worship, p. 212.
[2] King : The Gnostics and their Remains, p. 168, and Hist. Hindostan, vol. ii. p. 485. R. Spence Hardy says : "The body of the Queen was transparent, and the child could be distinctly seen, like a priest seated upon a throne in the act of saying bana, or like a golden image enclosed in a vase of crystal; so that it could be known how much he grew every succeeding day." (Hardy: Manual of Buddhism, p. 144.) The same thing was said of Mary, the mother of Jesus. Early art represented the infant distinctly visible in her womb. (See Inman's Ancient Pagan and Modern Christian Symbolism, and chap. xxix. this work.)
[3] See Bell's Pantheon, vol. ii. p. 84.
[4] Squire : Serpent Symbol. p. 185. See also Anacalypsis, vol. i. pp. 162 and 303.

southerly extremity of the peninsula of Hindostan, were surprised to find the inhabitants worshiping a Lord and Saviour whom they called *Salivahana.* They related that his father's name was Taishaca, but that he was *a divine child born of a Virgin*, in fact, an incarnation of the Supreme *Vishnu.*[1]

The belief in a virgin-born god-man is found in the religions of China. As Sir John Francis Davis remarks,[2] "China has her mythology in common with all other nations, and under this head we must range the persons styled *Fo-hi* (or Fuh-he), *Shin-noong*, *Hoang-ty* and their immediate successors, who, like the demi-gods and heroes of Grecian fable, rescued mankind by their ability or enterprise from the most primitive barbarism, and have since been invested with *superhuman* attributes. The most extravagant prodigies are related of these persons, and the most incongruous qualities attributed to them.".

Dean Milman, in his "History of Christianity" (Vol. i. p. 97), refers to the tradition, found among the Chinese, that *Fo-hi* was born of a virgin ; and remarks that, the first Jesuit missionaries who went to China were appalled at finding, in the mythology of that country, a counterpart of the story of the virgin of Judea.

Fo-hi is said to have been born 3468 years B. C., and, according to some Chinese writers, with him begins the historical era and the foundation of the empire. When his mother conceived him in her womb, a rainbow was seen to surround her.[3]

The Chinese traditions concerning the birth of Fo-hi are, some of them, highly poetical. That which has received the widest acceptance is as follows:

"Three nymphs came down from heaven to wash themselves in a river ; but scarce had they got there before the herb *lotus* appeared on one of their garments, with its coral fruit upon it. They could not imagine whence it proceeded, and one was tempted to taste it, whereby she became pregnant and was delivered of a boy, who afterwards became a great man, a founder of religion, a conqueror, and legislator."[4]

The sect of *Xaca*, which is evidently a corruption of Buddhism, claim that their master was also of supernatural origin. Alvarez Semedo, speaking of them, says:

"The third religious sect among the Chinese is from India, from the parts of Hindostan, which sect they call *Xaca*, from the founder of it, concerning whom they fable—that he was conceived by his mother Maya, from a white elephant,

---

[1] See Asiastic Res., vol. x., and Anac., vol. i. p. 662.

[2] Davis : Hist. China, vol. i. p. 161.

[3] Thornton : Hist. China, vol. i. pp. 21, 22.

[4] Squire: Serpent Symbol, p. 184.

which she saw in her sleep, and for more purity she brought him from one of her sides."[1]

Lao-kiun, sometimes called *Lao-tsze;* who is said to have been born in the third year of the emperor *Ting-wang,* of the Chow dynasty (604 B. C.), was another miraculously-born man. He acquired great reputation for sanctity, and marvelous stories were told of his birth. It was said that he had existed from all eternity; that he had descended on earth *and was born of a virgin,* black in complexion, described "marvelous and beautiful as jasper." Splendid temples were erected to him, and he was worshiped as a *god.* His disciples were called "Heavenly Teachers." They inculcated great tenderness toward animals, and considered strict celibacy necessary for the attainment of perfect holiness. Lao-kiun believed in *One God* whom he called *Tao,* and the sect which he formed is called *Tao-tse,* or "Sect of Reason." Sir Thomas Thornton, speaking of him, says:

"The mythological history of this 'prince of the doctrine of the *Taou*,' which is current amongst his followers, *represents him as a divine emanation incarnate in a human form.* They term him the 'most high and venerable prince of the portals of gold of the palace of the *genii*,' and say that he condescended to a contact with humanity when he became incorporated with the 'miraculous and excellent Virgin of jasper.' Like Buddha, he came out of his mother's side, and was born under a tree.

"The legends of the *Taou-tse* declare their founder to have existed antecedent to the birth of the elements, in the Great Absolute; that he is the 'pure essence of the tëen;' that he is the 'original ancestor of the prime breath of life;' and that he gave form to the heavens and the earth."[2]

M. Le Compte says:

"Those who have made this (the religion of Taou-tsze) their professed business, are called *Tien-se,* that is, 'Heavenly Doctors;' they have houses (Monasteries) given them to live together in society; they erect, in divers parts, temples to their master, and king and people honor him with *divine* worship."

Yu was another *virgin-born* Chinese sage, who is said to have lived upon earth many ages ago. Confucius—as though he had been questioned about him—says: "I see no defect in the character of Yu. He was sober in eating and drinking, and eminently pious toward spirits and ancestors."[3]

Háu-ki, the Chinese hero, was of supernatural origin.

The following is the history of his birth, according to the "Shih-King:"

[1] Semedo : Hist. China, p. 89, in Anac., vol. ii. p. 227.
[2] Thornton : Hist. China, vol. i. pp. 134–
137. See also Chambers's Encyclo., art. Lao-tsze.
[3] Prog. Relig. Ideas, vol. i. pp. 204, 205.

"His mother, who was childless, had presented a pure offering and sacrificed, that her childlessness might be taken away. She then trod on a toe-print
made by God, and was moved,[1] in the large place where she rested. She became
pregnant; she dwelt retired; she gave birth to and nourished a son, who was
Hâu-ki. When she had fulfilled her months, her first-born son came forth like a
lamb. There was no bursting, no rending, no injury, no hurt; showing how
wonderful he would be. Did not God give her comfort? Had he not accepted
her pure offering and sacrifice, so that thus easily she brought forth her son?"[2]

Even the sober Confucius (born B. C. 501) was of supernatural
origin. The most important event in Chinese literary and ethical
history is the birth of *Kung-foo-tsze* (Confucius), both in its effects
on the moral organization of this great empire, and the study of
Chinese philosophy in Europe.

Kung-foo-tsze (meaning "the sage Kung" or "the wise excellence") was of *royal descent;* and his family the most ancient in
the empire, as his genealogy was traceable directly up to Hwang-
te, the reputed organizer of the state, the first emperor of the semi-
historical period (beginning 2696 B. O.).

At his birth a prodigious quadruped, called the Ke-lin, appeared
and prophesied that the new-born infant "would be a king without throne or territory." Two dragons hovered about the couch
of *Yen-she* (his mother), and five celestial sages, or angels, entered
at the moment of the birth of the wondrous child; heavenly
strains were heard in the air, and harmonious chords followed
each other, fast and full. Thus was Confucius ushered into the
world.

His disciples, who were to expound his precepts, were seventy-
two in number, *twelve* of whom were his ordinary companions, the
depositories of his thoughts, and the witnesses of all his actions.
To them he minutely explained his doctrines, and charged them
with their propagation after his death. YAN-HWUY was his favorite
disciple, who, in his opinion, had attained the highest degree of
moral perfection. Confucius addressed him in terms of great
affection, which denoted that he relied mainly upon him for the
accomplishment of his work.[3]

Even as late as the seventeenth century of our era, do we find
the myth of the virgin-born God in China.[4]

---

1 "The '*toe-print made by God*' has occasioned much speculation of the critics. We
may simply draw the conclusion that the poet
meant to have his readers believe with him
that the conception of his hero was SUPER-
NATURAL." (James Legge.)
2 The Shih-King, Decade ii. Ode 1.
3 See Thornton's Hist. China, vol. i. pp. 199,
200, and Buckley's Cities of the Ancient World,
pp. 168–170.
4 " Le Dieu LA des LAMAS est né d'une
Vierge: plusieurs princes de l'Asie, entr'autres
l'Empereur Kienlong, aujourd'hui regnant à la
Chine, et qui est de la race de ces Tartares
Mandhuis, qui conquirent cet empire en 1644,
croit, et assure lui-même, être descendu d'une
Vierge." (D'Hancarville : Res. Sur l'Orig., p.
186, in Anac., vol. ii. p. 97.)

All these god-begotten and virgin-born men were called *Tien-tse*, *i. e.*, "Sons of Heaven."

If from China we should turn to Egypt we would find that, for ages before the time of Jesus of Nazareth, the mediating deity, born of a virgin, and without a worldly father, was a portion of the Egyptian belief.[1]

Horus, who had the epithet of "*Saviour*," was born of the virgin Isis. "His birth was one of the greatest Mysteries of the Egyptian religion. Pictures representing it appear on the walls of temples."[2] He is "the second emanation of *Amon*, the son whom he begot."[3] Egyptian monuments represent the infant Saviour in the arms of his virgin mother, or sitting on her knee.[4] An inscription on a monument, translated by Champollion, reads thus:

"O thou avenger, God, son of a God; O thou avenger, Horus, manifested by Osiris, engendered of the goddess Isis."[5]

The Egyptian god *Ra* was born from the side of his mother, *but was not engendered.*[6]

The ancient Egyptians also deified kings and heroes, in the same manner as the ancient Greeks and Romans. An Egyptian king became, in a sense, "the vicar of God on earth, the infallible, and the personated deity."[7]

P. Le Page Renouf, in his Hibbert Lectures on the Religion of Ancient Egypt, says:

"I must not quit this part of my subject without a reference to the belief that the ruling sovereign of Egypt was the living image and vicegerent of the Sun-god (*Ra*). *He was invested with the attributes of divinity*, and that in the earliest times of which we possess monumental evidence."[8]

Menes, who is said to have been the first king of Egypt, was believed to be a god.[9]

Almost all the temples of the left bank of the Nile, at Thebes, had been constructed in view of the worship rendered to the Pharaohs, their founders, after their death.[10]

On the wall of one of these Theban temples is to be seen a picture representing the god Thoth—the messenger of God—telling

[1] See Mahaffy : Proleg. to Anct. Hist., p. 416, and Bonwick's Egyptian Belief, p. 406.
[2] Bonwick : Egyptian Belief, p. 157.
[3] Renouf : Relig. Anct. Egypt, p. 162.
[4] See the chapter on "The Worship of the Virgin Mother."
[5] "O toi vengeur, Dieu fils d'un Dieu; O toi vengeur, Horus, manifesté par Osiris, en-

gendré d'Isis déesee." (Champollion, p. 190.)
[6] Bonwick : Egyptian Belief, p. 406.
[7] Ibid, p. 247.
[8] Renouf : Religion of Ancient Egypt, p. 161.
[9] See Bell's Pantheon, vol. ii. pp. 67 and 147.
[10] Bonwick : Egyptian Belief, p. 248.

the *maiden*, Queen Mautmes, that she is to give birth to a *divine son*, who is to be King *Amunothph* III.[1]

An inscription found in Egypt makes the god *Ra* say to his son Ramses III.:

"I am thy father; by me are begotten all thy members as divine; I have formed thy shape like the Mendesian god; I have begotten thee, impregnating thy venerable mother."[2]

Raam-ses, or *Ra-mé-ses*, means "Son of the Sun," and *Ramses Hek An*, a name of Ramses III., means "engendered by Ra (the Sun), Prince of An (Heliopolis)."[3]

" *Thotmes* III., on the tablet of Karnak, presents offerings to his predecessors; so does *Ramses* on the tablet of Abydos. Even during his life-time the Egyptian king was denominated '*Beneficent God.*' "[4]

The ancient Babylonians also believed that their kings were gods upon earth. A passage from Ménaut's translation of the great inscription of Nebuchadnezzar, reads thus:

"I am Nabu-kuder-usur . . . the first-born son of Nebu-pal-usur, King of Babylon. The god *Bel* himself created me, the god *Marduk* engendered me, and deposited himself the germ of my life in the womb of my mother."[5]

In the life of *Zoroaster*, the law-giver of the *Persians*, the common mythos is apparent. He was born in innocence, of an immaculate conception, of a ray of the Divine Reason. As soon as he was born the glory from his body enlightened the whole room.[6] Plato informs us that Zoroaster was said to be "the son of Oromasdes, which was the name the Persians gave to the Supreme God '"[7]—therefore he was the *Son of God.*

From the East we will turn to the West, and shall find that many of the ancient heroes of Grecian and Roman mythology were regarded as of divine origin, were represented as men, possessed of god-like form, strength and courage; were believed to have lived on earth in the remote, dim ages of the nation's history; to have been occupied in their life-time with thrilling adventures and extraordinary services in the cause of human civilization, and to have been after death in some cases translated to a life among the gods, and entitled to sacrifice and worship. In the hospitable Pantheon of the Greeks and Romans, a niche was always in readi-

[1] Bonwick : Egyptian Belief, p. 407.
[2] Renouf : Relig. of Anct. Egypt, p. 163.
[3] See Herbert Spencer's Principles of Sociology, vol. i. p. 420.
[4] Kenrick's Egypt, vol. i. p. 431.
[5] Spencer's Principles of Sociology, vol. i. p. 421.
[6] Malcolm : Hist. Persia, vol. i. p. 494.
[7] Anac. vol. i. p. 117.

ness for every new divinity who could produce respectable cre-
dentials.

The Christian Father Justin Martyr, says :

"It having reached the Devil's ears that the prophets had foretold the coming of Christ (*the Son of God*), he set the *Heathen Poets* to bring forward a great
many who should be called *the sons of Jove*. The Devil laying his scheme in
this, to get men to imagine that the *true* history of Christ was of the same character as the *prodigious fables* related of the sons of Jove."

Among these "sons of Jove" may be mentioned the following :
Hercules was the son of Jupiter by a mortal mother, Alcmene,
Queen of Thebes.[1] Zeus, the god of gods, spake of Hercules, his
son, and said: "This day shall a child be born of the race of
Perseus, who shall be the mightiest of the sons of men."[2]

Bacchus was the son of Jupiter and a mortal mother, Semele,
daughter of Kadmus, King of Thebes.[3] As Montfaucon says, "It
is the son of Jupiter and Semele which the poets celebrate, and
which the monuments represent."[4]

Bacchus is made to say :

"I, son of Deus, am come to this land of the Thebans, Bacchus, whom formerly Semele the daughter of Kadmus brings forth, being delivered by the
lightning-bearing flame: *and having taken a mortal form* instead of a god's, I
have arrived at the fountains of Dirce and the water of Ismenus."[5]

Amphion was the son of Jupiter and a mortal mother, Antiope,
daughter of Nicetus, King of Bœotia.[6]

Prometheus, whose name is derived from a Greek word signifying foresight and providence, was a deity who united the divine and
human nature in one person, and was confessedly both man and
god.[7]

Perseus was the son of Jupiter by the virgin Danae, daughter
of Acrisius, King of Argos.[8] Divine honors were paid him, and a
temple was erected to him in Athens.[9]

Justin Martyr (A. D. 140), in his Apology to the Emperor
Adrian, says :

"By declaring the Logos, the first-begotten of God, our Master, Jesus Christ,
to be born of a virgin, without any human mixture, we (Christians) *say no more
in this than what you* (Pagans) *say of those whom you style the Sons of Jove.* For

[1] Roman Antiq., p. 124. Bell's Panth., i.
328. Dupuis, p. 258.
[2] Tales of Anct. Greece, p. 55.
[3] Greek and Italian Mytho., p. 81. Bell's
Panth., i. 117. Roman Antiq., p. 71, and Murray's Manual Mytho., p. 118.
[4] L'Antiquité Expliquée, vol. i. p. 229.
[5] Euripides; Bacchae. Quoted by Dunlap:
Spirit Hist. of Man, p. 200.
[6] Bell's Pantheon, vol. i. p. 58. Roman Antiquities, p. 133.
[7] See the chapter on "The Crucifixion of
Jesus," and Bell's Pantheon, ii. 195.
[8] Bell's Pantheon, vol. ii. p. 170. Bulfinch:
The Age of Fable, p. 161.
[9] Bell's Pantheon, vol. ii. p. 171.

you need not be told what a parcel of sons the writers most in vogue among you assign to Jove. . . .

"As to the Son of God, called Jesus, should we allow him to be nothing more than man, yet the title of ' the Son of God ' is very justifiable, upon the account of his wisdom, considering that you (Pagans) have your Mercury in worship under the title of the Word, a messenger of God. . . .

"As to his (Jesus Christ's) being born of a virgin, *you have your Perseus to balance that.*"[1]

Mercury was the son of Jupiter and a mortal mother, Maia, daughter of Atlas. Cyllene, in Arcadia, is said to have been the scene of his birth and education, and a magnificent temple was erected to him there.[2]

Æolus, king of the Lipari Islands, near Sicily, was the son of Jupiter and a mortal mother, Acasta.[3]

Apollo was the son of Jupiter and a mortal mother, Latona.[4] Like Buddha and Lao-Kiun, Apollo, so the Ephesians said, was born under a tree ; Latona, taking shelter under an olive-tree, was delivered there.[5] Then there was joy among the undying gods in Olympus, and the Earth laughed beneath the smile of Heaven.[6]

Aethlius, who is said to have been one of the institutors of the Orphic games, was the son of Jupiter by a mortal mother, Protogenia.[7]

Arcas was the son of Jupiter and a mortal mother.[8]

Aroclus was the son of Jupiter and a mortal mother.[9]

We might continue and give the names of many more sons of Jove, but sufficient has been seen, we believe, to show, in the words of Justin, that Jove had a great " parcel of sons." " The images of self-restraint, of power used for the good of others, are prominent in the lives of all or almost all the Zeus-born heroes."[10]

This Jupiter, who begat so many sons, was the supreme god of the Pagans. In the words of *Orpheus :*

" Jupiter is omnipotent; the first and the last, the head and the midst; Jupiter, the giver of all things, the foundation of the earth, and the starry heavens."[11]

The ancient Romans were in the habit of deifying their living and departed emperors, and gave to them the title of Divus, or the Divine One. It was required throughout the whole empire that divine honors should be paid to the emperors.[12] They had a cere-

[1] Apol. 1, ch. xxii.
[2] Bell's Pantheon, vol. ii. p. 67. Bulfinch : The Age of Fable, p. 19.
[3] Bell's Pantheon, vol. i. p. 25.
[4] Ibid, p. 74, and Bulfinch : p. 248.
[5] Tacitus : Annals, iii. lxi.
[6] Tales of Anct. Greece, p. 4.
[7] Bell's Pantheon, vol. i. p. 31.
[8] Ibid. p. 81.
[9] Ibid. p. 16.
[10] Bell's Pantheon, ii. p. 30.
[11] Cox : Aryan Mythology, ii. 45.
[12] The Bible for Learners, vol. iii. p. 8.

mony called *Apotheosis*, or deification.   After this ceremony,
temples, altars, and images, with attributes of divinity, were erected
to the new deity.   It is related by Eusebius, Tertullian, and Chrysostom, that Tiberius proposed to the Roman Senate the Apotheosis
or deification of Jesus Christ.[1] Ælius Lampridius, in his Life of
Alexander Severus (who reigned A. D. 222–235), says:

> "This emperor had two private chapels, one more honorable than the other;
> and in the former were placed the deified emperors, and also some *eminent good*
> *men*, among them Abraham, Christ, and Orpheus."[2]

Romulus, who is said to have been the founder of Rome, was
believed to have been the son of God by a pure virgin, Rhea-Sylvia.[3]
One Julius Proculus took a solemn oath, that Romulus himself
appeared to him and ordered him to inform the Senate of his being called up to the assembly of the gods, under the name of Quiri-
nus.[4]

Julius Cæsar was supposed to have had a god for a father.[5]

Augustus Cæsar was also believed to have been of celestial origin, and had all the honors paid to him as to a divine person.[6]   His
divinity is expressed by Virgil, in the following lines:

> "—— Turn, turn thine eyes, see here thy race divine,
> Behold thy own imperial Roman Sire   :
> Cæsar, with all the Julian name survey;
> See where the glorious ranks ascend to-day !—
> This—this is he—*the chief so long foretold,*
> To bless the land where Saturn ruled of old,
> And give the Learnean realms a second eye of gold!
> The promised prince, *Augustus the divine,*
> Of Cæsar's race, and Jove's immortal line."[7]

"The honors due to the gods," says Tacitus, "were no longer
sacred: *Augustus* claimed equal worship.   Temples were built,
and statues were erected, to him; a mortal man was adored, and
priests and pontiffs were appointed to pay him impious homage."[8]

Divine honors were declared to the memory of Claudius, after
his death, and he was added to the number of the gods.   The titles
"Our Lord," "Our Master," and "Our God," were given to the
Emperors of Rome, even while living.[9]

---

[1] Bell's Pantheon, vol. i. p. 78.
[2] Quoted by Lardner, vol. iii. p. 157.
[3] Draper : Religion and Science, p. 8.
[4] Middleton's Letters from Rome, p. 37. In
the case of *Jesus,* one *Saul* of Tarsus, said to
be of a worthy and upright character, declared
most solemnly, that Jesus himself appeared
to him while on his way to Damascus, and
again while praying in the temple at Jerusalem.
(Acts xxii.)
[5] See Higgins : Anacalypsis, vol. ii. p. 345.
Gibbon's Rome, vol. i. pp. 84, 85.
[6] Higgins : Anacalypsis, vol. i. p. 611.
[7] Æneid, lib. iv.
[8] Tacitus : Annals, bk. i. ch. x.
[9] Ibid. bk. ii. ch. lxxxii. and bk. xiii. ch. ii.

In the deification of the Cæsars, a testimony upon oath, of an eagle's flying out of the funeral pile, toward heaven, which was supposed to convey the soul of the deceased, was the established proof of their divinity.[1]

. *Alexander the Great,* King of Macedonia (born 356 B. C.), whom genius and uncommon success had raised above ordinary men, was believed to have been a god upon earth.[2] He was believed to have been the son of Jupiter by a mortal mother, Olympias.

Alexander at one time visited the temple of Jupiter Ammon, which was situated in an oasis in the Libyan desert, and the *Oracle* there declared him to be a son of the god. He afterwards issued his orders, letters, decrees, &c., styling himself "*Alexander, son of Jupiter Ammon.*"[3]

The words of the oracle which declared him to be divine were as follows, says Socrates:

> " Let altars burn and incense pour, please Jove Minerva eke;
> The potent Prince though nature frail, his favor you must seek,
> , For Jove from heaven to earth him sent, lo! Alexander king,
> As God he comes the earth to rule, and just laws for to bring."[4]

Ptolemy, who was one of Alexander's generals in his Eastern campaigns, and into whose hands Egypt fell at the death of Alexander, was also believed to have been of divine origin. At the siege of Rhodes, Ptolemy had been of such signal service to its citizens that in gratitude they paid *divine honors* to him, and saluted him with the title of *Soter, i. e.,* Saviour. By that designation, "*Ptolemy Soter,*" he is distinguished from the succeeding kings of the Macedonian dynasty in Egypt.[5]

Cyrus, King of Persia, was believed to have been of *divine origin;* he was called the "*Christ,*" or the "*Anointed* of God," and God's messenger.[6]

Plato, born at Athens 429 B. C., was believed to have been the son of God by a *pure virgin,* called Perictione.[7]

The reputed father of Plato (Aris) was admonished in a dream to respect the person of his wife until after the birth of the child of which she was then pregnant by a god.[8]

Prof. Draper, speaking of Plato, says:

---

[1] See Middleton's Letters from Rome, pp. 37, 38.

[2] See Religion of the Ancient Greeks, p. 81, and Gibbon's Rome, vol. i. pp. 84, 85.

[3] Draper: Religion and Science, p. 8.

[4] Socrates: Eccl. Hist. Lib. 3, ch. xix.

[5] Draper: Religion and Science, p. 17.

[6] See Inman: Ancient Faiths, vol. i. p. 418. Bunsen: Bible Chronology, p. 5, and The Angel-Messiah, pp. 80 and 298.

[7] See Higgins: Anacalypsis, vol. ii. p. 113, and Draper: Religion and Science, p. 8.

[8] Hardy: Manual Budd., p. 141. Higgins: Anac., i. 618.

"The Egyptian disciples of Plato would have looked with anger on those who rejected the legend that Perictione, the mother of that great philosopher, a pure virgin, had suffered an immaculate conception through the influences of (the god) Apollo, *and that the god had declared to Aris, to whom she was betrothed, the parentage of the child.*"[1]

Here we have the legend of the angel appearing to Joseph—to whom Mary was betrothed—believed in by the disciples of Plato for centuries before the time of Christ Jesus, the only difference being that the virgin's name was Perictione instead of Mary, and the confiding husband's name Aris instead of Joseph. We have another similar case.

The mother of *Apollonius* (B. C. 41) was informed by a god, who appeared to her, *that he himself should be born of her.*[2] In the course of time she gave birth to Apollonius, who became a great religious teacher, and performer of miracles.[3]

Pythagoras, born about 570 B. C., had divine honors paid him. His mother is said to have become impregnated through a *spectre*, or Holy Ghost. His father—or foster-father—was also informed that his wife should bring forth a son, who should be a benefactor to mankind.[4]

Æsculapius, the great performer of miracles,[5] was supposed to be the son of a god and a worldly mother, Coronis. The Messenians, who consulted the oracle at Delphi to know where Æsculapius was born, and of what parents, were informed that a god was his father, Coronis his mother, and that their son was born at Epidaurus.

Coronis, to conceal her pregnancy from her father, went to Epidaurus, where she was delivered of a son, whom she exposed on a mountain. Aristhenes, a goat-herd, going in search of a goat and a dog missing from his fold, discovered the child, whom he would have carried to his home, had he not, upon approaching to lift him from the earth, *perceived his head encircled with fiery rays, which made him believe the child was divine.* The voice of fame soon published the birth of a miraculous infant, upon which the people flocked from all quarters *to behold this heaven-born child.*[6]

Being honored as a god in Phenicia and Egypt, his worship passed into Greece and Rome.[7]

---

[1] Draper : Religion and Science, p. 8. Compare Luke i. 26–35.

[2] Philostratus, p. 5.

[3] See the chapter on Miracles.

[4] See Higgins : Anacalypsis, vol. i. p. 151.

[5] See the chapter on Miracles.

[6] Bell's Pantheon, i. 27. Roman Ant., 136. Taylor's Diegesis, p. 150.

[7] Ibid.

Simon the Samaritan, surnamed " *Magus* " or the " Magician," who was contemporary with Jesus, was believed to be a *god*. In Rome, where he performed wonderful miracles, he was honored as a god, and his picture placed among the gods.[1]

Justin Martyr, quoted by Eusebius, tells us that Simon Magus attained great honor among the Romans. That he was believed to be a *god*, and that he was worshiped as such. Between two bridges upon the River Tibris, was to be seen this inscription: "Simoni Deo Sancto," *i. e.* "To Simon the Holy God."[2]

It was customary with all the heroes of the northern nations (Danes, Swedes, Norwegians and Icelanders), to speak of themselves as sprung from their supreme deity, *Odin*. The historians of those times, that is to say, the poets, never failed to bestow the same honor on all those whose praises they sang; and thus they multiplied the descendants of Odin as much as they found convenient. The first-begotten son of Odin was Thor, whom the Eddas call the most valiant of his sons. "Baldur the Good," the "Beneficent Saviour," was the son of the Supreme Odin and the goddess Frigga, whose worship was transferred to that of the Virgin Mary.[3]

In the mythological systems of *America*, a virgin-born god was not less clearly recognized than in those of the Old World. Among the savage tribes his origin and character were, for obvious reasons, much confused; but among the more advanced nations he occupied a well-defined position. Among the nations of Anahuac, he bore the name of *Quetzalcoatle*, and was regarded with the highest veneration.

For ages before the landing of Columbus on its shores, the inhabitants of ancient Mexico worshiped a "Saviour"—as they called him—(*Quetzalcoatle*) who was *born of a pure virgin*.[4] *A messenger from heaven announced to his mother that she should bear a son without connection with man.*[5] Lord Kingsborough tells us that the annunciation of the *virgin Sochiquetzal*, mother of Quetzalcoatle,—who was styled the " *Queen of Heaven* "[6]—was the subject of a Mexican hieroglyph.[7]

The embassador was sent from heaven to this virgin, who had two sisters, Tzochitlique and Conatlique. "These three being alone in the house, two of them, on perceiving the embassador from heaven, died of fright, Sochiquetzal remaining alive, to whom the

[1] Eusebius : Eccl. Hist., lib. 2, ch. xiii.
[2] Ibid. ch. xiii.
[3] See Mallet's Northern Antiquities.
[4] See Higgins : Anacalypsis, vol. ii. p. 32, Kingsborough : Mexican Antiquities, vol.

vi. 166 and 175–6.
[5] Ibid.
[6] See Kingsborough : Mexican Antiquities, vol. vi. p. 176.
[7] Ibid. p. 175.

embassador announced that it was the will of God that she should conceive a son."[1] She therefore, according to the prediction, "conceived a son, *without connection with man*, who was called Quetzalcoatle."[2]

Dr. Daniel Brinton, in his "Myths of the New World," says:

"The Central figure of Toltec mythology is *Quetzalcoatle*. Not an author on ancient Mexico, but has something to say about the glorious days when he ruled over the land. No one denies him to have been a god. *He was born of a virgin* in the land of *Tula* or *Tlopallan*."[3]

The Mayas of *Yucatan* had a virgin-born god, corresponding entirely with Quetzalcoatle, if he was not the same under a different name, a conjecture very well sustained by the evident relationship between the Mexican and Mayan mythologies. He was named *Zama*, and was the only-begotten son of their supreme god, Kinchahan.[4]

The *Muyscas* of Columbia had a similar hero-god. According to their traditionary history, he bore the name of *Bochica*. He was the incarnation of the Great Father, whose sovereignty and paternal care he emblematized.[5]

The inhabitants of *Nicaragua* called their principal god Thomathoyo; and said that he had a *son*, who came down to earth, whose name was Theotbilahe, and that he was their general instructor.[6]

We find a corresponding character in the traditionary history of *Peru*. The Sun—the god of the Peruvians—deploring their miserable condition, sent down his son, *Manco Capac*, to instruct them in religion, &c.[7]

We have also traces of a similar personage in the traditionary *Votan* of *Guatemala;* but our accounts concerning him are more vague than in the cases above mentioned.

We find this traditional character in countries and among tribes where we would be least apt to suspect its existence. In *Brazil,* besides the common belief in an age of violence, during which the world was destroyed by water, there is a tradition of a supernatural personage called *Zome*, whose history is similar, in some respects, to that of Quetzalcoatle.[8]

The semi-civilized agricultural tribes of *Florida* had like traditions. The *Cherokees*, in particular, had a priest and law-giver

---

[1] See Kingsborough : Mexican Antiquities, vol. vi p. 176.

[2] Ibid. p. 166.

[3] Brinton : Myths of the New World, pp. 180, 181.

[4] Squire : Serpent Symbol, p. 187.

[5] Ibid. p. 188.

[6] Ibid.

[7] Ibid.

[8] Ibid. p. 190.

essentially corresponding to Quetzalcoatle and Bochica. He was their great prophet, and bore the name of *Wasi.* "He told them what had been from the beginning of the world, and what would be, and gave the people in all things directions what to do. He appointed their feasts and fasts, and all the ceremonies of their religion, and enjoined upon them to obey his directions from generation to generation."[1]

Among the savage tribes the same notions prevailed. The *Edues* of the Californians taught that there was a supreme Creator, *Niparaya*, and that his son, *Quaagagp*, came down upon the earth and instructed the Indians in religion, &c. Finally, through hatred, the Indians killed him; but although dead, he is incorruptible and beautiful. To him they pay adoration, as the *mediatory power* between earth and the Supreme Niparaga.[2]

The *Iroquois* also had a beneficent being, uniting in himself the character of *a god and man,* who was called *Tarengawagan.* He imparted to them the knowledge of the laws of the Great Spirit, established their form of government, &c.[3]

Among the *Algonquins,* and particularly among the *Ojibways* and other remnants of that stock of the North-west, this intermediate great teacher (denominated, by Mr. Schoolcraft, in his "*Notes of the Iroquois,*" "the great incarnation of the North-west") is fully recognized. He bears the name of *Michabou,* and is represented as *the first-born son of a great celestial Manitou,* or *Spirit, by an earthly mother,* and is esteemed the friend and protector of the human race.[4]

I think we can now say with M. Dupuis, that "the idea of a God, who came down on earth to save mankind, is neither new nor peculiar to the Christians," and with Cicero, the great Roman orator and philosopher, that "brave, famous or powerful men, after death, came to be *gods,* and they are the very ones whom we are accustomed to worship, pray to and venerate."

Taking for granted that the synoptic Gospels are historical, there is no proof that Jesus ever claimed to be either God, or a god; on the other hand, it is quite the contrary.[5] As Viscount Amberly says: "The best proof of this is that Jesus never, at any period of his life,

---

[1] Squire: Serpent Symbol, p. 191.
[2] Ibid.
[3] Ibid.
[4] Ibid, p. 192.
[5] "If we seek, in the first three Gospels, to know what his biographers thought of Jesus, we find his *true humanity* plainly stated, and if

we possessed only the Gospel of *Mark* and the discourses of the Apostles in the *Acts,* the whole Christology of the New Testament would be reduced to this: that Jesus of Nazareth was '*a prophet mighty in deeds and in words,* made by God Christ and Lord.'" (Albert Réville.)

desired his followers to worship him, either as God, or as the Son of God," in the sense in which it is now understood. Had he believed of himself what his followers subsequently believed of him, that he was one of the constituent persons in a divine Trinity, he must have enjoined his Apostles both to address him in prayer themselves, and to desire their converts to do likewise. It is quite plain that he did nothing of the kind, and that they never supposed him to have done so.

Belief in Jesus *as the Messiah* was taught as the first dogma of Christianity, but adoration of Jesus *as God* was not taught at all.

But we are not left in this matter to depend on conjectural inferences. The words put into the mouth of Jesus are plain. Whenever occasion arose, *he asserted his inferiority to the Father*, though, as no one had then dreamt of his equality, it is natural that the occasions should not have been frequent.

He made himself *inferior in knowledge* when he said that of the day and hour of the day of judgment no one knew, neither the angels in heaven nor the Son; no one except the Father.[1]

He made himself *inferior in power* when he said that seats on his right hand and on his left in the kingdom of heaven were not his to give.[2]

He made himself *inferior in virtue* when he desired a certain man not to address him as " Good Master," for there was none good but God.[3]

The words of his prayer at Gethsemane, " all things are possible unto *thee*," imply that all things were *not* possible to *him*, while its conclusion " not what *I will*, but what *thou wilt*," indicates submission to a superior, not the mere execution of a purpose of his own.[4] Indeed, the whole prayer would have been a mockery, useless for any purpose but the deception of his disciples, if he had himself been identical with the Being to whom he prayed, and had merely been giving effect by his death to their common counsels. While the cry of agony from the cross, "*My God, my God! why hast thou forsaken me?*"[5] would have been quite unmeaning if *the person forsaken*, and *the person forsaking*, had been one and the same.

Either, then, we must assume that the language of Jesus has been misreported, or we must admit that he never for a moment pretended to be co-equal, co-eternal or consubstantial with God.

---

[1] Mark, xiii. 32.
[2] Mark, x. 40.
[3] Mark, x. 18.
[4] Mark, xiv. 36.
[5] Mark, xv. 34.

It also follows of necessity from *both the genealogies*,[1] that their compilers entertained no doubt that *Joseph* was the father of Jesus. Otherwise the descent of Joseph would not have been in the least to the point. All attempts to reconcile this inconsistency with the doctrine of the Angel-Messiah has been without avail, although the most learned Christian divines, for many generations past, have endeavored to do so.

So, too, of the stories of the Presentation in the Temple,[2] and of the child Jesus at Jerusalem,[3] *Joseph is called his father.* Jesus is repeatedly described as *the son of the carpenter*,[4] or the *son of Joseph*, without the least indication that the expression is not strictly in accordance with the fact.[5]

If his parents fail to understand him when he says, at twelve years old, that he must be about his Father's business;[6] if he afterwards declares that he finds no faith among his nearest relations;[7] if he exalts his faithful disciples above his *unbelieving mother* and brothers;[8] above all, if Mary and her other sons put down his prophetic enthusiasm to *insanity*;[9]—then the untrustworthy nature of these stories of his birth is absolutely certain. If even a *little* of what they tell us had been true, then *Mary at least* would have believed in Jesus, and would not have failed so utterly to understand him.[10]

The Gospel of Mark—which, in this respect, at least, abides most faithfully by the old apostolic tradition—says not a word about Bethlehem or *the miraculous birth*. The congregation of Jerusalem to which Mary and the brothers of Jesus belonged,[11] and over which the eldest of them, James, presided,[12] can have known nothing of it; for the later Jewish-Christian communities, the so-called Ebionites, who were descended from the congregation at Jerusalem, called Jesus *the son of Joseph*. Nay, the story that the *Holy Spirit* was the father of Jesus, must have risen among

---

[1] Matt. and Luke.
"The passages which appear most confirmatory of Christ's Deity, or Divine nature, are, in the first place, the narratives of the Incarnation and of the Miraculous Conception, as given by Matthew and Luke. Now, the two narratives do not harmonize with each other; they neutralize and negative the *genealogies* on which depend so large a portion of the proof of Jesus being the Messiah—the marvellous statement they contain is not referred to in any subsequent portion of the two Gospels, and is tacitly but positively negatived by several passages—it is never mentioned in the Acts or in the Epistles, and was evidently unknown to all the Apostles—and, finally, the tone of the narrative, especially in Luke, is poetical and legendary, and bears a marked similarity to the stories contained in the Apocryphal Gospels." (W. R. Greg: The Creed of Christendom, p. 229.)

[2] Luke, ii. 27. [3] Luke, ii. 41-48.
[4] Matt. xiii. 55.
[5] Luke, iv. 22. John, i. 46; vi. 42. Luke, iii. 23.
[6] Luke, ii. 50.
[7] Matt. xiii. 57. Mark, vi. 4.
[8] Matt. xii. 46-50. Mark, iii. 33-35.
[9] Mark, iii. 21.
[10] Dr. Hooykaas.
[11] Acts, i. 14.
[12] Acts, xxi. 18. Gal. ii. 10-21.

the *Greeks*, or elsewhere, and not among the first believers, who were Jews, for the Hebrew word for *spirit* is of the *feminine gender*.[1]

The immediate successors of the " congregation at Jerusalem " —to which Mary, the mother of Jesus, and his brothers belonged— were, as we have seen, the Ebionites. Eusebius, the first ecclesiastical historian (born A. D. 264), speaking of the *Ebionites* (*i. e.* " poor men ") ,tell us that they believed Jesus to be " *a simple and common man*," born as other men, " *of Mary and her husband.*"[2]

The views held by the Ebionites of Jesus were, it is said, derived from the Gospel of Matthew, *and what they learned direct from the Apostles.* Matthew had been a hearer of Jesus, a companion of the Apostles, and had seen and no doubt conversed with Mary. When he wrote his Gospel everything was fresh in his mind, and there could be no object, on his part, in writing the life of Jesus, to state falsehoods or omit important truths in order to deceive his countrymen. If what is stated in the *interpolated* first two chapters, concerning the miraculous birth of Jesus, were true, Matthew would have known of it ; and, knowing it, why should he omit it in giving an account of the life of Jesus ?[3]

The Ebionites, or Nazarenes, as they were previously called, were rejected by the Jews *as apostates*, and by the Egyptian and Roman Christians *as heretics*, therefore, until they completely disappear, their history is one of tyrannical persecution. Although some traces of that obsolete sect may be discovered as late as the fourth century, they insensibly melted away, either into the Roman Christian Church, or into the Jewish Synagogue,[4] and with them perished the *original* Gospel of Matthew, *the only Gospel written by an apostle.*

" Who, where masses of men are burning to burst the bonds of time and sense, to deify and to adore, wants what seems earth-born, prosaic fact? Woe to the man that dares to interpose it! Woe to the sect of faithful Ebionites even, and on the very soil of Palestine, that dare to maintain the earlier, humbler tradition ! Swiftly do they become heretics, revilers, blasphemers, though sanctioned by a James, brother of the Lord."

Edward Gibbon, speaking of this most unfortunate sect, says :

" A laudable regard for the honor of the first proselytes has countenanced the belief, the hope, the wish, that the Ebionites, or at least the Nazarenes, were

---

[1] See The Bible for Learners, vol. iii. p. 57.
[2] Eusebius : Eccl. Hist., lib. 3, ch. xxiv.
[3] Mr. George Reber has thoroughly investi-
gated this subject in his " Christ of Paul," to Which the reader is referred.
[4] See Gibbon's Rome, vol. i. pp. 515–517.

distinguished only by their obstinate perseverance in the practice of the Mosaic rites. Their churches have disappeared, *their books are obliterated,* their obscure freedom might allow a latitude of faith, and the softness of their infant creed would be variously moulded by the zeal of prejudice of three hundred years. Yet the most charitable criticism must refuse these sectaries any knowledge of the pure and proper *divinity of Christ.* Educated in the school of Jewish prophecy and prejudice, they had never been taught to elevate their hope above *a human* and temporal Messiah. If they had courage to hail their king when he appeared in a plebeian garb, their grosser apprehensions were incapable of discerning their God, *who had studiously disguised his celestial character under the name and person of a mortal.*

"The familiar companions of Jesus of Nazareth conversed with their friend and countryman, who, in all the actions of rational and human life, appeared of the same species with themselves. His progress from infancy to youth and manhood was marked by a regular increase in stature and wisdom; and after a painful agony of mind and body, he expired on the cross."[1]

The Jewish Christians then—the congregation of Jerusalem, and their immediate successors, the Ebionites or Nazarenes—saw in their master nothing more than *a man.* From this, and the other facts which we have seen in this chapter, it is evident that the man Jesus of Nazareth was deified long after his death, just as many other men had been deified centuries before his time, and even *after.* Until it had been settled by a council of bishops that Jesus was not only *a God,* but *"God himself in human form,"* who appeared on earth, as did Crishna of old, to redeem and save mankind, there were many theories concerning his nature.

Among the early Christians there were a certain class called by the later Christians *Heretics.* Among these may be mentioned the *"Carpocratians,"* named after one Carpocrates. They maintained that Jesus was a *mere man,* born of Joseph and Mary, *like other men,* but that he was good and virtuous. "Some of them have the vanity," says *Irenæus,* "to think that they may equal, or in some respects exceed, Jesus himself."[2]

These are called by the general name of *Gnostics, and comprehend almost all the sects of the first two ages.*[3] They said that "all the ancients, and even the Apostles themselves, received and taught the same things which they held; and that the truth of the Gospel had been preserved till the time of *Victor,* the thirteenth Bishop of Rome, but by his successor, *Zephyrinus,* the truth had been corrupted."[4]

Eusebius, speaking of *Artemon* and his followers, who denied the divinity of Christ, says:

[1] Gibbon's Rome, vol. iv. pp. 488, 489.   [3] Ibid. p. 306.
[2] See Lardner's Works, vol. viii. pp. 395, 396.   [4] Ibid. p. 571.

"They affirm that all our ancestors, yea, and the Apostles themselves, were
of the same opinion, and taught the same with them, and that this their true
doctrine (for so they call it) was preached and embraced unto the time of Victor,
the thirteenth Bishop of Rome after Peter, and corrupted by his successor
Zephyrinus."[1]

There were also the "*Cerinthians*," named after one Cerinthus,
who maintained that Jesus was *not* born of a virgin, which to them
appeared impossible, but that he was the son of Joseph and Mary,
born altogether as other men are; but he excelled all men in virtue, knowledge and wisdom. At the time of his baptism, "*the
Christ*" came down upon him in the shape of a dove, and *left
him* at the time of his crucifixion.[2]

Irenæus, speaking of Cerinthus and his doctrines, says:

"He represents Jesus as the son of Joseph and Mary, according to the ordinary course of human generation, and *not* as having been born of a virgin. He
believed nevertheless that he was more righteous, prudent and wise than most
men, and that *the Christ* descended upon, and entered into him, at the time
of his baptism."[3]

The *Docetes* were a numerous and learned sect of Asiatic Christians who invented the *Phantastic* system, which was afterwards promulgated by the Marcionites, the Manicheans, and various other sects.

They denied the truth and authenticity of the Gospels, as far as
they related to the conception of Mary, the birth of Jesus, and the
thirty years that preceded the exercise of his ministry.

Bordering upon the Jewish and Gentile world, the *Cerinthians*
labored to reconcile the *Gnostic* and the *Ebionite*, by confessing in
the *same Messiah* the supernatural union of a man and a god; and
this *mystic* doctrine was adopted, with many fanciful improvements, by many sects. The hypothesis was this: that Jesus of
Nazareth was a mere mortal, the legitimate son of Joseph and
Mary, but he was *the best* and wisest of the human race, selected as
the worthy instrument to restore upon earth the worship of the
true and supreme Deity. When he was baptized in the Jordan,
and not till then, he became *more than man.* At that time, *the
Christ,* the first of the *Æons,* the Son of God himself, descended
on Jesus in the form of a dove, *to inhabit his mind,* and direct his
actions during the allotted period of *his ministry.* When he was
delivered into the hands of the Jews, *the Christ* forsook him, flew
back to the world of spirits, and left the *solitary Jesus* to suffer, to

¹ Eusebius: Eccl. Hist., lib. 5, ch. xxv.   ² Lardner: vol. viii. p. 404.
³ Irenæus: Against Heresies, bk. i. c. xxiv.

complain, and to die. This is why he said, while hanging on the cross: "My God! My God! why hast thou forsaken me?"[1]

Here, then, we see the *first* budding out of—what was termed by the *true* followers of Jesus—*heretical doctrines.* The time had not yet come to make Jesus *a god,* to claim that he had been born of a virgin. As he *must,* however, have been different from other mortals—throughout the period of his ministry, at least—the Christ *must* have entered into him at the time of his baptism, and *as mysteriously* disappeared when he was delivered into the hands of the Jews.

In the course of time, the seeds of the faith, which had slowly arisen in the rocky and ungrateful soil of Judea, were transplanted, in full maturity, to the happier climes of the *Gentiles;* and the strangers of *Rome* and *Alexandria, who had never beheld the manhood,* were more ready to embrace the *divinity* of Jesus.

The polytheist and the philosopher, the Greek and the barbarian, were alike accustomed to receive—as we have seen in this chapter—a long succession and infinite chain of angels, or deities, or *æons,* or emanations, issuing from the throne of light. Nor could it seem strange and incredible *to them,* that the first of the *æons,* the Logos, or Word of God, of the same substance with the Father, should descend upon earth, to deliver the human race from vice and error. The histories of their countries, their odes, and their religions were teeming with such ideas, as happening in the past, and they were also *looking for and expecting an Angel-Messiah.*[2]

Centuries rolled by, however, before the doctrine of Christ Jesus, the Angel-Messiah, became a settled question, an established tenet in the Christian faith. The dignity of Christ Jesus was measured by *private judgment,* according to the indefinite *rule of Scripture,* or *tradition* or *reason.* But when his pure and proper divinity had been established *on the ruins of Arianism,* the faith of the Catholics trembled *on the edge of a precipice* where it was impossible to recede, dangerous to stand, dreadful to fall; and the *manifold inconveniences of their creed* were aggravated by the sublime character of their theology. They hesitated to pronounce that *God himself,* the second person of an equal and consubstantial Trinity, was *manifested in the flesh,*[3] that the Being who pervades the universe *had been confined in the womb of Mary;* that his

[1] See Gibbon's Rome, vol. iv. pp. 492-495.
[2] Not a *worldly Messiah,* as the Jews looked for, but an *Angel-Messiah,* such an one as always came at the end of a *cycle.* We shall treat of this subject anon, when we answer the question *why* Jesus was believed to be an *Avatar,* by the Gentiles, and not by the Jews; why, in fact, the doctrine of *Christ incarnate* in Jesus succeeded and prospered.
[3] "This strong expression might be justified

eternal duration had been marked by the days, and months, and years of human existence; *that the Almighty God had been scourged and crucified;* that his impassible essence *had felt pain and anguish;* that his omniscience was *not exempt from ignorance;* and that *the source of life and immortality expired on Mount Calvary.*

These alarming consequences were affirmed with unblushing simplicity by Apollinaris, Bishop of Laodicea, and one of the luminaries of the Church. The son of a learned grammarian, he was skilled in all the sciences of Greece; eloquence, erudition, and philosophy, conspicuous in the volumes of Apollinaris, were humbly devoted to the service of religion.

The worthy friend of Athanasius, the worthy antagonist of Julian, he bravely wrestled with the Arians and polytheists, *and though he affected the rigor of geometrical demonstration,* his commentaries revealed the literal and allegorical sense of the Scriptures.

A mystery, which had long floated in the looseness of popular belief, was defined by his perverse diligence in a technical form, *and he first proclaimed the memorable words, "One incarnate nature of Christ."*[1]

This was about A. D. 362, he being Bishop of Laodicea, in Syria, at that time.[2]

The recent zeal against the errors of Apollinaris reduced the Catholics to a seeming agreement with the *double-nature* of Cerinthus. But instead of a temporary and occasional alliance, they established, and Christians *still embrace,* the substantial, indissoluble, and everlasting *union of a perfect God with a perfect man,* of the second person of the Trinity with a reasonable soul and human flesh. In the beginning of the *fifth century,* the unity of the two natures was the prevailing doctrine of the church.[3] From that time, until a comparatively recent period, the cry was: *"May those who divide Christ*[4] *be divided with the sword; may*

---

by the language of St. Paul (*God* was manifest in the flesh, justified in the spirit, seen of angels, &c. I. Timothy, iii. 16), but we are deceived by our modern Bibles. The word *which* was altered to *God* at Constantinople in the beginning of the sixth century: the true meaning, which is visible in the Latin and Syriac versions, still exists in the reasoning of the Greek, as well as of the Latin fathers; and this fraud, with that of the *three witnesses of St. John* (I. John, v. 7), is admirably detected by Sir Isaac Newton." (Gibbon's Rome, iv. 496, *note.*) *Dean Milman* says: "The weight of au-

thority is so much against the common reading of both these points (*i. e.,* I. Tim. iii. 16, and I. John, v. 7), that they are no longer urged by prudent controversialists." (Note in Ibid.)

[1] Gibbon's Rome, vol. iv. pp. 492–497.
[2] See Chambers's Encyclopædia, art. "Apollinaris."
[3] Gibbon's Rome, vol. iv. p. 498.
[4] That is, separate *him* from God the Father, by saying that *he,* Jesus of Nazareth, was *not* really and truly God Almighty himself in human form.

they be hewn in pieces, may they be burned alive!" These were actually the words of a *Christian* synod.[1] Is it any wonder that after this came the *dark ages?* How appropriate is the name which has been applied to the centuries which followed! *Dark* indeed they were. Now and then, however, a ray of light was seen, which gave evidence of the coming *morn,* whose glorious light we now enjoy. But what a grand light is yet to come from the noon-day sun, which must shed its glorious rays over the whole earth, ere it sets.

---

[1] See Gibbon's Rome, vol. iv. p. 516

CHAPTER XIII.

BEING born in a miraculous manner, as other great personages had been, it was necessary that the miracles attending the births of these virgin-born gods should be added to the history of Christ Jesus, otherwise the legend would not be complete.

The first which we shall notice is the story of the *star* which is said to have heralded his birth, and which was designated " *his* star." It is related by the *Matthew* narrator as follows:[1]

" When Jesus was born in Bethlehem, of Judea, in the days of Herod the king, behold, there came wise men from the east to Jerusalem, saying: ' Where is he that is born King of the Jews ? for we have seen *his star* in the east, and are come to worship him.' "

Herod the king, having heard these things, he privately called the wise men, and inquired of them what time the star appeared, at the same time sending them to Bethlehem to search diligently for the young child. The wise men, accordingly, departed and went on their way towards Bethlehem. " The star which they saw in the east went before them, till it came *and stood over* where the young child was."

The general legendary character of this narrative—its similarity in style with those contained in the apocryphal gospels—and more especially its conformity with those *astrological notions* which, though prevalent in the time of the Matthew narrator, have been exploded by the sounder scientific knowledge of our days—all unite to stamp upon the story the impress of poetic or mythic fiction.

The fact that the writer of this story speaks not of *a star* but of *his* star, shows that it was the popular belief of the people among whom he lived, that each and every person was born under a star, and that this one which had been seen was *his star*.

All ancient nations were very superstitious in regard to the influence of the stars upon human affairs, and this ridiculous idea

---

[1] Matthew, ch. ii.

has been handed down, in some places, even to the present day. Dr. Hooykaas, speaking on this subject, says:

"In ancient times the Jews, like other peoples, might very well believe that there was some immediate connection between the stars and the life of man—an idea which we still preserve in the forms of speech that so-and-so was born under a lucky or under an evil star. They might therefore suppose that the birth of greatmen, such as Abraham, for instance, was announced in the heavens. In our century, however, if not before, all serious belief in astrology has ceased, and it would be regarded as an act of the grossest superstition for any one to have his horoscope drawn; for the course, the appearance and the disappearance of the heavenly bodies have been long determined with mathematical precision by science." [1]

The Rev. Dr. Geikie says, in his *Life of Christ:* [2]

"The Jews had already, long before Christ's day, dabbled in astrology, and the various forms of magic which became connected with it. . . . They were much given to cast horoscopes from the numerical value of a name. Everywhere throughout the whole Roman Empire, Jewish magicians, dream expounders, and sorcerers, were found.

" 'The life and portion of children,' says the *Talmud,* 'hang not on righteousness, but on *their* star.' 'The planet of the day has no virtue, but the planet of the hour (of nativity) has much.' 'When the Messiah is to be revealed,' says the book *Sohar,* 'a star will rise in the east, shining in great brightness, and *seven* other stars round it will fight against it on every side.' 'A star will rise in the east, which is the star of the Messiah, and will remain in the east fifteen days.' "

The moment of every man's birth being supposed to determine every circumstance in his life, it was only necessary to find out in what mode the *celestial bodies*—supposed to be the primary wheels to the universal machine—operated at that moment, in order to discover all that would happen to him afterward.

The regularity of the risings and settings of the fixed stars, though it announced the changes of the seasons and the orderly variations of nature, could not be adapted to the capricious mutability of human actions, fortunes, and adventures: wherefore the astrologers had recourse to the planets, whose more complicated revolutions offered more varied and more extended combinations. Their different returns to certain points of the Zodiac, their relative positions and conjunctions with each other, were supposed to influence the affairs of men; whence daring impostors presumed to foretell, not only the destinies of individuals, but also the rise and fall of empires, and the fate of the world itself. [3]

The inhabitants of *India* are, and have always been, very superstitious concerning the stars. The Rev. D. O. Allen, who resided

---

[1] Bible for Learners, vol. iii. p. 72.   [3] See Knight : Ancient Art and Mythology,
[2] Vol. i. p. 145.   p. 52.

in India for twenty-five years, and who undoubtedly became thoroughly acquainted with the superstitions of the inhabitants, says on this subject:

"So strong are the superstitious feelings of many, concerning the supposed influence of the stars on human affairs, that some days are *lucky*, and others again are *unlucky*, that no arguments or promises would induce them to deviate from the course which these *stars*, signs, &c., indicate, as the way of safety, prosperity, and happiness. The evils and inconveniences of these superstitions and prejudices are among the things that press heavily upon the people of India."[1]

The *Nakshatias*—twenty-seven constellations which in Indian astronomy separate the moon's path into twenty-seven divisions, as the signs of the Zodiac do that of the sun into twelve—are regarded as deities who exert a vast influence on the destiny of men, not only at the moment of their entrance into the world, but during their whole passage through it. These formidable constellations are consulted at births, marriages, and on all occasions of family rejoicing, distress or calamity. No one undertakes a journey or any important matter except on days which the aspect of the Nakshatias renders lucky and auspicious. If any constellation is unfavorable, it must by all means be propitiated by a ceremony called S'anti.

The *Chinese* were very superstitious concerning the stars. They annually published astronomical calculations of the motions of the planets, for every hour and minute of the year. They considered it important to be very exact, because the hours, and even the minutes, are lucky or unlucky, according to the aspect of the stars. Some days were considered peculiarly fortunate for marrying, or beginning to build a house; and the gods are better pleased with sacrifice offered at certain hours than they are with the same ceremony performed at other times.[2]

The ancient *Persians* were also great astrologers, and held the stars in great reverence. They believed and taught that the destinies of men were intimately connected with their motions, and therefore it was important to know under the influence of what star a human soul made its advent into this world. Astrologers swarmed throughout the country, and were consulted upon all important occasions.[3]

The ancient *Egyptians* were exactly the same in this respect. According to Champollion, the tomb of Ramses V., at Thebes, contains tables of the constellations, and of their influence on human beings, for every hour of every month of the year.[4]

---

[1] Allen's India, p. 456.   [2] Ibid. p. 261.
[3] See Prog. Relig. Ideas, vol. i. p. 221.   [4] See Kenrick's Egypt, vol. i. p. 456.

The Buddhists' sacred books relate that the birth of *Buddha* was announced in the heavens by an *asterim* which was seen rising on the horizon. It is called the "*Messianic star.*"[1]

The Fo-pen-hing says:

"The time of Bôdhisatwa's incarnation is, when the constellation *Kwei* is in conjunction with the Sun."[2]

"Wise men," known as "Holy Rishis," were informed by these celestial signs that the Messiah was born.[3]

In the *Rāmāyana* (one of the sacred books of the Hindoos) the horoscope of Rama's birth is given. He is said to have been born on the 9th Tithi of the month Caitra. *The planet Jupiter* figured at his birth; it being in Cancer at that time.[4] Rama was an incarnation of Vishnu. When *Crishna* was born "*his stars*" were to be seen in the heavens. They were pointed out by one Nared, a great prophet and astrologer.[5]

Without going through the list, we can say that the birth of every Indian *Avatar* was foretold by *celestial signs.*[6]

The same myth is to be found in the legends of China. Among others they relate that a star figured at the birth of *Yu*, the founder of the first dynasty which reigned in China,[7] who—as we saw in the last chapter—was of heavenly origin, having been born of a virgin. It is also said that a star figured at the birth of *Laou-tsze*, the Chinese sage.[8]

In the legends of the Jewish patriarchs and prophets, it is stated that a *brilliant star* shone at the time of the birth of *Moses*. It was seen by the *Magi* of Egypt, who immediately informed the king.[9]

When *Abraham* was born "*his star*" shone in the heavens, if we may believe the popular legends, and its brilliancy outshone all the other stars.[10] Rabbinic traditions relate the following:

"Abraham was the son of Terah, general of Nimrod's army. He was born at Ur of the Chaldees 1948 years after the Creation. On the night of his birth, Terah's friends—among whom were many of Nimrod's councillors and sooth-sayers—were feasting in his house. On leaving, late at night, *they observed an unusual star in the east*, it seemed to run from one quarter of the heavens to the other, and to devour four stars which were there. All amazed in astonishment

---

[1] See Bunsen's Angel-Messiah, pp. 22, 23, 33.
[2] See Beal : Hist. Buddha, pp. 23, 33, 35.
[3] See Bunsen's Angel-Messiah, p. 36.
[4] Williams's Indian Wisdom, p. 347.
[5] See Hist. Hindostan, ii. 336.
[6] See Higgins : Anacalypsis, vol. i. p. 56. For that of Crishna, see Vishnu Purana, book v.
ch. iii.
[7] See Ibid. P. 618.
[8] Thornton : Hist. China, vol. i. p. 137.
[9] See Annc., i. p. 560, and Geikie's Life of Christ, i. 559.
[10] See Ibid., and The Bible for Learners, vol. iii. p. 72, and Calmet's Fragments, art. "Abraham."

at this wondrous sight, ' Truly,' said they, '*this can signify nothing else but that Terah's new-born son will become great and powerful.*' "[1]

It is also related that Nimrod, in a dream, saw a star rising above the horizon, which was very brilliant. The soothsayers being consulted in regard to it, foretold that a child was born who would become a great prince.[2]

A brilliant star, which eclipsed all the other stars, was also to be seen at the birth of the Cæsars ; in fact, as Canon Farrar remarks, " The Greeks and Romans had *always* considered that the births and deaths of great men were symbolized by the appearance and disappearance of heavenly bodies, and the same belief has continued down to comparatively modern times."[3]

Tacitus, the Roman historian, speaking of the reign of the Emperor Nero, says :

" A comet having appeared, in this juncture, the phenomenon, according to the *popular opinion*, announced that governments were to be changed, and kings dethroned. In the imaginations of men, Nero was already dethroned, and who should be his successor was the question."[4]

According to Moslem authorities, the birth of *Ali*—Mohammed's great disciple, and the chief of one of the two principal sects into which Islam is divided—was foretold by celestial signs. " A light was distinctly visible, resembling a bright column, extending from the earth to the firmament."[5] Even during the reign of the Emperor Hadrian, a hundred years after the time assigned for the death of Jesus, a certain Jew who gave himself out as the " *Messiah*," and headed the last great insurrection of his country, assumed the name of *Bar-Cochba* — that is, " *Son of a Star.*"[6]

This myth evidently extended to the New World, as we find that the symbol of *Quetzalcoatle*, the virgin-born Saviour, was the " *Morning Star.*"[7]

We see, then, that among the ancients there seems to have been a very general idea that the birth of a great person would be announced by a star. The Rev. Dr. Geikie, who maintains to his utmost the truth of the Gospel narrative, is yet constrained to admit that :

" It was, indeed, universally believed, that extraordinary events, especially

---

[1] Baring-Gould : Legends of the Patriarchs, p. 149.
[2] Calmet's Fragments, art. " Abraham."
[3] Farrar's Life of Christ, p. 52.
[4] Tacitus : Annals, bk. xiv. ch. xxii.

[5] Amberly's Analysis of Religious Belief, p. 227.
[6] Bible for Learners, vol. iii. p. 78.
[7] Brinton : Myths of the New World, pp. 180, 181, and Squire : Serpent Symbol.

the birth and death of great men, were heralded by appearances of stars, and still more of comets, or by conjunctions of the heavenly bodies."[1]

The whole tenor of the narrative recorded by the *Matthew* narrator is the most complete justification of the science of *astrology;* that the first intimation of the birth of the Son of God was given to the worshipers of Ormuzd, who have the power of distinguishing with certainty *his* peculiar star; that from these *heathen* the tidings of his birth are received by the Jews at Jerusalem, *and therefore that the theory must be right which connects great events in the life of men with phenomena in the starry heavens.*

If this *divine sanction of astrology* is contested on the ground that this was an *exceptional* event, in which, simply to bring the Magi to Jerusalem, God caused the star to appear in accordance with their superstitious science, the difficulty is only pushed one degree backwards, for in this case God, it is asserted, wrought an event which was perfectly certain to strengthen the belief of the Magi, of Herod, of the Jewish priests, and of the Jews generally, in the truth of astrology.

If, to avoid the alternative, recourse be had to the notion that the star appeared *by chance,* or that this *chance* or *accident* directed the Magi aright, is the position really improved? Is *chance* consistent with any notion of supernatural interposition?

We may also ask the question, why were the Magi brought to Jerusalem at all? If they knew that the star which they saw was the star of Christ Jesus—as the narrative states[2]—and were by this knowledge conducted to Jerusalem, why did it not suffice to guide them *straight to Bethlehem,* and thus prevent the Slaughter of the Innocents? Why did the star desert them after its first appearance, not to be seen again till they issued from Jerusalem? or, if it did not desert them, why did they ask of Herod and the priests the road which they should take, when, by the hypothesis, the star was ready to guide them?[3]

It is said that in the oracles of Zoroaster there is to be found a prophecy to the effect that, *in the latter days,* a virgin would conceive and bear a son, and that, at the time of his birth, a star would shine at noonday. Christian divines have seen in this a prophecy of the birth of *Christ* Jesus, but when critically examined, it does not stand the test. The drift of the story is this:

Ormuzd, the Lord of Light, who created the universe in *six* periods of time, accomplished his work by making the first man

---

[1] Life of Christ, vol i. p 144.
[2] Matthew ii. 2.
[3] See Thomas Scott's English Life of Jesus for a full investigation of this subject.

and woman, and infusing into them the breath of life. It was not long before Ahriman, the evil one, contrived to seduce the first parents of mankind by pursuading them to eat of the forbidden fruit. Sin and death are now in the world; the principles of *good* and *evil* are now in deadly strife. Ormuzd then reveals to mankind his *law* through his prophet Zoroaster; the strife between the two principles continues, however, and will continue until the end of a destined term. During the last three thousand years of the period Ahriman is predominant. The world now hastens to its doom; religion and virtue are nowhere to be found; mankind are plunged in sin and misery. *Sosiosh* is born of a virgin, and redeems them, subdues the Devs, awakens the dead, *and holds the last judgment.* A comet sets the world in flames; the Genii of Light combat against the Genii of Darkness, and cast them into Duzakh, where Ahriman and the Devs and the souls of the wicked are thoroughly cleansed and purified by fire. Ahriman then submits to Ormuzd; evil is absorbed into goodness; the unrighteous, thoroughly purified, are united with the righteous, and *a new earth and a new heaven* arise, free from all evil, where peace and innocence will forever dwell.

Who can fail to see that this virgin-born *Sosiosh* was to come, *not eighteen hundred years ago*, but, in the "*latter days*," when the world is to be set on fire by a *comet*, the *judgment* to take place, and the "new heaven and new earth" is to be established? Who can fail to see also, by a perusal of the New Testament, that the idea of a *temporal Messiah* (a mighty king and warrior, who should liberate and rule over his people Israel), and the idea of an *Angel-Messiah* (who had come to announce that the "kingdom of heaven was at hand," that the "stars should fall from heaven," and that all men would shortly be judged according to their deeds), are both jumbled together in a heap?

CHAPTER XIV.

THE story of the Song of the Heavenly Host belongs exclusively to the *Luke* narrator, and, in substance, is as follows :

At the time of the birth of Christ Jesus, there were shepherds abiding in the fields, keeping watch over their flock by night. And the angel of the Lord appeared among them, and the glory of the Lord shone round about them, and the angel said : "I bring you good tidings of great joy, which shall be to all people ; for unto you is born this day in the city of David, a Saviour, which is Christ the Lord."

And suddenly there was with the angel a multitude of the Heavenly Host, praising God in song, saying : "Glory to God in the highest ; and on earth peace, good will towards men." After this the angels went *into heaven.*[1]

It is recorded in the *Vishnu Purana*[2] that while the virgin Devaki bore *Crishna*, " the protector of the world," in her womb, she was eulogized by the gods, and on the day of Crishna's birth, " the quarters of the horizon were irradiate with joy, as if moonlight was diffused over the whole earth." " *The spirits and the nymphs of heaven danced and sang*," and, " at *midnight*,[3] when the support of all was born, *the clouds emitted low pleasing sounds, and poured down rain of flowers.*"[4]

Similar demonstrations of celestial delight were not wanting at the birth of *Buddha*. All beings everywhere were full of joy. Music was to be heard all over the land, and, as in the case of Crishna, there fell from the skies a gentle shower of flowers and perfumes. Caressing breezes blew, and a marvellous light was produced.[5]

---

[1] Luke, ii. 8–15.

[2] Translated from the original Sanscrit by H. H. Wilson, M. D., F.R.S.

[3] All the virgin-born Saviours are born at *midnight or early dawn.*

[4] Vishnu Purana, book v. ch. iii. p. 502.

[5] See Amberly's Analysis, p. 226. Beal: Hist. Buddha, pp. 45, 46, 47, and Bunsen's Angel-Messiah, p. 35.

147

The Fo-pen-hing relates that:

"The attending spirits, who surrounded the Virgin Maya and the infant Saviour, singing praises of 'the Blessed One,' said: 'All joy be to you, Queen Maya, rejoice and be glad, for the child you have borne is holy.' Then the Rishis and Devas who dwelt on earth exclaimed with great joy: 'This day Buddha is born for the good of men, to dispel the darkness of their ignorance.' Then the four heavenly kings took up the strain and said: 'Now because Bôdhisatwa is born, to give joy and bring peace to the world, therefore is there this brightness.' Then the gods of the thirty-three heavens took up the burden of the strain, and the Yama Devas and the Tûsita Devas, and so forth, through all the heavens of the Kama, Rupa, and Arupa worlds, even up to the Akanishta heavens, all the Devas joined in this song, and said: ' *To-day Bôdhisatwa is born on earth, to give joy and peace to men and Devas, to shed light in the dark places, and to give sight to the blind.*"[1]

Even the sober philosopher *Confucius* did not enter the world, if we may believe Chinese tradition, without premonitory symptoms of his greatness.[2]

Sir John Francis Davis, speaking of Confucius, says:

"Various prodigies, *as in other instances*, were the forerunners of the birth of this extraordinary person. On the eve of his appearance upon earth, *celestial music* sounded in the ears of his mother; and when he was born, this inscription appeared on his breast: 'The maker of a rule for setting the World.' "[3]

In the case of *Osiris*, the Egyptian Saviour, at his birth, a voice was heard proclaiming that: "The Ruler of all the Earth is born."[4]

In Plutarch's "*Isis*" occurs the following:

" At the birth of Osiris, there was heard a voice that the Lord of all the Earth was coming in being; and some say that a woman named Pamgle, as she was going to carry water to the temple of Ammon, in the city of Thebes, heard that voice, which commanded her to proclaim it with a loud voice, that the great beneficent god Osiris was born."[5]

Wonderful demonstrations of delight also attended the birth of the heavenly-born *Apollonius*. According to Flavius Philostratus, who wrote the life of this remarkable man, a flock of swans surrounded his mother, and clapping their wings, as is their custom, they sang in unison, while the air was fanned by gentle breezes.

When the god *Apollo* was born of the virgin Latona in the Island of Delos, there was joy among the undying gods in Olympus, and the Earth laughed beneath the smile of Heaven.[6]

---

[1] See Beal : Hist. Buddha, pp. 43, 55, 56, and Bunsen's Angel-Messiah, p. 35.

[2] See Amberly : Analysis of Religious Belief, p. 84.

[3] Davis : History of China, vol. ii. p. 48. See also Thornton : Hist. China, i. 152.

[4] See Prichard's Egyptian Mythology, p. 56, and Kenrick's Egypt, vol. i. p. 408.

[5] Bonwick: Egyptian Belief, p. 424, and Kenrick's Egypt, vol. i. p. 408.

[6] See Tales of Ancient Greece, p. 4.

At the time of the birth of "*Hercules the Saviour*," his father Zeus, the god of gods, spake from heaven and said:

"This day shall a child be born of the race of Perseus, who shall be the mightiest of the sons of men."[1]

When *Æsculapius* was a helpless infant, and when he was about to be put to death, a voice from the god Apollo was heard, saying:

"Slay not the child with the mother; *he is born to do great things;* but bear him to the wise centaur Cheiron, and bid him train the boy in all his wisdom and teach him to do brave deeds, that men may praise his name in the generations that shall be hereafter."[2]

As we stated above, the story of the Song of the Heavenly Host belongs exclusively to the *Luke* narrator; none of the other writers of the synoptic Gospels know anything about it, which, if it really happened, seems very strange.

If the reader will turn to the apocryphal Gospel called *Protevangelion* " (chapter xiii.), he will there see one of the reasons why it was thought best to leave this Gospel out of the canon of the New Testament. It relates the "Miracles at Mary's labor," similar to the *Luke* narrator, but in a still more wonderful form. It is probably from this apocryphal Gospel that the Luke narrator copied.

---

[1] See Tales of Ancient Greece, p. 55.   [2] Ibid. p. 45.

CHAPTER XV.

THE next in order of the wonderful events which are related to have happened at the birth of Christ Jesus, is the recognition of the divine child, and the presentation of gifts.

We are informed by the *Matthew* narrator, that being guided by a star, the *Magi*[1] from the east came to where the young child was.

"And when they were come into the *house* (not *stable*) they saw the young child, with Mary his mother, and fell down and worshiped him. And when they had opened their treasures, they presented unto him gifts, gold, frankincense, and myrrh."[2]

The *Luke* narrator—who seems to know nothing about the Magi from the east—informs us that *shepherds* came and worshiped the young child. They were keeping their flocks by night when the angel of the Lord appeared before them, saying:

"Behold, I bring you good tidings—for unto you is born this day in the city of David a Saviour, which is Christ the Lord."

After the angel had left them, they said one to another:

"Let us go unto Bethlehem and see this thing which is come to pass, which the Lord hath made known to us. And they came with haste, and found Mary and Joseph, and the babe lying in a *manger*."[3]

The Luke narrator evidently borrowed this story of the *shepherds* from the " *Gospel of the Egyptians* " (of which we shall speak in another chapter), or from other sacred records of the biographies of Crishna or Buddha.

It is related in the legends of *Crishna* that the divine child

---

[1] "The original word here is ' *Magoi*,' from which comes our word ' *Magician*.' . . . The persons *here* denoted were philosophers, priests, or *astronomers*. They dwelt chiefly in Persia and Arabia. They were the learned men of the Eastern nations, devoted to *astronomy*. to religion, and to medicine. They were held in high esteem by the Persian court; were admitted as councilors, and followed the camps in war to give advice." (Barnes's Notes, vol. i. p. 25.)

[2] Matthew, ii. 2.   [3] Luke, ii. 8–16.

was cradled among shepherds, to whom were first made known the stupendous feats which stamped his character with marks of the divinity. He was recognized as the promised *Saviour* by Nanda, a shepherd, or cowherd, and his companions, who prostrated themselves before the heaven-born child. After the birth of Crishna, the Indian prophet Nared, having heard of his fame, visited his father and mother at Gokool, examined the stars, &c., and declared him to be of celestial descent.[1]

Not only was Crishna adored by the shepherds and Magi, and received with *divine honors*, but he was also *presented with gifts*. These gifts were "sandal wood and perfumes."[2] (Why not "frankincense and myrrh?")

Similar stories are related of the infant *Buddha*. He was visited, at the time of his birth, by *wise men*, who at once recognized in the marvellous infant all the characters of the divinity, and he had scarcely seen the day before he was hailed god of gods.[3]

> " 'Mongst the strangers came
> A grey-haired saint, Asita, one whose ears,
> Long closed to earthly things, caught heavenly sounds,
> And heard at prayer beneath his peepul-tree,
> The Devas singing songs at Buddha's birth."

Viscount Amberly, speaking of him, says:[4]

"He was visited and adored by a very eminent *Rishi*, or hermit, known as *Asita*, who predicted his future greatness, but wept at the thought that he himself was too old to see the day when the law of salvation would be taught by the infant whom he had come to contemplate."

"I weep (said Asita), because I am old and stricken in years, and shall not see all that is about to come to pass. The Buddha Bhagavat (God Almighty Buddha) comes to the world only after many kalpas. This bright boy will be Buddha. *For the salvation of the world* he will teach the law. He will succor the old, the sick, the afflicted, the dying. He will release those who are bound in the meshes of *natural corruption*. He will quicken the spiritual vision of those whose eyes are darkened by the thick darkness of ignorance. Hundreds of thousands of millions of beings will be carried by him to the 'other shore'— will put on immortality. And I shall not see this perfect Buddha—this is why I weep."[5]

He returns rejoicing, however, to his mountain-home, for his eyes had seen the promised and expected Saviour.[6]

Paintings in the *cave* of Ajunta represent Asita with the

[1] Higgins : Anacalypsis, vol. i. pp. 129, 130, and Maurice : Hist. Hindostan, vol. ii. pp. 256, 257 and 317. Also, The Vishnu Purana.
[2] Oriental Religions, pp. 500, 501. See also, Ancient Faiths, vol. ii. p. 353.
[3] Anacalypsis, vol. i. p. 157.
[4] Amberly's Analysis, p. 177. See also, Bunsen's Angel-Messiah, p. 36.
[5] Lillie : Buddha and Early Buddhism, p. 76.
[6] Bunsen's Angel-Messiah, p. 6, and Beal : Hist. Buddha, pp. 58, 60.

infant Buddha in his arms.[1] The marvelous gifts of this child had become known to this eminent ascetic by *supernatural signs*.[2]

Buddha, as well as Crishna and Jesus, was presented with "costly jewels and precious substances."[3] (Why not gold and perfumes?)

Rama—the seventh incarnation of Vishnu for human deliverance from evil—is also hailed by "*aged saints*"—(why not "*wise men*"?)—who die gladly when their eyes see the long-expected one.[4]

How-tseich, who was one of those personages styled, in China, "Tien-Tse," or "Sons of Heaven,"[5] and who came into the world in a miraculous manner, was laid in a narrow lane. When his mother had fulfilled her time:

> " Her first-born son (came forth) like a lamb.
> There was no bursting, no rending,
> No injury, no hurt—
> Showing how wonderful he would be."

When born, the sheep and oxen protected him with loving care.[6]

The birth of *Confucius* (B. C. 551), like that of all the demigods and saints of antiquity, is fabled to have been attended with allegorical prodigies, amongst which was the appearance of the *Ke-lin*, a miraculous quadruped, prophetic of happiness and virtue, which announced that the child would be "a king without a throne or territory." *Five celestial sages, or "wise men," entered the house at the time of the child's birth, whilst vocal and instrumental music filled the air.*[7]

Mithras, the Persian Saviour, and mediator between God and man, was also visited by "wise men" called Magi, at the time of his birth.[8] He was presented with gifts consisting of gold, frankincense and myrrh.[9]

According to Plato, at the birth of *Socrates* (469 B. C.) there came three Magi from the east to worship him, bringing gifts of gold, frankincense and myrrh.[10]

Æsculapius, the virgin-born Saviour, was protected by goatherds (why not shepherds?), who, upon seeing the child, knew at once that he was divine. The voice of fame soon published the

---

[1] Bunsen's Angel-Messiah, p. 36.
[2] See Amberly's Analysis. p. 231, and Bunsen's Angel-Messiah, p. 36.
[3] Beal : Hist. Buddha, p. 58.
[4] Oriental Religions, p. 491.
[5] See Prog. Relig. Ideas, vol. i. p. 200.

[6] See Amberly's Analysis of Religious Belief, p. 226.
[7] See Thornton's Hist. China, vol. i. p. 152.
[8] King : The Gnostics and their Remains, pp. 134 and 149.
[9] Inman : Ancient Faiths. vol. ii. p. 353.
[10] See Higgins : Anacalypsis, vol. ii. p. 96.

birth of this miraculous infant, upon which people flocked from all quarters to behold and worship this heaven-born child.[1]

Many of the Grecian and Roman demi-gods and heroes were either fostered by or worshiped by shepherds. Amongst these may be mentioned *Bacchus*, who was educated among shepherds,[2] and *Romulus*, who was found on the banks of the Tiber, and educated by shepherds.[3] *Paris*, son of Priam, was educated among shepherds,[4] and *Ægisthus* was exposed, like Æsculapius, by his mother, found by shepherds and educated among them.[5]

Viscount Amberly has well said that: "Prognostications of greatness in infancy are, indeed, among the stock incidents in the mythical or semi-mythical lives of eminent persons."

We have seen that the *Matthew* narrator speaks of the infant Jesus, and Mary, his mother, being in a "*house*"—implying that he had been born there; and that the *Luke* narrator speaks of the infant "lying in a *manger*"—implying that he was born in a stable. We will now show that there is still *another* story related of the *place* in which he was born.

---

[1] Taylor's Diegesis, p. 150. Roman Antiquities, p. 136, and Bell's Pantheon, vol. i. p. 27.
[2] Higgins: Anacalypsis, vol. i. p. 322.
[3] Bell's Pantheon, vol. ii. p. 213.
[4] Ibid. vol. i. p. 47.
[5] Ibid. p. 20.

CHAPTER XVI.

THE writer of that portion of the Gospel according to *Matthew* which treats of the *place* in which Jesus was born, implies, as we stated in our last chapter, that he was born in a *house*. His words are these:

"Now when Jesus was born in Bethlehem of Judea *in the days of Herod the king*, behold, there came wise men from the east" to worship him. "And when they were come *into the house*, they saw the young child with Mary his mother."[1]

The writer of the *Luke* version implies that he was born in *a stable*, as the following statement will show:

"The days being accomplished that she (Mary) should be delivered . . . she brought forth her first-born son, and wrapped him in swaddling clothes, and *laid him in a manger*, there being no room for him in the *inn*."[2]

If these accounts were contained in these Gospels in the time of Eusebius, the first ecclesiastical historian, who flourished during the Council of Nice (A. D. 327), it is very strange that, in speaking of the birth of Jesus, he should have omitted even mentioning them, and should have given an altogether different version. He tells us that Jesus was neither born in a *house*, nor in a *stable*, but in a *cave*, and that at the time of Constantine a magnificent temple was erected on the spot, so that the Christians might worship in the place where their Saviour's feet had stood.[3]

In the apocryphal Gospel called "*Protevangelion*," attributed to James, the brother of Jesus, we are informed that Mary and her husband, being away from their home in Nazareth, and when within three miles of Bethlehem, to which city they were going, Mary said to Joseph:

"Take me down from the ass, for that which is in me presses to come forth."

---

[1] Matthew, ii.
[2] Luke, ii.
[3] Eusebius's Life of Constantine, lib. 3, chs xl., xli. and xlii.

154

Joseph, replying, said:

"Whither shall I take thee, *for the place is desert?*"

Then said Mary again to Joseph:

"Take me down, for that which is within me mightily presses me."

Joseph then took her down from off the ass, and he found there a *cave* and put her into it.

Joseph then left Mary in the cave, and started toward Bethlehem for a midwife, whom he found and brought back with him. When they neared the spot a bright cloud overshadowed the cave.

"But on a sudden the cloud became *a great light in the cave,* so their eyes could not bear it. But the light gradually decreased, until the infant appeared and sucked the breast of his mother."[1]

Tertullian (A. D. 200), Jerome (A. D. 375) and other Fathers of the Church, also state that Jesus was born in a *cave,* and that the *heathen* celebrated, in their day, the birth and *Mysteries* of their Lord and Saviour Adonis in this very cave near Bethlehem.[2]

Canon Farrar says:

"That the actual place of Christ's birth was a *cave,* is a very ancient tradition, and this cave used to be shown as the scene of the event even so early as the time of Justin Martyr (A. D. 150)."[3]

Mr. King says:

"The place *yet* shown as the scene of their (the Magi's) adoration at Bethlehem is a *cave.*"[4]

The Christian ceremonies in the Church of the Nativity at Bethlehem are celebrated to this day in a *cave,*[5] and are undoubtedly nearly the same as were celebrated, *in the same place,* in honor of *Adonis,* in the time of Tertullian and Jerome; and as are yet celebrated in Rome every Christmas-day, *very early in the morning.*

We see, then, that there are *three* different accounts concerning the *place* in which Jesus was born. The first, and evidently true one, was that which is recorded by the *Matthew* narrator, namely, that he was born in a *house.* The stories about his being born in a *stable* or in a *cave*[6] were later inventions, caused from the desire to place him in as *humble* a position as possible in his infancy, and from the fact that the virgin-born Saviours who had *preceded*

[1] Protevangelion. Apoc. chs. xii., xiii., and xiv., and Lily of Israel, p. 95.
[2] See Higgins: Anacalypsis, vol. ii. pp. 98, 99.
[3] Farrar's Life of Christ, p. 38, and *note.* See also, Hist. Hindostan, ii. 311.
[4] King: The Gnostics and their Remains, p. 134.
[5] Higgins: Anacalypsis, vol. ii. p. 95.
[6] Some writers have tried to connect these by saying that it was a *cave-stable,* but why should a stable be in a *desert place,* as the narrative states?

him had almost all been born in a position the most humiliating —such as a cave, a cow-shed, a sheep-fold, &c.—or had been placed there after birth. This was a part of the *universal mythos*. As illustrations we may mention the following:

Crishna, the Hindoo virgin-born Saviour, was born in a *cave*,[1] fostered by an honest *herdsman*,[2] and, it is said, placed in a *sheep-fold* shortly after his birth.

How-Tseih, the Chinese "Son of Heaven," when an infant, was left unprotected by his mother, but the *sheep* and *oxen* protected him with loving care.[3]

Abraham, the Father of Patriarchs, is said to have been *born in a cave*.[4]

Bacchus, who was the son of God by the virgin Semele, is said to have been *born in a cave*, or placed in one shortly after his birth.[5] Philostratus, the Greek sophist and rhetorician, says, " the inhabitants of India had a tradition that Bacchus was born at *Nisa*, and was brought up in a *cave* on Mount Meros."

Æsculapius, who was the son of God by the virgin Coronis, was left exposed, when an infant, on a mountain, where he was found and cared for by a *goatherd*.[6]

Romulus, who was the son of God by the virgin Rhea-Sylvia, was left exposed, when an infant, on the banks of the river Tiber, where he was found and cared for by a *shepherd*.[7]

Adonis, the "Lord" and "Saviour," was placed in a *cave* shortly after his birth.[8]

Apollo (Phoibos), son of the Almighty Zeus, was born in a cave at early dawn.[9]

Mithras, the Persian Saviour, was born in a *cave or grotto*,[10] at early dawn.

Hermes, the son of God by the mortal *Maia*, was born early in the morning, in *a cave or grotto* of the Kyllemian hill.[11]

Attys, the god of the Phrygians,[12] was born in a *cave* or grotto.[13]

The *object* is the same in all of these stories, however they may differ in detail, which is to place the heaven-born infant in the most humiliating position in infancy.

We have seen it is recorded that, at the time of the birth

---

[1] Aryan Myths, vol. ii. p. 107.

[2] See Asiatic Researches, vol. i. p. 259.

[3] See Amberly's Analysis, p. 226.

[4] See Calmet's Fragments, art. "Abraham."

[5] See Higgins: Anacalypsis, vol. i. p. 321. Bell's Pantheon, vol. i. p. 118, and Dupuis, p. 234.

[6] See Taylor's Diegesis, p. 150, and Bell's Pantheon under "Æsculapius."

[7] See Bell's Pantheon, vol. ii. p. 213.

[8] See Ibid. vol. i. p. 12.

[9] Aryan Mythology, vol. i. pp. 72, 158.

[10] See Dunlap's Mysteries of Adoni, p. 124, and Aryan Mythology, vol. ii. p. 184.

[11] Ibid.

[12] See Dupuis: Origin of Religious Beliefs, p. 255.

[13] See Dunlap's Mysteries of Adoni, p. 124.

of Jesus "there was a *great light* in the cave, so that the eyes of Joseph and the midwife could not bear it." This feature is also represented in early Christian art. "Early Christian painters have represented the infant Jesus as welcoming three Kings of the East, *and shining as brilliantly as if covered with phosphuretted oil.*"[1] In all pictures of the Nativity, the light is made to arise from the body of the infant, and the father and mother are often depicted with glories round their heads. This too was a part of the old mythos, as we shall now see.

The moment *Crishna* was born, his mother became beautiful, and her form brilliant. The whole cave was splendidly illuminated, being filled with a *heavenly light*, and the countenances of his father and his mother emitted rays of glory.[2]

So likewise, it is recorded that, at the time of the birth of Buddha, "the Saviour of the World," which, according to one account, took place in an *inn*, "*a divine light diffused around his person*," so that "the Blessed One" was "heralded into the world by a supernatural light."[3]

When *Bacchus* was born, a *bright light* shone round him,[4] so that, "*there was a brilliant light in the cave.*"

When *Apollo* was born, *a halo of serene light encircled his cradle*, the nymphs of heaven attended, and bathed him in pure water, and girded a broad golden band around his form.[5]

When the Saviour *Æsculapius* was born, his countenance shone like the sun, and he was surrounded by a fiery ray.[6]

In the life of *Zoroaster* the common mythos is apparent. He was born in innocence of an immaculate conception of a Ray of the Divine Reason. As soon as he was born, *the glory arising from his body enlightened the whole room*, and he laughed at his mother.[7]

It is stated in the legends of the Hebrew Patriarchs that, at the birth of *Moses*, a bright light appeared and shone around.[8]

There is still another feature which we must notice in these narratives, that is, the contradictory statements concerning the *time* when Jesus was born. As we shall treat of this subject more fully in the chapter on "The Birthday of Christ Jesus," we shall allude to it here simply as far as necessary.

[1] Inman : Ancient Faiths, vol. ii. p. 460.
[2] Cox : Aryan Mythology, vol. ii. p. 133. Higgins : Anacalypsis. vol. i. p. 130. See also, Vishnu Purana, p. 502, where it says: "No person could bear to gaze upon Devaki from the light that invested her."
[3] See Beal : Hist. Buddha, pp. 43, 46, or Bunsen's Angel-Messiah, pp. 34, 35.
[4] See Higgins : Anacalypsis, vol. i. p. 322, and Dupuis : Origin of Relig. Belief, p. 119.
[5] Tales of Anct. Greece, p. xviii.
[6] Bell's Pantheon, vol. i. p. 27. Roman Antiquities, p. 136.
[7] Inman : Ancient Faiths, vol. ii. p. 460. Anacalypsis, vol. i. p. 649.
[8] See Hardy : Manual of Buddhism, p. 145

The *Matthew* narrator informs us that Jesus was born *in the days of Herod the King*, and the *Luke* narrator says he was born *when Cyrenius* was *Governor of Syria*, or later. This is a very awkward and unfortunate statement, as Cyrenius was not Governor of Syria until some *ten years after the time of Herod.*[1]

The cause of this dilemma is owing to the fact that the Luke narrator, after having interwoven into *his* story, of the birth of Jesus, the *old myth* of the tax or tribute, which is said to have taken place at the time of the birth of some *previous* virgin-born Saviours, looked among the records to see if a taxing had ever taken place in Judea, so that he might refer to it in support of his statement. He found the account of the taxing, referred to above, and without stopping to consider *when* this taxing took place, or whether or not it would conflict with the statement that Jesus was born *in the days of Herod*, he added to his narrative the words: "And this taxing was *first made* when Cyrenius was governor of Syria."[2]

We will now show the ancient myth of the taxing. According to the *Vishnu Purana*, when the infant Saviour *Crishna* was born, his foster-father, *Nanda*, had come to the city *to pay his tax or yearly tribute to the king*. It distinctly speaks of Nanda, and other cowherds, "*bringing tribute or tax to Kansa*" the reigning monarch.[3]

It also describes a scene which took place after the taxes had been paid.

Vasudeva, an acquaintance of Nanda's, "went to the wagon of Nanda, and found Nanda there, rejoicing that a son (Crishna) had been born to him.

"Vasudeva spoke to him kindly, and congratulated him *on having a son in his old age.*[4]

"'Thy yearly tribute,' he added, 'has been paid to the king . . . why do you delay, now that your affairs are settled? Up, Nanda, quickly, and set off to your own pastures.' . . . Accordingly Nanda and the other cowherds returned to their village."[5]

Now, in regard to *Buddha*, the same myth is found.

Among the thirty-two signs which were to be fulfilled by the mother of the expected Messiah (Buddha), the fifth sign was recorded to be, "*that she would be on a journey at the time of her*

---

[1] See the chapter on "Christmas."

[2] It may be that this verse was added by another hand some time after the narrative was written. We have seen it stated somewhere that, in the manuscript, this verse is in brackets.

[3] See Vishnu Purana, book v. chap. iii.

[4] Here is an exact counterpart to the story of Joseph—the foster-father, so-called—of Jesus. He too, had a son in his old age.

[5] Vishnu Purana, book v. chap. v.

child's birth." Therefore, "that it might be fulfilled which was spoken by the prophets," the virgin Maya, in the tenth month after her heavenly conception, was on a journey to her father, when lo, the birth of the Messiah took place under a tree. One account says that "she had alighted at an *inn* when Buddha was born."[1]

The mother of *Lao-tsze,* the Virgin-born Chinese sage, was away from home when her child was born. She stopped to rest *under a tree,* and there, like the virgin Maya, gave birth to her son.[2]

Pythagoras (B. C. 570), whose real father was the Holy Ghost,[3] was also born at a time when his mother was away from home on a journey. She was travelling with her husband, who was *about his mercantile concerns,* from Samos to Sidon.[4]

Apollo was born when his mother was away from home. The Ionian legend tells the simple tale that Leto, the mother of the unborn Apollo, could find no place to receive her in her hour of travail until she came to Delos. The child was born like Buddha and Lao-tsze—*under a tree.*[5] The mother knew that he was destined to be a being of mighty power, ruling among the undying gods and mortal men.[6]

Thus we see that the stories, one after another, relating to the birth and infancy of Jesus, are simply old myths, and are therefore not historical.

[1] Bunsen : The Angel-Messiah, p. 34. See also, Beal : Hist. Buddha, p. 32, and Lillie : Buddha and Early Buddhism, p. 73.
[2] Thornton : Hist. China, i. 188.
[3] As we saw in Chapter XII.
[4] Higgins : Anacalypsis, vol. i. p. 150.
[5] See Rhys David's Buddhism, p. 26.
[6] See Cox : Aryan Myths, vol. ii. p. 21.

CHAPTER XVII.

THE biographers of Jesus, although they have placed him in a position the most humiliating in his infancy, and although they have given him poor and humble parents, have notwithstanding made him to be of *royal descent*. The reasons for doing this were twofold. First, because, according to the Old Testament, the expected Messiah was to be of the seed of Abraham,[1] and second, because the Angel-Messiahs who had previously been on earth to redeem and save mankind had been of *royal descent*, therefore Christ Jesus must be so.

The following story, taken from Colebrooke's "*Miscellaneous Essays*,"[2] clearly shows that this idea was general:

"The last of the Jinas, Vardhamâna, was *at first* conceived by Devanandâ, a Brahmânâ. The conception was announced to her by a dream. Sekra, being apprised of his incarnation, prostrated himself and worshiped the future saint (who was in the womb of Devanandâ); but reflecting that *no great saint was ever born in an indigent or mendicant family*, as that of a Brahmânâ, Sekra commanded his chief attendant to remove the child from the womb of Devanandâ to that of Trisala, wife of Siddhartha, *a prince of the race of Jeswaca*, of the Kasyapa family."

In their attempts to accomplish their object, the biographers of Jesus have made such poor work of it, that all the ingenuity Christianity has yet produced, has not been able to repair their blunders.

The genealogies are contained in the first and third Gospels, and although they do not agree, yet, if either is right, then Jesus was *not* the son of God, engendered by the "Holy Ghost," but the legitimate son of Joseph and Mary. In any other sense they amount to nothing. That Jesus can be of royal descent, and yet

---

[1] That is, a passage in the Old Testament was construed to mean this, although another and more plausible meaning might be inferred. It is when Abraham is blessed by the Lord, who is made to say: "*In thy seed* shall all the nations of the earth be blessed, because thou hast obeyed my voice." (Genesis, xxii. 18.)

[2] Vol. ii. p. 214.

be the Son of God, in the sense in which these words are used, is a conclusion which can be acceptable to those only who believe in *alleged* historical narratives on no other ground than that they wish them to be true, and dare not call them into question.

The *Matthew* narrator states that *all* the generations from Abraham to David are *fourteen*, from David until the carrying away into Babylon are *fourteen*, and from the carrying away into Babylon unto Jesus are *fourteen* generations.[1] Surely nothing can have a more *mythological* appearance than this. But, when we confine our attention to the genealogy itself, we find that the generations in the third stage, including Jesus himself, amount to only *thirteen*. All attempts to get over this difficulty have been without success; the genealogies are, and have always been, hard nuts for theologians to crack. Some of the early Christian fathers saw this, and they very wisely put an *allegorical* interpretation to them.

Dr. South says, in Kitto's Biblical Encyclopædia:

"Christ's being the true Messiah depends upon his being the son of David and king of the Jews. *So that unless this be evinced the whole foundation of Christianity must totter and fall.*"

Another writer in the same work says:

"In these two documents (Matthew and Luke), which profess to give us the genealogy of Christ, there is no notice whatever of the connection of his only earthly parent with the stock of David. On the contrary, both the genealogies profess to give us the descent of Joseph, to connect our Lord with whom by natural generation, would be to falsify the whole story of his miraculous birth, and overthrow the Christian faith."

Again, when the idea that one of the genealogies is Mary's is spoken of:

. "One thing is certain, that our belief in Mary's descent from David is grounded on inference and tradition and not on any direct statement of the sacred writings. And there has been a ceaseless endeavor, both among ancients and moderns, to gratify the natural cravings for knowledge on this subject."

Thomas Scott, speaking of the genealogies, says:

"It is a favorite saying with those who seek to defend the history of the Pentateuch against the scrutiny of modern criticism, that the objections urged against it were known long ago. The objections to the *genealogy* were known long ago, indeed; and perhaps nothing shows more conclusively than this knowledge, the disgraceful dishonesty and willful deception of the most illustrious of Christian doctors."[2]

Referring to the two genealogies, Albert Barnes says :

" No two passages of Scripture have caused more difficulty than these, and various attempts have been made to explain them. . . . Most interpreters have supposed that Matthew gives the genealogy of Joseph, and Luke that of Mary. *But though this solution is plausible and may be true, yet it wants evidence.*"

Barnes furthermore admits the fallibility of the Bible in his remarks upon the genealogies; 1st, by comparing them to *our* fallible family records; and 2d, by the remark that "the only inquiry which can now be fairly made *is whether they copied these tables correctly.*"

Alford, Ellicott, Hervey, Meyer, Mill, Patritius and Wordsworth hold that both genealogies are Joseph's ; and Aubertin, Ebrard, Greswell, Kurtz, Lange, Lightfoot and others, hold that one is Joseph's, and the other Mary's.

When the genealogy contained in *Matthew* is compared with the Old Testament *they are found to disagree ;* there are omissions which any writer with the least claim to historical sense would never have made.

When the genealogy of the *third* Gospel is turned to, the difficulties greatly increase, instead of diminish. It not only contradicts the statements made by the *Matthew* narrator, but it does not agree with the Old Testament.

What, *according to the three first evangelists*, did Jesus think of himself? In the first place he made no allusion to any miraculous circumstances connected with his birth. He looked upon himself as belonging to *Nazareth*, not as the child of Bethlehem;[1] *he reproved the scribes for teaching that the Messiah must necessarily be a descendant of David,*[2] *and did not himself make any express claim to such descent.*[3]

As we cannot go into an extended inquiry concerning the genealogies, and as there is no real necessity for so doing, as many others have already done so in a masterly manner,[4] we will continue our investigations in another direction, and show that Jesus was not the only Messiah who was claimed to be of royal descent.

---

[1] Matthew, xiii. 54; Luke, iv. 24.
[2] Mark, ii. 35.
[3] "There is no doubt that the authors of the genealogies regarded him (Jesus), as did his countrymen and contemporaries generally, as the eldest son of Joseph, Mary's husband, and that they had no idea of anything miraculous connected with his birth. All the attempts of the old commentators to reconcile the in-

consistencies of the evangelical narratives are of no avail." (Albert Réville : Hist. Dogma, Deity, Jesus, p. 15.)
[4] The reader is referred to Thomas Scott's English Life of Jesus, Strauss's Life of Jesus, The Genealogies of Our Lord, by Lord Arthur Hervey, Kitto's Biblical Encyclopædia, and Barnes' Notes.

To commence with *Crishna*, the Hindoo Saviour, he was of *royal descent*, although born in a state the most abject and humiliating.[1] Thomas Maurice says of him:

" Crishna, in the *male* line, was of royal descent, being of the Yadava line, the oldest and noblest of India; and nephew, by his *mother's* side, to the reigning sovereign; but, though royally descended, he was actually born in a state the most abject and humiliating; and, though not in a stable, yet in a dungeon."[2]

Buddha was of *royal descent*, having descended from the house of Sakya, the most illustrious of the caste of Brahmans, which reigned in India over the powerful empire of Mogadha, in the Southern Bahr.[3]

R. Spence Hardy says, in his " Manual of Buddhism :"

" The ancestry of Gotama Buddha is traced from his father, Sodhódana, through various individuals and races, all of royal dignity, to Maha Sammata, the first monarch of the world. Several of the names, and some of the events, are met with in the Puranas of the Brahmins, but it is not possible to reconcile one order of statement with the other; and it would appear that the Buddhist historians have introduced races, and invented names, that they may invest their venerated sage with all the honors of heraldry, in addition to the attributes of divinity."

How remarkably these words compare with what we have just seen concerning the genealogies of Jesus!

Rama, another Indian *avatar*—the seventh incarnation of Vishnu—was also of *royal descent*.[4]

Fo-hi; or *Fuh-he*, the virgin-born " Son of Heaven," was of *royal descent*. He belonged to the oldest family of monarchs who ruled in China.[5]

Confucius was of *royal descent*. His pedigree is traced back in a summary manner to the monarch *Hoang-ty*, who is said to have lived and ruled more than two thousand years before the time of Christ Jesus.[6]

Horus, the Egyptian virgin-born Saviour, was of *royal descent*, having descended from a line of kings.[7] He had the title of " Royal Good Shepherd."[8]

Hercules, the Saviour, was of *royal descent*.[9]

---

[1] See Higgins : Anacalypsis, vol. i. p. 130. Asiatic Researches, vol. i. p. 259, and Allen's India, p. 379.

[2] Hist. Hindostan, ii. p. 310.

[3] See Higgins : Anacalypsis, vol. i. p. 157. Bunsen : The Angel-Messiah. Davis : Hist. of China, vol. ii. p. 80, and Huc's Travels, vol. i. p. 327.

[4] Allen's India, p. 379.

[5] See Prog. Relig. Ideas, vol. i. p. 200, and Chambers's Encyclo., art. " Fuh-he."

[6] Davis : History of China, vol. ii. p. 48, and Thornton : Hist. China, vol. i. p. 131.

[7] See almost any work on Egyptian history or the religions of Egypt.

[8] See Lundy : Monumental Christianity. p. 403.

[9] See Taylor's Diegesis, p. 152. Roman Antiquities, p. 124, and Bell's Pantheon, i. 382

Bacchus, although the Son of God, was of *royal descent.*[1]

Perseus, son of the virgin Danae, was of *royal descent.*[2]

Æsculapius, the great performer of miracles, although a son of God, was notwithstanding of *royal descent.*[3]

Many more such cases might be mentioned, as may be seen by referring to the histories of the virgin-born gods and demi-gods spoken of in Chapter XII.

---

[1] See Greek and Italian Mythology, p. 81. Bell's Pantheon, vol. i. p. 117. Murray: Manual of Mythology, p. 118, and Roman Antiquities, p. 71.

[2] See Bell's Pantheon, vol. ii. p. 170, and Bulfinch : The Age of Fable, p. 161.

[3] See Bell's Pantheon, vol. i. p. 27. Roman Antiquities, p. 136, and Taylor's Diegesis, p. 150.

CHAPTER XVIII.

INTERWOVEN with the miraculous conception and birth of Jesus, the star, the visit of the Magi, &c., we have a myth which belongs to a common form, and which, in this instance, is merely adapted to the special circumstances of the age and place. This has been termed "the myth of the dangerous child." Its general outline is this: A child is born concerning whose future greatness some prophetic indications have been given. But the life of the child is fraught with danger to some powerful individual, generally a monarch. In alarm at his threatened fate, this person endeavors to take the child's life, but it is preserved by divine care.

Escaping the measures directed against it, and generally remaining long unknown, it at length fulfills the prophecies concerning its career, while the fate which he has vainly sought to shun falls upon him who had desired to slay it. There is a departure from the ordinary type, in the case of Jesus, inasmuch as Herod does not actually die or suffer any calamity through his agency. But this failure is due to the fact that Jesus did not fulfill the conditions of the Messiahship, according to the Jewish conception which Matthew has here in mind. Had he—as was expected of the Messiah—become the actual sovereign of the Jews, he must have dethroned the reigning dynasty, whether represented by Herod or his successors. But as his subsequent career belied the expectations, the evangelist was obliged to postpone to a future time his accession to that throne of temporal dominion which the incredulity of his countrymen had withheld from him during his earthly life.

The story of the slaughter of the infants which is said to have taken place in Judea about the time of the birth of Jesus, is to be found in the second chapter of *Matthew*, and is as follows:

"When Jesus was born in Bethlehem of Judea, in the days of Herod the king, there came wise men from the East to Jerusalem, saying: 'Where is he that is born *king of the Jews?* for we have seen *his star* in the East and have come to worship him.' When Herod the king had heard these things, he was troubled and all Jerusalem with him. Then Herod, when he had privately called the wise men, enquired of them diligently what time the star appeared. And he sent them to Bethlehem, and said: 'Go and search diligently for the young child; and when ye have found him, bring me word.'"

The wise men went to Bethlehem and found the young child, but instead of returning to Herod as he had told them, they departed into their own country another way, having been warned of God *in a dream* that they should not return to Herod.

"Then Herod, when he saw that he was mocked of the wise men, was exceeding wroth, *and sent forth, and slew all the children that were in Bethlehem, and in all the coasts thereof, from two years old and under.*"

We have in this story, told by the *Matthew* narrator—which the writers of the other gospels seem to know nothing about,—almost a counterpart, if not an exact one, to that related of *Crishna* of India, which shows how closely the mythological history of Jesus has been copied from that of the Hindoo Saviour.

Joguth Chunder Gangooly, a "Hindoo convert to Christ," tells us, in his "Life and Religion of the Hindoos," that:

"A *heavenly voice* whispered to the foster-father of Crishna and told him to fly with the child across the river Jumna, which was immediately done.[1] This was owing to the fact that the reigning monarch, King Kansa, sought the life of the infant Saviour, and to accomplish his purpose, he sent messengers ' *to kill all the infants in the neighboring places.*'"[2]

Mr. Higgins says:

"Soon after Crishna's birth he was carried away by night and concealed in a region remote from his natal place, for fear of a tyrant whose destroyer it was foretold he would become; and who had, for that reason, ordered all the male children born at that period to be slain."[3]

Sir William Jones says of Crishna:

"He passed a life, according to the Indians, of a most extraordinary and incomprehensible nature. His birth was concealed through fear of the reigning tyrant Kansa, who, at the time of his birth, *ordered all new-born males to be slain, yet this wonderful babe was preserved.*"[4]

In the Epic poem Mahabarata, composed more than two thousand years ago, we have the whole story of this incarnate deity, born of a virgin, and miraculously escaping in his infancy from the reigning tyrant of his country, related in its original form.

---

[1] *A heavenly voice* whispered to the foster-father of Jesus, and told him to fly with the child into Egypt, which was immediately done. (See Matthew, ii. 13.)

[2] Life and Relig. of the Hindoos, p. 134.

[3] Anacalypsis, vol. i. p. 129. See, also, Cox : Aryan Mythology, vol. ii. p. 134, and Maurice : Hist. Hindostan, vol. ii. p. 331.

[4] Asiatic Researches, vol. i. pp. 273 and 259.

Representations of this flight with the babe at midnight are sculptured on the walls of ancient Hindoo temples.[1]

This story is also the subject of an immense sculpture in the cave-temple at Elephanta, where the children are represented as being slain. The date of this sculpture is lost in the most remote antiquity. It represents a person holding a drawn sword, surrounded by slaughtered *infant boys*. Figures of men and women are also represented who are supposed to be supplicating for their children.[2]

Thomas Maurice, speaking of this sculpture, says :

"The event of Crishna's birth, and the attempt to destroy him, took place by night, and therefore the shadowy mantle of darkness, *upon which mutilated figures of infants are engraved*, darkness (at once congenial with his crime and the season of its perpetration), involves the tyrant's bust; the string of *death heads* marks the multitude of infants slain by his savage mandate; and every object in the sculpture illustrates the events of that Avatar."[3]

Another feature which connects these stories is the following :

Sir Wm. Jones tells us that when Crishna was taken out of reach of the tyrant Kansa who sought to slay him, he was fostered at *Mathura* by Nanda, the herdsman;[4] and Canon Farrar, speaking of the sojourn of the Holy Family in Egypt, says :

"St. Matthew neither tells us where the Holy Family abode in Egypt, nor how long their exile continued; but ancient legends say that they remained two years absent from Palestine, and lived at Matareèh, a few miles north-east of Cairo."[5]

Chemnitius, out of Stipulensis, who had it from Peter Martyr, Bishop of Alexandria, in the third century, says, that the place in Egypt where Jesus was banished, is now called Matarea, about ten miles beyond Cairo, that the inhabitants constantly burn a lamp in remembrance of it, and that there is a garden of trees yielding a balsam, which was planted by Jesus when a boy.[6]

Here is evidently one and the same legend.

Salivahana, the virgin-born Saviour, anciently worshiped near Cape Comorin, the southerly part of the Peninsula of India, had the same history. It was attempted to destroy him in infancy by a tyrant who was afterward killed by him. Most of the other circumstances, with slight variations, are the same as those told of Crishna and Jesus.[7]

---

[1] See Prog. Relig. Ideas, vol. i. p. 61.

[2] See Higgins : Anacalypsis, vol. i. 130, 13 . and Maurice : Indian Antiquities, vol. i. pp. 112, 113, and vol. iii. pp. 45, 95.

[3] Indian Antiqu'ties, vol. i. pp. 112, 113.

[4] Asiatic Researches, vol. i. p. 259.

[5] Farrar's Life of Christ, p. 58.

[6] See Introduction to Gospel of Infancy Apoc.

[7] See vol. x. Asiatic Researches.

Buddha's life was also in danger when an infant. In the southern country of Magadha, there lived a king by the name of Bimbasara, who, being fearful of some enemy arising that might overturn his kingdom, frequently assembled his principal ministers together to hold discussion with them on the subject. On one of these occasions they told him that away to the north there was a respectable tribe of people called the Sâkyas, and that belonging to this race there was a youth newly-born, the first-begotten of his mother, &c. This youth, who was Buddha, they said was liable to overturn him, they therefore advised him to "at once raise an army and destroy the child."[1]

In the chronicles of the East Mongols, the same tale is to be found repeated in the following story :

"A certain king of a people called Patsala, had a son whose peculiar appearance led the Brahmins at court to prophesy that he would bring evil upon his father, and to advise his destruction. Various modes of execution having failed, *the boy was laid in a copper chest and thrown into the Ganges.* Rescued by an old peasant who brought him up as his son, he, in due time, learned the story of his escape, and returned to seize upon the kingdom destined for him from his birth."[2]

Hau-ki, the Chinese hero of supernatural origin, was exposed in infancy, as the "Shih-king" says :

"He was placed in a narrow lane, but the sheep and oxen protected him with loving care. He was placed in a wide forest, where he was met with by the wood-cutters. He was placed on the cold ice, and a bird screened and supported him with its wings," &c.[3]

Mr. Legge draws a comparison with this to the Roman legend of Romulus.

Horus, according to the Egyptian story, was born in the winter, and brought up secretly in the Isle of Buto, for fear of Typhon, who sought his life. Typhon at first schemed to prevent his birth and then sought to destroy him when born.[4]

Within historical times, *Cyrus*, king of Persia (6th cent. B. C.), is the hero of a similar tale. His grandfather, Astyages, had dreamed certain dreams which were interpreted by the Magi to mean that the offspring of his daughter Mandane would expel him from his kingdom.

Alarmed at the prophecy, he handed the child to his kinsman Harpagos to be slain ; but this man having entrusted it to a shepherd to be exposed, the latter contrived to save it by exhibiting to

[1] Beal : Hist. Buddha, pp. 103, 104.　　[3] The Shih-king. Decade ii, ode 1.
[2] Amberly's Analysis, p. 229.　　[4] Bonwick : Egyptian Belief, pp. 158 and 166.

the emissaries of Harpagos the body of a still-born child of which his own wife had just been delivered. Grown to man's estate Cyrus of course justified the prediction of the Magi by his successful revolt against Astyages and assumption of the monarchy.

Herodotus, the Grecian Historian (B. C. 484), relates that Astyages, in a vision, appeared to see a vine grow up from Mandane's womb, which covered all Asia. Having seen this and communicated it to the interpreters of dreams, he put her under guard, resolving to destroy whatever should be born of her; for the Magian interpreters had signified to him from his vision that the child born of Mandane would reign in his stead. Astyages therefore, guarding against this, as soon as Cyrus was born sought to have him destroyed. The story of his exposure on the mountain, and his subsequent good fortune, is then related.[1]

Abraham was also a " dangerous child." At the time of his birth, Nimrod, king of Babylon, was informed by his soothsayers that "a child should be born in Babylonia, who would shortly become a great prince, and that he had reason to fear him." The result of this was that Nimrod then issued orders that " all women with child should be guarded with great care, *and all children born of them should be put to death.*"[2]

The mother of Abraham was at that time with child, but, of course, *he* escaped from being put to death, although many children were slaughtered.

Zoroaster, the chief of the religion of the Magi, was a " dangerous child." Prodigies had announced his birth; he was exposed to dangers from the time of his infancy, and was obliged to fly into Persia, like Jesus into Egypt. Like him, he was pursued by a king, his enemy, who wanted to get rid of him.[3]

His mother had alarming dreams of evil spirits seeking to destroy the child to whom she was about to give birth. But a good spirit came to comfort her and said: "Fear nothing! Ormuzd will protect this infant. He has sent him as a prophet to the people. The world is waiting for him."[4]

Perseus, son of the Virgin Danae, was also a " dangerous child." Acrisius, king of Argos, being told by the oracle that a son born of his virgin daughter would destroy him, immured his daughter Danae in a tower, *where no man could approach her*, and by this means hoped to keep his daughter from

[1] Herodotus, bk. 1, ch. 110.

[2] Calmet's Fragments, art. "Abraham."

[3] See Dupuis : Origin of Religious Belief, p. 240.

[4] See Prog. Relig. Ideas, vol. i. "Religions of Persia."

becoming *enceinte.* The god Jupiter, however, visited her there, as it is related of the Angel Gabriel visiting the Virgin Mary,[1] the result of which was that she bore a son—*Perseus.* Acrisius, on hearing of his daughter's disgrace, caused both her and the infant to be shut up in a chest and cast into the sea. They were discovered by one Dictys, and liberated from what must have been anything but a pleasant position.[2]

Æsculapius, when an infant, was exposed on the Mount of Myrtles, and left there to die, but escaped the death which was intended for him, having been found and cared for by *shepherds.*[3]

Hercules, son of the virgin Leto, was left to die on a plain, but was found and rescued by a maiden.[4]

Œdipous was a "dangerous child." Laios, King of Thebes, having been told by the Delphic Oracle that Œdipous would be his destroyer, no sooner is Œdipous born than the decree goes forth that the child must be slain; but the servant to whom he is intrusted contents himself with exposing the babe on the slopes of Mount Kithairon, where a *shepherd* finds him, and carries him, like Cyrus or Romulus, to his wife, who cherishes the child with a mother's care.[5]

The Theban myth of Œdipous is repeated substantially in the Arcadian tradition of *Telephos.* He is exposed, when a babe, on Mount Parthenon, and is suckled by a doe, which represents the wolf in the myth of Romulus, and the dog of the Persian story of Cyrus. Like Moses, he is brought up in the palace of a king.[6]

As we read the story of Telephos, we can scarcely fail to think of the story of the Trojan *Paris,* for, like Telephos, Paris is exposed as a babe on the mountain-side.[7] Before he is born, there are portents of the ruin which he is to bring upon his house and people. Priam, the ruling monarch, therefore decrees that the child shall be left to die on the hill-side. But the babe lies on the slopes of *Ida* and is nourished by a she-bear. He is fostered, like Crishna and others, by *shepherds,* among whom he grows up.[8]

Iamos was left to die among the bushes and violets. Aipytos, the chieftain of Phaisana, had learned at Delphi that a child had been born who should become the greatest of all the seers and prophets of the earth, and he asked all his people where the babe

---

[1] In the Apocryphal Gospel of the Birth of Mary and "Protevangelion."
[2] See Bell's Pantheon, vol. i. p. 9. Cox: Aryan Mythology, vol. ii. p. 58, and Bulfinch: The Age of Fable, p. 161.
[3] Bell's Pantheon, vol. i. p. 27. Cox: Aryan Mytho. vol. ii. p. 34.
[4] Cox: Aryan Mytho. vol. ii. p. 44.
[5] Ibid, p. 69, and Tales of Ancient Greece, p. xlii.
[6] Cox: Aryan Mythology, vol. ii. p. 74.
[7] Ibid. p. 75. [8] Ibid. p. 78.

was: but none had heard or seen him, for he lay away amid the thick bushes, with his soft body bathed in the golden and pure rays of the violets. So when he was found, they called him Iamos, the "violet child;" and as he grew in years and strength, he went down into the Alpheian stream, and prayed to his father that he would glorify his son. Then the voice of Zeus was heard, bidding him come to the heights of Olympus, where he should receive the gift of prophecy.[1]

Chandragupta was also a "dangerous child." He is exposed to great dangers in his infancy at the hands of a tributary chief who has defeated and slain his suzerain. His mother, "relinquishing him to the protection of the Devas, places him in a vase, and deposits him at the door of a *cattle pen*." A *herdsman* takes the child and rears it as his own.[2]

Jason is another hero of the same kind. Pelias, the chief of Iolkos, had been told that one of the children of Aiolos would be his destroyer, and decreed, therefore, that all should be slain. Jason only is preserved, and brought up by Cheiron.[3]

Bacchus, son of the virgin Semele, was destined to bring ruin upon Cadmus, King of Thebes, who therefore orders the infant to be put into a chest and thrown into a river. He is found, and taken from the water by loving hands, and lives to fulfill his mission.[4]

Herodotus relates a similar story, which is as follows:

"The constitution of the *Corinthians* was formerly of this kind; it was an *oligarchy*, (a government in the hands of a selected few), and those who were called *Bacchiadæ* governed the city. About this time one Eetion, who had been married to a maiden called Labda, and having no children by her, went to Delphi to inquire of the oracle about having offspring. Upon entering the temple he was immediately saluted as follows: 'Eetion, no one honors thee, though worthy of much honor. Labda is pregnant and will bring forth a round stone; it will fall on monarchs, and vindicate Corinth.' This oracle, pronounced to Eetion, was by chance reported to the *Bacchiadæ*, who well knew that it prophesied the birth of a son to Eetion who would overthrow them, and reign in their stead; and though they comprehended, they kept it secret, purposing to destroy the offspring that should be born to Eetion. As soon as the woman brought forth, they sent ten persons to the district where Eetion lived, to put the child to death; but, the child, *by a divine providence*, was saved. His mother hid him in a chest, and as they could not find the ·child they resolved to depart, and tell those who sent them that they had done all that they had commanded. After this, Eetion's son grew up, and having escaped this danger, the name of Cypselus was given him, from the chest. When Cypselus reached man's estate, and consulted the oracle, an ambiguous answer was given him at Delphi; relying on which he attacked and got possession of Corinth."[5]

---

[1] Cox: Aryan Mytho. ii. p. 81.
[2] Ibid. p. 84.
[3] Ibid. p. 150.
[4] Bell's Pantheon, vol. i. p. 188. Cox: Aryan Mytho. vol. ii. p. 296.
[5] Herodotus: bk. v. ch. 92.

Romulus and *Remus*, the founders of Rome, were exposed on the banks of the Tiber, when infants, and left there to die, but escaped the death intended for them.

The story of the " dangerous child " was well known in ancient Rome, and several of their emperors, so it is said, were threatened with death at their birth, or when mere infants. Julius Marathus, in his life of the Emperor Augustus Cæsar, says that before his birth there was a prophecy in Rome that a king over the Roman people would soon be born. To obviate this danger to the republic, the Senate ordered that all the male children born in that year should be abandoned or exposed.[1]

The flight of the virgin-mother with her babe is also illustrated in the story of Astrea when beset by Orion, and of Latona, the mother of Apollo, when pursued by the monster.[2] It is simply the same old story, over and over again. Some one has predicted that a child born at a certain time shall be great, he is therefore a " dangerous child," and the reigning monarch, or some other interested party, attempts to have the child destroyed, but he invariably escapes and grows to manhood, and generally accomplishes the purpose for which he was intended. This almost universal mythos was added to the fictitious history of Jesus by its fictitious authors, who have made him escape in his infancy from the reigning tyrant with the usual good fortune.

When a marvellous occurrence is said to have happened *everywhere*, we may feel sure that it never happened anywhere. Popular fancies propagate themselves indefinitely, but historical events, especially the striking and dramatic ones, are rarely repeated. That this is a fictitious story is seen from the narratives of the birth of Jesus, which are recorded by the first and third Gospel writers, without any other evidence. In the one—that related by the *Matthew* narrator—we have a birth at Bethlehem—implying the ordinary residence of the parents there—and a *hurried flight* —almost immediately after the birth—from that place into Egypt,[3] the slaughter of the infants, and a journey, after many months, from Egypt to Nazareth in Galilee. In the other story—that told by the *Luke* narrator—the parents, who have lived in Nazareth, came to Bethlehem only for business of the State, and the casual birth in the cave or stable is followed by a quiet sojourn, during which the child is circumcised, and by a leisurely journey to Jerusalem ;

---

[1] See Farrar's Life of Christ, p. 60.
[2] Bonwick : Egyptian Belief, p. 168.
[3] There are no very early examples in

Christian art of the flight of the Holy Family into Egypt. (See Monmental Christianity, p. 239.)

whence, everything having gone off peaceably and happily, they return naturally to their own former place of abode, full, *it is said over and over again*, of wonder at the things that had happened, and deeply impressed with the conviction that their child had a special work to do, and was specially gifted for it. *There is no fear of Herod, who seems never to trouble himself about the child, or even to have any knowledge of him. There is no trouble or misery at Bethlehem, and certainly no mourning for children slain.* Far from flying hurriedly away by night, his parents *celebrate openly*, and at the usual time, the circumcision of the child; and when he is presented in the temple, there is not only no sign that enemies seek his life, *but the devout saints give public thanks for the manifestation of the Saviour.*

Dr. Hooykaas, speaking of the slaughter of the innocents, says:

"Antiquity in general delighted in representing great men, such as Romulus, Cyrus, and many more, as having been threatened in their childhood by fearful dangers. This served to bring into clear relief both the lofty significance of their future lives, and the special protection of the deity who watched over them.

"The brow of many a theologian has been bent over this (Matthew) narrative! For, as long as people believed in the miraculous inspiration of the Holy Scriptures, of course they accepted every page as literally true, and thought that there *could* not be any contradiction between the different accounts or representations of Scripture. The worst of all such pre-conceived ideas is, that they compel those who hold them to do violence to their own sense of truth. For when these so-called religious prejudices come into play, people are afraid to call things by their right names, and, without knowing it themselves, become guilty of all kinds of evasive and arbitrary practices; for what would be thought quite unjustifiable in any other case is here considered a duty, inasmuch as it is supposed to tend toward the maintenance of faith and the glory of God!"[1]

As we stated above, this story is to be found in the fictitious gospel according to Matthew only; contemporary history has nowhere recorded this audacious crime. It is mentioned neither by Jewish nor Roman historians. Tacitus, who has stamped forever the crimes of despots with the brand of reprobation, it would seem then, did not think such infamies worthy of his condemnation. Josephus also, who gives us a minute account of the atrocities perpetrated by Herod up to even the very last moment of his life, does not say a single word about this unheard-of crime, which must have been so notorious. Surely he must have known of it, and must have mentioned it, had it ever been committed. "We can readily imagine the Pagans," says Mr. Reber, "who composed the learned and intelligent men of their day, at work in exposing the story of Herod's cruelty, by showing that, considering the ex-

---

[1] Bible for Learners, vol. iii. pp. 71-74.

tent of territory embraced in the order, and the population within it, the assumed destruction of life stamped the story false and ridiculous.   A governor of a Roman province who dared make such an order would be so speedily overtaken by the vengeance of the Roman people, that his head would fall from his body before the blood of his victims had time to dry.   Archelaus, his son, was deposed for offenses not to be spoken of when compared with this massacre of the infants."

No wonder that there is no trace at all in the Roman catacombs, nor in Christian art, of this fictitious story, until about the beginning of the fifth century.[1]   Never would Herod dared to have taken upon himself the odium and responsibility of such a sacrifice. *Such a crime could never have happened at the epoch of its pro-fessed perpetration.*   To such lengths were the early Fathers led, by the servile adaptation of the ancient traditions of the East, they required a *second edition* of the tyrant Kansa, and their holy wrath fell upon Herod.   The Apostles of Jesus counted too much upon human credulity, they trusted too much that the future might not unravel their maneuvers, the sanctity of their object made them too reckless.   They destroyed all the evidence against themselves which they could lay their hands upon, but they did not destroy it all.

---

[1] See Monumental Christianity, p. 238.

CHAPTER XIX.

WE are informed by the *Matthew* narrator that, after being baptized by John in the river Jordan, Jesus was led by the spirit into the wilderness " *to be tempted of the devil.*"

" And when he had fasted *forty days and forty nights,* he was afterward an hungered. And when the *tempter* came to him he said: 'If thou be the Son of God, command that these stones be made bread.' . . . Then the devil taketh him up into the holy city, *and setteth him on a pinnacle of the temple,* and saith unto him: 'If thou be the Son of God, cast thyself down.' . . . Again, the devil taketh him up into an exceeding high mountain, *and showeth him all the kingdoms of the world,* and the glory of them, and saith unto him: ' *All these things will I give thee* if thou wilt fall down and worship me.' Then saith Jesus unto him, ' Get thee hence, Satan: for it is written, Thou shalt worship the Lord thy God, and him only shalt thou serve.' Then the devil leaveth him, and, behold, angels came and ministered unto him."[1]

This is really a very peculiar story; it is therefore not to be wondered at that many of the early Christian Fathers rejected it as being fabulous,[2] but this, according to orthodox teaching, cannot be done; because, in all consistent reason, " *we must accept the whole of the inspired autographs or reject the whole,*"[3] and, because, " the very foundations of our faith, the very basis of our hopes, the very nearest and dearest of our consolations, are taken from us, when *one line* of that sacred volume, on which we base everything, is declared to be untruthful and untrustworthy."[4]

The reason why we have this story in the New Testament is because the writer wished to show that Christ Jesus was proof against all temptations, that *he* too, as well as *Buddha* and others, could resist the powers of the prince of evil. This Angel-Messiah was tempted by the devil, and he fasted for forty-seven days and nights, without taking an atom of food.[5]

---

[1] Matthew, iv. 1-11.
[2] See Lardner's Works, vol. viii. p. 401.
[3] Words of the Rev. E. Garbett, M. A., in a sermon preached before the University of Oxford, England.
[4] The Bishop of Manchester (England), in the " Manchester Examiner and Times."
[5] See Lillie's Buddhism, p. 100.

The story of Buddha's temptation, presented below, is taken from the "*Siamese Life of Buddha*," by Moncure D. Conway, and published in his "*Sacred Anthology*," from which we take it.[1] It is also to be found in the *Fo-pen-hing*,[2] and other works on Buddha and Buddhism. Buddha went through a more lengthy and severe trial than did Jesus, having been tempted in many different ways. The portion which most resembles that recorded by the Matthew narrator is the following:

"The Grand Being (Buddha) applied himself to practice ascetcism of the extremest nature. *He ceased to eat* (that is, he *fasted*), and held his breath. . . . *Then it was that the royal Mara* (the Prince of Evil) *sought occasion to tempt him.* Pretending compassion, he said: 'Beware, O Grand Being, your state is pitiable to look on; you are attenuated beyond measure, . . . you are practicing this mortification in vain; I can see that you will not live through it. . . . Lord, that art capable of such vast endurance, go not forth to adopt a religious life, but return to thy kingdom, and in *seven* days thou shalt become *the Emperor of the World*, riding over the four great continents.'"

To this the Grand Being, Buddha, replied:

"'Take heed, O Mara; I also know that in seven days I might gain universal empire, but I desire not such possessions. I know that the pursuit of religion is better than the empire of the world. You, thinking only of evil lusts, would force me to leave all beings without guidance into your power. *Avaunt! Get thou away from me!*'

"The Lord (then) rode onwards, intent on his purpose. The skies rained flowers, and delicious odors pervaded the air."[3]

Now, mark the similarity between these two legends.

Was Jesus about "beginning to preach" when he was tempted by the evil spirit? So was Buddha about to go forth "to adopt a religious life," when he was tempted by the evil spirit.

Did Jesus fast, and was he "afterwards an hungered"? So did Buddha "cease to eat," and was "attenuated beyond measure."

Did the evil spirit take Jesus and show him "all the kingdoms of the world," which he promised to give him, provided he did not lead the life he contemplated, but follow him?

So did the evil spirit say to Buddha: "Go not forth to adopt a religious life, and in seven days thou shalt become an emperor of the world."

Did not Jesus resist these temptations, and say unto the evil one, "Get thee behind me, Satan"?

So did Buddha resist the temptations, and said unto the evil one, "Get thee away from me."

[1] Pp. 44 and 172, 173.
[2] Translated by Prof. Samuel Beal.
[3] See also Bunsen's Angel-Messiah, pp. 38, 39. Beal: Hist. Buddha, pp. xxviii., xxix., and 190, and Hardy: Buddhist Legends, p. xvii.

After the evil spirit left Jesus did not "angels come and minister unto him"?

So with Buddha. After the evil one had left him "the skies rained flowers, and delicious odors pervaded the air."

These parallels are too striking to be accidental.

Zoroaster, the founder of the religion of the Persians, was tempted by the devil, who made him magnificent promises, in order to induce him to become his servant and to be dependent on him, but the temptations were in vain.[1] "His temptation by the devil, forms the subject of many traditional reports and legends."[2]

Quetzalcoatle, the virgin-born Mexican Saviour, was also tempted by the devil, and the forty days' fast was found among them.[3]

Fasting and self-denial were observances practiced by all nations of antiquity. The *Hindoos* have days set apart for fasting on many different occasions throughout the year, one of which is when the birth-day of their Lord and Saviour Crishna is celebrated. On this occasion, the day is spent in fasting and worship. They abstain entirely from food and drink for more than thirty hours, at the end of which Crishna's image is worshiped, and the story of his miraculous birth is read to his hungry worshipers.[4]

Among the ancient *Egyptians*, there were times when the priests submitted to abstinence of the most severe description, being forbidden to eat even bread, and at other times they only ate it mingled with hyssop. "The priests in Heliopolis," says Plutarch, "have many fasts, during which they meditate on divine things."[5]

Among the *Sabians*, fasting was insisted on as an essential act of religion. During the month *Tammuz*, they were in the habit of fasting from sunrise to sunset, without allowing a morsel of food or drop of liquid to pass their lips.[6]

The Jews also had their fasts, and on special occasions they gave themselves up to prolonged fasts and mortifications.

Fasting and self-denial were observances required of the Greeks who desired initiation into the *Mysteries*. Abstinence from food, chastity and hard couches prepared the neophyte, who broke his fast on the third and fourth day only, on consecrated food.[7]

The same practice was found among the ancient *Mexicans* and *Peruvians*. Acosta, speaking of them, says:

---

[1] Dupuis : Origin of Religious Belief, p. 240.
[2] Chambers's Enclyclo. art. "Zoroaster."
[3] See Kingsborough : Mexican Antiquities, vol. vi. p. 200.
[4] Life and Relig. of the Hindoos, p. 184.
[5] Baring-Gould : Orig. Relig. Belief, vol. L p. 341.
[6] Ibid.   [7] Ibid. p. 340.

"These priests and religious men used great fastings, of five and ten days together, before any of their great feasts, and they were unto them as our four ember weeks. . . .

"They drank no wine, and slept little, for the greatest part of their exercises (of penance) were at night, committing great cruelties and martyring themselves for the devil, and all to be reputed great fasters and penitents."[1]

In regard to the number of days which Jesus is said to have fasted being specified as *forty*, this is simply owing to the fact that the number *forty* as well as *seven* was a sacred one among most nations of antiquity, particularly among the Jews, and because *others* had fasted that number of days. For instance; it is related[2] that *Moses* went up into a mountain, "and he was there with the Lord *forty days and forty nights, and he did neither eat bread, nor drink water,*" which is to say that he *fasted.*

In Deuteronomy[3] Moses *is made to say*—for he did not write it, "When I was gone up into the mount to receive the tables of stone, . . . then I abode in the mount *forty days and forty nights,* I neither did eat bread nor drink water."

Elijah also had a long fast, which, *of course,* was continued for a period of *forty days and forty nights.*[4]

St. Joachim, father of the "ever-blessed Virgin Mary," had a long fast, which was also continued for a period of *forty days and forty nights.* The story is to be found in the apocryphal gospel *Protevangelion.*[5]

The ancient *Persians* had a religious festival which they annually celebrated, and which they called the "Salutation of Mithras." During this festival, *forty days* were set apart for thanksgiving and sacrifice.[6]

The *forty days' fast* was found in the New World.

Godfrey Higgins tells us that:

"The ancient *Mexicans* had a *forty days' fast,* in memory of one of their sacred persons (Quetzalcoatle) who was tempted (and fasted) *forty days* on a mountain."[7]

Lord Kingsborough says:

"The temptation of Quetzalcoatle, and *the fast of forty days,* . . . are *very curious and mysterious.*"[8]

The ancient Mexicans were also in the habit of making their

1 Acosta : Hist. Indies, vol. ii. p. 339.
2 Exodus, xxiv. 28.
3 Deut. ix. 18.
4 1 Kings, xix. 8.
5 Chapter i.
6 See Prog. Relig. Ideas, vol. i. p. 272.
7 Anacalypsis, vol. ii. p. 19.
8 Mexican Antiquities, vol. vi. pp. 197-200.

prisoners of war fast for a term of *forty days* before they were put to death.[1]

Mr. Bonwick says:

"The Spaniards were surprised to see the *Mexicans* keep the vernal *forty days' fast.* The Tammuz month of Syria was in the spring. The *forty days* were kept for Proserpine. Thus does history repeat itself."[2]

The Spanish monks accounted for what Lord Kingsborough calls "very curious and mysterious" circumstances, by the agency of the devil, and burned all the books containing them, whenever it was in their power.

The forty days' fast was also found among some of the Indian tribes in the New World. Dr. Daniel Brinton tells us that "the females of the *Orinoco* tribes *fasted forty days* before marriage,"[3] and Prof. Max Müller informs us that it was customary for some of the females of the South American tribes of Indians "to fast before and after the birth of a child," and that, among the *Carib-Couduve* tribe, in the West Indies, "when a child is born the mother goes presently to work, but the father begins to complain, and takes to his hammock, and there he is visited as though he were sick. *He then fasts for forty days.*"[4]

The females belonging to the tribes of the Upper Mississippi, were held unclean for *forty days* after childbirth.[5] The prince of the Tezcuca tribes *fasted forty days* when he wished an heir to his throne, and the Mandanas supposed it required *forty days and forty nights* to wash clean the earth at the deluge.[6]

The number *forty* is to be found in a great many instances in the Old Testament; for instance, at the end of *forty days* Noah sent out a raven from the ark.[7] Isaac and Esau were each *forty years* old when they married.[8] *Forty days* were fulfilled for the embalming of Jacob.[9] The spies were *forty days* in search of the land of Canaan.[10] The Israelites wandered *forty years* in the wilderness.[11] The land "had rest" *forty years* on three occasions.[12] The land was delivered into the hand of the Philistines *forty years.*[13] Eli judged Israel *forty years.*[14] King David reigned *forty years.*[15]

---

[1] See Kingsborough's Mexican Antiquities, vol. vi. p. 223.

[2] Bonwick's Egyptian Belief, p. 370.

[3] Brinton : Myths of the New World, p. 94.

[4] Max Müller's Chips, vol. ii. p. 279.

[5] Brinton : Myths of the New World, p. 94.

[6] Ibid. According to Genesis, vii. 12, "the rain was upon the earth forty days and forty nights" at the time of the flood.

[7] Genesis, viii. 6.

[8] Gen. xxv. 20—xxvi. 34.

[9] Gen. i. 3.

[10] Numbers, xiii. 25.

[11] Numbers, xiii. 13.

[12] Jud. iii. 11 ; v. 31 ; viii. 28.

[13] Jud. xiii. 1.

[14] I. Samuel, iv. 18.

[15] I. Kings, ii. 11.

King Solomon reigned *forty years*.[1] Goliath presented himself *forty days*.[2] The rain was upon the earth *forty days* at the time of the deluge.[3] And, as we saw above, Moses was on the mount *forty days* and *forty nights* on each occasion.[4] Can anything be more mythological than this?

The number forty was used by the ancients in constructing temples. There were *forty* pillars around the temple of Chilminar, in Persia; the temple at Baalbec had *forty* pillars; on the frontiers of China, in Tartary, there is to be seen the "Temple of the *forty* pillars." *Forty* is one of the most common numbers in the Druidical temples, and in the plan of the temple of Ezekiel, the four oblong buildings in the middle of the courts have each *forty* pillars.[5] Most temples of antiquity were imitative—were microcosms of the Celestial Templum—and on this account they were surrounded with pillars recording *astronomical* subjects, and intended both to do honor to these subjects, and to keep them in perpetual remembrance. In the Abury temples were to be seen the cycles of 650–608–600–60–40–30–19–12, etc.[6]

---

[1] I. Kings, xi. 42.
[2] I. Samuel, xvii. 16.
[3] Gen. vii. 12.
[4] Exodus, xxiv. 18—xxxiv. 28.

[5] See Higgins' Anacalypsis, vol. i. p. 708; vol. ii. p. 402.
[6] See Ibid. vol. ii. p. 708.

THE punishment of an individual by crucifixion, for claiming to be "King of the Jews," "Son of God," or "The Christ;" which are the causes assigned by the Evangelists for the Crucifixion of Jesus, would need but a passing glance in our inquiry, were it not for the fact that there is much attached to it of a *dogmatic* and *heathenish* nature, which demands considerably more than a " passing glance." The doctrine of atonement for sin had been preached long before the doctrine was deduced from the Christian Scriptures, long before these Scriptures are pretended to have been written. Before the period assigned for the birth of Christ Jesus, the poet *Ovid* had assailed the demoralizing delusion with the most powerful shafts of philosophic scorn: " *When thou thyself art guilty,*" says he, "*why should a victim die for thee ? What folly it is to expect savlation from the death of another.*"

The idea of expiation by the sacrifice of a *god* was to be found among the Hindoos even in *Vedic* times. *The sacrificer was mystically identified with the victim,* which was regarded as the ransom for sin, and the instrument of its annulment. The *Rig - Veda* represents the gods as sacrificing *Purusha,* the primeval male, supposed to be coeval with the Creator. This idea is even more remarkably developed in the *Tāndya-brāhmanas,* thus:

"The lord of creatures (*prajā-pati*) *offered himself a sacrifice for the gods.*"

And again, in the *Satapatha-brāhmana :*

" He who, knowing this, sacrifices the *Purusha-medha,* or sacrifice of the primeval male, becomes everything."[1]

Prof. Monier Williams, from whose work on *Hindooism* we quote the above, says:

---

[1] Monier Williams: Hinduism, pp. 86-40.

"Surely, in these mystical allusions to the sacrifice of a representative man, we may perceive traces of the original institution of sacrifice as a *divinely-appointed ordinance typical of the one great sacrifice of the Son of God for the sins of the world.*"[1]

This idea of redemption from sin through the sufferings and death of a Divine Incarnate Saviour, is simply the crowning-point of the idea entertained by primitive man that the gods *demanded* a sacrifice of some kind, to atone for some sin, or avert some calamity.

In primitive ages, when men lived mostly on vegetables, they offered only grain, water, salt, fruit, and flowers to the gods, to propitiate them and thereby obtain temporal blessings. But when they began to eat meat and spices, and drink wine, they offered the same; naturally supposing the deities would be pleased with whatever was useful or agreeable to themselves. They imagined that some gods were partial to animals, others to fruits, flowers, etc. To the celestial gods they offered *white* victims at sunrise, or at open day. To the infernal deities they sacrificed *black* animals in the night. Each god had some creature peculiarly devoted to his worship. They sacrificed a *bull* to Mars, a *dove* to Venus, and to Minerva, a *heifer* without blemish, which had never been put to the yoke. If a man was too poor to sacrifice a living animal, he offered an image of one made of bread.

In the course of time, it began to be imagined that the gods demanded something more sacred as offerings or atonements for sin. This led to the sacrifice of *human beings*, principally slaves and those taken in war, then, their own children, even their most beloved "first-born." It came to be an idea that every sin must have its prescribed amount of punishment, *and that the gods would accept the life of one person as atonement for the sins of others.* This idea prevailed even in Greece and Rome : but there it mainly took the form of heroic self-sacrifice for the public good. Cicero says : " The force of religion was so great among our ancestors, that some of their commanders have, with their faces veiled, and with the strongest expressions of sincerity, *sacrificed themselves to the immortal gods to save their country.*"[2]

In Egypt, offerings of human sacrifices, for the atonement of sin, became so general that " if the eldest born of the family of Athamas entered the temple of the Laphystan Jupiter at Alos in Achaia, he was sacrificed, crowned with garlands like an animal victim."[3]

---

[1] Monier Williams: Hinduism, p. 36.   [2] See Prog. Relig. Ideas, vol. i. p. 303.
[3] Kenrick's Egypt, vol. i. p. 443.

When the Egyptian priests offered up a sacrifice to the gods, they pronounced the following imprecations on the head of the victim:

"If any evil is about to befall either those who now sacrifice, or Egypt in general, *may it be averted on this head.*"[1]

This idea of atonement finally resulted in the belief that the incarnate *Christ*, the *Anointed*, the *God among us*, was to *save* mankind from a curse by God imposed. Man had sinned, and God could not and did not forgive without a propitiatory *sacrifice*. The curse of God must be removed from the *sinful*, and the *sinless* must bear the load of that curse. It was asserted that *divine justice* required BLOOD.[2]

The belief of redemption from sin by the sufferings of a *Divine Incarnation*, whether by death on the cross or otherwise, was general and popular among the heathen, centuries before the time of Jesus of Nazareth, and this dogma, no matter how sacred it may have become, or how *consoling* it may be, must fall along with the rest of the material of which the Christian church is built.

Julius Firmicius, referring to this popular belief among the *Pagans*, says: "The *devil* has *his Christs.*"[3] This was the general off-hand manner in which the Christian Fathers disposed of such matters. Everything in the religion of the Pagans which corresponded to their religion was of the devil. Most Protestant divines have resorted to the *type* theory, of which we shall speak anon.

As we have done heretofore in our inquiries, we will first turn to *India*, where we shall find, in the words of M. l'Abbé Huc, that "*the idea of redemption by a divine incarnation*," who came into the world for the express purpose of redeeming mankind, was "general and popular."[4]

"A sense of *original corruption*," says Prof. Monier Williams,

---

[1] Herodotus : bk. ii. ch. 89.

[2] In the trial of Dr. Thomas (at Chicago) for "*doctrinal heresy*," one of the charges made against him (Sept. 8, 1881) was that he had said "the BLOOD of the Lamb had nothing to do with salvation." And in a sermon preached in Boston, Sept. 2, 1881, at the Columbus Avenue Presbyterian Church, by the Rev. Andrew A. Bonar, D.D., the preacher said : "No sinner dares to meet the holy God until his sin has been forgiven, or until he has received *remission*. The penalty of sin is death, *and this penalty is not remitted by anything the sinner can do for himself*, but only through the BLOOD of Jesus. If you have accepted Jesus as your Saviour, you can take the blood of Jesus, and with boldness present it to the Father *as payment in full of the penalties of all your sins.* Sinful man has no right to the benefits and the beauties and glories of nature. *These were all lost to him through Adam's sin*, but to the blood of Christ's sacrifice he has a right ; it was shed for him. It is Christ's death that does the blessed work of salvation for us. It was *not* his life nor his Incarnation. His Incarnation could not pay a farthing of our debt, but his *blood* shed in redeeming love. *pays it all.*' (See Boston Advertiser, Sept. 3, 1881.)

[3] *Habet ergo Diabolus Christos suos.*

[4] Huc's Travels, vol. i. pp. 326 and 327.

seems to be felt by all classes of Hindoos, as indicated by the following prayer used after the *Gāyatrī* by some Vaishnavas :

"'I am sinful, I commit sin, my nature is sinful, *I am conceived in sin.*
Save me, O thou lotus-eyed Heri (Saviour), the remover of sin.'"[1]

Moreover, the doctrine of *bhakti (salvation by faith)* existed
among the Hindoos from the earliest times.[2]

Crishna, the virgin-born, "the Divine Vishnu himself,"[3]
"he who is without beginning, middle or end,"[4] being moved
"to relieve the earth of her load,"[5] came upon earth and redeemed
man by his *sufferings*—to *save* him.

The accounts of the deaths of most all the virgin-born Saviours
of whom we shall speak, are conflicting. It is stated in one place
that such an one died in such a manner, and in another place we
may find it stated altogether differently. Even the accounts of the
death of Jesus, as we shall hereafter see, are conflicting; therefore,
until the chapter on "*Explanation*" is read, these myths cannot
really be thoroughly understood.

As the Rev. Geo. W. Cox remarks, in his *Aryan Mythology*,
Crishna is described, in one of his aspects, as a self-sacrificing and
unselfish hero, a being who is filled with divine wisdom and love,
who offers up a sacrifice which he alone can make.[6]

The *Vishnu Purana*[7] speaks of *Crishna* being shot in the *foot*
with an arrow, and states that *this* was the cause of his death. Other
accounts, however, state that he was suspended on a tree, or in
other words, *crucified.*

Mons. Guigniaut, in his "*Religion de l'Antiquité*," says :

"The death of Crishna is very differently related. One remarkable and convincing tradition makes him perish on a *tree*, to which he was *nailed* by the
stroke of an arrow."[8]

Rev. J. P. Lundy alludes to this passage of Guigniaut's in his
"Monumental Christianity," and translates the passage "un bois
fatal" (see note below) "*a cross.*" Although we do not think he
is justified in doing this, as M. Guigniaut has distinctly stated that
this "bois fatal" (which is applied to a gibbet, a cross, a scaffold,
etc.) was "un arbre" (a *tree*), yet, he is justified in doing so on
other accounts, for we find that *Crishna* is represented *hanging on
a cross*, and we know that a *cross* was frequently called the "ac-

---

[1] Hinduism, p. 214.
[2] Ibid. p. 115.
[3] Vishnu Purana, p. 440.
[4] Ibid.
[5] Ibid.
[6] Aryan Mythology, vol. ii. p. 132.

[7] Pages 274 and 612.
[8] "On reconte fort diversement la mort de
Crishna. Une tradition remarquable et avérée
le fait périr sur un bois fatal (un arbre), ou il
fut cloué d'un coup de flèche." (Quoted by
Higgins : Anacalypsis, vol. i. p. 144.)

cursed *tree.*" It was an ancient custom to use trees as gibbets for crucifixion, or, if artificial, to call the cross a tree.[1]

A writer in *Deuteronomy*[2] speaks of hanging criminals upon a *tree*, as though it was a general custom, and says:

"He that is hanged (on a tree) is accursed of God."

And *Paul* undoubtedly refers to this text when he says:

"Christ hath redeemed us from the *curse* of the law, being made a curse for us; for it is written, 'Cursed is every one that hangeth on a tree.'"[3]

It is evident, then, that to be hung on a cross was anciently called hanging on a *tree*, and to be hung on a tree was called crucifixion. We may therefore conclude from this, and from what we shall now see, that Crishna was said to have been *crucified*.

In the earlier copies of Moor's "*Hindu Pantheon*," is to be seen representations of Crishna (as *Wittoba*),[4] with marks of holes in both feet, and in others, of holes in the hands. In Figures 4 and 5 of Plate 11 (Moor's work), the figures have *nail-holes in both feet.* Figure 6 has a *round hole in the side;* to his collar or shirt hangs the emblem of a *heart* (which we often see in pictures of Christ Jesus) and on his head he has a *Yoni-Linga* (which we *do not* see in pictures of Christ Jesus.)

Our Figure No. 7 (next page), is a pre-Christian crucifix of *Asiatic* origin,[5] evidently intended to represent Crishna crucified. Figure No. 8 we can speak more positively of, it is surely Crishna crucified. It is unlike any Christian crucifix ever made, and, with that described above with the *Yoni-Linga* attached to the head, would probably not be claimed as such. Instead of the *crown of thorns* usually put on the head of the Christian Saviour, it has the turreted coronet of the Ephesian Diana, the ankles are tied together by a cord, *and the dress about the loins is exactly the style with which Crishna is almost always represented.*[6]

Rev. J. P. Lundy, speaking of the Christian crucifix, says:

[1] See Higgins: Anacalypsis, vol. i. p. 499, and Mrs. Jameson's "History of Our Lord in Art," ii. 317, where the cross is called the "accursed tree."

[2] Chap. xxi. 22, 23: "If a man have committed a sin worthy of death, and he be to be put to death, and thou hang him on a tree: his body shall not remain all night upon the tree, but thou shalt in any wise bury him that day; (for he that is hanged is accursed of God;) that thy land be not defiled, which the Lord thy God giveth thee for an inheritance."

[3] Galatians, iii. 13.

[4] See Higgins: Anacalypsis, vol. i. p. 146, and Inman's Ancient Faiths, vol. i. p. 402.

"The crucified god Wittoba is also called Balū. He is worshiped in a marked manner at Pander-poor or Bunder-poor, near Poonah." (Higgins: Anacalypsis, vol. i. p. 750, *note* 1.)

"A form of Vishnu (Crishna), called *Vithal* or *Vithobā*, is the popular god at Pandharpur in Mahā-rāshtrā, the favorite of the celebrated Marāthi poet Tukārāma." (Prof. Monier Williams: Indian Wisdom, p. xlviii.)

[5] See Lundy: Monumental Christianity, p. 160.

[6] This can be seen by referring to Calmet, Sonnerat, or Higgins, vol. ii., which contain plates representing Crishna.

"I object to the crucifix because it is an *image*, and liable to gross abuse, *just as the old Hindoo crucifix was an idol*."[1]

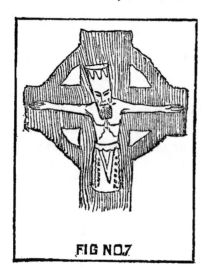

FIG NO.7

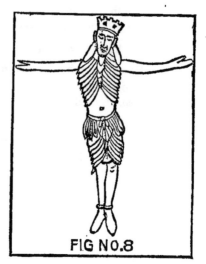

FIG NO.8

And Dr. Inman says:

"Crishna, whose history so closely resembles our Lord's, was also like him in his being crucified."[2]

The Evangelist[3] relates that when Jesus was crucified two others (malefactors) were crucified with him, one of whom, through his favor, went to heaven. One of the malefactors reviled him, but the other said to Jesus: "Lord, remember me when thou comest into thy kingdom." And Jesus said unto him: "Verily I say unto thee, to-day shalt thou be with me in paradise." According to the *Vishnu Purana*, the hunter who shot the arrow at Crishna afterwards said unto him: "Have pity upon me, who am consumed by my crime, for thou art able to consume me!" Crishna replied: "Fear not thou in the least. *Go, hunter, through my favor, to heaven, the abode of the gods.*" As soon as he had thus spoken, a celestial car appeared, and the hunter, ascending it, forthwith proceeded to heaven. Then the illustrious Crishna, having united himself with his own pure, spiritual, inexhaustible, inconceivable, unborn, undecaying, imperishable and universal spirit, which is one with *Vasudeva* (God),[4] abandoned his mortal body, and the condition of the threefold equalities.[5] One of the titles of Crishna

[1] Monumental Christianity, p. 128.
[2] Ancient Faiths, vol. i. p. 411.
[3] Luke, xxiii. 39–43.
[4] Vasudeva means God. See Vishnu Purana, p. 274.
[5] Vishnu Purana, p 612.

is " *Pardoner of sins*," another is " *Liberator from the Serpent of death*."[1]

The monk Georgius, in his *Tibetinum Alphabetum* (p. 203),

FIG 9

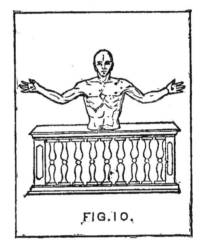

FIG. 10.

has given plates of *a crucified god* who was worshiped in *Nepal*. These crucifixes were to be seen at the corners of roads and on eminences. He calls it the god *Indra*. Figures No. 9 and No. 10 are taken from this work. They are also different from any Christian crucifix yet produced. Georgius says:

' If the matter stands as Beausobre thinks, then the inhabitants of India, and the Buddhists, whose religion is the same as that of the inhabitants of Thibet, have received these new portents of fanatics nowhere else than from the Manicheans. For those nations, especially in the city of Nepal, in the month of August, being about to celebrate the festival days of the god *Indra*, erect crosses, wreathed with *Abrotono*, to his memory, everywhere. You have the description of these in letter B, the picture following after; for A is the representation of *Indra* himself *crucified*, bearing on his forehead, hands and feet the signs *Telech*.'[2]

P. Andrada la Crozius, one of the first Europeans who went to Nepal and Thibet, in speaking of the god whom they worshiped there—*Indra*—tells us that they said *he spilt his blood for the salva-*

---

[1] See Prog. Relig. Ideas, vol. i. p. 72.

[2] "Si ita se res habet, ut existimat Beausobrius, *Indi*, et *Budistæ* quorum religio, eadem est ac Tibetana, nonnisi a Manichæis nova hæc deliriorum portenta acceperunt. Hænamque gentes præsertim in urbe Nepal, Luna XII. *Badr* seu *Bhadon Augusti* mensis, dies festos auspicaturæ Dei *Indræ*, erigunt ad illius memoriam ubique locorum *cruces* amictas *Abrotono*. Earum figuram descriptam habes ad lit. B, Tabula pone sequenti. Nam A effigies est ipsius *Indræ crucifixi* signa Telech in fronte manibus pedibusque gerentis." (Alph Tibet, p. 203. Quoted in Higgins' Anacalypsis, vol. i. p. 130.)

tion of the human race, and that he was pierced through the body with nails.   He further says that, although they do not say he suffered the penalty of the cross, yet they find, nevertheless, figures of it in their books.[1]

In regard to Beausobre's ideas that the religion of India is corrupted Christianity, obtained from the Manicheans, little need be said, as all scholars of the present day know that the religion of India is many centuries older than Mani or the Manicheans.[2]

In the promontory of India, in the South, at Tanjore, and in the North, at Oude or Ayoudia, was found the worship of the *crucified god Bal-li*.   This god, who was believed to have been an incarnation of Vishnu, was represented with holes in his hands and side.[3]

The incarnate god Buddha, although said to have expired peacefully at the foot of a tree, is nevertheless described as a suffering Saviour, who, "when his mind was moved by pity (for the human race) *gave his life like grass for the sake of others.*"[4]

A hymn, addressed to Buddha, says:

> " Persecutions without end,
> Revilings and many prisons,
> *Death and murder,*
> These hast thou suffered with love and patience
> (To secure the happiness of mankind),
> Forgiving thine executioners."[5]

He was called the " Great Physician,"[6] the " Saviour of the World,"[7] the " Blessed One,"[8] the " God among Gods,"[9] the " Anointed," or the " Christ,"[10] the " Messiah,"[11] the " Only Begotten,"[12] etc.   He is described by the author of the " Cambridge Key"[13] as sacrificing his life to wash away the offenses of mankind, and thereby to make them partakers of the kingdom of heaven.

---

[1] " Ils conviennent qu'il a répandu son sang pour le salut du genre humain, ayant été percé de clous par tout son corps.   Quoiqu'ils ne disent pas qu'il a souffert le supplice de la croix, on en trouve pourtant la figure dans leurs livres." (Quoted in Higgins' Anacalypsis, vol. ii. p. 118.)

[2] "Although the nations of Europe have changed their religions during the past eighteen centuries, the Hindoo has not done so, except very partially. . . .   The religious creeds, rites, customs, and habits of thought of the Hindoos generally, have altered little since the days of Manu, 500 years B. C." (Prof. Monier Williams : Indian Wisdom, p. iv.)

[3] See Higgins : Anacalypsis, vol. i. pp. 147,

572, 667 and 750 ; vol. ii. p. 122, and note 4, p. 185, this chapter.

[4] See Max Müller's Science of Religion, p. 224.

[5] Quoted in Lillie's Buddhism, p. 93.

[6] See Bunsen's Angel-Messiah, p. 20.

[7] See Bunsen's Angel-Messiah, pp. 20, 25, 35. Prog. Relig. Ideas, vol. i. p. 247. Huc's Travels, vol. i. pp. 326, 327, and almost any work on Buddhism.

[8] See Bunsen's Angel-Messiah, p. 20.

[9] Ibid.   Johnson's Oriental Religions, p. 604. See also Asiatic Researches, vol. iii., or chapter xii. of this work.

[10] See Bunsen's Angel-Messiah, p. 18.

[11] Ibid.

[12] Ibid.   [13] Vol. i p. 118.

This induces him to say "Can a Christian doubt that this Buddha was the TYPE of the Saviour of the World."[1]

As a spirit in the fourth heaven, he resolves to give up "all that glory, in order to be born into the world," "to rescue all men from their misery and every future consequence of it." He vows "to deliver all men, who are left as it were without a *Saviour.*"[2]

While in the realms of the blest, and when about to descend upon earth to be born as man, he said:

"I am now about to assume a body; not for the sake of gaining wealth, or enjoying the pleasures of sense, but I am about to descend and be born, among men, *simply to give peace and rest to all flesh; to remove all sorrow and grief from the world.*"[3]

M. l'Abbé Huc says:

"In the eyes of the Buddhists, this personage (Buddha) is sometimes a man and sometimes a god, or rather both one and the other—a divine incarnation, a man-god—who came into the world to enlighten men, to *redeem them,* and to indicate to them the way of safety. This idea of *redemption by a divine incarnation* is so general and popular among the Buddhists, that during our travels in Upper Asia we everywhere found it expressed in a neat formula. If we addressed to a Mongol or a Thibetan the question 'Who is Buddha?' he would immediately reply: '*The Saviour of Men!*'"[4]

According to Prof. Max Müller, Buddha is reported as saying:

"*Let all the sins that were committed in this world fall on me, that the world may be delivered.*"[5]

The *Indians* are no strangers to the doctrine of *original sin.* It is their invariable belief that *man is a fallen being;* admitted by them from time immemorial.[6] And what we have seen concerning their beliefs in *Crishna* and *Buddha* unmistakably shows a belief in a *divine Saviour,* who *redeems man,* and takes upon himself the sins of the world; so that "*Buddha* paid it all, all to him is due."[7]

[1] Quoted in Anacalypsis, vol. ii. p. 118.
[2] Bunsen's Angel-Messiah, p. 20.
[3] Beal: Hist. Buddha, p. 33.
[4] Huc's Travels, vol. i. pp. 326, 327.
[5] Müller: Hist. Sanscrit Literature, p. 80.
[6] See Maurice: Indian Antiquities, vol. v. p. 95, and Williams: Hinduism, p. 214.
[7] "He in mercy left paradise, and came down to earth, because he was filled with compassion for the sins and miseries of mankind. He sought to lead them into better paths, *and took their sufferings upon himself, that he might* expiate *their crimes,* and mitigate the punishment they must otherwise inevitably undergo." (Prog. Relig. Ideas, vol. ii. p. 86.)

"The object of his mission on earth was to instruct those who were straying from the right path, *expiate the sins of mortals by his own sufferings,* and produce for them a happy entrance into another existence by obedience to his precepts and prayers in his name. They always speak of him as one with God from all eternity. His most common title is '*The Saviour of the World.*'" (Ibid. vol. i. p. 247.)

The idea of redemption through the sufferings and death of a *Divine Saviour*, is to be found even in the ancient religions of China. One of their five sacred volumes, called the *Y-King*, says, in speaking of *Tien, the " Holy One ":*

" The *Holy One* will unite in himself all the virtues of heaven and earth. By his justice the world will be re-established in the ways of righteousness. He will labor and suffer much. He must pass the great torrent, whose waves shall enter into his soul; *but he alone can offer up to the Lord a sacrifice worthy of him.*"[1]

An ancient commentator says :

" The common people sacrifice their lives to gain bread; the philosophers to gain reputation; the nobility to perpetuate their families. The *Holy One* (*Tien*) does not seek himself, but the good of others. *He dies to save the world.*"[2]

Tien, the Holy One, is always spoken of as one with God, existing with him from all eternity, "before anything was made."

Osiris and *Horus*, the Egyptian virgin-born gods, suffered death.[3] Mr. Bonwick, speaking of *Osiris*, says :

"He is one of the *Saviours* or deliverers of humanity, to be found in almost all lands." "In his efforts to do good, he encounters evil; in struggling with that he is overcome; he is killed."[4]

Alexander Murray says :

" *The Egyptian Saviour Osiris* was gratefully regarded as the great exemplar of self-sacrifice, in *giving his life for others.*"[5]

Sir J. G. Wilkinson says of him :

" The sufferings and death of *Osiris* were the great Mystery of the Egyptian religion, and some traces of it are perceptible among other peoples of antiquity. His being the *Divine Goodness*, and the abstract idea of 'good,' his manifestation upon earth (like a Hindoo god), his death and resurrection, and his office as judge of the dead in a future state, *look like the early revelation of a future manifestation of the deity converted into a mythological fable.*"[6]

Horus was also called " The Saviour." "As Horus Sneb, he is the *Redeemer*. He is the Lord of Life and the Eternal One."[7] He is also called " The Only-Begotten."[8]

Attys, who was called the " *Only Begotten Son*"[9] and "*Saviour,*" was worshiped by the Phrygians (who were regarded as one of the

---

[1] Qnoted in Preg. Relig. Ideas, vol. i. p. 211.
[2] Ibid.
[3] See Renouf : Religions of Ancient Egypt, p. 178.
[4] Bonwick : Egyptian Belief, p. 155.
[5] Murray : Manual of Mythology, p. 348.
[6] In Rawlinson's Herodotus, vol. ii. p. 171. Quoted in Knight's Art and Mythology, p. 71.
[7] Bonwick : Egyptian Belief, p. 185.
[8] See Mysteries of Adoni, p. 88.
[9] See Knight : Ancient Art and Mythology, p. xxii. note.

oldest races of Asia Minor). He was represented by them as *a man tied to a tree*, at the foot of which was a *lamb*,[1] and, without doubt, also *as a man nailed to the tree, or stake*, for we find Lactantius making this Apollo of Miletus (anciently, the greatest and most flourishing city of Ionia, in Asia Minor) say that:

"He was a mortal according to the flesh; wise in miraculous works; but, being arrested by an armed force by command of the Chaldean judges, *he suffered a death made bitter with nails and stakes.*"[2]

In this god of the Phrygians, we again have the myth of the *crucified Saviour of Paganism.*

By referring to Mrs. Jameson's "History of Our Lord in Art,"[3] or to illustrations in chapter xl. this work, it will be seen that a common mode of representing a crucifixion was that of a man, tied with cords by the hands and feet, to an upright beam or stake. The *lamb*, spoken of above, which signifies considerable, we shall speak of in its proper place.

Tammuz, or *Adonis*, the Syrian and Jewish *Adonai* (in Hebrew " Our Lord "), was another *virgin-born* god, who suffered for mankind, and who had the title of *Saviour*. The accounts of his death are conflicting, just as it is with almost all of the so-called Saviours of mankind (*including the Christian Saviour*, as we shall hereafter see) one account, however, makes him a *crucified Saviour.*[4]

It is certain, however, that the ancients who honored him as their Lord and Saviour, celebrated, annually, a feast in commemoration of his death. An image, intended as a representation of their Lord, was laid on a bed or bier, and bewailed in mournful ditties—just as the Roman Catholics do at the present day in their " Good Friday " mass.

During this ceremony the priest murmured:

"*Trust ye in your Lord, for the pains which he endured, our salvation have procured.*"[5]

The Rev. Dr. Parkhurst, in his " Hebrew Lexicon," after referring to what we have just stated above, says:

"I find myself *obliged* to refer *Tammuz* to that class of idols which were originally designed to represent the promised Saviour, the Desire of all Nations. His other name, *Adonis*, is almost the very Hebrew *Adoni* or *Lord*, a well-known title of Christ."[6]

---

[1] Dupuis: Origin of Religious Belief, p. 255.
[2] Vol. ii.
[3] Lactant. Inst., div. iv. chap. xiii. in Anacalypsis, vol. i. p. 544.
[4] See chapter xxxix, this work.
[5] See Higgins: Anacalypsis, vol. ii. p. 114, and Taylor's Diegesis, p. 163.
[6] See the chapter on " The Resurrection of Jesus."

Prometheus was a crucified Saviour. He was "an immortal god, a friend of the human race, *who does not shrink even from sacrificing himself for their salvation.*"[1]

The tragedy of the crucifixion of Prometheus, written by Æschylus, was acted in Athens five hundred years before the Christian Era, and is by many considered to be the most ancient dramatic poem now in existence. The plot was derived from materials even at that time of an infinitely remote antiquity. Nothing was ever so exquisitely calculated to work upon the feelings of the spectators. No author ever displayed greater powers of poetry, with equal strength of judgment, in supporting through the piece the august character of the *Divine Sufferer.* The spectators themselves were unconsciously made a party to the interest of the scene: its hero was their friend, their benefactor, their creator, and their *Saviour;* his wrongs were incurred in their quarrel— *his sorrows were endured for their salvation;* " he was wounded for their transgressions, and bruised for their iniquities ; the chastisement of their peace was upon him, and by his stripes they were healed ;" " he was oppressed and afflicted, yet he opened not his mouth." The majesty of his silence, whilst the ministers of an offended god were *nailing him by the hands and feet to Mount Caucasus,*[2] could be only equaled by the modesty with which he relates, *while hanging with arms extended in the form of a cross,* his services to the human race, which had brought on him that horrible crucifixion.[3] "None, save myself," says he, " opposed his (Jove's) will,"

> " I dared;
> And boldly pleading saved them from destruction,
> Saved them from sinking to the realms of night.
> For this offense I bend beneath these pains,
> Dreadful to suffer, piteous to behold:
> For mercy to mankind I am not deem'd
> Worthy of mercy; but with ruthless hate
> In this uncouth appointment am fix'd here
> A spectacle dishonorable to Jove."[4]

---

[1] Chambers's Encyclo., art. "Prometheus."

[2] "*Prometheus* has been a favorite subject with the poets. He is represented as the friend of mankind, who interposed in their behalf when Jove was incensed against them." (Bulfinch : The Age of Fable, p. 32.)

" In the mythos relating to Prometheus, he always appears as the friend of the human race, suffering in its behalf the most fearful tortures." (John Fiske : Myths and Mythmakers, pp. 64, 65.) " Prometheus was *nailed* to the rocks on Mount Caucasus, *with arms*

extended." (Alexander Murray : Manual of Mythology, p. 82.) " Prometheus is said to have been *nailed up with arms extended,* near the Caspian Straits, on Mount Caucasus. The history of Prometheus on the Cathedral at Bordeaux (France) here receives its explanation." (Higgins : Anacalypsis, vol. ii. p. 113.)

[3] See Æschylus' "Prometheus Chained," Translated by the Rev. R. Potter : Harper & Bros., N. Y.

[4] Ibid. p. 82.

In the catastrophe of the plot, his especially professed friend, Oceanus, *the Fisherman*—as his name *Petræus* indicates,[1]—being unable to prevail on him to make his peace with Jupiter, by throwing the cause of human redemption out of his hands,[2] forsook him and fled. None remained to be witness of his dying agonies but the chorus of ever-amiable and ever-faithful which also bewailed and lamented him,[3] but were unable to subdue his inflexible philanthropy.[4]

In the words of Justin Martyr: "Suffering was common to all the sons of Jove." They were called the "Slain Ones," "Saviours," "Redeemers," &c.

Bacchus, the offspring of Jupiter and Semele,[5] was called the "*Saviour.*"[6] He was called the "*Only Begotten Son*,"[7] the "Slain One,"[8] the "Sin Bearer,"[9] the "Redeemer,"[10] &c. Evil having spread itself over the earth, through the inquisitiveness of Pandora, the Lord of the gods is begged to come to the relief of mankind. Jupiter lends a willing ear to the entreaties, "and wishes that his *son* should be the *redeemer* of the misfortunes of the world; *The Bacchus Saviour.* He promises to the earth a *Liberator* . . . The universe shall worship him, and shall praise in songs his blessings." In order to execute his purpose, Jupiter overshadows the beautiful young maiden—the virgin Semele—who becomes the mother of the *Redeemer.*[11]

"It is I (says the lord Bacchus to mankind), who guides you; it is I who protects you, and who saves you; I who am Alpha and Omega."[12]

Hercules, the son of Zeus, was called "The Saviour."[13] The words "Hercules the Saviour" were engraven on ancient coins and monuments.[14] He was also called "The Only Begotten," and the "Universal Word." He was re-absorbed into God. He was said by Ovid to be the "Self-produced," the Generator and Ruler of all things, and the Father of time.[15]

---

[1] Petræus was an interchangeable synonym of the name Oceanus.

[2] "Then Peter took him, and began to rebuke him, saying: Be it far from thee, Lord; this shall not be unto thee." (Matt. xvi. 22.)

[3] "And there followed him a great company of people, and of women, which also bewailed and lamented him." (Luke, xxiii. 27.)

[4] See Taylor's Diegesis, pp. 193, 194, or Potter's Æschylus.

[5] "They say that the god (Bacchus), the offspring of Zeus and Demeter, was torn to pieces." (Diodorus Siculus, in Knight, p. 156, *note*.)

[6] See Knight: Anct. Art and Mythology, p. 98, *note*. Dupuis: Origin of Religious Belief, 258. Higgins: Anacalypsis, vol. ii. p. 102.

[7] Knight: Ancient Art and Mythology, p.

xxii. *note*.

[8] Ibid.

[9] Bonwick: Egyptian Belief, p. 169.

[10] Dupuis: Origin of Religious Belief, p. 135.

[11] Ibid.

[12] Beausobre quotes the inscription on a monument of Bacchus, thus: "C'est moi, dit il, qui vous conduis, C'est moi, qui vous conserve, on qui vous sauve; Je sui Alpha et Omega, &c." (See chap. xxxix this work.)

[13] See Higgins: Anacalypsis, vol. i. p. 322. Dupuis: Origin of Religious Belief, p. 195. Bonwick: Egyptian Belief, p. 152. Dunlap: Mysteries of Adoni, p. 94.

[14] See Celtic Druids, Taylor's Diegesis, p. 153, and Montfaucon, vol. i.

[15] See Mysteries of Adoni, p. 91, and Higgins: Anac., vol. i. p. 322.

Æsculapius was distinguished by the epithet "The Saviour."[1] The temple erected to his memory in the city of Athens was called: "*The Temple of the Saviour.*"[2]

Apollo was distinguished by the epithet "*The Saviour.*"[3] In a hymn to *Apollo* he is called: "The willing *Saviour* of distressed mankind.'"[4]

Serapis was called "The Saviour."[5] He was considered by Hadrian, the Roman emperor (117–138 A. D.), and the Gentiles, to be the peculiar god of the Christians.[6] A *cross* was found under the ruins of his temple in Alexandria in Egypt.[7] Fig. No. 11 is a  representation of this Egyptian Saviour, taken from Murray's "Manual of Mythology." It certainly resembles the pictures of "the peculiar God of the Christians." It is very evident that the pictures of Christ Jesus, as we know them to-day, are simply the pictures of some of the Pagan gods, who were, for certain reasons which we shall speak of in a subsequent chapter, always represented with *long yellow or red hair, and a florid complexion.* If such a person as Jesus of Nazareth ever lived in the flesh, he was undoubtedly a *Jew*, and would therefore have *Jewish features;* this his pictures do not betray.[8]

FIG. 11.

Mithras, who was "Mediator between God and man,"[9] was called "The Saviour." He was the peculiar god of the Persians, who believed that he had, by his sufferings, worked their salvation, and on this account he was called their *Saviour*.[10] He was also called "*The Logos.*"[11]

The Persians believed that they were tainted with *original sin*, owing to the fall of their first parents who were tempted by the evil one in the form of a serpent.[12]

They considered their law-giver *Zoroaster* to be also a *Divine Messenger*, sent to redeem men from their evil ways, and they always worshiped his memory. To this day his followers mention him with the greatest reverence, calling him "*The Immortal Zoroaster*,"

[1] See Taylor's Diegesis, p. 153.
[2] See the chapter on "Miracles of Jesus."
[3] See Dupuis : Origin of Religious Belief, p. 264.
[4] See Monumental Christianity, p. 186.
[5] See Higgins : Anacalypsis, vol. ii. p. 15.
[6] See Giles : Hebrew and Christian Records, vol. ii. p. 86.
[7] See Anacalypsis, vol. ii. p. 15, and *our* chapter on Christian Symbols.
[8] This subject will be referred to again in chapter xxxix.
[9] See Dunlap's Spirit Hist., pp. 237, 241, 242, and Mysteries of Adoni, p. 123, *note*.
[10] See Higgins : Anacalypsis, vol. ii. p. 99.
[11] See Dunlap's Son of the Man, p. 20.
"According to the most ancient tradition of the East-Iranians recorded in the *Zend-Avesta*, the God of Light (Ormuzd) communicated his mysteries to some men through his *Word*." (Bunsen's Angel-Messiah, p. 75.)
[12] Wake : Phallism, &c., p. 47.

" *The Blessed Zoroaster*," " The First-Born of the Eternal One," &c.'

" In the life of Zoroaster the common mythos is apparent. He was born in innocence, of an immaculate conception, of a ray of the Divine Reason. As soon as he was born, the glory arising from his body enlightened the room, and he laughed at his mother. He was called a *Splendid Light from the Tree of Knowledge*, and, in fine, he or his soul was *suspensus a lingo*, hung upon a tree, and this was the Tree of Knowledge."²

How much this resembles " the mystery which hath been hid from ages and from generations, but now is made manifest to his saints."³

Hermes was called " *The Saviour*." On the altar of Pepi (B. C. 3500) are to be found prayers to Hermes—" *He who is the good Saviour*."⁴ He was also called " *The Logos*." The church fathers, Hippolytus, Justin Martyr, and Plutarch (*de Iside et Osir*) assert that the *Logos* is *Hermes*.⁵ The term " *Logos*" is Greek, and signifies literally " *Word*."⁶ He was also "*The Messenger of God*."⁷

Dr. Inman says :

"There are few words which strike more strongly upon the senses of an inquirer into the nature of ancient faiths, than *Salvation* and *Saviour*. Both were used long before the birth of Christ, and they are still common among those who never heard of Jesus, or of that which is known among us as the Gospels."⁸

He also tells us that there is a very remarkable figure copied in Payne Knight's work, in which we see on a man's shoulders a *cock's* head, whilst on the pediment are placed the words : " *The Saviour of the World*."⁹

Besides the titles of " God's First-Born," " Only Begotten," the " Mediator," the " Shepherd," the " Advocate," the " Paraclete or Comforter," the " Son of God," the " Logos," &c.,¹⁰ being applied to heathen virgin-born gods, before the time assigned for the birth of Jesus of Nazareth, we have also that of *Christ* and *Jesus*.

---

¹ Prog. Relig. Ideas, vol. i. pp. 258, 259.

² Malcom : Hist. Persia, vol. i. Ap. p. 494 ; Nimrod, vol. ii. p. 31. Anacalypsis, vol. i. p. 649.

³ Col. i. 26.

⁴ See Bonwick : Egyptian Belief, p. 102.

⁵ See Dunlap's Son of the Man, p. 39, *marginal note*.

⁶ " In the beginning was the *Word*, and the *Word* was with God, and the *Word* was God." (John, i. 1.)

⁷ See Bell's Pantheon, vol. ii. 69 and 71.

⁸ Inman : Ancient Faiths, vol. ii. p. 652.

⁹ Ibid. vol. i. p. 537.

¹⁰ See Bunsen's Angel-Messiah, p. 119. Knight's Ancient Art and Mythology, pp. xxii. and 98. Dunlap's Son of the Man, p. 71, and Spirit History, pp. 183, 205, 206, 249. Bible for Learners, vol. ii. p. 25. Isis Unveiled, vol. ii. pp. 195, 237, 516, besides the authorities already cited.

Cyrus, King of Persia, was called the "Christ," or the "Anointed of God."[1] As Dr. Giles says, "*Christ*" is "a name having no spiritual signification, and importing nothing more than an *ordinary surname.*"[2] The worshipers of *Serapis* were called "*Christians,*" and those devoted to Serapis were called "Bishops of Christ."[3] *Eusebius*, the ecclesiastical historian, says, that the names of "Jesus" and "Christ," were both known and honored among the ancients.[4]

Mithras was called the "Anointed" or the "Christ;"[5] and *Horus, Mano, Mithras, Bel-Minor, Iao, Adoni,* &c., were each of them "God of Light," "Light of the World," the "Anointed," or the "Christ."[6]

It is said that Peter called his Master *the Christ*, whereupon "he straightway charged them (the disciples), and commanded them to tell no man *that thing.*"[7]

The title of "*Christ*" or "The Anointed," was held by the kings of Israel. "Touch not my Christ and do my prophets no harm," says the Psalmist.[8]

The term "Christ" was applied to religious teachers, leaders of factions, necromancers or wonder-workers, &c. This is seen by the passage in *Matthew*, where the writer says:

'There shall arise false Christs and false prophets, and shall show great signs and wonders, insomuch that, if it were possible, they shall deceive the very elect."[9]

The virgin-born Crishna and Buddha were incarnations of Vishnu, called Avatars. An Avatar is an *Angel-Messiah*, a *God-man*, a CHRIST; for the word *Christ* is from the Greek *Christos*, an *Anointed One*, a *Messiah*.

The name *Jesus*, which is pronounced in Hebrew *Yezua*, and is sometimes Grecized into *Jason*, was very common. After the Captivity it occurs quite frequently, and is interchanged with the name *Joshua*. Indeed Joshua, the successor of Moses, is called Jesus in the New Testament more than once,[10] though the meaning of the two names is not really quite the same. We know of a Jesus, son of Sirach, a writer of proverbs, whose collection is

---

[1] See Bunsen's Bible Chronology, p. 5. Keys of St. Peter, 125. Volney's Ruins, p. 168.
[2] Giles : Hebrew and Christian Records, p. 64, vol. ii.
[3] Ibid. p. 86, and Taylor's Diegesis, pp. 202, 206, 407. Dupuis : p. 267.
[4] Eusebius : Eccl. Hist., lib. 1, ch. iv.
[5] See Dunlap's Son of the Man, p. 78.
[6] See Ibid. p. 39.

[7] Luke, iv. 21.
[8] Psalm, cv. 15. The term "an *Anointed One,*" which we use in English, is *Christos* in Greek, and *Messiah* in Hebrew. (See Bible for Learners, and Religion of Israel, p. 147.)
[9] Matthew, xxiv. 24.
[10] Acts, vii. 45 ; Hebrews, iv. 8 ; compare Nehemiah, viii. 17.

preserved among the apocryphal books of the Old Testament. The notorious *Barabbas*[1] or *son of Abbas*, was himself called Jesus. Among Paul's opponents we find a magician called Elymas, *the Son of Jesus*. Among the early Christians a certain Jesus, also called Justus, appears. Flavius Josephus mentions more than *ten* distinct persons—priests, robbers, peasants, and others—who bore the name of Jesus, all of whom lived during the last century of the Jewish state.[2]

To return now to our theme—*crucified gods before the time of Jesus of Nazareth.*

The holy Father *Minucius Felix*, in his *Octavius*, written as late as A. D. 211, indignantly *resents the supposition that the sign of the cross should be considered exclusively as a Christian symbol*, and represents his advocate of the Christian argument as retorting on an infidel opponent. His words are:

"As for the adoration of *crosses* which you (*Pagans*) object against us (*Christians*), I must tell you, *that we neither adore crosses nor desire them ; you it is, ye Pagans* . . . who are the most likely people to adore wooden crosses . . . for what else are your ensigns, flags, and standards, *but crosses gilt and beautiful.* Your victorious trophies not only represent a simple cross, *but a cross with a man upon it.*"[3]

The existence, in the writings of Minucius Felix, of this passage, is probably owing to an oversight of the destroyers of all evidences against the Christian religion that could be had. The practice of the Romans, here alluded to, of carrying *a cross with a man on it*, or, in other words, a *crucifix*, has evidently been concealed from us by the careful destruction of such of their works as alluded to it. The priests had everything their own way for centuries, and to destroy what was evidence against their claims was a very simple matter.

It is very evident that this celebrated Christian Father alludes to some Gentile mystery, of which the prudence of his successors has deprived us. When we compare this with the fact that for centuries after the time assigned for the birth of Christ Jesus, he was not represented as a man on a cross, and that the Christians did not have such a thing as a *crucifix*, we are inclined to think that the effigies of a black or *dark-skinned crucified man*, which were to be seen in many places in Italy even during the last century, may have had something to do with it.[4]

---

[1] He who, it is said, was liberated at the time of the crucifixion of Jesus of Nazareth.

[2] See Bible for Learners, vol. iii. p. 60.

[3] Octavius, c. xxix.

[4] See Anacalypsis, vol ii. p. 116.

While speaking of "*a cross with a man on it*" as being carried by the Pagan Romans as a *standard*, we might mention the fact, related by Arrian the historian,[1] that the troops of Porus, in their war with Alexander the Great, carried on their standards *the figure of a man*.[2] Here is evidently the *crucifix standard* again.

"This must have been (says Mr. Higgins) a Staurobates or Salivahana, and looks very like the figure of a man carried on their standards by the Romans. This was similar to the dove carried on the standards of the Assyrians. This must have been the crucifix of Nepaul."[3]

Tertullian, a Christian Father of the second and third centuries, writing to the Pagans, says:

"The origin of *your* gods is derived from *figures moulded on a cross*. All those rows of *images on your standards* are the appendages of crosses; those hangings on your standards and banners are the robes of crosses."[4]

We have it then, on the authority of a Christian Father, as late as A. D. 211, that the Christians "*neither adored crosses nor desired them*," but that the *Pagans* "adored crosses," and not that alone, but "*a cross with a man upon it*." This we shall presently find to be the case. Jesus, in those days, nor for centuries after, was *not* represented as a *man on a cross*. He was represented as a *lamb*, and the adoration of the crucifix, by the Christians, was a later addition to their religion. But this we shall treat of in its place.

We may now ask the question, who was this *crucified man* whom the Pagans "*adored*" before and after the time of Jesus of Nazareth? Who did the crucifix represent? It was, undoubtedly, "the Saviour crucified for the salvation of mankind," long before the Christian Era, *whose effigies were to be seen in many places all over Italy*. These Pagan crucifixes were either destroyed, corrupted, or adopted; the latter was the case with many ancient paintings of the *Bambino*,[5] on which may be seen the words *Deo Soli*. Now, these two words can never apply to Christ Jesus. He was *not Deus Solus*, in any sense, according to the idiom of the Latin language, and the Romish faith. Whether we construe the words to "the only God," or "God alone," they are equally heretical. No priest, in any age of the Church, would have thought of putting them there; *but finding them there*, they tolerated them.

In the "*Celtic Druids*," Mr. Higgins describes a *crucifix*, a *lamb*, and an *elephant*, which was cut upon the "fire tower"—so-

---

[1] In his *History of the Campaigns of Alexander.*
[2] See Anacalypsis, vol. ii. p. 118.
[3] Ibid.

[4] Apol. c. 16 ; Ad Nationes, c. xii.
[5] See the chapter on "The Worship of the Virgin."

called—at Brechin, a town of Forfarshire, in Scotland. Although they appeared to be of very ancient date, he supposed, at that time, that they were modern, and belonged to Christianity, but some years afterwards, he wrote as follows:

"I now doubt (the modern date of the tower), for we have, over and over again, seen the crucified man before Christ. We have also found 'The Lamb that taketh away the sins of. the world,' among the Carnutes of Gaul, before the time of Christ; and when I contemplate these, and the *Elephant* or *Ganesa*,[1] and the *Ring*[2] and its Cobra,[3] *Linga*,[4] *Iona*,[5] and Nandies, found not far from the tower, on the estate of Lord Castles, with the Colidei, the island of Iona, and Ii, . . . I am induced to doubt my former conclusions. The Elephant, the Ganesa of India, is a very stubborn fellow to be found here. The Ring, too, when joined with other matters, I cannot get over. *All these superstitions must have come from India.*"[6]

On one of the Irish "round towers" is to be seen *a crucifix of unmistakable Asiatic origin.*[7]

If we turn to the New World, we shall find, strange though it may appear, that the ancient *Mexicans* and *Peruvians* worshiped a *crucified Saviour.* This was the virgin-born *Quetzalcoatle* whose crucifixion is represented in the paintings of the "*Codex Borgianus*," and the "*Codex Vaticanus.*"

These paintings illustrate the religious opinions of the ancient Mexicans, and were copied from the hieroglyphics found in Mexico. The Spaniards destroyed nearly all the books, ancient monuments and paintings which they could find; had it not been for this, much more regarding the religion of the ancient Mexicans would have been handed down to us. Many chapters were also taken—by the Spanish authorities—from the writings of the first historians who wrote on ancient Mexico. *All manuscripts had to be inspected previous to being published.* Anything found among these heathens resembling the religion of the Christians, was destroyed when possible.[8]

The first Spanish monks who went to Mexico were surprised to find the *crucifix* among the heathen inhabitants, and upon inquiring what it meant, were told that it was a representation of

---

[1] *Ganesa* is the *Indian* God of Wisdom. (See Asiatic Researches. vol. i.)

[2] The *Ring* and circle was an emblem of god, or eternity, among the *Hindoos*. (See Lundy : Monumental Christianity, p. 87.)

[3] The Cobra, or hooded snake, is a native of the *East Indies*, where it is held as sacred. (See Knight : Anct. Art and Mytho., p. 16, and Fergusson's Tree and Serpent Worship.

[4] *Linga* denotes, in the sectarian worship of the *Hindoos*, the *Phallus*, an emblem of the male or generative power of nature.

[5] *Iona*, or *Yoni*, is the counterpart of Linga, *i. e.*, an emblem of the female generative power. We have seen that these were attached to the effigies of the *Hindoo* crucified Saviour, Crishna.

[6] Anacalypsis, vol. ii. p. 130.

[7] See Lundy : Monumental Christianity, pp. 253, 254, 255.

[8] See Kingsborough : Mexican Antiquities, vol. vi. pp. 165 and 179.

Bacob (Quetzalcoatle), the Son of God, who was put to death by *Eopuco.* They said that he was placed on a beam of wood, *with his arms stretched out,* and that he died there.[1]

Lord Kingsborough, from whose very learned and elaborate work we have taken the above, says:

"Being questioned as to the manner in which they became acquainted with these things, they replied that the lords instructed their sons in them, and that thus this doctrine descended from one to another."[2]

Sometimes Quetzalcoatle or Bacob is represented as *tied* to the cross—just as we have seen that *Attys* was represented by the Phrygians—and at other times he is represented "in the attitude of a person crucified, with impressions of nail-holes in his hands and feet, but not actually upon a cross"—just as we have found the Hindoo *Crishna,* and as he is represented in Fig. No. 8. Beneath *this* representation of Quetzalcoatle crucified, is an image of Death, which an angry serpent seems threatening to devour.[3]

On the 73d page of the Borgian MS., he is represented *crucified on a cross of the Greek form.* In this print there are also *impressions of nails* to be seen on the *feet and hands,* and his body is strangely covered with *suns.*[4]

In vol. ii. plate 75, the god is crucified in a circle of nineteen figures, and a *serpent* is depriving him of the organs of generation.

Lord Kingsborough, commenting on these paintings, says:

"It is remarkable that in these Mexican paintings the faces of many of the figures are *black,* and that the visage of Quetzalcoatle is frequently painted in a very deformed manner."[5]

His lordship further tells us that (according to the belief of the ancient Mexicans), "the death of Quetzalcoatle upon the cross" was "*an atonement for the sins of mankind.*"[6]

Dr. Daniel Brinton, in his "*Myths of the New World,*" tells us that the *Aztecs* had a feast which they celebrated "*in the early spring,*" when "*victims were nailed to a cross and shot with an arrow.*"[7]

Alexander Von Humboldt, in his "*American Researches,*" also speaks of this feast, when the Mexicans crucified a man, and pierced him with an arrow.[8]

---

[1] See Kingsborough : Mexican Antiquities, vol. vi. p. 166.

[2] Ibid. p. 162.

[3] Ibid. p. 161.

[4] Ibid. p. 167.

[5] Ibid. p. 167.

[6] Ibid. p. 166.

[7] Brinton : Myths of the New World, p. 95.

[8] See, also, Monumental Christianity, p. 393.

"Once a year the ancient Mexicans made an image of one of their gods, which was pierced by an arrow, shot by a priest of Quetzalcoatle." (Dunlap's Spirit Hist., 207.)

The author of *Monumental Christianity*, speaking of this, says :

" Here is the old story of the *Prometheus crucified* on the Caucasus, *and of all other Pagan crucifixions of the young incarnate divinities of India, Persia, Asia Minor and Egypt.*"[1]

This we believe ; *but how did this myth get there ?* He does not say, but we shall attempt to show, in a future chapter, how *this* and *other* myths of Eastern origin became known in the New World.[2]

It must not be forgotten, in connection with what we have seen concerning the Mexican crucified god being sometimes represented as *black*, and the feast when the *crucified man* was shot with an arrow, that effigies of a *black crucified man were found in Italy ;* that Crishna, the crucified, is very often represented *black ;* and that *Crishna* was shot with an arrow.

Crosses were also found in *Yucatan*, as well as Mexico, *with a man upon them.*[3] Cogolludo, in his " History of Yucatan," speaking of a crucifix found there, says :

" Don Eugenio de Alcantara (one of the true teachers of the Gospel), told me, not only once, that I might safely write that the Indians of Cozumel possessed this holy cross in the time of their paganism ; and that some years had elapsed since it was brought to Medira ; for having heard from many persons what was reported of it, he had made particular inquiries of some very old Indians who resided there, who assured him that it was the fact."

He then speaks of the difficulty in accounting for this crucifix being found among the Indians of Cozumel, and ends by saying :

"But if it be considered that these Indians believed that the Son of God, whom they called Bacob, *had died upon a cross, with his arms stretched out upon it*, it cannot appear so difficult a matter to comprehend that they should have formed his image according to the religious creed which they possessed."[4]

We shall find, in another chapter, that these virgin-born *"Saviours"* and "Slain Ones ;" Crishna, Osiris, Horus, Attys, Adonis, Bacchus, &c.—whether torn in pieces, killed by a boar, or crucified—*will all melt into* ONE.

We now come to a very important fact not generally known, namely : *There are no early representations of Christ Jesus suffering on the cross.*

---

[1] Monumental Christianity, p. 393.
[2] See Appendix A.
[3] See Monumental Christianity, p. 390, and

Mexican Antiquities, vol. vi. p. 169.
[4] Quoted by Lord Kingsborough : Mexican Antiquities, vol. vi. p. 172.

Rev. J. P. Lundy, speaking of this, says:

"Why should a fact so well known to the heathen as the crucifixion be concealed? *And yet its actual realistic representation never once occurs in the monuments of Christianity, for more than six or seven centuries.*"[1]

Mrs. Jameson, in her "History of Our Lord in Art," says:

"The crucifixion is *not* one of the subjects of early Christianity. The death of our Lord was represented by various *types*, but *never in its actual form.*

"The *earliest* instances of the *crucifixion* are found in illustrated manuscripts of various countries, and in those *ivory and enameled forms* which are described in the Introduction. Some of these are ascertained, by historical or by internal evidence, to have been executed in the *ninth century*, there is one also, of an extraordinary rude and fantastic character, in a MS. in the ancient library of St. Galle, which is ascertained to be of the *eighth century*. *At all events, there seems no just grounds at present for assigning an earlier date.*"[2]

"Early Christian art, such as it appears in the bas-reliefs on sarcophagi, gave but one solitary incident from the story of Our Lord's Passion, *and that utterly divested of all circumstances of suffering.* Our Lord is represented as young and beautiful, free from bonds, with no ' *accursed tree*' on his shoulders."[3]

The oldest representation of Christ Jesus was a figure of a *lamb*,[4] to which sometimes a vase was added, into which his blood flowed, and at other times couched at the foot of a cross. *This custom subsisted up to the year* 680, *and until the pontificate of Agathon, during the reign of Constantine Pogonat.* By the sixth synod of Constantinople (canon 82) it was ordained that instead of the ancient symbol, which had been the LAMB, *the figure of a man fastened to a cross* (such as the *Pagans* had adored), should be represented. All this was confirmed by Pope Adrian I.[5]

A simple cross, which was the symbol of eternal life, or of salvation, among the ancients, was sometimes, as we have seen, placed alongside of the *Lamb.* In the course of time, the *Lamb* was put on the cross, as the ancient *Israelites* had put the paschal lamb centuries before,[6] and then, as we have seen, they put a *man* upon it.

Christ Jesus is also represented in early art as the " Good Shepherd," that is, as a young man with a lamb on his shoulders.[7]

---

[1] Monumental Christianity, p. 246.
[2] History of Our Lord in Art, vol. ii. p. 137.
[3] Ibid. p. 317.
[4] See Illustrations in Ibid. vol. i.
[5] See Dupuis : Origin of Religious Belief, p. 252. Higgins : Anacalypsis, vol. ii. 111, and Monumental Christianity, p. 246, *et seq.*
[6] The paschal lamb was roasted on a *cross*, by ancient Israel, and is still so done by the Samaritans at Nablous. (See Lundy's Monumental Christianity, pp. 19 and 247.)
"The *lamb* slain (at the feast of the pass-

over) was roasted whole, with two spits thrust through it—one lengthwise, and one transversely —crossing each other near the fore legs ; so that the animal was, in a manner, *crucified.* Not a bone of it might be broken—a circumstance strongly representing the sufferings of our Lord Jesus. *the passover slain for us.*" (Barnes's Notes, vol. i. p. 292.)

[7] See King : The Gnostics and their Remains, p. 138. Also, Monumental Christianity, and Jameson's History of Our Lord in Art, for illustrations.

This is just the manner in which the Pagan Apollo, Mercury and others were represented centuries before.[1]

Mrs. Jameson says:

"*Mercury* attired as a *shepherd*, with a *ram* on his shoulders, borne in the same manner as in many of the Christian representations, was no unfrequent object (in ancient art) and in some instances led to a difficulty in distinguishing between the two,"[2] that is, between *Mercury* and *Christ Jesus*.

M. Renan says:

"The Good Shepherd of the catacombs in Rome is a copy from the *Aristeus*, or from the *Apollo Nomius*, which figured in the same posture on the *Pagan* sarcophagi; and still carries the flute of *Pan*, in the midst of the four half-naked seasons."[3]

The Egyptian Saviour *Horus* was called the "Shepherd of the People."[4]

The Hindoo Saviour *Crishna* was called the "Royal Good Shepherd."[5]

We have seen, then, on the authority of a Christian writer who has made the subject a special study, that, "there seems no just grounds at present for assigning an earlier date," for the "earliest instances of the crucifixion" of Christ Jesus, represented in art, than the *eighth* or *ninth* century. Now, a few words in regard to *what these crucifixes looked like*. If the reader imagines that the crucifixes which are familiar to us at the present day are similar to those early ones, we would inform him that such is not the case. The earliest artists of the crucifixion represent the Christian Saviour as *young and beardless*, always without the crown of thorns, alive, and erect, apparently elate; no signs of bodily suffering are there.[6]

On page 151, plate 181, of Jameson's "History of Our Lord in Art" (vol. ii.), he is represented standing on a foot-rest on the cross, alive, and eyes open. Again, on page 330, plate 253, he is represented standing "with body upright and arms extended straight, with *no nails, no wounds, no crown of thorns*—frequently clothed, and with a regal crown—a God, young and beautiful, hanging, as it were, without compulsion or pain."

On page 167, plate 188, are to be seen "the thieves *bound* to their

---

[1] See King's Gnostics, p. 178. Knight: Ancient Art and Mythology, p. xxii., and Jameson's History of Our Lord in Art, ii. 340.

[2] Jameson: Hist. of Our Lord in Art, p. 340, vol. ii.

[3] Quoted in Knight: Ancient Art and My-thology, p. xxii. *note*.

[4] Dunlap: Spirit Hist., p. 185.

[5] See chapter xvii. and vol. ii. Hist. Hindostan.

[6] See Jameson's Hist. of Our Lord in Art, vol. ii. p. 142.

cross (*which is simply an upright beam, without cross-bars*), with
the figure of the Lord *standing* between them." He is not bound
nor nailed to a cross; no cross is there. He is simply standing
erect in the form of a cross. This is a representation of what is
styled, "*Early crucifixion with thieves.*" On page 173, plate 190,
we have a representation of the crucifixion, in which Jesus and the
thieves are represented crucified on the Egyptian *tau* (see Fig.
No. 12). The thieves are *tied*, but the man-god is *nailed* to the
cross. A similar representation may be seen on page 189, plate
198.

On page 155, plate 183, there is a representation of what is
called " Virgin and St. John at foot of *cross*," but this *cross* is simply *an upright beam* (as Fig. No. 13). There are no cross-bars
attached. On page 167, plate 188, the thieves are *tied* to an upright beam (as Fig. 13), and Jesus stands between them, *with arms
extended in the form of a cross*, as the Hindoo Crishna is to be
seen in Fig. No. 8. On page 157, plate 185, Jesus is represented
crucified on the Egyptian cross (as No. 12).

Some ancient crucifixes represent the Christian Saviour crucified on a cross similar in form to the Roman figure which stands for
the number *ten* (see Fig. No. 14). Thus we see that there was
no uniformity in representing the " cross of Christ," among the
early Christians; even the cross which Constantine put on his
" Labarum," or sacred banner, was nothing more than the monogram of the Pagan god Osiris (Fig. No. 15),[1] as we shall see in a
subsequent chapter.

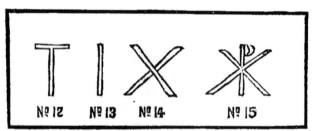

The dogma of the *vicarious atonement* has met with no success
whatever among the Jews. The reason for this is very evident.
The idea of vicarious atonement, in any form, is contrary to Jew-

---

[1] " It would be difficult to prove that the
cross of Constantine was of the simple construction as now understood. . . . As regards the *Labarum*, the coins of the time, in
which it is especially set forth, prove that the
so-called cross upon it was nothing else than
the same ever-recurring monogram of Christ"
(that is, the XP). (History of Our Lord in Art,
vol. ii. p. 316. See also, Smith's Bible Dictionary, art. "Labarum.")

ish ethics, but it is in full accord with the *Gentile.* The *law* ordains that[1] "every man shall be put to death for *his own* sin," and not for the sin or crime committed by any other person. No ransom should protect the murderer against the arm of justice.[2] The principle of equal rights and equal responsibilities is fundamental in the law. If the law of *God*—for as such it is received—denounces the vicarious atonement, viz., *to slaughter an innocent person to atone for the crimes of others,* then God must abhor it. What is more, Jesus is said to have sanctioned this law, for is he not made to say: "Think not that I am come to destroy the law, or the prophets: I am not come to destroy, but to fulfill. For verily I say unto you, Till heaven and earth pass, one jot or one tittle shall in no wise pass from the law."[3]

"Salvation is and can be nothing else than learning the laws of life and keeping them. There is, in the modern world, neither place nor need for any of the theological 'schemes of salvation' or theological 'Saviours.' No wrath of either God or devil stands in man's way; and therefore no 'sacrifice' is needed to get them out of the way. Jesus saves only as he helps men know and keep God's laws. Thousands of other men, in their degree, are Saviours in precisely the same way. As there has been no 'fall of man,' all the hundreds of theological devices for obviating its supposed effects are only imaginary cures for imaginary ills. What man does need is to be taught the necessary laws of life, and have brought to bear upon him adequate motives for obeying them. To know and keep God's laws is being reconciled to him. This is health; and out of health—that is, the perfect condition of the whole man, called holiness or wholeness—comes happiness, in this world and in all worlds."

---

[1] Deut. xxiv. 16.　　[2] Num. xxv. 31-34.　　[3] Matt. v. 17, 18.

CHAPTER XXI.

THE DARKNESS AT THE CRUCIFIXION.

THE *Luke* narrator informs us that at the time of the death of Christ Jesus, the sun was darkened, and there was darkness over the earth from the sixth until the ninth hour; also the veil of the temple was rent in the midst.[1]

The *Matthew* narrator, in addition to this, tells us that:

"The earth did quake, and the rocks were rent, and the graves were opened, *and many bodies of the saints which slept arose, and came out of their graves* . . . and went into the holy city and appeared unto many."[2]

" *His star* " having shone at the time of his birth, and his having been born in a miraculous manner, it was necessary that at the death of Christ Jesus, something miraculous should happen. Something of an unusual nature had happened at the time of the death of other supernatural beings, therefore something must happen at *his* death; *the myth would not have been complete without it.* In the words of Viscount Amberly : "The darkness from the sixth to the ninth hour, the rending of the temple veil, the earthquake, the rending of the rocks, *are altogether like the prodigies attending the decease of other great men.*"[3]

The Rev. Dr. Geikie, one of the most orthodox writers, says :[4]

"It is impossible to explain the *origin* of this darkness. The passover moon was then at the full, so that it could not have been an *eclipse.* The early Fathers, relying on a notice of *an* eclipse that *seemed* to coincide in time, though it really *did not,* fancied that the darkness was caused by it, but incorrectly."

Perhaps " the *origin* of this darkness " may be explained from what we shall now see.

At the time of the death of the Hindoo Saviour *Crishna,* there

---

[1] Luke, xxiii. 44, 45.
[2] Matthew, xxvii. 51-53.

[3] Amberly : Analysis of Religious Belief, p. 268. [4] Life of Christ, vol. ii. p. 643.

came calamities and bad omens of every kind. A black circle surrounded the moon, *and the sun was darkened at noon-day ;* the sky rained fire and ashes; flames burned dusky and livid; demons committed depredations on earth ; at sunrise and sunset, thousands of figures were seen skirmishing in the air; spirits were to be seen on all sides.[1]

When the conflict began between *Buddha,* the Saviour of the World, and the Prince of Evil, *a thousand appalling meteors fell; clouds and darkness prevailed.* Even this earth, with the oceans and mountains it contains, though it is unconscious, *quaked like a conscious being*—like a fond bride when forcibly torn from her bridegroom—like the festoons of a vine shaken under the blast of a whirlwind. The ocean rose under the vibration of this earthquake; rivers flowed back toward their sources; peaks of lofty mountains, where countless trees had grown for ages, rolled crumbling to the earth ; a fierce storm howled all around; the roar of the concussion became terrific ; *the very sun enveloped itself in awful darkness, and a host of headless spirits filled the air.*[2]

When *Prometheus* was crucified on Mount Caucasus, *the whole frame of nature became convulsed.* The earth did quake, thunder roared, lightning flashed, the wild winds rent the vexed air, the boisterous billows rose, and the dissolution of the universe seemed to be threatened.[3]

The ancient Greeks and Romans, says Canon Farrar,[4] had always considered that the *births* and *deaths* of great men were announced by *celestial signs.* We therefore find that at the death of *Romulus,* the founder of Rome, the sun was darkened, *and there was darkness over the face of the earth for the space of six hours.*[5]

When *Julius Cæsar,* who was the son of a god, was murdered, there was a darkness over the earth, *the sun being eclipsed for the space of six hours.*[6]

This is spoken of by *Virgil,* where he says:

" He (the Sun) covered his luminous head with a sooty darkness, And the impious ages feared eternal night."[7]

It is also referred to by Tibullus, Ovid, and Lucian (poets), Pliny, Appian, Dion Cassius, and Julius Obsequenes (historians.)[8]

---

[1] See Prog. Relig. Ideas, vol. i. p. 71.
[2] Rhys David's Buddhism, pp. 36, 37.
[3] See Potter's Æschylus, " Prometheus Chained," last stanza.
[4] Farrar's Life of Christ, p. 52.
[5] See Higgins: Anacalypsis, vol. i. pp.616,617.
[6] See Ibid. and Gibbon's Rome, vol. i. pp.

159 and 590, also Josephus : Jewish Antiquities, book xiv. ch. xii. and *note.*
[7] "Cum caput obscura nitidum ferrugine texit
Impiaque æternam timuerunt sæcula noctem."
[8] See Gibbon's Rome, vol. i. pp. 159 and 590.

When *Æsculapius* the Saviour was put to death, *the sun shone dimly from the heavens ;* the birds were silent in the darkened groves ; the trees bowed down their heads in sorrow ; and the hearts of all the sons of men fainted within them, because the healer of their pains and sickness lived no more upon the earth.[1]

When *Hercules* was dying, he said to the faithful female (Iole) who followed him to the last spot on earth on which he trod, " Weep not, my toil is done, and now is the time for rest. I shall see thee again in the bright land which is never trodden by the feet of night." Then, as the dying god expired, *darkness was on the face of the earth ;* from the high heaven came down the thick cloud, *and the din of its thunder crashed through the air.* In this manner, Zeus, the god of gods, carried his son home, and the halls of Olympus were opened to welcome the bright hero who rested from his mighty toil. There he now sits, clothed in a white robe, with a crown upon his head.[2]

When *Œdipus* was about to leave this world of pain and sorrow, he bade Antigone farewell, and said, " Weep not, my child, I am going to my home, and I rejoice to lay down the burden of my woe." Then there were *signs* in the heaven above and on the earth beneath, that the end was nigh at hand, *for the earth did quake, and the thunder roared* and echoed again and again through the sky.[3]

" The Romans had a god called *Quirinius.* His soul emanated from the sun, and was restored to it. He was begotten by the god of armies upon a *virgin* of the royal blood, and exposed by order of the jealous tyrant Amulius, and was preserved and educated among *shepherds.* He was torn to pieces at his death, when he ascended into heaven ; *upon which the sun was eclipsed or darkened.*"[4]

When *Alexander the Great* died, similar prodigies are said to have happened ; again, when foul murders were committed, it is said that the sun seemed to hide its face. This is illustrated in the story of *Atreus,* King of Mycenae, who foully murdered the children of his brother Thyestes. At that time, the sun, unable to endure a sight so horrible, *" turned his course backward and withdrew his light.*"[5]

At the time of the death of the virgin-born *Quetzalcoatle,* the

---

[1] Tales of Ancient Greece, p. 46.   [4] Anacalypsis, vol. i. p. 822.
[2] Ibid. pp. 61, 62.   [5] See Bell's Pantheon, vol. i. p. 106.
[3] Ibid. p. 270.

Mexican crucified Saviour, *the sun was darkened*, and withheld its light.[1]

Lord Kingsborough, speaking of this event, considers it very strange that the Mexicans should have preserved an account of it among their records, when "the great eclipse which sacred history records" is *not* recorded in profane history.

Gibbon, the historian, speaking of this phenomenon, says :

"Under the reign of Tiberius, the whole earth,[2] or at least a celebrated province of the Roman empire,[3] was involved in a perpetual darkness of three hours. Even this miraculous event, which ought to have excited the wonder, the curiosity, and the devotion of mankind, passed without notice in an age of science and history. It happened during the life-time of Seneca[4] and the elder Pliny,[5] who must have experienced the immediate effects, or received the earliest intelligence, of the prodigy. · Each of these philosophers, in a laborious work, has recorded all the great phenomena of nature, earthquakes, meteors, comets and eclipses, which his indefatigable curiosity could collect.[6] But the one and the other have omitted to mention the greatest phenomenon to which the mortal eye has been witness since the creation of the globe."[7]

This account of the darkness at the time of the death of Jesus of Nazareth, is one of the prodigies related in the New Testament which no Christian commentator has been able to make appear reasonable. The favorite theory is that it was a *natural* eclipse of the sun, which *happened* to take place at that particular time, but, if this was the case, there was nothing *supernatural* in the event, and it had nothing whatever to do with the death of Jesus. Again, it would be necessary to prove from other sources that such an event happened at that time, but this cannot be done. The argument from the duration of the darkness—*three hours*—is also of great force against such an occurrence having happened, *for an eclipse seldom lasts in great intensity more than six minutes.*

Even if it could be proved that an eclipse really happened at the time assigned for the crucifixion of Jesus, how about the earthquake, when the rocks were rent and the graves opened? and how about the "saints which slept" rising *bodily* and walking in the streets of the Holy City and *appearing to many?* Surely, the faith that would remove mountains,[8] is required here.

---

[1] See Kingsborough's Mexican Antiquities, vol. vi. p. 5.

[2] The Fathers of the Church seem to cover the whole earth with darkness, in which they are followed by most of the moderns. (Gibbon. Luke, xxiii. 44, says "*over all the earth.*")

[3] Origen (a Father of the third century) and a few modern critics, are desirous of confining it to the land of Judea. (Gibbon.)

[4] Seneca, a celebrated philosopher and historian, born in Spain a few years B. C., but educated in Rome, and became a "Roman."

[5] Pliny the elder, a celebrated Roman philosopher and historian, born about 23 A. D.

[6] Seneca : Quaest. Natur. l. i. 15, vi. l. vii. 17. Pliny : Hist. Natur. l. ii.

[7] Gibbon's Rome, i. 589, 590.

[8] Matt. xvi. 20.

Shakespeare has embalmed some traditions of the kind exactly analogous to the present case :

> " In the most high and palmy state of Rome,
> A little ere the mightiest Julius fell,
> The graves stood tenantless, and the sheeted dead
> Did squeak and gibber in the Roman streets."[1]

Belief in the influence of the *stars* over life and death, *and in special portents at the death of great men,* survived, indeed, to recent times. Chaucer abounds in allusions to it, and still later Shakespeare tells us :

> " When beggars die there are no comets seen;
> The heavens themselves blaze forth the death of princes."

It would seem that this superstition survives even to the present day, for it is well known that the dark and yellow atmosphere which settled over so much of the country, on the day of the removal of President Garfield from Washington to Long Branch, was sincerely held by hundreds of persons to be a death-warning sent from heaven, and there were numerous predictions that dissolution would take place before the train arrived at its destination.

As Mr. Greg remarks, there can, we think, remain little doubt in unprepossessed minds, that the whole legend in question was one of those intended to magnify Christ Jesus, which were. current in great numbers at the time the Matthew narrator wrote, and which he, with the usual want of discrimination and somewhat omnivorous tendency, which distinguished him as a compiler, admitted into his Gospel.

---

[1] Hamlet, act 1, s. 1.

CHAPTER XXII.

THE doctrine of Christ Jesus' descent into hell is emphatically part of the Christian belief, although not alluded to by Christian divines excepting when unavoidable.

In the first place, it is taught in the *Creed* of the Christians, wherein it says:

> "*He descended into hell, and on the third day he rose again from the dead.*"

The doctrine was also taught by the Fathers of the Church. St. Chrysostom (born 347 A. D.) asks:

> "Who but an infidel would deny that Christ was in hell?"[1]

And St. Clement of Alexandria, who flourished at the beginning of the third century, is equally clear and emphatic as to Jesus' descent into hell. He says:

> "The Lord preached the gospel to those in Hades, as well as to all in earth, in order that all might believe and be saved, wherever they were. If, then, the Lord descended to Hades for no other end but to preach the gospel, *as He did descend*, it was either to preach the gospel to all, or to the Hebrews only. If accordingly to all, then all who believe shall be saved, although they may be of the Gentiles, on making their profession there."[2]

Origen, who flourished during the latter part of the second, and beginning of the third centuries, also emphatically declares that Christ Jesus descended into hell.[3]

Ancient Christian works of art represent his descent into hell.[4]

The apocryphal gospels teach the doctrine of Christ Jesus' descent into hell, the object of which was to preach to those in bondage there, and to liberate the *saints* who had died before his advent on earth.

---

[1] Quoted by Bonwick: Egyptian Belief, p. 46.

[2] Strom. vi. c. 6.

[3] Contra Celsus. bk. ii. c. 43.

[4] See Jameson's Hist. of Our Lord in Art, vol. ii. pp. 354, 355.

On account of the sin committed by Adam in the Garden of Eden, all mankind were doomed, all had gone to hell—excepting those who had been translated to heaven—even those persons who were "after God's own heart," and who had belonged to his "chosen people." The coming of Christ Jesus into the world, however, made a change in the affairs of man. The *saints* were then liberated from their prison, and all those who believe in the efficacy of his name, shall escape hereafter the tortures of hell. This is the doctrine to be found in the apocryphal gospels, and was taught by the Fathers of the Church.[1]

In the "*Gospel of Nicodemus*" (apoc.) is to be found the whole story of Christ Jesus' descent into hell, and of his liberating the saints.

Satan, and the Prince of Hell, having heard that Jesus of Nazareth was about to descend to their domain, began to talk the matter over, as to what they should do, &c. While thus engaged, on a sudden, there was a voice as of thunder and the rushing of winds, saying: "Lift up your gates, O ye Princes, and be ye lifted up, O ye everlasting gates, and the King of Glory shall come in."

When the Prince of Hell heard this, he said to his impious officers: "Shut the brass gates . . . and make them fast with iron bars, and fight courageously."

The *saints* having heard what had been said on both sides, immediately spoke with a loud voice, saying: "Open thy gates, that the King of Glory may come in." The divine prophets, *David* and *Isaiah*, were particularly conspicuous in this protest against the intentions of the Prince of Hell.

Again the voice of Jesus was heard saying: "Lift up your gates, O Prince; and be ye lifted up, ye gates of hell, and the King of Glory will enter in." The Prince of Hell then cried out : "Who is the King of Glory?" upon which the prophet *David* commenced to reply to him, but while he was speaking, the mighty Lord Jesus appeared in the form of a man, and broke asunder the fetters which before could not be broken, and crying aloud, said: "Come to me, all ye saints, who were created in my image, who were condemned by the tree of the forbidden fruit . . . live now by the word of my cross."

Then presently all the saints were joined together, hand in hand, and the Lord Jesus laid hold on Adam's hand, and ascended from hell, and all the saints of God followed him.[2]

---

[1] See Jameson's Hist. of Our Lord in Art,   [2] Nicodemus : Apoc. ch. xvi. and xix.
vol. ii. pp. 250, 251.

When the saints arrived in paradise, two "very ancient men" met them, and were asked by the saints: "Who are ye, who have not been with us in hell, and have had your bodies placed in paradise?" One of these "very ancient men" answered and said: "I am *Enoch*, who was translated by the word of God, and this man who is with me is Elijah the Tishbite, who was translated in a fiery chariot."[1]

The doctrine of the descent into hell may be found alluded to in the *canonical* books; thus, for instance, in I. Peter:

"It is better, if the will of God be so, that ye suffer for well doing, than for evil doing. For Christ also hath suffered for sins, the just for the unjust, that he might bring us to God, being put to death in the flesh, but quickened by the spirit: *by which also he went and preached unto the spirits in prison*."[2]

Again, in "Acts," where the writer is speaking of David as a *prophet*, he says:

"He, seeing this before, spake of the resurrection of Christ, *that his soul was not left in hell*, neither his flesh did see corruption."[3]

The reason why Christ Jesus has been made to descend into hell, is because *it is a part of the universal mythos*, even the *three days'* duration. The *Saviours* of mankind had all done so, *he* must therefore do likewise.

Crishna, the Hindoo Saviour, *descended into hell*, for the purpose of raising the dead (the doomed),[4] before he returned to his heavenly seat.

Zoroaster, of the Persians, *descended into hell*.[5]

Osiris, the Egyptian Saviour, *descended into hell*.[6]

Horus, the virgin-born Saviour, *descended into hell*.[7]

Adonis, the virgin-born Saviour, *descended into hell*.[8]

Bacchus, the virgin-born Saviour, *descended into hell*.[9]

Hercules, the virgin-born Saviour, *descended into hell*.[10]

Mercury, the *Word* and Messenger of God, *descended into hell*.[11]

---

[1] Nicodemus: Apoc. ch. xx.
[2] I. Peter, iii. 17–19.
[3] Acts, ii. 31.
[4] See Asiatic Researches, vol. i. p. 237. Bonwick's Egyptian Belief, p. 168, and Maurice: Indian Antiquities, vol. ii. p. 85.
[5] See Monumental Christianity, p. 286.
[6] See Dupuis: Origin of Religious Belief, p. 258, Bonwick's Egyptian Belief, and Dunlap's Mysteries of Adoni, pp. 125, 152.
[7] See Chap. XXXIX.
[8] See Bell's Pantheon, vol. i. p. 12.
[9] See Higgins: Anacalypsis, vol. i. p. 322. Dupuis: Origin of Religious Belief, p. 257, and Dunlap's Mysteries of Adoni, p. 33.
[10] See Taylor's Mysteries, p. 40, and Mysteries of Adoni, pp. 94–96.
[11] See Bell's Pantheon, vol. ii. p. 72. Our Christian writers discover considerable apprehension, and a jealous caution in their language, when the resemblance between *Paganism* and *Christianity* might be apt to strike the mind too cogently. In quoting Horace's account of Mercury's descent into hell, and his causing a cessation of the sufferings there, Mr. Spence, in "Bell's Pantheon," says: "As this, perhaps, may be a mythical part of his character, *we had better let it alone*."

Baldur, the Scandinavian god, after being killed, *descended into hell.*[1]

Quetzalcoatle, the Mexican crucified Saviour, *descended into hell.*[2]

All these gods, and many others that might be mentioned, *remained in hell for the space of three days and three nights.* "They descended into hell, and on the third day rose again."[3]

---

[1] See Bonwick : Egyptian Belief, p. 169, and Mallet, p. 448.

[2] See Mexican Antiquities, vol. vi. p. 166.

[3] See the chapter on *Explanation.*

CHAPTER XXIII.

THE story of the resurrection of Christ Jesus is related by the four Gospel narrators, and is to the effect that, after being crucified, his body was wrapped in a linen cloth, laid in a tomb, and a " great stone " rolled to the door. The sepulchre was then made sure by " sealing the stone " and " setting a watch."

On the first day of the week some of Jesus' followers came to see the sepulchre, when they found that, in spite of the " sealing " and the " watch," the angel of the Lord had descended from heaven, had rolled back the stone from the door, and that " *Jesus had risen from the dead*."[1]

The story of his *ascension* is told by the *Mark*[2] narrator, who says " he was received up into heaven, and sat on the right hand of God ; " by *Luke*,[3] who says " he was carried up into heaven ; " and by the writer of the *Acts*,[4] who says " he was taken up (to heaven) and a cloud received him out of sight."

We will find, in stripping Christianity of its robes of Paganism, that these miraculous events must be put on the same level with those we have already examined.

Crishna, the crucified Hindoo Saviour, *rose from the dead*,[5] and *ascended bodily into heaven*.[6] At that time a great light enveloped the earth and illuminated the whole expanse of heaven. Attended by celestial spirits, and luminous as on that night when he was born in the house of Vasudeva, *Crishna* pursued, by his own light, the journey between earth and heaven, to the bright paradise from whence he had descended. All men saw him, and exclaimed, " *Lo, Crishna's soul ascends its native skies !* "[7]

---

[1] See Matthew, xxviii. Mark, xvi. Luke, xxiv. and John, xx.   [2] Mark, xvi. 19.

[3] Luke, xxiv. 51.   [4] Acts, i. 9.

[5] See Dupuis : Origin of Religious Belief, p. 240. Higgins : Anacalypsis, vol. ii. pp. 142 and 145.

[6] See Higgins : Anacalypsis, vol. i. p. 131. Bonwick's Egyptian Belief, p. 168. Asiatic Researches, vol. i. pp. 259 and 261.

[7] See Prog. Relig. Ideas, vol. i. p. 72. Hist. Hindostan, ii. pp. 466 and 473.

" In Hindu pictures, Vishnu, who is identi-

Samuel Johnson, in his "Oriental Religions," tells us that *Râma* —an incarnation of Vishnu—after his manifestations on earth, "*at last ascended to heaven*," "resuming his divine essence."

"By the blessings of Râma's name, and through previous faith in him, all sins are remitted, and every one who shall at death pronounce his name with sincere worship shall be forgiven."[1]

The mythological account of *Buddha*, the son of the Virgin Maya, who, as the God of Love, is named *Cam-deo, Cam,* and *Cama,* is of the same character as that of other virgin-born gods. When he died there were tears and lamentations. Heaven and earth are said equally to have lamented the loss of "*Divine Love*," insomuch that *Maha-deo* (the supreme god) was moved to pity, and exclaimed, "*Rise, holy love!*" on which *Cama* was restored and the lamentations changed into the most enthusiastic joy. The heavens are said to have echoed back the exulting sound; then the deity, supposed to be lost (*dead*), was restored, "*hell's great dread and heaven's eternal admiration.*"[2]

The coverings of the body unrolled themselves, and the lid of his coffin was opened by supernatural powers.[3]

Buddha also ascended bodily to the celestial regions when his mission on earth was fulfilled, and marks on the rocks of a high mountain are shown, and believed to be the last impression of his footsteps on this earth. By prayers in his name his followers expect to receive the rewards of paradise, and finally to become one with him, as he became one with the Source of Life.[4]

Lao-Kiun, the virgin-born, he who had existed from all eternity, when his mission of benevolence was completed on earth, *ascended bodily into the paradise above.* Since this time he has been worshiped as a *god,* and splendid temples erected to his memory.[5]

Zoroaster, the founder of the religion of the ancient Persians, who was considered "a divine messenger sent to redeem men from their evil ways," *ascended to heaven* at the end of his earthly career. To this day his followers mention him with the greatest reverence, calling him "The Immortal Zoroaster," "The Blessed Zoroaster," "The Living Star," &c.[6]

fied with Crishna, is often seen mounted on the Eagle Garuda." (Moore : Hindu Panth. p. 214.) And M. Sonnerat noticed "two basso-relievos pinced at the entrance of the choir of Bordeaux Cathedral, one of which represents the ascension of our Saviour to heaven on an Eagle." (Higgins : Anac., vol. i. p. 273.)
[1] Oriental Religions, pp. 404, 495.

[2] Asiatic Res., vol. x. p. 129. Anacalypsis, vol. ii. p. 103.
[3] Bunsen : The Angel-Messiah, p. 49.
[4] Prog. Relig. Ideas, vol. i. p. 86. See also. Higgins : Anacalypsis, vol. i. p. 159.
[5] Prog. Relig. Ideas, vol. i. p. 214.
[6] Ibid. p. 258.

Æsculapius, the Son of God, the Saviour, after being put to death, *rose from the dead.* His history is portrayed in the following lines of *Ovid's*, which are prophecies foretelling his life and actions :

> " Once, as the sacred infant she surveyed,
> The god was kindled in the raving maid;
> And thus she uttered her prophetic tale:
> Hail, great Physician of the world ! all hail !
> Hail, mighty infant, who in years to come
> Shalt heal the nations, and defraud the tomb !
> Swift be thy growth, thy triumphs unconfined,
> Make kingdoms thicker, and increase mankind.
> Thy daring art shall animate the dead,
> And draw the thunder on thy guilty head;
> *Then shalt thou die, but from the dark abode*
> *Shalt rise victorious, and be twice a god.*"[1]

The Saviour *Adonis* or *Tammuz*, after being put to death, *rose from the dead.* The following is an account given of the rites of Tammuz or of Adonis by Julius Firmicius (who lived during the reign of Constantine):

> " On a certain night (while the ceremony of the Adonia, or religious rites in honor of Adonis, lasted), an image was laid upon a bed (or bier) and bewailed in doleful ditties. After they had satiated themselves with fictitious lamentations, light was brought in: then the mouths of all the mourners were anointed by the priests (*with oil*), upon which he, with a gentle murmur, whispered :
>
> > ' Trust, ye Saints, your God restored.
> > Trust ye, *in your risen Lord ;*
> > For the pains which he endured
> > Our salvation have procured.'
>
> " Literally, ' Trust, ye *communicants :* the God having been saved, there shall be to us out of pain, *Salvation.*' "[2]

Upon which their sorrow was turned into joy.

Godwyn renders it :

> " *Trust ye in God, for out of pains,*
> *Salvation is come unto us.*"[3]

Dr. Prichard, in his " *Egyptian Mythology*," tells us that the Syrians celebrated, *in the early spring*, this ceremony in honor of *the resurrection of Adonis.* After lamentations, his restoration was commemorated with joy and festivity.[4]

Mons. Dupuis says :

> " The obsequies of *Adonis* were celebrated at *Alexandria* (in Egypt) with the utmost display. His image was carried with great solemnity to a tomb, which served the purpose of rendering him the last honors. Before singing his return

[1] Ovid's Metamorphoses, as rendered by Addison. Quoted in Taylor's Diegesis, p. 148.
[2] Quoted by Higgins : Anacalypsis, vol. ii. p. 114. See also, Taylor's Diegesis, pp. 163, 164.
[3] Taylor's Diegesis, p. 164.
[4] Prichard's Egyptian Mythology, pp. 66, 67.

to life, there were mournful rites celebrated in honor of his suffering and his death. The large wound he had received was shown, just as the wound was shown which was made to Christ by the thrust of the spear. *The feast of his resurrection was fixed at the 25th of March.*"[1]

In Calmet's "Fragments," the resurrection of *Adonis* is referred to as follows:

"In these *mysteries*, after the attendants had for a long time bewailed the death of this *just person*, he was at length understood to be *restored to life*, to have experienced a *resurrection ;* signified by the re-admission of light. On this the priest addressed the company, saying, 'Comfort yourselves, all ye who have been partakers of the mysteries of the deity, thus preserved: for we shall now enjoy some respite from our labors:' to which were added these words: 'I have scaped a sad calamity, and my lot is greatly mended.' The people answered by the invocation: 'Hail to the Dove l the Restorer of Light l '"[2]

Alexander Murray tells us that the ancient Greeks also celebrated this festival in honor of the resurrection of Adonis, in the course of which a figure of him was produced, and the ceremony of burial, with weeping and songs of wailing, gone through. After these a joyful shout was raised: "*Adonis lives and is risen again.*"[3]

Plutarch, in his life of Alcibiades and of Nicias, tells us that it was at the time of the celebration of the death of *Adonis* that the Athenian fleet set sail for its unlucky expedition to Sicily ; that nothing but images of dead Adonises were to be met with in the streets, and that they were carried to the sepulchre in the midst of an immense train of women, crying and beating their breasts, and imitating in every particular the lugubrious pomp of interments. Sinister omens were drawn from it, which were only too much realized by subsequent events.[4]

It was in an oration or address delivered to the Emperors Constans and Constantius that Julius Firmicius wrote concerning the rites celebrated by the heathens in commemoration of the resurrection of Adonis. In his tide of eloquence he breaks away into indignant objurgation of the priest who officiated in those *heathen mysteries*, which, he admitted, resembled the *Christian sacrament* in honor of the death and resurrection of Christ Jesus, so closely that there was really no difference between them, except that no sufficient proof had been given to the world of the resurrection of Adonis, *and no divine oracle had borne witness to his resurrection,*

---

[1] Dupuis : Origin of Religious Belief, p. 161. See also, Dunlap's Mysteries of Adoni, p. 23, and Spirit Hist. of Man, p. 216.

[2] Calmet's Fragments, vol. ii. p. 21.
[3] Murray : Manual of Mythology, p. 86.
[4] See Dupuis : Origin of Religious Beliefs, p. 261.

nor had he shown himself alive after his death to those who were concerned to have assurance of the fact that they might believe.

The *divine oracle,* be it observed, which Julius Firmicius says had borne testimony to Christ Jesus' resurrection, *was none other than the answer of the god Apollo, whom the Pagans worshiped at Delphos,* which this writer derived from Porphyry's books " *On the Philosophy of Oracles.*"[1]

Eusebius, the celebrated ecclesiastical historian, has also condescended to quote this claimed testimony from *a Pagan oracle,* as furnishing one of the most convincing proofs that could be adduced in favor of the resurrection of Christ Jesus.

"But thou at least (says he to the Pagans), *listen to thine own gods, to thy oracular deities themselves,* who have borne witness, and ascribed to our Saviour (Jesus Christ) not imposture, but piety and wisdom, and ascent into heaven."

This was vastly obliging and liberal of the god Apollo, but, it happens awkwardly enough, that the whole work (consisting of several books) ascribed to Porphyry, in which this and other admissions equally honorable to the evidences of the Christian religion are made, was *not* written by Porphyry, but is altogether the pious fraud of Christian hands, who have kindly fathered the great philosopher with admissions, which, as he would certainly never have made himself, they have very charitably made for him.[2]

The festival in honor of the resurrection of Adonis was observed in Alexandria in Egypt—*the cradle of Christianity*—in the time of St. Cyril, Bishop of Alexandria (A. D. 412), and at Antioch—the ancient capital of the Greek Kings of Syria—even as late as the time of the Emperor Julian (A. D. 361–363), whose arrival there, during the solemnity of the festival, was taken as an ill omen.[3]

It is most curious that the arrival of the Emperor Julian at Antioch—where the followers of Christ Jesus, it is said, were first called Christians—at that time, should be considered an *ill omen.* Why should it have been so ? He was not a Christian, but a known apostate from the Christian religion, and a zealous patron of *Paganism.* The evidence is very conclusive ; *the celebration in honor of the resurrection of Adonis had become to be known as a Christian festival, which has not been abolished even unto this day.* The ceremonies held in Roman Catholic countries on Good Friday and on Easter Sunday, are nothing more than the festival of the death and resurrection of Adonis, as we shall presently see.

---

[1] See Dupuis : Origin of Religious Beliefs, p. 247, and Taylor's Diegesis, p. 164.

[2] See Taylor's Diegesis, p. 164. We shall speak of *Christian* forgeries anon.

[3] See Bell's Pantheon, vol. i. p. 2.

Even as late as the year A. D. 386, the resurrection of Adonis was celebrated in *Judea*. St. Jerome says:

"Over Bethlehem (in the year 386 after Christ) the grove of Tammuz, that is, of Adonis, was casting its shadow! And in the *grotto* where formerly the infant Anointed (*i. e., Christ Jesus*) cried, the lover of Venus was being mourned."[1]

In the idolatrous worship practiced by the *children of Israel* was that of the worship of *Adonis*.

Under the designation of *Tammuz*, this god was worshiped, and had his altar even in the Temple of the Lord which was at Jerusalem. Several of the Psalms of David were parts of the liturgical service employed in his worship; the 110th, in partic- ular, is an account of a friendly alliance between the two gods, Jehovah and Adonis, in which Jehovah adorns Adonis for his priest, as sitting at his right hand, and promises to fight for him against his enemies. This god was worshiped at Byblis in Phœ- nicia with precisely the same ceremonies: the same articles of faith as to his mystical incarnation, his precious death and burial, and his glorious resurrection and ascension, and even in the very same words of religious adoration and homage which are now, with the slightest degree of variation that could well be conceived, addressed to the Christ of the Gospel.

The prophet Ezekiel, when an exile, painted once more the scene he had so often witnessed of the Israelitish women in the Temple court bewailing the death of Tammuz.[2]

Dr. Parkhurst says, in his "Hebrew Lexicon":

"I find myself *obliged* to refer Tammuz, as well as the Greek and Roman Her- cules, to that class of idols *which were originally designed to represent the prom- ised Saviour* (Christ Jesus), the desire of all nations. His other name, Adonis, is almost the very Hebrew word 'Our Lord,' a well-known title of Christ."[4]

So it seems that the ingenious and most learned orthodox Dr. Parkhurst was *obliged* to consider Adonis a type of "the promised Saviour (Christ Jesus), the desire of all nations." This is a very favorite way for Christian divines to express themselves, when pushed thereto, by the striking resemblance between the Pagan, virgin-born, crucified, and resurrected gods and Christ Jesus.

If the reader is satisfied that all these things are types or sym- bols of what the "*real Saviour*" was to do and suffer, he is welcome

---

[1] Quoted in Dunlap's Son of the Man, p. vii. See also, Knight: Ancient Art and My- thology, p. xxvii.

"From the days of the prophet Daniel, down to the time when the red cross knights gave no quarter (fighting for *the Christ*) in the streets

of Jerusalem, the Anointed was worshiped in Babylon, Basan, Galilee and Palestine." (Son of the Man, p. 38.)

[2] Ezekiel, viii. 14.

[4] Quoted in Taylor's Diegesis, p. 162, and Higgins: Anacalypsis, vol. ii. p. 114.

to such food. The doctrine of Dr. Parkhurst and others comes with but an ill grace, however, from Roman Catholic priests, *who have never ceased to suppress information when possible*, and when it was impossible for them to do so, they claimed these things to be the work of the devil, in imitation of their predecessors, the Christian Fathers.

Julius Firmicius has said : "The devil has his Christs," and does not deny that *Adonis* was one. Tertullian and St. Justin explain all the conformity which exists between *Christianity* and *Paganism*, by asserting "that a long time before there were Christians in existence, the devil had taken pleasure to have their future mysteries and ceremonies copied by his worshipers."[1]

Osiris, the Egyptian Saviour, after being put to death, *rose from the dead*,[2] and bore the title of " *The Resurrected One.*"[3]

Prof. Mahaffy, lecturer on ancient history in the University of Dublin, observes that :

' The *Resurrection* and reign over an eternal kingdom, by an *incarnate mediating deity* born of a virgin, was a theological conception which pervaded the oldest religion of Egypt."[4]

The ancient Egyptians celebrated annually, in early spring, about the time known in Christian countries as Easter, the resurrection and ascension of Osiris. During these mysteries the misfortunes and tragical death of the "*Saviour*" were celebrated in a species of drama, in which all the particulars were exhibited, accompanied with loud lamentations and every mark of sorrow. At this time his image was carried in a procession, covered—as were those in the temples—*with black veils*. On the 25th of March his *resurrection from the dead* was celebrated with great festivity and rejoicings.[5]

Alexander Murray says:

" The worship of *Osiris* was universal throughout Egypt, where he was gratefully regarded as the great exemplar of *self-sacrifice*—in giving his life for others —as the manifestor of good, as the opener of truth, and as being full of goodness and truth. *After being dead, he was restored to life.*"[6]

Mons. Dupuis says on this subject :

"The Fathers of the Church, and the writers of the Christian sect, speak frequently of these feasts, celebrated in honor of Osiris, *who died and arose from*

---

[1] See Justin : Cum. Typho, and Tertullian: De Bap.

[2] See Higgins : Anacalypsis, vol. ii. p. 16, and vol. i. p. 19. Also, Prichard's Egyptian Mythology, p. 66, and Bonwick's Egyptian Belief, p. 163.

[3] See Bonwick's Egyptian Belief, p. 166, and Dunlap's Mysteries of Adoni, pp. 124, 125.

[4] Prolegomena to Ancient History.

[5] See Higgins: Anacalypsis, vol. ii. p. 102.

[6] Murray : Manual of Mythology, pp. 347, 348.

the dead, and they draw a parallel with the adventurers of *their* Christ. Athanasius, Augustin, Theophilus, Athenagoras, Minucius Felix, Lactantius, Firmicius, as also the ancient authors who have spoken of *Osiris* . . . all agree in the description of the universal mourning of the Egyptians at the festival, when the commemoration of that death took place. They describe the ceremonies which were practiced at his sepulchre, the tears, which were there shed during several days, and the festivities and rejoicings, which followed after that mourning, at the moment when his resurrection was announced."[1]

Mr. Bonwick remarks, in his " Egyptian Belief," that :

"It is astonishing to find that, at least, five thousand years ago, men trusted an *Osiris* as the ' *Risen Saviour*,' and confidently hoped to rise, as he arose, from the grave."[2]

Again he says :

"Osiris was, unquestionably, the popular god of Egypt. . . . Osiris was dear to the hearts of the people. He was pre-eminently ' *good*.' He was in life and death their friend. His birth, death, burial, resurrection and ascension, embraced the leading points of Egyptian theology." "In his efforts to do good, he encounters evil. In struggling with that, he is overcome. He is killed. The story, entered into in the account of the Osiris myth, is a circumstantial one. Osiris is buried. His tomb was the object of pilgrimage for thousands of years. *But he did not rest in his grave. At the end of three days, or forty, he arose again,* and ascended to heaven. This is the story of his humanity." "As the *invictus Osiris*, his tomb was illuminated, as is the holy sepulchre of Jerusalem now. The mourning song, whose plaintive tones were noted by Herodotus, and has been compared to the ' *miserere* ' of Rome, was followed, *in three days*, by the language of triumph."[3]

Herodotus, who had been initiated into the Egyptian and Grecian " *Mysteries*," speaks thus of them :

"At Sais (in Egypt), in the sacred precinct of Minerva; behind the chapel and joining the wall, is the tomb of one whose name I consider it impious to divulge on such an occasion; and in the inclosure stand large stone obelisks, and there is a lake near, ornamented with a stone margin, formed in a circle, and in size, as appeared to me, much the same as that in Delos, which is called the circular. In this lake they perform by night the representation of that person's adventures, which they call *mysteries*. On these matters, however, though accurately acquainted with the particulars of them, ·*I must observe a discreet silence ;* and respecting the sacred rites of Ceres, which the Greeks call Thesmyphoria, although I am acquainted with them, I must observe silence except so far as is lawful for me to speak of them."[4]

Horus, son of the virgin *Isis*, experienced similar misfortunes. The principal features of this sacred romance are to be found in the writings of the Christian Fathers. They give us a description of the grief which was manifested at his death, and of the rejoicings at his *resurrection*, which are similar to those spoken of above.[5]

---

[1] Dupuis : Origin of Religious Belief, p. 256.
[2] Bonwick's Egyptian Belief, p. vi.
[3] Ibid. pp. 150–155, 178.
[4] Herodotus, bk. ii. chs. 170, 171.
[5] See Dupuis : Origin of Religious Belief, p. 263, and Higgins : Anacalypsis, vol. ii. 102.

Atys, the Phrygian Saviour, was put to death, *and rose again from the dead.* Various histories were given of him in various places, but all accounts terminated in the usual manner. He was one of the " Slain Ones " who rose to life again on the 25th of March, or the " *Hilaria* " or primitive Easter.[1]

Mithras, the Persian Saviour, and mediator between God and man, was believed by the inhabitants of Persia, Asia Minor and Armenia, to have been put to death, *and to have risen again from the dead.* In their mysteries, the body of a young man, apparently dead, was exhibited, which was feigned to be restored to life. By his sufferings he was believed to have worked their salvation, and on this account he was called their " *Saviour.*" His priests watched his tomb to the midnight of the veil of the 25th of March, *with loud cries, and in darkness ;* when all at once the lights burst forth from all parts, and the priest cried:

" *Rejoice, Oh sacred Initiated, your god is risen. His death, his pains, his sufferings, have worked our salvation.*"[2]

Mons. Dupuis, speaking of the resurrection of this god, says:

" It is chiefly in the religion of *Mithras.* . . . that we find mostly these features of analogy with the death and resurrection of Christ, and with the mysteries of the Christians. *Mithras*, who was also born on the 25th of December, like Christ, died as he did; and he had his sepulchre, over which his disciples came to shed tears. During the night, the priests carried his image to a tomb, expressly prepared for him; he was laid out on a litter, like the Phœnician *Adonis.*

"These funeral ceremonies, like those on Good Friday (in Roman Catholic churches), were accompanied with funeral dirges and groans of the priests; after having spent some time with these expressions of feigned grief; after having lighted the sacred *flambeau*, or their paschal candle, and anointed the image with *chrism* or perfumes, one of them came forward and pronounced with the gravest mien these words: ' *Be of good cheer, sacred band of Initiates, your god has risen from the dead. His pains and his sufferings shall be your salvation.*' "[3]

In King's " *Gnostics and their Remains* " (Plate XI.), may be seen the representation of a bronze medal, or rather disk, engraved

---

[1] See Bonwick's Egyptian Belief, p. 169. Higgins : Anacalypsis, vol. ii. p. 104. Dupuis : Origin of Religious Belief, p. 255. Dunlap's Mysteries of Adoni, p. 110, and Knight : Anct. Art and Mythology, p. 86.

[2] Higgins : Anacalypsis, vol. ii. p. 99. *Mithras* remained in the grave a period of *three days*, as did Christ *Jesus*, and the other Christs. "The Persians believed that the soul of man remained yet *three days* in the world after its separation from the body." (Dunlap : Mysteries of Adoni, p. 63.)

"In the Zoroastrian religion, after soul and body have separated, the souls, *in the third night* after death—as soon as the shining sun ascends—come over the Mount Berezaiti upon the bridge Tshinavat which leads to Garonmana, the dwelling of the good gods." (Dunlap's Spirit Hist., p. 216, and Mysteries of Adoni, 60.)

The Ghost of Polydore says :

" Being raised up this *third day*—light, Having deserted my body !" (Euripides, Hecuba, 31, 32.)

[3] Dupuis : Origin of Religious Beliefs, pp. 246, 247.

in the coarsest manner, on which is to be seen a female figure, standing in the attitude of adoration, the object of which is expressed by the inscription—ORTVS SALVAT, "*The Rising of the Saviour*"—*i. e.*, of *Mithras*.[1]

"This medal" (says Mr. King), "doubtless had accompanied the interment of some individual initiated into the Mithraic mysteries; and is certainly the most curious relic of that faith that has come under my notice."[2]

Bacchus, the Saviour, son of the virgin Semele, after being put to death, also *arose from the dead.* During the commemoration of the ceremonies of this event the dead body of a young man was exhibited with great lamentations, in the same manner as the cases cited above, and at dawn on the 25th of March his resurrection from the dead was celebrated with great rejoicings.[3] After having brought solace to the misfortunes of mankind, he, after his resurrection, *ascended into heaven.*[4]

Hercules, the Saviour, the son of Zeus by a mortal mother, was put to death, but arose from the funeral pile, *and ascended into heaven* in a *cloud,* 'mid peals of thunder. His followers manifested gratitude to his memory by erecting an altar on the spot from whence he ascended.[5]

Memnon is put to death, but rises again to life and immortality. His mother Eos weeps tears at the death of her son—as Mary does for Christ Jesus—but her prayers avail to bring him back, like Adonis or Tammuz, and Jesus, from the shadowy region, to dwell always in Olympus.[6]

The ancient Greeks also believed that *Amphiaraus*—one of their most celebrated prophets and demi-gods—*rose from the dead.* They even pointed to the place of his resurrection.[7]

Baldur, the Scandinavian Lord and Saviour, is put to death, but does not rest in his grave. He too rises again to life and immortality.[8]

When "Baldur the Good," the beneficent god, descended into hell, Hela (Death) said to Hermod (who mourned for Baldur): "If all things in the world, both living and lifeless, weep for him, then shall he return to the Æsir (the gods)." Upon hearing this, messengers were dispatched throughout the world to beg every-

[1] King's Gnostics and their Remains, p. 225.
[2] Ibid. p. 226.
[3] See Higgins: Anacalypsis, vol. ii. p. 102. Dupuis: Origin of Religious Belief, pp. 256, 257, and Bonwick's Egyptian Belief, p. 169.
[4] See Dupuis: Origin of Religious Belief, p. 135, and Higgins: Anacalypsis, vol. i. 322.

[5] Prog. Relig. Ideas, vol. i. p. 294. See also, Goldzhier's Hebrew Mythology, p. 127. Higgins : Anacalypsis, vol. i. p. 322, and Chambers's Encyclo., art. "Hercules."
[6] Aryan Mytho., vol. ii. p. 90.
[7] See Bell's Pantheon, vol. i. p. 56.
[8] Aryan Mytho., vol. ii. p. 94.

thing to weep in order that Baldur might be delivered from hell. All things everywhere willingly complied with this request, both men and every other living being, so that *wailing* was heard in all quarters.[1]

Thus we see the same myth among the northern nations. As Bunsen says:

"The tragedy of the *murdered and risen god* is familiar to us from the days of ancient Egypt: must it not be of equally primeval origin here?" [In Teutonic tradition.]

The ancient Scandinavians also worshiped a god called *Frey*, who was put to death, *and rose again from the dead*.[2]

The ancient *Druids* celebrated, in the British Isles, in heathen times, the rites of the resurrected Bacchus, and other ceremonies, similar to the Greeks and Romans.[3]

Quetzalcoatle, the Mexican crucified Saviour, after being put to death, *rose from the dead*. His resurrection was represented in Mexican *hieroglyphics*, and may be seen in the *Codex Borgianus*.[4]

The Jews in Palestine celebrated their *Passover* on the same day that the Pagans celebrated the resurrection of their gods.

Besides the resurrected gods mentioned in this chapter, who were believed in for centuries before the time assigned for the birth of Christ Jesus, many others might be named, as we shall see in our chapter on " Explanation." In the words of Dunbar T. Heath :

"We find men taught everywhere, from Southern Arabia to Greece, by hundreds of symbolisms, the birth, death, and resurrection of deities, and a resurrection too, apparently after the second day, *i. e., on the third*."[5]

And now, to conclude all, *another god* is said to have been born on the *same day*[6] as these Pagan deities ; he is crucified and buried, and on the *same day*[7] rises again from the dead. Christians of Europe and America celebrate annually the resurrection of *their*

---

[1] Mallet's Northern Antiquities, p. 449.

[2] See Knight: Ancient Art and [Mythology, p. 85.

[3] See Davies: Myths and Rites of the British Druids, pp. 89 and 208.

[4] See Kingsborough's Mexican Antiquities, vol. vi. p. 166.

[5] Quoted in Bonwick's Egyptian Belief, p. 174.

[6] As we shall see in the chapter on " The Birth-day of Christ Jesus."

[7] *Easter*, the triumph of Christ, was originally solemnized on the 25th of March, the very day upon which the Pagan gods were believed to have risen from the dead.' (See Dupuis: Origin of Religious Belief, pp. 244, 255.)

A very long and terrible schism took place in the Christian Church upon the question whether *Easter*, the day of the resurrection, was to be celebrated on the 14th day of the first month, after the Jewish custom, or on the Lord's day afterward; and it was at last decided in favor of the Lord's day. (See Higgins: Anacalypsis, vol. ii. p. 90, and Chambers's Encyclopædia, art. " Easter.")

The day upon which Easter should be celebrated was not settled until the Council of Nice. (See Euseb. Life of Constantine, lib. 3, ch. xvi. Also, Socrates' Eccl. Hist. lib. 1, ch. vi.)

Saviour in almost the identical manner in which the Pagans celebrated the resurrection of *their* Saviours, centuries before the God
of the Christians is said to have been born. In Roman Catholic
churches, in Catholic countries, the body of a young man is laid on
a bier, and placed before the altar; the wound in his side is to be
seen, and his death is bewailed in mournful dirges, and the verse,
Gloria Patri, is discontinued in the mass. All the images in the
churches and the altar *are covered with black*, and the priest and
attendants are robed in black; nearly all lights are put out, and the
windows are darkened. This is the "Agonie," the "Miserere,"
the "Good Friday" mass. On Easter Sunday' all the drapery has
disappeared; the church is *illuminated*, and rejoicing, in place of
sorrow, is manifest. The Easter hymns partake of the following
expression:

> "*Rejoice, Oh sacred Initiated, your God is risen. His death, his pains, his suf-
> ferings, have worked our salvation.*"

Cedrenus (a celebrated Byzantine writer), speaking of the 25th
of March, says:

> "The first day of the first month, is the first of the month *Nisan;* it corre-
> sponds to the 25th of March of the *Romans*, and the *Phamenot* of the *Egyptians*.
> On that day Gabriel saluted Mary, in order to make her conceive the Saviour.
> I observe that it is the same month, *Phamenot*, that *Osiris* gave fecundity to *Isis*,
> according to the Egyptian theology. *On the very same day, our God Saviour*
> (Christ Jesus), *after the termination of his career, arose from the dead;* that is,
> what our forefathers called the *Pass-over*, or the passage of the Lord. It is also
> on the *same day*, that our ancient theologians have fixed his return, or his
> second advent."[2]

We have seen, then, that a festival celebrating the resurrection
of their several gods was annually held among the Pagans, before
the time of Christ Jesus, and that it was almost universal. That
it dates to a period of great antiquity is very certain. The adventures of these incarnate gods, exposed in their infancy, put to death,
and rising again from the grave to life and immortality, were acted
on the *Deisuls* and in the sacred theatres of the ancient Pagans,[3]
just as the "Passion Play" is acted to-day.

Eusebius relates a *tale* to the effect that, at one time, the Chris-

---

[1] Even the name of "EASTER" is derived
from the heathen goddess, *Ostrt*, of the Saxons,
and the *Eostre* of the Germans.

"Many of the popular observances con-
nected with Easter are clearly of *Pagan origin*.
The goddess Ostara or Eastre seems to have
been the personification of the morning or
East, and also of the opening year or Spring.
. . . With her usual policy, the church en-

deavored to give a Christian significance to
such of the rites as could not be rooted out;
and in this case the conversion was practically easy." (Chambers's Encyclo., art.
"Easter.")

[2] Quoted in Dupuis: Origin of Religious
Belief, p. 244.

[3] See Higgins: Anacalypsis, vol. II. p. 340.

tians were about to celebrate " the solemn vigils of Easter," when, to their dismay, they found that *oil* was wanted. Narcissus, Bishop of Jerusalem, who was among the number, " commanded that such as had charge of the *lights*, speedily to bring unto him water, drawn up out of the next well." This water Narcissus, " by the wonderful power of God," changed into *oil,* and the celebration was continued.[1]

This tells the whole story. Here we see the *oil*—which the Pagans had in their ceremonies, and with which the priests anointed the lips of the Initiates—and the *lights*, which were suddenly lighted when the god was feigned to have risen from the dead.

With her usual policy, the Christian Church endeavored to give a *Christian* significance to the rites borrowed from Paganism, and in this case, as in many others, the conversion was particularly easy.

In the earliest times, the Christians did not celebrate the resurrection of their Lord from the grave. They made the *Jewish Passover* their chief festival, celebrating it on the same day as the Jews, the 14th of Nisan, no matter in what part of the week that day might fall. Believing, according to the tradition, that Jesus on the eve of his death had eaten the Passover with his disciples, they regarded such a solemnity as a commemoration of the Supper and not as a memorial of the Resurrection. But in proportion as Christianity more and more separated itself from Judaism and imbibed paganism, this way of looking at the matter became less easy. A new tradition gained currency among the Roman Christians to the effect that Jesus before his death had not eaten the Passover, but had died on the very day of the Passover, thus substituting himself for the Paschal Lamb. The great Christian festival was then made the Resurrection of Jesus, and was celebrated on the first pagan holiday—*Sun-day*—after the Passover.

This *Easter* celebration was observed in *China*, and called a " Festival of Gratitude to Tien."[4] From there it extended over the then known world to the extreme West.

The ancient Pagan inhabitants of Europe celebrated annually this same feast, which is yet continued over all the Christian world. This festival began with a week's indulgence in all kinds of sports, called the *carne-vale,* or the taking *a farewell to animal* food, because it was followed by a fast of forty days. This was in honor of the Saxon goddess *Ostrt* or *Eostre* of the Germans, whence our *Easter*.[2]

---

[1] Eccl. Hist., lib. 6, c. viii.   [2] Anacalypsis, ii. 59.

The most characteristic Easter rite, and the one most widely diffused, is the use of *Easter eggs*. They are usually stained of various colors with dye-woods or herbs, and people mutually make presents of them ; sometimes they are kept as *amulets*, sometimes eaten. Now, " dyed eggs were sacred Easter offerings in *Egypt ;*"[1] the ancient *Persians*, "when they kept the festival of the solar new year (in March), mutually presented each other with colored eggs ;"[2] " the *Jews* used eggs in the feast of the Passover ;" and the custom prevailed in Western countries.[3]

The stories of the resurrection written by the Gospel narrators are altogether different. This is owing to the fact that the story, as related by one, was written to correct the mistakes and to endeavor to reconcile with common sense the absurdities of the other. For instance, the "*Matthew*" narrator says : " And when they saw him (after he had risen from the dead) they worshiped him ; *but some doubted.*"[4]

To leave the question where this writer leaves it would be fatal. In such a case there must be no doubt. Therefore, the "*Mark*" narrator makes Jesus appear *three times*, under such circumstances as to render a mistake next to impossible, and to silence the most obstinate skepticism. He is first made to appear to Mary Magdalene, who was convinced that it was Jesus, because she went and told the disciples that he had risen, and that she had seen him. They—*notwithstanding that Jesus had foretold them of his resurrection*[5]—disbelieved, nor could they be convinced until he appeared to *them*. They in turn told it to the other disciples, who were also skeptical ; and, that they might be convinced, Jesus also appeared to *them* as they sat at meat, when he upbraided them for their unbelief.

This story is much improved in the hands of the "*Mark*" narrator, but, in the anxiety to make a clear case, it is overdone, as often happens when the object is to remedy or correct an oversight or mistake previously made. In relating that the disciples *doubted* the words of Mary Magdalene, he had probably forgotten Jesus had promised them that he should rise, for, if he had told them this, *why did they doubt ?*

Neither the "*Matthew*" nor the "*Mark*" narrator says in what *way* Jesus made his appearance—whether it was in the *body* or only in the *spirit*. If in the latter, it would be fatal to the whole theory

---

[1] See Bonwick's Egyptian Belief, p. 24.
[2] See Chambers's Encyclo., art. "Easter."
[3] Ibid.
[4] Matthew, xxviii. 17.
[5] See xii. 40 ; xvi. 21 ; Mark, ix. 31 ; xiv. 28 ; John, ii. 19.

of the resurrection, as it is a *material* resurrection that Christianity taught—just like their neighbors the Persians—and not a spiritual.[1]

To put this disputed question in its true light, and to silence the objections which must naturally have arisen against it, was the object which the " *Luke* " narrator had in view. He says that when Jesus appeared and spoke to the disciples they were afraid: " But they were terrified and affrighted, and *supposed* they had seen a *spirit*."[2] Jesus then—to show that he was *not* a spirit— showed the wounds in his hands and feet. " And they gave him a piece of a broiled fish, and of a honeycomb. And he took it, *and did eat before them*."[3] After this, who is there that can doubt? but, if the *fish* and *honeycomb* story was true, why did the " *Matthew* " and " *Mark* " narrators fail to mention it ?

The " *Luke* " narrator, like his predecessors, had also overdone the matter, and instead of convincing the skeptical, he only excited their ridicule.

The " *John* " narrator now comes, and endeavors to set matters right. He does not omit entirely the story of Jesus eating fish, *for that would not do, after there had been so much said about it.* He might leave it to be inferred that the " *Luke* " narrator made a mistake, so he modifies the story and omits the ridiculous part. The scene is laid on the shores of the Sea of Tiberias. Under the direction of Jesus, Peter drew his net to land, full of fish. " Jesus said unto them : Come and dine. And none of the disciples durst ask him, Who art thou? knowing that it was the Lord. Jesus then cometh, and taketh *bread*, and *giveth them*, and *fish* likewise."[4]

It does not appear from *this* account that Jesus ate the fish at all. He took the fish and *gave to the disciples;* the inference is that *they* were the ones that ate. In the " *Luke* " narrator's account, *the statement is reversed;* the disciples gave the fish to Jesus, *and he ate*. The " *John* " narrator has taken out of the story that which was absurd, but he leaves us to infer that the " *Luke* " narrator was *careless* in stating the account of what took place. If we leave out of the " *Luke* " narrator's account the part that relates to the fish and honeycomb, he fails to prove what it really

---

[1] " And let not any one among you say, that *this very flesh* is not judged, neither raised up. Consider, in what were ye saved ? in what did ye look up, if not whilst ye were in this flesh ? We must, therefore, keep our flesh as the temple of God. For in like manner as ye were called in the flesh, *ye shall also come to judgment* in the flesh. Our one Lord Jesus Christ, who has saved us, being first a spirit, was made flesh, and so called us : *even so we also in this flesh, shall receive the reward (of heaven).* (H. Corinthians, ch. iv. *Apoc.* See also the Christian Creed : " I believe in the resurrection of the *body*.")

[2] Luke, xxiv. 37.

[3] Luke, xxiv. 42, 43.   [4] John, xxi. 12, 13.

was which appeared to the disciples, as it seems from this that the disciples could not be convinced that Jesus was not a spirit until he had actually eaten something.

Now, if the *eating* part is struck out—which the "*John*" narrator does, and which, no doubt, the ridicule cast upon it drove him to do—the "*Luke*" narrator leaves the question *just where he found it.* It was the business of the "*John*" narrator to attempt to leave it clean, and put an end to all cavil.

Jesus appeared to the disciples when they assembled at Jerusalem. "And when he had so said, he shewed unto them his hands and his side."[1] They were satisfied, and no doubts were expressed. But Thomas was not present, and when he was told by the brethren that Jesus had appeared to them, he refused to believe; nor would he, "Except I shall see in his hands the print of the nails, and put my finger into the print of the nails, and thrust my hand into his side, I will not believe."[2] Now, if Thomas could be convinced, with all *his* doubts, it would be foolish after *that* to deny that Jesus was not in the *body* when he appeared to his disciples.

After eight days Jesus again appears, for no other purpose—as it would seem—but to convince the doubting disciple Thomas. Then said he to Thomas: "Reach hither thy finger, and behold my hands; and reach hither thy hand, and thrust it into my side; and be not faithless, but believing."[3] This convinced Thomas, and he exclaimed: "My Lord and my God." After *this evidence,* if there were still unbelievers, they were even more skeptical than Thomas himself. We should be at a loss to understand *why the writers of the first three Gospels entirely omitted the story of Thomas,* if we were not aware that when the "*John*" narrator wrote the state of the public mind was such that proof of the most unquestionable character was demanded that Christ Jesus had risen in the body. The "*John*" narrator selected a person who claimed he was hard to convince, and if the evidence was such as to satisfy *him,* it ought to satisfy the balance of the world.[4]

The first that we knew of the fourth Gospel—attributed to *John*—is from the writings of *Irenæus* (A. D. 177–202), and the evidence is that *he is the author of it.*[5] That controversies were rife in his day concerning the resurrection of Jesus, is very evident from other sources. We find that at this time the resurrection of

[1] John, xx. 20.
[2] John, xx. 25.
[3] John, xx. 27.
[4] See, for a further account of the resurrec-
tion, Reber's Christ of Paul; Scott's English Life of Jesus; and Greg's Creed of Christendom.
[5] See the Chapter xxxviii.

the dead (according to the accounts of the Christian forgers) was very far from being esteemed an uncommon event; that the miracle was frequently performed on necessary occasions by great fasting and the joint supplication of the church of the place, and that the persons thus restored by their prayers had lived afterwards among them many years. At such a period, when faith could boast of so many wonderful victories over death, it seems difficult to account for the skepticism of those philosophers, who still rejected and derided the doctrine of the resurrection. A noble Grecian had rested on this important ground the whole controversy, and promised Theophilus, bishop of Antioch, *that if he could be gratified by the sight of a single person who had been actually raised from the dead, he would immediately embrace the Christian religion.*

"It is somewhat remarkable," says Gibbon, the historian, from whom we take the above, "that the prelate of the first Eastern Church, however anxious for the conversion of his friend, thought proper to *decline* this fair and reasonable challenge."[1]

This Christian *saint*, Irenæus, had invented many stories of others being raised from the dead, for the purpose of attempting to strengthen the belief in the resurrection of Jesus. In the words of the Rev. Jeremiah Jones:

"Such *pious frauds* were very common among Christians even in the first three centuries; and a forgery of this nature, with the view above-mentioned, *seems natural and probable.*"

One of these "*pious frauds*" is the "*Gospel of Nicodemus the Disciple, concerning the Sufferings and Resurrection of our Master and Saviour Jesus Christ.*" Although attributed to Nicodemus, a disciple of Jesus, it has been shown to be a forgery, written towards the close of the second century—during the time of *Irenæus*, the well-known pious forger. In this book we find the following:

"And now hear me a little. We all know the blessed Simeon, the high-priest, who took Jesus when an infant into his arms in the temple. This same Simeon had two sons of his own, *and we were all present at their death and funeral.* Go therefore and see their *tombs,* for these are open, *and they are risen;* and behold, they are in the city of Arimathæa, spending their time together in offices of devotion."[2]

The purpose of this story is very evident. Some "zealous believer," observing the appeals for proof of the resurrection, wishing to make it appear that resurrections from the dead were

---

common occurrences, invented this story *towards the close of the
second century*, and fathered it upon Nicodemus.

We shall speak, anon, more fully on the subject of the frauds
of the early Christians, the "lying and deceiving *for the cause of
Christ*," which is carried on even to the present day.

As President Cheney of Bates College has lately remarked,
" *The resurrection is the doctrine of Christianity and the foundation of the entire system*,"[1] but outside of the four spurious gospels this greatest of all recorded miracles is hardly mentioned.
"We have epistles from Peter, James, John, and Jude—all of
whom are said by the evangelists to have *seen* Jesus after he rose
from the dead, in none of which epistles is the fact of the resurrection even stated, much less that Jesus was seen by the writer after
his resurrection."[2]

Many of the early Christian sects denied the resurrection of
Christ Jesus, but taught that he will rise, when there shall be a
general resurrection.

No actual representation of the resurrection of the Christian's
Saviour has yet been found among the monuments of *early* Christianity. The earliest representation of this event that has been
found is an ivory carving, and belongs to the *fifth or sixth*
century.[3]

[1] Baccalaureate Sermon, June 26th, 1881.
[2] Greg : The Creed of Christendom, p. 284.
[3] See Jameson's Hist. of Our Lord in Art, vol. ii., and Lundy's Monumental Christianity.

CHAPTER XXIV.

THE second coming of Christ Jesus is clearly taught in the canonical, as well as in the apocryphal, books of the New Testament. Paul teaches, or *is made to teach it*,[1] in the following words:

> "If we believe that Jesus died and rose again, even so them also which sleep in Jesus will God bring with him. For this we say unto you by the word of the Lord, that we which are alive *and remain unto the coming of the Lord*, shall not prevent them which are asleep. *For the Lord himself shall descend from heaven* with a shout, with the voice of the archangel, and with the trump of God, and the dead in Christ shall rise first: Then we which are alive and remain shall be *caught up* together with them in the clouds, to meet the Lord *in the air:* and so shall we ever be with the Lord."[2]

He further tells the Thessalonians to "abstain from all appearance of evil," and to "be preserved blameless *unto the coming of our Lord Jesus Christ.*"[3]

James,[4] in his epistle to the brethren, tells them not to be in too great a hurry for the coming of their Lord, but to "be patient" and wait for the "coming of the Lord," as the "husbandman waiteth for the precious fruit of the earth." But still he assures them that "the coming of the Lord draweth nigh."[5]

Peter, in his first epistle, tells his brethren that "the end of all things is at hand,"[6] and that when the "chief shepherd" does appear, they "shall receive a crown of glory that fadeth not away."[7]

John, in his first epistle, tells the Christian community to "abide

---

[1] We say "is made to teach it," for the probability is that Paul never wrote this passage. The authority of *both* the Letters to the *Thessalonians*, attributed to Paul, is undoubtedly spurious. (See The Bible of To-Day, pp. 211, 212.)

[2] I. Thessalonians, iv. 14–17.

[3] Ibid. v. 22, 23.

[4] We say "James," but, it is probable that we have, in this epistle of James, another pseudonymous writing which appeared after the time that James must have lived. (See The Bible of To-Day, p. 225.)

[5] James, v. 7, 8.

[6] I. Peter, iv. 7.

[7] I. Peter, v. 7. This Epistle is not authentic. (See The Bible of To-Day, pp. 226, 227, 228.)

in him" (Christ), so that, "when he shall appear, we may have confidence, and not be ashamed before him."[1]

He further says:

"Behold, now are we the sons of God, and it doth not yet appear what we
shall be, but we know that, *when he shall appear*, we shall be like him, for we
shall see him as he is."[2]

According to the writer of the book of "The Acts," when
Jesus ascended into heaven, the Apostles stood looking *up* towards
heaven, where he had gone, and while thus engaged: "behold, two
men stood by them (dressed) in white apparel," who said unto them:

"Ye men of Galilee, why stand ye gazing up into heaven? This same Jesus
which is *taken up* from you into heaven, *shall so come in like manner as ye have
seen him go* (up) *into heaven*."[3]

The one great object which the writer of the book of Revelations wished to present to view, was "*the second coming of Christ*."
This writer, who seems to have been anxious for that time, which
was "surely" to come "quickly;" ends his book by saying:
"Even so, come Lord Jesus."[4]

The two men, dressed in white apparel, who had told the
Apostles that Jesus should "come again," were not the only persons whom they looked to for authority. He himself (according
to the Gospel) had told them so:

"The Son of man shall come (again) in the glory of his Father with his
angels."

And, as if to impress upon their minds that his second coming
should not be at a distant day, he further said:

"Verily I say unto you, there be some standing here, which shall not taste of
death, *till they see the Son of man coming in his kingdom*."[5]

This, surely, is very explicit, but it is not the only time he
speaks of his second advent. When foretelling the destruction
of the temple, his disciples came unto him, saying:

"Tell us when shall these things be, *and what shall be the sign of thy coming?*"[6]

His answer to this is very plain:

"Verily I say unto you, *this generation shall not pass till all these things be
fulfilled* (i. e., the destruction of the temple and his second coming), but of that
day and hour knoweth no man, no, not the angels of heaven, but my Father
only."[7]

---

[1] L John, ii. 28. This epistle is not authentic. (See Ibid. p. 231.)
[2] I. John, v. 2.
[3] Acts, i. 10, 11.
[4] Rev. xxii. 20.
[5] Matt. xvi. 27, 28.
[6] Ibid. xxiv. 3.
[7] Ibid. xxiv. 34–36.

In the second Epistle *attributed* to Peter, which was written after that generation had passed away,[1] there had begun to be some impatience manifest among the *believers,* on account of the long delay of Christ Jesus' second coming. " Where is the promise of his coming ? " say they, " for since the fathers fell asleep all things continue as they were from the beginning of the creation."[2] In attempting to smoothe over matters, this writer says : " There shall come in the last days scoffers, saying : ' Where is the promise of his coming ? '" to which he replies by telling them that they were ignorant of all the ways of the Lord, and that : " One day is with the Lord as a thousand years, and a thousand years as one day." He further says : " The Lord is not slack concerning his promise ;" and that " the day of the Lord *will come.*" This coming is to be " as a thief in the night," that is, when they least expect it.[3]

No wonder there should have been scoffers—as this writer calls them—the generation which was not to have passed away before his coming, had passed away ; all those who stood there had been dead many years ; the sun had not yet been darkened ; the stars were still in the heavens, and the moon still continued to reflect light. None of the predictions had yet been fulfilled.

Some of the early Christian Fathers have tried to account for the words of Jesus, where he says : " Verily I say unto you, there be some standing here which shall not taste of death, till they see the Son of man coming in his kingdom," by saying that he referred to *John* only, and that that Apostle was not dead, but sleeping. This fictitious story is related by Saint Augustin, " from the re- port," as he says, " of credible persons," and is to the effect that :

" At Ephesus, where St. John the Apostle lay buried, he was not believed to be dead, *but to be sleeping only in the grave,* which he had provided for himself till our Saviour's second coming: in proof of which, they affirm, that the earth, under which he lay, was seen to heave up and down perpetually, in conformity to the motion of his body, in the act of breathing."[4]

This story clearly illustrates the stupid credulity and superstition of the primitive age of the church, and the faculty of imposing any fictions upon the people, which their leaders saw fit to inculcate.

The doctrine of the *millennium* designates a certain period in the history of the world, lasting for a long, indefinite space (vaguely a *thousand years,* as the word " *millennium* " implies) during which the kingdom of *Christ Jesus* will be visibly established on the earth. The idea undoubtedly originated proximately in the Messianic ex-

---

[1] Towards the close of the second century. (See Bible of To-Day.)   [2] II. Peter, iii. 4.   [3] II. Peter, iii. 8-10.   [4] See Middleton's Works, vol. 1. p. 188.

pectation of the Jews (as Jesus *did not* sit on the throne of David and become an earthly ruler, it *must be* that he is *coming again* for this purpose), but more remotely in the Pagan doctrine of the final triumph of the several " Christs " over their adversaries.

In the first century of the Church, *millenarianism* was a *whis-pered* belief, to which the book of Daniel, and more particularly the predictions of the *Apocalypse*[1] gave an apostolical authority, but, when the church imbibed *Paganism*, their belief on this subject lent it a more vivid coloring and imagery.

The unanimity which the early Christian teachers exhibit in regard to *millenarianism*, proves how strongly it had laid hold of the imagination of the Church, to which, in this early stage, immortality and future rewards were to a great extent things of this world as yet.   Not only did Cerinthus, but even the orthodox doctors—such as Papias (Bishop of Hierapolis), Irenæus, Justin Martyr and others—delighted themselves with dreams of the glory and magnificence of the millennial kingdom.   Papias, in his collection of traditional sayings of Christ Jesus, indulges in the most monstrous representations of the re-building of Jerusalem, and the colossal vines and grapes of the millennial reign.

According to the general opinion, the millennium was to be preceded by great calamities, after which the Messiah, *Christ Jesus*, would appear, and would bind Satan for a thousand years, annihilate the godless heathen, or make them slaves of the believers, overturn the Roman empire, from the ruins of which a new order of things would spring forth, in which " the dead in Christ " would rise, and along with the surviving saints enjoy an incomparable felicity in the city of the " New Jerusalem."   Finally, all nations would bend their knee to *him*, and acknowledge *him only* to be *the Christ*—his religion would reign supreme.   This is the " Golden Age " of the future, which all nations of antiquity believed in and looked forward to.

We will first turn to *India*, and shall there find that the *Hindoos* believed their "*Saviour*," or "*Preserver*" *Vishnu*, who appeared in mortal form as *Crishna*, is *to come again in the latter days.*   Their sacred books declare that in the last days, when the fixed stars have all apparently returned to the point whence they started, at the beginning of all things, in the month *Scorpio*, Vishnu will appear among mortals, in the form of an armed warrior, riding a winged *white horse*.[2]   In one hand he will carry a

---

[1] Chapters xx. and xxi. in particular.
[2] The *Christian Saviour*, as well as the *Hin-*

doo *Saviour*, will appear " in the latter days " among mortals " in the form of an armed war-

scimitar, "blazing like a comet," to destroy all the impure who shall then dwell on the face of the earth. In the other hand he will carry a large shining ring, to signify that the great circle of *Yugas* (ages) is completed, and that the end has come. At his approach *the sun and moon will be darkened, the earth will tremble, and the stars fall from the firmament.*[1]

The Buddhists believe that *Buddha* has repeatedly assumed a human form to facilitate the reunion of men with his own universal soul, so they believe that "*in the latter days*" *he will come again.* Their sacred books predict this coming, and relate that his mission will be to restore the world to order and happiness.[2] This is exactly the Christian idea of the millennium.

The *Chinese* also believe that "*in the latter days*" there is to be a *millennium* upon earth. Their five sacred volumes are full of prophesies concerning this "Golden Age of the Future." It is the universal belief among them that a "*Divine Man*" will establish himself on earth, and everywhere restore peace and happiness.[3]

The ancient *Persians* believed that in the last days, there would be a millennium on earth, when the religion of Zoroaster would be accepted by all mankind. The Parsees of to-day, who are the remnants of the once mighty Persians, have a tradition that a holy personage is waiting in a region called Kanguedez, for a summons from the Ized Serosch, who in the last days will bring him to Persia, to restore the ancient dominion of that country, and spread the religion of Zoroaster over the whole earth.[4]

The Rev. Joseph B. Gross, in his "Heathen Religion,"[5] speaking of the belief of the ancient Persians in the millennium, says:

"The dead would be raised,[6] and he who has made all things, cause the earth and the sea to return again the remains of the departed.[7] Then Ormuzd shall clothe them with flesh and blood, while they that live at the time of the resurrection, must die in order to likewise participate in its advantage.

"Before this momentous event takes place, three illustrious prophets shall appear, who will announce their presence by the performance of miracles.

"During this period of its existence, and till its final removal, the earth will be afflicted with pestilence, tempests, war, famine, and various other baneful calamities."[8]

rior, riding a *white horse.*" St. John sees this in his *vision*, and prophecies it in his "Revelation" thus: "And I saw, and behold a *white horse:* and he that sat on him had a *bow*; and a *crown* was given unto him: and he went forth conquering, and to conquer." (Rev. vi. 2.)

[1] Prog. Relig. Ideas, vol. i. p. 75. Hist. Hindostan, vol. ii. pp. 497-503. See also, Williams: Hinduism, p. 108.

[2] Prog. Relig. Ideas, i. 247, and Bunsen's Angel-Messiah, p. 48.

[3] See Prog. Relig. Ideas. vol. i. p. 209.

[4] See Ibid. p. 279. The Angel-Messiah, p. 287, and chap. xiii. this work.

[5] Pp. 122, 123.

[6] "And I saw the *dead*, small and great, stand before God." (Rev. xx. 12.)

[7] "And the *sea* gave up the dead which were in it." (Rev. xx. 13.)

[8] "And ye shall hear of wars, and rumors of wars." "Nation shall rise against nation, and

"After the resurrection, every one will be apprised of the good or evil which he may have done, and the righteous and the wicked will be separated from each other.[1] Those of the latter whose offenses have not yet been expiated, will be cast into hell during the term of three days and three nights,[2] in the presence of an assembled world, in order to be purified in the burning stream of liquid ore.[3] After this, they enjoy endless felicity in the society of the blessed, and the pernicious empire of Ahriman (the devil), is fairly exterminated.[4] Even this lying spirit will be under the necessity to avail himself of this fiery ordeal, and made to rejoice in its expurgating and cleansing efficacy. Nay, hell itself is purged of its mephitic impurities, and washed clean in the flames of a universal regeneration.[5]

"The earth is now the habitation of bliss, all nature glows in light; and the equitable and benignant laws of Ormuzd reign supremely through the illimitable universe.[6] Finally, after the resurrection, mankind will recognize each other again; wants, cares, and passions will cease;[7] and everything in the paradisian and all-embracing empire of light, shall rebound to the praise of the benificent God."[8]

The disciples of *Bacchus* expected his *second advent*. They hoped he would assume at some future day the government of the universe, and that he would restore to man his primary felicity.[9]

The *Esthonian* from the time of the German invasion lived a life of bondage under a foreign yoke, and the iron of his slavery entered into his soul. He told how the ancient hero Kalewipoeg sits in the realms of shadows, waiting until his country is in its extremity of distress, when he will *return to earth* to avenge the injuries of the Esths, and elevate the poor crushed people into a mighty power.[10]

The suffering *Celt* has his Brian Boroihme, or Arthur, *who will come again*, the first to inaugurate a Fenian millennium, the second to regenerate Wales. Olger Dansk waits till the time arrives when he is to start from sleep to the assistance of the *Dane* against the hated Prussian. The Messiah is to come and restore the kingdom

---

kingdom against kingdom, and there shall be famines, pestilences, and earthquakes in divers places." (Matt. xxiv. 6, 7.)

[1] "And before him shall be gathered all nations : and he shall separate them one from another, as a shepherd divideth his sheep from the goats; (Matt. xxv. 32, 33.)

[2] "He descended into hell, the third day he rose (again) from the dead." (Apostles' Creed.)

[3] Purgatory—a place in which souls are supposed by the papists to be purged by fire from carnal impurities, before they are received into heaven.

[4] "And he laid hold on the dragon, that old serpent, which is the Devil, and Satan, and bound him a thousand years." (Rev. xx. 2.)

[5] "And death and hell were cast into the lake of fire." (Rev. xx. 14.)

[6] "And I saw a new heaven and a new earth ; for the first earth, and the first heaven were passed away." (Rev. xxi. 1.)

[7] "And God shall wipe away all tears from their eyes ; and there shall be no more death, neither sorrow, nor crying, neither shall there be any more pain : for the former things are passed away." (Rev. xxi. 4.)

[8] "And after these things I heard a great voice of much people in heaven, saying, 'Alleluia; salvation, and glory, and honor, and power, unto the Lord, our God.'" (Rev. xix. 1.) "For the Lord God omnipotent reigneth." (Rev. xix. 6.)

[9] Dupuis : Orig. Relig. Belief.

[10] Baring-Gould : Orig. Relig. Belief, vol. L p. 407.

of the *Jews*.	Charlemagne was the Messiah of mediæval Teuton-
dom. He.it was who founded the great German empire, and shed
over it the blaze of Christian truth, and now he sleeps in the Kyff-
hauserberg, waiting till German heresy has reached its climax and
Germany is wasted through internal conflicts, to rush to earth once
more, and revive the great empire and restore the Catholic faith.[1]

The ancient *Scandinavians* believed that in the " latter days "
great calamities would befall mankind. The earth would tremble,
and the stars fall from heaven. After which, the great *serpent*
would be chained, and the religion of Odin would reign supreme.[2]

The disciples of *Quetzalcoatle*, the Mexican Saviour, expected
his second advent. Before he departed this life, he told the inhabitants of Cholula that he would return again to govern them.[3]
This remarkable tradition was so deeply cherished in their hearts,
says Mr. Prescott in his " Conquest of Mexico," that " the Mexicans
looked confidently to the return of their benevolent deity."[4]

So implicitly was this believed by the subjects, that when the
Spaniards appeared on the coast, they were joyfully hailed as the
returning god and his companions. Montezuma's messengers reported to the Inca that "it was Quetzalcoatle who was coming,
bringing his temples (ships) with him." All throughout New
Spain they expected the reappearance of this " Son of the Great
God." into the world, who would renew all things.[5]

Acosta alludes to this, in his " History of the Indies," as follows :

"In the beginning of the year 1518, they (the Mexicans), discovered a fleet at
sea, in the which was the Marques del Valle, Don Fernando Cortez, with his companions, a news which much troubled Montezuma, and conferring with his
council, they all said, that without doubt, their great and ancient lord Quetzalcoatle was come, who had said that he would return from the East, whither he
had gone."[6]

The doctrine of the millennium and the second advent of Christ
Jesus, has been a very important one in the Christian church. The
ancient Christians were animated by a contempt for their present
existence, and by a just confidence of immortality, of which the
doubtful and imperfect faith of modern ages cannot give us any
adequate notion. In the primitive church, the influence of truth
was powerfully strengthened by an opinion, which, however much
it may deserve respect for its usefulness and antiquity, has not been

---

[1] Baring-Gould : Orig. Relig. Belief, vol. i.
p. 407.
[2] See Mallet's Northern Antiquities.
[3] Humboldt : Amer. Res., vol. i. p. 91.

[4] Prescott : Con. of Mexico, vol. i. p. 60.
[5] Fergusson : Tree and Serpent Worship, p.
37. Squire : Serpent Symbol, p. 187,
[6] Acosta : Hist. Indies, vol. ii.p. 513.

found agreeable to experience. *It was universally believed, that the end of the world and the kingdom of heaven were at hand.*[1] The near approach of this wonderful event had been predicted, as we have seen, by the Apostles ; the tradition of it was preserved by their earliest disciples, and those who believed that the discourses *attributed* to Jesus were really uttered by him, were *obliged* to expect the second and glorious coming of the " Son of Man " in the clouds, *before that generation was totally extinguished* which had beheld his humble condition upon earth, and which might still witness the calamities of the Jews under Vespasian or Hadrian. The revolution of seventeen centuries has instructed us not to press too closely the *mysterious* language of prophecy and revelation ; but as long as this error was permitted to subsist in the church, it was productive of the most salutary effects on the faith and practice of Christians, who lived in the awful expectation of that moment when the globe itself and all the various races of mankind, *should tremble at the appearance of their divine judge.* This expectation was countenanced—as we have seen—by the twenty-fourth chapter of St. Matthew, and by the first epistle of Paul to the Thessalonians. Erasmus (one of the most vigorous promoters of the Reformation) removes the difficulty by the help of *allegory* and *metaphor ;* and the learned Grotius (a learned theologian of the 16th century) ventures to insinuate, that, for wise purposes, *the pious deception was permitted to take place.*

The ancient and popular doctrine of the millennium was intimately connected with the second coming of Christ Jesus. As the works of the creation had been fixed in *six days,* their duration in the present state, according to a tradition which was attributed to the prophet Elijah, was fixed to *six thousand years.*[2] By the same analogy it was inferred, that this long period of labor and contention, which had now almost elapsed, would be succeeded by a joyful Sabbath of *a thousand years,* and that Christ Jesus, with the triumphant band of the saints and the elect who had escaped death, or who had been miraculously revived, would reign upon earth until the time appointed for the last and general resurrection. So pleasing was this hope to the mind of the believers, that the " New Jerusalem," the

---

[1] Over all the Higher Asia there seems to have been diffused an immemorial tradition relative to a second grand convulsion of nature, and the final dissolution of the earth by the terrible agency of FIRE, as the first is said to have been by that of WATER. It was taught by the Hindoos, the Egyptians, Plato, Pythagoras, Zoroaster, the Stoics, and others, and was afterwards adopted by the Christians. (II. Peter, iii. 9. Hist. Hindostan, vol. ii. pp. 498–500.)

[2] " And God made, in six days, the works of his hands, . . . the meaning of it is this ; that in *six thousand years* the Lord will bring all things to an end." (Barnabas. *Apoc.* c. xiii.)

seat of this blissful kingdom, was quickly adorned with all the gayest colors of the imagination. A felicity consisting only of pure and spiritual pleasure would have been too refined for its inhabitants, who were still supposed to possess their human nature and senses. A "Garden of Eden," with the amusements of the pastoral life, was no longer suited to the advanced state of society which prevailed under the Roman empire. A city was therefore erected of gold and precious stones, and a supernatural plenty of corn and wine was bestowed on the adjacent territory; in the free enjoyment of whose spontaneous productions, the happy and benevolent people were never to be restrained by any jealous laws of exclusive property. Most of these pictures were borrowed from a misrepresentation of Isaiah, Daniel, and the Apocalypse. One of the grossest images may be found in Irenæus (l. v.) the disciple of Papias, who had seen the Apostle St. John. Though it might not be universally received, it appears to have been the reigning sentiment of the orthodox believers; and it seems so well adapted to the desires and apprehensions of mankind, that it must have contributed in a very considerable degree to the progress of the Christian faith. But when the edifice of the church was almost completed, the temporary support was laid aside. The doctrine of Christ Jesus' reign upon earth was at first treated as a profound *allegory*, was considered by degrees as a *doubtful* and *useless* opinion, and was at length rejected as the absurd invention of heresy and fanaticism. But although this doctrine had been " laid aside," and " rejected," it was again resurrected, and is alive and rife at the present day, even among those who stand as the leaders of the orthodox faith.

The expectation of the " last day " in the year 1000 A. D., reinvested the doctrine with a transitory importance; but it lost all credit again when the hopes so keenly excited by the *crusades* faded away before the stern reality of Saracenic success, and the predictions of the "Everlasting Gospel," a work of Joachim de Floris, a Franciscan abbot, remained unfulfilled.[1]

At the period of the *Reformation*, millenarianism once more experienced a partial revival, because it was not a difficult matter

---

[1] After the devotees and followers of the new gospel had in vain expected the *Holy One* who was to come, they at last pitched upon St. Francis as having been the expected one, and, of course, the most surprising and absurd miracles were said to have been performed by him. Some of the fanatics who believed in this man, maintained that St. Francis was " wholly and entirely transformed into the person of Christ "—*Totum Christo configuratum*. Some of them maintained that the gospel of Joachim was expressly preferred to the gospel of Christ. (Mosheim : Hist. Cent., xiii. pt. ii. sects. xxxiv. and xxxvi. Anacalypsis, vol. i. p. 695,)

16

to apply some of its symbolism to the papacy. The Pope, for example, was *Antichrist*—a belief still adhered to by some extreme
Protestants.   Yet the doctrine was not adopted by the great body
of the reformers, but by some fanatical sects, such as the Anabaptists,
and by the Theosophists of the seventeenth century.

During the civil and religious wars in France and England,
when great excitement prevailed, it was also prominent.   The
" Fifth Monarchy Men " of Cromwell's time were millenarians of the
most exaggerated and dangerous sort.   Their peculiar tenet was that
the millennium *had* come, and that *they* were the saints who were
to inherit the earth.   The excesses of the French Roman Catholic
Mystics and Quietists terminated in *chiliastic*[1] views.   Among the
Protestants it was during the " Thirty Years' War " that the most enthusiastic and learned chiliasts flourished.   The awful suffering and
wide-spread desolation of that time led pious hearts to solace themselves with the hope of a peaceful and glorious future.   Since then
the *penchant* which has sprung up for expounding the prophetical
books of the Bible, and particularly the *Apocalypse*, with a view to
present events, has given the doctrine a faint semi-theological life,
very different, however, from the earnest faith of the first Christians.

Among the foremost chiliastic teachers of modern centuries are
to be mentioned Ezechiel Meth, Paul Felgenhauer, Bishop Co-
menius, Professor Jurien, Seraris, Poiret, J. Mede; while Thomas
Burnet and William Whiston endeavored to give chiliasm a geological foundation, but without finding much favor.   Latterly, especially since the rise and extension of missionary enterprise, the
opinion has obtained a wide currency, that after the conversion of
the whole world to Christianity, a blissful and glorious era will en-
sue; but not much stress—except by extreme literalists—is now
laid on the nature or duration of this far-off felicity.

Great eagerness, and not a little ingenuity have been exhibited
by many persons in fixing a *date* for the commencement of the
millennium.   The celebrated theologian, Johann Albrecht Bengel,
who, in the eighteenth century, revived an earnest interest in the
subject amongst orthodox Protestants, asserted from a study of the
prophecies that the millennium would begin in 1836.   This date
was long popular.   Swedenborg held that the last judgment *took
place* in 1757, and that the new church, or "*Church of the New
Jerusalem*," as his followers designate themselves—in other words,
the millennial era—*then began.*

---

[1] *Chiliasm*—the thousand years when Satan is bound.

In America, considerable agitation was excited by the preaching of one William Miller, who fixed the second advent of Christ Jesus about 1843. Of late years, the most noted English millenarian was Dr. John Cumming, who placed the end of the *present dispensation* in 1866 or 1867 ; but as that time passed without any millennial symptoms, he modified his original views considerably, before he died, and conjectured that the beginning of the millennium would not differ so much after all from the years immediately preceding it, as people commonly suppose.

CHAPTER XXV.

CHRIST JESUS AS JUDGE OF THE DEAD.

ACCORDING to Christian dogma, "God the Father" is not to be the judge at the last day, but this very important office is to be held by "God the Son." This is taught by the writer of "The Gospel according to St. John"—whoever he may have been—when he says:

> "For the Father judgeth no man, *but· hath committed all judgment unto the Son.*"[1]

Paul also, in his "Epistle to the Romans" (or some other person who has interpolated the passage), tells us that:

> "In the day when God shall judge the secrets of men," this judgment shall be done "by *Jesus Christ*," his son.[2]

Again, in his "Epistle to Timothy,"[3] he says:

> "*The Lord Jesus Christ* shall judge the quick and the dead, at his appearing and his kingdom."[4]

The writer of the "Gospel according to St. Matthew," also describes Christ Jesus as judge at the last day.[5]

Now, the question arises, *is this doctrine original with Christianity?* To this we must answer *no*. It was taught, for ages before the time of Christ Jesus or Christianity, that the Supreme Being—whether "Brahmá," "Zeruâné Akeréné," "Jupiter," or "Yahweh,"[6]—was not to be the judge at the last day, but that their *sons* were to hold this position.

The sectarians of *Buddha* taught that he (who was the *Son of God* (Brahmá) and the Holy Virgin Maya), is to be the judge of the dead.[7]

---

[1] John, v. 22.
[2] Romans, ii. 16.
[3] Not authentic. (See The Bible of To-Day, p. 212.)
[4] II. Timothy, iv. 1.

[5] Matt. xxv. 31–46.
[6] Through an error we pronounce this name *Jehovah*.
[7] See Dupuis : Origin of Religious Relief, p 366.

According to the religion of the Hindoos, *Crishna* (who was the *Son of God*, and the Holy Virgin Devaki), is to be the judge at the last day.[1] And *Yama* is the god of the departed spirits, and the judge of the dead, according to the *Vedas*.[2]

Osiris, the Egyptian "Saviour" and son of the "Immaculate Virgin" Neith or Nout, was believed by the ancient Egyptians to be the judge of the dead.[3] He is represented on Egyptian monuments, seated on his throne of judgment, bearing a staff, and carrying the *crux ansata*, or cross with a handle.[4] *St. Andrew's cross* is upon his breast. His *throne* is in checkers, to denote the good and evil over which he presides, or to indicate the good and evil who appear before him as the judge."[5]

Among the many hieroglyphic titles which accompany his figure in these sculptures, and in many other places on the walls of temples and tombs, are "Lord of Life," "The Eternal Ruler," "Manifester of Good," "Revealer of Truth," "Full of Goodness and Truth," &c.[6]

Mr. Bonwick, speaking of the Egyptian belief in the last judgment, says:

"A perusal of the twenty-fifth chapter of Matthew will prepare the reader for the investigation of the Egyptian notion of the last judgment."[7]

Prof. Carpenter, referring to the Egyptian Bible—which is by far the most ancient of all holy books[8]—says:

"In the 'Book of the Dead,' there are used the very phrases we find in the New Testament, *in connection with the day of judgment*."[9]

According to the religion of the *Persians*, it is *Ormuzd*, "*The First Born of the Eternal One*," who is judge of the dead. He had the title of "The All-Seeing," and "The Just Judge."[10]

Zeruâné Akeréné is the name of him who corresponds to "God the Father" among other nations. He was the "One Supreme essence," the "Invisible and Incomprehensible."[11]

Among the ancient *Greeks*, it was *Aeacus*—Son of the Most High God—who was to be judge of the dead.[12]

The Christian Emperor Constantine, in his oration to the clergy, speaking of the ancient poets of Greece, says:

---

[1] See Samuel Johnson's Oriental Religions, p. 504.
[2] See Williams' Hinduism, p. 25.
[3] See Bonwick's Egyptian Belief, p. 120. Renouf : Religions of the Ancient Egyptians, p. 110, and Prog. Relig. Ideas, vol. i. p. 152.
[4] See Bonwick's Egyptian Belief, p. 151, and Prog. Relig. Ideas, vol. i. p. 152.
[5] See Bonwick's Egyptian Belief, p. 151.
[6] See Prog. Relig. Ideas, vol. i. p. 154.
[7] Egyptian Belief, p. 419.
[8] See Ibid. p. 185.
[9] Quoted in Ibid. p. 419.
[10] Prog. Relig. Ideas, vol. i. p. 259.
[11] Ibid. p. 258.
[12] See Bell's Pantheon, vol. ii. p. 16.

"They affirm that men who are the *sons of the gods*, do judge departed souls."[1]

Strange as it may seem, "there are no examples of Christ Jesus conceived as judge, or the last judgment, in the *early* art of Christianity."[2]

The author from whom we quote the above, says, "It would be difficult to define the *cause* of this, though many may be conjectured."[3]

Would it be unreasonable to "conjecture" that the *early* Christians did not teach this doctrine, but that it was imbibed, in after years, with many other heathen ideas?

---

[1] Constantine's Oration to the Clergy, ch. x.   vol. ii. p. 392.
[2] Jameson: History of Our Lord in Art,   [3] Ibid.

CHAPTER XXVI.

CHRIST JESUS AS CREATOR, AND ALPHA AND OMEGA.

CHRISTIAN dogma also teaches that it was not "God the Father," but "God the Son" who created the heavens, the earth, and all that therein is.

The writer of the fourth Gospel says:

"*All things were made by him*, and without him was not anything made that was made."[1]

Again:

"He was in the world *and the world was made by him*, and the world knew him not."[2]

In the "Epistle to the Colossians," we read that:

"By *him* were all things created. that are in heaven, and that are in earth, visible and invisible, whether they be thrones or dominions, or principalities, or powers; *all things were created by him.*"[3]

Again, in the "Epistle to the Hebrews," we are told that:

"God hath spoken unto us by *his son*, whom he hath appointed heir of all things, *by whom also he made the world.*"[4]

Samuel Johnson, D. O. Allen,[5] and Thomas Maurice,[6] tell us that, according to the religion of the *Hindoos*, it is *Crishna*, the Son, and the second person in the ever-blessed Trinity,[7] "who is the origin and end of all the worlds; *all this universe came into being through him, the eternal maker.*"[8]

In the holy book of the Hindoos, called the *"Bhagvat Geeta,"* may be found the following words of *Crishna*, addressed to his "beloved disciple" Ar-jouan:

"I am *the Lord of all created beings.*"[9] "*Mankind was created by me* of four kinds, distinct in their principles, and in their duties; *know me then to be the Creator of mankind*, uncreated, and without decay."[10]

---

[1] John, i. 3.
[2] John, i. 10.
[3] Colossians, i.
[4] Hebrews, i. 2.
[5] Allen's India, pp. 137 and 380.
[6] Indian Antiq., vol. ii. p. 288.
[7] See the chapter on the Trinity.
[8] Oriental Religions, p. 502.
[9] Lecture iv. p. 51.
[10] Geeta, p. 52.

247

In Lecture VII., entitled : " Of the Principles of Nature, and the Vital Spirit," he also says :

' I am the 'creation and the dissolution of the whole universe.   There is not anything greater than I, and all things hang on me."

Again, in Lecture IX., entitled, " Of the Chief of Secrets and Prince of Science," Crishna says :

' The whóle world was spread abroad by me in my invisible form.   All things are dependent on me."   " I am the Father and the Mother of this world, the Grandsire and the Preserver.   I am the Holy One worthy to be known; the mystic figure OM.[1]   .   .   .   I am the journey of the good; the *Comforter ;* the *Creator ;* the *Witness ;* the *Resting-place ;* the *Asylum* and the *Friend.*"[2]

In Lecture X., entitled, " Of the diversity of the Divine Nature," he says :

"*I am the Creator of all things*, and all things proceed from me.   Those who are endued with spiritual wisdom, believe this and worship me; their very hearts and minds are in me; they rejoice amongst themselves, and delight in speaking of my name, and teaching one another my doctrine."[3]

Innumerable texts, similar to these, might be produced from the Hindoo Scriptures, but these we deem sufficient to show, in the words of Samuel Johnson quoted above, that, "According to the religion of the Hindoos, it is Crishna who is the origin and the end of all the worlds ;" and that "all this universe came into being through him, the Eternal Maker."   The *Chinese* believed in One Supreme God, to whose honor they burnt incense, but of whom they had no image.   This " God the Father " was *not* the Creator, according to their theology or mythology; but they had another god, of whom they had statues or idols, called *Natigai,* who was the god of allterrestrial things ; in fact, God, *the Creator of this world* —inferior or subordinate to the Supreme Being—from whom they petition for fine weather, or whatever else they want—a sort of *mediator.*[4]

Lanthu, who was born of a " pure, spotless virgin," is believed by his followers or disciples to be the Creator of all things ;[5] and *Taou,* a deified hero, who is mentioned about 560 B. C., is believed by some sects and affirmed by their books, to be " the original source and first productive cause of all things."[6]

In the *Chaldean* oracles, the doctrine of the " Only Begotten Son," I A O, as *Creator,* is plainly taught.

---

[1] O. M. or A. U. M. is the Hindoo ineffable name ; the mystic emblem of the deity.   It is never uttered aloud, but only mentally by the devout.   It signifies Brahma, Vishnou, and Siva, the *Hindoo Trinity.*   (See Charles Wilkes in Geeta, p. 142, and King's Gnostics and their Remains, p. 163.)

[2] Geeta, p. 80.
[3] Geeta, p. 84.
[4] See Higgins : Anacalypsis, vol i. p. 48.
[5] See Bell's Pantheon, vol. ii. p. 85.
[6] See Davis : Hist. China, vol. ii. pp. 109 and 113, and Thornton, vol. i. p. 187.

According to ancient *Persian* mythology, there is one supreme essence, invisible and incomprehensible, named "*Zeruâné Akerêné*," which signifies "unlimited time," or "the eternal." From him emanated *Ormuzd*, the "King of Light," the "First-born of the Eternal One," &c. Now, this "First-born of the Eternal One" is he by whom all things were made, all things came into being through him; *he is the Creator.*[1]

A large portion of the *Zend-Avesta*—the Persian Sacred Book or Bible—is filled with prayers to Ormuzd, God's First-Born. The following are samples:

"I address my prayer to Ormuzd, *Creator of all* things; who always has been, who is, and who will be forever; who is wise and powerful; who made the great arch of heaven, the sun, the moon, stars, winds, clouds, waters, earth, fire, trees, animals and men, whom Zoroaster adored. Zoroaster, who brought to the world knowledge of the law, who knew by natural intelligence, and by the ear, what ought to be done, all that has been, all that is, and all that will be; the science of sciences, *the excellent word*, by which souls pass the luminous and radiant bridge, separate themselves from the evil regions, and go to light and holy dwellings, full of fragrance. *O Creator*, I obey thy laws, I think, act, speak, according to thy orders. I separate myself from all sin. I do good works according to my power. I adore thee with purity of thought, word, and action. I pray to Ormuzd, who recompenses good works, who delivers unto the end all those who obey his laws. Grant that I may arrive at paradise, where all is fragrance, light, and happiness."[2]

According to the religion of the ancient *Assyrians*, it was *Narduk*, the Logos, the WORD, "the eldest son of Hea," "the Merciful One," "the Life-giver," &c., who created the heavens, the earth, and all that therein is.[3]

Adonis, the Lord and Saviour, was believed to be the Creator of men, and god of the resurrection of the dead.[4]

Prometheus, the Crucified Saviour, is the divine forethought, existing before the souls of men, and the creator Hominium.[5]

The writer of "The Gospel according to St. John," has made Christ Jesus *co-eternal* with God, as well as Creator, in these words:

"In the beginning was the *Word*, and the Word was with God." "The same was in the beginning with God."[6]

Again, in praying to his Father, he makes Jesus say:

"And now, O Father, glorify thou me with thine own self with the glory *which I had with thee before the world was.*"[7]

---

[1] See Prog. Relig. Ideas, vol. i. p. 259. In the most ancient parts of the Zend-Avesta, Ormuzd is said to have created the world by his WORD. (See Bunsen's Angel-Messiah, p. 104, and Gibbon's Rome, vol. ii. p. 302, Note by Guizot.) In the beginning was the WORD, and the WORD was with God, and the WORD was God." (John, i. 1.)

[2] Quoted in Prog. Relig. Ideas, vol. i. p. 267.
[3] See Bonwick's Egyptian Belief, p. 404.
[4] See Dunlap's Mysteries of Adoni, p. 156.
[5] See Ibid. p. 156, and Bulfinch, Age of Fable.
[6] John, i. 1, 2.
[7] John, xvii. 5.

Paul is made to say:

"And he (Christ) is before all things."[1]

Again:

"Jesus Christ, the same yesterday, to-day, and forever."[2]

St. John the Divine, in his "Revelation," has made Christ Jesus say:

"I am Alpha and Omega, the beginning and the end"—"which is, and which was, and which is to come, the Almighty,"[3] "the first and the last."[4]

Hindoo scripture also makes *Crishna* "the first and the last," "the beginning and the end." We read in the "Geeta," where Crishna is reported to have said:

"I myself never was not."[5] "Learn that he by whom all things were formed" (meaning himself) "is incorruptible."[6] "I am eternity and non-eternity."[7] "I am before all things, and the mighty ruler of the universe."[8] "I am the beginning, the middle and the end of all things."[9]

Arjouan, his disciple, addresses him thus:

"Thou art the Supreme Being, incorruptible, worthy to be known; thou art prime supporter of the universal orb; thou art the never-failing and eternal guardian of religion; *thou art from all beginning*, and I esteem thee."[10] Thou art "the Divine Being, before all other gods."[11]

Again he says:

"Reverence! Reverence be unto thee, before and behind! Reverence be unto thee on all sides, O thou who art all in all! Infinite in thy power and thy glory! Thou includest all things, wherefore thou art all things."[12]

In another Holy Book of the Hindoos, called the "Vishnu Purana," we also read that Vishnu—in the form of Crishna—"who descended into the womb of the (virgin) Devaki, and was born as her son" was "*without beginning, middle or end.*"[13]

Buddha is also Alpha and Omega, without beginning or end, "The Lord," "the Possessor of All," "He who is Omnipotent and Everlastingly to be Contemplated," "the Supreme Being, the Eternal One."[14]

Lao-kiun, the Chinese virgin-born God, who came upon earth about six hundred years before Jesus, was without beginning. It was said that he had existed from all eternity."[15]

---

[1] Col. i. 17.
[2] Hebrews, xiii. 8.
[3] Rev. i. 8, 22, 13.
[4] Rev. i. 77; xii. 18.
[5] Geeta, p. 35.
[6] Geeta, p. 36.
[7] Lecture ix. p. 80.
[8] Lecture x. p. 83.
[9] Lecture x. p. 85.
[10] Lecture ix. p. 91.
[11] Lecture x. p. 84.
[12] Lecture xi. p. 95.
[13] See Vishnu Purana, p. 440.
[14] See chapter xii.
[15] See Prog. Relig. Ideas, vol. i. p. 200.

The legends of the Taou-tsze sect in China declare their founder to have existed antecedent to the birth of the elements, in the Great Absolute; that he is the "pure essence of the *teen;*" that he is the original ancestor of the prime breath of life; that he gave form to the heavens and the earth, and caused creations and annihilations to succeed each other, in an endless series, during innumerable periods of the world. He himself is made to say:

"I was in existence prior to the manifestation of any corporeal shape; I appeared anterior to the supreme being, or first motion of creation."[1]

According to the *Zend Avesta,* Ormuzd, the first-born of the Eternal One, is he "who is, always has been, and who will be forever."[2]

Zeus was Alpha and Omega. An Orphic line runs thus:

"Zeus is the beginning, Zeus the middle, out of Zeus all things have been made."[3]

Bacchus was without beginning or end. An inscription on an ancient medal, referring to him, reads thus:

"It is I who leads you; it is I who protects you, and who saves you. I am Alpha and Omega."

Beneath this inscription is a serpent with his tail in his mouth, thus forming a *circle,* which was an emblem of *eternity* among the ancients.[4]

Without enumerating them, we may say that the majority of the virgin-born gods spoken of in Chapter XII. were like Christ Jesus—without beginning or end—and that many of them were considered Creators of all things. This has led M. Dridon to remark (in his Hist. de Dieu), that in *early works of art,* Christ Jesus is made to take the place of his Father in *creation* and in similar labors, just as in heathen religions an inferior deity does the work under a superior one.

[1] Thornton: Hist. China, vol. i. p. 137.
[2] Prog. Relig. Ideas. ii. p. 267.
[3] Müller's Chips, vol. ii. p. 15.
[4] "C'est moi qui vous conduis, vous et tout ce qui vous regarde. C'est moi, qui vous conserve, ou qui vous sauve. Je suis Alpha et Omega. Il y a au dessons de l'inscription un serpent qui tient sa queue dans sa gueule et dans la cercle qu'il décrit, cest trois lettrs Greques TEE, qui sont le nombre 365. Le serpent, qui est'ordinaire un emblème de l'éternité est ici celui de soleil et de ses revolutions." Beausobre: Hist. de Manichee, Tom. ii. p. 56.
"I say that I am immortal, Dionysus (Bacchus) son of Deus." (*Aristophanes,* in Myst. of Adoni, pp. 80 and 105.)

CHAPTER XXVII.

THE MIRACLES OF CHRIST JESUS AND THE PRIMITIVE CHRISTIANS.

THE legendary history of Jesus of Nazareth, contained in the books of the New Testament, is full of prodigies and wonders. These alleged prodigies, and the faith which the people seem to have put in such a tissue of falsehoods, indicate the prevalent disposition of the people to believe in everything, and it was among such a class that Christianity was propagated. All leaders of religion had the reputation of having performed miracles ; the biographers of Jesus, therefore, not wishing *their* Master to be outdone, have made him also a wonder-worker, and a performer of miracles ; without them Christianity could not prosper. Miracles were needed in those days, on all special occasions. " There is not a single historian of antiquity, whether Greek or Latin, who has not recorded oracles, prodigies, prophecies, and *miracles*, on the occasion of some memorable events, or revolutions of states and kingdoms. Many of these are attested in the gravest manner by the gravest writers, *and were firmly believed at the time by the people.*"[1]

Hindoo sacred books represent *Crishna*, their Saviour and Redeemer, as in constant strife against the evil spirit. He surmounts extraordinary dangers ; strews his way with miracles ; raising the dead, healing the sick, restoring the maimed, the deaf and the blind ; everywhere supporting the weak against the strong, the oppressed against the powerful. The people crowded his way and adored him as a GOD, and these miracles were the evidences of his divinity for centuries before the time of Jesus.

The learned Thomas Maurice, speaking of Crishna, tells us that he passed his innocent hours at the home of his foster-father, in rural diversions, his divine origin not being suspected, *until repeated miracles soon discovered his celestial origin ;*[2] and Sir William Jones speaks of his *raising the dead*, and saving multitudes *by his*

---

[1] Dr. Conyers Middleton : Free Enquiry, p. 177.   [2] Indian Antiquities, vol. iii. p. 46,

miraculous powers.[1] To enumerate the miracles of Crishna would be useless and tedious; we shall therefore mention but a few, of which the Hindoo sacred books are teeming.

When Crishna was born, his life was sought by the reigning monarch, Kansa, who had the infant Saviour and his father and mother locked in a dungeon, guarded, and barred by seven iron doors. While in this dungeon the father heard a secret voice distinctly utter these words: "Son of Yadu, take up this child and carry it to Gokool, to the house of Nanda." Vasudeva, struck with astonishment, answered: "How shall I obey this injunction, thus vigilantly guarded and barred by seven iron doors that prohibit all egress?" The unknown voice replied: "The doors shall open of themselves to let thee pass, and behold, I have caused a deep slumber to fall upon thy guards, which shall continue till thy journey be accomplished." Vasudeva immediately felt his chains miraculously loosened, and, taking up the child in his arms, hurried with it through all the doors, the guards being buried in profound sleep. When he came to the river Yumna, which he was obliged to cross to get to Gokool, the waters immediately rose up to kiss the child's feet, and then respectfully retired on each side to make way for its transportation, so that Vasudeva passed dry-shod to the opposite shore.[2]

When Crishna came to man's estate, one of his first miracles was the cure of a leper.

A passionate Brahman, having received a slight insult from a certain Rajah, on going out of his doors, uttered this curse: "That he should, from head to foot, be covered with boils and leprosy;" which being fulfilled in an instant upon the unfortunate king, he prayed to Crishna to deliver him from his evil. At first, Crishna did not heed his request, but finally he appeared to him, asking what his request was? He replied, "To be freed from my distemper." The Saviour then cured him of his distemper.[3]

Crishna was one day walking with his disciples, when "they met a poor cripple or lame woman, having a vessel filled with spices, sweet-scented oils, sandal-wood, saffron, civet and other perfumes. Crishna making a halt, she made a certain sign with her finger on his forehead, *casting the rest upon his head.* Crishna asking her what it was she would request of him, the woman replied, nothing but the use of my limbs. Crishna, then, setting his foot upon hers, and taking her by the hand, raised her from the ground, and not

[1] Asiatic Researches, vol. i. p. 237.   [2] Hist. Hindostan, vol. ii. p. 331.   [3] Ibid. p. 319.

only restored her limbs, but renewed her age, so that, instead of a wrinkled, tawny skin, she received a fresh and fair one in an instant. At her request, Crishna and his company lodged in her house."[1]

On another occasion, Crishna having requested a learned Brahman to ask of him whatever boon he most desired, the Brahman said, "Above all things, I desire to have my two dead sons restored to life." Crishna assured him that this should be done, and immediately the two young men were restored to life and brought to their father.[2]

The learned Orientalist, Thomas Maurice, after speaking of the miracles performed by Crishna, says:

"In regard to the numerous miracles wrought by Crishna, it should be remembered that miracles are never wanting to the decoration of an Indian romance; they are, in fact, the life and soul of the vast machine; nor is it at all a subject of wonder that the dead should be raised to life in a history expressly intended, like all other sacred fables of Indian fabrication, for the propagation and support of the whimsical doctrine of the Metempsychosis."[3]

To speak thus of the miracles of Christ Jesus, would, of course, be heresy—although what applies to the miracles of Crishna apply to those of Jesus—we, therefore, find this gentleman branding as "*infidel*" a learned French orientalist who was guilty of doing this thing.

Buddha performed great miracles for the good of mankind, and the legends concerning him are full of the most extravagant prodigies and wonders.[4] "By miracles and preaching," says Burnouf, "was the religion of Buddha established."

R. Spence Hardy says of Buddha:

"All the principal events of his life are represented as being attended by incredible prodigies. He could pass through the air at will, and know the thoughts of all beings."[5]

Prof. Max Müller says:

"The Buddhist legends teem with miracles attributed to Buddha and his disciples—miracles which in wonderfulness certainly surpass the miracles of any other religion."[6]

Buddha was at one time going from the city of Rohita-vastu to the city of Benares, when, coming to the banks of the river Ganges, and wishing to go across, he addressed himself to the owner of a

[1] Hist. Hindostan, vol. ii. p. 320. Vishnu Purana, bk. v. ch. xx.
[2] Prog. Relig. Ideas, vol. i. p. 68.
[3] Hist. Hindostan, vol. ii. p. 269.
[4] See Hardy's Buddhist Legends, and Eastern Monachism. Beal's Romantic Hist. Buddha. Bunsen's Angel-Messiah, and Huc's Travels, &c.
[5] Hardy: Buddhist Legends, pp. xxi. xxii.
[6] The Science of Religion, p. 27.

terry-boat, thus; "Hail! respectable sir! I pray you take me across the river in your boat!" To this the boatman replied, "If you can pay me the fare, I will willingly take you across the river." Buddha said, "Whence shall I procure money to pay you your fare, I, who have given up all worldly wealth and riches, &c." The boatman still refusing to take him across, Buddha, pointing to a flock of geese flying from the south to the north banks of the Ganges, said:

> "See yonder geese in fellowship passing o'er the Ganges,
> They ask not as to fare of any boatman,
> But each by his inherent strength of body
> Flies through the air as pleases him.
> So, by my power of spiritual energy,
> Will I transport myself across the river,
> Even though the waters on this southern bank
> Stood up as high and firm as (Mount) Semeru."[1]

He then floats through the air across the stream.

In the *Lalita Vistara* Buddha is called the "Great Physician" who is to "dull all human pain." At his appearance the "sick are healed, the deaf are cured, the blind see, the poor are relieved." He visits the sick man, Su-ta, and heals soul as well as body.

At Vaisali, a pest like modern cholera was depopulating the kingdom, due to an accumulation of festering corpses. Buddha, summoned, caused a strong rain which carried away the dead bodies and cured every one. At Gaudhârâ was an old mendicant afflicted with a disease so loathsome that none of his brother monks could go near him on account of his fetid humors and stinking condition. The "Great Physician" was, however, not to be deterred; he washed the poor old man and attended to his maladies. A disciple had his feet hacked off by an unjust king, and Buddha cured even him. To convert certain skeptical villagers near Srâvastî, Buddha showed them a man walking across the deep and rapid river without immersing his feet. Pûrna, one of Buddha's disciples, had a brother in imminent danger of shipwreck in a "black storm." The "spirits that are favorable to Pûrna and Arya" apprised him of this and he at once performed the miracle of transporting himself to the deck of the ship. "Immediately the black tempest ceased, as if Sumera arrested it."[2]

When Buddha was told that a woman was suffering in severe labor, unable to bring forth, he said, Go and say: "I have never knowingly put any creature to death since I was born; by the vir-

[1] Beal: Hist. Buddha, pp. 246, 247.
[2] Dhammapada, pp. 47, 50 and 90. Bigan-
det, pp. 186 and 192. Bournouf: Intro. p. 156. In Lillie's Buddhism, pp. 139, 140.

tue of this obedience may you be free from pain!" When these words were repeated in the presence of the mother, the child was instantly born with ease.[1]

Innumerable are the miracles ascribed to Buddhist saints, and to others who followed their example. Their garments, and the staffs with which they walked, are supposed to imbibe some mysterious power, and blessed are they who are allowed to touch them.[2] A Buddhist saint who attains the power called "*perfection*," is able to rise and float along through the air.[3] Having this power, the saint exercises it by mere determination of his will, his body becoming imponderous, as when a man in the common human state determines to leap, and leaps. Buddhist annals relate the performance of the miraculous suspension by Gautama Buddha, himself, as well as by other *saints*.[4]

In the year 217 B. C., a Buddhist missionary priest, called by the Chinese historians Shih-le-fang, came from "the west" into Shan-se, accompanied by eighteen other priests, with their sacred books, in order to propagate the faith of Buddha. The emperor, disliking foreigners and exotic customs, imprisoned the missionaries; but an angel, genii, or spirit, came and opened the prison door, and liberated them.[5]

Here is a third edition of " Peter in prison," for we have already seen that the Hindoo sage Vasudeva was liberated from prison in like manner.

Zoroaster, the founder of the religion of the Persians, opposed his persecutors by performing miracles, in order to confirm his divine mission.[6]

Bochia of the Persians also performed miracles; the places where he performed them were consecrated, and people flocked in crowds to visit them.[7]

Horus, the Egyptian Saviour, performed great miracles, among which was that of raising the dead to life.[8]

Osiris of Egypt also performed great miracles;[9] and so did the virgin goddess *Isis*.

Pilgrimages were made to the temples of Isis, in Egypt, by the sick. Diodorus, the Grecian historian, says that:

[1] Hardy : Manual of Buddhism.
[2] See Prog. Relig. Ideas, vol. i. p. 229.
[3] See Tylor : Primitive Culture, vol. i. p. 135, and Hardy : Buddhist Legends, pp. 98, 126, 137.
[4] See Tylor : Primitive Culture, vol. i. p. 135.
[5] Thornton : Hist. China, vol. i. p. 341.

[6] See Dupuis : Origin of Religious Belief, p. 240, and Inman's Ancient Faiths, vol. ii. p. 460.
[7] See Higgins : Anacalypsis, vol. ii. p. 34.
[8] See Lundy : Monumental Christianity, pp. 303-405.
[9] See Bonwick's Egyptian Belief.

"Those who go to consult in dreams the goddess Isis recover perfect health. Many whose cure has been despaired of by physicians have by this means been saved, and others who have long been deprived of sight, or of some other part of the body, by taking refuge, so to speak, in the arms of the goddess, have been restored to the enjoyment of their faculties."[1]

Serapis, the Egyptian Saviour, performed great miracles, principally those of healing the sick. He was called "The Healer of the World."[2]

Marduk, the Assyrian God, the "Logos," the "Eldest Son of Hea;" "He who made Heaven and Earth;" the "Merciful One;" the "Life-Giver," &c., performed great miracles, among which was that of raising the dead to life.[3]

Bacchus, son of Zeus by the virgin Semele, was a great performer of miracles, among which may be mentioned his changing water into wine,[4] as it is recorded of Jesus in the Gospels.

"In his gentler aspects he is the giver of joy, the healer of sicknesses, the guardian against plagues. As such he is even a law-giver and a promoter of peace and concord. As kindling new or strange thoughts in the mind, he is a giver of wisdom and the revealer of hidden secrets of the future."[5]

The legends related of this god state that on one occasion Pantheus, King of Thebes, sent his attendants to seize Bacchus, the "vagabond leader of a faction"—as he called him. This they were unable to do, as the multitude who followed him were too numerous. They succeeded, however, in capturing one of his disciples, Acetes, who was led away and shut up fast in prison; but while they were getting ready the instruments of execution, *the prison doors came open of their own accord, and the chains fell from his limbs,* and when they looked for him he was nowhere to be found.[6] Here is still another edition of "Peter in prison."

Æsculapius was another great performer of miracles. The ancient Greeks said of him that he not only cured the sick of the most malignant diseases, *but even raised the dead.*

---

[1] Quoted by Baring-Gould : Orig. Relig. Belief, vol. i. p. 397.

[2] See Prichard's Mythology, p. 347.

[3] See Bonwick's Egyptian Belief, p. 404.

[4] See Dupuis : Origin of Religious Belief, 258, and Anacalypsis, vol. ii. p. 102. Compare John, ii. 7.

A *Grecian* festival called THYIA was observed by the Eleans *in honor of Bacchus.* The priests conveyed three empty vessels into a chapel, in the presence of a large assembly, after which the doors were shut and *sealed.*

"On the morrow the company returned, and after every man had looked upon his own seal, and seen that it was unbroken, the doors being opened, the vessels were found full of wine." The god himself is said to have appeared in person and filled the vessels. (Bell's Pantheon.)

[5] Cox : Aryan Mytho., vol. ii. p. 295.

[6] Bulfinch : The Age of Fable, p. 225. "And they laid their hands on the apostles, and put them in the common prison ; but the angel of the Lord by night opened the prison doors, and brought them forth." (Acts, v. 18, 19.)

A writer in Bell's Pantheon says :

"As the Greeks always carried the encomiums of their great men beyond the truth, so they feigned that Æsculapius was so expert in medicine as not only to cure the sick, but even to raise the dead."[1]

Eusebius, the ecclesiastical historian, speaking of Æsculapius, says :

"He sometimes appeared unto them (the Cilicians) in dreams and visions, and sometimes restored the sick to health."

He claims, however, that this was the work of the DEVIL, "who by this means did withdraw the minds of men from the knowledge of the *true* SAVIOUR."[2]

For many years after the death of Æsculapius, miracles continued to be performed by the efficacy of faith in his name. Patients were conveyed to the temple of Æsculapius, and there cured of their disease. A short statement of the symptoms of each case, and the remedy employed, were inscribed on tablets and hung up in the temples.[3] There were also a multitude of eyes, ears, hands, feet, and other members of the human body, made of wax, silver, or gold, and presented by those whom the god had cured of blindness, deafness, and other diseases.[4]

Marinus, a scholar of the philosopher Proclus, relates one of these remarkable cures, in the life of his master. He says :

"Asclipigenia, a young maiden who had lived with her parents, was seized with a grievous distemper, incurable by the physicians. All help from the physicians failing, the father applied to the philosopher, earnestly entreating him to pray for his daughter. Proclus, full of faith, went to the temple of Æsculapius, intending to pray for the sick young woman to the god—for the city (Athens) was at that time blessed in him, and still enjoyed the undemolished temple of THE SAVIOUR—but while he was praying, a sudden change appeared in the damsel, and she immediately became convalescent, for the *Saviour*, Æsculapius, as being God, easily healed her."[5]

Dr. Conyers Middleton says :

"Whatever proof the primitive (Christian) Church might have among themselves, of the miraculous gift, yet it could have but little effect towards making proselytes among those who pretended to the same gift—possessed more largely and exerted more openly, than in the private assemblies of the Christians. For in the temples of *Æsculapius*, all kinds of diseases were believed to be publicly cured, by the pretended help of that deity, in proof of which there were erected in each temple, columns or tables of brass or marble, on which a distinct narrative of each particular cure was inscribed. Pausanias[6] writes that in the temple

---

[1] Bell's Pantheon, vol. i. p. 28.

[2] Eusebius: Life of Constantine, lib. 3, ch. liv.

"*Æsculapius*, the son of Apollo, was endowed by his father with such skill in the healing art that he even restored the dead to life." (Bulfinch: The Age of Fable. p. 246.)

[3] Murray : Manual of Mythology, pp. 179, 180.

[4] See Prog. Relig. Ideas, vol. i. p. 304.

[5] Marinus : Quoted in Taylor's Diegesis, p. 151.

[6] Pausanias was one of the most eminent Greek geographers and historians.

at Epidaurus there were many columns anciently of this kind, and six of them remaining to his time, *inscribed with the names of men and women who had been cured by the god*, with an account of their several cases, and the method of their cure ; and that there was an old pillar besides, which stood apart, dedicated to the memory of Hippolytus, *who had been raised from the dead*. Strabo, also, another grave writer, informs us that these temples were constantly filled with the sick, imploring the help of the god, and that they had tables hanging around them, in which all the miraculous cures were described. There is a remarkable fragment of one of these tables still extant, and exhibited by Gruter in his collection, as it was found in the ruins of Æsculapius's temple in the Island of the Tiber, in Rome, which gives an account of two blind men restored to sight by Æsculapius, in the open view,[1] and with the loud acclamation of the people, acknowledging the manifest power of the god."[2]

Livy, the most illustrious of Roman historians (born B. C. 61), tells us that temples of *heathen gods* were rich in the number of offerings *which the people used to make in return for the cures and benefits which they received from them.*[3]

A writer in *Bell's Pantheon* says :

"Making presents to the gods was a custom even from the earliest times, either to deprecate their wrath, obtain some benefit, or acknowledge some favor. These donations consisted of garlands, garments, cups of gold, or whatever conduced to the decoration or splendor of their temples. They were sometimes laid on the floor, sometimes hung upon the walls, doors, pillars, roof, or any other conspicuous place. Sometimes the occasion of the dedication was inscribed, either upon the thing itself, or upon a tablet hung up with it."[4]

No one custom of antiquity is so frequently mentioned by ancient historians, as the practice which was so common among the *heathens*, of making votive offerings to their deities, and hanging them up in their temples, many of which are preserved to this day, viz., images of metal, stone, or clay, as well as legs, arms, and other parts of the body, *in testimony of some divine cure effected in that particular member.*[5]

Horace says :

"——Me tabula sacer
Votivâ paries indicat humida
Suspendisse potenti
Vestimenta maris Deo." (Lib. 1, Ode V.)

It was the custom of offering *ex-votos* of *Priapic* forms, at the church of Isernia, in the *Christian* kingdom of Naples, during the last century, which induced Mr. R. Payne Knight to compile his remarkable work on Phallic Worship.

---

[1] "And when Jesus departed thence, *two blind men* followed him, crying and saying : thou son of David, have mercy on us. . . . And Jesus said unto them : Believe ye that I am able to do this ? They said unto him, Yea, Lord. Then touched he their eyes, saying ; According to your faith be it unto you, and their eyes were opened." (Matt. ix. 27-30.)

[2] Middleton's Works, vol. i. pp. 63, 64.

[3] Ibid. p. 48.

[4] Bell's Pantheon, vol. i. p. 62.

[5] See Middleton's Letters from Rome, p. 76.

Juvenal, who wrote A. D. 81-96, says of the goddess *Isis*, whose religion was at that time in the greatest vogue at Rome, that the painters get their livelihood out of her. This was because " the most common of all offerings (made by the heathen to their deities) were *pictures* presenting the history of the miraculous cure or deliverance, vouchsafed upon the vow of the donor."[1] One of their prayers ran thus :

"Now, Goddess, help, for thou canst help bestow,
   As all these pictures round thy altars show."[2]

In *Chambers's Encyclopœdia* may be found the following :

"Patients that were cured of their ailments (by *Æsculapius*, or through faith in him) hung up a tablet in his temple, recording the name, the disease, and the manner of cure. *Many of these votive tablets are still extant.*"[3]

Alexander S. Murray, of the department of Greek and Roman Antiquities in the British Museum, speaking of the miracles performed by *Æsculapius*, says :

"A person who had recovered from a local illness would dictate a sculptured representation of the part that had been affected. *Of such sculptures there are a number of examples in the British Museum.*"[4]

Justin Martyr, in his *Apology* for the Christian religion, addressed to the Emperor Hadrian, says :

"As to *our* Jesus curing the lame, and the paralytic, and such as were crippled from birth, this is little more than what you say of your *Æsculapius.*"[5]

At a time when the Romans were infested with the plague, having consulted their sacred books, they learned that in order to be delivered from it, they were to go in quest of *Æsculapius* at Epidaurus; accordingly, an embassy was appointed of ten senators, at the head of whom was Quintus Ogulnius, and the worship of Æsculapius was established at Rome, A. U. C. 462, that is, B. C. 288. But the most remarkable coincidence is that the worship of this god continued with scarcely any diminished splendor, for several hundred years after the establishment of Christianity.[6]

Hermes or Mercury, the Lord's Messenger, was a wonder-worker. The staff or rod which Hermes received from Phoibos (Apol-

---

[1] See Middleton's Letters from Rome, p. 76.
[2] "Nunc Dea, nunc succurre mihi, nam posse mederi
   Picta docet temptes multa tabella tuis."
(Horace: Tibull. lib, 1, Eleg. iii. In Ibid.)
[3] Chambers's Encyclo., art. "Æsculapius."
[4] Murray : Manual of Mythology, p. 180.
[5] Apol. 1, ch. xxii.
[6] Deane: Serp. Wor. p. 204. See also, Bell's Pantheon, vol. i. p. 29.

"There were numerous oracles of Æsculapius, but the most celebrated one was at Epidaurus. Here the sick sought responses and the recovery of their health by sleeping in the temple. . . . The worship of Æsculapius was introduced into Rome in a time of great sickness, and an embassy sent to the temple Epidaurus to entreat the aid of the god." (Bulfinch : The Age of Fable, p. 397.)

lo), and which connects this myth with the special emblem of Vishnu (the Hindoo Saviour), was regarded as denoting his heraldic
office. It was, however, always endowed with magic properties, and
had the power even of raising the dead.[1]

Herodotus, the Grecian historian, relates a wonderful miracle
which happened among the *Spartans*, many centuries before the
time assigned for the birth of Christ Jesus. The story is as follows:

A Spartan couple of great wealth and influence, had a daughter born to them
who was a cripple from birth. Her nurse, perceiving that she was misshapen,
and knowing her to be the daughter of opulent persons, and deformed, and seeing, moreover, that her parents considered her form a great misfortune, considering these several circumstances, devised the following plan. She carried her
every day to the temple of the Goddess *Helen*, and standing before her image,
prayed to the goddess to free the child from its deformity. One day, as the
nurse was going out of the temple, a woman appeared to her, and having appeared, asked what she was carrying in her arms; and she answered that she
was carrying an infant; whereupon she bid her show it to her, but the nurse refused, for she had been forbidden by the parents to show the child to any one.
The woman, however—who was none other than the Goddess herself—urged
her by all means to show it to her, and the nurse, seeing that the woman was so
very anxious to see the child, at length showed it; upon which she, stroking the
head of the child with her hands, said that she would surpass all the women in
Sparta in beauty. From that day her appearance began to change, her deformed
limbs became symmetrical, and when she reached the age for marriage she was
the most beautiful woman in all Sparta.[2]

Apollonius of Tyana, in Cappadocia, who was born in the
latter part of the reign of Augustus, about four years before the
time assigned for the birth of Jesus, and who was therefore contemporary with him, was celebrated for the wonderful miracles he
performed. Oracles in various places declared that he was endowed
with a portion of Apollo's power to cure diseases, and foretell
events; and those who were affected were commanded to apply to
him. The priests of Iona made over the diseased to his care, and
his cures were considered so remarkable, that divine honors were
decreed to him.[3]

He at one time went to Ephesus, but as the inhabitants did not
hearken to his preaching, he left there and went to Smyrna, where
he was well received by the inhabitants. While there, ambassadors

[1] Aryan Mytho. vol. ii. p. 238.
[2] Herodotus: bk. vi. ch. 61.
[3] See Philostratus: Vie d'Apo.

Gibbon, the historian, says of him: "Apollonius of Tyana, born about the same time as
Jesus Christ. His life (that of the former) is
related in so fabulous a manner by his disciples, that we are at a loss to discover whether
he was a sage, an impostor, or a fanatic."
(Gibbon's Rome, vol. i. p. 353, *note*.) What
this learned historian says of Apollonius applies
to Jesus of Nazareth. *His* disciples have related his life in so fabulous a manner, that
some consider him to have been an impostor,
others a fanatic, others a sage, and others a
God.

came from Ephesus, begging him to return to that city, where a
terrible plague was raging, *as he had prophesied.* He went immo-
diately, and as soon as he arrived, he said to the Ephesians : " Be
not dejected, I will this day put a stop to the disease." According
to his words, the pestilence was stayed, and the people erected a
statue to him, in token of their gratitude.[1]

In the city of Athens, there was one of the dissipated young
citizens, who laughed and cried by turns, and talked and sang to
himself, without apparent cause. His friends supposed these habits
were the effects of early intemperance, but Apollonius, who happened to meet the young man, told him he was possessed of a
demon ; and, as soon as he fixed his eyes upon him, the demon
broke out into all those horrid, violent expressions used by people
on the rack, and then swore he would depart out of the youth, and
never enter another.[2] The young man had not been aware that
he was possessed by a devil, but from that moment, his wild, disturbed looks changed, he became very temperate, and assumed the
garb of a Pythagorean philosopher.

Apollonius went to Rome, and arrived there after the emperor
Nero had passed very severe laws against *magicians.* He was met
on the way by a person who advised him to turn back and not enter
the city, saying that all who wore the philosopher's garb were in
danger of being arrested as magicians. He heeded not these words
of warning, but proceeded on his way, and entered the city. It
was not long before he became an object of suspicion, was closely
watched, and finally arrested, but when his accusers appeared before the tribunal and unrolled the parchment on which the charges
against him had been written, they found that all the characters had
disappeared. Apollonius made such an impression on the magistrates
by the bold tone he assumed, that he was allowed to go where he
pleased.[3]

Many miracles were performed by him while in Rome, among
others may be mentioned his restoring a *dead maiden to life.*

She belonged to a family of rank, and was just about to be
married, when she died suddenly. Apollonius met the funeral procession that was conveying her body to the tomb. He asked them
to set down the bier, saying to her betrothed : " I will dry up the
tears you are shedding for this maiden." They supposed he was
going to pronounce a funeral oration, but he merely *took her hand,*
bent over her, and uttered a few words in a low tone. She opened

[1] See Philostratus, p. 146.   [2] Ibid. p. 158.   [3] See Ibid. p. 182.

her eyes, and began to speak, and was carried back alive and well to her father's house.[1]

Passing through Tarsus, in his travels, a young man was pointed out to him who had been bitten thirty days before by a mad dog, and who was then running on all fours, barking and howling. Apollonius took his case in hand, and it was not long before the young man was restored to his right mind.[2]

Domitian, Emperor of Rome, caused Apollonius to be arrested, during one of his visits to that city, on charge of allowing himself to be worshiped (the people having given him *divine honors*), speaking against the reigning powers, and pretending that his words were inspired by the gods. He was taken, loaded with irons, and cast into prison. " I have bound you," said the emperor, " and you will not escape me."

Apollonius was one day visited in his prison by his steadfast disciple, Damus, who asked him when he thought he should recover his liberty, whereupon he answered : " This instant, if it depended upon myself," and drawing his legs out of the shackles, he added : " Keep up your spirits, you see the freedom I enjoy." He was brought to trial not long after, and so defended himself, that the emperor was induced to acquit him, but forbade him to leave Rome. Apollonius then addressed the emperor, and ended by saying : " You cannot kill me, because I am not mortal ;" and as soon as he had said these words, *he vanished from the tribunal.*[3] Damus (the disciple who had visited him in prison) had previously been sent away from Rome, with the promise of his master that he would soon rejoin him. Apollonius vanished from the presence of the emperor (at Rome) at noon. *On the evening of the same day, he suddenly appeared before Damus and some other friends who were at Puteoli, more than a hundred miles from Rome.* They started, being doubtful whether or not it was his spirit, but he stretched out his hand, saying : " Take it, and if I escape from you regard me as an apparition."[4]

---

[1] Compare Matt. ix. 18-25. "There came a certain ruler and worshiped him, saying : ' My daughter is even now dead, but come and lay thy hand upon her, and she shall live,' And Jesus arose and followed him, and so did his disciples. . . . And when Jesus came into the ruler's house, and saw the minstrels and the people making a noise, he said unto them: ' Give peace, for the maid is not dead, but sleepeth.' And they laughed him to scorn. But when the people were put forth, he went in, *and took her by the hand*, and the maid 'arose."

[2] See Philostratus, pp. 285-286.

[3] " He could render himself invisible, evoke departed spirits, utter predictions, and discover the thoughts of other men." (Hardy : Eastern Monachism, p. 380.)

[4] "And as they thus spoke, Jesus himself stood in the midst of them, and said unto them : ' Peace be unto you.' But they were terrified and affrighted, and supposed that they

When Apollonius had told his disciples that he had made his defense in Rome, only a few hours before, they marveled how he could have performed the journey so rapidly. He, in reply, said that they must ascribe it to a god.[1]

The Empress Julia, wife of Alexander Severus, was so much interested in the history of Apollonius, that she requested Flavius Philostratus, an Athenian author of reputation, to write an account of him. The early Christian Fathers, alluding to this life of Apollonius, do not deny the miracles it recounts, but attribute to them the aid of evil spirits.[2]

Justin Martyr was one of the believers in the miracles performed by Apollonius, and by others through him, for he says:

"How is it that the talismans of Apollonius have power in certain members of creation ? for they prevent, *as we see*, the fury of the waves, and the violence of the winds, and the attacks of wild beasts, and whilst *our* Lord's miracles *are preserved by tradition alone, those of Apollonius are most numerous, and actually manifested in present facts, so as to lead astray all beholders.*"[3]

So much for Apollonius. We will now speak of another miracle performer, *Simon Magus.*

Simon the Samaritan, generally called Simon *Magus*, produced marked effects on the times succeeding him ; being the progenitor of a large class of sects, which long troubled the Christian churches.

In the time of Jesus and Simon Magus it was almost universally believed that men could foretell events, cure diseases, and obtain control over the forces of nature, by the aid of spirits, if they knew how to invoke them. It was Simon's proficiency in this occult science which gained him the surname of *Magus*, or *Magician.*

The writer of the eighth chapter of " *The Acts of the Apostles* " informs us that when Philip went into Samaria, " to preach Christ unto them," he found there " a certain man called Simon, which beforetime in the same city used sorcery, and bewitched the people of Samaria, giving out that himself was some great one. To whom they all gave heed, from the least to the greatest, saying : This man is the great power of God."[4]

Simon traveled about preaching, and made many proselytes. He professed to be " *The Wisdom of God,*" " *The Word of God,*"

---

had seen a spirit. And he said unto them : 'Why are ye troubled ? and why do thoughts arise in your hearts ? Behold my hands and my feet, that it is myself ; handle me and see ; for a spirit hath not flesh and bones, as ye see me have." (Luke, xxiv. 36–39.)

[1] See Philostratus, p. 342.
[2] Ibid. p. 5.
[3] Justin Martyr's " *Quæst,*" xxiv. Quoted in King's Guostics, p. 242.
[4] Acts, viii. 9, 10.

"*The Paraclete,* or *Comforter*," "*The Image of the Eternal Father, Manifested in the Flesh,*" and his followers claimed that he was "*The First Born of the Supreme.*"[1] All of these are titles, which, in after years, were applied to Christ Jesus. His followers had a gospel called "*The Four Corners of the World,*" which reminds us of the reason given by Irenæus, for there being *four* Gospels among the Christians. He says:

"It is impossible that there could be more or less than *four*. For there are *four* climates, and *four* cardinal winds; but the *Gospel* is the pillar and foundation of the Church, and its breath of life. The Church, therefore, was to have *four pillars*, blowing immortality from every quarter, and giving life to men."[2]

Simon also composed some works, of which but slight fragments remain, Christian authority having evidently destroyed them. That he made a lively impression on his contemporaries is indicated by the subsequent extension of his doctrines, under varied forms, by the wonderful stories which the Christian Fathers relate of him, and by the strong dislike they manifested toward him.

Eusebius, the ecclesiastical historian, says of him:

"The malicious power of *Satan*, enemy to all honesty, and foe to all human salvation, brought forth at that time this monster Simon, a father and worker of all such mischiefs, *as a great adversary unto the mighty and holy Apostles.*

"Coming into the city of Rome, he was so aided by that power which prevaileth in this world, that in short time he brought his purpose to such a pass, that his picture was there placed with others, and he honored as a god."[3]

Justin Martyr says of him:

"After the ascension of *our* Savior into heaven, the DEVIL brought forth certain men which called themselves gods, who not only suffered no vexation of you (Romans), but attained unto honor amongst you, by name one *Simon*, a Samaritan, born in the village of Gitton, who (under Claudius Cæsar) by the art of *devils*, through whom he dealt, wrought devilish enchantments, was esteemed and counted in your regal city of Rome for a *god*, and honored by you as a *god*, with a picture between two bridges upon the river Tibris, having this Roman inscription : '*Simoni deo Sancto*' (To Simon the Holy God). And in manner all the Samaritans, and certain also of other nations, do worship him, acknowledging him for their chief god."[4]

According to accounts given by several other Christian Fathers, he could make his appearance wherever he pleased to be at any moment; could poise himself on the air; make inanimate things

---

[1] See Mosheim, vol. i. pp. 137, 140.
[2] Irenæus: Against Heresies, bk. iii. ch. xi. The *authorship* of the fourth gospel, attributed to John, has been traced to this same *Irenæus*. He is the *first* person who speaks of it; and adding this fact to the statement that "it is impossible that there could be more or less than *four*," certainly makes it appear very suspicious. We shall allude to this again.
[3] Eusebius: Eccl. Hist. lib. 2, ch. xiv.
[4] Apol. 1, ch. xxiv.

move without visible assistance ; produce trees from the earth suddenly ; cause a stick to reap without hands ; change himself into
the likeness of any other person, or even into the forms of animals ;
fling himself from high precipices unhurt, walk through the streets
accompanied by spirits of the dead ; and many other such like per-
formances.[1]

Simon went to Rome, where he gave himself out to be an " Incarnate Spirit of God."[2]   He became a favorite with the Emperor
Claudius, and afterwards with Nero.   His Christian opponents, as
we have seen in the cases cited above, did not deny the miracles
attributed to him, but said they were done through the agency of
evil spirits, which was a common opinion among the Fathers.   They
claimed that every *magician* had an attendant evil spirit, who came
when summoned, obeyed his commands, and taught him ceremonies
and forms of words, by which he was able to do supernatural
things.   In this way they were accustomed to account for all the
miracles performed by Gentiles and heretics.[3]

Menander—who was called the " Wonder-Worker"—was another great performer of miracles.   Eusebius, speaking of him, says
that he was skilled in magical art, and performed *devilish* operations ;
and that "as yet there be divers which can testify the same of
him."[4]

Dr. Conyers Middleton, speaking on this subject, says:

"It was universally received and believed through all ages of the primitive
church, that there was a number of magicians, necromancers, or conjurors,
both among the *Gentiles*, and the *heretical Christians*, who had each their peculiar
demon or evil spirit, for their associates, perpetually attending on their persons
and obsequious to their commands, by whose help they could perform miracles,
foretell future events, call up the souls of the dead, exhibit them to open view,
and infuse into people whatever dreams or visions they saw fit, all which is
constantly affirmed by the primitive writers and apologists, and commonly applied by them to prove the immortality of the soul."[5]

After quoting from Justin Martyr, who says that these *magicians*
could convince any one " that the souls of men exist still after
death," he continues by saying :

' Lactantius, speaking of certain philosophers who held that the soul perished
with the body, says : 'they durst not have declared such an opinion, in the
presence of any *magician*, for if they had done it, he would have confuted them

---

[1] See Prog. Relig. Ideas, vol. ii. pp. 241, 242.

[2] According to Hieronymus (a Christian Father, born A. D. 346), Simon Magus applied to himself these words: "I am the Word (or Logos) of God ; I am the Beautiful, I the Ad-vocate, I the Omnipotent ; I am all things

that belong to God." (See "Son of the Man," p. 67.)

[3] See Prog. Relig. Ideas, vol. ii. p. 316, and Middleton's Free Inquiry, p. 62.

[4] Eusebius : Ecc. Hist., lib. 3, ch. xiv.

[5] Middleton's Works, vol. i. p. 54.

upon the spot, by sensible experiments; *by calling up souls from the dead, and rendering them visible to human eyes, and making them speak and foretell future events.*"[1]

The Christian Father Theophilus, Bishop of Antioch, who was contemporary with Irenæus· (A. D. 177-202), went so far as to declare that it was evil spirits who inspired the old poets and prophets of Greece and Rome. He says :

"The truth of this is manifestly shown; because those who are possessed by devils, even at this day, are sometimes exorcised by us in the name of God; and the seducing spirits confess themselves to be the same demons who before inspired the Gentile poets."[2]

Even in the second century after Christianity, foreign conjurors were professing to exhibit miracles among the Greeks. Lucian gives an account of one of these "foreign barbarians"—as he calls them[3]—and says :

"I believed and was overcome in spite of my resistance, for what was I to do when I saw him carried through the air in daylight, and walking on the water,[4] and passing leisurely and slowly through the fire ?"[5]

He further tells us that this "foreign barbarian". was able to raise the dead to life.[6]

Athenagoras, a Christian Father who flourished during the latter part of the second century, says on this subject :

"We (Christians) do not deny that in several places, cities, and countries, there are some extraordinary works performed in the name of *idols*," *i. e.*, heathen gods.[7]

Miracles were not uncommon things among the Jews before and during the time of Christ Jesus. Casting out devils was an every-day occurrence,[8] and miracles frequently happened to confirm the sayings of Rabbis. One cried out, when his opinion was disputed, "May this tree prove that I am right!" and forthwith the tree was torn up by the roots, and hurled a hundred ells off. But

1 Middleton's Works, vol. i. p. 54.
2 Prog. Relig. Ideas, vol. ii. p. 312, and Middleton's Works, vol. i. p. 10.
3 "The Egyptians call all men 'barbarians' who do not speak the same language as themselves." (Herodotus, book ii. ch. 158.)
"By 'barbarians' the Greeks meant all who were not sprung from themselves—all foreigners." (Henry Cary, translator of *Herodotus*.)
The Chinese call the English, and all foreigners from western countries, "*western barbarians* ;" the Japanese were called by them the "*eastern barbarians*." (See Thornton's History of China, vol. i.)
The Jews considered all who did not belong to their race to be *heathens* and *barbarians*.

The Christians consider those who are not followers of Christ Jesus to be *heathens* and *barbarians*.
The Mohammedans consider all others to be *dogs, infidels*, and *barbarians*.
4 "And in the fourth watch of the night, Jesus went unto them, walking on the sea." (Matt. xiv. 25.)
5 Prog. Relig. Ideas, vol. ii. p. 236. We have it on the authority of *Strabo* that Roman priests walked barefoot over burning coals, without receiving the slightest injury. This was done in the presence of crowds of people. *Pliny* also relates the same story.
6 Prog. Relig. Ideas, vol. ii. p. 236.
7 Athenagoras, Apolog. p. 25. Quoted in Middleton's Works, vol. i. p. 62.
8 Geikie : Life of Christ, vol. ii. p. 610.

his opponents declared that a tree could prove nothing. "May this stream, then, witness for me!" cried Eliezar, and at once it flowed the opposite way.[1]

Josephus, the Jewish historian, tells us that *King Solomon* was expert in casting out devils who had taken possession of the body of mortals. This gift was also possessed by many Jews throughout different ages. He (Josephus) relates that he saw one of his own countrymen (Eleazar) casting out devils, in the presence of a vast multitude.[2]

Dr. Conyers Middleton says:

"It is remarkable that all the Christian Fathers, who lay so great a stress on the particular gift of *casting out devils*, allow the same power both to the Jews and the Gentiles, *as well before as after our Saviour's coming.*"[3]

Vespasian, who was born about ten years after the time assigned for the birth of Christ Jesus, performed wonderful miracles, for the good of mankind. Tacitus, the Roman historian, informs us that he cured a *blind man* in Alexandria, by means of his spittle, and a *lame man* by the mere touch of his foot.

The words of Tacitus are as follows:

"Vespasian passed some months at Alexandria, having resolved to defer his voyage to Italy till the return of summer, when the winds, blowing in a regular direction, afford a safe and pleasant navigation. During his residence in that city, a number of incidents, out of the ordinary course of nature, seemed to mark him as the peculiar favorite of the gods. A man of mean condition, born at Alexandria, had lost his sight by a defluxion on his eyes. He presented himself before Vespasian, and, falling prostrate on the ground, implored the emperor to administer a cure for his blindness. He came, he said, by the admonition of Serapis, the god whom the superstition of the Egyptians holds in the highest veneration. The request was, that the emperor, with his spittle, would condescend to moisten the poor man's face and the balls of his eyes.[4] Another, who had lost the use of his hand, inspired by the same god, begged that he would tread on the part affected. . . . In the presence of a prodigious multitude, all erect with expectation, he advanced with an air of serenity, and hazarded the experiment. The paralytic hand recovered its functions, and the blind man saw the light of the sun.[5] By living witnesses, who were actually on the spot, both events are confirmed at this hour, when deceit and flattery can hope for no reward."[6]

The striking resemblance between the account of these miracles, and those attributed to Jesus in the Gospels "*according to*"

---

[1] Geikie: Life of Christ, vol. i. p. 75.
[2] Jewish Antiqiities, bk. viii. ch. ii.
[3] Middleton's Works, vol. i. p. 68.
[4] "And he cometh to Bethsaida, and they bring a *blind man* unto him, and besought him to touch him. And he took the blind man by the hand . . . *and when he had spit on his eyes*, . . . he looked up and said: 'I see men and trees,' . . . and he was restored." (Mark, viii. 22-25.)

[5] "And behold there was a man *which had his hand withered.* . . . Then said he unto the man, 'Stretch forth thine hand;' and he stretched it forth, and it was restored whole, like as the other." (Matt. xii. 10-13.)

[6] Tacitus: Hist., lib. iv. ch. lxxxi.

Matthew and Mark, would lead us to think that one had been copied from the other, but when we find that Tacitus wrote his history A. D. 98,[1] and that the "*Matthew*" and Mark narrators' works were not known until *after* that time,[2] the evidence certainly is that Tacitus was *not* the plagiarist, but that this charge must fall on the shoulders of the Christian writers, whoever they may have been.

To come down to earlier times, even the religion of the Mahometans is a religion of miracles and wonders. Mahomet, like Jesus of Nazareth, did not claim to perform miracles, but the votaries of Mahomet are more assured than himself of his miraculous gifts ; and their confidence and credulity increase as they are farther removed from the time and place of his spiritual exploits. They believe or affirm that trees went forth to meet him ; that he was saluted by stones ; that water gushed from his fingers ; that he fed the hungry, cured the sick, and raised the dead ; that a beam groaned to him ; that a camel complained to him ; that a shoulder of mutton informed him of its being poisoned ; and that both animate and inanimate nature were equally subject to the apostle of God. His dream of a nocturnal journey is seriously described as a real and corporeal transaction. A mysterious animal, the Borak, conveyed him from the temple of Mecca to that of Jerusalem ; with his companion Gabriel he successively ascended the seven heavens, and received and repaid the salutations of the patriarchs, the prophets, and the angels in their respective mansions. Beyond the seventh heaven, Mahomet alone was permitted to proceed ; he passed the veil of unity, approached within two bow-shots of the throne, and felt a cold that pierced him to the heart, when his shoulder was touched by the hand of God. After a familiar, though important conversation, he descended to Jerusalem, remounted the Borak, returned to Mecca, and performed in the tenth part of a night the journey of many thousand years. His resistless word split asunder the orb of the moon, and the obedient planet stooped from her station in the sky.[3]

These and many other wonders, similar in character to the story of Jesus sending the demons into the swine, are related of Mahomet by his followers.

It is very certain that the same circumstances which are claimed to have taken place with respect to the Christian religion, are also claimed to have taken place in the religions of Crishna, Bud-

---

[1] See Chambers's Encyclo., art. "Tacitus." [2] See The Bible of To-Day, pp. 273, 278.
[3] See Gibbon's Rome, vol. i. pp. 539–541.

dha, Zoroaster, Æsculapius, Bacchus, Apollonius, Simon Magus, &c. Histories of these persons, with miracles, relics, circumstances of locality, suitable to them, were as common, as well authenticated (if not better), and as much believed by the devotees as were those relating to Jesus.

All the Christian theologians which the world has yet produced have not been able to procure any evidence of the miracles recorded in the *Gospels*, half so strong as can be procured in evidence of miracles performed by heathens and heathen gods, both before and after the time of Jesus; and, as they cannot do this, let them give us a reason why we should reject the one and receive the other. And if they cannot do this, let them candidly confess that we must either admit them all, or reject them all, for they all stand on the same footing.

In the early times of the Roman republic, in the war with the Latins, the gods Castor and Pollux are said to have appeared on white horses in the Roman army, which by their assistance gained a complete victory: in memory of which, the General Posthumius vowed and built a temple to these deities; and for a proof of the fact, there was shown, we find, in Cicero's time (106 to 43 B. C.), the marks of the horses' hoofs on a rock at Regillum, where they first appeared.[1]

Now this miracle, with those which have already been mentioned, and many others of the same kind which could be mentioned, has as authentic an attestation, if not more so, as any of the Gospel miracles. It has, for instance: The decree of a senate to confirm it; visible marks on the spot where it was transacted; and all this supported by the best authors of antiquity, amongst whom Dionysius, of Halicarnassus, who says that there was subsisting in his time at Rome many evident proofs of its reality, besides a yearly festival, with a solemn sacrifice and procession, in memory of it.[2]

With all these evidences in favor of this miracle having really happened, it seems to us so ridiculous, that we wonder how there could ever have been any so simple as to believe it, yet we should believe that Jesus raised Lazarus from the dead, after he had been in the tomb four days, our only authority being that *anonymous* book known as the "Gospel according to St. John," which was not

---

[1] Middleton's Letters from Rome, p. 102. See also, Bell's Pantheon, vol. i. p. 16.

[2] Dionysius of Halicarnassus, one of the most accurate historians of antiquity, says: "In the war with the Latins, Castor and Pollux appeared visibly on white horses, and fought on the side of the Romans, who by their assistance gained a complete victory. As a perpetual memorial of it, a temple was erected and a yearly festival instituted in honor of these deities." (Prog. Relig. Ideas, vol. i. p. 323, and Middleton's Letters from Rome, p. 103.)

known until after A. D. 173. Albert Barnes, in his "Lectures on the Evidences of Christianity," speaking of the authenticity of the Gospel miracles, makes the following damaging confession:

"An important question is, whether there is any stronger evidence in favor of miracles, than there is in favor of witchcraft, or sorcery, or the re-appearance of the dead, of ghosts, of apparitions ? Is not the evidence in favor of these as strong as any that can be adduced in favor of miracles ? Have not these things been matters of universal belief ? In what respect is the evidence in favor of the miracles of the Bible stronger than that which can be adduced in favor of witchcraft and sorcery ? Does it differ in nature and degrees; and if it differs, is it not in favor of witchcraft and sorcery ? Has not the evidence in favor of the latter been derived from as competent and reliable witnesses ? Has it not been brought to us from those who saw the facts alleged ? Has it not been subjected to a close scrutiny in the courts of justice, to cross-examination, to tortures ? Has it not convinced those of highest legal attainments; those accustomed to sift testimony; those who understood the true principles of evidence? Has not the evidence in favor of witchcraft and sorcery had, what the evidence in favor of miracles has not had, the advantage of strict judicial investigation? and been subjected to trial, where evidence should be, before courts of law? Have not the most eminent judges in the most civilized and enlightened courts of Europe and America admitted the force of such evidence, and on the ground of it committed great numbers of innocent persons to the gallows and to the stake? *I confess that of all the questions ever asked on the subject of miracles, this is the most perplexing and the most difficult to answer.* It is rather to be wondered at that it has not been pressed with more zeal by those who deny the reality of miracles, and that they have placed their objections so extensively on other grounds."

It was a common adage among the Greeks, "*Miracles for fools*," and the same proverb obtained among the shrewder Romans, in the saying: "*The common people like to be deceived—deceived let them be.*"

St. Chrysostom declares that "miracles are proper only to excite sluggish and vulgar minds, *men of sense have no occasion for them ;*" and that "they frequently carry some untoward suspicion along with them ;" and Saint Chrysostom, Jerome, Euthemius, and Theophylact, prove by several instances, that *real miracles* had been performed by those who were not Catholic, but heretic, Christians.[1]

Celsus (an Epicurean philosopher, towards the close of the second century), the first writer who entered the lists against the claims of the Christians, in speaking of the miracles which were claimed to have been performed by Jesus, says :

"His miracles, *granted to be true*, were nothing more than the common works of those *enchanters*, who, for a few *oboli*, will perform greater deeds in the midst of the Forum, calling up the souls of heroes, exhibiting sumptuous banquets, and tables covered with food, which have no reality. Such things do not prove these jugglers to be sons of God; nor do Christ's miracles."[2]

---

[1] See Prefatory Discourse to vol. iii. Middleton's Works, p. 64.   [2] See Origen: Contra Celus, bk. 1, ch. lxviii

Celsus, in common with most of the Grecians, looked upon Christianity as a *blind faith*, that shunned the light of reason. In speaking of the Christians, he says:

"They are forever repeating: 'Do not examine. *Only believe*, and thy *faith* will make thee blessed. *Wisdom* is a bad thing in life; *foolishness* is to be preferred.'"[1]

He jeers at the fact that *ignorant men* were allowed to preach, and says that "weavers, tailors, fullers, and the most illiterate and rustic fellows," set up to teach strange paradoxes. "They openly declared that none but the ignorant (were) fit disciples for the God they worshiped," and that one of their rules was, "let no man that is learned come among us."[2]

The *miracles* claimed to have been performed by the Christians, he attributed to *magic*,[3] and considered—as we have seen above—their miracle performers to be on the same level with all Gentile magicians. He says that the "wonder-workers" among the Christians "rambled about to play tricks at fairs and markets," that they never appeared in the circles of the wiser and better sort, but always took care to intrude themselves among the ignorant and uncultured.[4]

"The magicians in Egypt (says he), cast out evil spirits, cure diseases by a breath, call up the spirits of the dead, make inanimate things move as if they were alive, and so influence some uncultured men, that they produce in them whatever sights and sounds they please. But because they do such things shall we consider them the sons of God? Or shall we call such things the tricks of pitiable and wicked men?"[5]

He believed that Jesus was like all these other wonder-workers, that is, simply a *necromancer*, and that he learned his magical arts in Egypt.[6] All philosophers, during the time of the Early Fathers, answered the claims that Jesus performed miracles, in the same manner. "They even ventured to call him a *magician* and a deceiver of the people," says Justin Martyr,[7] and St. Augustine asserted that it was generally believed that Jesus had been initiated in *magical art* in Egypt, and that he had written books concerning magic, one of which was called "*Magia Jesu Christi.*"[8] In the Clementine Recognitions, the charge is brought against Jesus that he did not perform his miracles as a Jewish prophet, but as a magician, an initiate of the heathen temples.[9]

---

[1] See Origen: Contra Celsus, bk. 1, ch. ix.
[2] Ibid. bk. iii. ch. xliv.
[3] Ibid.
[4] Ibid. bk. 1, ch. lxviii.
[5] Ibid.
[6] Ibid.
[7] Dial. Cum. Typho. ch. lxix.

[8] See Isis Unveiled, vol. ii. p. 148.
[9] See Baring-Gould's Lost and Hostile Gospels. A knowledge of magic had spread from Central Asia into Syria, by means of the return of the Jews from Babylon, and had afterwards extended widely, through the mixing of nations produced by Alexander's conquests.

The casting out of devils was the most frequent and among the most striking and the oftenest appealed to of the miracles of Jesus; yet, in the conversation between himself and the Pharisees (Matt. xii. 24–27), he speaks of it as one that was constantly and habitually performed by their own *exorcists;* and, so far from insinuating any difference between the two cases, *expressly puts them on a level.*

One of the best proofs, and most unquestionable, that Jesus was accused of being a *magician*, or that some of the early Christians believed him to have been such, may be found in the representations of him performing miracles. On a *surcophagus* to be found in the *Museo Gregoriano*, which is paneled with bas-reliefs, is to be seen a representation of Jesus raising Lazarus from the grave. He is represented as a young man, beardless, and equipped with a *wand* in the received guise of a *necromancer*, whilst the corpse of Lazarus is swathed in bandages exactly as an Egyptian mummy.[1]   On other Christian monuments representing the miracles of Jesus, he is pictured in the same manner. For instance, when he is represented as turning the water into wine, and multiplying the bread in the wilderness, he is a necromancer with a *wand* in his hand.[2]

Horus, the Egyptian Saviour, is represented on the ancient monuments of Egypt, *with a wand in his hand raising the dead to life*, "just as we see Christ doing the same thing," says J. P. Lundy, "in the same way, to Lazarus, in our Christian monuments."[3]

Dr. Conyers Middleton, speaking of the primitive Christians, says :

" In the performance of their miracles, they were always charged with fraud and imposture, by their adversaries. Lucian (who flourished during the second century), tells us that whenever any crafty juggler, expert in his trade, and who knew how to make a right use of things, went over to the Christians, he was sure to grow rich immediately, by making a prey of their simplicity. And Celsus represents all the Christian wonder-workers as mere vagabonds and common cheats, who rambled about to play their tricks at fairs and markets; not in the circles of the wiser and the better sort, for among such they never ventured to appear, but wherever they observed a set of raw young fellows, slaves or fools, there they took care to intrude themselves, and to display all their arts."[4]

The same charge was constantly urged against them by Julian, Porphyry and others. Similar sentiments were entertained by Polybius, the Pagan philosopher, who considered all miracles as fables, invented to preserve in the unlearned a due sense of respect for the deity.[5]

---

[1] See King's Gnostics, p. 145. Monumental Christianity, pp. 100 and 402, and Jameson's Hist. of Our Lord in Art, vol. i. p. 16.

[2] See Monumental Christianity, p. 402, and

Hist. of Our Lord, vol. i. p. 16.

[3] Monumental Christianity, pp. 403–405.

[4] Middleton's Works, vol. i. p. 19.

[5] See Taylor's Diegesis, p. 59.

Edward Gibbon, speaking of the miracles of the Christians, writes in his familiar style as follows:

"How shall we excuse the supine inattention of the Pagan and philosophic world, to those evidences which were represented by the hand of Omnipotence, not to their reason, but to their senses? During the age of Christ, of his apostles, and of their first disciples, the doctrine which they preached was confirmed by innumerable prodigies. The lame walked, the blind saw, the sick were healed, the dead were raised, demons were expelled, and the laws of nature were frequently suspended for the benefit of the church. But the sages of Greece and Rome turned aside from the awful spectacle, and, pursuing the ordinary occupations of life and study, appeared unconscious of any alterations in the moral or physical government of the world."[1]

The learned Dr. Middleton, whom we have quoted on a preceding page, after a searching inquiry into the miraculous powers of the Christians, says:

"From these short hints and characters of the primitive wonder-workers, as given both by friends and enemies, we may fairly conclude, that the celebrated gifts of these ages were generally engrossed and exercised by the primitive Christians, chiefly of the laity, who used to travel about from city to city, to assist the ordinary pastors of the church, and preachers of the Gospel, in the conversion of Pagans, by the extraordinary gifts with which they were supposed to be indued by the spirit of God, and the miraculous works which they pretended to perform. . . .

"We have just reason to suspect that there was some original fraud in the case; and that the strolling wonder-workers, by a dexterity of jugglery which art, not heaven, had taught them, imposed upon the credulity of the pious Fathers, whose strong prejudices and ardent zeal for the interest of Christianity would dispose them to embrace, without examination, whatever seemed to promote so good a cause. That this was really the case in some instances, is certain and notorious, and that it was so in all, will appear still more probable, when we have considered the particular characters of the several Fathers, on whose testimony the credit of these wonderful narratives depends."[2]

Again he says:

"The pretended miracles of the primitive church were all mere fictions, which the pious and zealous Fathers, partly from a weak credulity, and partly from reasons of policy, believing some perhaps to be true, and knowing all of them to be useful, were induced to espouse and propagate, for the support of a righteous cause."[3]

Origen, a Christian Father of the third century, uses the following words in his answer to Celsus:

"A vast number of persons who have left those horrid debaucheries in which they formerly wallowed, and have professed to embrace the Christian religion,

[1] Gibbon's Rome, vol. i. p. 588. An eminent heathen challenged his Christian friend Theophilus, Bishop of Antioch, a champion of the Gospel, to show him but one person who had been raised from the dead, on the condition of turning Christian himself upon it. *The Christian bishop was unable to give* *him that satisfaction.* (See Gibbon's Rome, vol. i. p. 541, and Middleton's Works, vol. i. p. 60.)

[2] Middleton's Works, vol. i. pp. 20, 21.

[3] Ibid. p. 62. The Christian Fathers are noted for their frauds. Their writings are full of falsehoods and deceit.

shall receive a bright and massive crown when this frail and short life is ended, *though they don't stand to examine the grounds on which their faith is* built, nor defer their conversion till they have a fair opportunity and capacity to apply themselves to rational and learned studies. And since our adversaries are continually making such a stir about our *taking things on trust*, I answer, that we, who see plainly and have found the vast advantage that the common people do manifestly and frequently reap thereby (who make up by far the greater number), I say, we (the Christian clergy), who are so well advised of these things, *do professedly teach men to believe without examination.*"[1]

Origen flourished and wrote A. D. 225–235, which shows that at that early day there was no rational evidence for Christianity, but it was professedly taught, and men were supposed to believe "*these things*" (*i. e.* the Christian legends) *without severe examination.*

The primitive Christians were perpetually reproached for their gross credulity, by all their enemies. Celsus, as we have already seen, declares that they cared neither to receive nor give any reason for their faith, and that it was a usual saying with them: "Do not examine, but believe only, and thy faith will save thee;" and Julian affirms that, "the sum of all their wisdom was comprised in the single precept, '*believe.*'"

Arnobius, speaking of this, says:

"The Gentiles make it their constant business to laugh at our faith, and to lash our credulity with their facetious jokes."

The Christian Fathers defended themselves against these charges by declaring that they did nothing more than the heathens themselves had always done; and reminds them that they too had found the same method useful with the uneducated or common people, who were not at leisure to examine things, and whom they taught therefore, to believe without reason.[2]

This "believing without reason" is illustrated in the following words of Tertullian, a Christian Father of the second century, who reasons on the evidence of Christianity as follows:

"I find no other means to prove myself to be impudent with success, and happily a fool, than by my contempt of shame; as, for instance—I maintain that the son of God was born: why am I not ashamed of maintaining such a thing? Why! but because it is a shameful thing. I maintain that the son of God died: well, *that* is wholly credible because it is monstrously absurd. I maintain that after having been buried, he rose again: and *that* I take to be absolutely true, because it was manifestly impossible."[3]

According to the very books which record the miracles of Jesus, he never claimed to perform such deeds, and Paul declares that the great reason why Israel did not believe Jesus to be the Messiah was

[1] Contra Celsus, bk. 1, ch. ix. x.   [3] On The F\ h of Christ, ch. v.
[2] See Middleton's Works, pp. 62, 63, 64.

that " the Jews required a sign.''[1] He meant : " Signs and wonders are the only proofs they will admit that any one is sent by God and is preaching the truth. If they cannot have this palpable, external proof, they withhold their faith."

A writer of the second century (John, in ch. iv. 18) makes Jesus aim at his fellow-countrymen and contemporaries, the reproach : " Unless you see signs and wonders, you do not believe." In connection with Paul's declaration, given above, these words might be paraphrased : " The reason why the Jews never believed in Jesus was that they never saw him do signs and wonders."

Listen to the reply he (Jesus) made when told that if he wanted people to believe in him he must first prove his claim by a miracle : " A wicked and adulterous generation asks for a *sign,* and no sign shall be given it except the sign of the prophet Jonas.''[2] Of course, this answer did not in the least degree satisfy the questioners ; so they presently came to him again with a more direct request : " If the kingdom of God is, as you say, close at hand, show us at least some *one* of the signs in heaven which are to precede the Messianic age." What could appear more reasonable than such a request? Every one knew that the end of the present age was to be heralded by fearful signs in heaven. The light of the sun was to be put out, the moon turned to blood, the stars robbed of their brightness, and many other fearful signs were to be shown![3] If any *one* of these could be produced, they would be content ; but if not, they must decline to surrender themselves to an idle joy which must end in a bitter disappointment ; and surely Jesus himself could hardly expect them to believe in him on his bare word.

Historians have recorded miracles said to have been performed by other persons, but not a word is said by *them* about the miracles claimed to have been performed by Jesus.

Justus of Tiberias, who was born about five years after the time assigned for the crucifixion of Jesus, wrote a *Jewish History.* Now, if the miracles attributed to Christ Jesus, and his death and resurrection, had taken place in the manner described by the Gospel narrators, he could not have failed to allude to them. But Photius, Patriarch of Constantinople, tells us that it contained " *no mention of the coming of Christ, nor of the events concerning him, nor of the prodigies he wrought.*" As Theodore Parker has remarked : " The miracle is of a most *fluctuating* character. The miracle-worker of to-day is a matter-of-fact juggler to-morrow.

---

[1] I. Corinthians, i. 22, 23.
[2] Matt. xii. 29.
[3] See, for example, Joel, ii. 10, 31 ; iii. 15 ;

Matt. xxiv. 29, 30 ; Acts, ii. 19, 20 ; Revelations, vi. 12, 13 ; xvi. 18, *et seq.*

Science each year adds new wonders to our store. The master of a locomotive steam-engine would have been thought greater than Jupiter Tonans, or the Elohim, thirty centuries ago."

In the words of Dr. Oort: " Our increased knowledge of nature has gradually undermined the belief in the possibility of miracles, and the time is not far distant when in the mind of every man, of any culture, all accounts of miracles will be banished together to their proper region—*that of legend.*"

What had been said to have been done in *India* was said by the "*half Jew*"[1] writers of the Gospels to have been done in Palestine. The change of names and places, with the mixing up of various sketches of *Egyptian, Phenician, Greek* and *Roman* mythology, was all that was necessary. They had an abundance of material, and with it they built. A long-continued habit of imposing upon others would in time subdue the minds of the impostors themselves, and cause them to become at length the dupes of their own deception.

---

[1] The writers of the Gospels were "I know not what sort of *half* Jews, not even agreeing with themselves." (Bishop Faustus.)

CHAPTER XXVIII.

BELIEVING and affirming, that the *mythological portion* of the history of Jesus of Nazareth, contained in the books forming the Canon of the New Testament, is nothing more or less than a copy of the mythological histories of the Hindoo Saviour *Crishna,* and the Buddhist Saviour *Buddha,*[1] with a mixture of mythology borrowed from the Persians and other nations, we shall in this and the chapter following, compare the histories of these *Christs,* side by side with that of Christ Jesus, the Christian Saviour.

In comparing the history of Crishna with that of Jesus, we have the following remarkable parallels:

1. "Crishna was born of a chaste virgin, called Devaki, who was selected by the Lord for this purpose on account of her purity."[2]

2. A chorus of Devatas celebrated with song the praise of Devaki, exclaiming: "In the delivery of this favored woman all nature shall have cause to exult."[4]

3. The birth of Crishna was announced in the heavens by *his star.*[6]

1. Jesus was born of a chaste virgin, called Mary, who was selected by the Lord for this purpose, on account of her purity.[3]

2. The angel of the Lord saluted Mary, and said: "Hail Mary! the Lord is with you, you are blessed above all women, . . . for thou hast found favor with the Lord."[5]

3. The birth of Jesus was announced in the heavens by *his star.*[7]

---

[1] It is also very evident that the history of Crishna—or that part of it at least which has a *religious aspect*—is taken from that of Buddha. Crishna, in the ancient epic poems, is simply a great hero, and it is not until about the fourth century B. C., that he is *deified* and declared to be an incarnation of Vishnu, or Vishnu himself in human form. (See Monier Williams' Hinduism, pp. 102, 103.)

"If it be urged that the attribution to Crishna of qualities or powers belonging to the other deities is a mere device by which his devotees sought to supersede the more ancient gods, *the answer must be that nothing is done in his case which has not been done in the case of almost every other member of the great company of the gods,* and that the systematic adoption of this method is itself conclusive proof of the looseness and flexibility of the materials of which the cumbrous mythology of the Hindu epic poems is composed." (Cox : Aryan Mythology, vol. ii. p. 130.) These words apply very forcibly to the history of Christ Jesus. He being attributed with qualities and powers belonging to the deities of the heathen is a mere device by which *his* devotees sought to supersede the more ancient gods.

[2] See ch. xii.
[3] See The Gospel of Mary, *Apoc.*, ch. vii.
[4] Hist. Hindostan, vol. ii. p. 329.
[5] Mary, *Apoc.*, vii. Luke, i. 28-30.
[6] Hist. Hindostan, vol. ii. pp. 317 and 336.
[7] Matt. ii. 2.

4. On the morn of Crishna's birth, "the quarters of the horizon were irradiate with joy, as if moonlight was diffused over the whole earth;" "the spirits and nymphs of heaven danced and sang," and "the clouds emitted low pleasing sounds."[1]

5. Crishna, though royally descended, was actually born in a state the most abject and humiliating, having been brought into the world in a *cave*.[3]

6. "The moment Crishna was born, the whole cave was splendidly illuminated, and the countenances of his father and his mother emitted rays of glory."[5]

7. "Soon after Crishna's mother was delivered of him, and while she was weeping over him *and lamenting his unhappy destiny*, the compassionate infant assumed the power of speech, and soothed and comforted his afflicted parent."[7]

8. The divine child—Crishna—was recognized, and adored by cowherds, who prostrated themselves before the heaven-born child.[9]

9. Crishna was received with divine honors, and presented with gifts of sandal-wood and perfumes.[11]

10. "Soon after the birth of Crishna, the holy Indian prophet Nared, hearing of the fame of the infant Crishna, pays him a visit at Gokul, examines the *stars*, and declares him to be of celestial descent."[13]

11. Crishna was born at a time when Nanda—his foster-father—was away from home, having come to the city to pay his tax or yearly tribute, to the king.[15]

4. When Jesus was born, the angels of heaven sang with joy, and from the clouds there came pleasing sounds.[2]

5. "The birth of Jesus, the King of Israel, took place under circumstances of extreme indigence; and the place of his nativity, according to the united voice of the ancients, and of oriental travelers, was in a *cave*."[4]

6. The moment Jesus was born, ' there was a great light in the cave, so that the eyes of Joseph and the midwife could not bear it.[6]"

7. " Jesus spake even when he was in his cradle, and said to his mother: 'Mary, I am Jesus, the Son of God, that *Word* which thou didst bring forth according to the declaration of the Angel Gabriel unto thee, and my Father hath sent me for the salvation of the world.' "[8]

8. The divine child—Jesus—was recognized, and adored by shepherds, who prostrated themselves before the heaven-born child.[10]

9. Jesus was received with divine honors, and presented with gifts of frankincense and myrrh.[12]

10. "Now when Jesus was born in Bethlehem of Judea, behold, there came wise men from the East, saying: Where is he that is born King of the Jews, for we have seen his *star* in the East and have come to worship him."[14]

11. Jesus was born at a time when Joseph—his foster-father—was away from home, having come to the city to pay his tax or tribute to the governor.[16]

---

[1] Vishnu Purana, p. 502.
[2] Luke, ii. 13.
[3] See ch. xvi.
[4] Hist. Hindostan, vol. ii. p. 311. See also, chap. xvi.
[6] See ch. xvi.
[6] Protevangelion, *Apoc.*, chs. xii. and xiii.
[7] Hist. Hindostan, vol. ii. 311.
[8] Infancy, *Apoc.*, ch. i. 2, 3.
[9] See ch. xv.
[10] Luke, ii. 8–10.
[11] See Oriental Religions, p. 500, and Inman's Ancient Faiths, vol. ii. p. 353.
[12] Matt. ii. 2.
[13] Hist. Hindostan, vol. ii. p. 317.
[14] Matt., ii. 1, 2.
[15] Vishnu Purana, bk. v. ch. iii.
[16] Luke, ii. 1–17.

12. Crishna, although born in a state the most abject and humiliating, was of royal descent.[1]

13. Crishna's father was warned by a "heavenly voice," to "fly with the child to Gacool, across the river Jumna," as the reigning monarch sought his life.[3]

14. The ruler of the country in which Crishna was born, having been informed of the birth of the divine child, sought to destroy him. For this purpose, he ordered "the massacre in all his states, of all the children of the male sex, born during the night of the birth of Crishna."[5]

15. "Mathura (pronounced Mattra), was the city in which Crishna was born, where his most extraordinary miracles were performed, and which continues at this day the place where his name and *Avatar* are held in the most sacred veneration of any province in Hindostan."[7]

16. Crishna was preceded by *Rama*, who was born a short time before him, and whose life was sought by Kansa, the ruling monarch, at the time he attempted to destroy the infant Crishna.[9]

17. Crishna, being brought up among shepherds, wanted the advantage of a preceptor to teach him the sciences. Afterwards, when he went to Mathura, a tutor, profoundly learned, was obtained for him; but, in a very short time, he became such a scholar as utterly to astonish and perplex his master with a variety of the most intricate questions in Sanscrit science.[11]

12. Jesus, although born in a state the most abject and humiliating, was of royal descent.[2]

13. Jesus' father was warned "in a dream" to "take the young child and his mother, and flee into Egypt," as the reigning monarch sought his life.[4]

·14. The ruler of the country in which Jesus was born, having been informed of the birth of the divine child, sought to destroy him. For this purpose, he ordered "all the children that were in Bethlehem, and in all the coasts thereof," to be slain.[6]

15. Matarea, near Hermopolis, in Egypt, is said to have been the place where Jesus resided during his absence from the land of Judea. At this place he is reported to have wrought many miracles.[8]

16. Jesus was preceded by *John* the "divine herald," who was born a short time before him, and whose life was sought by Herod, the ruling monarch, at the time he attempted to destroy the infant Jesus.[10]

17. Jesus was sent to Zaccheus the schoolmaster, who wrote out an alphabet for him, and bade him say *Aleph*. "Then the Lord Jesus said to him, Tell me first the meaning of the letter Aleph, and then I will pronounce Beth, and when the master threatened to whip him, the Lord Jesus explained to *him* the meaning of the letters Aleph and Beth; also which where the straight figures of the letters, which the oblique, and what letters had

[1] Asiatic Researches, vol. i. p. 259. Hist. Hindostan, vol. ii. p. 810.

[2] See the Genealogies in Matt. and Luke.

[3] See ch. xviii.

[4] Matt. ii. 13.

[5] See ch. xviii.

[6] Matt. ii. 16.

[7] Hist. Hindostan, vol. ii. p. 317. Asiatic Researches, vol. i. p. 259.

[8] Introduc. to Infancy, Apoc. Higgins: Anacalypsis, vol. i. p. 130. Savary: Travels in

Egypt, vol. i. p. 126, in Hist. Hindostan, vol. ii. p. 318.

[9] Hist. Hindostan, vol. ii. p. 316.

[10] "Elizabeth, hearing that her son John was about to be searched for (by Herod), took him and went up into the mountains, and looked around for a place to hide him. . . . But Herod made search after John, and sent servants to Zacharias," &c. (Protevangelion, Apoc. ch. xvi.)

[11] Hist. Hindostan. vol. ii. p. 321.

double figures; which had points, and which had none ; why one letter went before another; and many other things he began to tell him and explain, of which the master himself had never heard, nor read in any book."[1]

18. "At a certain time, Crishna, taking a walk with the other cowherds, they chose him their *King*, and every one had his place assigned him under the new King."[2]

18. "In the month Adar, Jesus gathered together the boys, and ranked them as though he had been a KING. . . . And if any one happened to pass by, they took him by force, and said, Come hither, and worship the King."[3]

19. Some of Crishna's play-fellows were stung by a serpent, and he, filled with compassion at their untimely fate, "and casting upon them an eye of divine mercy, they immediately rose," and were restored.[4]

19. When Jesus was at play, a boy was stung by a serpent, "and he (Jesus) touched the boy with his hand," and he was restored to his former health.[5]

20. Crishna's companions, with some calves, were stolen, and hid in a cave, whereupon Crishna, "by his power, created other calves and boys, in all things, perfect resemblances of the others."[6]

20. Jesus' companions, who had hid themselves in a furnace, were turned into kids, whereupon Jesus said: "Come hither, O boys, that we may go and play; and immediately the kids were changed into the shape of boys."[7]

21. "One of the first miracles performed by Crishna, when mature, was the curing of a leper."[8]

21. One of the first miracles performed by Jesus, when mature, was the curing of a leper.[9]

22. A poor cripple, or lame woman, came, with "a vessel filled with spices, sweet-scented oils, sandal-wood, saffron, civet, and other perfumes, and made a certain sign on his (Crishna's) forehead, *casting the rest upon his head.*"[10]

22. "Now, when Jesus was in Bethany, in the house of Simon the leper, there came unto him a woman having an alabaster box of very precious ointment, *and poured it on his head,* as he sat at meat."[11]

23. Crishna was crucified, and he is represented with arms extended, hanging on a cross.[12]

23. Jesus was crucified, and he is represented with arms extended, hanging on a cross.

24. At the time of the death of Crishna, there came calamities and bad omens of every kind. A black circle surrounded the moon, and the sun was darkened at noon-day ; the sky rained fire and ashes ; flames burned dusky and livid; demons committed depreda-

24. At the time of the death of Jesus, there came calamities of many kinds. The veil of the temple was rent in twain from the top to the bottom, the sun was darkened from the sixth to the ninth hour, and the graves were opened, and many bodies of the

1 Infancy, Apoc., ch. xx. 1-8.
2 Hist. Hindostan, vol. ii. p. 321.
3 Infancy, Apoc., ch. xviii. 1-3.
4 Hist. Hindostan, vol. ii. p. 343.
5 Infancy, Apoc., ch. xviii.
6 Hist. Hindostan, vol. ii. p. 340. Aryan Mytho., vol. ii. p. 136.
7 Infancy, Apoc., ch. xvii.
8 Hist. Hindostan, vol. ii. p. 319, and ch. xxvii. this work.
9 Matthew, viii. 2.
10 Hist. Hindostan, vol. ii. p. 320.
11 Matt. xxvi. 6 7.
12 See ch. xx.

tions on earth ; at sunrise and sunset, thousands of figures were seen skirmishing in the air; spirits were to be seen on all sides.[1]

25. Crishna was pierced with an arrow.[3]

26. Crishna said to the hunter who shot him: "Go, hunter, through my favor, to heaven, the abode of the gods."[5]

27. Crishna descended into hell.[7]

28. Crishna, after being put to death, rose again from the dead.[9]

29. Crishna ascended bodily into heaven, and many persons witnessed his ascent.[11]

30. Crishna is to come again on earth in the latter days. He will appear among mortals as an armed warrior, riding a white horse. At his approach the sun and moon will be darkened, the earth will tremble, and the stars fall from the firmament.[13]

31. Crishna is to be judge of the dead at the last day.[15]

32. Crishna is the creator of all things visible and invisible; "all this universe came into being through him, the eternal maker."[17]

33. Crishna is Alpha and Omega, "the beginning, the middle, and the end of all things."[19]

34. Crishna, when on earth, was in constant strife against the evil spirit.[21] He surmounts extraordinary dangers, strews his way with miracles, raising the dead, healing the sick, restoring the maimed, the deaf and the blind, every-

saints which slept arose and came out of their graves.[2]

25. Jesus was pierced with a spear

26. Jesus said to one of the malefactors who was crucified with him : "Verily I say unto thee, this day shalt thou be with me in paradise."[6]

27. Jesus descended into hell.[8]

28. Jesus, after being put to death, rose again from the dead.[10]

29. Jesus ascended bodily into heaven, and many persons witnessed his ascent.[12]

30. Jesus is to come again on earth in the latter days. He will appear among mortals as an armed warrior, riding a white horse. At his approach, the sun and moon will be darkened, the earth will tremble, and the stars fall from the firmament.[14]

31. Jesus is to be judge of the dead at the last day.[16]

32. Jesus is the creator of all things visible and invisible; "all this universe came into being through him, the eternal maker."[18]

33. Jesus is Alpha and Omega, the beginning, the middle, and the end of all things.[20]

34. Jesus, when on earth, was in constant strife against the evil spirit.[22] He surmounts extraordinary dangers, strews his way with miracles, raising the dead, healing the sick, restoring the maimed, the deaf and the blind,

[1] Prog. Relig. Ideas, vol. i. p. 71.
[2] Matt. xxii. Luke, xxviii.
[3] See ch. xx.
[4] John, xix. 34.
[5] See Vishnu Purana, p. 612.
[6] Luke, xxiii. 43.
[7] See ch. xxii.
[8] See Ibid.
[9] See ch. xxiii.
[10] Matt. xxviii.
[11] See ch. xxiii.
[12] See Acts, i. 9–11.
[13] See ch. xxiv.
[14] See passages quoted in ch. xxiv.
[15] See Oriental Religions, p. 504.
[16] Matt. xxiv. 31. Rom. xiv. 10.
[17] See ch. xxvi.

[18] John, i. 3. I. Cor. viii. 6. Eph. iii. 9.
[19] See Geeta, lec. x. p. 85.
[20] Rev. i. 8, 11 ; xxii. 13 ; xxi. 6.
[21] He is described as a superhuman organ of light, to whom the superhuman organ of darkness, the evil serpent, was opposed. He is represented " bruising the head of the serpent," and standing upon him. (See illustrations in vol. i. Asiatic Researches ; vol. ii. Higgins' Anacalypsis ; Calmet's Fragments, and other works illustrating Hindoo Mythology.)
[22] Jesus, "the Sun of Righteousness," is also described as a superhuman organ of light, opposed by Satan, "the old serpent." He is claimed to have been the seed of the woman who should " bruise the head of the serpent." (Genesis, iii. 15.)

where supporting the weak against the strong, the oppressed against the powerful. The people crowded his way, and adored him as a *God.*[1]

35. Crishna had a beloved disciple —*Arjuna.*[3]

36. Crishna was transfigured before his disciple Arjuna. "All in an instant, with a thousand suns, blazing with dazzling luster, so beheld he the glories of the universe collected in the one person of the God of Gods."[5]

Arjuna bows his head at this vision, and folding his hands in reverence, says:

"Now that I see thee as thou really art, I thrill with terror! Mercy! Lord of Lords, once more display to me thy human form, thou habitation of the universe."[6]

37. Crishna was "the meekest and best tempered of beings." "He preached very nobly indeed, and sublimely." "He was pure and chaste in reality,"[8] and, as a lesson of humility, "he even condescended to wash the feet of the Brahmins."[9]

38. "Crishna is the very Supreme Brahma, though it be a *mystery* how the Supreme should assume the form of a man."[11]

39. Crishna is the second person in the Hindoo Trinity.[13]

everywhere supporting the weak against the strong, the oppressed against the powerful. The people crowded his way and adored him as a *God.*[2]

35. Jesus had a beloved disciple —*John.*[4]

36. And after six days, Jesus taketh Peter, James, and John his brother, and bringeth them up into a high mountain apart, and was transfigured before them. And his face did shine as the sun, and his raiment was white as the light. . . While he yet spake, behold, a bright cloud overshadowed them, and behold, a voice out of the cloud, which said: &c." "And when the disciples heard it, they fell on their faces, and were sore afraid."[7]

37. Jesus was the meekest and best tempered of beings. He preached very nobly indeed, and sublimely. He was pure and chaste, and he even condescended to wash the feet of his disciples, to whom he taught a lesson of humility.[10]

38. Jesus is the very Supreme Jehovah, though it be a *mystery* how the Supreme should assume the form of a man, for "Great is the mystery of Godliness."[12]

39. Jesus is the second person in the Christian Trinity.[14]

---

[1] See ch. xxvii.
[2] According to the New Testament.
[3] See Bhagavat Geeta.
[4] John, xiii. 23.
[5] Williams' Hinduism, p. 215.
[6] Ibid. p. 216.   [7] Matt. xvii. 1-6.
[b] "He was pure and chaste in *reality*," although represented as sporting amorously, when a youth, with cowherdesses. According to the pure Vaishnava faith, however, Crishna's love for the Gopis, and especially for his favorite Radhā, is to be explained allegorically, as symbolizing the longing of the human soul for the Supreme. (Prof. Monier Williams: Hinduism, p. 144.) Just as the amorous "*Song of Solomon*" is said to be *allegorical*, and to mean "Christ's love for his church."
[9] See Indian Antiquities, iii. 46, and Asiatic Researches, vol. i. p. 273.
[10] John, xiii.
[11] Vishnu Purana, p. 492, *note* 3.
[12] I. Timothy, iii. 16.
[13] Brahma, Vishnu, and Siva. *Crishna is Vishnu in human form.* "A more personal,

and, so to speak, *human* god than Siva was needed for the mass of the people—a god who could satisfy the yearnings of the human heart for religion of faith (*bhakti*)—a god who could sympathize with, and condescend to human wants and necessities. Such a god was found in the second member of the Tri-mūtri. It was as *Vishnu* that the Supreme Being was supposed to exhibit his sympathy with human trials, and his love for the human race. "If *Siva* is the great god of the Hindu Pantheon, to whom adoration is due from all indiscriminately, *Vishnu* is certainly its most popular deity. He is the god selected by far the greater number of individuals as their Saviour, protector and friend, who rescues them from the power of evil, interests himself in their welfare, and finally admits them to his heaven. But it is not so much *Vishnu* in his own person as *Vishnu* in his *incarnations*, that effects all this for his votaries." (Prof. Monier Williams: Hinduism, p. 100.)

[14] Father, Son, and Holy Ghost. Jesus is the Son in human form.

40. Crishna said: "Let him if seeking God by deep abstraction, abandon
his possessions and his hopes, betake
himse'f to some secluded spot, and fix
his heart and thoughts on God alone.[1]

41. Crishna said : "Whate'er thou
dost perform, whate'er thou eatest,
whate'er thou givest to the poor,
whate'er thou offerest in sacrifice,
whate'er thou doest as an act of holy
presence, do all as if to me, O Arjuna.
I am the great Sage, without beginning ; I am the Ruler and the All-
sustainer."[3]

42. Crishna said : "I am the cause
of the whole universe; through me it is
created and dissolved; on me all things
within it hang and suspend, like pearls
upon a string."[5]

43. Crishna said: "I am the light
in the Sun and Moon, far, far beyond
the darkness. I am the brilliancy in
flame, the radiance in all that's radiant,
and the light of lights."[7]

44. Crishna said: "I am the sustainer of the world, its friend and Lord. I
am its way and refuge."[9]

45. Crishna said : "I am the Goodness of the good; l am Beginning,
Middle, End, Eternal Time, the Birth,
the Death of all."[11]

46. Crishna said : "Then be not
sorrowful, from all thy sins I will
deliver thee. Think thou on me, have
faith in me, adore and worship me,
and join thyself in meditation to me ;
thus shalt thou come to me, O Arjuna ;
thus shalt thou rise to my supreme
abode, where neither sun nor moon
hath need to shine, for know that all
the lustre they possess is mine."[13]

40. Jesus said: "But thou, when
thou prayest, enter into thy closet, and
when then hast shut thy door, pray to
thy Father, which is in secret."[3]

41. Jesus said: "Whether therefore
ye eat, or drink, or whatsoever ye do,
do all to the glory of God "[4] who is the
great Sage, without beginning ; the
Ruler and the All-sustainer.

42. "Of him, and through him, and
unto him, are all things." "All things
were made by him ; and without him
was not anything made that was made."[6]

43. "Then spoke Jesus again unto
them, saying : I am the light of the
world; he that followeth me shall not
walk in darkness, but shall have the
light of life."[8]

44. "Jesus said unto them, I am
the way, the truth, and the life. No
man cometh unto the Father, but by
me."[10]

45. "I am the first and the last;
and have the keys of hell and of
death."[12]

46. Jesus said: "Be of good cheer;
thy sins be forgiven thee."[14] "My
son, give me thine heart."[15] "The
city had no need of the sun, neither of
the moon, to shine in it ; for the glory
of God did lighten it."[16]

. Many other remarkable passages might be adduced from the
Bhagavad-gita, the following of which may be noted :[17]

[1] Williams' Hinduism, p. 211.
[2] Matt. vi. 6.
[3] Williams' Hinduism, p. 212.
[4] I. Cor. x. 31.
[5] Williams' Hinduism, p. 213.
[6] John, i. 3.
[7] Williams' Hinduism, p. 213.
[8] John, viii. 12.
[9] Williams' Hinduism, p. 213.
[10] John, xiv. 6.
[11] Williams' Hinduism, p. 213.
[12] Rev. i. 17, 18.
[13] Williams' Hinduism, p. 214.
[14] Matt. ix. 2.
[15] Prov. xxiii. 26.
[16] Rev. xxi. 23.
[17] Quoted from Williams' Hinduism pp.
217-219.

"He who has brought his members under subjection, but sits with foolish minds thinking in his heart of sensual things, is called a hypocrite." (Compare Matt. v. 28.)

"Many are my births that are past ; many are thine too, O Arjuna. I know them all, but thou knowest them not." (Comp. John, viii. 14.)

"For the establishment of righteousness am I born from time to time." (Comp. John, xviii. 37 ; I. John, iii. 3.)

"I am dearer to the wise than all possessions, and he is dearer to me." (Comp. Luke, xiv. 33 ; John, xiv. 21.)

"The ignorant, the unbeliever, and he of a doubting mind perish utterly." (Comp. Mark, xvi. 16.)

"Deluded men despise me when I take human form." (Comp. John, i. 10.)

Crishna had the titles of " Saviour," " Redeemer," " Preserver," " Comforter," " Mediator," &c. He was called " The Resurrection and the Life," " The Lord of Lords," " The Great God," " The Holy One," " The Good Shepherd," &c. All of which are titles applied to Christ Jesus.

Justice, humanity, good faith, compassion, disinterestedness, in fact, all the virtues, are said[1] to have been taught by Crishna, both by precept and example.

The Christian missionary Georgius, who found the worship of the crucified God in India, consoles himself by saying : " That which P. Cassianus Maceratentis had told me before, I find to have been observed more fully in French by the living De Guignes, a most learned man ; i. e., that *Crishna* is the very name corrupted of Christ the Saviour."[2] Many others have since made a similar statement, but unfortunately for them, the name *Crishna* has nothing whatever to do with " Christ the Saviour." It is a purely Sanscrit word, and means " *the dark god* " or " *the black god.*"[3] The word *Christ* (which is not a name, but a title), as we have already seen, is a Greek word, and means " the Anointed," or " the Messiah." The fact is, the history of Christ Crishna is older than that of Christ Jesus.

Statues of Crishna are to be found in the very oldest cave temples throughout India, and it has been satisfactorily proved, on the authority of a passage of *Arrian*, that the *worship* of Crishna was practiced in the time of Alexander the Great at what still remains one of the most famous temples of India, the temple of Mathura, on the Jumna river,[4] which shows that he was considered a *god* at

[1] It is said in the Hindoo sacred books that Crishna was a religious teacher, but, as we have previously remarked, this is a later addition to his legendary history. In the ancient epic poems he is simply a great hero and warrior. The portion pertaining to his religious career, is evidently a copy of the history of Buddha.

[2] " Est Crishna (quod ut mihi pridem indi-caverat P. Cassianus Maceratentis, sic nunc uberius in Galliis observatum intelligo avivo litteratissimo De Guignes) nomen ipsum cor-ruptum Christi Servatoris."

[3] See Williams' Hinduism, and Maurice : Hist. Hindostan, vol. ii. p. 269.

[4] See Celtic Druids, pp. 256, 257.

that time.[1] We have already seen that, according to Prof. Monier Williams, he was *deified* about the fourth century B. C.

Rev. J. P. Lundy says:

"If we may believe so good an authority as Edward Moor (author of Moor's "Hindu Pantheon," and "Oriental Fragments"), both the name of Crishna, and the general outline of his history, were long anterior to the birth of our Saviour, *as very certain things*, and probably extended to the time of Homer, nearly nine hundred years before Christ, or more than a hundred years before Isaiah lived and prophesied."[2]

In the Sanscrit Dictionary, compiled more than two thousand years ago, we have the whole story of Crishna, the incarnate deity, born of a virgin, and miraculously escaping in his infancy from Kansa, the reigning monarch of the country.[3]

The Rev. J. B. S. Carwithen, known as one of the "Brampton Lecturers," says:

"Both the name of Crishna and the general outline of his story are long an-terior to the birth of our Saviour; and this we know, *not on the presumed anti-quity of the Hindoo records alone.* Both Arrian and Strabo assert that the god Crishna was anciently worshiped at Mathura, on the river Jumna, where he is worshiped at this day. But the emblems and attributes essential to this deity are also transplanted into the mythology of the West."[4]

On the walls of the most ancient Hindoo temples, are sculptured representations of the flight of Vasudeva and the infant Saviour Crishna, from King Kansa, who sought to destroy him. The story of the slaughtered infants is also the subject of an immense sculpture in the cave temple of Elephanta. A person with a drawn sword is represented surrounded by slaughtered infant boys, while men and women are supplicating for their children. The date of this sculpture is lost in the most remote antiquity.[5]

The *flat roof* of this cavern-temple, and that of Ellora, and every other circumstance connected with them, prove that their origin must be referred to a very remote epoch. The *ancient* temples can easily be distinguished from the more modern ones—such as those of Solsette—by the shape of the roof. The ancient are flat, while the more modern are arched.[6]

---

[1] "Alexander the Great made his expedition to the banks of the Indus about 327 B. C., and to this invasion is due the first trustworthy information obtained by Europeans concern-ing the north-westerly portion of India and the region of the five rivers, down which the Grecian troops were conducted in ships by Nearchus. Megasthenes, who was the embas-sador of Seleukos Nikator (Alexander's succes-sor, and ruler over the whole region between the Euphrates and Indus, B. C. 312), at the court of Candra-gupa (Sandrokottus), in Pataliputra (Patna), during a long sojourn in that city col-lected further information, of which Strabo, Pliny, *Arrian*, and others availed themselves." (Williams' Hinduism, p. 4.)

[2] Monumental Christianity, p. 151. See also, Asiatic Researches, i. 273.

[3] See Asiatic Researches, vol. i. pp. 259–273.

[4] Quoted in Monumental Christianity, pp. 151, 152.

[5] See chapter xviii.

[6] See Prichard's Egyptian Mythology, p. 112.

The *Bhagavad gita*, which contains so mar y sentiments akin to Christianity, and which was not written until about the first or second century,[1] has led many *Christian* scholars to believe, and attempt to prove, that they have been borrowed from the New Testament, but unfortunately for them, their premises are untenable. Prof. Monier Williams, *the* accepted authority on Hindooism, and a thorough Christian, writing for the "Society for Promoting Christian Knowledge," knowing that he could not very well overlook this subject in speaking of the *Bhagavad-gita*, says :

"To any one who has followed me in tracing the outline of this remarkable philosophical dialogue, and has noted the numerous parallels it offers to passages in *our* Sacred Scriptures, it may seem strange that I hesitate to concur to any theory which explains these coincidences by supposing that the author had access to the New Testament, or that he derived some of his ideas from the first propagaters of Christianity. Surely it will be conceded that the probability of contact and interaction between Gentile systems and the Christian religion of the first two centuries of our era must have been greater in Italy than in India. Yet, if we take the writings and sayings of those great Roman philosophers, Seneca, Epictetus, and Marcus Aurelius, we shall find them full of resemblances to passages in our Scriptures, while their appears to be no ground whatever for supposing that these eminent Pagan writers and thinkers derived any of their ideas from either Jewish or Christian sources. In fact, the Rev. F. W. Farrar, in his interesting and valuable work 'Seekers after God,' has clearly shown that 'to say that Pagan morality kindled its faded taper at the Gospel light, whether furtively or unconsciously, that it dissembled the obligation and made a boast of the splendor, as if it were originally her own, is to make an assertion wholly untenable.' He points out that the attempts of the Christian Fathers to make out Pythagoras a debtor to Hebraic wisdom, Plato an 'Atticizing Moses,' Aristote a picker-up of ethics from a Jew, Seneca a correspondent of St. Paul, were due 'in some cases to ignorance, in some to a want of perfect honesty in controversial dealing.'[2]

"*His arguments would be even more conclusive if applied to the Bhagavad-gita*, the author of which was probably contemporaneous with Seneca.[3] It must, indeed, be admitted that the flames of true light which emerge from the mists of pantheism in the writings of Indian philosophers, must spring from the same source of light as the Gospel itself ; but it may reasonably be questioned whether there could have been any actual contact of the Hindoo systems with Christianity with-

---

[1] In speaking of the antiquity of the *Bhagavad-gita*, Prof. Monier Williams says : "The author was probably a Brahman and nominally a Vishnava, but really a philosopher whose mind was cast in a broad and comprehensive mould. He is supposed to have lived in India during the first and second century of our era. Some consider that he lived as late as the third century, and some place him even later, *but with these I cannot agree*." (Indian Wisdom, p. 137.)

[2] In order that the resemblances to Christian Scripture in the writings of Roman philosophers may be compared, Prof. Williams refers the reader to "Seekers after God," by the Rev. F. W. Farrar, and Dr. Ramage's "Beautiful Thoughts." The same sentiments are to be found in *Manu*, which, says Prof. Williams, "few will place later than the fifth century B.C." The *Mahabhrata*, written many centuries B. C., contains numerous parallels to New Testament sayings. (See our chapter on "Paganism in Christianity.")

[3] Seneca, the celebrated Roman philosopher, was born at Corduba, in Spain, a few years B.C. When a child, he was brought by his father to Rome, where he was initiated in the study of eloquence.

out a more satisfactory result in the modification of pantheistic and anti-Christian ideas."[1]

Again he says:

" It should not be forgotten that although the nations of Europe have changed their religions during the past eighteen centuries, *the Hindu has not done so, except very partially.* Islam converted a certain number by force of arms in the eighth and following centuries, and Christian truth is at last slowly creeping onwards and winning its way by its own inherent energy in the nineteenth; *but the religious creeds, rites, customs, and habits of thought of the Hindus generally, have altered little since the days of Manu, five hundred years* B. C."[2]

These words are conclusive; comments, therefore, are unnecessary.

Geo. W. Cox, in his " Aryan Mythology," speaking on this subject says :

"It is true that these myths have been crystallized around the name of Crishna in ages subsequent to the period during which the earliest *vedic* literature came into existence; *but the myths themselves are found in this older literature associated with other gods,* and not always only in germ. *There is no more room for inferring foreign influence in the growth of any of these myths than, as Bunsen rightly insists, there is room for tracing Christian influence in the earlier epical literature of the Teutonic tribes.* Practically the myths of Crishna seems to have been fully developed in the days of Megasthenes (fourth century B. C.) who identifies him with the Greek Hercules."[3]

It should be remembered, in connection with this, that Dr. Parkhurst and others have considered *Hercules* a type of Christ Jesus.

In the ancient epics Crishna is made to say :

"I am Vishnu, Brahma, Indra, and the source as well as the destruction of things, the creator and the annihilator of the whole aggregate of existences. While all men live in unrighteousness, I, the unfailing, build up the bulwark of righteousness, as the ages pass away."[4]

These words are almost identical with what we find in the *Bhagavad-gita.* In the *Maha-bharata,* Vishnu is associated or identified with Crishna, just as he is in the *Bhagavad-gita* and *Vishnu Purana,* showing, in the words of Prof. Williams, that : the *Puranas,* although of a comparatively modern date, are nevertheless composed of matter to be found in the two great epic poems the *Ramayana* and the *Maha-bharata.*

---

[1] Indian Wisdom, pp. 153, 154. Similar sentiments are expressed in his Hinduism, pp. 212-220.

[2] Indian Wisdom, p. iv.

[3] Cox : Aryan Mythology, vol. ii. pp. 137, 138.

[4] Ibid. p. 131.

[5] Williams' Hinduism, pp. 119-110. It was from these sources that the doctrine of *incarnation* was first evolved by the Brahman. They were written many centuries B. C. (See Ibid.)

CHAPTER XXIX.

CHRIST BUDDHA AND CHRIST JESUS COMPARED.

"The more I learn to know Buddha the more I admire him, and the sooner all mankind shall have been made acquainted with his doctrines the better it will be, for he is certainly one of the heroes of humanity." *Fausböll.*

THE *mythological* portions of the histories of Buddha and Jesus are, without doubt, nearer in resemblance than that of any two characters of antiquity. The *cause* of this we shall speak of in our chapter on "Why Christianity Prospered," and shall content ourselves for the present by comparing the following analogies:

1. Buddha was born of the Virgin Mary,[1] who conceived him without carnal intercourse.[2]

2. The incarnation of Buddha is recorded to have been brought about by the descent of the divine power called the "*Holy* Ghost," upon the Virgin Maya.[4]

3. When Buddha descended from

1. Jesus was born of the Virgin Mary, who conceived him without carnal intercourse.[3]

2. The incarnation of Jesus is recorded to have been brought about by the descent of the divine power called the "Holy Ghost," upon the Virgin Mary.[3]

3. When Jesus descended from his

---

[1] Maya, and Mary, as we have already seen, are one and the same name.

[2] See chap. xii. Buddha is considered to be an incarnation of Vishnu, although he preached against the doctrines of the Brahmans. The adoption of Buddha as an incarnation of Vishnu was really owing to the desire of the Brahmans to effect a compromise with Buddhism. (See Williams' Hinduism, pp. 82 and 108.)

"Buddha was brought forth not from the matrix, but from the right side, of a virgin." (De Guignes: Hist. des Huns, tom. i. p. 224.)

"Some of the (Christian) heretics maintained that Christ was born from the side of his mother." (Anacalypsis, vol. i. p. 157.)

"In the eyes of the Buddhists, this personage is sometimes a man and sometimes a god, or rather both one and the other, a divine incarnation, a man-god; who came into the world to enlighten men, to redeem them, and to indicate to them the way of safety. This idea of redemption by a divine incarnation is so gen-

eral and popular among the Buddhists, that during our travels in Upper Asia, we everywhere found it expressed in a neat formula. If we addressed to a Mongol or Thibetan the question, 'Who is Buddha?' he would immediately reply, 'The Saviour of Men.'" (M. L'Abbé Huc: Travels, vol. i. p. 326.)

"The miraculous birth of Buddha, his life and instructions, contain a great number of the moral and dogmatic truths professed in Christianity." (Ibid. p. 327.)

"He in mercy left paradise, and came down to earth because he was filled with compassion for the sins and misery of mankind. He sought to lead them into better paths, and took their sufferings upon himself, that he might expiate their crimes, and mitigate the punishment they must otherwise inevitably undergo." (L. Maria Child.)

[3] Matt. ch. i.

[4] See Bunsen's Angel-Messiah, pp. 10, 25 and 44. Also, ch. xiii. this work.

the regions of the souls,[1] and entered the body of the Virgin Maya, her womb assumed the appearance of clear transparent crystal, in which Buddha appeared, beautiful as a flower.[2]

4. The birth of Buddha was announced in the heavens by an *asterim* which was seen rising on the horizon. It is called the "Messianic Star."[4]

5. "The son of the Virgin Maya, on whom, according to the tradition, the 'Holy Ghost' had descended, was said to have been born on Christmas day."[6]

6. Demonstrations of celestial delight were manifest at the birth of Buddha. The *Devas*[8] in heaven and earth sang praises to the "Blessed One," and said: "To day, *Bodhisatwa* is born on earth, to give joy and peace to men and Devas, to shed light in the dark places, and to give sight to the blind."[9]

7. "Buddha was visited by wise men who recognized in this marvelous infant all the characters of the divinity, and he had scarcely seen the day before he was hailed God of Gods."[11]

8. The infant Buddha was presented with "costly jewels and precious substances."[13]

9. When Buddha was an infant, just born, he spoke to his mother, and said: "I am the greatest among men."[15]

heavenly seat, and entered the body of the Virgin Mary, her womb assumed the appearance of clear transparent crystal, in which Jesus appeared beautiful as a flower.[3]

4. The birth of Jesus was announced in the heavens by "his star," which was seen rising on the horizon.[5] It might properly be called the "Messianic Star."

5. The Son of the Virgin Mary, on whom, according to the tradition, the 'Holy Ghost' had descended, was said to have been born on Christmas day.[7]

6. Demonstrations of celestial delight were manifest at the birth of Jesus. The angels in heaven and earth sang praises to the "Blessed One," saying: "Glory to God in the highest, and on earth peace, good will toward men."[10]

7. Jesus was visited by wise men who recognized in this marvelous infant all the characters of the divinity, and he had scarcely seen the day before he was hailed God of Gods.[12]

8. The infant Jesus was presented with gifts of gold, frankincense, and myrrh.[14]

9. When Jesus was an infant in his cradle, he spoke to his mother, and said: "I am Jesus, the Son of God."[16]

---

[1] "As a spirit in the fourth heaven he resolves to give up all that glory in order to be born in the world for the purpose of rescuing all men from their misery and every future consequence of it: he vows to deliver all men who are left as it were without a *Saviour*." (Bunsen: The Angel-Messiah, p. 20.)

[2] See King's Gnostics, p. 168, and Hardy's Manual of Buddhism, p. 144.

[3] See chap. xii. *note* 2, page 117.
"On a painted glass of the sixteenth century, found in the church of Jouy, a little village in France, the Virgin is represented standing, her hands clasped in prayer, and the naked body of the child in the same attitude appears upon her stomach, apparently supposed to be seen through the garments and body of the mother. M. Drydon saw at Lyons a Salutation painted on shutters, in which the two infants (Jesus and John) likewise depicted on their mothers' stomachs, were also saluting each other. This precisely corresponds to

Buddhist accounts of the Boddhisattvas antenatal proceedings." (Viscount Amberly: Analysis of Relig. Belief, p. 224, *note*.)

[4] See chap. xiii.

[5] Matt. ii. 1, 2.

[6] Bunsen: The Angel-Messiah, p. x.

[7] We show, in our chapter on "The Birth-Day of Christ Jesus," that this was not the case. This day was adopted by his followers long after his death.

[8] "*Devas*," *i. e.*, angels.

[9] See chap. xiv.

[10] Luke, ii. 13, 14.

[11] See chap. xv.

[12] Matt. ii. 1–11.

[13] See chap. xi.

[14] Matt. ii. 11.

[15] See Hardy's Manual of Buddhism, pp. 145, 146.

[16] Gospel of Infancy, *Apoc.*, i. 8. No sooner was *Apollo* born than he spoke to his virgin-mother, declaring that he should teach to men

10. Buddha was a "dangerous child." His life was threatened by King Bimbasara. who was advised to destroy the child, as he was liable to overthrow him.[1]

11. When sent to school, the young Buddha surprised his masters. Without having ever studied, he completely worsted all his competitors, not only in writing, but in arithmetic, mathematics, metaphysics, astrology, geometry, &c.[4]

12. "When *twelve* years old the child Buddha is presented in the temple. He explains and asks learned questions; he excels all those who enter into competition with him."[6]

13. Buddha entered a temple, on which occasion forthwith all the statues rose and threw themselves at his feet, in act of worship.[8]

14. "The ancestry of Gotama Buddha is traced from his father, *Sodhōdana*, through various individuals and races, all of royal dignity, to *Maha Sammata*, the first monarch of the world. Several of the names and some of the events are met with in the Puranas of the Brahmans, but it is not possible to reconcile one order of statement with the other; and it would appear that the Buddhist historians

10. Jesus was a "dangerous child." His life was threatened by King Herod,[2] who attempted to destroy the child, as he was liable to overthrow him.[3]

11. When sent to school, Jesus surprised his master Zaccheus, who, turning to Joseph, said: "Thou hast brought a boy to me to be taught, who is more learned than any master."[5]

12. "And when he was *twelve* years old, they brought him to (the temple at) Jerusalem . . . . While in the temple among the doctors and elders, and learned men of Israel, he proposed several questions of learning, and also gave them answers."[7]

13. "And as Jesus was going in by the ensigns, who carried the standards, the tops of them bowed down and worshiped Jesus."[9]

14. The ancestry of Jesus is traced from his father, Joseph, through various individuals, nearly all of whom were of royal dignity, to Adam, the first monarch of the world. Several of the names, and some of the events, are met with in the sacred Scriptures of the Hebrews, but it is not possible to reconcile one order of statement with the other; and it would appear that the Christian historians have invented

---

the councils of his heavenly father Zeus. (See Cox : Aryan Mythology, vol. ii. p. 22.) *Hermes* spoke to his mother as soon as he was born, and, according to Jewish tradition, so did *Moses.* (See Hardy's Manual of Buddhism, p. 145.)

[1] See Beal : Hist. Buddha, pp. 103, 104.

[2] See Matt. ii. 1.

[3] That is, provided he was the expected Messiah, who was to be a mighty prince and warrior, and who was to rule his people Israel.

[4] See Hardy's Manual of Buddhism ; Bunsen's Angel-Messiah ; Beal's Hist. Buddha, and other works on Buddhism.
This was a common myth. For instance : A Brahman called *Dashthaka*, a "*heaven descended mortal*," after his birth, *without any human instruction whatever*, was able thoroughly to explain the four *Vedas*, the collective body of the sacred writings of the Hindoos, which were considered as directly revealed by Brahma. (See Beal's Hist. Buddha, p. 48.)

Confucius, the miraculous-born Chinese sage, was a wonderful child. At the age of seven he went to a public school, the superior of which was a person of eminent wisdom and piety. The faculty with which Confucius imbibed the lessons of his master, the ascendency which he acquired amongst his fellow pupils, and the superiority of his genius and capacity, raised universal admiration. He appeared to acquire knowledge *intuitively*, and his mother found it superfluous to teach him what " heaven had already engraven upon his heart." (See Thornton's Hist. China, vol. i. p. 153.)

[6] See Infancy, *Apoc.*, xx. 11, and Luke, ii. 46, 47.

[6] See Bunsen's Angel-Messiah, p. 37, and Beal : Hist. Buddha, pp. 67–69.

[7] See Infancy, *Apoc.*, xxi. 1, 2, and Luke, ii. 41–48.

[8] See Bunsen's Angel-Messiah, p. 37, and Beal : Hist. Bud. 67–69.

[9] Nicodemus, *Apoc.*, ch. i. 20.

have introduced races, and invented names, that they may invest their venerated Sage with all the honors of heraldry, in addition to the attributes of divinity."[1]

15. When Buddha was about to go forth "to adopt a religious life," *Mara*[3] appeared before him, to tempt him.[4]

16. *Mara* said unto Buddha: "Go not forth to adopt a religious life, and in seven days thou shalt become an emperor of the world."[6]

17. Buddha would not heed the words of the Evil One, and said to him: "Get thee away from me."[8]

18. After *Mara* had left Buddha, 'the skies rained flowers, and delicious odors pervaded the air."[10]

19. Buddha fasted for a long period.[12]

20. Buddha, the Saviour, was baptized, and at this recorded water-baptism the Spirit of God was present; that is, not only the highest God, but also the "Holy Ghost," through whom the incarnation of Gautama Buddha is recorded to have been brought about by the descent of that Divine power upon the Virgin Maya.[14]

21. "On one occasion toward the end of his life on earth, Gautama Buddha is reported to have been *transfigured*. When *on a mountain* in Ceylon, suddenly a flame of light descended upon him and encircled the crown of his head with a circle of light. The mount is called *Pandava*, or yellow-white color. It is said that 'the glory of his person shone forth with double power,' that his body was 'glorious as a bright golden image,' that he 'shone as the brightness of the sun and moon,' that bystanders expressed their opinion, that he could not be 'an every-day person,' or 'a

and introduced names, that they may invest their venerated Sage with all the honors of heraldry, in addition to the attributes of divinity.[2]

15. When Jesus was about "beginning to preach," the *devil* appeared before him, to tempt him.[5]

16. The *devil* said to Jesus: If thou wilt fall down and worship me, I will give thee all the kingdoms of the world.[7]

17. Jesus would not heed the words of the Evil One, and said to him: "Get thee behind me, Satan."[9]

18. After the *devil* had left Jesus, "angels came and ministered unto him."[11]

19. Jesus fasted forty days and nights.[13]

20. Jesus was baptized by John in the river Jordan, at which time the Spirit of God was present; that is, not only the highest God, but also the "Holy Ghost," through whom the incarnation of Jesus is recorded to have been brought about, by the descent of that Divine power upon the Virgin Mary.[15]

21. On one occasion during his career on earth, Jesus is reported to have been transfigured: "Jesus taketh Peter, James, and John his brother, and bringeth them up into a *high mountain* apart. And was transfigured before them: and his face did shine as the sun, and his raiment as white as the light."[16]

---

[1] R. Spence Hardy, in Manual of Buddhism.
[2] See chap. xvii.
[3] "*Mara*" is the "Author of Evil," the "King of Death," the "God of the World of Pleasure," &c., *i. e.*, the *Devil*. (See Beal: Hist. Buddha, p. 36.)
[4] See ch. xix.
[5] Matt. iv. 1-18.
[6] See ch. xix.
[7] Matt. iv. 8-19.
[8] See ch. xix.
[9] Luke, iv. 8.
[10] See ch. xix.
[11] Matt. iv. 11.
[12] See ch. xix.
[13] Matt. iv. 2.
[14] Bunsen: The Angel-Messiah, p. 45.
[15] Matt. iii. 13-17.   [16] Matt. xvii. 1, 2.

mortal man,' and that his body was divided into *three*[1] parts, from each of which a ray of light issued forth."[2]

22. "Buddha performed great miracles for the good of mankind, and the legends concerning him are full of the greatest prodigies and wonders."[3]

23. By prayers in the name of Buddha, his followers expect to receive the rewards of paradise.[5]

24. When Buddha died and was buried, "the coverings of the body unrolled themselves, and the lid of his coffin was opened by supernatural powers."[6]

25. Buddha ascended bodily to the celestial regions, when his mission on earth was fulfilled.[8]

26. Buddha is to come upon the earth again in the latter days, his mission being to restore the world to order and happiness.[10]

27. Buddha is to be judge of the dead.[12]

28. Buddha is Alpha and Omega, without beginning or end, "the Supreme Being, the Eternal One."[14]

29. Buddha is represented as saying: "Let all the sins that were committed in this world fall on me, that the world may be delivered."[17]

30. Buddha said: "Hide your good deeds, and confess before the world the sins you have committed."[19]

22. Jesus performed great miracles for the good of mankind, and the legends concerning him are full of the greatest prodigies and wonders.[4]

23. By prayers in the name of Jesus, his followers expect to receive the rewards of paradise.

24. When Jesus died and was buried, the coverings of his body were unrolled from off him, and his tomb was opened by supernatural powers.[7]

25. Jesus ascended bodily to the celestial regions, when his mission on earth was fulfilled.[9]

26. Jesus is to come upon the earth again in the latter days, his mission being to restore the world to order and happiness.[11]

27. Jesus is to be the judge of the dead.[13]

28. Jesus is Alpha and Omega, without beginning or end,[15] the Supreme Being, the Eternal One.[16]

29. Jesus is represented as the Saviour of mankind, and all sins that are committed in this world may fall on him, that the world may be delivered.[18]

30. Jesus taught men to hide their good deeds,[20] and to confess before the world the sins they had committed.[21]

---

[1] This has evidently an allusion to the Trinity. Buddha, as an incarnation of Vishnu, would be one god and yet three, three gods and yet one. (See the chapter on the *Trinity*.)

[2] See Bünsen's Angel-Messiah, p. 45, and Beal : Hist. Buddha, p. 177.

Iamblichus, the great *Neo-Platonic mystic*, was at one time *transfigured*. According to the report of his servants, *while in prayer to the gods*, his body and clothes were changed to a beautiful gold color, but after he ceased from prayer, his body became as before. He then returned to the society of his followers. (Primitive Culture, i. 136, 137.)

[3] See ch. xxvii.

[4] See that recorded in Matt. viii. 28–34.

[5] See ch. xxiii.

[6] Bunsen's Angel-Messiah, p. 49.

[7] See Matt. xxviii. John, xx.

[8] See chap. xxiii.   [9] See Acts, i. 9–12.

[10] See ch. xxiv.   [11] See Ibid.

[12] See ch. xxv. [13] Matt. xvi. 27; John, v. 22.

[14] "Buddha, the Angel-Messiah, was regarded as the divinely chosen and incarnate messenger, the vicar of God, and God himself on earth." (Bunsen : The Angel-Messiah, p. 33. See also, our chap. xxvi.)

[15] Rev. i. 8 ; xxii. 13.

[16] John, i. 1. Titus, ii. 13. Romans, ix. 5. Acts, vii. 59, 60.

[17] Müller : Hist. Sanscrit Literature, p. 80.

[18] This is according to Christian dogma :

"Jesus paid it all,
    All to him is due,
Nothing. either great or small,
    Remains for me to do."

[19] Müller : Science of Religion, p. 28.

[20] "Take heed that ye do not your alms before men, to be seen of them : otherwise ye have no reward of your father which is in heaven." (Matt. vi. 1.)

[12] "Confess your faults one to another, and pray one for another, that ye may be healed." (James, v. 16.)

31. "Buddha was described as a superhuman organ of light, to whom a superhuman organ of darkness, Mara or Naga, the Evil Serpent, was opposed."[1]

32. Buddha came, not to destroy, but to fulfill, the law. He delighted in "representing himself as a *mere link* in a long chain of enlightened teachers."[4]

33. "One day Ananda, the disciple of Buddha, after a long walk in the country, meets with Mâtangî, a woman of the low caste of the Kândâlas, near a well, and asks her for some water. She tells him what she is, and that she must not come near him. But he replies, 'My sister, I ask not for thy caste or thy family, I ask only for a draught of water.' She afterwards became a disciple of Buddha."[6]

34. "According to Buddha, the motive of all our actions should be *pity* or *love* for our neighbor."[8]

35. During the early part of his career as a teacher, "Buddha went to the city of Benares, and there delivered a discourse, by which Kondanya, and afterwards *four* others, were induced to become his disciples. From that period, whenever he preached, multitudes of men and women embraced his doctrines."[10]

36. Those who became disciples of Buddha were told that they must "renounce the world," give up all their riches, and avow poverty.[13]

31. Jesus was described as a superhuman organ of light—"the *Sun* of Righteousness"[2] — opposed by "the old Serpent," the Satan, hinderer, or adversary.[3]

32. Jesus said: "Think not that I am come to destroy the law, or the prophets: I am not come to destroy, but to fulfill."[5]

33. One day Jesus, after a long walk, cometh to the city of Samaria, and being wearied with his journey, sat on a well. While there, a woman of Samaria came to draw water, and Jesus said unto her: "give me to drink." "Then said the woman unto him: How is it that thou, being a Jew, asketh drink of me, which am a woman of Samaria? For the Jews have no dealings with the Samaritans."[7]

34. "Love your enemies, bless them that curse you, do good to them that hate you."[9]

35. During the early part of his career as a teacher, Jesus went to the city of Capernaum, and there delivered a discourse. It was at this time that *four* fishermen were induced to become his disciples.[11] From that period, whenever he preached, multitudes of men and women embraced his doctrines.[12]

36. Those who became disciples of Jesus were told that they must renounce the world, give up all their riches, and avow poverty.[14]

---

[1] Bunsen : The Angel-Messiah, pp. x. and 39.
[2] "That was the true light, which lighteth every man that cometh into the world." (John, i. 9.)
[3] Matt. iv. 1 ; Mark, i. 13 ; Luke, iv. 2.
[4] Müller : Science of Religion, p. 140.
[5] Matt. v. 17.
[6] Müller : Science of Religion, p. 243. See also, Bunsen's Angel-Messiah, pp. 47, 48, and Amberly's Analysis, p. 285.
[7] John, iv. 1-11.
Just as the Samaritan woman wondered that Jesus, a Jew, should ask drink of *her*, one of a nation with whom the Jews had no dealings, so this young Matangi warned Ananda of her caste, which rendered it unlawful for her to approach a monk. And as Jesus continued, nevertheless, to converse with the woman, so Ananda did not shrink from this outcast damsel. And as the disciples "marvelled" that Jesus should have conversed with this member of a despised race, so the respectable Brahmans and householders who adhered to Brahmanism were scandalized to learn that the young Matangi had been admitted to the order of mendicants.
[8] Müller : Religion of Science, p. 249.
[9] Matt. v. 44.
[10] Hardy : Eastern Monachism, p. 6.
[11] See Matt. iv. 13-25.
[12] "And there followed him great multitudes of people." (Matt. iv. 25.)
[13] Hardy : Eastern Monachism, pp. 6 and 62 *et seq.*
While at Rajageiha Buddha called together his followers and addressed them at some length on the means requisite for Buddhist salvation. This sermon was summed up in the celebrated verse :

" To cease from all sin,
To get virtue,
To cleanse one's own heart—
This is the religion of the Buddhas."
                —(Rhys David's Buddha, p. 62.)
[14] See Matt. viii. 19, 20 ; xvi. 25-28.

37. It is recorded in the "Sacred Canon" of the Buddhists that the multitudes "*required a sign*" from Buddha "that they might believe."[1]

38. When Buddha's time on earth was about coming to a close, he, "foreseeing the things that would happen in future times," said to his disciple Ananda: "Ananda, when I am gone, you must not think there is no Buddha; the *discourses* I have delivered, and the *precepts* I have enjoined, *must be my successors*, or representatives, and be to you as Buddha."[3]

39. In the Buddhist *Somadeva*, is to be found the following: "To give away our riches is considered the most difficult virtue in the world; he who gives away his riches is like a man who gives away his life: for our very life seems to cling to our riches. But Buddha, when his mind was moved by pity, *gave his life* like grass, for the sake of others; why should we think of miserable riches! By this exalted virtue, Buddha, when he was freed from all desires, and had obtained divine knowledge, attained unto Buddhahood. Therefore let a wise man, after he has turned away his desires from all pleasures, do good to all beings, even unto sacrificing his own life, that thus he may attain to true knowledge."[6]

40. Buddha's aim was to establish

37. It is recorded in the "Sacred Canon" of the Christians that the multitudes required a sign from Jesus that they might believe.[3]

38. When Jesus' time on earth was about coming to a close, he told of the things that would happen in future times,[4] and said unto his disciples: "Go ye therefore, and teach all nations, teaching them to observe all things whatsoever I have commanded you; and, lo, I am with you alway, even unto the end of the world."[5]

39. "And behold, one came and said unto him, Good Master, what good thing shall I do, that I may have eternal life? . . . Jesus said unto him, If thou wilt be perfect, go and sell that thou hast, and give to the poor, and thou shalt have treasure in heaven: and come and follow me."[7] "Lay not up for yourselves treasures upon earth, where moth and rust doth corrupt, and where thieves break through and steal: But lay up for yourselves treasures in heaven, where neither moth nor rust doth corrupt, and where thieves do not break through nor steal."[8]

40. "From that time Jesus began

---

[1] Müller : Science of Religion, p. 27.

[3] Hardy : Eastern Monachism, p. 230.

"Gautama Buddha is said to have announced to his disciples that the time of his departure had come : 'Arise, let us go hence, my time is come.' Turned toward the East and with folded arms he prayed to the highest spirit who inhabits the region of purest light, to Maha-Brahma, to the king in heaven, to Devaraja, who from his throne looked down on Gautama, and appeared to him in a self-chosen personality." (Bunsen: The Angel-Messiah. Compare with Matt. xxvi. 36-47.)

[2] "Then certain of the scribes and Pharisees answered, saying. Master, we would see a sign from thee." (Matt. xii. 38.)

[4] See Matt. xxiv ; Mark, viii. 31 ; Luke, ix. 18.

[5] Mark, xxviii. 18-20.

Buddha at one time said to his disciples : "Go ye now, and preach the most excellent law, expounding every point thereof, and un-

folding it with care and attention in all its bearings and particulars. Explain the beginning, the middle, and the end of the law, to all men without exception ; let everything respecting it be made publicly known and brought to the broad daylight." (Rhys David's Buddhism, p. 55, 56.)

When Buddha, just before his death, took his last formal farewell of his assembled followers, he said unto them : "Oh mendicants, thoroughly learn, and practice, and perfect, and spread abroad the law thought out and revealed by me, in order that this religion of mine may last long, and be perpetuated for the good and happiness of the great multitudes, out of pity for the world, to the advantage and prosperity of gods and men." (Ibid. p. 172.)

[6] Müller : Science of Religion, p. 244.

[7] Matt. xix. 16-21.

[8] Matt. vi. 19, 20.

a "Religious Kingdom," a " *Kingdom of Heaven.*"[1]

41. Buddha said: "I now desire to turn the wheel of the excellent law.[8] For this purpose am I going to the city of Benares,[4] to give light to those enshrouded in darkness, and to open the gate of Immortality to man."[5]

42. Buddha said: "Though the heavens were to fall to earth, and the great world be swallowed up and pass away: Though Mount Sumera were to crack to pieces, and the great ocean be dried up, yet, Ananda, be assured, the words of Buddha are true."[7]

43. Buddha said: "There is no passion more violent than voluptuousness. Happily there is but one such passion. If there were two, not a man in the whole universe could follow the truth." "Beware of fixing your eyes upon women. If you find yourself in their company, let it be as though you were not present. If you speak with them, guard well your hearts."[10]

44. Buddha said: "A wise man should avoid married life as if it were

to preach, and to say, Repent: for the Kingdom of Heaven is at hand."[2]

41. Jesus, after his temptation by the devil, began to establish the dominion of his religion, and he went for this purpose to the city of Capernaum. "The people which sat in darkness saw great light, and to them which sat in the region and shadow of death, light is sprung up."[6]

42. "The law was given by Moses, but grace and *truth* came by Jesus Christ."[8]

"*Verily* I say unto you . . . heaven and earth shall pass away, *but my words shall not pass away.*"[9]

43. Jesus said: "Ye have heard that it was said by them of old time. Thou shalt not commit adultery: But I say unto you, that whosoever looketh on a woman to lust after her, hath committed adultery with her already in his heart."[11]

44. "It is good for a man not to touch a woman," "but if they cannot

---

[1] Beal : Hist. Buddha, p. x. *note.*
[2] Matt. iv. 17.
[8] *i. e.,* to establish the dominion of religion. (See Beal : p. 244, *note.*)
[4] The Jerusalem, the Rome, or the Mecca of India.
This celebrated city of Benares, which has a population of 200,000, out of which at least 25,000 are Brahmans, was probably one of the first to acquire a fame for sanctity, and it has always maintained its reputation as the most sacred spot in all India. Here, in this fortress of Hindooism, Brahmanism displays itself in all its plentitude and power. Here the degrding effect of idolatry is visibly demonstrated as it is nowhere else except in the extreme south of India. Here, temples, idols, and symbols, sacred wells, springs, and pools, are multiplied beyond all calculation. Here every particle of ground is believed to be hallowed, and the very air holy. The number of temples is at least two thousand, not counting innumerable smaller shrines. In the principal temple of Siva, called Visvesvara, are collected in one spot several thousand idols and symbols, the whole number scattered throughout the city, being, it is thought, at least half a million.
Benares, indeed, must always be regarded

as the Hindoo's Jerusalem. The desire of a pious man's life is to accomplish at least one pilgrimage to what he regards as a portion of heaven let down upon earth ; and if he can die within the holy circuit of the Pancakosi stretching with a radius of ten miles around the city—nay, if any human being die there, be he Asiatic or European—no previously incurred guilt, however heinous, can prevent his attainment of celestial bliss.
[5] Beal : Hist. Buddha, p. 245.
[6] Matt. iv. 13–17.
[7] Beal : Hist. Buddha, p. 11.
[8] John, i. 17.
[9] Luke, xxi. 32, 33.
[10] Prog. Relig. Ideas, vol. i. p. 228.
[11] Matt. v. 27, 28.
On one occasion Buddha preached a sermon on the five senses and the heart (which he regarded as a sixth organ of sense), which pertained to guarding against the passion of lust. Rhys Davids, who, in speaking of this sermon, says : "One may pause and wonder at finding such a sermon preached so early in the history of the world—more than 400 years before the rise of Christianity—and among a people who have long been thought peculiarly idolatrous and sensual." (Buddhism, p. 60.)

a burning pit of live coals. One who is not able to live in a state of celibacy should not commit adultery."[1]

45. "Buddhism is convinced that if a man reaps sorrow, disappointment, pain, he himself, and no other, must at some time have sown folly, error, sin; and if not in this life then in some former birth."[3]

46. Buddha knew the thoughts of others: "By directing his mind to the thoughts of others, he can know the thoughts of all beings."[5]

47. In the *Somadeva* a story is related of a Buddhist ascetic whose eye offended him, he therefore plucked it out, and cast it away.[7]

48. When Buddha was about to become an ascetic, and when riding on the horse "Kantako," his path was strewn with flowers, thrown there by Devas.[9]

contain let them marry, for it is better to marry than to burn." "To avoid fornication, let every man have his own wife and let every woman have her own husband."[2]

45. "And as Jesus passed by, he saw a man which was *blind from his birth*. And his disciples asked him, saying, Master, who did sin, this man, or his parents, that he was born blind."[4]

46. Jesus knew the thoughts of others. By directing his mind to the thoughts of others, he knew the thoughts of all beings.[6]

47. It is related in the New Testament that Jesus said: "If thy right eye offend thee, pluck it out, and cast it from thee."[8]

48. When Jesus was entering Jerusalem, riding on an ass, his path was strewn with palm branches, thrown there by the multitude.[10]

Never were devotees of any creed or faith as fast bound in its thraldom as are the disciples of Gautama Buddha. For nearly two thousand four hundred years it has been the established religion of Burmah, Siam, Laos, Pega, Cambodia, Thibet, Japan, Tartary, Ceylon and Loo-Choo, and many neighboring islands, beside about two-thirds of China and a large portion of Siberia; and at the present day no inconsiderable number of the simple peasantry of Swedish Lapland are found among its firm adherents."[11]

---

[1] Rhys Davids' Buddhism, p. 138.
[2] I. Corinth. vii. 1-7.
[3] Rhys Davids' Buddhism, p. 103.
[4] John, ix. 1, 2.
This is the doctrine of transmigration clearly taught. If this man was born blind, as punishment for some sin committed by him, this sin must have been committed in *some former birth*.
[5] Hardy: Buddhist Legends, p. 181.
[6] See the story of his conversation with the woman of Samaria. (John, iv. 1.) And with the woman who was cured of the "bloody issue." (Matt. ix. 20.)
[7] Müller: Science of Religion, p. 245.
[8] Matt. v. 29.
[9] Hardy: Buddhist Legends, p. 134.
[10] Matt. xxi. 1-9.
Bacchus rode in a triumphal procession, on approaching the city of *Thebes*. "Pantheus, the king, who had no respect for the new worship (instituted by Bacchus) forbade

its rites to be performed. But when it was known that Bacchus was advancing, men and women, but chiefly the latter, young and old, poured forth to meet him and to join his triumphal march. . . . It was in vain Pantheus remonstrated, commanded and threatened. 'Go,' said he to his attendants, 'seize this vagabond leader of the rout and bring him to me. I will soon make him confess his false claim of heavenly parentage and renounce his counterfeit worship.'" (Bulfinch: Age of Fable, p. 222. Compare with Matt. xxvi.; Luke, xxii.; John xviii.)
[14] "There are few names among the men of the West, that stand forth as saliently as Gotama Buddha, in the annals of the East. In little more than two centuries from his decease the system he established had spread throughout the whole of India, overcoming opposition the most formidable, and binding together the most discordant elements; and at the present moment Buddhism is the pre-

"Well authenticated records establish indisputably the facts, that together with a noble physique, superior mental endowments, and high moral excellence, there were found in Buddha a purity of life, sanctity of character, and simple integrity of purpose, that commended themselves to all brought under his influence. Even at this distant day, one cannot listen with tearless eyes to the touching details of his pure, earnest life, and patient endurance under contradiction, often fierce persecution for those he sought to benefit. Altogether he seems to have been one of those remarkable examples, of genius and virtue occasionally met with, unaccountably superior to the age and nation that produced them.

There is no reason to believe that he ever arrogated to himself any higher authority than that of a teacher of religion, but, *as in modern factions*, there were readily found among his followers those who carried his peculiar tenets much further than their founder. These, not content with lauding during his life-time the noble deeds of their teacher, exalted him, within a quarter of a century after his death, to a place among their deities—worshiping as a God one they had known only as a simple-hearted, earnest, truth-seeking philanthropist.[1]

This worship was at first but the natural upgushing of the veneration and love Gautama had inspired during his noble life, and his sorrowing disciples, mourning over the desolation his death had occasioned, turned for consolation to the theory that he still lived.

Those who had known him in life cherished his name as the very synonym of all that was generous and good, and it required but a step to exalt him to divine honors ; and so it was that Gautama Buddha became a God, and continues to be worshiped as such.

For more than forty years Gautama thus dwelt among his followers, instructing them daily in the sacred law, and laying down

vailing religion, under various modifications, of Tibet, Nepal, Siam, Burma, Japan, and South Ceylon ; and in China it has a position of at least equal prominence with its two great rivals, Confucianism and Taouism. A long time its influence extended throughout nearly three-fourths of Asia ; from the steppes of Tartary to the palm groves of Ceylon, and from the vale of Cashmere to the isles of Japan." (R. Spence Hardy : Buddhist Leg. p. xi.)

[1] "Gautama was *very early* regarded as omniscient, and absolutely sinless. His perfect wisdom is declared by the ancient epithet of *Samma-sambuddha*, ' the Completely Enlightened One ;' found at the commencement of every Pali text ; and at the present day, in Ceylon, the usual way in which Gautama is styled is *Sarwajnan-wahanse*, ' the Venerable Omniscient One.' From his perfect wisdom, according to Buddhist belief, *his sinlessness would follow as a matter of course.* He was the first and the greatest of the Arahats. *At a consequence of this doctrine* the belief soon sprang up that he could not have been, that he was not, born as ordinary men are ; that he had no earthly father ; that he descended of his own accord into his mother's womb from his throne in heaven ; and that he gave unmistakable signs, immediately after his birth of his high character and of his future great ness." (Rhys Davids' Buddhism, p. 162.)

many rules for their guidance when he should be no longer with them.[1]

He lived in a style the most simple and unostentatious, bore uncomplainingly the weariness aud privations incident to the many long journeys made for the propagation of the new faith; and performed countless deeds of love and mercy.

When the time came for him to be perfected, he directed his followers no longer to remain together, but to go out in companies, and proclaim the doctrines he had taught them, found schools and monasteries, build temples, and perform acts of charity, that they might 'obtain merit,' and gain access to the blessed shade of Nigban, which he told them he was about to enter, and where they believe he has now reposed more than two thousand years."

To the pious Buddhist it seems irreverent to speak of Gautama by his mere ordinary and human name, and he makes use therefore, of one of those numerous epithets which are used only of the Buddha, " the Enlightened One." Such are *Sakya-sinha*, " the Lion of the Tribe of Sakya ;" *Sakya-muni*, " the Sakya Sage ;" *Sugata*, " the Happy One ;" *Sattha*, " the Teacher ;" *Jina*, " the Conqueror ;" *Bhagavad*, " the Blessed One ;" *Loka-natha*, " the Lord of the World ;" *Sarvajna*, " the Omniscient One ;" *Dharma-raja*, " the King of Righteousness ;" he is also called " the Author of Happiness," " the Possessor of All," " the Supreme Being," " the Eternal One," " the Dispeller of Pain and Trouble," " the Guardian of the Universe," " the Emblem of Mercy," " the Saviour of the World," " the Great Physician," " the God among Gods," " the Anointed " or " the Christ," " the Messiah," " the Only-Begotten," " the Heaven-Descended Mortal," " the Way of Life, and of Immortality," &c.[2]

At no time did Buddha receive his knowledge from a human

---

[1] Gautama Buddha left behind him no written works, but the Buddhists believe that he composed works which his immediate disciples learned by heart in his life-time, and which were handed down by memory in their original state until they were committed to writing. This is not impossible : it is known that the *Vedas* were handed down in this manner for many hundreds of years, and none would now dispute the enormous powers of memory to which Indian priests and monks attained, when written books were not invented, or only used as helps to memory. Even though they are well acquainted with writing, the monks in Ceylon do not use books in their religious services, but, repeat, for instance, the whole of the *Patimokkha* on Uposatha (Sabbath)

days by heart. (See Rhys Davids' Buddhism, pp. 9, 10.)

[2] Compare this with the names, titles, and characters given to Jesus. He is called the " Deliverer," (Acts, vii. 35) ; the " First Begotten " (Rev. i. 5); " God blessed forever" (Rom. ix. 5); the " Holy One " (Luke, iv. 34 ; Acts, iii. 14); the " King Everlasting " (Luke, i. 33); " King of Kings " (Rev. xvii. 14); " Lamb of God " (John, i. 29, 36); " Lord of Glory " (I. Cor. ii. 8); " Lord of Lords " (Rev. xvii. 14); " Lion of the tribe of Judah " (Rev. v. 5); " Maker and Preserver of all things " (John, i. 3, 10 ; I. Cor. viii. 6; Col. i. 16); " Prince of Peace " (Isai. ix. 6); " Redeemer," " Saviour," " Mediator," " Word," &c., &c.

source, that is, from flesh and blood. His source was the power of
his divine wisdom, the spiritual power of Maya, which he already
possessed before his incarnation. It was by this divine power,
which is also called the "Holy Ghost," that he became the Saviour,
the Kung-teng, the Anointed or Messiah, to whom prophecies had
pointed. Buddha was regarded as the supernatural light of the
world ; and this world to which he came was his own, his possession, for he is styled: "The Lord of the World."[1]

"Gautama Buddha taught that all men are brothers[2] that
charity ought to be extended to all, even to enemies; that men
ought to love truth and hate the lie; that good works ought not be
done openly, but rather in secret; that the dangers of riches are to
be avoided; that man's highest aim ought to be purity in thought,
word and deed, since the higher beings are pure, whose nature is
akin to that of man."[3]

"Sakya-Muni healed the sick, performed miracles and taught
his doctrines to the poor. He selected his first disciples among lay-
men, and even two women, the mother and wife of his first convert,
the sick Yasa, became his followers. He subjected himself to the
religious obligations imposed by the recognized authorities, avoided
strife, and illustrated his doctrines by his life."[4]

It is said that eighty thousand followers of Buddha went forth
from Hindostan, as missionaries to other lands ; and the traditions
of various countries are full of legends concerning their benevolence, holiness, and miraculous power. His religion has never been
propagated by the sword. It has been effected entirely by the influence of peaceable and persevering devotees.[5] The era of the
Siamese is the death of Buddha. In Ceylon, they date from the introduction of his religion into their island. It is supposed to be
more extensively adopted than any religion that ever existed. Its
votaries are computed at four hundred millions ; more than one-
third of the whole human race.[6]

There is much contradiction among writers concerning the *date*

---

[1] Bunsen : The Angel-Messiah, p. 41.

[2] "He joined to his gifts as a thinker a prophetic ardor and missionary zeal which
prompted him to popularize his doctrine, and
to preach to all without exception, men and
women, high and low, ignorant and learned
alike." (Rhys Davids' Buddhism, p. 53.)

[3] Bunsen : The Angel-Messiah, p. 45.

[4] Ibid. p. 46.

[5] "The success of Buddhism was in great
part due to the reverence the Buddha inspired
by his own personal character. He practiced
honestly what he preached enthusiastically.

He was sincere, energetic, earnest, self-sacrificing, and devout. Adherents gathered in
thousands around the person of the consistent
preacher, and the Buddha himself became the
real centre of Buddhism." (Williams' Hinduism, p. 102.)

[6] "It may be said to be the prevailing religion of the world. Its adherents are estimated
at four hundred millions, more than a third of
the human race." (Chambers's Encyclo., art.
"Buddhism." See also, Bunsen's Angel-Messiah, p. 251.)

of the Buddhist religion. This confusion arises from the fact that there are several Buddhas,' objects of worship; because the word is not a name, but a title, signifying an extraordinary degree of holiness. Those who have examined the subject most deeply have generally agreed that Buddha Sakai, from whom the religion takes its name, must have been a real, historical personage, who appeared many centuries before the time assigned for the birth of Christ Jesus.' There are many things to confirm this supposition. In some portions of India, his religion appears to have flourished for a long time side by side with that of the Brahmans. This is shown by the existence of many ancient temples, some of them cut in subterranean rock, with an immensity of labor, which it must have required a long period to accomplish. In those old temples, his statues represent him with hair knotted all over his head, which was a very ancient custom with the anchorites of Hindostan, before the practice of shaving the dead was introduced among their devotees.' His religion is also mentioned in one of the very ancient epic poems of India. The severity of the persecution indicates that their numbers and influence had became formidable to the Brahmans, who had everything to fear from a sect which abolished hereditary priesthood, and allowed the holy of all castes to become teachers.'

It may be observed that in speaking of the pre-existence of Buddha in heaven—his birth of a virgin—the songs of the angels at his birth—his recognition as a divine child—his disputation with the doctors—his temptation in the wilderness—his transfiguration on the Mount—his life of preaching and working miracles—and finally, his ascension into heaven, we referred to Prof. Samuel Beal's "History of Buddha," as one of our authorities. This work is simply a translation of the "Fo-pen-hing," made by Professor Beal from a Chinese copy, in the "Indian Office Library."

---

[1] It should be understood that the Buddha of this chapter, and in fact, the Buddha of *this* work, is *Gautama* Buddha, the Sakya Prince. According to Buddhist belief there have been many different Buddhas on earth. *The names of twenty-four* of the Buddhas who appeared previous to Gautama have been handed down to us. The *Buddhavansa* or " History of the Buddhas," gives the lives of all the previous Buddhas before commencing the account of Gautama himself. (See Rhys Davids' Buddhism, pp. 179, 180.)

[2] "The date usually fixed for Buddha's death is 543 B. C. Whether this precise year for one of the greatest epochs in the religious history of the human race can be accepted is doubtful, but it is tolerably certain that Buddhism arose in Behar and Eastern Hindustan about five centuries B. C.; and that it spread with great rapidity, *not by force of arms, or coercion of any kind*, like Muhammedanism, but by the sheer persuasiveness of its doctrines." (Monier Williams' Hinduism, p. 72.)

[3] " Of the high antiquity of Buddhism there is much collateral as well as direct evidence—evidence that neither internecine nor foreign strife, not even religious persecution, has been able to destroy. . . . Witness the gigantic images in the caves of Elephanta, near Bombay and those of Lingi Sara, in the interior of Java, all of which are known to have been in existence at least four centuries prior to our Lord's advent." (The Mammoth Religion.)

[4] Bunsen's Angel-Messiah, p. 250.

Now, in regard to the antiquity of this work, we will quote the words of the translator in speaking on this subject.

First, he says:

We know that the Fo-pen-hing was translated into Chinese from Sanscrit (the ancient language of Hindostan) so early as the eleventh year of the reign of Wing-ping (Ming-ti), of the Han dynasty, i. e., 69 or 70 A. D. We may, therefore, safely suppose that the original work was in circulation in India for some time previous to this date."[1]

Again, he says:

"There can be no doubt that the present work (i. e. the Fo-pen-hing, or Hist. of Buddha) contains as a woof (so to speak) some of the earliest verses (Gâthas) in which the History of Buddha was sung, long before the work itself was penned.

These Gâthas were evidently composed in different Prakrit forms (during a period of disintegration) before the more modern type of Sanscrit was fixed by the rules of Panini, and the popular epics of the Mâhabharata and the Ramâyana."[2]

Again, in speaking of the points of resemblance in the history of Buddha and Jesus, he says:

"These points of agreement with the Gospel narrative naturally arouse curiosity and require explanation. If we could prove that they (the legends related of Buddha) were unknown in the East for some centuries after Christ, the explanation would be easy. But all the evidence we have goes to prove the contrary.

It would be a natural inference that many of the events in the legend of Buddha were borrowed from the Apocryphal Gospels, if we were quite certain that these Apocryphal Gospels had not borrowed from it. How then may we explain the matter? It would be better at once to say that in our present state of knowledge there is no complete explanation to offer."[3]

There certainly is no "complete explanation" to be offered by one who attempts to uphold the historical accuracy of the New Testament. The "Devil" and "Type" theories having vanished, like all theories built on sand, nothing now remains for the honest man to do but acknowledge the truth, which is, *that the history of Jesus of Nazareth as related in the books of the New Testament, is simply a copy of that of Buddha,·with a mixture of mythology borrowed from other nations.* Ernest de Bunsen almost acknowledges this when he says:

"With the remarkable exception of the death of Jesus on the cross, and of the doctrine of atonement by vicarious suffering, which is absolutely excluded by Buddhism, the most ancient of the Buddhistic records known to us contain statements about the life and the doctrines of Gautama Buddha which correspond in a remarkable manner, and impossibly by mere chance, with the traditions recorded in the Gospels about the life and doctrines of Jesus Christ. It is still more strange that these Buddhistic legends about Gautama as the Angel-Messiah refer to a doctrine which we find only in the Epistles of Paul and in the

---

[1] Beal: Hist. Buddha. p. vi.   [2] Ibid. pp. x. and xi.   [3] Ibid. pp. viii., ix. and note:

fourth Gospel. This can be explained by the assumption of a common source of revelation; but then the serious question must be considered, why the doctrine of the Angel-Messiah, supposing it to have been revealed, and which we find in the East and in the West, is not contained in any of the Scriptures of the Old Testament which can possibly have been written before the Babylonian Captivity, nor in the first three Gospels. *Can the systematic keeping-back of essential truth be attributed to God or to man?*"[1]

Beside the work referred to above as being translated by Prof. Beal, there is another copy originally composed in verse. This was translated by the learned Fonceau, who gives it an antiquity of *two thousand years*, "although the original treatise must be attributed to an earlier date."[2]

In regard to the teachings of Buddha, which correspond so strikingly with those of Jesus, Prof. Rhys Davids, says:

"With regard to Gautama's teaching we have more reliable authority than we have with regard to his life. It is true that none of the books of the Three Pitakas can at present be satisfactorily traced back before the Council of Asoka, held at Patna, about 250 B. c., that is to say, at least one hundred and thirty years after the death of the teacher; but they undoubtedly contain a great deal of much older matter."[3]

Prof. Max Müller says:

"Between the language of Buddha and his disciples, and the language of Christ and his apostles, there are strange coincidences. Even some of the Buddhist legends and parables sound as if taken from the New Testament; *though we know that many of them existed before the beginning of the Christian Era.*"[4]

Just as many of the myths related of the Hindoo Saviour Crishna were *previously current* regarding some of the Vedic gods, so likewise, many of the myths *previously current* regarding the god *Sumana*, worshiped both on Adam's peak, and at the cave of Dambulla, *were added to the Buddha myth.*[5] Much of the legend which was transferred to the Buddha, had previously existed, and had clustered around the idea of a *Chakrawarti.*[6] Thus we see that the legend of *Christ* Buddha, as with the legend of *Christ* Jesus, *existed before his time.*[7]

---

[1] Bunsen's Angel-Messiah, p. 50.

[2] Quoted by Prof. Beal: Hist. Buddha, p. viii.

[3] Rhys Davids' Buddhism, p. 86.

[4] Science of Religion, p. 243.

[5] Rhys Davids' Buddhism.

[6] Ibid. p. 184.

"It is surprising," says Rhys Davids, "that, like Romans worshiping Augustus, or Greeks adding the glow of the sun-myth to the glory of Alexander, the Indians should have formed an ideal of their Chakravarti, and transferred to this new ideal many of the dimly sacred and half understood traits of the Vedic heroes? Is it surprising that the Buddhists should have found it edifying to recognize in *their* hero the Chakravarti of Righteousness, and that the story of the Buddha should be tinged with the coloring of these Chakravarti myths?" (Ibid. Buddhism, p. 230.)

[7] In Chapter xxxix., we shall explain the origin of these myths.

We have established the fact then—*and no man can produce better authorities*—that Buddha and Buddhism, which correspond in such a remarkable manner with Jesus and Christianity, were long anterior to the Christian era. Now, as Ernest de Bunsen says, this remarkable similarity in the histories of the founders and their religion, could not possibly happen by chance.

Whenever two religious or legendary histories of mythological personages resemble each other so completely as do the histories and teachings of Buddha and Jesus, the older must be the parent, and the younger the child. We must therefore conclude that, since the history of Buddha and Buddhism is very much older than that of Jesus and Christianity, the Christians are incontestably *either sectarians or plagiarists of the religion of the Buddhists.*

CHAPTER XXX.

WE are informed by the *Matthew* narrator that when Jesus was eating his last supper with the disciples,

"He took bread and blessed it, and brake it, and gave it to the disciples, and said, Take, eat, *this is my body*. And he took the cup, and gave thanks, and gave it to them, saying, drink ye all of it, *for this is my blood* of the New Testament, which is shed for many for the remission of sins."[1]

According to Christian belief, Jesus *instituted* this "*Sacrament*"[2]—as it is called—and it was observed by the primitive Christians, as he had enjoined them; but we shall find that this breaking of bread, and drinking of wine,—*supposed to be the body and blood of a god*—is simply another piece of Paganism imbibed by the Christians.

The *Eucharist* was instituted many hundreds of years before the time assigned for the birth of Christ Jesus. Cicero, the greatest orator of Rome, and one of the most illustrious of her statesmen, born in the year 106 B. C., mentions it in his works, and wonders at the strangeness of the rite. "How can a man be so stupid," says he, "as to imagine that which he eats to be a God?" There had been an esoteric meaning attached to it from the first establishment of the *mysteries* among the Pagans, and the Eucharistia is one of the oldest rites of antiquity.

The adherents of the Grand Lama in Thibet and Tartary offer to their god a sacrament of *bread and wine*.[4]

---

[1] Matt. xxvi. 26. See also, Mark, xiv. 22.

[2] At the heading of the chapters named in the above note may be seen the words : "Jesus keepeth the Passover (and) *instituteth* the Lord's Supper."

[3] According to the Roman Christians, the Eucharist is the natural body and blood of Christ Jesus *verè et realiter*, but the Protestant sophistically explains away these two plain words *verily* and *indeed*, and by the grossest abuse of language, makes them to mean *spiritually by grace and efficacy*. "In the sacrament of the altar," says the Protestant divine, "is the *natural* body and blood of Christ *verè et realiter*, verily and indeed, if you take these terms for *spiritually by grace and efficacy*; but if you mean *really and indeed*, so that thereby you would include a lively and movable body under the form of bread and wine, then in that sense it is *not* Christ's body in the sacrament really and indeed."

[4] See Inman's Ancient Faiths, vol. ii. p. 203, and Anacalypsis, i. 232.

P. Andrada La Crozius, a French missionary, and one of the first Christians who went to Nepaul and Thibet, says in his "History of India :"

" Their Grand Lama celebrates a species of sacrifice with *bread* and *wine*, in which, after taking a small quantity himself, he distributes the rest among the Lamas present at this ceremony."[1]

In certain rites both in the *Indian* and the *Parsee* religions, the devotees drink the juice of the Soma, or *Haoma* plant. They consider it a *god* as well as a plant, just as the wine of the Christian sacrament is considered both the juice of the grape, and the blood of the Redeemer.[2] Says Mr. Baring-Gould :

" Among the ancient Hindoos, *Soma* was a chief deity; he is called 'the Giver of Life and of health,' the 'Protector,' he who is 'the Guide to Immortality.' He became incarnate among men, was taken by them and slain, and brayed in a mortar. But he rose in flame to heaven, to be the 'Benefactor of the World,' and the 'Mediator between God and Man.' Through communion with him in his sacrifice, man, (who partook of this god), has an assurance of immortality, for by that *sacrament* he obtains union with his divinity."[3]

The ancient *Egyptians*—as we have seen—annually celebrated the *Resurrection* of their God and Saviour *Osiris*, at which time they commemorated his death by the *Eucharist*, eating the sacred cake, or wafer, *after it had been consecrated by the priest, and become veritable flesh of his flesh.*[4] The bread, after sacerdotal rites, became mystically the body of *Osiris*, and, in such a manner, *they ate their god.*[5] Bread and wine were brought to the temples by the worshipers, as offerings.[6]

The *Therapeutes* or *Essenes*, whom we believe to be of Buddhist origin, and who lived in large numbers in Egypt, also had the ceremony of the sacrament among them.[7] Most of them, however, being temperate, substituted water for wine, while others drank a mixture of water and wine.

Pythagoras, the celebrated Grecian philosopher, who was born about the year 570 B. C., performed this ceremony of the *sacrament.*[8] He is supposed to have visited Egypt, and there availed himself of all such mysterious lore as the priests could be induced to impart. He and his followers practiced asceticism, and peculiarities of diet and clothing, similar to the Essenes, which has led some scholars to

---

[1] " Leur grand Lama célèbre une espèce de sacrifice avec du pain et du vin dont il prend une petite quantité, et distribue le reste aux Lamas présens à cette cérémonie." (Quoted in Anacalypsis, vol. ii. p. 118.)

[2] Viscount Amberly's Analysis, p. 46.

[3] Baring-Gould : Orig. Relig. Belief, vol. i. p. 401.

[4] See Bonwick's Egyptian Belief, p. 163.

[5] See Ibid. p. 417.

[6] See Prog. Relig. Ideas, vol. i. p. 179.

[7] See Bunsen's Keys of St. Peter, p. 199; Anacalypsis, vol. ii. p. 60, and Lillie's Buddhism, p. 136.

[8] See Higgins : Anacalypsis, vol. ii. p. 60.

believe that he instituted the order, but this is evidently not the case.

The Kenite "King of Righteousness," *Melchizedek*, "a priest of the Most High God," brought out BREAD *and* WINE as a *sign* or *symbol* of worship ; as *the mystic elements of Divine presence.* In the visible symbol of *bread and wine* they worshiped *the invisible presence of the Creator of heaven and earth.*[1]

To account for this, Christian divines have been much puzzled. The Rev. Dr. Milner says, in speaking of this passage :

"It was in offering up a sacrifice of bread and wine, instead of slaughtered animals, that Melchizedek's sacrifice differed from the generality of those in the old law, and that he *prefigured* the sacrifice which Christ was to *institute* in the new law from the same elements. No other sense than this can be elicited from the Scripture as to this matter ; and accordingly the holy fathers unanimously adhere to this meaning."[2]

This style of reasoning is in accord with the TYPE theory concerning the Virgin-born, Crucified and Resurrected Saviours, but it is not altogether satisfactory. If it had been said that the religion of Melchizedek, and the religion of the Persians, were the *same*, there would be no difficulty in explaining the passage.

Not only were bread and wine brought forth by Melchizedek when he blessed Abraham, but it was offered to God and eaten before him by Jethro and the elders of Israel, and some, at least, of the *mourning* Israelites broke bread and drank "the cup of consolation," in remembrance of the departed, "to comfort them for the dead."[3]

It is in the ancient religion of Persia—the religion of Mithra, the Mediator, the Redeemer and Saviour—that we find the nearest resemblance to the sacrament of the Christians, and from which it was evidently borrowed. Those who were initiated into the mysteries of Mithra, or became *members*, took the sacrament of bread and wine.[4]

M. Renan, speaking of *Mithraicism*, says:

"It had its mysterious meetings: its chapels, which bore a strong resemblance to little churches. It forged a very lasting bond of brotherhood between its initiates: it had a *Eucharist*, a Supper so like the Christian Mysteries, that good Justin Martyr, the Apologist, can find only one explanation of the apparent identity, namely, that Satan, in order to deceive the human race, determined to imitate the Christian ceremonies, and so stole them."[5]

---

[1] See Bunsen's Keys of St. Peter, p. 55, and Genesis, xiv. 18, 19.

[2] St. Jerome says : "Melchizédek in typo Christi panem et vinum obtulit : et mysterium Christianum in Salvatoris sanguine et corpore dedicavit."

[3] See Bunsen's Angel-Messiah, p. 227.

[4] See King's Gnostics and their Remains, p. xxv., and Higgins' Anacalypsis, vol. ii. pp. 58, 59.

[5] Renan's Hibbert Lectures, p. 35.

The words of St. Justin, wherein he alludes to this ceremony, are as follows :

"The apostles, in the commentaries written by themselves, which we call Gospels, have delivered down to us how that Jesus thus commanded them : He having taken bread, *after he had given thanks,*1 said, Do this in commemoration of me; this is my body.   And having taken a cup, and returned thanks, he said: This is my blood, and delivered it to them alone.   Which thing indeed the evil spirits have taught to be done out of mimicry in the Mysteries and Initiatory rites of Mithra.

For you either know, or can know, that bread and a cup of water (or wine) are given out, with certain incantations, in the consecration of the person who is being initiated in the Mysteries of Mithra." 2

This food they called the Eucharist, of which no one was allowed to partake but the persons who believed that the things they taught were true, and who had been washed with the washing that is for the remission of sin.3 Tertullian, who flourished from 193 to 220 A. D., also speaks of the Mithraic devotees celebrating the Eucharist.4

The Eucharist of the Lord and Saviour, as the Magi called Mithra, the second person in their Trinity, or their Eucharistic sacrifice, was always made exactly and in every respect the same as that of the orthodox Christians, for both sometimes used water instead of wine, or a mixture of the two.5

The Christian Fathers often liken their rites to those of the Therapeuts (Essenes) and worshipers of Mithra.   Here is Justin Martyr's account of Christian initiation :

'But we, after we have thus washed him who has been-convinced and assented to our teachings, bring him to the place where those who are called *brethren* are assembled, in order that we may offer hearty prayers in common for ourselves and the *illuminated* person.   Having ended our prayers, we salute one another with a kiss.   There is then brought to the president of the brethren *bread and a cup of wine mixed with water.*   When the president has given thanks, and all the people have expressed their assent, those that are called by us *deacons* give to each of those present to partake of the bread and wine mixed with water."6

---

1 In the words of Mr. King: "This expression shows that the notion of blessing or consecrating the elements was *as yet* unknown to the Christians."

2 Apol. 1. ch. lxvi.

3 Ibid.

4 De Præscriptione Hæreticorum, ch. xl. Tertullian explains this conformity between Christianity and Paganism, by asserting that the devil copied the Christian mysteries.

5 De Tinctione, de oblatione pauis, et de imagine resurrectionis, videatur doctiss, de la Cerda ad ea Tertulliani loca ubi de hiscerebus agitur.   Gentiles citra Christum, talia celebradant Mithriaca quæ videbautur cum doctrinâ *eucharistæ* et *resurrectionis* et aliis ritibus

Christianis convenire, quæ fecerant ex industria ad imitationem Christianismi; unde Tertulliani et Patres aiunt eos talia fecisse, duce diabolo, quo vult esse simia Christi, &c. Volunt itaque eos res suas ita compârasse, ut *Mithræ mysteria essent eucharistiæ Christiunæ imago.* Sic Just. Martyr (p. 98), et Tertullianus et Chrysostomus.   In suis etiam sacris habebant Mithriaci lavacra (quasi regenerationis) in quibus tingit et ipse (sc. sacerdos) quosdam utique credentes et fideles suos, et expiatoria delictorum de lavacro repromittit et sic adhuc initiat Mithræ." (Hyde : De Relig. Vet. Persian. p. 113.)

6 Justin : 1st Apol., ch. lvi.

In the service of Edward the Sixth of England, water is directed to be mixed with the wine.[1] This is a union of the two; not a half measure, but a double one. If it be correct to take it with wine, then they were right; if with water, they still were right; as they took both, they could not be wrong.

The *bread*, used in these Pagan Mysteries, was carried in *baskets*, which practice was also adopted by the Christians. St. Jerome, speaking of it, says:

"Nothing can be richer than one who carries *the body of Christ* (viz.: *the bread*) in a basket made of twigs."[2]

The Persian Magi introduced the worship of Mithra into Rome, and his mysteries were solemnized in a *cave*. In the process of initiation there, candidates were also administered the sacrament of *bread and wine*, and were marked on the forehead with the sign of the cross.[3]

The ancient *Greeks* also had their "*Mysteries*," wherein they celebrated the sacrament of the Lord's Supper. The Rev. Robert Taylor, speaking of this, says:

"The *Eleusinian* Mysteries, or, Sacrament of the Lord's Supper, was the most august of all the Pagan ceremonies celebrated, more especially by the Athenians, every fifth year,[4] in honor of *Ceres*, the goddess of corn, who, in allegorical language, *had given us her flesh to eat;* as *Bacchus*, the god of wine, in like sense, *had given us his blood to drink*. . . .

"From these ceremonies is derived the very name attached to our *Christian* sacrament of the Lord's Supper,—'*those holy Mysteries;*'—and not one or two, but absolutely all and every one of the observances used in our Christian solemnity. Very many of our forms of expression in that solemnity are precisely the same as those that appertained to the Pagan rite."[5]

Prodicus (a Greek sophist of the 5th century B. C.) says that, the ancients worshiped *bread* as Demeter (*Ceres*) and *wine* as Dionysos (*Bacchus*);[6] therefore, when they ate the bread, and drank the wine, after it had been consecrated, they were doing as the Romanists claim to do at the present day, *i. e.*, *eating the flesh and drinking the blood of their god.*[7]

Mosheim, the celebrated ecclesiastical historian, acknowledges that:

---

[1] Dr. Grabes' Notes on Irenæus, lib. v. c. 2, in Anac., vol. i. p. 60.

[2] Quoted in Monumental Christianity, p. 370.

[3] See Prog. Relig. Ideas, vol. i. p. 369.

"The Divine Presence called his angel of mercy and said unto him: 'Go through the midst of the city, through the midst of Jerusalem, and set the mark of Tau (T, the headless cross) upon the foreheads of the men that sigh and that cry for all the abominations that are done in the midst thereof.'" (Bunsen: The Angel-Messiah, p. 305.

[4] They were celebrated every fifth year at *Eleusis*, a town of Attica, from whence their name.

[5] Taylor's Diegesis, p. 212.

[6] Müller: Origin of Religion, p. 181.

[7] "In the *Bacchic* Mysteries a consecrated cup (of wine) was handed around after supper, called the cup of the *Agathodaemon*." (Cousin: Lec. on Modn. Phil. Quoted in Isis Unveiled, ii. 513. See also, Dunlap's Spirit Hist., p. 217.)

"The profound respect that was paid to the Greek and Roman *Mysteries*, and the extraordinary sanctity that was attributed to them, induced the Christians of the second century, to give *their* religion a *mystic* air, in order to put it upon an equal footing in point of dignity, with that of the Pagans. For this purpose they gave the name of *Mysteries* to the institutions of the Gospels, and decorated particularly the 'Holy Sacrament' with that title; they used the very terms employed in the *Heathen Mysteries,* and adopted some of the rites and ceremonies of which those renowned mysteries consisted. This imitation began in the eastern provinces; but, after the time of Adrian, who first introduced the mysteries among the Latins, it was followed by the Christians who dwelt in the western part of the empire. A great part, therefore, of the service of the Church in this—the second—century, had a certain air of the Heathen Mysteries, and resembled them considerably in many particulars."[1]

Eleusinian Mysteries and *Christian Sacraments Compared.*

1. "But as the benefit of Initiation was great, such as were convicted of witchcraft, murder, even though unintentional, or any other heinous crimes, were debarred from those mysteries."[2]

2. "At their entrance, purifying themselves, by washing their hands in *holy water*, they were at the same time admonished to present themselves with pure minds, without which the external cleanness of the body would by no means be accepted."[4]

3. "The priests who officiated in these sacred solemnities, were called Hierophants, or '*revealers of holy things.*'"[6]

4. The Pagan Priest dismissed their congregation with these words:
"*The Lord be with you.*"[7]

1. "For as the benefit is great, if, with a true penitent heart and lively faith, we receive that holy sacrament, &c., if any be an open and notorious evil-liver, or hath done wrong to his neighbor, &c, that he presume not to come to the Lord's table."[3]

2. See the fonts of *holy water* at the entrance of every Catholic chapel in Christendom for the same purpose.
"Let us draw near with a true heart in full assurance of faith, having our hearts sprinkled from an evil conscience, and our bodies washed with pure water."[5]

3. The priests who officiate at these Christian solemnities are supposed to be 'revealers of holy things.'

4. The Christian priests dismiss their congregation with these words:
"*The Lord be with you.*"

These Eleusinian Mysteries were accompanied with various rites, expressive of the purity and self-denial of the worshiper, and were therefore considered to be an expiation of past sins, and to place the initiated under the special protection of the awful and potent goddess who presided over them.[8]

These *mysteries* were, as we have said, also celebrated in honor of *Bacchus* as well as *Ceres.* A consecrated cup of wine was handed around after supper, called the "Cup of the Agathodae-

---

[1] Eccl. Hist. cent. ii. pt. 2, sec. v.
[2] Bell's Pantheon, vol. i. p. 282.
[3] Episcopal Communion Service.
[4] Bell's Pantheon, vol. i. p. 232.

[5] Hebrews, x. 22.
[6] See Taylor's Diegesis, p. 213.
[7] See Ibid.
[8] Kenrick's Egypt, vol. i. p. 471.

mon"—the Good Divinity.¹ Throughout the whole ceremony, the name of the *Lord* was many times repeated, and his brightness or glory not only exhibited to the eye by the rays which surrounded his name (or his monogram, I. H. S.), but was made the peculiar theme or subject of their triumphant exultation.²

The mystical wine and bread were used during the Mysteries of *Adonis*, the Lord and Saviour.³ In fact, the communion of bread and wine was used in the worship of nearly every important deity.⁴

The rites of *Bacchus* were celebrated in the British Islands in heathen times,⁵ and so were those of *Mithra*, which were spread over Gaul and Great Britain.⁶ We therefore find that the ancient *Druids* offered the sacrament of bread and wine, during which ceremony they were dressed in white robes,⁷ just as the Egyptian priests of Isis were in the habit of dressing, and as the priests of many Christian sects dress at the present day.

Among some negro tribes in Africa there is a belief that " on eating and drinking consecrated food they eat and drink the god himself."⁸

The ancient *Mexicans* celebrated the mysterious sacrament of the Eucharist, called the "most holy supper," during which they ate the flesh of their god. The bread used at their Eucharist was made of *corn* meal, which they mixed with *blood*, instead of wine. This was *consecrated* by the priest, and given to the people, who ate it with humility and penitence, *as the flesh of their god.*⁹

Lord Kingsborough, in his *"Mexican Antiquities,"* speaks of the ancient Mexicans as performing this sacrament; when they made a cake, which they called *Tzoalia*. The high priest blessed it in his manner, after which he broke it into pieces, and put it into certain very clean vessels. He then took a thorn of *maguery*, which resembles a thick needle, with which he took up with the utmost reverence single morsels, *which he put into the mouth of each individual, after the manner of a communion.*¹⁰

The writer of the "Explanation of Plates of the *Codex Vaticanus*,"—which are copies of Mexican *hieroglyphics*—says:

" I am disposed to believe that these poor people have had the knowledge of our mode of communion, or of the annunciation of the gospel; or perhaps the

¹ See Dunlap's Spirit Hist., p. 217, and Isis Unveiled, vol. ii. p. 513.
² See Taylor's Diegesis, p. 214.
³ See Isis Unveiled, vol. ii. p. 189.
⁴ See Ibid. p. 513.
⁵ See Myths of the British Druids, p. 89.
⁶ See Dupuis: Origin of Relig. Belief, p. 228.
⁷ See Myths of the British Druids, p. 280, and Prog. Relig. Ideas, vol. i. p. 876.
⁸ Herbert Spencer: Principles of Sociology, vol. i. p. 299.
⁹ See Monumental Christianity, pp. 390 and 393.
¹⁰ Mexican Antiquities, vol. vi. p. 220.

devil, most envious of the honor of God, may have led them into this superstition, in order that by this ceremony he might be adored and served as Christ our Lord."[1]

The Rev. Father Acosta says:

"That which is most admirable in the hatred and presumption of Satan is, that he hath not only counterfeited in idolatry and sacrifice, but also in certain ceremonies, *our Sacraments*, which Jesus Christ our Lord hath instituted and the holy Church doth use, having especially pretended to imitate in some sort the *Sacrament of the Communion*, which is the most high and divine of all others."

He then relates how the *Mexicans* and *Peruvians*, in certain ceremonies, ate the flesh of their god, and called certain morsels of paste, "the flesh and bones of *Vitzilipuzlti*."

"After putting themselves in order about these morsels and pieces of paste, · they used certain ceremonies with singing, by means whereof they (the pieces of paste) were blessed and consecrated for the flesh and bones of this idol."[2]

These facts show that the *Eucharist* is another piece of Paganism adopted by the Christians. The story of Jesus and his disciples being at supper, where the Master did break bread, may be true, but the statement that he said, "Do this in remembrance of me,"— "this is my body," and "this is my blood," was undoubtedly invented to give authority to the *mystic* ceremony, which had been borrowed from Paganism.

Why should they do this in remembrance of Jesus? . Provided he took this supper with his disciples—which the *John* narrator denies[3]—he did not do anything on that occasion new or unusual among Jews. To pronounce the benediction, break the bread, and distribute pieces thereof to the persons at table, was, and is now, a common usage of the Hebrews. Jesus could not have commanded born Jews to do in remembrance of him what they already practiced, and what every religious Jew does to this day. The whole story is evidently a myth, as a perusal of it with the eye of a critic clearly demonstrates.

The *Mark* narrator informs us that Jesus sent two of his disciples to the city, and told them this:

"Go ye into the city, and there shall meet you a man bearing a pitcher of water; follow him. And wheresoever he shall go in, say ye to the *goodman* of the house, The Master saith, Where is the guest-chamber, where I shall eat the

---

[1] Quoted in Mexican Antiquities, vol. vi. p. 221.

[2] Acosta : Hist. Indies, vol. ii. chs. xiii. and xiv.

[3] According to the "*John*" narrator, Jesus ate no Paschal meal, but was captured the evening before Passover, and was crucified

before the feast opened. According to the *Synoptics*, Jesus partook of the Paschal supper, was captured the first night of the feast, and executed on the first day thereof, which was on a Friday. If the *John* narrator's account is true, that of the *Synoptics* is not, or *vice versa*.

passover with my disciples? And he will show you a large upper room *furnished and prepared :* there make ready for us. And his disciples went forth, and came into the city, and found as he had said unto them: and they made ready the passover."[1]

The story of the passover or the last supper, seems to be introduced in this unusual manner to make it manifest that a divine power is interested in, and conducting the whole affair, parallels of which we find in the story of Elieser and Rebecca, where Rebecca is to identify herself in a manner pre-arranged by Elieser with God ;[2] and also in the story of Elijah and the widow of Zarephath, where by God's directions a journey is made, and the widow is found.[3]

It suggests itself to our mind that that this style of connecting a supernatural interest with human affairs was not entirely original with the Mark narrator. In this connection it is interesting to note that a man in Jerusalem should have had an unoccupied and *properly* furnished room just at *that* time, when two millions of pilgrims sojourned in and around the city. The man, it appears, was not distinguished either for wealth or piety, for his *name* is not mentioned; he was not present at the supper, and no further reference is made to him. It appears rather that the Mark narrator imagined an ordinary man who had a furnished room to let for such purposes, and would imply that Jesus knew it *prophetically.* He had only to pass in his mind from Elijah to his disciple Elisha, for whom the great woman of Shunem had so richly furnished an upper chamber, to find a like instance.[4] *Why should not somebody have furnished also an upper chamber for the Messiah ?*

The Matthew narrator's account is free from these embellishments, and simply runs thus : Jesus said to some of his disciples— the number is not given—

'Go into the city to such a man, and say unto him, The Master saith, My time is at hand; I will keep the passover at thy house with my disciples. And the disciples did as Jesus had appointed them; and *they* made ready the passover."[5]

In this account, no pitcher, no water, no prophecy is mentioned.[6]

It was many centuries before the genuine heathen doctrine of *Transubstantiation*—a change of the elements of the Eucharist into

---

[1] Mark, xiv. 13–16.
[2] Gen. xxiv.
[3] I. Kings, xvii. 8.
[4] II. Kings, iv. 8.
[5] Matt. xxvi. 18, 19.

[6] For further observations on this subject, see Dr. Isaac M. Wise's "Martyrdom of Jesus of Nazareth," a valuable little work, published at the office of the American Israelite, Cincinnati, Ohio.

the *real* body and blood of Christ Jesus—became a tenet of the Christian faith. This greatest of mysteries was developed gradually. As early as the second century, however, the seeds were planted, when we find Ignatius, Justin Martyr, and Irenæus advancing the opinion, that the mere bread and wine became, in the Eucharist, *something higher*—the earthly, something heavenly—without, however, ceasing to be bread and wine. Though these views were opposed by some eminent individual Christian teachers, yet both among the people and in the ritual of the Church, the miraculous or supernatural view of the Lord's Supper gained ground. After the third century the office of presenting the bread and wine came to be confined to the *ministers* or *priests*. This practice arose from, and in turn strengthened, the notion which was gaining ground, that in this act of presentation by the priest, a sacrifice, similar to that once offered up in the death of Christ Jesus, though bloodless, was ever anew presented to God. This still deepened the feeling of *mysterious* significance and importance with which the rite of the Lord's Supper was viewed, and led to that gradually increasing splendor of celebration which took the form of the *Mass*. As in Christ Jesus two distinct natures, the divine and the human, were wonderfully combined, so in the Eucharist there was a corresponding union of the earthly and the heavenly.

For a long time there was no formal declaration of the mind of the Church on the *real presence* of Christ Jesus in the Eucharist. At length a *discussion* on the point was raised, and the most distinguished men of the time took part in it. One party maintained that "the bread and wine are, in the act of consecration, transformed by the omnipotence of God into the *very body* of Christ which was once born of Mary, nailed to the cross, and raised from the dead." According to this conception, nothing remains of the bread and wine but the outward form, the taste and the smell; while the other party would only allow that there is *some change* in the bread and wine themselves, but granted that an actual transformation of their power and efficacy takes place.

The greater accordance of the first view with the credulity of the age, its love for the wonderful and magical, the interest of the priesthood to add lustre, in accordance with the heathens, to a rite which enhanced their own office, resulted in the doctrine of Transubstantiation being declared an article of faith of the Christian Church.

Transubstantiation, the invisible change of the bread and wine into the body and blood of Christ, is a tenet that may defy the powers of argument and pleasantry; but instead of consulting the evidence of their senses, of their sight, their feeling, and their taste, the first Protestants were entangled in their own scruples, and awed by the reputed words of Jesus in the institution of the sacrament. Luther maintained a *corporeal*, and Calvin a *real* presence of Christ in the Eucharist; and the opinion of Zuinglius, that it is no more than a spiritual communion, a simple memorial, has slowly prevailed in the reformed churches.[1]

Under Edward VI. the reformation was more bold and perfect, but in the fundamental articles of the Church of England, a strong and explicit declaration against the real presence was *obliterated* in the original copy, to please the people, or the Lutherans, or Queen Elizabeth. At the present day, the Greek and Roman Catholics alone hold to the original doctrine of the *real presence*.

Of all the religious observances among heathens, Jews, or Turks, none has been the cause of more hatred, persecution, outrage, and bloodshed, than the Eucharist. Christians persecuted one another like relentless foes, and thousands of Jews were slaughtered on account of the Eucharist and the Host.

[1] See Gibbon's Rome. vol. v. pp. 399, 400. Calvin, after quoting *Matt.* xxvi. 26, 27, says: 'There is no doubt that as soon as these words are added to the bread and the wine, the bread and the wine become the *true* body and the *true* blood of Christ, so that the substance of bread and wine is transmuted into the *true* body and blood of Christ. He who denies this calls the omnipotence of Christ in question, and charges Christ himself with foolishness." (Calvin's Tracts, p. 214. Translated by Henry Beveridge, Edinburgh, 1851.) In other parts of his writings, Calvin seems to contradict this statement, and speaks of the bread and wine in the Eucharist as being *symbolical*. Gibbon evidently refers to the passage quoted above.

CHAPTER XXXI.

BAPTISM.

BAPTISM, or purification from sin by water, is supposed by many to be an exclusive *Christian* ceremony. The idea is that circumcision was given up, but *baptism took its place* as a compulsory form indispensable to salvation, and was declared to have been instituted by Jesus himself or by his predecessor John.[1] That Jesus was baptized by John may be true, or it may not, but that he never directly enjoined his followers to call the *heathen* to a share in the privileges of the *Golden Age* is gospel doctrine;[2] and this saying:

"Go out into *all the world* to preach the gospel to every creature. And whoever believes and is baptized shall be saved, but whoever believes not shall be damned,"

must therefore be of comparatively late origin, dating from a period at which the mission to the heathen was not only fully recognized, but even declared to have originated with the followers of Jesus.[3] When the early Christians received members among them they were *not* initiated by baptism, but with prayer and laying on of hands. This, says *Eusebius*, was the "*ancient custom*," which was followed until the time of Stephen. During his bishopric controversies arose as to whether members should be received "after the ancient Christian custom" or by baptism,[4] after the heathen custom. Rev. J. P. Lundy, who has made ancient religions a special study, and who, being a thorough Christian writer, endeavors to get over the difficulty by saying that:

"John the Baptist simply *adopted* and practiced the *universal custom* of sacred bathing *for the remission of sins.* Christ sanctioned it; the church inherited it from his example."[5]

---

[1] The Rev. Dr. Geikie makes the assertion that: "With the call to repent, John united a significant rite for all who were willing to own their sins, and promise amendment of life. It was the *new* and striking requirement of baptism, *which John had been sent by divine appointment to* INTRODUCE." (Life of Christ, vol. i. p. 394.)

[2] See Galatians, ii. 7-9. Acts, x. and xi.

[3] See The Bible for Learners, vol. iii. pp. 658 and 472.

[4] See Eusebius: Eccl. Hist., lib. 7, ch. ii.

[5] Monumental Christianity, p. 385.

316

When we say that baptism is a *heathen* rite adopted by the Christians, we come near the truth. Mr. Lundy is a strong advocate of the *type* theory—of which we shall speak anon—therefore the above mode of reasoning is not to be wondered at.

The facts in the case are that baptism by immersion, or sprinkling in infancy, *for the remission of sin*, was a common rite, to be found in countries the most widely separated on the face of the earth, and the most unconnected in religious genealogy.[1]

If we turn to India we shall find that in the vast domain of the Buddhist faith the birth of children is regularly the occasion of a ceremony, at which the priest is present. In Mongolia and Thibet this ceremony assumes the special form of *baptism*. Candles burn and incense is offered on the domestic altar, the priest reads the prescribed prayers, *dips the child three times in water, and imposes on it a name.*[2]

Brahmanism, from the very earliest times, had its initiatory rites, similar to what we shall find among the ancient Persians, Egyptians, Greeks and Romans. Mr. Mackenzie, in his " Royal Masonic Cyclopædia," (*sub voce* " Mysteries of Hindustan,") gives a capital digest of these mysteries from the " Indische Alterthum-Skunde " of Lassen. After an invocation to the sun, an oath was demanded of the aspirant, to the effect of implicit obedience to superiors, purity of body, and inviolable secrecy. *Water was then sprinkled over him*, suitable addresses were made to him, &c. This was supposed to constitute the *regeneration* of the candidate, and he was now invested with the white robe and the tiara. A peculiar cross was marked on his forehead, and the Tau cross on his breast. Finally, he was given the sacred word, A. U. M.[3]

The Brahmans had also a mode of baptism similar to the Christian sect of Baptists, the ceremony being performed in a river.

[1] "Among all nations, and from the very earliest period, WATER has been used as a species of religious sacrament. . . . Water was the agent by means of which everything was *regenerated or born again.* Hence, in all nations, we find the Dove, or Divine Love, operating by means of its agent, water, and all nations using the ceremony of plunging, or, as we call it, baptizing, for the remission of sins, to introduce the candidate to a regeneration, to a new birth unto righteousness." (Higgins : Anacalypsis, vol. i. p. 529.)

" Baptism is a very ancient rite pertaining to *heathen* religions, whether of Asia, Africa, Europe or America." (Bonwick : Egyptian Belief, p. 416.)

" Baptism, or purification by water, was a ceremony common to all religions of antiquity. It consists in being made clean from some supposed pollution or defilement." (Bell's Pantheon, vol. ii. p. 201.)

" L'usage de ce *Baptême* par immersion, qui subsista dans l'Occident jusqu' au 8e ciècle, se maintient encore dans l'Eglise Greque : c'est celui que Jean le *Précurseur* administra, dans le Jourdain, à Jesus Christ même. Il fut pratiqué chez les Juifs, chez les Grecs, *et chez presque tous les peuples*, bien des siècles *avant* l'existence de la religion Chrétienne." (D'Ancarville : Res., vol. i. p. 292.)

[2] See Amberly's Analysis, p. 61. Bunsen's Angel-Messiah, p. 42. Higgins' Anacalypsis, vol. ii. p. 69, and Lillie's Buddhism, pp. 55 and 134. [3] Lillie's Buddhism, p. 134.

The officiating Brahman priest, who was called Gooroo, or Pastor,[1] rubbed mud on the candidate, *and then plunged him three times into the water.* During the process the priest said :

"O Supreme Lord, this man is impure, like the mud of this stream; but as water cleanses him from this dirt, *do thou free him from his sin.*"[2]

Rivers, as sources of fertility and purification, were at an early date invested with a sacred character. Every great river was supposed to be permeated with the divine essence, and its waters held to cleanse from all moral guilt and contamination. And as the Ganges was the most majestic, so it soon became the holiest and most revered of all rivers. No sin too heinous to be removed, no character too black to be washed clean by its waters. Hence the countless temples, with flights of steps, lining its banks; hence the array of priests, called "Sons of the Ganges," sitting on the edge of its streams, ready to aid the ablutions of conscience-stricken bathers, and stamp them as white-washed when they emerge from its waters. Hence also the constant traffic carried on in transporting Ganges water in small bottles to all parts of the country.[3]

The ceremony of baptism was a practice of the followers of *Zoroaster*, both for infants and adults.

M. Beausobre tells us that :

"The ancient *Persians* carried their infants to the temple a few days after they were born, and presented them to the priest before the sun, and before the fire, which was his symbol. *Then the priest took the child and baptized it for the purification of the soul.* Sometimes he plunged it into a great vase full of water: it was in the same ceremony that the father gave a name to the child."[4]

The learned Dr. Hyde also tells us that infants were brought to the temples and baptized by the priests, sometimes by sprinkling and sometimes by immersion, plunging the child into a large vase filled with water. This was to them a regeneration, or a purification of their souls. A name was at the same time imposed upon the child, as indicated by the parents.[5]

[1] Life and Religion of the Hindus, p. 94.
[2] Prog. Relig. Ideas, vol. i. p. 125.
"Every orthodox Hindu is perfectly persuaded that the dirtiest water, if taken from a *sacred stream* and applied to his body, either externally or internally, *will purify his soul.*" (Prof. Monier Williams : Hinduism, p. 157.) The Egyptians bathed in the water of the Nile ; the Chaldeans and Persians in the Euphrates, and the Hindus, as we have seen, in the Ganges, all of which were considered as "sacred waters" by the different nations. The Jews looked upon the Jordan in the same manner. Herodotus, speaking of the Persians' manners, says :

"They (the Persians) neither make water, nor spit, nor wash their hands in a river, nor defile the stream with urine, nor do they allow any one else to do so, but they pay extreme veneration to all rivers." (Hist. lib. i. ch. 138.)
[3] Williams' Hinduism, p. 176.
[4] Hist. Manichee, lib. ix. ch. vi. sect. xvi. in Anac., vol. ii. p. 65. See also, Dupuis : Orig. Relig. Belief, p. 249, and Baring-Gould : Orig. Relig. Belief, vol. i. p. 392.
[5] "Pro infantibus non utuntur circumcisione, sed tantum baptismo seu lotione ad animæ purificationem internam. Infantem ad

The rite of baptism was also administered to adults in the *Mithraic* mysteries during initiation. The foreheads of the initiated being marked at the same time with the "*sacred sign*," which was none other than the sign of the CROSS.[1] The Christian Father Tertullian, who believed it to be the work of the devil, says :

"He BAPTIZES his believers and followers; he promises the remission of sins at the *sacred fount*, and thus initiates them into the religion of *Mithra ;* he *marks on the forehead* his own soldiers," &c.[2]

" He marks on the forehead," *i. e.,* he marks *the sign of the cross* on their foreheads, just as priests of Christ Jesus do at the present day to those who are initiated into the Christian mysteries.

Again, he says :

" The nations who are strangers to all spiritual powers (the heathens), ascribe to their idols (gods) the power of impregnating the waters with the same efficacy as in Christian baptism." For, "in certain sacred rites of theirs, the mode of initiation is by baptism," and "whoever had defiled himself with murder, expiation was sought in purifying water."[3]

He also says that :

"The devil signed his soldiers in the forehead, in imitation of the Christians."[4]

And St. Augustin says :

" The *cross* and *baptism* were never parted."[5]

The ancient *Egyptians* performed their rite of baptism, and those who were initiated into the mysteries of Isis were baptized.[6]

Apuleius of Madura, in Africa, who was initiated into these mysteries, shows that baptism was used; that the ceremony was performed by the attending priest, and that purification and forgiveness of sin was the result.[7]

---

sacerdotem in ecclesiam adductum sistunt coram sole et igne, quâ factâ ceremoniâ, eundem sanctiorem existimant. D. Lord dicit quod aquam ad hoc afferunt in cortice arboris Holm : ea autem arbor revera est Haum Magorum, cujus mentionem aliâ occasione suprâ fecimus. Alias, aliquando fit immergendo in magnum vas aquæ, ut dicit Tavernier. Post talem lotionem seu baptismum, sacerdos imponit nomen à parentibus inditum." (Hyde de Rel. Vet. Pers., p. 414.) After this Hyde goes on to say, that when he comes to be fifteen years of age he is confirmed by receiving the girdle, and the sudra or cassock.

[1] See Knight : Anct. Art and Mytho., p. xxv. Higgins : Anac., vol. i. pp. 218 and 222. Dunlap : Mysteries of Adoni, p. 139. King : The Gnostics and their Remains, p. 51.

[2] De Præscrip. ch. xi.

[3] Ibid.

[4] " Mithra signat illic in frontibus milites suos."

[5] " Semper enim cruci baptismus jungitur." (Aug, Temp. Ser. ci.)

[6] See Anacalypsis, vol. ii. p. 69, and Monumental Christianity, p. 385.

[7] "Sacerdos, stipatum me religiosa cohorte.

The custom of baptism in Egypt is known by the hieroglyphic term of "*water of purification.*" The water so used in immersion absolutely cleansed the soul, *and the person was said to be regenerated.*[1]

They also believed in baptism *after death,* for it was held that the dead were washed from their sins by Osiris, the beneficent saviour, in the land of shades, and the departed are often represented (on the sarcophagi) kneeling before Osiris, who pours over them water from a pitcher.[2]

The ancient *Etruscans* performed the rite of baptism. In *Tab.* clxxii. Gorius gives two pictures of ancient Etruscan baptism by water. In the first, the youth is held in the arms of one priest, and another is pouring water upon his head. In the second, the young person is going through the same ceremony, kneeling on a kind of altar. At the time of its baptism the child was named, blessed and marked on the forehead with *the sign of the cross.*[3]

Baptism, or the application of water, was a rite well known to the Jews before the time of Christ Jesus, and was practiced by them when they admitted proselytes to their religion from heathenism. When children were baptized they received the sign of the cross, were anointed, and fed with milk and honey.[4] "It was not customary, however, among them, to baptize those who were converted to the Jewish religion, *until after the Babylonish captivity.*"[5] This clearly shows that they learned the rite from their heathen oppressors.

Baptism was practiced by the ascetics of Buddhist origin, known as the *Essenes.*[6] John the Baptist was, evidently, nothing more than a member of this order, with which the deserts of Syria and the Thebais of Egypt abounded.

The idea that man is restrained from perfect union with God by his imperfection, uncleanness and sin, was implicitly believed by the ancient *Greeks* and *Romans.* In Thessaly was yearly celebrated a great festival of cleansing. A work bearing the name of "*Museus*" was a complete ritual of purifications. The usual mode of purification was dipping in water (immersion), or

deducit ad proximas balucas; et prius sueto lavraco traditum, proefatus deûm veniam, purissimê circumrorans abluit." (Apuleius: Milesi, ii. citat. a Higgins: Anac., vol. ii. p. 69.)

[1] Bonwick: Egyptian Belief, p. 416. Dunlap: Mysteries Adoni, p. 139.

[2] Baring-Gould: Orig. Relig. Belief, vol. i.

p. 392.

[3] See Higgins: Anac., vol. ii. pp. 67-69.

[4] Barnes: Notes, vol. i. p. 38. Higgins: Anacalypsis, vol. ii. p. 65.

[5] Barnes: Notes, vol. i. p. 41.

[6] See Bunsen's Angel-Messiah, p. 121, Gainsburgh's Essenes, and Higgins' Anacalypsis, vol. ii. pp. 66, 67.

it was performed by aspersion. These sacraments were held to have virtue independent of the dispositions of the candidates, an opinion which called forth the sneer of Diogenes, the Grecian historian, when he saw some one undergoing baptism by aspersion.:

"Poor wretch I do you not see that since these sprinklings cannot repair your grammatical errors, they cannot repair either, the faults of your life."[1]

And the belief that water could wash out the stains of original sin, led the poet *Ovid* (43 B. C.) to say :

"Ah, easy fools, to think that a whole flood
Of water e'er can purge the stain of blood."

These ancient Pagans had especial gods and goddesses who presided over the birth of children. The goddess *Nundina* took her name from the ninth day, *on which all male children were sprinkled with holy water,*[2] as females were on the eighth, at the same time receiving their name, of which *addition* to the ceremonial of Christian baptism we find no mention in the Christian Scriptures. When all the forms of the Pagan nundination were duly complied with, the priest gave a certificate to the parents of the regenerated infant ; it was, therefore, duly recognized as a legitimate member of the family and of society, and the day was spent in feasting and hilarity.[3]

Adults were also baptized; and those who were initiated in the sacred rites of the *Bacchic* mysteries were regenerated and admitted by baptism, just as they were admitted into the mysteries of Mithra.[4] Justin Martyr, like his brother Tertullian, claimed that this ablution was invented by demons, in imitation of the *true* baptism, that their votaries might also have their pretended purification by water.[5]

Infant Baptism was practiced among the ancient inhabitants of northern Europe—the Danes, Swedes, Norwegians and Icelanders —long before the first dawn of Christianity had reached those parts. Water was poured on the head of the new-born child, and

---

[1] Baring-Gould : Orig. Relig. Belief, vol. i. p. 391.

[2] " *Holy Water* "—water wherein the person is baptized, in the name of the Father, and the Son, and of the Holy Ghost. (Church of England Catechism.)

[3] See Taylor's Diegesis, pp. 333, 334, and Higgins' Anacalypsis, ii. p. 65.

[4] See Taylor's Diegesis, pp. 80 and 232, and Baring-Gould's Orig. Relig. Belief, vol. i. p. 391.

"De-la-vint, que pour devenir capable d'entendre les secrets de la création, révélés dans ces mêmes mystères, il fallut se faire *régénérer* par *l'initiation.* Cette cérémonie, par laquelle, *on apprenoit les vrais principes de la vie,* s'opéroit par le moyen de *l'eau* qui voit été celui de la *régénération* du monde. On conduisoit sur les bords de l'Ilissus le candidat qui devoit être initié ; apres l'avoir purifié avec le sel et l'eau de lar mer. on repandoit de l'orge sur lui, ou le couronoit de fleurs, et *l'Hydranos* ou le *Baptiseur* le pongeoit dans le fleure." (D'Ancarville : Res., vol. i. p. 292. Anac., ii. p. 65.)

[5] Taylor's Diegesis, p. 232.

a name was given it at the same time. Baptism is expressly mentioned in the *Hava-mal* and *Rigs-mal*, and alluded to in other epic poems.[1]

The ancient *Livonians* (inhabitants of the three modern Baltic provinces of Courland, Livonia, and Esthonia), observed the same ceremony; which also prevailed among the ancient *Germans*. This is expressly stated in a letter which the famous Pope Gregory III. sent to their apostle Boniface, directing him how to act in respect to it.[2]

The same ceremony was performed by the ancient Druids of Britain.[3]

Among the *New Zealanders* young children were baptized. After the ceremony of baptism had taken place, prayers were offered to make the child sacred, and clean from all impurities.[4]

The ancient *Mexicans* baptized their children shortly after birth. After the relatives had assembled in the court of the parents' house, the midwife placed the child's head to the east, and prayed for a blessing from the *Saviour* Quetzacoatle, and the goddess of the water. The breast of the child was then touched with the fingers dipped in water, and the following prayer said:

"May it (the water) destroy and separate from thee all the evil that was beginning in thee before the beginning of the world."

After this the child's body was washed with water, and all things that might injure him were requested to depart from him, "that now he may live again and be born again."[5]

Mr. Prescott alludes to it as follows, in his "Conquest of Mexico:"[6]

"The lips and bosom of the infant were sprinkled with water, and the Lord was implored to permit the holy drops to wash away that sin that was given to it before the foundation of the world, so that the child might be born anew." "This interesting rite, usually solemnized with great formality, in the presence of assembled friends and relations, is detailed with minuteness by Sahagun and by Zuazo, both of them eyewitnesses."

Rev. J. P. Lundy says:

"Now, as baptism of some kind has been the *universal custom* of all religious nations and peoples for purification and regeneration, it is not to be wondered at that it had found its way from high Asia, the centre of the Old World's religion and civilization, into the American continent. . . .

---

[1] See Mallet's Northern Antiquities, pp. 306, 313, 320, 366. Baring-Gould's Orig. Relig. Belief, vol. i. pp. 392, 393, and Dupuis, p. 242.

[2] Mallet: Northern Antiquities, p. 206.

[3] Baring-Gould: Orig. Relig. Belief, vol. i. p. 393. Higgins: Anac., vol. ii. p. 67, and Davies: Myths of the British Druids.

[4] Sir George Grey: Polynesian Mytho., p. 32, in Baring-Gould: Orig. Relig. Belief, vol. i. p. 392.

[5] See Viscount Amberly's Analysis Relig Belief, p. 59.

[6] Vol. i. p. 64.

"American priests were found in Mexico, beyond Darien, baptizing boys and girls a year old in the temples at the cross, pouring the water upon them from a small pitcher."[1]

The water which they used was called the "WATER OF REGEN-ERATION."[2]

The Rev. Father Acosta alludes to this baptism by saying:

"The Indians had an infinite number of other ceremonies and customs which resembled to the ancient law of Moses, and some to those which the Moores use, and some approaching near to the Law of the Gospel, as the baths or *Opacuna*, as they called them; *they did wash themselves in water to cleanse themselves from sin.*"[3]

After speaking of "*confession which the Indians used*," he says:

"When the Inca had been confessed, he made a certain bath to cleanse himself, in a running river, saying these words: '*I have told my sins to the Sun* (his god); *receive them, O thou River, and carry them to the Sea, where they may never appear more.*'"[4]

He tells us that the Mexicans also had a baptism for infants, which they performed with great ceremony.[5]

Baptism was also practiced in Yucatan. They administered it to children three years old; and called it REGENERATION.[6]

The ancient Peruvians also baptized their children.[7]

History, then, records the fact that all the principal nations of antiquity administered the rite of baptism to their children, and to adults who were initiated into the sacred mysteries. The words "*regenerationem et impunitatem perjuriorum suorum*"—used by the heathen in this ceremony—prove that the doctrines as well as the outward forms were the same. The giving of a name to the child, the marking of him with the *cross* as a sign of his being a soldier of Christ, followed at fifteen years of age by his admission into the mysteries of the ceremony of *confirmation*, also prove that the two institutions are identical. But the most striking feature of all is the *regeneration*—and consequent forgiveness of sins—the being "*born again.*" This shows that the Christian baptism in *doctrine* as well as in *outward ceremony*, was precisely that of the heathen. We have seen that it was supposed to destroy all the evil in him, and all things that might injure him were requested to depart from him. So likewise among the Christians; the priest, looking upon the child, and baptizing him, was formerly accustemed to say:

[1] Monumental Christianity, pp. 389, 390.
[2] Kingsborough: Mex. Antiq., vol. vi. p. 114.
[3] Hist. Indies, vol. ji. p. 369.
[4] Ibid. p. 361.
[5] Ibid. p. 369.
[6] Monumental Christianity, p. 390.
[7] Bonwick: Egyptian Belief, p. 416.

"I command thee, unclean spirit, in the name of the Father, of the Son, and of the Holy Ghost, that thou come out and depart from this infant, whom our Lord Jesus Christ has vouchsafed to call to this holy baptism, to be made member of his body and of his holy congregation. And presume not hereafter to exercise any tyranny towards this infant, whom Christ hath bought with his precious blood, and by this holy baptism called to be of his flock."

The ancients also baptized with *fire* as well as water. This is what is alluded to many times in the gospels; for instance, Matt. (iii. 11) makes John say, "I, indeed, baptize you with water; he shall baptize you with the Holy Ghost and with FIRE."

The baptism by *fire* was in use by the Romans; it was performed by jumping *three times* through the flames of a sacred fire. This is still practiced in India. Even at the present day, in some parts of Scotland, it is a custom at the baptism of children to swing them in their clothes over a fire *three times*, saying, "*Now, fire, burn this child, or never.*" Here is evidently a relic of the heathen *baptism by fire*.

Christian baptism was not originally intended to be administered to unconscious infants, but to persons in full possession of their faculties, and responsible for their actions. Moreover, it was performed, as is well known, not merely by sprinkling the forehead, but by causing the candidate to descend naked into the water, the priest joining him there, and pouring the water over his head. The catechumen could not receive baptism until after he understood something of the nature of the faith he was embracing, and was prepared to assume its obligations. A rite more totally unfitted for administration to *infants* could hardly have been found. Yet such was the need that was felt for a solemn recognition by religion of the entrance of a child into the world, that this rite, in course of time, completely lost its original nature, and, as with the heathen, *infancy* took the place of maturity: sprinkling of immersion. But while the age and manner of baptism were altered, the ritual remained under the influence of the primitive idea with which it had been instituted. The obligations were no longer confined to the persons baptized, hence they must be undertaken for them. Thus was the Christian Church landed in the absurdity —unparalleled, we believe, in any other natal ceremony—of requiring the most solemn promises to be made, not by those who were thereafter to fulfill them, *but by others in their name;* these others having no power to enforce their fulfillment, and neither those actually assuming the engagement, nor those on whose behalf it was assumed, being morally responsible in case it should be broken. Yet this strange incongruity was forced upon the church by an imperious want of human nature itself, and the insignificant sects who have adopted the baptism of adults only, have failed, in their zeal for historical consistency, to recognize a sentiment whose roots lie far deeper than the chronological foundation of Christian rites, and stretch far wider than the geographical boundaries of the Christian faith.

The intention of all these forms of baptism is identical. Water, as the natural means of physical cleansing, is the universal symbol of spiritual purification. Hence immersion, or washing, or sprinkling, implies the deliverance of the infant from the stain of original sin.[1] The *Pagan* and *Christian* rituals, as we have seen, are perfectly clear on this head. In both, the avowed intention is to wash away the sinful nature common to humanity; in both, the infant is declared to be born again by the agency of water. Among the early Christians, as with the Pagans, the sacrament of baptism was supposed to contain a full and absolute expiation of sin; and the soul was instantly restored to its original purity, and entitled to the promise of eternal salvation. Among the proselytes of Christianity, there were many who judged it imprudent to precipitate a salutary rite, which could not be repeated; to throw away an inestimable privilege, which could never be recovered. By the delay of their baptism, they could venture freely to indulge their passions in the enjoyments of this world, while they still retained in their own hands the means of a sure and easy absolution. St. Constantine was one of these.

---

[1] That man is born in *original sin* seems to have been the belief of all nations of antiquity, especially the Hindus. This sense of original corruption is expressed in the following prayer, used by them:

"I am sinful, I commit sin, my nature is sinful, *I am conceived in sin*. Save me, O thou lotus-eyed Heri, the remover of Sin." (Williams' Hinduism, p. 214.)

CHAPTER XXXII.

THE WORSHIP OF THE VIRGIN MOTHER.

THE worship of the "Virgin," the "Queen of Heaven," the "Great Goddess," the "Mother of God," &c., which has become one of the grand features of the Christian religion—the Council of Ephesus (A. D. 431) having declared Mary "Mother of God," her

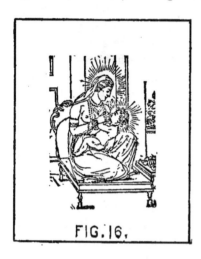

FIG. 16,

assumption being declared in 813, and her Immaculate Conception by the Pope and Council in 1851[1]— was almost universal, for ages before the birth of Jesus, and "the *pure virginity* of the celestial mother was a tenet of faith for two thousand years before the virgin now adored was born."[2]

In *India,* they have worshiped, for ages, *Devi, Maha-Devi*—"The One Great Goddess"[3]—and have temples erected in honor of her.[4] Gonzales states that among the Indians he found

a temple "*Pariturœ Virginis*"—of the Virgin about to bring forth.[5]

Maya, the mother of Buddha, and *Devaki* the mother of Crishna, were worshiped as *virgins,*[6] and represented with the infant Saviours in their arms, just as the virgin of the Christians is represented at the present day. Maya was so pure that it was impossible for God, man, or Asura to view her with carnal desire. Fig. No. 16 is

---

[1] See Bonwick's Egyptian Belief, p. 115, and Monumental Christianity, pp. 206 and 226.

[2] Inman : Ancient Faiths, vol. i. p. 159.

[3] See Williams' Hinduism.

[4] See Higgins : Anacalypsis, vol. i. p. 540.

[5] See Taylor's Diegesis, p. 185.

[6] *St. Jerome* says : "It is handed down as a tradition among the Gymnosophists of India,

a representation of the Virgin Devaki, with the infant Saviour Crishna, taken from Moor's "Hindu Pantheon."[1] "No person could bear to gaze upon Devaki, because of the light that invested her." "The gods, invisible to mortals, celebrated her praise continually from the time that *Vishnu* was contained in her person."[2]

"Crishna and his mother are almost always represented *black*,"[3] and the word "*Crishna*" means "*the black.*"

The *Chinese*, who have had several *avatars*, or virgin-born gods, among them, have also worshiped a Virgin Mother from time immemorial. Sir Charles Francis Davis, in his "History of China," tells us that the Chinese at Canton worshiped an idol, to which they gave the name of "The Virgin."[4]

The Rev. Joseph B. Gross, in his "Heathen Religion," tells us that:

'Upon the altars of the Chinese temples were placed, behind a screen, an image of *Shin-moo*, or the 'Holy Mother,' *sitting with a child in her arms*, in an alcove, with rays of glory around her head, and tapers constantly burning before her."[5]

Shin-moo is called the "Mother Goddess," and the "Virgin." Her child, who was exposed in his infancy, was brought up by poor fishermen. He became a great man, and performed wonderful miracles. In wealthy houses the sacred image of the "Mother Goddess" is carefully kept in a recess behind an altar, veiled with a silken screen.[6]

The Rev. Mr. Gutzlaff, in his "Travels," speaking of the Chinese people, says:

"Though otherwise very reasonable men, they have always showed themselves bigoted heathens. . . . They have everywhere built splendid temples, chiefly in honor of *Ma-tsoo-po*, the 'Queen of Heaven.'"[7]

Isis, mother of the Egyptian Saviour, Horus, was worshiped as a virgin. Nothing is more common on the religious monuments of Egypt than the infant Horus seated in the lap of his virgin mother. She is styled "Our Lady," the "Queen of Heaven," "Star of the Sea," "Governess," "Mother of God," "Intercessor," "Immacu-

---

that *Buddha*, the founder of their system was brought forth by a virgin from her side." (*Contra Jovian*, bk. i. Quoted in Rhys Davids' Buddhism, p. 183.)

[1] Plate 59.
[2] Monumental Christianity, p. 218.
Of the Virgin *Mary* we read: "Her face was shining as snow, and its brightness could

hardly be borne. Her conversation was with the angels, &c." (Nativity of Mary, *Apoc.*)
[3] See Ancient Faiths, i. 401.
[4] Davis' China, vol. ii. p. 95.
[5] The Heathen Relig., p. 60.
[6] Barrows: Travels in China, p. 467.
[7] Gutzlaff's Voyages, p. 154.

late Virgin," &c.;[1] all of which epithets were in after years applied
to the Virgin Mother worshiped by the Christians.[2]

"The most common representation of Horus is being nursed on
the knee of Isis, or suckled at her breast."[3] In *Monumental
Christianity* (Fig. 92), is to be seen a representation of "Isis and
Horus." The infant Saviour is sitting on his mother's knee, while
she gazes into his face. A cross is on the back of the seat. The
author, Rev. J. P. Lundy, says, in speaking of it:

"Is this Egyptian mother, too, meditating her son's conflict, suffering, and
triumph, as she holds him before her and gazes into his face? And is this cross
meant to convey the idea of life through suffering, and conflict with Typho or
Evil?"

In some statues and *basso-relievos*, when Isis appears alone, she
is entirely veiled from head to foot, in common with nearly every
other goddess, as a symbol of a mother's chastity. No mortal man
hath ever lifted her veil.

Isis was also represented standing on the *crescent* moon, with
twelve stars surrounding her head.[4] In almost every Roman
Catholic Church on the continent of Europe may be seen pictures
and statues of *Mary*, the "Queen of Heaven," standing on the
crescent moon, and her head surrounded with *twelve* stars.

Dr. Inman, in his "Pagan and Christian Symbolism," gives a
figure of the Virgin Mary, with her infant, standing on the *crescent
moon*. In speaking of this figure, he says:

"In it the Virgin is seen as the 'Queen of Heaven,' nursing her infant, and
identified with the crescent moon. . . . Than this, nothing could more completely identify the Christian mother and child, with Isis and Horus."[5]

This *crescent moon* is the symbol of Isis and Juno, and is the
Yoni of the Hindoos.[6]

The priests of Isis yearly dedicated to her a new ship (emblematic of the YONI), laden with the first fruits of spring. Strange
as it may seem, the carrying in procession of ships, in which the
Virgin Mary takes the place of the heathen goddesses, has not yet
wholly gone out of use.[7]

Isis is also represented, with the infant Saviour in her arms,
enclosed in a framework of the flowers of the Egyptian bean, or
lotus.[8] The Virgin *Mary* is very often represented in this
manner, as those who have studied mediæval art well know.

[1] Bonwick's Egyptian Belief, p. 141.
[2] See The Lily of Israel, p. 14.
[3] Kenrick's Egypt, vol. i. p. 425.
[4] See Draper's Science and Religion, pp. 47,
48 and Higgins' Anacalypsis, vol. i. p. 304.
[5] Pagan and Christian Symbolism, p. 50.

[6] See Monumental Christianity, p. 307, and
Dr. Inman's Ancient Faiths.
[7] See Cox's Aryan Mytho., vol. ii. p. 119,
note.
[8] See Pagan and Christian Symbolism, pp.
13, 14.

Dr. Inman, describing a painting of the Virgin Mary, which is to be seen in the South Kensington Museum, and which is enclosed in a framework of flowers, says:

"It represents the Virgin and Child precisely as she used to be represented in Egypt, in India, in Assyria, Babylonia, Phœnicia, and Etruria."[1]

The lotus and poppy were sacred among all Eastern nations, and were consecrated to the various virgins worshiped by them. These virgins are represented holding this plant in their hands, just as the Virgin, adored by the Christians, is represented at the present day.[2] Mr. Squire, speaking of this plant, says:

FIG. 17

"It is well known that the 'Nymphe' — lotus or water-lily — is held sacred throughout the East, and the various sects of that quarter of the globe represented their deities either decorated with its flowers, holding it as a sceptre, or seated on a lotus throne or pedestal. Lacshmi, the beautiful Hindoo goddess, is associated with the lotus. The Egyptian Isis is often called the 'Lotus-crowned,' in the ancient invocations. The Mexican goddess Corieotl, is often represented with a water-plant resembling the lotus in her hand."[3]

In Egyptian and Hindoo mythology, the offspring of the virgin is made to bruise the head of the serpent, but the Romanists have given this office to the mother. Mary is often seen represented standing on the serpent. Fig. 17 alludes to this, and to her *immaculate conception*, which, as we have seen, was declared by the Pope and council in 1851. The notion of the divinity of Mary was broached by some at the Council of Nice, and they were thence named Marianites.

The Christian Father Epiphanius accounts for the fact of the Egyptians worshiping a virgin and child, by declaring that the prophecy—"Behold, a virgin shall conceive and bring forth a son" —must have been revealed to them.[4]

In an ancient Christian work, called the "Chronicle of Alexandria," occurs the following:

[1] Pagan and Christian Symbolism, pp. 4, 5.
[2] See Knight: Ancient Art and Mythology, pp. 45, 104, 105.
"We see, in pictures, that the Virgin and Child are associated in modern times with the split apricot, the pomegranate, rimmon, and the Viue, just as was the ancient Venus." (Dr. Inman: Ancient Faiths, vol. i. p. 528.)
[3] Serpent Symbol, p. 39.
[4] Taylor's Diegesis, p. 185.

" Watch how Egypt has constructed the childbirth of a virgin, and the birth of her son, *who was exposed in a crib to the adoration of the people.*"[1]

We have another Egyptian Virgin Mother in Neith or Nout, mother of "Osiris the Saviour." She was known as the "Great Mother," and yet "Immaculate Virgin."[2]   M. Beauregard speaks of

" The Immaculate Conception of the Virgin (Mary), who can henceforth, as well as the Egyptian Minerva, the mysterious Neith, boast of having come from herself, and of having given birth to god."[3]

What is known in Christian countries as "Candlemas day," or the Purification of the Virgin Mary, is of Egyptian origin.   The feast of Candlemas was kept by the ancient Egyptians in honor of the goddess Neith, and on the very day that is marked on our Christian almanacs as "Candlemas day."[4]

The ancient *Chaldees* believed in a celestial virgin, who had purity of body, loveliness of person, and tenderness of affection; and who was one to whom the erring sinner could appeal with more chance of success than to a stern father. She was portrayed as a mother, although a virgin, with a child in her arms.[5]

The ancient Babylonians and Assyrians worshiped a goddess mother, and son, who was represented in pictures and in images as an infant in his mother's arms (see Fig. No. 18). Her name was *Mylitta*, the divine son was *Tammuz*, the Saviour, whom we have seen rose from the dead. He was invested with all his father's attributes and glory, and identified with him. He was worshiped as *mediator*.[6]

There was a temple at Paphos, in Cyprus, dedicated to the Virgin Mylitta, and was the most celebrated one in Grecian times.[7]

The ancient *Etruscans* worshiped a Virgin Mother and Son, who was represented in pictures and images in the arms of his mother. This was the goddess *Nutria*, to be seen in Fig. No. 19. On the arm of the mother is an inscription in Etruscan letters. This goddess was also worshiped in Italy. Long before the Christian era temples and statues were erected in memory of her. "To the Great Goddess Nutria," is an inscription which has been found among the ruins of a temple dedicated to her. No doubt the Roman Church would have claimed her for a

1 Bonwick's Egyptian Belief, p. 143.
2 Ibid. p. 115.
3 Quoted in Ibid. p. 115.
4 Ibid., and Kenrick's Egypt.

5 Inman's Ancient Faiths, vol. i. p. 59.
6 See Monumental Christianity, p. 211, and Ancient Faiths, vol. ii. p. 350.
7 Ancient Faiths, vol. i. p. 213.

Madonna, but most unluckily for them, she has the name "*Nutria*," in Etruscan letters on her arm, after the Etruscan practice.

The Egyptian *Isis* was also worshiped in Italy, many centuries before the Christian era, and all images of her, with the infant Horus in her arms, have been adopted, as we shall presently see, by the Christians, even though they represent her and her child as *black* as an Ethiopian, in the same manner as we have seen that Devaki and Crishna were represented.

FIG NO. 18

FIG. 19

The children of Israel, who, as we have seen in a previous chapter, were idolaters of the worst kind—worshiping the sun, moon and stars, and offering human sacrifices to their god, Moloch—were also worshipers of a Virgin Mother, whom they styled the "Queen of Heaven."

Jeremiah, who appeared in Jerusalem about the year 625 B.C., and who was one of the prophets and reformers, rebukes the Israelites for their idolatry and worship of the "Queen of Heaven," whereupon they answer him as follows:

"As for the word that thou hast spoken unto us, in the name of the Lord, we will not hearken unto thee. But we will certainly do whatsoever thing goeth forth out of our own mouth, to burn incense unto the *Queen of Heaven*, and to pour out drink offerings unto her, *as we have done, we, and our fathers, our kings, and our princes, in the city of Judah, and in the streets of Jerusalem :* for then we had plenty of victuals, and were well, and saw no evil.

"But since we left off to burn incense to the *Queen of Heaven*, and to pour out drink offerings unto her, we have wanted all things, and have been consumed by the sword and by the famine. And when we burned incense to the *Queen of*

Heaven, and poured out drink offerings unto her, did we make her *cakes* to worship her, and pour out drink offerings unto her, without our men ?"[1]

The "*cakes*" which were offered to the "Queen of Heaven" by the Israelites were marked with a *cross*, or other symbol of sun worship.[2]   The ancient Egyptians also put a cross on their "sacred cakes."[3]   Some of the early Christians offered "sacred cakes" to the Virgin Mary centuries after.[4]

The ancient Persians worshiped the Virgin and Child. On the monuments of Mithra, the Saviour, the Mediating and Redeeming God of the Persians, the Virgin Mother of this god is to be seen suckling her infant.[5]

The ancient Greeks and Romans worshiped the Virgin Mother and Child for centuries before the Christian era. One of these was *Myrrha,*[6] the mother of *Bacchus,* the Saviour, who was represented with the infant in her arms. She had the title of "Queen of Heaven."[7]   At many a *Christian* shrine the infant Saviour Bacchus may be seen reposing in the arms of his deified mother. The names are changed—the ideas remain as before.[8]

The Rev. Dr. Stuckley writes:

"Diodorus says Bacchus was born of Jupiter, the Supreme God, and Ceres (Myrrha). Both Ceres and Proserpine were called *Virgo* (Virgin). The story of this woman being deserted by a man, and espoused by a god, has somewhat so exceedingly like that passage, Matt. i. 19, 20, of the blessed Virgin's history, that we should wonder at it, *did we not see the parallelism infinite between the sacred and the profane history before us.*

"There are many similitudes between the Virgin (Mary) and the mother of Bacchus (also called Mary—see note 6 below)—in all the old fables. Mary, or Miriam, St. Jerome interprets Myrrha Maris. Orpheus calls the mother of Bacchus a *Sea Goddess* (and the mother of Jesus is called ' *Mary, Star of the Sea.* ")[9]

Thus we see that the reverend and learned Dr. Stuckley has clearly

---

[1] Jeremiah, xliv. 16-22.
[2] See Colenso's Lectures, p. 297, and Bonwick's Egyptian Belief, p. 148.
[3] See the Pentateuch Examined, vol. vi. p. 115, App., and Bonwick's Egyptian Belief, p. 148.
[4] See King's Gnostics, p. 91, and Monumental Christianity, p. 224.
[5] See Dupuis: Origin of Relig. Belief, p. 237.
[6] It would seem more than chance that so many of the virgin mothers and goddesses of antiquity should have the same name. The mother of *Bacchus* was Myrrha; the mother of Mercury or Hermes was Myrrha or Maia (See Ferguson's Tree and Serpent Worship, p. 186, and Inman's Ancient Faiths, vol. ii. p. 253); the mother of the Siamese Saviour—Sommona Cadom—was called Maya Maria, i. e., "the Great Mary;" the mother of Adonis was Myrrha

(See Anacalypsis, vol. i. p. 314, and Inman's Ancient Faiths, vol. ii. p. 253); the mother of Buddha was Maya; now, all these names, whether Myrrha, Maia or Maria, are the same as *Mary,* the name of the mother of the Christian Saviour. (See Inman's Ancient Faiths, vol. ii. pp. 353 and 780. Also, Dunlap's Mysteries of Adoni, p. 124.) The month of *May* was sacred to these goddesses, so likewise is it sacred to the Virgin Mary at the present day, *She* was also called Myrrha and Maria, as well as Mary. (See Anacalypsis, vol. i. p. 304, and Son of the Man, p. 26.)
[7] Higgins: Anacalypsis, vol. i. pp. 303, 304.
[8] Prof. Wilder, in "Evolution," June, '77. Isis Unveiled, vol. ii.
[9] Stuckley: Pal. Sac. No. 1. p. 34, in Anacalypsis, i. p. 304.

made out that the story of Mary, the "Queen of Heaven," the "Star of the Sea," the mother of the Lord, with her translation to heaven, &c., was an *old story* long before Jesus of Nazareth was born. After this Stuckley observes that the *Pagan* "Queen of Heaven" has upon her head a crown of twelve stars. This, as we have observed above, is the case of the *Christian* "Queen of Heaven" in almost every Romish church on the continent of Europe.

The goddess *Cybele* was another. She was equally called the "Queen of Heaven" and the "Mother of God." As devotees now collect alms in the name of the Virgin Mary, so did they in ancient times in the name of Cybele. The *Galli* now used in the churches of Italy, were anciently used in the worship of Cybele (called *Galliambus*, and sang by her priests). "Our Lady Day," or the day of the Blessed Virgin of the Roman Church, was heretofore dedicated to Cybele.[1]

Minerva, who was distinguished by the title of "Virgin Queen,"[2] was extensively worshiped in ancient Greece. Among the innumerable temples of Greece, the most beautiful was the *Parthenon*, meaning, the *Temple of the Virgin Goddess*. It was a magnificent Doric edifice, dedicated to Minerva, the presiding deity of Athens.

Juno was called the "Virgin Queen of Heaven."[3] She was represented, like *Isis* and *Mary*, standing on the crescent moon,[4] and was considered the special protectress of women, from the cradle to the grave, just as Mary is considered at the present day.

Diana, who had the title of "Mother," was nevertheless famed for her virginal purity.[5] She was represented, like *Isis* and *Mary*, with stars surrounding her head.[6]

The ancient *Muscovites* worshiped a sacred group, composed of a woman with a *male child* in her lap, and another *standing by her*. They had likewise another idol, called *the golden heifer*, which, says Mr. Knight, "seems to have been the animal *symbol* of the same personage."[7] Here we have the Virgin and infant Saviour, with the companion (John the Baptist), and "The *Lamb* that taketh away the sins of the world," among the ancient *Musco-*

[1] Higgins : Anacalypsis, vol. i. p. 805.
[2] See Bell's Pantheon, and Knight : Ancient Art and Mytho., p. 175.
[3] See Roman Antiquities, p. 73. Anacalypsis, vol. ii. p. 82, and Bell's Pantheon, vol. ii. p. 160.
[4] See Monumental Christianity, p. 808—Fig. 144.
[5] See Knight : Anct. Art and Mytho., pp. 175, 176.
[6] See Montfaucon, vol. i. plate xcii.
[7] Knight's Anct. Art and Mytho., p. 147.

vites before the time of Christ Jesus. This goddess had also the title of " Queen of Heaven.'

The ancient *Germans* worshiped a virgin goddess under the the name of *Hertha*, or Ostara, who was fecundated by the active spirit, *i.e.*, the " Holy Spirit."² She was represented in images as a woman with a child in her arms. This image was common in their consecrated forests, and was held peculiarly sacred.³ The Christian celebration called *Easter* derived its *name* from this goddess.

The ancient *Scandinavians* worshiped a virgin goddess called Disa. Mr. R. Payne Knight tells us that :

"This goddess is delineated on the sacred drums of the Laplanders, *accompanied by a child*, similar to the *Horus* of the Egyptians, who so often appears in the lap of Isis on the religious monuments of that people."⁴

The ancient *Scandinavians* also worshiped the goddess Frigga. She was mother of " Baldur the Good," his father being Odin, the supreme god of the northern nations. It was she who was addressed, as Mary is at the present day, in order to obtain happy marriages and easy childbirths. The Eddas style her the most favorable of the goddesses.⁵

In *Gaul*, the ancient Druids worshiped the *Virgo-Paritura* as the " Mother of God," and a festival was annually celebrated in honor of this virgin.⁶

In the year 1747 a monument was found at Oxford, England, of pagan origin, on which is exhibited a female nursing an infant.⁷ Thus we see that the Virgin and Child were worshiped, in pagan times, from China to Britain, and, if we turn to the New World, we shall find the same thing there ; for, in the words of Dr. Inman, " even in Mexico the ' Mother and Child ' were worshiped."⁸

This mother, who had the title of " Virgin," and " Queen of Heaven,"⁹ was Chimalman, or Sochiquetzal, and the infant was Quetzalcoatle, the crucified Saviour. Lord Kingsborough says :

"She who represented ' Our Lady ' (among the ancient Mexicans) had her hair tied up in the manner in which the Indian women tie and fasten their hair,

¹ Anacalypsis, vol. ii. pp. 109, 110.
² See Knight's Anct. Art and Mytho., p. 21.
³ See Prog. Relig. Ideas, vol. i. p. 374, and Mallet : Northern Antiquities.
⁴ Knight : Anct. Art and Mytho., p. 147.
⁵ See Mallet's Northern Antiquities.
⁶ See Higgins : Anacalypsis, vol. ii. pp. 108, 109, 259. Dupuis : Orig. Relig. Belief, p. 257.

Celtic Druids, p. 163, and Taylor's Diegesis, p. 184.
⁷ See Celtic Druids, p. 163, and Dupuis, p. 237.
⁸ Ancient Faiths, vol. i. p. 100.
⁹ See Anacalypsis, vol. ii. p. 33, and Mexican Antiquities, vol. vi. p. 176.

and in the knot behind was inserted a small *cross,* by which it was intended to show that she was the Most Holy."[1]

The Mexicans had pictures of this "Heavenly Goddess" on long pieces of leather, which they rolled up.[2]

The annunciation to the Virgin Chimalman, that she should become the mother of the Saviour Quetzalcoatle, was the subject of a Mexican hieroglyphic, and is remarkable in more than one respect. She appears to be receiving a bunch of flowers from the embassador or angel,[3] which brings to mind the *lotus,* the sacred plant of the East, which is placed in the hands of the Pagan and Christian virgins.

The 25th of March, which was celebrated throughout the ancient Grecian and Roman world, in honor of "the Mother of the Gods," was appointed to the honor of the Christian "Mother of God," and is now celebrated in Catholic countries, and called "Lady day."[4] The festival of the conception of the "Blessed Virgin Mary" is also held on the very day that the festival of the miraculous conception of the "Blessed Virgin Juno" was held among the pagans,[5] which, says the author of the "Perennial Calendar," "is a remarkable coincidence."[6] It is not such a very "remarkable coincidence" after all, when we find that, even as early as the time of St. Gregory, Bishop of Neo-Cæsarea, who flourished about A.D. 240–250, Pagan festivals were changed into Christian holidays. This saint was commended by his namesake of Nyssa for changing the Pagan festivals into Christian holidays, the better to draw the heathens to the religion of Christ.[7]

The month of *May,* which was dedicated to the heathen Virgin Mothers, is also the month of Mary, the Christian Virgin.

Now that we have seen that the worship of the Virgin and Child was universal for ages before the Christian era, we shall say a few words on the subject of pictures and images of the Madonna—so called.

The most ancient pictures and statues in Italy and other parts of Europe, of what are supposed to be representations of the Virgin *Mary* and the infant Jesus, are *black.* The infant god, in the arms of his black mother, his eyes and drapery white, is himself perfectly black.[8]

Godfrey Higgins, on whose authority we have stated the above, informs us that, at the time of his writing—1825–1835—images and

[1] Mexican Antiquities, vol. vi. p. 176.
[2] Ibid.
[3] Ibid.
[4] Higgins : Anacalypsis, vol. i. p. 304.
[5] Ibid. vol. ii. p. 82.
[6] Quoted in Ibid.
[7] See Middleton's Letters from Rome, p. 236.
[8] Higgins : Anacalypsis, vol. i. p. 138.

paintings of this kind were to be seen at the cathedral of Moulins; the famous chapel of "the Virgin" at Loretto; the church of the Annunciation, the church of St. Lazaro, and the church of St. Stephens, at *Genoa;* St. Francis, at *Pisa;* the church at *Brixen*, in the Tyrol; the church at *Padua;* the church of St. Theodore, at *Munich*—in the two last of which the white of the eyes and teeth, and the studied redness of the lips, are very observable.[1]

"The *Bambino*[2] at *Rome* is black," says Dr. Inman, "and so are the Virgin and Child at Loretto."[3] Many more are to be seen in Rome, and in innumerable other places; in fact, says Mr. Higgins,

FIG. 20.

"There is scarcely an old church in Italy where some remains of the worship of the *black Virgin*, and *black child*, are not met with;" and that "pictures in great numbers are to be met with, where the white of the eyes, and of the teeth, and the lips a little tinged with red, like the black figures in the museum of the Indian company."[4]

Fig. No. 20 is a copy of the image of the Virgin of Loretto. Dr. Conyers Middleton, speaking of it, says:

"The mention of Loretto puts me in mind of the surprise that I was in at the first sight of the Holy Image, for its face is as black as a negro's. But I soon recollected, that this very circumstance of its complexion made it but resemble the more exactly the *old idols of Paganism*."[5]

The reason assigned by the Christian priests for the images being black, is that they are made so by smoke and incense, but, we may ask, if they became black by smoke, why is it that the *white* drapery, *white* teeth, and the *white* of the eyes have not changed in color? Why are the lips of a bright red color? Why, we may also ask, are the black images crowned and adorned with jewels, just as the images of the Hindoo and Egyptian virgins are represented?

When we find that the Virgin Devaki, and the Virgin Isis were represented just as these so-called *ancient Christian* idols represent Mary, we are led to the conclusion that they are Pagan idols adopted by the Christians.

[1] Higgins: Anacalypsis, vol. i. p. 138.
[2] *Bambino*—a term in art, descriptive of the swaddled figure of the infant Saviour.
[3] Ancient Faiths, vol. i. p. 401.
[4] Higgins: Anacalypsis, vol. i. p. 138.
[5] Letters from Rome, p. 84

We may say, in the words of Mr. Lundy, " what jewels are doing on the neck of this poor and lowly maid, it is not easy to say."[1] The *crown* is also foreign to early representations of the Madonna and Child, but not so to Devaki and Crishna,[2] and Isis and Horus. The *coronation* of the Virgin Mary is unknown to primitive Christian art, but is common in Pagan art.[3] " It may be well," says Mr. Lundy, " to compare some of the oldest *Hindoo* representations of the subject with the Romish, and see how complete the resemblance is ; "[4] and Dr. Inman says that, " the head-dress, as put on the head of the Virgin Mary, is of Grecian, Egyptian, and Indian origin."[5]

The whole secret of the fact of these early representations of the Virgin Mary and Jesus—so-called—being *black*, crowned, and covered with jewels, is that they are of pre-Christian origin ; they are *Isis* and *Horus*, and perhaps, in some cases, Devaki and Crishna, baptized anew.

The Egyptian " Queen of Heaven " was worshiped in Europe for centuries before and after the Christian Era.[6] Temples and statues were also erected in honor of Isis, one of which was at Bologna, in Italy.

Mr. King tells us that the Emperor Hadrian zealously strove to reanimate the forms of that old religion, whose spirit had long since passed away, and it was under his patronage that the creed of the Pharaohs blazed up for a moment with a bright but fictitious lustre.[7] To this period belongs a beautiful sard, in Mr. King's collection, representing Serapis[8] and Isis, with the legend : " Immaculate is Our Lady Isis."[9]

Mr. King further tells us that :

" The ' *Black Virgins* ' so highly reverenced in certain French cathedrals during the long night of the middle ages, proved, when at last examined critically, basalt figures of Isis."[10]

And Mr. Bonwick says :

" We may be surprised that, as Europe has *Black* Madonnas, Egypt had *Black*

---

[1] Monumental Christianity, p. 208.
[2] See Ibid. p. 229, and Moore's Hindu Pantheon, Inman's Christian and Pagan Symbolism, Higgins' Anacalypsis, vol. ii., where the figures of Crishna and Devaki may be seen, crowned, laden with jewels, and a ray of glory surrounding their heads.
[3] Monumental Christianity, p. 227.
[4] Ibid.
[5] Ancient Faiths, vol. ii. p. 767.
[6] In King's Gnostics and their Remains, p. 109, the author gives a description of a procession, given during the second century by Apuleius, in honor of *Isis*, the " Immaculate Lady."

[7] King's Gnostics, p. 71.
[8] " Serapis does not appear to be one of the native gods, or monsters, who sprung from the fruitful soil of Egypt. The first of the Ptolemies had been commanded, by a dream, to import the mysterious stranger from the coast of Pontus, where he had been long adored by the inhabitants of Sinope ; but his attributes and his reign were so imperfectly understood, that it became a subject of dispute, whether he represented the bright orb of day, or the gloomy monarch of the subterraneous regions." (Gibbon's Rome, vol. iii. p. 143.)
[9] Ibid.
[10] King's Gnostics, p. 71, *note.*

22

images and pictures of Isis.   At the same time it is a little odd that the Virgin Mary copies most honored should not only be *Black*, but have a decided *Isis cast* of feature."[1]

The shrine now known as that of the " Virgin in Amadon," in France, was formerly an old Black *Venus*.[2]

" To this we may add," (says Dr. Inman), " that at the Abbey of Einsiedelen, on Lake Zurich, the object of adoration is an old *black doll*, dressed in gold brocade, and glittering with jewels.   She is called, apparently, the Virgin of the Swiss Mountains.   My friend, Mr. Newton, also tells me that he saw, over a church door at Ivrea, in Italy, twenty-nine miles from Turin, the fresco of a *Black* Virgin and child, the former bearing a *triple crown*."[3]

This *triple crown* is to be seen on the heads of Pagan gods and goddesses, especially those of the Hindoos.

Dr. Barlow says :

" The doctrine of the Mother of God was of Egyptian origin.   It was brought in along with the worship of the Madonna by Cyril (Bishop of Alexandria, and the Cyril of Hypatia) and the monks of Alexandria, in the fifth century.   The earliest representations of the Madonna have quite a Greco-Egyptian character, and there can be little doubt that Isis nursing Horus was the origin of them all."[4]

And Arthur Murphy tells us that:

" The superstition and religious ceremonies of the *Egyptians* were diffused over Asia, Greece, *and the rest of Europe*.   Brotier says, that inscriptions of Isis and Serapis (Horus ?) have been frequently found in *Germany*. . . .   The missionaries who went in the eighth and ninth centuries to propagate the Christian religion in those parts, *saw many images and statues of these gods*."[5]

These " many images and statues of these gods" were evidently baptized anew, given other names, and allowed to remain where they were.

In many parts of Italy are to be seen pictures of the Virgin with her infant in her arms, inscribed with the words : " Deo Soli."   This betrays their Pagan origin.

[1] Bonwick's Egyptian Belief, p. 141. "*Black* is the color of the Egyptian Isis." (The Rosecrucians, p. 154.)

[2] Ancient Faiths, vol. i. p. 159. In Montefaucon, vol. i. plate xcv., may be seen a representation of a *Black* Venus.

[3] Ancient Faiths, vol. ii. p. 264.

[4] Quoted in Bonwick's Egyptian Belief, p. 142.

[5] Notes 3 and 4 to Tacitus' Manners of the Germans.

CHAPTER XXXIII.

CHRISTIAN SYMBOLS.

A THOROUGH investigation of this subject would require a volume, therefore, as we can devote but a chapter to it, it must necessarily be treated somewhat slightingly.

The first of the Christian Symbols which we shall notice is the CROSS.

Overwhelming historical facts show that the cross was used, *as a religious emblem*, many centuries before the Christian era, by every nation in the world. Bishop Colenso, speaking on this subject, says:—

"From the dawn of organized Paganism in the Eastern world, to the final establishment of Christianity in the West, the cross was undoubtedly one of the commonest and most sacred of symbolical monuments. Apart from any distinctions of social or intellectual superiority, of caste, color, nationality, or location in either hemisphere, it appears to have been the aboriginal possession of every people in antiquity.

"Diversified forms of the symbol are delineated more or less artistically, according to the progress achieved in civilization at the period, on the ruined walls of temples and palaces, on natural rocks and sepulchral galleries, on the hoariest monoliths and the rudest statuary; on coins, medals, and vases of every description; and in not a few instances, are preserved in the architectural proportions of subterranean as well as superterranean structures of tumuli, as well as fanes.

"Populations of essentially different culture, tastes, and pursuits—the highly-civilized and the semi-civilized, the settled and the nomadic—vied with each other in their superstitious *adoration* of it, and in their efforts to extend the knowledge of its exceptional import and virtue amongst their latest posterities.

"Of the several varieties of the cross still in vogue, as national and ecclesiastical emblems, and distinguished by the familiar appellations of St. George, St. Andrew, the Maltese, the Greek, the Latin, &c., &c., *there is not one amongst them the existence of which may not be traced to the remotest antiquity. They were the common property of the Eastern nations.*

"That each known variety has been derived from a common source, and is emblematical of one and the same truth may be inferred from the fact of forms identically the same, whether simple or complex, cropping out in contrary directions, in the Western as well as the Eastern hemisphere."[1]

---

[1] The Pentateuch Examined, vol. vi. p. 113.

The cross has been adored in *India* from time immemorial, and was a symbol of mysterious significance in Brahmanical iconography. It was the symbol of the Hindoo god Agni, the "Light of the World."[1]

In the Cave of Elephanta, over the head of the figure represented as destroying the infants, whence the story of Herod and the infants of Bethlehem (which was unknown to all the Jewish, Roman, and Grecian historians) took its origin, may be seen the Mitre, the Crosier, and the Cross.[2]

It is placed by Muller in the hand of Siva, Brahma, Vishnu, Crishna, Tvashtri and Jama. To it the worshipers of Vishnu attribute as many virtues as does the devout Catholic to the Christian cross.[3] Fra Paolino tells us it was used by the ancient kings of India as a sceptre.[4]

Two of the principal pagodas of India—Benares and Mathura—were erected in the forms of vast crosses.[5] The pagoda at Mathura was sacred to the memory of the Virgin-born and crucified Saviour Crishna.[6]

The cross has been an object of profound veneration among the Buddhists from the earliest times. One is the sacred Swastica (Fig. No. 21). It is seen in the old Buddhist Zodiacs, and is one of the symbols in the Asoka inscriptions. It is the sectarian mark of the Jains, and the distinctive badge of the sect of Xaca Japonicus. The Vaishnavas of India have also the same sacred sign.[7] And, according to Arthur Lillie,[8] "*the only Christian cross in the catacombs is this Buddhist Swastica.*"

FIG Nº 21

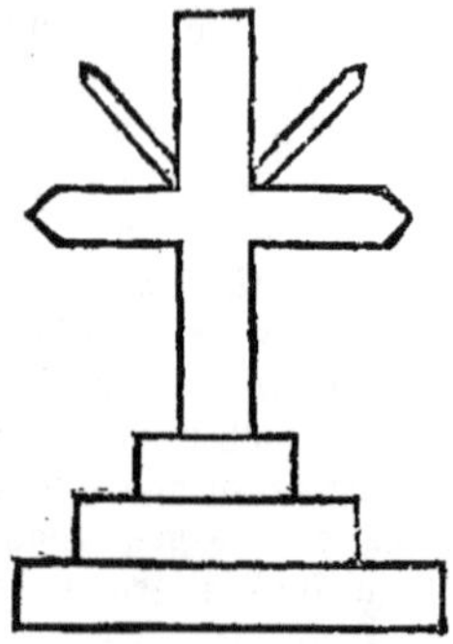

The cross is adored by the followers of the Lama of Thibet.[9] Fig. No. 22 is a representation of the most familiar form of Buddhist cross. The close

FIG. 22

[1] Monumental Christianity, p. 14.
[2] Baring-Gould : Curious Myths, p. 301. Higgins : Anac., vol. i. p. 220.
[3] Curious Myths, p. 301.
[4] Ibid. p. 302.
[5] Maurice ; Indian Antiquities, vol. ii. p. 359.

[6] Ibid. vol. iii. p. 47.
[7] Curious Myths, pp. 280-282. Buddha and Early Buddhism, pp. 7, 9, and 22, and Anacalypsis, vol. i. p. 223.
[8] Buddha and Early Buddhism, p. 227.
[9] Inman : Ancient Faiths, vol. i. p. 409. Higgins : Anac., vol. i. p. 230.

resemblance between the ancient religion of Thibet and that of the Christians has been noticed by many European travellers and missionaries, among whom may be mentioned Pere Grebillon, Pere Grueber, Horace de la Paon, D'Orville, and M. L'Abbé Huc. The Buddhists, and indeed all the sects of India, marked their followers on the head with the sign of the cross.[1] This was undoubtedly practiced by almost all heathen nations, as we have seen in the chapter on the *Eucharist* that the initiates into the Heathen mysteries were marked in that manner.

The ancient *Egyptians* adored the cross with the profoundest veneration. This sacred symbol is to be found on many of their ancient monuments, some of which may be seen at the present day in the British Museum.[2] In the museum of the London University, a cross upon a Calvary is to be seen upon the breast of one of the Egyptian mummies.[3] Many of the Egyptian images hold a cross in their hand. There is one now extant of the Egyptian Saviour Horus holding a cross in his hand,[4] and he is represented as an infant sitting on his mother's knee, with a cross on the back of the seat they occupy.[5]

The commonest of all the Egyptian crosses, the CRUX ANSATA (Fig. No. 23) was adopted by the Christians. Thus, beside one of the Christian inscriptions at Phile (a celebrated island lying in the midst of the Nile) is seen both a *Maltese cross* and a *crux ansata*.[6] In a painting covering the end of a church in the cemetery of El-Khargeh, in the Great Oasis, are three of these crosses round the principal subject, which seems to have been a figure of a saint.[7] In an inscription in a

FIG. Nº 23.

Christian church to the east of the Nile, in the desert, these crosses are also to be seen. Beside, or in the hand of, the Egyptian gods, this symbol is generally to be seen. When the Saviour Osiris is represented holding out the *crux ansata* to a mortal, it signifies that the person to whom he presents it has put off mortality, and entered on the life to come.[8]

The Greek cross, and the cross of St. Anthony, are also found

[1] See Ibid.
[2] See Celtic Druids, p. 126 ; Anacalypsis, vol. i. p. 217, and Bonwick's Egyptian Belief, pp. 216, 217 and 219.
[3] Anacalypsis, vol. i. p. 217.
[4] Knight: Anct. Art and Mytho., p. 58.

[5] See Inman's "Symbolism," and Lundy's Monu. Christianity, Fig. 92.
[6] Baring-Gould : Curious Myths, p. 285.
[7] Hoskins' Visit to the great Oasis, pl. xii. in Curious Myths, p. 286.
[8] Curious Myths, p. 286.

on Egyptian monuments. A figure of a Shari (Fig. No. 24), from Sir Gardner Wilkinson's book, has a necklace round his throat, from which depends a pectoral cross. A third Egyptian cross is

that represented in Fig. No. 25, which is apparently intended for a Latin cross rising out of a heart, like the mediæval emblem of " *Cor in Cruce, Crux in Corde:* " it is the hierogylph of goodness.[1]

FIG N.º 24

FIG N.º 25

It is related by the ecclesiastical historians Socrates and Sozomon, that when the temple of Serapis, at Alexandria, in Egypt, was demolished by one of the Christian emperors, beneath the foundation was discovered a cross. The words of Socrates are as follows :

"In the temple of Serapis, now overthrown and rifled throughout, there were found engraven in the stones certain letters . . . resembling the form of the cross. The which when both Christians and Ethnics beheld, every one applied to his proper religion. The Christians affirmed that the cross was a sign or token of the passion of Christ, and the proper cognizance of their profession. *The Ethnics avouched that therein was contained something in common, belonging as well to Serapis as to Christ.*"[2]

It should be remembered, in connection with this, that the Emperor Hadrian saw no difference between the worshipers of Serapis and the worshipers of Christ Jesus. In a letter to the Consul Servanus he says :

"There are there (in Egypt) *Christians* who worship *Serapis*, and devoted to Serapis are those who call themselves ' *Bishops of Christ.*' "[3]

The ancient Egyptians were in the habit of putting a cross on their sacred cakes, just as the Christians of the present day do on Good Friday.[4] The plan of the chamber of some Egyptian sepulchres has the form of a cross,[5] and the cross was worn by Egyptian ladies as an ornament, in precisely the same manner as Christian ladies wear it at the present day.[6]

The ancient Babylonians honored the cross as a religious symbol. It is to be found on their oldest monuments. Anu, a deity who stood at the head of the Babylonian mythology, had a cross for his

---

[1] Curious Myths, p. 287.
[2] Socrates: Eccl. Hist., lib. v. ch. xvii.
[3] Quoted by Rev. Dr. Giles: Hebrew and Christian Records, vol. ii. p. 86, and Rev. Robert Taylor: Diegesis, p. 202.
[4] See Colenso's Pentateuch Examined vol. vi. p. 115.
[5] Bonwick: Egyptian Belief, p. 12.
[6] Ibid. p. 219.

sign or symbol.[1] It is also the symobl of the Babylonian god Bal.[2] A cross hangs on the breast of Tiglath Pileser, in the colossal tablet from Nimroud, now in the British Museum. Another king, from the ruins of Ninevah, wears a Maltese cross on his bosom. And another, from the hall of Nisroch, carries an emblematic necklace, to which a Maltese cross is attached.[3] The most common of crosses, the *crux ansata* (Fig. No. 21) was also a sacred symbol among the Babylonians. It occurs repeatedly on their cylinders, bricks and gems.[4]

The ensigns and standards carried by the Persians during their wars with Alexander the Great (B. c. 335), were made in the form of a cross—as we shall presently see was the style of the ancient *Roman* standards—and representations of these cross-standards have been handed down to the present day.

Sir Robert Ker Porter, in his very valuable work entitled: "Travels in Georgia, Persia, Armenia, and Ancient Babylonia,"[5] shows the representation of a *bas-relief*, of very ancient antiquity, which he found at Nashi-Roustam, or the Mountain of Sepulchres. It represents a combat between two horsemen—Babaram-Gour, one of the old Persian kings, and a Tartar prince. Baharam-Gour is in the act of charging his opponent with a spear, and behind him, scarcely visible, appears an almost effaced form, which must have been his standard-bearer, as the *ensign* is very plainly to be seen. *This ensign is a cross.* There is another representation of the same subject to be seen in a *bas-relief*, which shows the standard-bearer and his *cross* ensign very plainly.[6] This *bas-relief* belongs to a period when the Arsacedian kings governed Persia,[7] which was within a century after the time of Alexander, and consequently more than two centuries B. c.

Sir Robert also found at this place, sculptures cut in the solid rock, which are in the form of crosses. These belong to the early race of Persian monarchs, whose dynasty terminated under the sword of Alexander the Great.[8] At the foot of Mount Nakshi-Rajab, he also found *bas-reliefs*, among which were two figures carrying a cross-standard. Fig. No. 26 is a representation of this.[9] It is coeval with the sculptures found at Nashi-Roustam,[10] and therefore belongs to a period before the time of Alexander's invasion.

 The cross is represented frequently and prominently on the coins

---

[1] Bonwick: Egyptian Belief, p. 218, and Smith's Chaldean Account of Genesis, p. 54.
[2] Egyptian Belief, p. 218.
[3] Bonomi: Ninevah and Its Palaces, in Curious Myths, p. 287.
[4] Curious Myths, p. 287.
[5] Vol. i. p. 337, pl. xx.
[6] Travels in Persia, vol. i. p. 545, pl. xxi.
[7] Ibid. p. 529, and pl. xvi.
[8] Ibid., and pl. xvii.
[9] Ibid. pl. xxvii.
[10] Ibid. p. 573.

of Asia Minor.   Several have a ram or lamb on one side, and a cross on the other.[1]   On some of the early coins of the Phenicians, the cross is found attached to a chaplet of beads placed in a circle, so as

to form a complete rosary, such as the Lamas of Thibet and China, the Hindoos, and the Roman Catholics, now tell over while they pray.[2]   On a Phenician medal, found in the ruins of Citium, in Cyprus, and printed in Dr. Clark's "Travels" (vol. ii. c. xi.), are engraved a cross, a rosary, and a lamb.[3]   This is the "Lamb of God who taketh away the sins of the world."

The ancient Etruscans revered the cross as a religious emblem.   This sacred sign, accompanied with the heart, is to be seen on their monu-

FIG. 26

ments.   Fig. No. 27, taken from the work of Gorrio (Tab. xxxv.), shows an ancient tomb with angels and the cross thereon.   It would answer perfectly for a Christian cemetery.

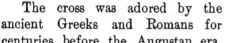

FIG. 27

FIG. 28

The   cross   was   adored   by   the ancient   Greeks   and   Romans   for centuries before the Augustan era.   An ancient inscription in Thessaly is accompanied by a Calvary cross (Fig. No. 28); and Greek crosses of equal arms adorn the tomb of Midas (one of the ancient kings), in Phrygia.[4]

[1] Curious Myths, p. 290.   [3] See Illustration in Anacalypsis, vol. i. p.
[2] Knight: Anct. Art and Mytho., p. 31.   224.
                     [4] Baring-Gould : Curious Myths, p. 291.

The adoration of the cross by the Romans is spoken of by the Christian Father Minucius Felix, when denying the charge of idolatry which was made against his sect.

" As for the adoration of cross," (says he to the Romans), "which you object against us, I must tell you that we neither adore crosses nor desire them. You it is, ye Pagans, who worship wooden gods, who are the most likely people to adore wooden crosses, as being part of the same substance with your deities. For what else are your ensigns, flags, and standards, but crosses, gilt and beautiful. Your victorious trophies not only represent a cross, but a cross with a man upon it."[1]

The principal silver coin among the Romans, called the *denarius*, had on one side a personification of Rome as a warrior with a helmet, and on the reverse, a chariot drawn by four horses. The driver had a cross-standard in one hand. This is a representation of a denarius of the earliest kind, which was first coined 296 B. C.[2] The cross was used on the roll of the Roman soldiery as the sign of *life*.[3]

But, long before the Romans, long before the Etruscans, there lived in the plains of Northern Italy a people to whom the cross was a religious symbol, the sign beneath which they laid their dead to rest ; a people of whom history tells nothing, knowing not their name ; but of whom antiquarian research has learned this, that they lived in ignorance of the arts of civilization, that they dwelt in villages built on platforms over lakes, and that they trusted to the cross to guard, and may be to revive, their loved ones whom they committed to the dust.

The examination of the tombs of Golasecca proves, in a most convincing, positive, and precise manner that which the terramares of Emilia had only indicated, but which had been confirmed by the cemetery of Villanova, that above a thousand years B. C., the cross was already a religious emblem of frequent employment.[4]

"It is more than a coincidence," (says the Rev. S. Baring-Gould), "that Osiris by the cross should give life eternal to the spirits of the just; that with the cross Thor should smite the head of the great Serpent, and bring to life those who were slain; that beneath the cross the Muysca mothers should lay their babes, trusting to that sign to secure them from the power of evil spirits; that with that symbol to protect them, the ancient people of Northern Italy should lay them down in the dust."[5]

The cross was also found among the ruins of Pompeï.[6]

It was a sacred emblem among the ancient Scandinavians.

---

[1] Octavius, ch. xxix.
[2] See Chambers's Encyclo., art. " Denarius."
[3] Curious Myths, p. 291.
[4] Ibid. pp. 291, 296.
[5] Ibid. p. 311.
[6] The Pentateuch Examined, vol. vi. p. 115.

"It occurs" (says Mr. R. Payne Knight), "on many Runic monuments found in Sweden and Denmark, which are of an age long anterior to the approach of Christianity to those countries, and, probably, to its appearance in the world."[1]

Their god Thor, son of the Supreme god Odin, and the goddess Freyga, had the hammer for his symbol. It was with this hammer that Thor crushed the head of the great Mitgard serpent, that he destroyed the giants, that he restored the dead goats to life, which drew his car, that he consecrated the pyre of Baldur. *This hammer was a cross.*[2]

The cross of Thor is still used in Iceland as a magical sign in connection with storms of wind and rain.

King Olaf, Longfellow tells us, when keeping Christmas at Drontheim :

> " O'er his drinking-horn, the sign
> He made of the Cross Divine,
> And he drank, and mutter'd his prayers;
> But the Berserks evermore
> Made the sign of the hammer of Thor
> 			Over theirs."

Actually, they both made the same symbol.

This we are told by Snorro Sturleson, in the Heimskringla (Saga iv. c. 18), when he describes the sacrifice at Lade, at which King Hakon, Athelstan's foster-son, was present :

"Now when the first full goblet was filled, Earl Sigurd spoke some words over it, and blessed it in Odin's name, and drank to the king out of the horn; and the king then took it, and made the sign of the cross over it. Then said Kaare of Greyting, 'What does the king mean by doing so? will he not sacrifice?' But Earl Sigurd replied, 'The King is doing what all of you do who trust in your power and strength; for he is blessing the full goblet in the name of Thor, by making the sign of his hammer over it before he drinks it.'"[3]

The cross was also a *sacred* emblem among the *Laplanders.* " In solemn sacrifices, all the Lapland idols were marked with it from the blood of the victims."[4]

It was adored by the ancient *Druids* of Britain, and is to be seen on the so-called " fire towers " of Ireland and Scotland. The "consecrated trees" of the Druids had a *cross beam* attached to them, making the figure of a cross. On several of the most curious and most ancient monuments of Britain, the cross is to be seen, evidently cut thereon by the Druids. Many large stones throughout Ireland have these Druid crosses cut in them.[5]

[1] Anct. Art and Mytho., p. 30.
[2] Curious Myths, pp. 280, 281.
[3] Ibid. pp. 281, 282.
[4] Knight : Ancient Art and Mytho., p. 30.
[5] See Celtic Druids, pp. 126, 130, 131.

Cleland observes, in his " Attempt to Revive Celtic Literature,"
that the Druids taught the doctrine of an overruling providence, and
the immortality of the soul : that they had also their Lent, their
Purgatory, their Paradise, their Hell, their Sanctuaries, and the
similitude of the May-pole *in form to the cross.*[1]

" In the Island of I-com-kill, at the monastery of the Culdees,
at the time of the Reformation, there were three hundred and sixty
crosses."[2] The Caaba at Mecca was surrounded by three hundred
and sixty crosses.[3] This number has nothing whatever to do with
Christianity, but is to be found everywhere among the ancients.
It represents the number of days of the ancient year.[4]

When the Spanish missionaries first set foot upon the soil of
America, in the fifteenth century, they were amazed to find that
the *cross* was as devoutly worshiped by the red Indians as by themselves. The hallowed symbol challenged their attention on every
hand, and in almost every variety of form. And, what is still more
remarkable, the cross was not only associated with other objects corresponding in every particular with those delineated on Babylonian
monuments ; but it was also distinguished by the Catholic appellations, " the tree of subsistence," " the wood of health," " the emblem
of life," &c.[5]

When the Spanish missionaries found that the cross was no new
object of veneration to the red men, they were in doubt whether to
ascribe the fact to the pious labors of St. Thomas, whom they thought
might have found his way to America, or the sacrilegious subtlety
of Satan. It was the central object in the great temple of Coza-
mel, and is still preserved on the *bas-reliefs* of the ruined city of
Palenque. From time immemorial it had received the prayers
and sacrifices of the Aztecs and Toltecs, and was suspended as an
august emblem from the walls of temples in Popogan and Cundin-
amarca.[6]

The ruined city of Palenque is in the depths of the forests of
Central America. It was not inhabited at the time of the conquest
of Mexico by the Spaniards. They discovered the temples and palaces of Chiapa, but of Palenque they knew nothing. According to
tradition it was founded by Votan in the ninth century before the
Christian era. The principal building in this ruined city is the
palace. A noble tower rises above the courtyard in the centre. In

[1] Cleland, p. 102, in Anac.. i. p. 716.
[2] Celtic Druids, p. 242, and Chambers's Encyclo., art. "Cross."
[3] Ibid.
[4] See Maurice : Indian Antiquities, vol. ii. 103.
[5] The Pentateuch Examined, vol. vi. p. 114.
[6] Brinton : Myths of the New World, p. 95.

this building are several small temples or chapels, with altars standing. At the back of one of these altars is a slab of gypsum, on
which are sculptured two figures, one on each side of a cross (Fig.
No. 29). The cross is surrounded with rich feather-work, and orna-
mental chains.[1] "The style of scripture," says Mr. Baring-Gould,
"and the accompanying hieroglyphic inscriptions, leave no room
for doubting it to be a heathen representation."[2]

The same cross is represented on old pre-Mexican MSS., as in
the Dresden Codex, and that in the possession of Herr Fejervary, at

the end of which is a colossal cross, in
the midst of which is represented a bleed-
ing deity, and figures stand round a *Tau*
cross, upon which is perched the sacred
bird.[3]

The cross was also used in the north
of Mexico. It occurs among the Mix-
tecas and in Queredaro. Siguenza speaks
of an Indian cross which was found in
the cave of Mixteca Baja. Among the
ruins on the island of Zaputero, in Lake
Nicaragua, were also found old crosses
reverenced by the Indians. White marble
crosses were found on the island of St.
Ulloa, on its discovery. In the state of

Fig. 29.

Oaxaca, the Spaniards found that wooden crosses were erected
as sacred symbols, so also in Aguatoleo, and among the Zapa-
tecas. The cross was venerated as far as Florida on one side, and
Cibola on the other. In South America, the same sign was considered symbolical and sacred. It was revered in Paraguay. In Peru
the Incas honored a cross made out of a single piece of jasper; it
was an emblem belonging to a former civilization.[4]

Among the Muyscas at Cumana the cross was regarded with
devotion, and was believed to be endowed with power to drive away
evil spirits; consequently new-born children were placed under the
sign.[5]

The Toltecs said that their national deity Quetzalcoatle—whom
we have found to be a virgin-born and crucified Saviour—had intro-

[1] Stephens : Central America, vol. ii. p. 346, ous Myths, pp. 298, 299.
in Curious Myths, p. 296.   [4] Curious Myths, p. 299.
[2] Curious Myths, p. 298.   [5] Müller : Geschichte der Amerikanischen
[3] Klemm Kulturgeschichte, v. 142, in Curi-   Urreligionen, in Ibid.

duced the sign and ritual of the cross, and it was called the "Tree of Nutriment," or "Tree of Life."[1]

Malcom, in his "Antiquities of Britain," says .

"Gomara tells that St. Andrew's cross, which is the same with that of Burgundy, was in great veneration among the Cumas, in South America, and that they fortified themselves with the cross against the incursions of evil spirits, and were in use to put them upon new-born infants; which thing very justly deserves admiration."[2]

Felix Cabrara, in his "Description of the Ancient City of Mexico," says:

"The adoration of the cross has been more general in the world, than that of any other emblem. It is to be found in the ruins of the fine city of Mexico, near Palenque, where there are many examples of it among the hieroglyphics on the buildings."[3]

In "Chambers's Encyclopædia" we find the following:

"It appears that the sign of the *cross* was in use *as an emblem having certain religious and mystic meanings attached to it, long before the Christian era;* and the Spanish conquerors were astonished to find it *an object of religious veneration* among the nations of Central and South America."[4]

Lord Kingsborough, in his "Antiquities of Mexico," speaks of crosses being found in Mexico, Peru, and Yucatan.[5] He also informs us that the *banner* of Montezuma was a cross, and that the historical paintings of the "Codex Vaticanus" represent him carrying a cross as his banner.[6]

A very fine and highly polished marble cross which was taken from the Incas, was placed in the Roman Catholic cathedral at Cuzco.[7]

Few cases have been more powerful in producing mistakes in ancient history, than the idea, hastily taken by Christians in all ages, that every monument of antiquity marked with a cross, or with any of those symbols which they conceived to be monograms of their god, was of Christian origin. The early Christians did not adopt it as one of their symbols; it was not until Christianity began to be paganized that it became a Christian monogram, and even then it was not the cross as we know it to-day. "It is not until the middle of the *fifth* century that the pure form of the cross emerges to light."[8] The cross of Constantine was nothing more than the ⚹, the monogram of Osiris, and afterwards of Christ.[9] This is seen

[1] Curious Myths, p. 301.
[2] Quoted in Anacalypsis, vol. ii. p. 80.
[3] Quoted in Celtic Druids, p. 131.
[4] Chambers's Encyclo., art. "Cross."
[5] Mexican Antiquities, vol. vi. pp. 165, 180.
[6] Ibid. p. 179.
[7] Higgins: Anacalypsis, vol. ii. p. 82.
[8] Jameson's Hist. of Our Lord in Art, vol. ii. p. 318.
[9] "These two letters in the old Samaritan, as found on coins, stand, the first for 400, the second for 200—600. This is the staff of Osiris.

from the fact that the "*Labarum*," or sacred banner of Constantine —on which was placed the sign by which he was to conquer—was inscribed with this sacred monogram. Fig. No. 30 is a representation of the Labarum, taken from Smith's Dictionary of the Bible. The author of "The History of Our Lord in Art" says:

> "It would be difficult to prove that the cross of Constantine was of the simple construction as now understood. As regards the Labarum, the coins of the time, in which it is expressly set forth, proves that the so-called cross upon it was nothing else than the same ever-recurring monogram of Christ."[1]

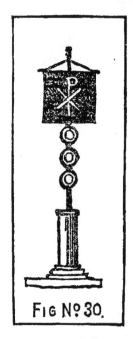

FIG No. 30.

Now, this so-called monogram of Christ, like everything else called Christian, is of Pagan origin. It was the monogram of the Egyptian Saviour, Osiris, and also of Jupiter Ammon.[2] As M. Basnage remarks in his *Hist. de Juif :*[3]

> "Nothing can be more opposite to Jesus Christ, than the Oracle of *Jupiter Ammon*. And yet the *same cipher* served the false god as well as the true one ; for we see a medal of Ptolemy, King of Cyrene, having an eagle carrying a thunderbolt, *with the monogram of Christ to signify the Oracle of Jupiter Ammon.*"

Rev. J. P. Lundy says :

> "Even the P.X., which I had thought to be exclusively Christian, are to be found in combination thus: ☧ (just as the early Christians used it), on coins of the Ptolemies, and on those of Herod the Great, struck forty years before our era, together with this other form, so often seen on the early Christian monuments, viz.: ⳩ ?"[4]

·This monogram is also to be found on the coins of Decius, a Pagan Roman emperor, who ruled during the commencement of the third century.[5]

Another form of the same monogram is ⳨ and X H. The monogram of the *Sun* was ♀ . P. H. All these are now called monograms of Christ, and are to be met with in great numbers in almost

---

It is also the monogram of Osiris, and has been adopted by the Christians, and is to be seen in the churches in Italy in thousands of places. See Basnage (lib. iii. c. xxxiii.), where several other instances of this kind may be found. In Addison's 'Travels in Italy' there is an account of a medal, at Rome, of Constantine, with this inscription ; *In hoc signo*

Victor eris ☧." (Anacalypsis, vol. i. p. 222.)
[1] Hist. of Our Lord in Art, vol. ii. p. 316.
[2] See Celtic Druids, p. 127, and Bonwick's Egyptian Belief, p. 218.
[3] Bk. iii. c. xxiii. in Anac., i. p. 219.
[4] Monumental Christianity. p. 125.
[5] See Celtic Druids, pp. 127, 128.

every church in Italy.' The monogram of Mercury was a cross.'
The monogram of the Egyptian Taut was formed by three crosses.'
The monogram of Saturn was a cross and a ram's horn; it was also
a monogram of Jupiter.' The monogram of Venus was a cross
and a circle.' The monogram of the Phenician Astarte, and the
Babylonian Bal, was also a cross and a circle.' It was also that of
Freya, Holda, and Aphrodite.' Its true significance was the Linga
and Yoni.

The cross, which was so universally adored, in its different forms
among heathen nations, was intended as an emblem or symbol of the
Sun, of *eternal life*, the *generative powers*, &c.'

As with the cross, and the X. P., so likewise with many other
so-called Christian symbols — they are borrowed from Paganism.
Among these may be mentioned the mystical three letters I. H. S.,
to this day retained in some of our Protestant, as well as Roman
Catholic churches, and falsely supposed to stand for "*Jesu Hominium Salvator*," or "In Hoc Signo." It is none other than the identical monogram of the heathen god *Bacchus*,' and was to be seen
on the coins of the Maharajah of *Cashmere*.'' Dr. Inman says:

"For a long period I. H. S., I. E. E. S, was a monogram of Bacchus; letters
now adopted by Romanists. *Hesus* was an old divinity of Gaul, possibly left by
the Phenicians. We have the same I. H. S. in *Jazabel*, and reproduced in our
Isabel. The idea connected with the word is '*Phallic Vigor*.'"¹¹

The TRIANGLE, which is to be seen at the present day in Christian churches as an emblem of the "Ever-blessed Trinity," is also
of Pagan origin, and was used by them for the same purpose.

Among the numerous symbols, the Triangle is conspicuous in
India. Hindoos attached a mystic signification to its *three* sides,
and generally placed it in their temples. It was often composed of
lotus plants, with an eye in the center.'' It was sometimes represented in connection with the mystical word AUM'' (Fig. No. 31),
and sometimes surrounded with rays of glory.''

This symbol was engraved upon the tablet of the ring which the
religious chief, called the *Brahm-âtma* wore, as one of the signs of

---

¹ See Ibid. and Monumental Christianity,
pp. 15, 92, 123, 126, 127.
² See Celtic Druids, p. 101. Anacalypsis,
vol. I. p. 220. Indian Antiq., ii. 68.
³ See Celtic Druids, p. 101. Bonwick's
Egyptian Belief, p. 103.
⁴ See Celtic Druids, p. 127, and Taylor's
Diegesis, p. 201.
⁵ See Celtic Druids, p. 127.
⁶ See Bonwick's Egyptian Belief, p. 218.
⁷ See Cox: Aryan Mythology, vol. ii. 115.

⁸ See The Pentateuch Examined, vol. vi.
pp. 113-115.
⁹ See Higgins: Anacalypsis, vol. i. pp. 291
and 328. Taylor's Diegesis, p. 187. Celtic
Druids, p. 127, and Isis Unveiled, p. 527, vol. ii.
¹⁰ See Bonwick's Egyptian Belief, p. 212.
¹¹ Ancient Faiths, vol. i. pp. 518, 519.
¹² See Prog. Relig. Ideas, vol. i. p. 94.
¹³ This word—AUM—stood for Brahma,
Vishnu and Siva, the Hindoo Trinity.
¹⁴ See Isis Unveiled, vol. ii. p. 81.

his dignity, and it was used by the Buddhists as emblematic of the Trinity.[1]

The ancient *Egyptians* signified their divine *Triad* by a single *Triangle.*[2]

Mr. Bonwick says:

> "The *Triangle* was a religious form from the first. It is to be recognized in the Obelisk and Pyramid (of Egypt). To this day, in some Christian churches, the priest's blessing is given as it was in Egypt, by the sign of a triangle; viz.: two fingers and a thumb. An Egyptian god is seen with a triangle over his shoulders. This figure, in ancient Egyptian theology, was the type of the Holy Trinity—three in one."[3]

And Dr. Inman says:

> "The Triangle is a sacred symbol in our modern churches, and it was the sign used in ancient temples before the initiated, to indicate the Trinity—three persons 'co-eternal together, and co-equal.'"[4]

The Triangle is found on ancient Greek monuments.[5] An an-

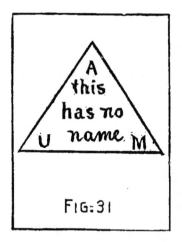

FIG: 31

cient seal (engraved in the Mémoires de l'Académie royale des Inscriptions et Belles Lettres), supposed to be of Phenician origin, "has as subject a standing figure between two stars, beneath which are handled crosses. Above the head of the deity is the TRIANGLE, or symbol of the Trinity."[6]

One of the most conspicuous among the symbols intended to represent the Trinity, to be seen in Christian churches, is the compound leaf of the *trefoil*. Modern story had attributed to St. Patrick the idea of demonstrating a trinity in unity, by showing the *shamrock* to his hearers; but, says Dr. Inman, "like many other things attributed to the moderns, the idea belongs to the ancients."[7]

The *Trefoil* adorned the head of *Osiris*, the Egyptian Saviour, and is to be found among the Pagan symbols or representations of

---

[1] See Isis Unveiled, vol. ii. p. 31.
[2] Knight: Anct. Art and Mytho., p. 196.
[3] Bonwick's Egyptian Belief, p. 213.
[4] Ancient Faiths, vol. i. p. 328.

[5] See Knight: Anct. Art and Mytho., p. 196.
[6] Curious Myths, p. 289.
[7] Inman's Ancient Faiths, vol. i. pp. 153, 154.

the *three-in-one* mystery.[1] Fig. No. 32 is a representation of the *Trefoil* used by the ancient Hindoos as emblematic of their celestial Triad — Brahma, Vishnu and Siva — and afterwards adopted by the Christians.[2] The leaf of the *Vila,* or *Bel-tree,* is typical of Siva's attributes, because *triple* in form.[3]

The *Trefoil* was a sacred plant among the ancient Druids of Britain. It was to them an emblem of the mysterious *three in one*.[4] It is to be seen on their *coins.*[5]

The *Tripod* was very generally employed among the ancients as an emblem of the *Trinity,* and is found composed in an endless variety of ways. On the coins of Menecratia, in Phrygia, it is represented between two asterisks, with a serpent wreathed around a battle-axe, inserted into it, as an accessory symbol, signifying preservation and destruction. In the ceremonial of worship, the number *three* was employed with mystic solemnity.[6]

The three lines, or three human legs, springing from a central disk or circle, which has been called a *Trinacria,* and supposed to allude to the

FIG. 32.

island of Sicily, is simply an ancient emblem of the *Trinity.* "It is of *Asiatic* origin; its earliest appearance being upon the very ancient coins of Aspendus in Pamphylia; sometimes alone in the square incuse, and sometimes upon the body of an eagle or the back of a lion."[7]

We have already seen, in the chapter on the *crucifixion,* that the earliest emblems of the Christian Saviour were the "Good Shepherd" and the "Lamb." Among these may also be mentioned the *Fish.* "The only satisfactory explanation why Jesus should be represented as a *Fish,*" says Mr. King, in his Gnostics and their Remains,[8] "seems to be the circumstance that in the quaint jargon of the Talmud the Messiah is often designated 'Dag,' or 'The Fish;'" and Mr. Lundy, in his "Monumental Christianity," says:

---

[1] See Bonwick's Egyptian Belief, p. 242.
[2] See Inman's Pagan and Christian Symbolism, p. 30.
[3] See Williams' Hinduism, p. 99.
[4] See Myths of the British Druids, p. 448.
[5] Ibid. p. 601.
[6] Knight: Anct. Art and Mytho., p. 170.
[7] Ibid. pp. 169, 170.
[8] Page 188.

"Next to the sacred monogram (the ☧) the *Fish* takes its place in import-ance as a sign of Christ in his special office of *Saviour*." "In the Talmud the Messiah is called 'Dag' or 'Fish.'" "Where did the Jews learn to apply 'Dag' to their Messiah? And why did the primitive Christians adopt it as a sign of Christ?" "I cannot disguise facts. Truth demands no concealment or apology. *Paganism* has its types and prophecies of Christ as well as Judaism. What then is the Dag-on of the old Babylonians? The *fish*-god or being that taught them all their civilization."[1]

As Mr. Lundy says, "truth demands no concealment or apol-ogy," therefore, when the truth is exposed, we find that *Vishnu*, the Hindoo Messiah, Preserver, Mediator and *Saviour*, was repre-sented as a "dag," or fish. The *Fish* takes its place in importance as a sign of *Vishnu* in his special office of *Saviour*.

Prof. Monier Williams says:

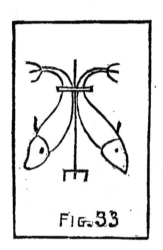

FIG. 33

"It is as *Vishnu* that the Supreme Being, according to the Hindoos, exhibited his sympa-thy with human trials, his love for the human race. Nine principal occasions have already occurred in which the god has thus interposed for the salvation of his creatures. The first was *Matsaya*, the *Fish*. In this Vishnu became a fish to save the seventh Manu, the progenitor of the human race, from the universal deluge."[2]

We have already seen, in Chap. IX., the identity of the Hindoo *Matsaya* and the Babylonian Dagon.

The fish was sacred among the Babylonians, Assyrians and Phenicians, as it is among the Romanists of to-day. It was sacred also to *Venus*, and the Romanists still eat it on the very day of the week which was called "*Dies veneris*," Venus' day; fish day.[3] It was an emblem of *fecundity*. The most ancient symbol of the productive power was a fish, and it is accordingly found to be the universal symbol upon many of the earliest coins.[4] Pythagoras and his followers did not eat fish. They were ascetics, and the eat-ing of fish was supposed to tend to carnal desires. This ancient superstition is entertained by many even at the present day.

The fish was the earliest symbol of Christ Jesus. Fig. No. 33 is a design from the catacombs.[5] This cross-fish is not unlike the sacred monogram.

---

[1] Monumental Christianity, pp. 130, 132, 133.
[2] Indian Wisdom, p. 329.
[3] Inman: Anct. Faiths, vol. i. pp. 528, 529, and Müller: Science of Relig., p. 315.
[4] Knight: Anct. Art and Mytho., p. 111.
[5] Lillie: Buddha and Early Buddhism, p. 227.

That the Christian Saviour should be called a fish, may at first appear strange, but when the mythos is properly understood (as we shall endeavor to make it in Chap. **XXXIX.**), it will not appear so. The Rev. Dr. Geikie, in his "Life and Words of Christ," says that a fish stood for his *name*, from the significance of the Greek letters in the word that expresses the idea, and for this reason he was called a fish. But, we may ask, why was Buddha not only called Fo, or Po, but *Dag-Po*, which was literally the Fish Po, or Fish Buddha? The fish did not stand for his name. The idea that Jesus was called a fish because the Messiah is designated "Dag" in the Talmud, is also an unsatisfactory explanation.

Julius Africanus (an early Christian writer) says :

"Christ is the great Fish taken by the fish-hook of God, and whose flesh nourishes the whole world."[1]

> " The fish fried
> Was Christ that died,"

is an old couplet.[2]

Prosper Africanus calls Christ,

"The great fish who satisfied for himself the disciples on the shore, and offered himself as a fish to the whole world."[3]

The *Serpent* was also an emblem of Christ Jesus, or in other words, represented Christ, among some of the early Christians.

Moses *set up* a brazen *serpent* in the wilderness, and Christian divines have seen in this a type of Christ Jesus. Indeed, the Gospels sanction this; for it is written :

" As Moses lifted up the serpent in the wilderness, so must the Son of man be lifted up."

From this serpent, Tertullian asserts, the early sect of Christians called *Ophites* took their rise. Epiphanius says, that the " Ophites sprung out of the Nicolaitans and Gnostics, who were so called from the *serpent*, which they worshiped." "The Gnostics," he adds, "*taught that the ruler of the world was of a dracontic form.*" The Ophites preserved live serpents in their sacred chest, and looked upon them as the *mediator* between them and God. Manes, in the third century, taught serpent worship in Asia Minor, under the name of Christianity, promulgating that

" *Christ was an incarnation of the Great Serpent, who glided over the cradle of the Virgin Mary, when she was asleep, at the age of a year and a half.*"[4]

" The Gnostics," says Irenaeus, " represented the Mind (the Son,

[1] Quoted in Monumental Christianity, p. 134.   [2] Ibid. p. 135.   [3] Ibid. p. 372.   [4] Squire : Serpent Symbol, p. 246.

the Wisdom) in the form of a serpent," and " the Ophites," says
Epiphanius, " have a veneration for the serpent ; they esteem him
the same as Christ." " They even quote the Gospels," says Tertullian, " to prove that Christ was an imitation of the serpent."[1]

The question now arises, Why was the Christian Saviour represented as a serpent? Simply because the heathen Saviours were
represented in like manner.

From the earliest times of which we have any historical notice,
the serpent has been connected with the preserving gods, or Saviours ; the gods of goodness and of wisdom. In Hindoo mythology, the serpent is intimately associated with Vishnu, the preserving
god, the Saviour.[2] Serpents are often associated with the Hindoo
gods, as emblems of eternity.[3] It was a very sacred animal among
the Hindoos.[4]

Worshipers of Buddha venerate serpents. " This animal,"
says Mr. Wake, " became equal in importance as Buddha himself."
And Mr. Lillie says :

"That God was worshiped at an early date by the Buddists under the symbol
of the *Serpent* is proved from the sculptures of oldest topes, where worshipers
are represented so doing."[5]

The Egyptians also venerated the serpent. It was the special
symbol of Thoth, a primeval deity of Syro-Egyptian mythology,
and of all those gods, such as Hermes and Seth, who can be connected with him.[6] Kneph and Apap were also represented as
serpents.[7]

Herodotus, when he visited Egypt, found sacred serpents in the
temples. Speaking of them, he says :

"In the neighborhood of Thebes, there are sacred serpents, not at all hurtful
to men: they are diminutive in size, and carry two horns that grow on the top
of the head. When these serpents die, they bury them in the temple of Jupiter;
for they say they are sacred to that god."[8]

The third member of the Chaldean triad, Héa, or Hoa, was represented by a serpent. According to Sir Henry Rawlinson, the
most important titles of this deity refer " to his functions as the
source of all knowledge and science." Not only is he " The Intelligent Fish," but his name may be read as signifying both " Life "
and a " Serpent," and he may be considered as "figured by the
great serpent which occupies so conspicuous a place among the

1 Fergusson : Tree and Serpent Worship, p. 9.   5 Wake, p. 73. Lillie : p. 20.
2 Wake : Phallism in Ancient Religs., p. 72.   6 Wake, p. 40, and Bunsen's Keys, p.
3 Williams' Hinduism, p. 169.   101.
4 Knight : Anct. Art and Mytho., p. 16, and   7 Champollion, pp. 144, 145.
Fergusson : Tree and Serpent Worship.   8 Herodotus, bk. ii. ch. 74.

symbols of the gods on the black stones recording Babylonian benefactors."[1]

The Phenicians and other eastern nations venerated the serpent as symbols of their beneficent gods.[2]

As god of medicine, Apollo, the central figure in Grecian mythology, was originally worshiped under the form of a serpent, and men invoked him as the "Helper." He was the Solar Serpent-god.[3]

Æsculapius, the healing god, the Saviour, was also worshiped under the form of a serpent.[4] "Throughout Hellas," says Mr. Cox, "Æsculapius remained the 'Healer,' and the 'Restorer of Life,' and accordingly the serpent is everywhere his special emblem."[5]

Why the serpent was the symbol of the Saviours and beneficent gods of antiquity, will be explained in Chap. XXXIX.

The *Dove*, among the Christians, is the symbol of the Holy Spirit. The Matthew narrator relates that when Jesus went up out of the water, after being baptized by John, "the heavens were opened unto him; and he saw the Spirit of God descending like a *dove*, and lighting upon him."

Here is another piece of Paganism, as we find that the *Dove* was the symbol of the Holy Spirit among all nations of antiquity. Rev. J. P. Lundy, speaking of this, says:

"It is a remarkable fact that this spirit (*i. e.*, the Holy Spirit) has been symbolized among all religious and civilized nations by the *Dove*."[6]

And Earnest De Bunsen says:

"The symbol of the Spirit of God was the *Dove*, in Greek, *peleia*, and the Samaritans had a brazen fiery dove, instead of the brazen fiery serpent. Both referred to fire, the symbol of the Holy Ghost."[7]

Buddha is represented, like Christ Jesus, with a dove hovering over his head.[8]

The virgin goddess Juno is often represented with a dove on her head. It is also seen on the heads of the images of Astarte, Cybele, and Isis; it was sacred to Venus, and was intended as a symbol of the Holy Spirit.[9]

Even in the remote islands of the Pacific Ocean, a *bird* is believed to be an emblem of the Holy Spirit.[10]

R. Payne Knight, in speaking of the "mystic Dove," says:

[1] Wake : Phallism in Anct. Religs., p. 30.
[2] See Knight : Anct. Art and Mytho., p. 16. Cox : Aryan Mytho., vol. ii. p. 128. Ferguson's Tree and Serpent Worship, and Squire's Serpent Symbol.
[3] Deane : Serpent Worship, p. 218.
[4] Tree and Serpent Worship, p. 7, and Bulfinch : Age of Fable, p. 397.
[5] Aryan Mytho., vol. ii. p. 36.
[6] Monumental Christianity, p. 293.
[7] Bunsen's Angel-Messiah, p. 44.
[8] See ch. xxix.
[9] Monumental Christianity, pp. 323 and 293.
[10] Knight : Anct. Art and Mytho., p 169

"A bird was probably chosen for the emblem of the third person (*i. e.*, the Holy Ghost) to signify incubation, by which was figuratively expressed the fructification of inert matter, caused by the vital spirit moving upon the waters.

"The *Dove* would naturally be selected in the East in preference to every other species of bird, on account of its domestic familiarity with man; it usually lodging under the same roof with him, and being employed as his messenger from one remote place to another. Birds of this kind were also remarkable for the care of their offspring, and for a sort of conjugal attachment and fidelity to each other, as likewise for the peculiar fervency of their sexual desires, whence they were sacred to Venus, and emblems of love."[1]

Masons' marks are conspicuous among the Christian symbols. On some of the most ancient Roman Catholic cathedrals are to be found figures of Christ Jesus with Mason's marks about him.

Many are the so-called Christian symbols which are direct importations from paganism. To enumerate them would take, as we have previously said, a volume of itself. For further information on this subject the reader is referred to Dr. Inman's "Ancient Pagan and Modern Christian Symbolism," where he will see how many ancient Indian, Egyptian, Etruscan, Grecian and Roman symbols have been adopted by Christians, a great number of which are *Phallic* emblems.[2]

---

[1] Knight's Ancient Art and Mythology, p. 170.

[2] See also, R. Payne Knight's Worship of Priapus, and the other works of Dr. Thomas Inman.

CHAPTER XXXIV.

THE BIRTH-DAY OF CHRIST JESUS.

CHRISTMAS — December the 25th — is a day which has been set apart by the Christian church on which to celebrate the birth of their Lord and Saviour, Christ Jesus, and is considered by the majority of persons to be really the day on which he was born. This is altogether erroneous, as will be seen upon examination of the subject.

There was no uniformity in the period of observing the Nativity among the early Christian churches; some held the festival in the month of May or April, others in January.[1]

The *year* in which he was born is also as uncertain as the month or day. "The year in which it happened," says Mosheim, the ecclesiastical historian, "has not hitherto been fixed with certainty, notwithstanding the deep and laborious researches of the learned."[2]

According to IRENÆUS (A. D. 190), on the authority of "The Gospel," and "all the elders who were conversant in Asia with John, the disciple of the Lord," Christ Jesus lived to be nearly, if not quite, *fifty years of age.* If this celebrated Christian father is correct, and who can say he is not, Jesus was born some twenty years before the time which has been assigned as that of his birth.[3]

The Rev. Dr. Giles says:

"Concerning the *time* of Christ's birth there are even greater doubts than about the *place;* for, though the four Evangelists have noticed several contemporary facts, which would seem to settle this point, yet on comparing these dates with the general history of the period, we meet with serious discrepancies, which involve the subject in the greatest uncertainty."[4]

Again he says:

---

[1] See Bible for Learners vol. iii. p. 66; Chambers's Encyclo., art. "*Christmas.*"

[2] Eccl. Hist., vol. i. p. 53. Quoted in Taylor's Diegesis, p. 104.

[3] See Chapter XL., this work.

[4] Hebrew and Christian Records, vol. ii. p. 189.

" Not only do we date our time from the exact year in which Christ *is said to-have been born,* but our ecclesiastical calendar has determined with scrupulous minuteness the day and almost the hour at which every particular of Christ's wonderful life is stated to have happened.   All this is implicitly believed by millions; *yet all these things are among the most uncertain and shadowy that history has recorded.   We have no clue to either the day or the time of year, or even the year itself, in which Christ was born.*"[1]

Some Christian writers fix the year 4 B. C., as the time when he was born, others the year 5 B. C., and again others place his time of birth at about 15 B. C.   The Rev. Dr. Geikie, speaking of this, in his *Life of Christ,* says :

" The whole subject is *very uncertain.*   Ewald appears to fix the date of the birth at *five* years earlier than our era.   Petavius and Usher fix it on the 25th of December, *five* years before our era.   Bengel on the 25th of December, *four* years before our era; Anger and Winer, *four* years before our era, *in the Spring;* Scaliger, *three* years before our era, in *October;* St. Jerome, *three* years before our era, on December 25th; Eusebius, *two* years before our era, on *January* 6th; and Idler, *seven* years before our era, in *December.*"[2]

Albert Barnes writes in a manner which implies that he knew all about the *year* (although he does not give any authorities), but knew nothing about the *month.*   He says :

" The birth of Christ took place *four* years before the common era.   That cra began to be used about A.D. 526, being first employed by Dionysius, and is supposed to have been placed about four years too late.   Some make the difference two, others three, four, five, and even eight years.   He was born at the commencement of the last year of the reign of Herod, or at the close of the year preceding."[3]

" The Jews sent out their flocks into the mountainous and desert regions during the summer months, and took them up in the latter part of October or the first of November, when the cold weather commenced. . . .   It is clear from this that our Saviour was born before the 25th of December, or before what we call *Christmas.*   At that time it is cold, and especially in the high and mountainous regions about Bethlehem.   *God has concealed the time of his birth.   There is no way to ascertain it.*   By different learned men it has been fixed at each month in the year."[4]

Canon Farrar writes with a little more caution, as follows :

" Although the date of Christ's birth cannot be fixed with absolute certainty, there is at least a large amount of evidence to render it *probable* that he was born *four* years before our present era.   It is universally admitted that our received chronology, which is not older than Dionysius Exignus, in the sixth century, is wrong.   But all attempts to discover the *month* and the *day* are useless.   No data whatever exists to enable us to determine them with even approximate accuracy."[5]

---

[1] Hebrew and Christian Records, p. 194.   [4] Ibid. p. 25.
[2] Life of Christ, vol. i. p. 559.   [5] Farrar's Life of Christ, App., pp. 673, 4.
[3] Barnes' Notes, vol. ii. p. 402.

Bunsen attempts to show (on the authority of *Irenæus*, above quoted), that Jesus was born some *fifteen* years before the time assigned, and that he lived to be nearly, if not quite, fifty years of age.[1]

According to Basnage,[2] the Jews placed his birth near a century sooner than the generally assumed epoch. Others have placed it even in the *third century* B. C. This belief is founded on a passage in the "*Book of Wisdom*,"[3] written about 250 B. C., which is supposed to refer to Christ *Jesus*, and none other. In speaking of some individual who lived *at that time*, it says:

"He professeth to have the knowledge of God, and he calleth himself *the child of the Lord*. He was made to reprove our thoughts. He is grievous unto us even to behold; for his life is not like other men's, his ways are of another fashion. We are esteemed of him as counterfeits; he abstaineth from our ways as from filthiness; he pronounceth the end of the just to be blessed, *and maketh his boast that God is his father*. Let us see if his words be true; and let us prove what shall happen in the end of him. For if the *just man* be the son of God, he (God) will help him, and deliver him from the hand of his enemies. Let us examine him with despitefulness and torture, that we may know his meekness, and prove his patience. Let us condemn him with a shameful death; for by his own saying he shall be respected."

This is a very important passage. Of course, the church claim it to be a *prophecy* of what Christ Jesus was to do and suffer, but this does not explain it.

If the writer of the "*Gospel according to Luke*" is correct, Jesus was not born until about A. D. 10, for he explicitly tells us that this event did not happen until Cyrenius was governor of Syria.[4] Now it is well known that Cyrenius was not appointed to this office until long after the death of Herod (during whose reign the Matthew narrator informs us Jesus was born[5]), and that the taxing spoken of by the Luke narrator as having taken place at this time, did not take place until about ten years after the time at which, according to the Matthew narrator, Jesus was born.[6]

Eusebius, the first ecclesiastical historian,[7] places his birth at the time Cyrenius was governor of Syria, and therefore at about A. D. 10. His words are as follows:

"It was the two and fortieth year after the reign of Augustus the Emperor, and the eight and twentieth year after the subduing of Egypt, and the death of Antonius and Cleopatra, when last of all the Ptolemies in Egypt ceased to bear

---

1 Bible Chronology, pp. 73, 74.
2 Hist. de Juif.
3 Chap. ii. 13–20.
4 Luke, ii. 1–7.
5 Matt. ii. 1.
6 See Josephus : Antiq.,bk. xviii. ch. i. sec. i.

7 Eusebius was Bishop of Cesarea from A.D. 315 to 340, in which he died, in the 70th year of his age, thus playing his great part in life chiefly under the reigns of Constantine the Great and his son Constantius.

rule, when our Saviour and Lord Jesus Christ, at the time of the first taxing—
Cyrenius, then President of Syria—was born in Bethlehem, a city of Judea,
according unto the prophecies in that behalf premised."[1]

Had the Luke narrator known anything about Jewish history,
he never would have made so gross a blunder as to place the taxing
of Cyrenius in the days of Herod, and would have saved the immense amount of labor that it has taken in endeavoring to explain
away the effects of his ignorance. One explanation of this mistake
is, that there were *two* assessments, one about the time Jesus was
born, and the other ten years after; but this has entirely failed.
Dr. Hooykaas, speaking of this, says:

"The Evangelist (Luke) falls into the most extraordinary mistakes throughout. In the first place, history is silent as to a census of the whole (Roman)
world ever having been made at all. In the next place, though Quirinius certainly did make such a register in Judea and Samaria, it did not extend to
Galilee ; so that Joseph's household was not affected by it. Besides, *it did not
take place until ten years after the death of Herod*, when his son Archelaus was
deposed by the emperor, and the districts of Judea and Samaria were thrown
into a Roman province. Under the reign of Herod, nothing of the kind took
place, nor was there any occasion for it. Finally, at the time of the birth of
Jesus, the Governor of Syria was not Quirinius, but Quintus Sentius Saturni-
nus."[2]

The institution of the festival of the Nativity of Christ Jesus
being held on the 25th of December, among the Christians, is attributed to Telesphorus, who flourished during the reign of Antonius Pius (A. D. 138–161), but the first *certain* traces of it are found
about the time of the Emperor Commodus (A. D. 180–192).[3]

For a long time the Christians had been trying to discover upon
what particular day Jesus had possibly or probably come into the
world; and conjectures and traditions that rested upon absolutely
no foundation, led one to the 20th of May, another to the 19th or
20th of April, and a third to the 5th of January. At last the opinion of the *community at Rome* gained the upper hand, and the 25th
of December was fixed upon.[4] It was not until the *fifth* century,
however, that this day had been *generally* agreed upon.[5] *How it
happened* that this day finally became fixed as the birthday of
Christ Jesus, may be inferred from what we shall now see.

On the first moment after midnight of the 24th of December
(*i. e.*, on the morning of the 25th), nearly all the nations of the earth,

[1] Eusebius : Eccl. Hist., lib. 1, ch. vi.
[2] Bible for Learners, vol. iii. p. 56.
[3] See Chambers's Encyclo., art. "*Christmas.*"
[4] See Bible for Learners, vol. iii. p. 66.
[5] "By the fifth century, however, whether
from the influence of some tradition, or from
the desire to supplant *Heathen Festivals* of that
period of the year, such as the Saturnalia, the
25th of December had been generally agreed
upon." (Encyclopædia Brit., art. "Christmas."

as if by common consent, celebrated the accouchement of tho *"Queen of Heaven,"* of the *"Celestial Virgin"* of the sphere, and the birth of the god *Sol.*

In *India* this is a period of rejoicing everywhere.[1] It is a great religious festival, and the people *decorate their houses with garlands,* and *make presents to friends and relatives.* This custom is of very great antiquity.[2]

In *China,* religious solemnities are celebrated at the time of the *winter solstice,* the last week in *December,* when all shops are shut up, and the courts are closed.[3]

Buddha, the son of the Virgin Mâya, on whom, according to Chinese tradition, "the Holy Ghost" had descended, was said to have been born on Christmas day, December 25th.[4]

Among the ancient *Persians* their most splendid ceremonials were in honor of their Lord and Saviour *Mithras;* they kept his birthday, with many rejoicings, on the 25th of December.

The author of the *"Celtic Druids"* says:

"It was the custom of the heathen, long before the birth of Christ, to celebrate the birth-day of their gods," and that, "the 25th of December was a great festival with the *Persians,* who, in very early times, celebrated the birth of their god *Mithras.*"[5]

The Rev. Joseph B. Gross, in his *"Heathen Religion,"* also tells us that:

"The ancient Persians celebrated a festival in honor of *Mithras* on the first day succeeding the *Winter Solstice,* the object of which was to *commemorate the birth of Mithras.*"[6]

Among the ancient *Egyptians,* for centuries before the time of Christ Jesus, the 25th of December was set aside as the birthday of their gods. M. Le Clerk De Septehenes speaks of it as follows:

"The ancient Egyptians fixed the pregnancy of *Isis* (the *Queen of Heaven,* and the *Virgin Mother* of the Saviour Horus), on the last days of March, and towards the end of *December* they placed the commemoration of her delivery."[7]

Mr. Bonwick, in speaking of *Horus,* says:

"He is the great God-loved of Heaven. His birth was one of the greatest mysteries of the Egyptian religion. Pictures representing it appeared on the

1 See Monier Williams: Hinduism, p. 181.
2 See Prog. Relig. Ideas, vol. i. p. 126.
3 Ibid. 216.
4 See Bunsen: The Angel-Messiah, pp. x.-25, and 110, and Lillie: Buddha and Buddhism, p. 73.
Some writers have asserted that *Crishna* is said to have been born on December 25th, but this is not the case. His birthday is held in July–August. (See Williams' Hinduism, p. 183, and Life and Religion of the Hindoos, p. 134.)
5 Celtic Druids, p. 163. See also, Prog. Relig. Ideas, vol. i. p. 272; Monumental Christianity, p. 167; Bible for Learners, iii. pp. 66, 67.
6 The Heathen Religion, p. 287. See also, Dupuis: p. 246.
7 Relig. of the Anct. Greeks, p. 214. See also, Higgins: Anacalypsis, vol. ii. p. 99.

walls of temples.   One passed through the holy *Adytum*[1] to the still more
sacred quarter of the temple known as the birth-place of Horus. He was pre-
sumably the child of Deity. *At Christmas time*, or that answering to our festival, his image was brought out of that sanctuary with peculiar ceremonies,
as the image of the infant *Bambino*[2] is still brought out and exhibited in
Rome."[3]

Rigord observes that the Egyptians not only worshiped a *Virgin Mother* "prior to the birth of our Saviour, but exhibited the
effigy of her son lying in the manger, in the manner the infant Jesus was afterwards laid in the cave at Bethlehem."[4]

The "Chronicles of Alexandria," an ancient Christian work,
says :

"Watch how Egypt has constructed the childbirth of a Virgin, and the birth
of her son, *who was exposed in a crib to the adoration of the people.*"[5]

Osiris, son of the "*Holy Virgin*," as they called Ceres, or
Neith, his mother, was born on the 25th of December.[6]

This was also the time celebrated by the ancient *Greeks* as being
the birthday of *Hercules*.   The author of "*The Religion of the Ancient Greeks*" says :

"The night of the *Winter Solstice*, which the Greeks named the triple night,
was that which they thought gave birth to *Hercules*."[7]

He further says :

"It has become an epoch of singular importance in the eyes of the Christian,
who has destined it to celebrate the birth of the Saviour, the *true* Sun of Justice,
who alone came to dissipate the darkness of ignorance."[8]

Bacchus, also, was born at early dawn on the 25th of December.
Mr. Higgins says of him :

"The birth-place of Bacchus, called Sabizius or Sabaoth, was claimed by
several places in Greece ; but on Mount Zelmissus, in Thrace, his worship seems
to have been chiefly celebrated. He was born of a virgin on the 25th of December, and was always called the SAVIOUR. In his Mysteries, he was shown to
the people, as an infant is by the Christians at this day, on Christmas-day morning, in Rome."[9]

The birthday of *Adonis* was celebrated on the 25th of December.   This celebration is spoken of by Tertullian, Jerome, and other

[1] "*Adytum*"—the interior or sacred part of a heathen temple.
[2] "*Bambino*"—a term used for representations of the infant Saviour, Christ Jesus, in *swaddlings*.
[3] Bonwick's Egyptian Belief, p. 157. See also, Dupuis, p. 237.
[4] "Deinceps Egyptii PARITURAM VIRGINEM magno in honore habuerunt ; quin soliti sunt puerum effingere jacentem in præsepe, quali POSTEA in Bethlehemeticâ speluncâ natus est." (Quoted in Anacalypsis, p. 102, of vol. ii.)
[5] Quoted by Bonwick, p. 143.
[6] Anacalypsis, vol. ii. p. 99.
[7] Relig. Anct. Greece, p. 215.
[8] Ibid.
[9] Anacalypsis, vol. ii. p. 102 ; Dupuis, p. 237, and Baring-Gould : Orig. Relig. Belief, vol. i. p. 322.

Fathers of the Church,[1] who inform us that the ceremonies took place in a cave, and that the cave in which they celebrated his mysteries in Bethlehem, was that in which Christ Jesus was born.

This was also a great holy day in ancient Rome. The Rev. Mr. Gross says:

"In *Rome*, before the time of Christ, a festival was observed on the 25th of December, under the name of '*Natalis Solis Invicti*' (Birthday of Sol the Invincible). It was a day of universal rejoicings, illustrated by illuminations and public games."[2] "All public business was suspended, declarations of war and criminal executions were postponed, *friends made presents to one another*, and the slaves were indulged with great liberties."[3]

A few weeks before the winter solstice, the Calabrian shepherds came into Rome to play on the pipes. Ovid alludes to this when he says:

> "Ante Deûm matrem cornu tibicen adunco
> Cum canit, exiguæ quis stipis aera neget."
> —(Epist. i. l. ii.)
>
> *i. e.*, "When to the mighty mother pipes the swain,
> Grudge not a trifle for his pious strain."

This practice is kept up to the present day.

The ancient *Germans*, for centuries before "the *true* Sun of Justice" was ever heard of, celebrated annually, at the time of the *Winter solstice*, what they called their Yule-feast. At this feast agreements were renewed, the gods were consulted as to the future, sacrifices were made to them, and the time was spent in jovial hospitality. Many features of this festival, such as burning the yule-log on Christmas-eve, still survive among us.[4]

Yule was the old name for Christmas. In French it is called *Noel*, which is the Hebrew or Chaldee word *Nule*.[5]

The greatest festival of the year celebrated among the ancient *Scandinavians*, was at the *Winter solstice*. They called the night upon which it was observed, the "*Mother-night*." This feast was named *Jul* — hence is derived the word *Yule* — and was celebrated in honor of *Freyr* (son of the Supreme God Odin, and the goddess Frigga), who was born on that day. Feasting, nocturnal assemblies, and all the demonstrations of a most dissolute joy, were then authorized by the general usage. At this festival the principal guests *received presents* — generally horses, swords, battle-axes, and gold rings—at their departure.[6]

---

[1] Anacalypsis, vol. ii. p. 99.
[2] The Heathen Religion, p. 287; Dupuis, p. 283.
[3] Bulfinch, p. 21.
[4] See Bible for Learners, vol. iii. p. 67, and

Chambers, art. "Yule."
[5] See Chambers's, art. "Yule," and "Celt'c Druids," p. 162.
[6] Mallet's Northern Antiquities, pp. 110 and 355. Knight: p. 87.

The festival of the 25th of December was celebrated by the ancient *Druids*, in Great Britain and Ireland, with great fires lighted on the tops of hills.[1]

Godfrey Higgins says :

" Stuckley observes that the worship of Mithra was spread all over Gaul and Britain. The Druids kept this night as a great festival, and called the day following it Nolagh or Noel, or the day of regeneration, and celebrated it with great fires on the tops of their mountains, which they repeated on the day of the Epiphany or twelfth night. The Mithraic monuments, which are common in Britain, have been attributed to the Romans, but this festival proves that the Mithraic worship was there prior to their arrival."[2]

This was also a time of rejoicing in Ancient Mexico. Acosta says :

" In the first month, which in Peru they call Rayme, and answering to our *December*, they made a solemn feast called *Capacrayme* (the Winter Solstice), wherein they made many sacrifices and ceremonies, which continued many days."[3]

The evergreens, and particularly the mistletoe, which are used all over the Christian world at Christmas time, betray its heathen origin. Tertullian, a Father of the Church, who flourished about A. D. 200, writing to his brethren, affirms it to be " *rank idolatry* " to deck their doors " *with garlands or flowers, on festival days, according to the custom of the heathen.*"[4]

This shows that the heathen in those days, did as the Christians do now. What have evergreens, and garlands, and Christmas trees, to do with Christianity ? Simply *nothing*. It is the old Yule-feast which was held by all the northern nations, from time immemorial, handed down to, and observed at the present day. In the greenery with which Christians deck their houses and temples of worship, and in the Christmas-trees laden with gifts, we unquestionably see a relic of the symbols by which our heathen forefathers signified their faith in the powers of the returning sun to clothe the earth again with green, and hang new fruit on the trees. Foliage, such as the laurel, myrtle, ivy, or oak, and in general, *all evergreens*, were *Dionysiac plants*, that is, symbols of the generative power, signifying perpetuity of youth and vigor.[5]

Among the causes, then, that co-operated in fixing this period—December 25th — as the birthday of Christ Jesus, was, as we have seen, that almost every ancient nation of the earth held a festival on this day in commemoration of the birth of *their* virgin-born god.

---

[1] Dupuis, 160 ; Celtic Druids, and Monumental Christianity, p. 167.

[2] Anacalypsis, vol. ii. p. 99.

[3] Hist. Indies, vol. ii. p. 354.

[4] See Middleton's Works, vol. i. p. 80.

[5] Knight : Anct. Art and Mytho., p. 32.

On this account the Christians *adopted it* as the time of the birth of *their* God. Mr. Gibbon, speaking of this in his "Decline and Fall of the Roman Empire," says:

"The Roman Christians, ignorant of the real date of his (Christ's) birth, fixed the solemn festival to the 25th of December, the *Brumalia*, or Winter Solstice, when the Pagans annually celebrated the birth of *Sol*."[1]

And Mr. King, in his "Gnostics and their Remains," says:

"The ancient festival held on the 25th of December in honor of the 'Birthday of the Invincible One,' and celebrated by the 'great games' at the circus, was afterwards transferred to the commemoration of the birth of Christ, the precise day of which many of the Fathers confess was then unknown."[2]

St. Chrysostom, who flourished about A. D. 390, referring to this Pagan festival, says:

"*On this day, also, the birth of Christ was lately fixed at Rome,* in order that whilst the heathen were busy with their *profane* ceremonies, the Christians might perform their *holy rites* undisturbed."[3]

Add to this the fact that St. Gregory, a Christian Father of the third century, was instrumental in, and commended by other Fathers for, changing *Pagan festivals* into Christian *holidays*, for the purpose, as they said, of drawing the heathen to the religion of Christ.[4]

As Dr. Hooykaas remarks, the church was always anxious to meet the heathen *half way*, by allowing them to retain the feasts they were accustomed to, only giving them a *Christian dress*, or attaching a new or Christian signification to them.[5]

In doing these, and many other such things, which we shall speak of in our chapter on "*Paganism in Christianity*," the Christian Fathers, instead of drawing the heathen to their religion, drew themselves into Paganism.

---

[1] Gibbon's Rome, vol. ii. p. 383.
[2] King's Gnostics, p. 49.
[3] Quoted in Ibid.
[4] See the chapter on "Paganism in Christianity."
[5] Bible for Learners, vo. iii. p. 67.

CHAPTER XXXV.

THE TRINITY.

" Say not there are three Gods, God is but One God."—(Koran.)

THE doctrine of the Trinity is the highest and most mysterious doctrine of the Christian church. It declares that there are *three* persons in the Godhead or divine nature — the Father, the Son, and the Holy Ghost — and that " these three are *one* true, eternal God, the same in substance, equal in power and glory, although distinguished by their personal propensities." The most celebrated statement of the doctrine is to be found in the Athanasian creed,[1] which asserts that :

' The Catholic[2] faith is this: That we worship *One* God as Trinity, and Trinity in Unity—neither confounding the persons, nor dividing the substance—for there is One person of the Father, another of the Son, and another of the Holy Ghost. But the Godhead of the Father, and of the Son, and of the Holy Ghost, *is all one ;* the glory equal, the majesty co-eternal."

As M. Reville remarks :

" The dogma of the Trinity displayed its contradictions with true bravery. The Deity divided into.*three* divine persons, *and yet* these *three* persons forming only *One* God ; of these three *the first only* being self-existent, the two others *deriving their existence* from the first, *and yet* these three persons being considered as *perfectly equal ;* each having his special, distinct character, his individual qualities, wanting in the other two, *and yet* each one of the three being supposed to possess the fullness of perfection—here, it must be confessed, we have the deification of the contradictory."[3]

We shall now see that this very peculiar doctrine of three in one, and one in three, is of *heathen* origin, and that it must fall with all the other dogmas of the Christian religion.

---

[1] The celebrated passage (I. John, v. 7) " For there are three that bear record in heaven, the Father, the Word, and the Holy Ghost, and these three are one," is now admitted on all hands to be an interpolation into the epistle many centuries after the time of Christ Jesus.

(See Giles' Hebrew and Christian Records, vol. ii. p. 12. Gibbon's Rome, vol. iii. p. 556. Inman's Ancient Faiths, vol. ii. p. 886. Taylor's Diegesis and Reber's Christ of Paul.)

[2] That is, the *true* faith.

[3] Dogma Deity Jesus Christ, p. 95.

The number *three* is sacred in all theories derived from oriental sources. Deity is always a trinity of some kind, or the successive emanations proceeded in threes.[1]

If we turn to *India* we shall find that one of the most promi-nent features in the Indian theology is the doctrine of a divine triad, governing all things. This triad is called *Tri-murti* — from the Sanscrit word *tri* (three) and *murti* (form) — and consists of Brahma, Vishnu, and Siva. It is an *inseparable* unity, though three in form.[2]

" When the universal and infinite being Brahma — the only re-ally existing entity, wholly without form, and unbound and unaf-fected by the three Gunas or by qualities of any kind — wished to create for his own entertainment the phenomena of the universe, he assumed the quality of activity·and became a male person, as *Brahma* the creator. Next, in the progress of still further self-evolution, he willed to invest himself with the second quality of goodness, as *Vishnu* the preserver, and with the third quality of darkness, as *Siva* the destroyer. This development of the doctrine of triple manifestation (*tri-murti*), which appears first in the Brah-manized version of the Indian Epics, had already been adumbrated in the Veda in the triple form of fire, and in the triad of gods, Agni, Sūrya, and Indra; and in other ways."[3]

This divine *Tri-murti*—says the Brahmans and the sacred books —is indivisible in essence, and indivisible in action; mystery pro-found! which is explained in the following manner:

Brahma represents the *creative* principle, the unreflected or un-evolved protogoneus state of divinity — the *Father*.

Vishnu represents the *protecting* and *preserving* principle, the evolved or reflected state of divinity — the *Son*.[4] .

Siva is the principle that presides at destruction and re-con-struction — the Holy Spirit.[5]

---

[1] " The notion of a *Triad* of Supreme Pow-ers is indeed common to most ancient relig-ions." (Prichard's Egyptian Mytho., p. 285.)

" Nearly all the Pagan nations of antiquity, in their various theological systems, acknowl-edged a trinity in the divine nature." (Maur-ice : Indian Antiquities, vol. vi. p. 35.)

" The ancients imagined that their *triad* of gods or persons, only constituted one god." (Celtic Druids, p. 197.)

[2] The three attributes called Brahmā, Vishnu and Siva, are indicated by letters correspond-ing to our A. U. M., generally pronounced OM. This mystic word is never uttered except in prayer, and the sign which represents it in their tem-

ples is an object of profound adoration.

[3] Monier Williams' Indian Wisdom, p. 324.

[4] That is, the Lord and Saviour *Crishna*. The Supreme Spirit, in order to preserve the world, produced Vishnu. Vishnu came upon earth, for this purpose, in the form of Crishna. He was believed to be an incarnation of the Su-preme Being, one of the persons of their holy and mysterious trinity, to use their language, " The Lord and Savior—three persons and one god." In the Geita, Crishna is made to say: " I am the Lord of all created beings." " I am the mystic figure O. M." " I am Brahmā, Vishnu, and Siva, three gods in one."

[5] See The Heathen Religion, p. 124.

24

The third person was the Destroyer, or, in his good capacity, the Regenerator. The dove was the emblem of the Regenerator. As the *spiritus* was the passive cause (brooding on the face of the waters) by which all things sprang into life, the dove became the emblem of the Spirit, or Holy Ghost, the third person.

These three gods are the first and the highest manifestations of the Eternal Essence, and are typified by the three letters composing the mystic syllable OM or AUM. They constitute the well known Trimurti or Triad of divine forms which characterizes Hindooism. It is usual to describe these three gods as Creator, Preserver and Destroyer, but this gives a very inadequate idea of their complex characters. Nor does the conception of their relationship to each other become clearer when it is ascertained that their functions are constantly interchangeable, and that each may take the place of the other, according to the sentiment expressed by the greatest of Indian poets, Kalidasa (Kumara-sambhava, Griffith, vii. 44):

> " In those three persons the One God was shown—
> Each first in place, each last—not one alone ;
> Of Siva, Vishnu, Brahmā, each may be
> First, second, third, among the blessed three."

A devout person called Attencin, becoming convinced that he should worship but *one* deity, thus addressed Brahma, Vishnu and Siva :

"O you *three* Lords ; know that I recognize only *One* God ; inform me therefore, *which of you is the true divinity*, that I may address to him alone my vows and adorations."

The three gods became manifest to him, and replied:

"Learn, O devotee, that there is no real distinction between us ; what to you *appears* such is only by semblance ; *the Single Being appears under three forms, but he is One.*"[1]

Sir William Jones says:

" Very respectable natives have assured me, that one or two missionaries have been absurd enough in their zeal for the conversion of the Gentiles, to urge that the Hindoos were even now almost Christians ; because their Brahmā, Vishnou, and Mahesa (Siva), were no other than the Christian Trinity."[2]

Thomas Maurice, in his " Indian Antiquities," describes a magnificent piece of Indian sculpture, of exquisite workmanship, and of stupendous antiquity, namely :

"A bust composed of *three heads*, united to *one body*, adorned with the *oldest* symbols of the Indian theology, and thus expressly fabricated according to the

---

[1] Allen's India, pp. 382, 383.   [2] Asiatic Researches, vol. i. p. 272.

unanimous confession of the sacred sacerdotal tribe of India, to indicate *the Creator*, the *Preserver*, and the *Regenerator*, of mankind ; which *establishes the solemn fact, that from the remotest eras, the Indian nations had adored a triune deity.*"[1]

Fig. No. 34 is a representation of an Indian sculpture, intended to represent the Triune God,[2] evidently similar to the one described above by Mr. Maurice. It is taken from "a very ancient granite" in the museum at the "Indian House," and was dug from the ruins of a temple in the island of Bombay.

The Buddhists, as well as the Brahmans, have had their Trinity from a very early period.

Mr. Faber, in his "Origin of Heathen Idolatry," says :

FIG. 34

"Among the Hindoos, we have the Triad of Brahmā, Vishnu, and Siva; so, among the votaries of Buddha, we find the self-triplicated Buddha declared to be the same as the Hindoo Trimurti. Among the Buddhist sect of the Jainists, we have the triple Jiva, in whom the Trimurti is similarly declared to be incarnate."

In this Trinity *Vajrapani* answers to Brahmā, or Jehovah, the "All-father," *Manjusri* is the "deified teacher," the counterpart of Crishna or Jesus, and *Avalokitesvara* is the "Holy Spirit."

Buddha was believed by *his* followers to be, not only an incarnation of the deity, but "God himself in human form"—as the followers of Crishna believed him to be—and therefore "three gods in one." This is clearly illustrated by the following address delivered to Buddha by a devotee called Amora :

"Reverence be unto thee, O God, in the form of the God of mercy, the dispeller of pain and trouble, the Lord of all things, the guardian of the universe, the emblem of mercy towards those who serve thee—OM ! the possessor of all things in vital form. Thou art Brahma, Vishnu, and Mahesa ; thou art Lord of all the universe. Thou art under the proper form of all things, movable and immovable, the possessor of the whole, and thus I adore thee. I adore thee, who art celebrated by a thousand names, and under various forms ; in the shape of Buddha, the god of mercy."[3]

The inhabitants of *China* and *Japan*, the majority of whom are Buddhists, worship God in the form of a Trinity. Their name

[1] Indian Antiquities, vol. iv. p. 372.
[2] Taken from Moore's "Hindoo Pantheon," plate 81.
[3] Asiatic Researches, vol. iii. pp. 285, 286 See also, King's Gnostics, 167.

for him (Buddha) is Fo, and in speaking of the Trinity they say:
"The three pure, precious or honorable Fo."[1]   This triad is represented in their temples by images similar to those found in the
pagodas of India, and when they speak of God they say: "*Fo is
one person, but has three forms.*"[2]

In a chapel belonging to the monastery of Poo-ta-la, which was
found in Manchow-Tartary, was to be seen representations of Fo, in
the form of three persons.[3]

Navarette, in his account of China, says:

"This sect (of Fo) has another idol they call *Sanpao*. It consists of *three*,
equal in all respects. This, which has been represented as an image of the Most
Blessed Trinity, is exactly the same with that which is on the high altar of the
monastery of the Trinitarians at Madrid. If any Chinese whatsoever saw it, he
would say that *Sanpao* of his country was worshiped in these parts."

And Mr. Faber, in his "Origin of Heathen Idolatry," says:

"Among the Chinese, who worship Buddha under the name of *Fo*, we find
this God mysteriously multiplied into *three persons*."

The mystic syllable O. M. or A. U. M. is also reverenced by the
Chinese and Japanese,[4] as we have found it reverenced by the inhabitants of India.

The followers of Laou-tsze, or Laou-keum-tsze—a celebrated
philosopher of China, and deified hero, born 604 B. C. — known as
the Taou sect, are also worshipers of a Trinity.[5] It was the leading
feature in Laou-keun's system of philosophical theology, that Taou,
the eternal reason, produced *one ;* one produced *two ;* two produced
three ; and three produced all things.[6]   This was a sentence which
Laou-keun continually repeated, and which Mr. Maurice considers,
"a most singular axiom for a *heathen* philosopher."[7]

The sacred volumes of the Chinese state that:

"The Source and Root of all is *One*. This self-existent unity necessarily
produced a *second*. The first and second, by their union, produced a *third*.
These *Three* produced all."[8]

The ancient emperors of China solemnly sacrificed, every three
years, to "Him who is One and Three."[9]

The ancient *Egyptians* worshiped God in the form of a Trinity,

---

[1] Davis' China, vol. ii. p. 104.
[2] Ibid. pp. 103 and 81.
[3] Ibid. pp. 105, 106.
[4] Ibid. pp. 103, 81.
[5] Ibid. 110, 111. Bell's Pantheon, vol. ii. p.
36. Dunlap's Spirit Hist., 150.
[6] Indian Antiquities, vol. v. p. 41.   Dupuis,
p. 285. Dunlap's Spirit Hist., 150.
[7] Indian Antiquities, vol. v. p. 41.

This Taou sect, according to John Francis
Davis, and the Rev. Charles Gutzlaff, both of
whom have resided in China—call their trinity
"the three pure ones," or "the three precious
ones in heaven." (See Davis' China, vol. ii. p.
110, and Gutzlaff's Voyages, p. 307.)
[8] See Prog. Relig. Ideas, vol. i. p. 210.
[9] Ibid.

which was represented in sculptures on the most ancient of their temples. The celebrated symbol of the wing, the globe, and the serpent, is supposed to have stood for the different attributes of God.[1]

The priests of Memphis, in Egypt, explained this mystery to the novice, by intimating that the premier (first) *monad* created the *dyad*, who engendered the *triad*, and that it is this triad which shines through nature.

Thulis, a great monarch, who at one time reigned over all Egypt, and who was in the habit of consulting the oracle of Serapis, is said to have addressed the oracle in these words:

"Tell me if ever there was before one greater than I, or will ever be one greater than me?"

The oracle answered thus:

"First *God*, afterward the *Word*, and with them the *Holy Spirit*, all these are of the same nature, and make but *one* whole, of which the power is eternal. Go away quickly, *mortal*, thou who hast but an uncertain life."[2]

The idea of calling the second person in the Trinity the *Logos*, or *Word*,[3] is an Egyptian feature, and was engrafted into Christianity many centuries after the time of Christ Jesus.[4] *Apollo*, who had his tomb at Delphi in Egypt, was called the Word.[5]

Mr. Bonwick, in his "Egyptian Belief and Modern Thought," says:

"Some persons are prepared to admit that the most astonishing development of the old religion of Egypt was in relation to the *Logos* or Divine *Word*, by whom all things were made, and who, though from God, was God. It had long been known that Plato, Aristotle, and others before the Christian era, cherished the idea of this Demiurgus; but it was not known till of late that Chaldeans and Egyptians recognized this mysterious principle."[6]

---

[1] Indian Antiquities, vol. i. p. 127.

[2] Higgins: Anacalypsis, vol. ii. p. 14. The following answer is stated by Manetho, an Egyptian priest, to have been given by an Oracle to Sesostris: "On his return through Africa he entered the sanctuary of the Oracle, saying: 'Tell me, O thou strong in fire, who before me could subjugate all things? and who shall after me?' But the Oracle rebuked him, saying, 'First, God; then the Word; and with them, the Spirit.'" (Nimrod, vol. i. p. 119, in Ibid. vol. i. p. 805.) Here we have distinctly enumerated God, the Logos, and the Spirit or Holy Ghost, in a very early period, long previous to the Christian era.

[3] I. John, v. 7. John i. 1.

[4] The *Alexandrian* theology, of which the celebrated *Plato* was the chief representative, taught that the *Logos* was "*the second God*;"

a being of divine essence, but distinguished from the Supreme God. It is also called "*the first-born Son of God*."

"The *Platonists* furnished brilliant recruits to the Christian churches of Asia Minor and Greece, and brought with them their love for system and their idealism." "It is in the Platonizing, or Alexandrian, branch of Judaism that we must seek for the antecedents of the Christian doctrine of the *Logos*." (A. Revillé: Dogma Deity Jesus, p. 29.)

[5] Higgins: Anacalypsis, vol. ii. p. 102. *Mithras*, the Mediator, and Saviour of the Persians, was called the *Logos*. (See Dunlap's Son of the Man, p. 20. Bunsen's Angel-Messiah, p. 75.) *Hermes* was called the *Logos*. (See Dunlap's Son of the Man, p. 39, *marginal note*.)

[6] Bonwick's Egyptian Belief, p. 402.

"The *Logos* or *Word* was a great mystery (among the Egyptians), in whose sacred books the following passages may be seen: 'I know the mystery of the divine Word;' 'The Word of the Lord of All, which was the maker of it;' 'The Word—this is the first person after himself, uncreated, infinite ruling over all things that were made by him.' "[1]

The Assyrians had Marduk for their Logos;[2] one of their sacred addresses to him reads thus:

"Thou art the powerful one—Thou art the life-giver—Thou also the prosperer—Merciful one among the gods—Eldest son of Hea, who made heaven and earth—Lord of heaven and earth, who an equal has not—Merciful one, who dead to life raises."[3]

The Chaldeans had their *Memra* or "Word of God," corresponding to the Greek *Logos*, which designated that being who organized and who still governs the world, and is inferior to God only.[4]

The Logos was with Philo a most interesting subject of discourse, tempting him to wonderful feats of imagination. There is scarcely a personifying or exalting epithet that he did not bestow on the Divine Reason. He described it as a distinct being; called it "a Rock," "The Summit of the Universe," "Before all things," "First-begotten Son of God," "Eternal Bread from Heaven," "Fountain of Wisdom," "Guide to God," "Substitute for God," "Image of God," "Priest," "Creator of the Worlds," "Second God," "Interpreter of God," "Ambassador of God," "Power of God," "King," "Angel," "Man," "Mediator," "Light," "The Beginning," "The East," "The Name of God," "The Intercessor."[5]

This is exactly the Logos of John. It becomes a man, "is made flesh;" appears as an *incarnation;* in order that the God whom "no man has seen at any time," may be manifested.

The worship of God in the form of a Trinity was to be found among the ancient *Greeks*. When the priests were about to offer up a sacrifice to the gods, the altar was *three times* sprinkled by dipping a laurel branch in holy water, and the people assembled around it were *three times* sprinkled also. Frankincense was taken from the censer with *three fingers*, and strewed upon the altar *three times*. This was done because an oracle had declared that *all sacred things ought to be in threes*, therefore, that number was scrupulously observed in most religious ceremonies.[6]

Orpheus[7] wrote that:

[1] Bonwick's Egyptian Belief, p. 404.
[2] Ibid.
[3] Ibid.
[4] Ibid. p. 28.
[5] Frothingham's Cradle of the Christ, p. 112.

[6] See Prog. Relig. Ideas, vol. i. p. 307.
[7] Orpheus is said to have been a native of Thracia, the oldest poet of Greece, and to have written before the time of Homer; but he is evidently a mythological character.

"All things were made by *One* godhead in *three* names, and that this god is all things."[1]

This Trinitarian view of the Deity he is said to have brought from Egypt, and the Christian Fathers of the third and fourth centuries claimed that Pythagoras, Heraclitus, and Plato — who taught the doctrine of the Trinity — had drawn their theological philosophy from the writings of Orpheus.[2]

The works of Plato were extensively studied by the Church Fathers, one of whom joyfully recognizes in the great teacher, the schoolmaster who, in the fullness of time, was destined to educate the heathen for Christ, as Moses did the Jews.[3]

The celebrated passage : "In the beginning was the Word, and the Word was with God, and the Word was God,"[4] is a fragment of some Pagan treatise on the Platonic philosophy, evidently written by Irenæus.[5] It is quoted by *Amelius*, a Pagan philosopher, as strictly applicable to the Logos, or Mercury, the Word, apparently as an honorable testimony borne to the Pagan deity by a barbarian—for such is what he calls the writer of John i. 1. His words are :

"This plainly was the Word, by whom all things were made, he being himself eternal, as Heraclitus also would say ; and by Jove, the same whom the *barbarian* affirms to have been in the place and dignity of a principal, and to be with God, and to be God, by whom all things were made, and in whom everything that was made has its life and being."[6]

The Christian Father, Justin Martyr, *apologizing* for the Christian religion, tells the Emperor Antoninus Pius, that the Pagans need not taunt the Christians for worshiping the Logos, which " was with God, and was God," as *they were also guilty of the same act.*

"If we (Christians) hold," says he, "some opinions near of kin to the poets and philosophers, in great repute among you, why are we thus unjustly hated?" "There's *Mercury*, Jove's interpreter, in imitation of the Logos, in worship among you," and "as to the Son of God, called Jesus, should we allow him to be nothing more than man, yet the title of the 'Son of God' is very justifiable, upon the account of his wisdom, considering *you* have your *Mercury*, (also called the 'Son of God') in worship under the title of the *Word* and Messenger of God."[7]

We see, then, that the title "Word" or "Logos," being applied to Jesus, is another piece of Pagan amalgamation with Chris-

[1] See Indian Antiquities, vol. iv. p. 332, and Taylor's Diegesis, p. 189.
[2] See Chambers's Encyclo., art. "Orpheus."
[3] Ibid., art. "Plato."
[4] John, i. 1.
[5] The first that we know of this gospel for certain is during the time of Irenæus, the great Christian forger.
[6] See Taylor's Diegesis, p. 185.
[7] Apol. 1. ch. xx.-xxii.

tianity. *It did not receive its authorized Christian form until the middle of the second century after Christ.*[1]

The ancient Pagan *Romans* worshiped a Trinity. An oracle is said to have declared that there was, "first God, then the Word, and with them the Spirit."[2]

Here we see distinctly enumerated, God, the Logos, and the Spirit or Holy Ghost, in ancient Rome, where the most celebrated temple of this capital — that of Jupiter Capitolinus — was dedicated to *three* deities, which three deities were honored with joint worship.[3]

The ancient *Persians* worshiped a Trinity.[4] This trinity consisted of Oromasdes, Mithras, and Ahriman.[5] It was virtually the same as that of the Hindoos: Oromasdes was the Creator, Mithras was the "Son of God," the "Saviour," the "Mediator" or "Intercessor," and Ahriman was the Destroyer. In the oracles of Zoroaster the Persian lawgiver, is to be found the following sentence:

"A *Triad* of Deity shines forth through the whole world, of which a *Monad* (an invisible thing) is the head."[6]

Plutarch, "De Iside et Osiride," says:

"Zoroaster is said to have made a *threefold* distribution of things: to have assigned the first and highest rank to Oromasdes, who, *in the Oracles*, is called the *Father*; the lowest to Ahrimanes; and the middle to Mithras; who, in the same Oracles, is called the *second Mind*."

The *Assyrians* and *Phenicians* worshiped a Trinity.[7]

"It is a curious and instructive fact, that the Jews had symbols of the divine Unity in Trinity as well as the Pagans."[8] The *Cabbala* had its Trinity: "the *Ancient*, whose name is sanctified, is with *three* heads, which make but *one*."[9]

Rabbi Simeon Ben Jocbai says:

"Come and see the *mystery* of the word *Elohim*: there are *three degrees*, and each degree by itself alone, and yet, notwithstanding, *they are all One*, and *joined together in One*, and cannot be divided from each other."

According to Dr. Parkhurst:

"The *Vandals*[10] had a god called Triglaff. One of these was found at Her-

---

[1] See Fiske : Myths and Myth-makers, p. 205. *Celsus* charges the Christians with a *re-coinage* of the misunderstood doctrine of the Logos.

[2] See Higgins' Anacalypsis, vol. i. p. 105.

[3] See Indian Antiquities, vol. iii. p. 158.

[4] See Indian Antiquities, vol. vi. p. 346. Monumental Christianity, p. 65. and Ancient Faiths, vol. ii. p. 819.   [5] Ibid.

[6] Indian Antiquities, vol. iv. p. 259.

[7] See Monumental Christianity, p. 65, and Ancient Faiths, vol. ii. p. 819.

[8] Monumental Christianity, p. 923. See also, Maurice's Indian Antiquities.

[9] Idra Suta, Sohar, iii. 288. B. Franck, 138. Son of the Man, p. 78.

[10] *Vandals*—a race of European barbarians, either of Germanic or Slavonic origin.

tungerberg, near Brandenburg (in Prussia). He was represented with *three* *heads*. This was apparently the *Trinity of Paganism*."[1]

The ancient *Scandinavians* worshiped a triple deity who was yet one god. It consisted of Odin, Thor, and Frey. A triune statue representing this Trinity in Unity was found at Upsal in Sweden.[2] The three principal nations of Scandinavia (Sweden, Denmark, and Norway) vied with each other in erecting temples, but none were more famous than the temple at Upsal in Sweden. It glittered on all sides with gold. It seemed to be particularly consecrated to the *Three Superior Deities*, Odin, Thor and Frey. The statues of these gods were placed in this temple on three thrones, one above the other. *Odin* was represented holding a sword in his hand : *Thor* stood at the left hand of Odin, with a crown upon his head, and a scepter in his hand ; *Frey* stood at the left hand of Thor, and was represented of both sexes. Odin was the supreme God, the *Al-fader ;* Thor was the first-begotten son of this god, and Frey was the bestower of fertility, peace and riches. King Gylfi of Sweden is supposed to have gone at one time to *As-gard* (the abode of the gods), where he beheld three thrones raised one above another, with a man sitting on each of them. Upon his asking what the names of these lords might be, his guide answered : " He who sitteth on the lowest throne is *the Lofty One ;* the second is *the equal to the Lofty One ;* and he who sitteth on the highest throne is called *the Third*."[3]

The ancient *Druids* also worshiped : " *Ain Treidhe Dia ainm Taulac, Fan, Mollac ;* " which is to say : " Ain triple God, of name Taulac, Fan, Mollac."[4]

The ancient inhabitants of *Siberia* worshiped a triune God. In remote ages, wanderers from India directed their eyes northward, and crossing the vast Tartarian deserts, finally settled in Siberia, bringing with them the worship of a triune God. This is clearly shown from the fact stated by Thomas Maurice, that :

"The first Christian missionaries who arrived in those regions, found the people already in possession of that fundamental doctrine of the true religion, which, among others, they came to impress upon their minds, and universally adored an idol fabricated to resemble, as near as possible, *a Trinity in Unity*."

This triune God consisted of, first " the Creator of all things," second, " the God of Armies," third, " the Spirit of Heavenly Love," and yet these three were but *one* indivisible God.[5]

---

[1] Parkhurst : Hebrew Lexicon, Quoted in Taylor's Diegesis, p. 216.
[2] See Knight: Anct. Art and Mytho., p. 169. Maurice : Indian Antiq., vol. v. p. 14, and Gross : The Heathen Religion, p. 210.
[3] See Mallet's Northern Antiquities.
[4] Celtic Druids, p. 171; Anacalypsis, vol. i. p. 123; and Myths of the British Druids, p. 448.
[5] Indian Antiquit'es, vol. v. pp. 8, 9.

The *Tartars* also worshiped God as a Trinity in Unity. On one of their medals, which is now in the St. Petersburgh Museum, may be seen a representation of the triple God seated on the lotus.[1]

Even in the remote islands of the Pacific Ocean, the supreme deities are God the Father, God the Son, and God the Spirit, the latter of which is symbolized as a bird.[2]

The ancient *Mexicans* and *Peruvians* had their Trinity. The supreme God of the Mexicans (*Tezcatlipoca*), who had, as Lord Kingsborough says, "all the attributes and powers which were assigned to Jehovah by the Hebrews," had associated with him two other gods, *Huitzlipochtli* and *Tlaloc ;* one occupied a place upon his left hand, the other on his right. This was the Trinity of the Mexicans.[3]

When the bishop Don Bartholomew de las Casas proceeded to his bishopric, which was in 1545, he commissioned an ecclesiastic, whose name was Francis Hernandez, who was well acquainted with the language of the Indians (as the natives were called), to visit them, carrying with him a sort of catechism of what he was about to preach. In about one year from the time that Francis Hernandez was sent out, he wrote to Bishop las Casas, stating that :

" The Indians believed in the God who was in heaven; that this God was the Father, Son, and Holy Ghost, and that the Father was named *Yzona*, the Son *Bacab*, who was born of a Virgin, and that the Holy Ghost was called *Echiah*."[4]

The Rev. Father Acosta says, in speaking of the *Peruvians :*

"It is strange that the devil after his manner hath brought a Trinity into idolatry, for the three images of the Sun called *Apomti, Churunti,* and *Intiquaoqui,* signifieth Father and Lord Sun, the Son Sun, and the Brother Sun.

" Being in Chuquisaca, an honorable priest showed me an information, which I had long in my hands, where it was proved that there was a certain oratory, whereat the Indians did worship an idol called *Tangatanga,* which they said was 'One in Three, and Three in One.' And as this priest stood amazed thereat, I said that the devil by his infernal and obstinate pride (whereby he always pretends to make himself God) did steal all that he could from the truth, to employ it in his lying and deceits."[5]

The doctrine was recognized among the Indians of the Californian peninsula. The statue of the principal deity of the New Granadian Indians had "three heads on one body," and was understood to be "three persons with one heart and one will."[6]

---

[1] Isis Unveiled, vol. ii. p. 48.
[2] Knight : Anct. Art and Mytho., p. 169.
[3] Squire : Serpent Symbol, pp. 179, 180. Mexican Ant., vol. vi. p. 164.
[4] Kingsborough : Mexican Antiquities, vol.

vi. p. 164.
[5] Acosta : Hist. Indies, vol. ii. p. 373. See also, Indian Antiq., vol. v. p. 26, and Squire's Serpent Symbol, p. 181.
[6] Squire : Serpent Symbol, p. 181.

The result of our investigations then, is that, for ages before the time of Christ Jesus or Christianity, God was worshiped in the form of a TRIAD, and that this doctrine was extensively diffused through all nations. That it was established in regions as far distant as China and Mexico, and immemorially acknowledged through the whole extent of Egypt and India. That it flourished with equal vigor among the snowy mountains of Thibet, and the vast deserts of Siberia. That the barbarians of central Europe, the Scandinavians, and the Druids of Britain and Ireland, bent their knee to an idol of a *Triune God.* What then becomes of "the Ever-Blessed Trinity" of Christianity? It must fall, together with all the rest of its dogmas, and be buried with the Pagan débris.

The learned Thomas Maurice imagined that this mysterious doctrine must have been revealed by God to Adam, or to Noah, or to Abraham, or to somebody else. Notice with what caution he wrote (A. D. 1794) on this subject. He says:

"In the course of the wide range which I have been compelled to take in the field of Asiatic mythology, certain topics have arisen for discussion, *equally delicate and perplexing.* Among them, in particular, a species of Trinity forms a constant and prominent feature in nearly all the systems of Oriental theology."

After saying, "*I venture with a trembling step,*" and that, "It was not from *choice,* but from *necessity,* that I entered thus upon this subject," he concludes:

" This extensive and interesting subject engrosses a considerable portion of this work, *and my anxiety to prepare the public mind to receive it,* my efforts to elucidate so *mysterious* a point of theology, induces me to remind the candid reader, that visible traces of this doctrine are discovered, not only in the *three* principals of the Chaldaic theology ; in the *Triplasios* Mithra of Persia ; in the *Triad,* Brahmā, Vishnu, and Siva, of India—where it was evidently promulgated in the Geeta, *fifteen hundred years before the birth of Plato;*[1] but in the Numen Triplex of Japan ; in the inscription upon the famous medal found in the deserts of Siberia, "To the Triune God," to be seen at this day in the valuable cabinet of the Empress, at St. Petersburgh ; in the Tanga-Tanga, or Three in One, of the South Americans ; and, finally, without mentioning the vestiges of it in Greece, in the Symbol of the Wing, the Globe, and the Serpent, conspicuous on most of the ancient temples of Upper Egypt."[2]

It was a long time after the followers of Christ Jesus had made him *a* God, before they ventured to declare that he was " *God him-*

[1] The ideas entertained concerning the antiquity of the Geeta, at the time Mr. Maurice wrote his Indian Antiquities, were erroneous. This work, as we have elsewhere seen, is not as old as he supposed. The doctrine of the *Trimurti* in India, however, is to be found in the *Veda,* and epic poems, which are of an antiquity long anterior to the rise of Christianity, preceding it by many centuries. (See Monier Williams' Indian Wisdom, p. 324, and Hinduism, pp. 109, 110–115.)
"The grand cavern pagoda of Elephanta, the oldest and most magnificent temple in the world, is neither more nor less than a superb temple of a Triune God." (Maurice : Indian Antiquities, vol. iii. p. ix.)

[2] Indian Antiquities, vol. i. pp. 125–127.

self in human form," and, *" the second person in the Ever-Blessed Trinity."* It was *Justin Martyr, a Christian convert from the Platonic school,*[1] who, about the middle of the second century, first promulgated the opinion, that Jesus of Nazareth, the " Son of God," was the second principle in the Deity, and the Creator of all material things. He is the earliest writer to whom the opinion can be traced. This knowledge, he does not ascribe to the Scriptures, but to the special favor of God.[2]

The passage in I. John, v. 7, which reads thus : " For there are three that bear record in heaven, the Father, the Word, and 'the Holy Ghost, and these three are one," is *one of the numerous interpolations which were inserted into the books of the New Testament, many years after these books were written.*[3] These passages are retained and circulated as the *word of God,* or as of equal authority with the rest, though known and admitted by the learned on all hands, to be forgeries, willful and wicked interpolations.

The subtle and profound questions concerning the nature, generation, the distinction, and the quality of the three divine persons of the mysterious triad, or Trinity, were agitated in the philosophical and in the Christian schools of *Alexandria in Egypt,*[4] but it was not a part of the established Christian faith until as late as A. D. 327, when the question was settled at the Councils of Nice and Constantinople. *Up to this time there was no understood and recognized doctrine on this high subject.* The Christians were for the most part accustomed to us escriptural expressions in speaking of the Father, and the Son, and the Spirit, without defining articulately their relation to one another.[5]

In these trinitarian controversies, which first broke out in Egypt — *Egypt, the land of Trinities* — the chief point in the discussion was to define the position of " the Son."

There lived in *Alexandria* a presbyter of the name of *Arius,* a disappointed candidate for the office of bishop. He took the

---

[1] We have already seen that Plato and his followers taught the doctrine of the Trinity centuries before the time of Christ Jesus.

[2] Israel Worsley's Enquiry, p. 54. Quoted in Higgins' Anacalypsis, vol. i. p. 116.

[3] " The memorable text (I. John v. 7) which asserts the unity of the three which bear witness in heaven, is condemned by the universal silence of the orthodox Fathers, ancient versions, and authentic manuscripts. It was first alleged by the Catholic Bishop whom Hunneric summoned to the Conference of Carthage (A.D. 254), or, more properly, by the four bishops who composed and published the profession of faith in the name of their brethren." (Gibbon's Rome, vol. iii. p. 556, and note 117.) None of the ancient manuscripts now extant, above four-score in number, *contain this passage.* (Ibid. note 116.) In the eleventh and twelfth centuries, the Bible was corrected. Yet, notwithstanding these corrections, the passage is still wanting in twenty-five Latin manuscripts. (Ibid. note 116. See also. Dr. Giles' Hebrew and Christian Records, vol. ii. p. 12. Dr. Inman's Ancient Faiths, vol. ii. p. 886. Rev. Robert Taylor's Diegesis, p. 421, and Reber's Christ of Paul.)

[4] See Gibbon's Rome, ii. 309.

[5] Chambers's Encyclo., art. " Trinity."

ground that there was a time when, from the very nature of *Sonship*, the Son did not exist, and a time at which he commenced to be, asserting that it is the necessary condition of the filial relation *that a father must be older than his son*. But this assertion evidently denied the *co-eternity* of the three persons of the Trinity, it suggested a *subordination* or *inequality* among them, and indeed implied a time when the Trinity did not exist. Hereupon, the bishop, who had been the successful competitor against Arius, displayed his rhetorical powers in public debates on the question, and, the strife spreading, the Jews and Pagans, who formed a very large portion of the population of Alexandria, *amused themselves with theatrical representations of the contest on the stage — the point of their burlesques being the equality of age of the Father and the Son*. Such was the violence the controversy at length assumed, that the matter had to be referred to the emperor (Constantine).

At first he looked upon the dispute as altogether frivolous, and perhaps in truth inclined to the assertion of Arius, that in the very nature of the thing a father must be older than his son. So great, however, was the pressure laid upon him, that he was eventually compelled to summon the Council of Nicea, which, to dispose of the conflict, set forth a formulary or creed, and attached to it this anathema :

" The Holy Catholic and Apostolic Church anathematizes those who say that there was a time when the Son of God was not, and that, before he was begotten, he was not, and that, he was made out of nothing, or out of another substance or essence, and is created, or changeable, or alterable."

Constantine at once *enforced* the decision of the council by the civil power.[1]

Even after this " subtle and profound question " had been settled at the Council of Nice, those who settled it did not understand the question they had settled. Athanasius, who was a member of the first general council, and who is said to have written the *creed* which bears his name, which asserts that the true Catholic faith is this :

" That we worship *One* God as Trinity, and Trinity in Unity—neither confounding the persons nor dividing the substance—for there is one person of the Father, another of the Son, and another of the Holy Ghost, but the Godhead of the Father, and of the Son, and of the Holy Ghost *is all one*, the glory equal, the majesty co-eternal,"

—also confessed that whenever he forced his understanding to

---

meditate on the divinity of the Logos, his toilsome and unavailing efforts recoiled on themselves; *that the more he thought the less he comprehended; and the more he wrote the less capable was he of expressing his thoughts.*[1]

We see, then, that this great question was settled, not by the consent of all members of the council, but simply because the *majority* were in favor of it. Jesus of Nazareth was " God himself in human form ;" " one of the persons of the Ever-Blessed Trinity," who " had no beginning, and will have no end," *because the majority of the members of this council said so.* Hereafter—so it was decreed—*all must believe it;* if not, they must not oppose it, but forever hold their peace.

The Emperor Theodosius declared his resolution of expelling from all the churches of his dominions, the bishops and their clergy who should obstinately refuse to believe, *or at least to profess,* the doctrine of the Council of Nice. His lieutenant, Sapor, was armed with the ample powers of a general law, a special commission, *and a military force;* and this ecclesiastical resolution was conducted *with so much discretion and vigor, that the religion of the Emperor was established.*[2]

Here we have the historical fact, that bishops of the Christian church, and their clergy, *were forced to profess their belief in the doctrine of the Trinity.*

We also find that:

" This orthodox Emperor (Theodosius) considered every heretic (as he called those who did not believe as he and his ecclesiastics professed) as a rebel against the supreme powers of heaven and of earth (he being one of the supreme powers of earth) *and each of the powers* might exercise their peculiar jurisdiction *over the soul and body of the guilty.*

" The decrees of the Council of Constantinople had ascertained the *true* standard of the faith, *and the ecclesiastics, who governed the conscience of Theodosius, suggested the most effectual methods of persecution.* In the space of fifteen years he promulgated at least fifteen severe edicts against the heretics, *more especially against those who rejected the doctrine of the Trinity.*"[3]

Thus we see one of the many reasons why the " most holy Christian religion " spread so rapidly.

Arius—who declared that in the nature of things a father must be older than his son—was excommunicated for his so-called heretical notions concerning the Trinity. His followers, who were very

---

[1] Athanasius, tom. i. p. 808. Quoted in Gibbon's Rome, vol. ii. p. 310.
Gennadius, Patriarch of Constantinople, was so much amazed by the extraordinary composition called " Athanasius' Creed," that he frankly pronounced it to be the work of a drunken man. (Gibbon's Rome, vol. iii. p. 555, note 114.)

[2] Gibbon's Rome, vol. iii. p. 87.

[3] Ibid. pp. 91, 92.

numerous, were called Arians. Their writings, if they had been permitted to exist,[1] would undoubtedly contain the lamentable story of the persecution which affected the church under the reign of the impious Emperor Theodosius.

[1] All their writings were ordered to be destroyed, and any one found to have them in his possession was severely punished.

CHAPTER XXXVI.

PAGANISM IN CHRISTIANITY.

Our assertion that that which is called Christianity is nothing more than the religion of Paganism, we consider to have been fully verified. We have found among the heathen, centuries before the time of Christ Jesus, the belief in an incarnate God born of a virgin; his previous existence in heaven; the celestial signs at the time of his birth; the rejoicing in heaven; the adoration by the magi and shepherds; the offerings of precious substances to the divine child; the slaughter of the innocents; the presentation at the temple; the temptation by the devil; the performing of miracles; the crucifixion by enemies; and the death, resurrection, and ascension into heaven. We have also found the belief that this incarnate God was from all eternity; that he was the Creator of the world, and that he is to be Judge of the dead at the last day. We have also seen the practice of Baptism, and the sacrament of the Lord's Supper or Eucharist, added to the belief in a Triune God, consisting of Father, Son, and Holy Ghost. Let us now compare the Christian creed with ancient Pagan belief.

Christian Creed.	*Ancient Pagan Belief.*
1. I believe in God the Father Almighty, maker of heaven and earth :	1. I believe in God the Father Almighty, maker of heaven and earth :[1]
2. And in Jesus Christ, his only Son, Our Lord.	2. And in his only Son, our Lord.[2]
3. Who was conceived by the Holy Ghost, born of the Virgin Mary,	3. Who was conceived by the Holy Ghost, born of the Virgin Mary.[3]
4. Suffered under Pontius Pilate, was crucified, dead and buried.	4. Suffered under (whom it might be), was crucified, dead, and buried.[4]

---

[1] "Before the separation of the Aryan race, before the existence of Sanscrit, Greek, or Latin, before the gods of the Veda had been worshiped, ONE SUPREME DEITY had been found, had been named, and had been invoked by the ancestors of our race." (Prof. Max Müller : The Science of Religion, p. 67.)

[2] See Chap. XII. and Chap. XX., for Only-begotten Sons.

[3] See Chap. XII. and Chap. XXXII., where we have shown that many other virgin-born gods were conceived by the Holy Ghost, and that the name MARY is the same as Maia, Maya, Myrra, &c.

[4] See Chap. XX., for Crucified Saviours.

5. He descended into Hell ;	5. He descended into Hell ;[1]
6. The third day he rose again from the dead ;	6. The third day he rose again from the dead ;[2]
7. He ascended into Heaven, and sitteth on the right hand of God the Father Almighty ;	7. He ascended into Heaven, and sitteth on the right hand of God the Father Almighty ;[3]
8. From thence he shall come to judge the quick and the dead.	8. From thence he shall come to judge the quick and the dead.[4]
9. I believe in the Holy Ghost ;	9. I believe in the Holy Ghost ;[5]
10. The Holy Catholic Church, the Communion of Saints ;	10. The Holy Catholic Church,[6] the Communion of Saints ;
11. The forgiveness of sins ;	11. The forgiveness of sins ;[7]
12. The resurrection of the body ; and the life everlasting.	12. The resurrection of the body ; and the life everlasting.[8]

The above is the so-called "*Apostles' Creed*," as it now stands in the book of common prayer of the United Church of England and Ireland, as by law established.

It is affirmed by Ambrose, that:

" The twelve apostles, as skilled artificers, assembled together, and made a key by their common advice, that is, the Creed, by which the darkness of the devil is disclosed, that the light of Christ may appear."

Others fable that every Apostle inserted an article, by which the Creed is divided into twelve articles.

The earliest account of its origin we have from Ruffinus, an historical compiler and traditionist of the *fourth* century, but not in the form in which it is known at present, it having been added to since that time. The most important addition is that which affirms that Jesus descended into hell, which has been added since A.D. 600.[9]

[1] See Chap. XXII.
[2] See Chaps. XXII. and XXXIX., for Resurrected Saviours.
[3] See Ibid.
[4] See Chap. XXIV., and Chap. XXV.
[5] See Chap. XII., and Chap. XXXV.
[6] That is, the holy *true* Church. All peoples who have had a religion believe that *theirs* was the *Catholic* faith.
[7] There was no nation of antiquity who did not believe in "the forgiveness of sins," especially if some innocent creature *redeemed* them by the shedding of his blood (see Chap. IV., and Chap. XX.), and as far as *confession* of sins is concerned, and thereby being forgiven, this too is almost as old as humanity. Father Acosta found it even among the Mexicans, and said that "the father of lies (the Devil) counterfeited the sacrament of confession, so that he might be honored with ceremonies very like the Christians." (See Acosta, vol. ii. p. 360.)
[8] "No doctrine except that of a supreme

and subtly-pervading deity, is so extended, and has retained its primitive form so distinctly, *as a belief in immortality*, and a future state of rewards and punishments. Among the most savage races, the idea of a future existence in a place of delight is found." (Kenneth R. H. Mackenzie.)
"Go back far as we may in the history of the Indo-European race, of which the Greeks and Italians are branches, and we do not find that this race has ever thought that after this short life all was finished for man. The most ancient generations, long before there were philosophers, believed in a second existence after the present. They looked upon death not as a dissolution of our being, but simply as a change of life." (M. De Coulanges: The Ancient City, p. 15.)
[9] For full information on this subject see Archbishop Wake's Apostolic Fathers, p. 103, Justice Bailey's Common Prayer, Taylor's Diegesis, p. 10, and Chambers's Encyclo., art. " Creeds."

25

Beside what we have already seen, the ancient Pagans had
many beliefs and ceremonies which are to be found among the
Christians.   One of these is the story of "*The War in Heaven.*"
The New Testament version is as follows :

" There was a war in heaven : Michael and his angels fought against the
dragon, and the dragon fought, and his angels, and prevailed not, neither was
their place found any more in heaven.   And the great dragon was cast out, that
old serpent, called the devil, and Satan, which deceiveth the whole world, he was
cast out into the earth, and his angels were cast out with him."[1]

The cause of the revolt, it is said, was that Satan,·who was then
an angel, desired to be as great as God.   The writer of Isaiah, xiv.
13, 14, is supposed to refer to it when he says :

" Thou hast said in thine heart, I will ascend into heaven, I will exalt my
throne above the stars of God ; I will sit also upon the mount of the congregation in the sides of the North ; I will ascend before the heights of the clouds ;
I will be like the Most High."

The Catholic theory of the fall of the angels is as follows :

" In the beginning, before the creation of heaven and earth, God made the
angels, free intelligences, and free wills, out of his love He made them, that they
might be eternally happy.   And that their happiness might be complete, he gave
them the perfection of a created nature, that is, he gave them freedom.   But
happiness is only attained by the free will agreeing in its freedom to accord with
the will of God.   Some of the angels by an act of free will obeyed the will of
God, and in such obedience found perfect happiness.   Other angels, by an act of
free will, rebelled against the will of God, and in such disobedience found
misery."[2]

They were driven out of heaven, after having a combat with
the obedient angels, and cast into hell.   The writer of second *Peter*
alludes to it in saying that God spared not the angels that sinned,
but cast them down into hell.[3]

The writer of *Jude* also alludes to it in saying :

" The angels which kept not their first estate, but left their own habitation,
he hath reserved in everlasting chains under darkness unto the judgment of the
great day."[4]

According to the *Talmudists*, Satan, whose proper name is
Sammael, was one of the Seraphim of heaven, with six wings.

" He was not driven out of heaven until after he had led Adam and Eve into sin;
then Sammael and his host were precipitated out of the place of bliss, with God's
curse to weigh them down.   In the struggle between Michael and Sammael, the
falling Seraph caught the wings of Michael, and tried to drag him down with
him, but God saved him, when Michael derived his name,—the Rescued."[5]

[1] Rev. xi. 7–9.
[2] S. Baring-Gould : Legends of Patriarchs,
p 25.
[3] II. Peter, ii. 4.
[4] Jude, 6.
[5] S. Baring-Gould : Legends of Patriarchs,
p. 16.

Sammael was formerly chief among the angels of God, and now he is prince among devils. His name is derived from Simmē, which means, to blind and deceive. He stands on the left side of men. He goes by various names ; such as " The Old Serpent," " The Unclean Spirit," " Satan," " Leviathan," and sometimes also " Asael."[1]

According to *Hindoo* mythology, there is a legion of evil spirits called *Rakshasas*, who are governed by a prince named *Ravana*. These Rakshasas are continually aiming to do injury to mankind, and are the same who fought desperate battles with *Indra*, and his Spirits of Light. They would have taken his paradise by storm, and subverted the whole order of the universe, if Brahmā had not sent *Vishnou* to circumvent their plans.

In the *Aitareya-brahmana* (Hindoo) written, according to Prof. Monier Williams, seven or eight centuries B. C., we have the following legend:

> " The gods and demons were engaged in warfare.
> The evil demons, like to mighty kings,
> Made these worlds castles ; then they formed the earth
> Into an iron citadel, the air
> Into a silver fortress, and the sky
> Into a fort of gold. Whereat the gods
> Said to each other, ' Frame me other worlds
> In opposition to these fortresses.'
> Then they constructed sacrificial places,
> Where they performed a triple burnt oblation.
> By the first sacrifice they drove the demons
> Out of their earthly fortress, by the second
> Out of the air, and by the third oblation
> Out of the sky. Thus were the evil spirits
> Chased by the gods in triumph from the worlds."[2]

The ancient *Egyptians* were familiar with the tale of the war in heaven; and the legend of the revolt against the god Rā, the Heavenly Father, and his destruction of the revolters, was discovered by M. Naville in one of the tombs at Biban-el-moluk.[3]

The same story is to be found among the ancient *Persian* legends, and is related as follows :

" Ahriman, the devil, was not created evil by the eternal one, but he became evil by revolting against his will. This revolt resulted in a ' war in heaven.' In this war the *Iveds* (good angels) fought against the *Divs* (rebellious ones) headed by *Ahriman*, and flung the conquered into Douzahk or hell."[4]

---

[1] S. Baring-Gould : Legends of Patriarchs, p. 17.
[2] Indian Wisdom, p. 32.
[3] See Renouf's Hibbert Lectures, p. 105.

Dupuis : Origin of Relig. Beliefs, p. 73, and Baring-Gould's Legends of the Prophets, p. 19.
[4] S. Baring-Gould's Legends of Patriarchs, p. 19.

An extract from the Persian *Zend-avesta* reads as follows:

" *Ahriman* interrupted the order of the universe, raised an army against *Ormuzd*, and having maintained a fight against him during ninety days, was at
length vanquished by Honover, the divine Word."[1]

The *Assyrians* had an account of a war in heaven, which was
like that described in the book of Enoch and the Revelation.[2]

This legend was also to be found among the ancient Greeks, in
the struggle of the *Titans* against *Jupiter*. Titan and all his rebellious host were cast out of heaven, and imprisoned in the dark
abyss.[3]

Anong the legends of the ancient *Mexicans* was found this same
story of the war in heaven, and the downfall of the rebellious
angels.[4]

" The natives of the *Caroline Islands* (in the North Pacific
Ocean), related that one of the inferior gods, named *Merogrog*, was
driven by the other gods out of heaven."[5]

We see, therefore, that this also was an almost universal legend.

The belief in *a future life* was almost universal among nations
of antiquity. The *Hindoos* have believed from time immemorial
that man has an invisible body within the material body; that is, a
soul.

Among the ancient *Egyptians* the same belief was to be found.
All the dead, both men and women, were spoken of as " *Osiriana;* "
by which they intended to signify " gone to Osiris."

Their belief in One Supreme Being, and the immortality of
the soul, must have been very ancient; for on a monument, which
dates ages before Abraham is said to have lived, is found this
epitaph: " May thy soul attain to the Creator of all mankind."
Sculptures and paintings in these grand receptacles of the dead, as
translated by Champollion, represent the deceased ushered into the
world of spirits by funeral deities, who announce, " A soul arrived
in Amenti."[6]

The Hindoo idea of a subtile invisible body within the material
body, reappeared in the description of Greek poets. They represented the constitution of man as consisting of three principles:
the soul, the invisible body, and the material body. The invisible
body they called the ghost or shade, and considered it as the material portion of the soul. At death, the soul, clothed in this sub-

---

[1] Priestley, p. 35.
[2] See Bonwick's Egyptian Belief, p. 411.
[3] See Inman's Ancient Faiths, vol. ii. p. 819.
Taylor's Diegesis, p. 215, and Dupuis: Origin
of Relig. Beliefs, p. 73.

[4] See Higgins' Anacalypsis, vol. ii. p. 31.
[5] S. Baring-Gould's Legends of Patriarchs,
p. 20.
[6] See Bunsen's Angel-Messiah, p. 159, and
Kenrick's Egypt, vol. i. ·

tile body, went to enjoy paradise for a season, or suffer in hell till its sins were expiated. This paradise was called the "Elysian Fields," and the hell was called Tartarus.

The paradise, some supposed to be a part of the lower world, some placed them in a middle zone in the air, some in the moon, and others in far-off isles in the ocean. There shone more glorious sun and stars than illuminated this world. The day was always serene, the air forever pure, and a soft, celestial light clothed all things in transfigured beauty. Majestic groves, verdant meadows, and blooming gardens varied the landscape. The river Eridanus flowed through winding banks fringed with laurel. On its borders lived heroes who had died for their country, priests who had led a pure life, artists who had embodied genuine beauty in their work, and poets who had never degraded their muse with subjects unworthy of Apollo. There each one renewed the pleasures in which he formerly delighted. Orpheus, in long white robes, made enrapturing music on his lyre, while others danced and sang. The husband rejoined his beloved wife; old friendships were renewed, the poet repeated his verses, and the charioteer managed his horses.

Some souls wandered in vast forests between Tartarus and Elysium, not good enough for one, or bad enough for the other. Some were purified from their sins by exposure to searching winds, others by being submerged in deep waters, others by passing through intense fires. After a long period of probation and suffering, many of them gained the Elysian Fields. This belief is handed down to our day in the Roman Catholic idea of *Purgatory*.

A belief in the existence of the soul after death was indicated in all periods of history of the world, by the fact that man was always accustomed to address prayers to the spirits of their ancestors.[1]

These *heavens* and *hells* where men abode after death, vary, in different countries, according to the likes and dislikes of each nation.

All the Teutonic nations held to a fixed Elysium and a hell, where the valiant and the just were rewarded, and where the cowardly and the wicked suffered punishment. As all nations have made a god, and that god has resembled the persons who made it, so have all nations made a heaven, and that heaven corresponds to the fancies of the people who have created it.

In the prose Edda there is a description of the joys of *Valhalla*

---

[1] This subject is most fully entered into by Mr. Herbert Spencer, in vol. 1. of "Principles of Sociology."

(the Hall of the Chosen), which states that : "All men who have fallen in fight since the beginning of the world are gone to Odin (the Supreme God), in Valhalla." A mighty band of men are there, "and every day, as soon as they have dressed themselves, they ride out into the court (or field), and there fight until they cut each other into pieces. This is their pastime, but when the meal-tide approaches, they remount their steeds, and return to drink in *Valhalla*. As it is said (in Vafthrudnis-mal) :

'The Einherjar all
On Odin's plain
Hew daily each other,
While chosen the slain are.
From the frey they then ride,
And drink ale with the Æsir.' "[1]

This description of the palace of Odin is a natural picture of the manners of the ancient Scandinavians and Germans. Prompted by the wants of their climate, and the impulse of their own temperament, they formed to themselves a delicious paradise in their own way ; where they were to eat and drink, and fight. The women, to whom they assigned a place there, were introduced for no other purpose but to fill their cups.

The Mohammedan paradise differs from this. Women *there*, are for man's pleasure. The day is always serene, the air forever pure, and a soft celestial light clothes all things in transfigured beauty. Majestic groves, verdant meadows, and blooming gardens vary the landscape. There, in radiant halls, dwell the departed, ever blooming and beautiful, ever laughing and gay.

The American Indian calculates upon finding successful chases after wild animals, verdant plains, and no winter, as the characteristics of his "future life."

The red Indian, when told by a missionary that in the "promised land" they would neither eat, drink, hunt, nor marry a wife, contemptuously replied, that instead of wishing to go there, he should deem his residence in such a place as the greatest possible calamity. Many not only rejected such a destiny for themselves, but were indignant at the attempt to decoy their children into such a comfortless region.

All nations of the earth have had their heavens. As Moore observes :

"A heaven, too, ye must have, ye lords of dust—
A splendid paradise, poor souls, ye must:

---

[1] See Mallet's Northern Antiquities, p. 429.

That prophet ill sustains his holy call
Who finds not heavens to suit the tastes of all.
Vain things ! as lust or *vanity* inspires,
The heaven of each is but what each desires."

Heaven was born of the sky,[1] and nurtured by cunning priests, who made man a coward and a slave.

Hell was built by priests, and nurtured by the fears and servile fancies of man during the ages when dungeons of torture were a recognized part of every government, and when God was supposed to be an infinite tyrant, with infinite resources of vengeance.

The devil is an imaginary being, invented by primitive man to account for the existence of evil, and relieve God of his responsibility. The famous Hindoo *Rakshasas* of our Aryan ancestors— the dark and evil *clouds* personified—are the originals of all devils. The cloudy shape has assumed a thousand different forms, horrible or grotesque and ludicrous, to suit the changing fancies of the ages.

But strange as it may appear, the god of one nation became the devil of another.

The rock of Behistun, the sculptured chronicle of the glories of Darius, king of Persia, situated on the western frontier of Media, on the high-road from Babylon to the eastward, was used as a "holy of holies." It was named *Bagistane* — "the place of the *Baga*" — referring to Ormuzd, chief of the Bagas. When examined with the lenses of linguistic science, the "*Bogie*" or "*Bug-a-boo*" or "*Bugbear*" of nursery lore, turns out to be identical with the Slavonic "*Bog*" and the "*Baga*" of the cuneiform inscriptions, both of which are names of the *Supreme Being*. It is found also in the old Aryan "*Bhaga*," who is described in a commentary of the *Rig-Veda* as the lord of life, the giver of bread, and the bringer of happiness. Thus, the same name which, to the *Vedic* poet, to the Persian of the time of Xerxes, and to the modern Russian, suggests the supreme majesty of deity, is in English associated with an ugly and ludicrous fiend. Another striking illustration is to be found in the word *devil* itself. When traced back to its primitive source, it is found to be a name of the Supreme Being.[2]

The ancients had a great number of festival days, many of which are handed down to the present time, and are to be found in Christianity.

We have already seen that the 25th of December was almost a universal festival among the ancients; so it is the same with the *spring* festivals, when days of fasting are observed.

---

[1] See Appendix C.   [2] See Fiske, pp. 104–107.

The *Hindoos* hold a festival, called *Siva-ratri*, in honor of *Siva*, about the middle or end of February. *A strict fast is observed during the day.* They have also a festival in April, when a strict fast is kept by some.[1]

At the *spring equinox* most nations of antiquity set apart a day to implore the blessings of their god, or gods, on the fruits of the earth. At the autumnal equinox, they offered the fruits of the harvest, and returned thanks. In China, these religious solemnities are called "Festivals of gratitude to Tien."[2] The last named corresponds to *our* "Thanksgiving" celebration.

One of the most considerable festivals held by the ancient *Scandinavians* was the *spring* celebration. This was held in honor of Odin, at the beginning of spring, in order to welcome in that pleasant season, and to obtain of their god happy success in their projected expeditions.

Another festival was held toward the autumn equinox, when they were accustomed to kill all their cattle in good condition, and lay in a store of provision for the winter. This festival was also attended with religious ceremonies, when Odin, the supreme god, was thanked for what he had given them, by having his altar loaded with the fruits of their crops, and the choicest products of the earth.[3]

There was a grand celebration in Egypt, called the "Feast of Lamps," held at Sais, in honor of the goddess Neith. Those who did not attend the ceremony, as well as those who did, burned lamps before their houses all night, filled with oil and salt: thus all Egypt was illuminated. It was deemed a great irreverence to the goddess for any one to omit this ceremony.[4]

The *Hindoos* also held a festival in honor of the goddesses Lakshmi and Bhavanti, called "*The feast of Lamps.*"[5] This festival has been handed down to the present time in what is called "Candlemas day," or the purification of the Virgin Mary.

The most celebrated Pagan festival held by modern Christians is that known as "*Sunday*," or the "Lord's day."[6]

All the principal nations of antiquity kept the *seventh* day of the week as a "holy day," just as the ancient Israelites did. This was owing to the fact that they consecrated the days of the week to the Sun, the Moon, and the five planets, Mercury, Venus, Mars, Jupiter, and Saturn. *The seventh day was sacred to Saturn from time im-*

---

[1] Williams' Hinduism, pp. 182, 183.
[2] See Prog Relig. Ideas, vol. i. p. 216.
[3] See Mailet's Northern Antiquities, p. 111.
[4] See Kenrick's Egypt, vol. i. p. 466.
[5] Williams' Hinduism, p. 184.

memorial. Homer and Hesiod call it the "Holy Day."[1] The people generally visited the temples of the gods, on that day, and offered up their prayers and supplications.[2] The Acadians, thousands of years ago, kept holy the 7th, 14th, 21st, and 28th of each month as *Salum* (rest), on which certain works were forbidden.[3] The *Arabs* anciently worshiped Saturn under the name of Hobal. In his hands he held *seven* arrows, symbols of the planets that preside over the seven days of the week.[4] The *Egyptians* assigned a day of the week to the sun, moon, and five planets, and the number *seven* was held there in great reverence.[5]

The planet *Saturn* very early became the chief deity of Semitic religion. Moses consecrated the number seven to him.[6]

In the *old* conception, which finds expression in the Decalogue in Deuteronomy (v. 15), the Sabbath has a purely theocratic significance, and is intended to remind the Hebrews of their miraculous deliverance from the land of Egypt and bondage. When the story of *Creation* was borrowed from the *Babylonians*, the celebration of the Sabbath was established on entirely new grounds (Ex. xx. 11), for we find it is because the "Creator," after his six days of work, rested on the seventh, that the day should be kept holy.

The Assyrians kept this day holy. Mr. George Smith says :

" In the year 1869, I discovered among other things a curious religious calendar of the Assyrians, in which every month is divided into four weeks, and the *seventh* days or ' *Sabbaths*,' are marked out as days on which no work should be undertaken.[7]

The ancient *Scandinavians* consecrated one day in the week to their Supreme God, *Odin* or *Wodin*.[8] Even at the present time we call this day *Odin's-day*.[9]

The question now arises, how was the great festival day changed

---

[1] " The *Seventh* day was sacred to *Saturn* throughout the East." (Dunlap's Spirit Hist., pp. 35, 36.

" Saturn's day was made sacred to God, and the planet is now called cochab shabbath, 'The Sabbath Star.'

" The sanctification of the Sabbath is clearly connected with the word Shabua or Sheba, *i. e.*, *seven*." (Inman's Anct. Faiths, vol. ii. p. 504.) " The Babylonians, Egyptians, Chinese, and the natives of India, were acquainted with the *seven* days' division of time, as were the ancient Druids." (Bonwick's Egyptian Belief, p. 412.) " With the Egyptians the *Seventh* day was consecrated to God the Father." (Ibid.) " Hesiod, Herodotus, Philostratus, &c., mention that day. Homer, Callimachus, and other ancient writers call the *Seventh* day the *Holy One.* Eusebius confesses its observance

by almost all philosophers and poets." (Ibid.)

[2] Ibid.

[3] Ibid. p. 413.

[4] Pococke Specimen : Hist. Arab., p. 97. Quoted in Dunlap's Spirit Hist., p. 274. " Some of the families of the Israelites worshiped *Saturn* under the name of Kiwan, which may have given rise to the religious observance of the Seventh day." (Bible for Learners, vol. i. p. 317.)

[5] Kenrick's Egypt, vol. i. p. 283.

[6] Movers Phönizier, vol. i. p. 313. Quoted in Dunlap's Spirit Hist., p. 36.

[7] Assyrian Discoveries.

[8] Mallet's Northern Antiquities, p. 92.

[9] Old Norse, *Odinsdagr ;* Swe. and Danish, *Onsdag ;* Ang. Sax., *Wodensdeg ;* Dutch, *Woensdag ;* Eng., *Wednesday.*

from the *seventh* — Saturn's day — to the *first* — *Sun*-day — among the Christians?

"If we go back to the founding of the church, we find that the most marked feature of that age, so far as the church itself is concerned, is the grand division between the 'Jewish faction,' as it was called, and the followers of Paul. This division was so deep, so marked, so characteristic, that it has left its traces all through the New Testament itself. It was one of the grand aspects of the time, and the point on which they were divided was simply this: the followers of Peter, those who adhered to the teachings of the central church in Jerusalem, held that all Christians, both converted Jews and Gentiles, were under obligation to keep the Mosaic law, ordinances, and traditions. That is, a Christian, according to their definition, was first a Jew; Christianity was something *added to* that, not something taking the place of it.

"We find this controversy raging violently all through the early churches, and splitting them into factions, so that they were the occasion of prayer and counsel. Paul took the ground distinctly that Christianity, while it might be spiritually the lineal successor of Judaism, was not Judaism; and that he who became a Christian, whether a converted Jew or Gentile, was under no obligation whatever to keep the Jewish law, so far as it was separate from practical matters of life and character. We find this intimated in the writings of Paul; for we have to go to the New Testament for the origin of that which, we find, existed immediately after the New Testament was written. Paul says: 'One man esteemeth one day above another: another man esteemeth every day alike' (Rom. xiv. 5–9). He leaves it an open question; they can do as they please. Then: 'Ye observe days, and months, and times, and years. I am afraid of you, lest I have bestowed upon you labor in vain' (Gal. iv. 10, 11). And if you will note this Epistle of Paul to the Galatians, you will find that the whole purpose of his writing it was to protest against what he believed to be the viciousness of the Judaizing influences. That is, he says: 'I have come to preach to you the perfect truth, that Christ hath made us free; and you are going back and taking upon yourselves this yoke of bondage. My labor is being thrown away; my efforts have been in vain.' Then he says, in his celebrated Epistle to the Colossians, that has never yet been explained away or met: 'Let no man therefore judge you any more in meat, or in drink, or in respect of an holy day, or of the new moon, or of the Sabbath days' (Col. ii. 16, 17), distinctly abrogating the binding authority of the Sabbath on the Christian church. So that, if Paul's word anywhere means anything—if his authority is to be taken as of binding force on any point whatever — then Paul is to be regarded as authoritatively and distinctly abrogating the Sabbath, and declaring that it is no longer binding on the Christian church."[1]

This breach in the early church, this controversy, resulted at last in Paul's going up to Jerusalem "to meet James and the representatives of the Jerusalem church, to see if they could find any common platform of agreement—if they could come together so that they could work with mutual respect and without any further bickering. What is the platform that they met upon? It was distinctly understood that those who wished to keep up the observance of Judaism should do so; and the church at Jerusalem gave Paul this grand freedom, substantially saying to him: 'Go back to your missionary work, found churches, and teach them that they are perfectly free in regard to all Mosaic and Jewish observances, save only these four: Abstain from pollutions of idols, from fornication, from things strangled, and from blood.'"[2]

The point to which our attention is forcibly drawn is, that the question of Sabbath-keeping is one of those that is left out. The point that Paul had been fighting for was conceded by the central church at Jerusalem, and he was to go out thenceforth free, so far as that was concerned, in his teaching of the churches that he should found.

There is no mention of the Sabbath, or the Lord's day, as binding in the New Testament. What, then, was the actual condition of affairs? What did the churches do in the first three hundred years of their existence? Why, they did just what Paul and the Jerusalem church had agreed upon. Those who wished to keep the Jewish Sabbath did so; and those who did not wish to, did not do so. This is seen from the fact that Justin Martyr, a Christian Father who flourished about A.D. 140, did not observe the day. In his "Dialogue" with Typho, the Jew reproaches the Christians for not keeping the "Sabbath." Justin admits the charge by saying:

"Do you not see that the Elements keep no Sabbaths, and are never idle? Continue as you were created. If there was no need of circumcision before Abraham's time, and no need of the Sabbath, of festivals and oblations, before the time of Moses, *neither of them are necessary after the coming of Christ.* If any among you is guilty of perjury, fraud, or other crimes, let him cease from them and repent, and he will have kept *the* kind of Sabbath pleasing to God."

---

[1] Rev. M. J. Savage.   [2] Acts, xv. 20.

There was no binding authority then, among the Christians, as to whether they should keep the first or the seventh day of the week holy, or not, until the time of the first Christian Roman Emperor. "*Constantine, a Sun worshiper, who had, as other Heathen, kept the Sun-day, publicly ordered this to supplant the Jewish Sabbath.*"[1] He commanded that this day should be kept holy, throughout the whole Roman empire, and sent an edict to all governors of provinces to this effect.[2] *Thus we see how the great Pagan festival, in honor of Sol the invincible, was transformed into a Christian holy-day.*

Not only were Pagan festival days changed into Christian holy-days, but Pagan idols were converted into Christian saints, and Pagan temples into Christian churches.

A Pagan temple at Rome, formerly sacred to the "*Bona Dea*" (the "Good Goddess"), was Christianized and dedicated to the Virgin Mary. In a place formerly sacred to Apollo, there now stands the church of Saint Apollinaris. Where there anciently stood the temple of Mars, may now be seen the church of Saint Martine.[3] A Pagan temple, originally dedicated to "*Cœlestis Dea*" (the "Heavenly Goddess"), by one Aurelius, a Pagan high-priest, was converted into a Christian church by another Aurelius, created Bishop of Carthage in the year 390 of Christ. He placed his episcopal chair in the very place where the statue of the Heavenly Goddess had stood.[4]

The noblest heathen temple now remaining in the world, is the *Pantheon* or *Rotunda*, which, as the inscription over the portico informs us, having been *impiously* dedicated of old by Agrippa to "Jove and all the gods," was *piously* reconsecrated by Pope Boniface the Fourth, to "The Mother of God and all the Saints."[5]

The church of Saint Reparatae, at Florence, was formerly a Pagan temple. An inscription was found in the foundation of this church, of these words: "To the Great Goddess Nutria."[6] The church of St. Stephen, at Bologna, was formed from heathen temples, one of which was a temple of Isis.[7]

At the southern extremity of the present Forum at Rome, and just under the Palatine hill — where the noble babes, who, miraculously preserved, became the founders of a state that was to command the world, were exposed—stands the church of St. Theodore.

[1] Bonwick : Egyptian Belief, p. 182.
[2] See Eusebius' Life of Constantine, lib. iv. chs. xviii. and xxiii.
[3] See Taylor's Diegesis, p. 237.
[4] See Bell's Pantheon, vol. i. p. 187, and
Gibbon's Rome, vol. iii. pp. 142, 143.
[5] See Taylor's Diegesis, p. 226, and Gibbon's Rome, vol. iii. pp. 142, 143
[6] Higgins' Anacalypsis, vol. i. p. 137.
[7] Ibid. p. 307.

This temple was built in honor of Romulus, and the brazen wolf—commemorating the curious manner in which the founders of Rome were nurtured — occupied a place here till the sixteenth century. And, as the Roman matrons of old used to carry their children, when ill, to the temple of Romulus, so too, the women still carry their children to St. Theodore on the same occasions.

In *Christianizing* these Pagan temples, free use was made of the sculptured and painted stones of heathen monuments. In some cases they evidently painted over one name, and inserted another. This may be seen from the following

INSCRIPTIONS FORMERLY IN PAGAN *and* TEMPLES.	INSCRIPTIONS NOW IN CHRISTIAN CHURCHES.
1.	**1.**
To Mercury and Minerva, Tutelary Gods.	To St. Mary and St. Francis, My Tutelaries.
2.	**2.**
To the Gods who preside over this Temple.	To the Divine Eustrogius, who presides over this Temple.
3.	**3.**
To the Divinity of Mercury the Availing, the Powerful, the Unconquered.	To the Divinity of St. George the Availing, the Powerful, the Unconquered.
4.	**4.**
Sacred to the Gods and Goddesses, with Jove the best and greatest.	Sacred to the presiding helpers, St. George and St. Stephen, with God the best and greatest.
5.	**5.**
Venus' Pigeon.	The Holy Ghost represented as a Pigeon.
6.	**6.**
The Mystical Letters I. H. S.[1]	The Mystical Letters I. H. S.[2]

In many cases the *Images* of the Pagan gods were allowed to remain in these temples, and, after being *Christianized,* continued to receive divine honors.[3]

"In St. Peter's, Rome, is a statue of *Jupiter*, deprived of his thunderbolt, which is replaced by the emblematic keys. In like manner, much of the religion of the lower orders, which we regard as essentially *Christian*, is ancient *heathenism*, refitted with Christian symbols."[4] We find that as early as the time of St. Gregory, Bishop of Neo-Cesarea (A. D. 243), the "simple" and "unskilled"

---

[1] Gruter's Inscriptions. Quoted in Taylor's Diegesis, p. 237.
[3] Boldonius' Epigraphs. Quoted in Ibid.
[3] See Bell's Pantheon, vol. ii. p. 237. Tay-lor's Diegesis, p. 48, and Middleton's Letters from Rome.
[4] Baring-Gould's Curious Myths, p. 426.

multitudes of Christians were allowed to pay divine honors to these images, hoping that in the process of time they would learn better.[1] In fact, as Prof. Draper says:

"Olympus was restored, but the divinities passed under other names. The more powerful provinces insisted upon the adoption of their time-honored conceptions. . . . Not only was the adoration of *ISIS* under a new name restored, but even her image, standing on the crescent moon, reappeared. The well-known effigy of that goddess with the infant Horus in her arms, has descended to our days in the beautiful, artistic creations of the Madonna and child. Such restorations of old conceptions under novel forms were everywhere received with delight. When it was announced to the Ephesians, that the Council of that place, headed by Cyril, had declared that the Virgin (Mary) should be called the ' *Mother of God*,' with tears of joy they embraced the knees of their bishop ; it was the old instinct cropping out ; their ancestors would have done the same for Diana."[2]

> "O bright goddess ; once again
> Fix on earth thy heav'nly reign ;
> Be thy sacred name ador'd,
> Altars rais'd, and rites restor'd."

Nestorius, Bishop of Constantinople from 428 A. D., refused to call Mary " *the mother of God*," on the ground that she could be the mother of the human nature only, which the divine Logos used as its organ. Cyril, Bishop of Alexandria, did all in his power to stir up the minds of the people against Nestorius; the consequence was that, both at Rome and at Alexandria, Nestorius was accused of heresy. The dispute grew more bitter, and Theodosius II. thought it necessary to convoke an Œcumenical Council at Ephesus in 431. On this, as on former occasions, the affirmative party overruled the negative. The person of Mary began to rise in the new empyrean. The paradoxical name of " *Mother of God*" pleased the popular piety. Nestorius was condemned, and died in exile.

The shrine of many an old hero was filled by the statue of some imaginary saint.

"They have not always" (says Dr. Conyers Middleton), "as I am well informed, given themselves the trouble of making even this change, but have been contented sometimes to take up with the *old image*, just as they found it ; after baptizing it only, as it were, or consecrating it anew, by the imposition of a Christian name. This their antiquaries do not scruple to put strangers in mind of, in showing their churches, as it was, I think, in that of St. Agnes, where they showed me an antique statue of a young *BACCHUS*, which, with a new name, and some little change of drapery, stands now worshiped under the title of a female saint."[3]

In many parts of Italy are to be seen pictures of the "Holy Family," of extreme antiquity, the grounds of them often of gold.

---

[1] Mosheim, Cent. ii. p. 202. Quoted in Taylor's Diegesis, p. 48.

[2] Draper : Religion and Science, pp. 48, 49.
[3] Middleton's Letters from Rome, p. 84.

These pictures represent the mother with a child on her knee, and
a little boy standing close by her side; the *Lamb* is generally seen
in the picture. They are inscribed "*Deo Soli*," and are simply
ancient representations of Isis and Horus. The *Lamb* is "The
Lamb that taketh away the sins of the world," which, as we have
already seen, was believed on in the Pagan world centuries before
the time of Christ Jesus.[1] Some half-pagan Christian went so far
as to forge a book, which he attributed to Christ Jesus himself,
which was for the purpose of showing that he—Christ Jesus—
was in no way against these heathen gods.[2]

The *Icelanders* were induced to embrace Christianity, with its
legends and miracles, and sainted divinities, as the Christian monks
were ready to substitute for Thor, their warrior-god, Michael, the
warrior-angel; for Freyja, their goddess, the Virgin Mary; and for
the god Vila, a St. Valentine—probably manufactured for the occasion.

"The statues of Jupiter, Apollo, Mercury, Orpheus, did duty
for *The Christ*.[3] The Thames River god officates at the baptism
of Jesus in the Jordan. Peter holds the keys of Janus.[4] Moses
wears the horns of Jove. Ceres, Cybele, Demeter assume new
names, as '*Queen of Heaven*,' '*Star of the Sea*,' '*Maria Illumin-
atrix*;' Dionysius is St. Denis; Cosmos is St. Cosmo; Pluto and
Proserpine resign their seats in the hall of final judgment to the
Christ and his mother. The Parcæ depute one of their number,
Lachesis, the disposer of lots, to set the stamp of destiny upon the
deaths of Christian believers. The *aura placida* of the poets, the
gentle breeze, is personified as Aura and Placida. The *perpetua
felicitas* of the devotee becomes a lovely presence in the forms of
St. Perpetua and St. Felicitas, guardian angels of the pious soul.
No relic of Paganism was permitted to remain in its casket. The
depositories were all ransacked. The shadowy hands of Egyptian
priests placed the urn of holy water at the porch of the basilica,
which stood ready to be converted into a temple. Priests of the

[1] See Higgins' Anacalypsis.
[2] Jones on the Canon, vol. i. p. 11.
Diegesis, p. 40.
[3] Compare "Apollo among the Muses," and
"The Vine and its Branches" (that is, Christ
Jesus and his Disciples), in Lundy's *Monumental Christianity*, pp. 141-143. As Mr. Lundy
says, there is so striking a resemblance between the two, that one looks very much like
a copy of the other. Apollo is also represented
as the "*Good Shepherd*," with a lamb upon
his back, just exactly as Christ Jesus is represented in Christian Art. (See Lundy's Mon-

umental Christianity, and Jameson's Hist. of
Our Lord in Art.)
[4] The Roman god Jonas, or Janus, with his
keys, was changed into Peter, who was surnamed Bar-Jonas. Many years ago a statue
of the god Janus, in bronze, being found in
Rome, he was perched up in St. Peter's with
his keys in his hand : the very identical god,
in all his native ugliness. This statue sits as
St. Peter, under the cupola of the church of
St. Peter. It is looked upon with the most
profound veneration : the toes are nearly kissed
away by devotees

most ancient faiths of Palestine, Assyria, Babylon, Thebes, Persia,
were permitted to erect the altar at the point where the transverse
beam of the cross meets the main stem.   The hands that constructed
the temple in cruciform shape had long become too attenuated to
cast the faintest shadow.   There Devaki with the infant Crishna,
Maya with the babe Buddha, Juno with the child Mars, represent
Mary with Jesus in her arms.   Coarse emblems are not rejected ;
the Assyrian dove is a tender symbol of the Holy Ghost. The rag-
bags and toy boxes were explored.   A bauble which the Roman
schoolboy had thrown away was picked up, and called an ' *agnus
dei*.'   The musty wardrobes of forgotten hierarchies furnished cos-
tumes for the officers of the new prince.   Alb and chasuble recalled
the fashions of Numa's day.   The cast-off purple habits and shoes
of Pagan emperors beautified the august persons of Christian popes.
The cardinals must be contented with the robes once worn by senators.   Zoroaster bound about the monks the girdle he invented as
a protection against evil spirits, and clothed them in the frocks he
had found convenient for his ritual.   The pope thrust out his foot
to be kissed, as Caligula, Heliogabalus, and Julius Cesar had thrust
out theirs.   Nothing came amiss to the faith that was to discharge
henceforth the offices of spiritual impression."[1]

The ascetic and monastic life practiced by some Christians of
the present day, is of great antiquity.   Among the Buddhists there
are priests who are ordained, tonsured, live in monasteries, and
make vows of celibacy.   There are also nuns among them, whose
vows and discipline are the same as the priests.[2]

The close resemblance between the ancient religion of *Thibet* and
Nepaul — where the worship of a crucified God was found — and
the Roman Catholic religion of the present day, is very striking.
In Thibet was found the pope, or head of the religion, whom they
called the "Dalai Lama ; "[3] they use holy water, they celebrate a
sacrifice with bread and wine; they give extreme unction, pray for
the sick ; they have monasteries, and convents for women ; they
chant in their services, have fasts; they worship one God in a trinity, believe in a hell, heaven, and a half-way place or purgatory ;
they make prayers and sacrifices for the dead, have confession, adore
the cross ; have chaplets, or strings of beads to count their prayers,
and many other practices common to the Roman Catholic Church.[4]

[1] Frothingham : The Cradle of the Christ, p. 179.
[2] See Hardy's Eastern Monachism.
[3] The "Grand Lama" is the head of a priestly order in Thibet and Tartary.   The office is not hereditary, but, like the Pope of Rome, he is elected by the priests. (Inman's Ancient Faiths, vol. ii. p. 203. See also, Bell's Pantheon, vol. ii. pp. 32–34.)
[4] See Higgins' Anacalypsis, vol. i. p. 233.

The resemblance between Buddhism and Christianity has been re-marked by many travelers in the eastern countries. Sir John Francis Davis, in his "History of China," speaking of Buddhism in that country, says:

" Certain it is—and the observance may be daily made even at Canton—that they (the Buddhist priests) practice the ordinances of celibacy, fasting, and prayers for the dead ; they have holy water, rosaries of beads, which they count with their prayers, the worship of relics, and a monastic habit resembling that of the Franciscans " (an order of Roman Catholic monks).

Père Premere, a Jesuit missionary to China, was driven to con-clude that the devil had practiced a trick to perplex his friends, the Jesuits. To others, however, it is not so difficult to account for these things as it seemed for the good Father. Sir John continues his account as follows:

' These priests are associated in monasteries attached to the temples of Fo. They are in China precisely a society of mendicants, and go about, like monks of that description in the Romish Church, asking alms for the support of their establishment. Their tonsure extends to the hair of the whole head. There is a regular gradation among the priesthood ; and according to his reputation for sanctity, his length of service and other claims, each priest may rise from the lowest rank of servitor—whose duty it is to perform the menial offices of the temple—to that of officiating priest—and ultimately of 'Tae Hoepang,' Abbot or head of the establishment."

The five principal precepts, or rather interdicts, addressed to the Buddhist priests are :

1. Do not kill.
2. Do not steal.
3. Do not marry.
4. Speak not falsely.
5. Drink no wine.

Poo-ta-la is the name of a monastery, described in Lord Macart-ney's mission, and is an extensive establishment, which was found in Manchow-Tartary, beyond the great wall. This building offered shelter to no less than eight hundred Chinese Buddhist priests.[1]

The Rev. Mr. Gutzlaff, in his " Journal of Voyages along the coast of China," tells us that he found the Buddhist " Monasteries, nuns, and friars very numerous ;" and adds that : " their priests are generally very ignorant."[2]

This reminds us of the fact that, for centuries during the " dark ages " of Christianity, Christian bishops and prelates, the teachers, spiritual pastors and masters, were mostly *marksmen*, that is, they

---

Inman's Ancient Faiths, vol. ii. p. 203, and Isis Unveiled, vol. i². p. 211.

[1] Davis : Hist. China, vol. ii. pp. 105, 106.
[2] Gutzlaff's Voyages, p. 309.

supplied, by the sign of the cross, their inability to write their own name.[1] Many of the bishops in the Councils of Ephesus and Chalcedon, it is said, could not write their names. Ignorance was not considered a disqualification for ordination. A cloud of ignorance overspread the whole face of the Church, hardly broken by a few glimmering lights, who owe almost the whole of their distinction to the surrounding darkness.[2]

One of the principal objects of curiosity to the Europeans who first went to China, was a large monastery at Canton. This monastery, which was dedicated to Fo, or Buddha, and which is on a very large scale, is situated upon the southern side of the river. There are extensive grounds surrounding the building, planted with trees, in the center of which is a broad pavement of granite, which is kept very clean. An English gentleman, Mr. Bennett, entered this establishment, which he fully describes. He says that after walking along this granite pavement, they entered a temple, where the priesthood happened to be assembled, worshiping. They were arranged in rows, chanting, striking gongs, &c. These priests, with their shaven crowns, and arrayed in the yellow robes of the religion, appeared to go through the mummery with devotion. As soon as the mummery had ceased, the priests all flocked out of the temple, adjourned to their respective rooms, divested themselves of their official robes, and the images — among which were evidently representations of Shin-moo, the "Holy Mother," and "Queen of Heaven," and "The Three Pure Ones," — were left to themselves, with lamps burning before them.

To expiate sin, offerings made to these priests are — according to the Buddhist idea — sufficient. To facilitate the release of some unfortunate from purgatory, they said masses. Their prayers are counted by means of a rosary, and they live in a state of celibacy.

Mr. Gutzlaff, in describing a temple dedicated to Buddha, situated on the island of Poo-ta-la, says:

"We were present at the vespers of the priests, which they chanted in the Pali language, not unlike the Latin service of the Romish church. They held their rosaries in their hands, which rested folded upon their breasts. One of them had a small bell, by the tingling of which the service was regulated."

The Buddhists in *India* have similar institutions. The French missionary, M. L'Abbé Huc, says of them:

"The Buddhist ascetic not aspiring to elevate himself only, he practiced virtue and applied himself to perfection to make other men share in its belief; and

[1] See Taylor's Diegesis, p. 84.　　　[2] See Hallam's Middle Ages.

by the institution of an order of religious mendicants, which increased to an immense extent, he attached towards him, and restored to society, the poor and unfortunate. It was, indeed, precisely because Buddha received among his disciples miserable creatures who were outcasts from the respectable class of India,
that he became an object of mockery to the Brahmins. But he merely replied to
their taunts, 'My law is a law of mercy for all.' "[1]

In the words of Viscount Amberly, we can say that, "Monasticism, in countries where Buddhism reigns supreme, is a vast and
powerful institution."

The *Essenes*, of whom we shall speak more fully anon, were an
order of ascetics, dwelling in monasteries. Among the order of
Pythagoras, which was very similar to the Essenes, there was an
order of nuns.[2] The ancient Druids admitted females into their
sacred order, and initiated them into the mysteries of their religion.[3]
The priestesses of the Saxon Frigga devoted themselves to perpetual
virginity.[4] The vestal virgins[5] were bound by a solemn vow to preserve their chastity for a space of thirty years.[6]

The Egyptian priests of Isis were obliged to observe perpetual
chastity.[7] They were also tonsured like the Buddhist priests.[8] The
Assyrian, Arabian, Persian and Egyptian priests wore *white* sur-
plices,[9] and so did the ancient Druids. The Corinthian Aphrodite
had her Hierodoulio, the pure Gerairai ministered to the goddess of
the Parthenon, the altar of the Latin Vesta was tended by her chosen
virgins, and the Romish "Queen of Heaven" has her nuns.

When the Spaniards had established themselves in Mexico and
Peru, they were astonished to find, among other things which closely
resembled their religion, *monastic institutions* on a large scale.

The Rev. Father Acosta, in his "Natural and Moral History of
the Indies," says :

"There is one thing worthy of special regard, the which is, how the Devil, by
his pride, hath opposed himself to God ; and that which God, by his wisdom,
hath decreed for his honor and service, and for the good and health of man, the
devil strives to imitate and pervert, to be honored, and to cause men to be
damned: for as we see the great God hath Sacrifices, Priests, Sacraments, Religious Prophets, and Ministers, dedicated to his divine service and holy ceremonies, so likewise the devil hath his Sacrifices, Priests, his kinds of Sacraments, his Ministers appointed, his secluded and feigned holiness, with a thousand sorts of false prophets."[10]

"We find among all the nations of the world, men especially dedicated to
the service of the true God, or to the false, which serve in sacrifices, and declare

[1] Huc's Travels, vol. i. p. 329.
[2] See Hardy's Eastern Monachism, p. 163.
[3] Ibid.
[4] Ibid.
[5] "Vestal Virgins," an order of virgins
consecrated to the goddess Vesta.
[6] Hardy : Eastern Monachism, p. 163.
[7] Ibid. p. 48.
[8] See Herodotus, b. ii. ch. 36.
[9] Dunlap : Son of the Man, p. x.
[10] Acosta, vol. ii. p. 324.

unto the people what their gods command them. There was in Mexico a
strange curiosity upon this point. And the devil, counterfeiting the use of the
church of God, hath placed in the order of his Priests, some greater or superiors, and some less, the one as Acolites, the other as Levites, and that which hath
made most to wonder, was, that the devil would usurp to himself the service of
God ; yea, and use the same name : for the Mexicans in their ancient tongue call
their high priests *Papes*, as they should say sovereign bishops, as it appears
now by their histories."[1]

In Mexico, within the circuit of the great temple, there were
two monasteries, one for virgins, the other for men, which they
called religious. These men lived poorly and chastely, and did the
office of Levites.[2]

' These priests and religious men used great fastings, of five or ten days together, before any of their great feasts, and they were unto them as our four
ember week ; they were so strict in continence that some of them (not to fall
into any sensuality) slit their members in the midst, and did a thousand things
to make themselves unable, lest they should offend their gods."[3]

" There were in Peru many monasteries of virgins (for there are no other admitted), at the least one in every province. In these monasteries there were two
sorts of women, one ancient, which they called Mamacomas (mothers), for the
instruction of the young, and the other was of young maidens placed there for a
certain time, and after they were drawn forth, either for their gods or for the
Inca." "If any of the Mamacomas or Acllas were found to have trespassed
against their honor, it was an inevitable chastisement to bury them alive or
to put them to death by some other kind of cruel torment."[4]

The Rev. Father concludes by saying :

"In truth it is very strange to see that this false opinion of religion hath so
great force among these young men and maidens of Mexico, that they will serve
the devil with so great rigor and austerity, which many of us do not in the service
of the most high God, the which is a great shame and confusion."[5]

The religious orders of the ancient Mexicans and Peruvians are
described at length in Lord Kingsborough's " Mexican Antiquities,"
and by most every writer on ancient Mexico. Differing in minor
details, the grand features of self-consecration are everywhere the
same, whether we look to the saintly Rishis of ancient India, to the
wearers of the yellow robe in China or Ceylon, to the Essenes
among the Jews, to the devotees of Vitziliputzli in pagan Mexico,
or to the monks and nuns of Christian times in Africa, in Asia, and
in Europe. Throughout the various creeds of these distant lands
there runs the same unconquerable impulse, producing the same remarkable effects.

The " *Sacred Heart*," was a great mystery with the ancients.

[1] Acosta, vol. ii. p. 330.
[2] Ibid. p. 336.
[3] Ibid. p. 338.
[4] Ibid. pp. 332, 333.
[5] Ibid. p. 337

Horus, the Egyptian virgin-born Saviour, was represented carrying the sacred heart outside on his breast. *Vishnu*, the Mediator and Preserver of the Hindoos, was also represented in that manner. So was it with *Bel* of Babylon.[1] In like manner, Christ Jesus, the Christian Saviour, is represented at the present day.

The amulets or charms which the Roman Christians wear, to drive away diseases, and to protect them from harm, are other relics of paganism. The ancient pagans wore these charms for the same purpose. The name of their favorite god was generally inscribed upon them, and we learn by a quotation from Chrysostom that the Christians at Antioch used to bind brass coins of Alexander the Great about their heads, to keep off or drive away diseases.[2] The Christians also used amulets with the name or monogram of the god *Serapis* engraved thereon, which show that it made no difference whether the god was their own or that of another. Even the charm which is worn by the Christians at the present day, has none other than the monogram of *Bacchus* engraved thereon, *i. e.*, I. H. S.[3]

The ancient Roman children carried around their necks a small ornament in the form of a heart, called *Bulla*. This was imitated by the early Christians. Upon their ancient monuments in the Vatican, the heart is very common, and it may be seen in numbers of old pictures. After some time it was succeeded by the *Agnus Dei*, which, like the ancient *Bulla*, was supposed to avert dangers from the children and the wearers of them. Cardinal Baronias (an eminent Roman Catholic ecclesiastical historian, born at Sora, in Naples, A. D. 1538) says, that those who have been baptized carry pendent from their neck an *Agnus Dei*, in imitation of a devotion of the Pagans, who hung to the neck of their children little bottles in the form of a heart, which served as preservatives against charms and enchantments. Says Mr. Cox:

"That ornaments in the shape of a *vesica* have been popular in all countries as preservatives against dangers, and especially from evil spirits, can as little be questioned as the fact that they still retain some measure of their ancient popularity in England, where horse-shoes are nailed to walls as a safeguard against unknown perils, where a shoe is thrown by way of good-luck after newly-married couples, and where the villagers have not yet ceased to dance round the May-pole on the green."[4]

All of these are emblems of either the Lingha or Yoni.

The use of amulets was carried to the most extravagant excess

1 Bonwick's Egyptian Belief, p. 241.   3 See Chap. XXXIII.
2 See Lardner's Works, vol. viii. pp. 375, 376.   4 Cox : Aryan Mythology, vol. ii. p. 127.

in ancient Egypt, and their Sacred Book of the Dead, even in its earliest form, shows the importance attached to such things.[1]

We can say with M. Renan that:

"Almost all our superstitions are the remains of a religion anterior to Christianity, and which Christianity has not been able entirely to root out."[2]

Baptismal fonts were used by the pagans, as well as the little cisterns which are to be seen at the entrance of Catholic churches. In the temple of Apollo, at Delphi, there were two of these; one of silver, and the other of gold.[3]

Temples always faced the east, to receive the rays of the rising sun. They contained an outer court for the public, and an inner sanctuary for the priests, called the "*Adytum.*" Near the entrance was a large vessel, of stone or brass, filled with water, made holy by plunging into it a burning torch from the altar. All who were admitted to the sacrifices were sprinkled with this water, and none but the unpolluted were allowed to pass beyond it. In the center of the building stood the statue of the god, on a pedestal raised above the altar and enclosed by a railing. On festival occasions, the people brought laurel, olive, or ivy, to decorate the pillars and walls. Before they entered they always washed their hands, as a type of purification from sin.[4] A story is told of a man who was struck dead by a thunderbolt because he omitted this ceremony when entering a temple of Jupiter. Sometimes they crawled up the steps on their knees, and bowing their heads to the ground, kissed the threshold. Always when they passed one of these sacred edifices they kissed their right hand to it, in token of veneration.

In all the temples of Vishnu, Crishna, Rama, Durga, and Kali, in India, there are to be seen idols before which lights and incense are burned. Moreover, the idols of these gods are constantly decorated with flowers and costly ornaments, especially on festive occasions.[5] The ancient Egyptian worship had a great splendor of ritual. There was a morning service, a kind of mass, celebrated by a priest, shorn and beardless; there were sprinklings of holy water, &c., &c.[6] All of this kind of worship was finally adopted by the Christians.

The sublime and simple theology of the primitive Christians

---

[1] Renouf: Hibbert Lectures, p. 191.
[2] Renan: Hibbert Lectures, p. 32.
[3] See Taylor's Diegesis, p. 232.
[4] "At their entrance, purifying themselves by washing their hands in *holy water*, they were at the same time admonished to present themselves with pure minds, without which the external cleanness of the body would by no means be accepted." (Bell's Pantheon, vol. ii. p. 282.)
[5] See Williams' Hinduism, p. 99.
[6] See Renan's Hibbert Lectures, p. 35.

was gradually corrupted and degraded by the introduction of a popular mythology, which tended to restore the reign of poly theism.

As the objects of religion were gradually reduced to the standard of the imagination, the rites and ceremonies were introduced that seemed most powerfully to affect the senses of the vulgar. If, in the beginning of the fifth century, Tertullian, or Lactantius, had been suddenly raised from the dead, to assist at the festival of some popular saint or martyr, they would have gazed with astonishment and indignation on the profane spectacle, which had succeeded to the pure and spiritual worship of a Christian congregation.[1]

Dr. Draper, in speaking of the early Christian Church, says:

"Great is the difference between Christianity under Severus (born 146) and Christianity under Constantine (born 274). Many of the doctrines which at the latter period were pre-eminent, in the former were unknown. Two causes led to the amalgamation of Christianity with Paganism. 1. The political necessities of the new dynasty : 2. The policy adopted by the new religion to insure its spread.

"Though the Christian party had proved itself sufficiently strong to give a master to the empire, it was never sufficiently strong to destroy its antagonist, Paganism. The issue of the struggle between them *was an amalgamation of the principles of both.* In this, Christianity differed from Mohammedanism, which absolutely annihilated its antagonist, and spread its own doctrines without adulteration.

"Constantine continually showed by his acts that he felt he must be the impartial sovereign of all his people, not merely the representative of a successful faction. Hence, if he built Christian churches, he also restored Pagan temples ; if he listened to the clergy, he also consulted the haruspices ; if he summoned the Council of Nicea, he also honored the statue of Fortune ; if he accepted the rite of Baptism, he also struck a medal bearing his title of 'God.' His statue, on top of the great porphyry pillar at Constantinople, consisted of an ancient image of Apollo, whose features were replaced by those of the emperor, and its head surrounded by the nails feigned to have been used at the crucifixion of Christ, arranged so as to form a crown of glory.

"Feeling that there must be concessions to the defeated Pagan party, in accordance with its ideas, he looked with favor on the idolatrous movements of his court. In fact, the leaders of these movements were persons of his own family.

To the emperor,—a mere worldling—a man without any religious convictions, doubtless it appeared best for himself, best for the empire, and best for the contending parties, Christian and Pagan, to promote their *union or amalgamation as much as possible.* Even sincere Christians do not seem to have been averse to this; perhaps they believed that the new doctrines would diffuse most thoroughly by incorporating in themselves ideas borrowed from the old; that Truth would assert herself in the end, and the impurities be cast off. In accomplishing this amalgamation, Helen, the Empress-mother, aided by the court ladies, led the way.

---

[1] Edward Gibbon : Decline and Fall, vol. iiL p. 161.

"As years passed on, the faith described by Tertullian (A.D. 150–195) was transformed into one more fashionable and more debased. It was incorporated with the old Greek mythology. Olympus was restored, but the divinities passed under new names. . . . .

"Heathen rites were adopted, a pompous and splendid ritual, gorgeous robes, mitres, tiaras, wax-tapers, processional services, lustrations, gold and silver vases, were introduced.

"The festival of the Purification of the Virgin was invented to remove the uneasiness of heathen converts on account of the loss of their Lupercalia, or feasts of Pan.

"The apotheosis of the old Roman times was replaced by canonization; tutelary *saints* succeeded to local mythological divinities. Then came the mystery of *transubstantiation*, or the conversion of bread and wine by the priest into the flesh and blood of Christ. As centuries passed, the *paganization* became more and more complete."[1]

The early Christian saints, bishops, and fathers, *confessedly* adopted the liturgies, rites, ceremonies, and terms of heathenism ; making it their boast, that the pagan religion, properly explained, really was nothing else than Christianity ; that the best and wisest of its professors, in all ages, had been Christians all along; that Christianity was but a name more recently acquired to a religion which had previously existed, and had been known to the Greek philosophers, to Plato, Socrates, and Heraclitus ; and that " if the writings of Cicero had been read as they ought to have been, there would have been no occasion for the Christian Scriptures."

And our Protestant, and most orthodox Christian divines, the best learned on ecclesiastical antiquity, and most entirely persuaded of the truth of the Christian religion, unable to resist or to conflict with the constraining demonstration of the data that prove the absolute sameness and identity of Paganism and Christianity, and unable to point out so much as one single idea or notion, of which they could show that it was peculiar to Christianity, or that Christianity had it, and Paganism had it not, have invented the apology of an hypothesis, that the Pagan religion was *typical*, and that Crishna, Buddha, Bacchus, Hercules, Adonis, Osiris, Horus, &c., were all of them *types* and forerunners of the *true* and *real* Saviour, Christ Jesus. Those who are satisfied with this kind of reasoning are certainly welcome to it.

That Christianity is nothing more than Paganism under a new name, has, as we said above, been admitted over and over again by the Fathers of the Church, and others. Aringhus (in his account of subterraneous Rome) acknowledges the conformity between the Pagan and Christian form of worship, and defends the admission

---

[1] Draper : Science and Religion, pp. 46–49.

of the ceremonies of heathenism into the service of the Church, by the authority of the wisest prelates and governors, whom, he says, found it necessary, in the conversion of the Gentiles, to dissemble, and wink at many things, and yield to the times; and not to use force against customs which the people were so obstinately fond of.[1]

Melito (a Christian bishop of Sardis), in an *apology* delivered to the Emperor Marcus Antoninus, in the year 170, claims the patronage of the emperor, for the *now* called Christian religion, which he calls "*our philosophy*," "on account of its *high antiquity*, as having been *imported* from countries lying beyond the limits of the Roman empire, in the region of his ancestor Augustus, who found its *importation* ominous of good fortune to his government."[2] This is an absolute demonstration that Christianity did *not* originate in Judea, which was a Roman province, but really was an exotic oriental fable, *imported* from India, and that Paul was doing as he claimed, viz.: preaching a God manifest in the flesh who had been "believed on in the world" centuries before his time, and a doctrine which had already been preached "unto every creature under heaven."

Baronius (an eminent Catholic ecclesiastical historian) says:

"It is permitted to the Church to use, *for the purpose of piety*, the ceremonies which the pagans used *for the purpose of impiety* in a superstitious religion, after having first expiated them by consecration—to the end, that the devil might receive a greater affront from employing, in honor of Jesus Christ, that which his enemy had destined for his own service."[3]

Clarke, in his "Evidences of Revealed Religion," says:

"Some of the ancient writers of the church have not scrupled expressly to call the Athenian *Socrates*, and some others of the best of the *heathen moralists*, by the name of *Christians*, and to affirm, as the law was as it were a schoolmaster, to bring the Jews unto Christ, so true moral philosophy was to the Gentiles a preparative to receive the gospel."[4]

Clemens Alexandrinus says:

"Those who lived according to the *Logos* were really *Christians*, though they have been thought to be atheists ; as Socrates and Heraclitus were among the Greeks, and such as resembled them."[5]

And St. Augustine says:

"*That*, in our times, is the *Christian religion*, which to know and follow is the most sure and certain health, called according to that name, but not accord-

[1] See Taylor's Diegesis, p. 237.
[2] Quoted in Taylor's Diegesis, p. 249. See also, Eusebius : Eccl. Hist., book iv. ch. xxvi. who alludes to it.
[3] Baronius' Annals, An. 36.
[4] Quoted by Rev. R. Taylor, Diegesis p. 41.
[5] Strom. bk. i. ch. xix.

ing to the thing itself, of which it is the name ; for the thing itself which is now called the *Christian religion,* really was known to the ancients, nor was wanting at any time from the beginning of the human race, until the time when Christ came in the flesh, from whence the true religion, *which had previously existed,* began to be called *Christian ;* and this in our days is the Christian religion, not as having been wanting in former times, but as having in later times received this name."[1]

Eusebius, the great champion of Christianity, admits that that which is called the Christian religion, is neither new nor strange, but—if it be lawful to testify the truth—was known to the *ancients.*[2]

How the common people were Christianized, we gather from a remarkable passage which Mosheim, the ecclesiastical historian, has preserved for us, in the life of Gregory, surnamed " *Thaumaturgus,*" that is, "the wonder worker." The passage is as follows :

" When Gregory perceived that the simple and unskilled multitude persisted in their worship of images, on account of the pleasures and sensual gratifications which they enjoyed at the Pagan festivals, *he granted them a permission to indulge themselves in the like pleasures,* in celebrating the memory of the holy martyrs, hoping that in process of time, they would return of their own accord, to a more virtuous and regular course of life."[3]

The historian remarks that there is no sort of doubt, that by this permission, Gregory allowed the Christians to dance, sport, and feast at the tombs of the martyrs, upon their respective festivals, and to do everything which the Pagans were accustomed to do in their temples, during the feasts celebrated in honor of their gods.

The learned Christian advocate, M. Turretin, in describing the state of Christianity in the fourth century, has a well-turned rhetoricism, the point of which is, that " it was not so much the empire that was brought over to the faith, as the faith that was brought over to the empire ; not the Pagans who were converted to Christianity, but Christianity that was converted to Paganism."[4]

Edward Gibbon says:

---

[1] " Ea est nostris temporibus Christiana religio, quam cognoscere ac sequi securissima et certissima salus est : secundum hoc nomen dictum est non secundum ipsam rem cujus hoc nomen est : nam res ipsa quæ nunc Christiana religio nuncupatur erat et apud antiquos, nec defuit ab initio generis humani, quousque ipse Christus veniret in carne, unde vera religio quæ jam erat cœpit appellari Christiana. Hæc est nostris temporibus Christiana religio, non quia prioribus temporibus non fuit, sed quia posterioribus hoc nomen accepit." (Opera Augustini, vol. i. p. 12. Quoted in Taylor's Diegesis, p. 42.)

[2] See Eusebius : Eccl. Hist., lib. 2, ch. v.

[3] " Cum animadvertisset Gregorius quod ob

corporeas delectationes et voluptates, simplex et imperitum vulgus in simulacrorum cultus errore permaneret—permisit eis, ut in memoriam et recordationem sanctorum martyrum sese oblectarent, et in lætitiam effunderentur, quod successu temporis aliquando futurum esset, ut sua sponte, ad honestiorem et accuratiorem vitæ rationem, transirent." (Mosheim, vol. i. cent. 2, p. 202.

[4] " Non imperio ad fidem adducto, sed et imperii pompa ecclesiam inficiente. Non ethnicis ad Christum conversis, sed et Christi religione ad Ethnicæ formam depravata." (Orat. Academ. De Variis Christ. Rel. fatis.)

"It must be confessed that the ministers of the Catholic church imitated the profane model which they were impatient to destroy. The most respectable bishops had persuaded themselves, that the ignorant rusties would more cheerfully renounce the superstitions of Paganism, if they found some resemblance, some compensation, in the bosom of Christianity. The religion of Constantine achieved, in less than a century, the final conquest of the Roman empire : *but the victors themselves were insensibly subdued by the arts of their vanquished rivals.*"[1]

Faustus, writing to St. Augustine, says:

" You have substituted your agapæ for the sacrifices of the Pagans ; for their idols your martyrs, whom you serve with the very same honors. You appease the shades of the dead with wine and feasts ; you celebrate the solemn festivities of the *Gentiles*, their calends, and their solstices ; and, as to their manners, those you have retained without any alteration. *Nothing distinguishes you from the Pagans, except that you hold your assemblies apart from them.*"[2]

Ammonius Saccus (a Greek philosopher, founder of the Neoplatonic school) taught that :

"Christianity and Paganism, when rightly understood, differ in no essential points, but had a common origin, *and are really one and the same thing.*"[3]

Justin explains the thing in the following manner :

' "It having reached the devil's ears that the prophets had foretold that Christ would come . . . he (the devil) set the heathen poets to bring forward a great many who should be called sons of Jove, (*i.e.*, " The Sons of God.") The devil laying his scheme in this, to get men to imagine that the *true* history of Christ was of the same character as the prodigious fables and poetic stories."[4]

Cæcilius, in the Octavius of Minucius Felix, says :

" All these fragments of crack-brained opiniatry and silly solaces played off in the sweetness of song by (the) deceitful (Pagan) poets, by you too credulous creatures (*i.e.*, the Christians) have been shamefully reformed and made over to your own god."[5]

Celsus, the Epicurean philosopher, wrote that :

"The Christian religion contains nothing but what Christians hold in common with heathens ; nothing new, or truly great."[6]

This assertion is fully verified by Justin Martyr, in his apology to the Emperor Adrian, which is one of the most remarkable admissions ever made by a Christian writer. He says:

" In saying that all things were made in this beautiful order by God, what do we seem to say more than Plato ? When we teach a general conflagration, what do we teach more than the Stoics ? By opposing the worship of the works of men's hands, we concur with Menander, the comedian ; and by declaring the

---

[1] Gibbon's Rome, vol. iii. p. 163.
[2] Quoted by Draper : Science and Religion, p. 48.
[3] See Taylor's Diegesis, p. 329.
[4] Justin: Apol. 1, ch. lix.
[5] Octavius, ch. xi.
[6] See Origen: Contra Celsus.

Logos, the first begotten of God, our master Jesus Christ, to be born of a v rgin, without any human mixture, to be crucified and dead, and to have rose again, and ascended into heaven : *we say no more in this, than what you say of those whom you style the Sons of Jove.* For you need not be told what a parcel of sons, the writers most in vogue among you, assign to Jove ; there's Mercury, Jove's interpreter, in imitation of the Logos, in worship among you. There's Æsculapius, the physician, smitten by a thunderbolt, and after that ascending into heaven. There's Bacchus, torn to pieces ; and Hercules, burnt to get rid of his pains. There's Pollux and Castor, the sons of Jove by Leda, and Perseus by Danae ; and not to mention others, I would fain know why you always deify the departed emperors and have a fellow at hand to make affidavit that he saw Cæsar mount to heaven from the funeral pile?

"As to the son of God, called Jesus, should we allow him to be nothing more than man, yet the title of the son of God is very justifiable, upon the account of his wisdom, considering that you have your Mercury in worship, under the title of the Word and Messenger of God.

"*As to the objection of our Jesus's being crucified,* I say, that suffering was common to all the forementioned sons of Jove, but only they suffered another kind of death. As to his being born of a virgin, you have your Perseus to balance that. As to his curing the lame, and the paralytic, and such as were cripples from birth, this is little more than what you say of your Æsculapius."[1]

The most celebrated Fathers of the Christian church, the most frequently quoted, and those whose names stand the highest were nothing more nor less than Pagans, being born and educated Pagans. Pantaenus (A. D. 193) was one of these half-Pagan, half-Christian, Fathers. He at one time presided in the school of the faithful in *Alexandria* in Egypt, and was celebrated on account of his learning. He was brought up in the Stoic philosophy.[2]

Clemeus Alexandrinus (A. D. 194) or St. Clement of Alexandria, was another Christian Father of the same sort, being originally a Pagan. He succeeded Pantaenus as president of the *monkish* university at Alexandria. His works are very extensive, and his authority very high in the church.[3]

Tertullian (A. D. 200) may next be mentioned. He also was originally a Pagan, and at one time Presbyter of the Christian church of Carthage, in Africa. The following is a specimen of his manner of reasoning on the evidences of Christianity. He says:

' I find no other means to prove myself to be impudent with success, and happily a fool, than by my contempt of shame ; as, for instance—I maintain that the Son of God was born ; why am I not ashamed of maintaining such a thing? Why ! but because it is itself a shameful thing. I maintain that the Son of God died: well, that is wholly credible because it is monstrously absurd. I maintain that after having been buried, he rose again : and that I take to be absolutely true, because it was manifestly impossible."[4]

---

[1] Apol. 1, ch. xx, xxi, xxii
[2] See Taylor's Diegesis, p 323.
[3] See Ibid. p. 324.
[4] On the Flesh of Christ, ch. v.

Origen (A. D. 230), one of the shining lights of the Christian church, was another Father of this class. Porphyry (a Neo-platonist philosopher) objects to him on this account.[1]

He also was born in the great cradle and nursery of superstition —Egypt—and studied under that celebrated philosopher, Ammonius Saccus, who taught that "Christianity and Paganism, when rightly understood, differed in no essential point, but had a common origin." This man was so sincere in his devotion to the cause of monkery, or Essenism, that he made himself an eunuch "for the kingdom of heaven's sake."[2] The writer of the twelfth verse of the nineteenth chapter of Matthew, was without doubt an Egyptian monk. The words are put into the mouth of the *Jewish* Jesus, which is simply ridiculous, when it is considered that the Jews did not allow an eunuch so much as to enter the congregation of the Lord.[3]

St. Gregory (A. D. 240), bishop of Neo-Cæsarea in Pontus, was another celebrated Christian Father, born of Pagan parents and educated a Pagan. He is called Thaumaturgus, or the wonder-worker, and is said to have performed miracles when still a Pagan.[4] He, too, was an Alexandrian student. This is the Gregory who was commended by his namesake of Nyssa for changing the Pagan festivals into Christian holidays, the better to draw the heathen to the religion of Christ.[5]

Mosheim, the ecclesiastical historian, in speaking of the Christian church during the second century, says:

"The profound respect that was paid to the Greek and Roman *mysteries*, and the extraordinary sanctity that was attributed to them, induced the Christians to give their religion a *mystic* air, in order to put it upon an equal footing, in point of dignity, with that of the Pagans. For this purpose they gave the name of *mysteries* to the institutions of the gospel, and decorated, particularly the holy sacrament, with that solemn title. They used, in that sacred institution, as also in that of baptism, several of the terms employed in the heathen mysteries, and proceeded so far at length, as even to adopt some of the rites and ceremonies of which those renowned mysteries consisted."[6]

We have seen, then, that the only difference between Christianity and Paganism is that Brahma, Ormuzd, Osiris, Zeus, Jupiter, etc., are called by another name; Crishna, Buddha, Bacchus, Adonis, Mithras, etc., have been turned into Christ Jesus: Venus' pigeon into the Holy Ghost; Diana, Isis, Devaki, etc., into the

---

[1] See Taylor's Diegesis, p. 328.
[2] Matt. xix. 12.
[3] Deut. xxiii. 1.
[4] See Taylor's Diegesis, p. 339.

[5] See Middleton's Letters from Rome, p. 236; Mosheim, vol. i. cent. 2, pt. 2, ch. 4.
[6] Eccl. Hist. vol. 1. p. 199.

Virgin Mary ; and the demi-gods and heroes into saints.   The exploits of the one were represented as the miracles of the other.
Pagan festivals became Christian holidays, and Pagan temples became Christian churches.

Mr. Mahaffy, Fellow and Tutor in Trinity College, and Lecturer
on Ancient History in the University of Dublin, ends his " Prolegomena to Ancient History " in the following manner:

"There is indeed, hardly a great or fruitful idea in the Jewish or Christian
systems, which has not its analogy in the (ancient) Egyptian faith.   The development of the one God into a *trinity ;* the incarnation of the mediating deity in a
Virgin, and without a father; his conflict and his momentary defeat by the powers
of darkness ; his partial victory (for the enemy is not destroyed); his resurrection and reign over an eternal kingdom with his justified saints ; his distinction
from, and yet identity with, the uncreate incomprehensible Father, whose form
is unknown, and who dwelleth not in temples made with hands—*all these theological conceptions pervade the oldest religion of Egypt.*   So, too, the contrast and
even the apparent inconsistencies between our moral and theological beliefs—
the vacillating attribution of sin and guilt partly to moral weakness, partly to
the interference of evil spirits, and likewise of righteousness to moral worth,
and again to the help of good genii or angels ; the immortality of the soul and its
final judgment—*all these things have met us in the Egyptian ritual and moral
treatises.*   So, too, the purely human side of morals, and the catalogue of virtues and vices, are by natural consequences as like as are the theological systems.
*But I recoil from opening this great subject now ; it is enough to have lifted the veil
and shown the scene of many a future contest.*"1

In regard to the *moral sentiments* expressed in the books of
the New Testament, and believed by the majority of Christians to
be peculiar to Christianity, we shall touch them but lightly, as this
has already been done so frequently by many able scholars.

The moral doctrines that appear in the New Testament, even the
sayings of the Sermon on the Mount and the Lord's Prayer, are
found with slight variation, among the Rabbins, who have certainly
borrowed nothing out of the New Testament.

Christian teachers have delighted to exhibit the essential superiority of Christianity to Judaism, have quoted with triumph the maxims
that are said to have fallen from the lips of Jesus, and which, they
surmised, could not be paralleled in the elder Scriptures, and have
put the least favorable construction on such passages in the ancient
books as seemed to contain the thoughts of evangelists and apostles.
A more ingenious study of the Hebrew law, according to the oldest
traditions, as well as its later interpretations by the prophets, re-
duces these differences materially by bringing into relief sentiments
and precepts whereof the New Testament morality is but an echo.

---

1 Prolegomena to Ancient History, pp. 416, 417.

There are passages in Exodus, Leviticus, Deuteronomy, even tenderer in their humanity than anything in the Gospels. The preacher from the Mount, the prophet of the Beatitudes, does but repeat with persuasive lips what the law-givers of his race proclaimed in mighty tones of command. Such an acquaintance with the later literature of the Jews as is really obtained now from popular sources, will convince the ordinarily fair mind that the originality of the New Testament has been greatly over-estimated.

"To feed the hungry, give drink to the thirsty, clothe the naked, bury the dead, loyally serve the king, forms the first duty of a pious man and faithful subject,"

is an abstract from the Egyptian "Book of the Dead," the oldest Bible in the world.

Confucius, the Chinese philosopher, born 551 B. C., said:

"Obey Heaven, and follow the orders of Him who governs it. *Love your neighbor as yourself.* Do to another what you would he should do unto you; and do not unto another what you would should not be done unto you; thou only needest this law alone, it is the foundation and principle of all the rest. Acknowledge thy benefits by the return of other benefits, *but never revenge injuries.*"[1]

The following extracts from Manu and the *Maha-bharata*, an Indian epic poem, written many centuries before the time of Christ Jesus,[2] compared with similar sentiment contained in the books of the New Testament, are very striking.

"An evil-minded man is quick to see his neighbor's faults, though small as mustard-seed; but when he turns his eyes towards his own, though large as Bilva fruit, he none descries." (Maha-bharata.)

"And why beholdest thou the mote that is in thy brother's eye, but considerest not the beam that is in thine own eye?" (Matt. vii. 3.)

"Conquer a man who never gives by gifts; subdue untruthful men by truthfulness; vanquish an angry man by gentleness; and overcome the evil man by goodness." (Ibid.)

"Be not overcome of evil, but overcome evil with good." (Romans, xii. 21.)

"To injure none by thought or word or deed, to give to others, and be kind to all—this is the constant duty of the good. High-minded men delight in doing good, without a thought of their own interest; when they confer a benefit on others, they reckon not on favors in return." (Ibid.)

"Love your enemies, and do good, and lend, hoping for nothing again; and your reward shall be great, and ye shall be the children of the Highest: for he is kind unto the unthankful and to the evil." (Luke, vii. 35.)

"Two persons will hereafter be exalted above the heavens—the man with

"And Jesus sat over against the treasury, and beheld how people cast

---

[1] Tindal: Christianity as Old as the Creation.

[2] Manu's works were written during the sixth century B. C. (see Williams' Indian Wisdom, p. 215), and the Maha-bharata about the same time.

boundless power, who yet forbears to use it indiscreetly, and he who is not rich, and yet can give." (Ibid.)

"Just heaven is not so pleased with costly gifts, offered in hope of future recompense, as with the merest trifle set apart from honest gains, and sanctified by faith." (Ibid.)

"To curb the tongue and moderate the speech, is held to be the hardest of all tasks. The words of him who talk too volubly have neither substance nor variety." (Ibid.)

"Even to foes who visit us as guests due hospitality should be displayed ; the tree screens with its leaves, the man who fells it." (Ibid.)

"In granting or refusing a request, a man obtains a proper rule of action by looking on his neighbor as himself." (Ibid.)

" Before infirmities creep o'er thy flesh ; before decay impairs thy strength and mars the beauty of thy limbs ; before the Ender, whose charioteer is sickness, hastes towards thee, breaks up thy fragile frame and ends thy life, lay up the only treasure: Do good deeds ; practice sobriety and self-control ; amass that wealth which thieves cannot abstract, nor tyrants seize, which follows thee at death, which never wastes away, nor is corrupted." (Ibid.)

"This is the sum of all true righteousness—Treat others as thou wouldst thyself be treated. Do nothing to thy neighbor, which hereafter thou would'st not have thy neighbor do to thee. In causing pleasure, or in giving pain, in doing good or injury to others, in granting or refusing a request, a man obtains a proper rule of action by looking on his neighbor as himself." (Ibid.)

money into the treasury : and many that were rich cast in much. And there came a certain poor widow, and she threw in two mites, which make a farthing. And he called unto him his disciples, and saith unto them, Verily I say unto you, that this poor widow hath cast more in, than all they which have cast into the treasury : For all *they* did cast in of their abundance, but she of her want did cast all that she had, even all her living." (Mark, xii. 41-44.)

" But the tongue can no man tame ; it is an unruly evil, full of deadly poison. (James, iii. 8.)

" Therefore, if thine enemy hunger, feed him ; if he thirst, give him drink; for in so doing thou shalt heap coals of fire on his head." (Rom. xii. 20.)

"Thou shalt love thy neighbor as thyself." (Matt. xxii. 39.)

" And as ye would that men should do to you, do ye also to them likewise." (Luke vi. 31.)

"Remember now thy creator in the days of thy youth, while the evil days come not, nor the years draw nigh, when thou shalt say: I have no pleasure in them." (Ecc. xii. 1.)

"Lay not up for yourselves treasures upon earth, where moth and rust doth corrupt, and where thieves break through and steal: But lay up for yourselves treasures in heaven, where neither moth nor rust doth corrupt, and where thieves do not break through and steal." (Matt. vi. 19–20.)·

"Ye have heard that it hath been said : Thou shalt love thy neighbor, and hate thine enemy. But I say unto you, love your enemies, bless them that curse you, do good to them that hate you, and pray for them which despitefully use you, and persecute you." (Matt. v. 43–44.)

" A new commandment I give unto you, that ye love one another : as I have loved you, that ye also love one another." (John, xii. 34.)

"Thou shalt love thy neighbor as thyself." (Matt. xi. 39.)

" Think constantly, O Son, how thou mayest please
Thy father, mother, teacher,—these obey.
By deep devotion seek thy debt to pay.
This is thy highest duty and religion."   (Manu.)

" Wound not another, though by him provoked.
Do no one injury by thought or deed.
Utter no word to pain thy fellow-creatures."   (Ibid.)

" Treat no one with disdain, with patience bear
Reviling language ; with an angry man
Be never angry ; blessings give for curses."   (Ibid.)

" E'en as a driver checks his restive steeds,
Do thou, if thou art wise, restrain thy passions,
Which, running wild, will hurry thee away."   (Ibid.)

"Pride not thyself on thy religious works.
Give to the poor, but talk not of thy gifts.
By pride religious merit melts away,
The merit of thy alms by ostentation."   (Ibid.)

" Good words, good deeds, and beautiful expressions
A wise man ever culls from every quarter,
E'en as a gleaner gathers ears of corn."   (Maha-bharata.)

" Repeated sin destroys the understanding,
And he whose reason is impaired, repeats
His sins.   The constant practice of virtue
Strengthens the mental faculties, and he
Whose judgment stronger grows, acts always right.   (Ibid.)

" If thou art wise seek ease and happiness
In deeds of virtue and of usefulness ;
And ever act in such a way by day
That in the night thy sleep may tranquil be ;
And so comport thyself when thou art young
That when thou art grown old, thy age may pass
In calm serenity.   So ply thy talk
Through thy life, that when thy days are ended,
Thou may'st enjoy eternal bliss hereafter."   (Ibid.)

" Do naught to others which if done to thee
Would cause thee pain ; this is the sum of duty."   (Ibid.)

" No sacred lore can save the hypocrite,—
Though he employ it craftily,—from hell ;
When his end comes, his pious texts take wings,
Like fledglings eager to forsake their nest."   (Ibid.)

" Iniquity once practiced, like a seed,
Fails not to yield its fruit to him who wrought it,
If not to him, yet to his sons and grandsons."   (Manu.)

27

" Single is every living creature born,
    Single he passes to another world,
    Single he eats the fruit of evil deeds,
    Single, the fruit of good ; and when he leaves
    His body like a log or heap of clay
    Upon the ground, his kinsmen walk away ;
    Virtue alone stands by him at the tomb,
    And bears him through the dreary, trackless gloom."   (Ibid.)

" Thou canst not gather what thou dost not sow ;
    As thou dost plant the tree so will it grow."   (Ibid.)

" He who pretends to be what he is not,
    Acts a part, commits the worst of crimes,
    For, thief-like, he abstracts a good man's heart."   (Ibid.)

CHAPTER XXXVII.

WE now come to the question, Why did Christianity prosper, and why was Jesus of Nazareth believed to be a divine incarnation and Saviour?

There were many causes for this, but as we can devote but one chapter to the subject, we must necessarily treat it briefly.

For many centuries before the time of Christ Jesus there lived a sect of religious monks known as *Essenes*, or *Therapeutæ ;*[1] these *entirely disappeared from history shortly after the time assigned for the crucifixion of Jesus.* There were thousands of them, and their *monasteries* were to be counted by the score. Many have asked the question, "What became of them?" We now propose to show, 1. That they were expecting the advent of an *Angel-Messiah ;* 2. That they considered Jesus of Nazareth to be *the* Messiah; 3. That they came over to Christianity in a body; and, 4. That they brought the legendary histories of the former Angel-Messiahs with them.

The origin of the sect known as *Essenes* is enveloped in mist, and will probably never be revealed. To speak of all the different ideas entertained as to their origin would make a volume of itself, we can therefore but glance at the subject. It has been the object of Christian writers up to a comparatively recent date, to claim that almost everything originated with God's chosen people, the *Jews*, and that even all languages can be traced to the *Hebrew*. Under these circumstances, then, it is not to be wondered at that we find they have also traced the Essenes to Hebrew origin.

Theophilus Gale, who wrote a work called "The Court of the

---

[1] "Numerous bodies of ascetics (Therapeutæ), especially near Lake Mareotis, devoted themselves to discipline and study, abjuring society and labor, and often forgetting. it is said, the simplest wants of nature, in contemplating the hidden wisdom of the *Scriptures*. Eusebius even claimed them as *Christians ;* and some of the forms of monasticism were evidently modeled after the *Therapeutæ*." (Smith's Bible Dictionary, art. " *Alexandria*."

Gentiles" (Oxford, 1671), to demonstrate that "the origin of *all
human literature*, both philology and philosophy, is from the Scriptures and the Jewish church," undoubtedly hits upon the truth when
he says:

> " Now, the origination or rise of these Essenes (among the Jews) I conceive
> by the best conjectures I can make from antiquity, *to be in or immediately after
> the Babylonian captivity*, though some make them later."

Some Christian writers trace them to Moses or some of the
prophets, but that they originated in *India*, and were a sort of
Buddhist sect, we believe is their true history.

Gfrörer, who wrote concerning them in 1835, and said that "*the
Essenes and the Therapeutœ are the same sect, and hold the same
views*," was undoubtedly another writer who was touching upon
historical ground.

The identity of many of the precepts and practices of *Essenism*
and those of the *New Testament* is unquestionable. Essenism urged
on its disciples to seek first the kingdom of God and his righteousness.[1] The Essenes forbade the laying up of treasures upon earth.[2]
The Essenes demanded of those who wished to join them to sell all
their possessions, and to divide it among the poor brethren.[3] The
Essenes had all things in common, and appointed one of the brethren as steward to manage the common bag.[4] Essenism put all its
members on the same level, forbidding the exercise of authority of
one over the other, and enjoining mutual service.[5] Essenism commanded its disciples to call no man master upon the earth.[6] Essenism laid the greatest stress upon being meek and lowly in spirit.[7]
The Essenes commended the poor in spirit, those who hunger and
thirst after righteousness, the merciful, the pure in heart, and the
peacemaker. They combined the healing of the body with that of
the soul. They declared that the power to cast out evil spirits, to
perform miraculous cures, &c., should be possessed by their disciples as signs of their belief.[8] The Essenes did not swear at all;
their answer was yea, yea, and nay, nay.[9] When the Essenes started
on a mission of mercy, they provided neither gold nor silver, neither
two coats, neither shoes, but relied on hospitality for support.[10] The
Essenes, though repudiating offensive war, yet took weapons with

---

[1] Comp. Matt. vi. 33 ; Luke, xii. 31.
[2] Comp. Matt. vi. 19–21.
[3] Comp. Matt. xix. 21 ; Luke, xii. 33.
[4] Comp. Acts, ii. 44, 45 ; iv. 32–34 ; John,
xii. 6 ; xiii. 29.
[5] Comp. Matt. xx. 25–28 ; Mark, ix. 35–37 ;
x. 42–45.
[6] Comp. Matt. xxiii. 8–10.
[7] Comp. Matt. v. 5 ; xi. 29.
[8] Comp. Mark, xvi. 17 ; Matt. x. 8 ; Luke,
ix. 1, 2 ; x. 9.
[9] Comp. Matt. v. 34.
[10] Comp. Matt. x. 9, 10.

them when they went on a perilous journey.[1] The Essenes abstained from connubial intercourse.[2] The Essenes did not offer animal sacrifices, but strove to present their bodies a living sacrifice, holy and acceptable unto God, which they regarded as a reasonable service.[3] It was the great aim of the Essenes to live such a life of purity and holiness as to be the temples of the Holy Spirit, and to be able to prophesy.[4]

Many other comparisons might be made, but these are sufficient to show that there is a great similarity between the two.[5] These similarities have led many Christian writers to believe that Jesus belonged to this order. Dr. Ginsburg, an advocate of this theory, says :

"It will hardly be doubted that *our* Saviour himself belonged to this holy brotherhood. This will especially be apparent when we remember that the whole Jewish community, at the advent of Christ, was divided into three parties, the Pharisees, the Sadducees, and the Essenes, and that every Jew had to belong to one of these sects. Jesus, who, in all things, conformed to the Jewish law, and who was holy, harmless, undefiled, and separate from sinners, would therefore naturally associate himself with that order of Judaism which was most congenial to his holy nature. Moreover, the fact that Christ, with the exception of once, was not heard of in public until his thirtieth year, implying that he lived in seclusion with this fraternity, and that though he frequently rebuked the scribes, Pharisees and Sadducees, he never denounced the Essenes, strongly confirms this conclusion."[6]

The *facts* — as Dr. Ginsburg calls them — which confirm his conclusions, are simply *no facts at all*. Jesus may or may not have been a member of this order; but when it is stated as a fact that he never rebuked the Essenes, it is implying too much. We know not whether the words *said to have been* uttered by Jesus were ever uttered by him or not, and it is almost certain that *had he* rebuked the Essenes, and had his words been written in the Gospels, *they would not remain there long*. We hear very little of the Essenes after A. D. 40,[7] therefore, when we read of the "*primitive Christians*," we are reading of *Essenes*, and others.

The statement that, with the exception of once, Jesus was not heard in public life till his *thirtieth* year, is also uncertain. One of the early Christian Fathers (Irenæus) tells us that he did not begin

---

[1] Comp. Luke, xxii. 26.
[2] Comp. Matt. xix. 10–12 ; I. Cor. viii.
[3] Comp. Rom. xii. 1.
[4] Comp. I. Cor. xiv. 1, 39.
[5] The above comparisons have been taken from Ginsburg's "Essenes," to which the reader is referred for a more lengthy observation on the subject.

[6] Ginsburg's Essenes, p. 24.
[7] "We hear very little of them after A.D. 40; and there can hardly be any doubt that, owing to the great similarity existing between their precepts and practices and those of primitive Christians, the Essenes *as a body* must have embraced Christianity." (Dr. Ginsburg, p. 27.)

to teach until he was *forty* years of age, or thereabout, and that he lived to be nearly *fifty* years old.[1] " *The records of his life are very scanty ; and these have been so shaped and colored and modified by the hands of ignorance and superstition and party prejudice and ecclesiastical purpose, that it is hard to be sure of the original outlines.*"

The similarity of the sentiments of the Essenes, or Therapeutæ, to those of the Church of Rome, induced the learned Jesuit, Nicolaus Serarius, to seek for them an honorable origin. He contended therefore, that they were Asideans, and derived them from the Rechabites, described so circumstantially in the thirty-fifth chapter of Jeremiah ; at the same time, he asserted that the first Christian monks were Essenes.[2]

Mr. King, speaking of the *Christian* sect called Gnostics, says:

"Their chief doctrines had been held for centuries before (their time) in many of the cities of Asia Minor. There, it is probable, they first came into existence as 'Mystæ,' *upon the establishment of a direct intercourse with India under the Seleucidæ and the Ptolemies.* The colleges of *Essenes* and Megabyzae at Ephesus, the Orphics of Thrace, the Curetes of Crete, *are all merely branches of one antique and common religion, and that originally Asiatic.*"[3]

Again :

" The introduction of *Buddhism* into Egypt and Palestine *affords the only true solution of innumerable difficulties in the history of religion.*"[4]

Again :

" That Buddhism had actually been planted in the dominions of the Seleucidæ and Ptolemies (Palestine belonging to the former) before the beginning of the third century B. C., is *proved to demonstration* by a passage in the Edicts of Asoka, grandson of the famous Chandragupta, the Sandracottus of the Greeks. These edicts are engraven on a rock at Girnur, in Guzerat."[5]

Eusebius, in quoting from Philo concerning the Essenes, seems to take it for granted that *they and the Christians were one and the same,* and from the manner in which he writes, it would appear that it was generally understood so. He says that Philo called them " Worshipers," and concludes by saying :

"But whether he himself gave them this name, or whether at the *beginning* they were so called, *when as yet the name of Christians was not everywhere published,* I think it not needful curiosity to sift out."[6]

---

[1] This will be alluded to in another chapter.

[2] It was believed by some that the order of *Essenes* was instituted by Elias, and some writers asserted that there was a regular succession of hermits upon Mount Carmel from the time of the prophets to that of Christ, and that the hermits embraced Christianity at an early period. (See Ginsburgh's Essenes, and Hardy's Eastern Monachism, p. 358.)

[3] King's Gnostics and their Remains, p. 1.

[4] Ibid. p. 6.

[5] King's Gnostics, p. 23.

[6] Eusebius : Eccl. Hist., lib. 2, ch. xvii.

This celebrated ecclesiastical historian considered it very probable that the writings of the Essenic Therapeuts in Egypt had been incorporated into the gospels of the New Testament, and into some Pauline epistles. His words are:

> "It is very likely that the commentaries (Scriptures) which were among them (the Essenes) were the Gospels, and the works of the apostles, and certain expositions of the ancient prophets, such as partly that epistle unto the Hebrews, and also the other epistles of Paul do contain."[1]

The principal doctrines and rites of the Essenes can be connected with the *East*, with Parsism, and especially with *Buddhism*. Among the doctrines which Essenes and Buddhists had in common was that of the *Angel-Messiah*.[2]

Godfrey Higgins says:

> "The *Essenes* were called physicians of the soul, or *Therapeutæ;* being resident both in Judea and Egypt. they probably spoke or had their sacred books in Chaldee. They were *Pythagoreans*, as is proved by all their forms, ceremonies, and doctrines, and they called themselves sons of Jesse. If the Pythagoreans or Conobitæ, as they are called by Jamblicus, were Buddhists, the Essenes were Buddhists. The Essenes lived in Egypt, on the lake of Parembole or Maria, in *monasteries*. These are the very places in which we formerly found the *Gymnosophists*, or *Samaneans*, or *Buddhist* priests to have lived ; which Gymnosophistæ are placed also by Ptolemy in north-eastern India."

> "Their (the Essenes) parishes, churches, bishops, priests, deacons, festivals are all identically the same (as the Christians). They had apostolic founders ; the manners which distinguished the immediate apostles of Christ ; scriptures divinely inspired ; the same allegorical mode of interpreting them, which has since obtained among Christians, and the same order of performing public worship. They had missionary stations or colonies of their community established in Rome, Corinth, Galatia, Ephesus, Phillippi, Colosse, and Thessalonica, precisely such, and in the same circumstances, as were those to whom St. Paul addressed his letters in those places. All the fine moral doctrines which are attributed to the Samaritan Nazarite, and I doubt not justly attributed to him, are to be found among the doctrines of these ascetics."[3]

And Arthur Lillie says:

> "It is asserted by calm thinkers like Dean Mansel that within two generations of the time of Alexander the Great, the missionaries of Buddha made their

[1] Eusebius : Eccl. Hist., lib. 2, ch. xvii.

[2] Bunsen : The Angel-Messiah, p. vii. "The New Testament is the Essene-Nazarene Glad Tidings 1 Adon, Adoni, Adonis, style of worship." (S. F. Dunlap : Son of the Man, p. iii.)

[3] Anacalypsis, vol. i. p. 747 ; vol. ii. p. 34.

[4] "In this," says Mr. Lillie, "he was supported by philosophers of the calibre of Schilling and Schopenhauer, and the great Sanscrit authority, Lassen. Renan also sees traces of this Buddhist propagandism in Palestine before the Christian era. Hilgenfeld, Mutter, Bohlen, King, all admit the Buddhist influence. Colebrooke saw a striking similarity between the Buddhist philosophy and that of the Pythagoreans. Dean Milman was convinced that the Therapeuts sprung from the 'contemplative and indolent fraternities' of India.' And, he might have added, the Rev. Robert Taylor in his "*Diegesis*," and Godfrey Higgins in his "Anacalypsis," have brought strong arguments to bear in support of this theory.

appearance at *Alexandria.*[4] This theory is confirmed—in the east by the Asoka monuments—in the west by Philo. He expressly maintains the identity in creed of the higher Judaism and that of the *Gymnosophists* of India who abstained from the 'sacrifice of living animals'—in a word, the BUDDHISTS. It would follow from this that the priestly religion of Babylonia, Palestine, Egypt, and Greece were undermined by certain kindred mystical societies organized by Buddha's missionaries under the various names of Therapeutes, Essenes, Neo-Pythagoreans, Neo-Zoroastrians, &c. *Thus Buddhism prepared the way for Christianity.*"[1]

The Buddhists have the "eight-fold holy path" (Dhammapada), eight spiritual states leading up to Buddhahood. The first state of the Essenes resulted from baptism, and it seems to correspond with the first Buddhistic state, those who have entered the (mystic) stream. Patience, purity, and the mastery of passion were aimed at by both devotees in the other stages. In the last, magical powers, healing the sick, casting out evil spirits, etc., were supposed to be gained. Buddhists and Essenes seem to have doubled up this eight-fold path into four, for some reason or other. Buddhists and Essenes had three orders of ascetics or monks, but this classification is distinct from the spiritual classifications.[2]

The doctrine of the *"Anointed Angel,"* of the man from heaven, the Creator of the world, the doctrine of the atoning sacrificial death of Jesus by the blood of his cross, the doctrine of the Messianic antetype of the Paschal lamb of the Paschal omer, and thus of the resurrection of Christ Jesus, the third day, according to the Scriptures, these doctrines of Paul can, with more or less certainty, be connected with the Essenes. It becomes almost a certainty that Eusebius was right in surmising that *Essenic writings have been used by Paul and the evangelists.* Not Jesus, but Paul, is the cause of the separation of the Jews from the Christians.[3]

The probability, then, that that sect of vagrant quack-doctors, the Therapeutæ, who were established in Egypt and its neighborhood many ages before the period assigned by later theologians as that of the birth of Christ Jesus, were the original fabricators of the writings contained in the New Testament, becomes a certainty on the basis of evidence, than which history has nothing more certain, furnished by the unguarded, but explicit, unwary, but most unqualified and positive statement of the historian Eusebius, that "*those ancient Therapeutæ were Christians, and that their ancient writings were our gospels and epistles.*"

The Essenes, the Therapeuts, the Ascetics, the Monks, the Ec-

[1] Buddha and Early Buddhism, p. vi. [2] Bunsen's Angel-Messiah, p. 121. [3] Ibid. p. 240.

clesiastics, and the Eclectics, are but different names for one and the self-same sect.

The word "*Essene*" is nothing more than the Egyptian word for that of which Therapeut is the Greek, each of them signifying "healer" or "doctor," and designating the character of the sect as professing to be endued with the miraculous gift of healing; and more especially so with respect to diseases of the mind.

Their name of "*Ascetics*" indicated the severe discipline and exercise of self-mortification, long fastings, prayers, contemplation, and even making of themselves eunuchs for the kingdom of heaven's sake, as did Origen, Melito, and others who derived their Christianity from the same school; Jesus himself is represented to have recognized and approved their practice.

Their name of "*Monks*" indicated their delight in solitude, their contemplative life, and their entire segregation and abstraction from the world, which Jesus, in the Gospel, is in like manner represented as describing, as characteristic of the community of which he was a member.

Their name of "*Ecclesiastics*" was of the same sense, and indicated their being called out, elected, separated from the general fraternity of mankind, and set apart to the more immediate service and honor of God.

They had a flourishing university, or corporate body, established upon these principles, at Alexandria in Egypt, long before the period assigned for the birth of Christ Jesus.[1]

From this body they sent out missionaries, and had established colonies, auxiliary branches, and affiliated communities, in various cities of Asia Minor, which colonies were in a flourishing condition, before the preaching of St. Paul.

"*The very ancient and Eastern doctrine of an Angel-Messiah had been applied to Gautama-Buddha, and so it was applied to Jesus Christ by the Essenes of Egypt and of Palestine, who introduced this new Messianic doctrine into Essenic Judaism and Essenic Christianity.*"[2]

In the Pali and Sanscrit texts the word *Buddha* is always used as a *title*, not as a name. It means "The Enlightened One." Gautama Buddha is represented to have taught that he was only one of a long series of Buddhas, who appear at intervals in the world, and who all teach the same system. After the death of each Buddha his religion flourishes for a time, but finally wickedness and vice

---

[1] "The Essenes abounded in Egypt, especially about Alexandria." (Eusebius: Eccl. Hist., lib. 2, ch. xvii.

[2] Bunsen's Angel-Messiah, p. 255.

again rule over the land.   Then a *new* Buddha appears, who again
preaches the lost *Dharma* or truth.   The names of twenty-four of
these Buddhas who appeared previous to Gautama have been handed down to us.   The *Buddhavansa*, or " History of the Buddhas,"
the last book of the *Khuddaka Nikaya* in the second Pitca, gives
the lives of all the previous Buddhas before commencing its account of Gautama himself; and the Pali commentary on the *Jata-
kas* gives certain details regarding each of the twenty-four.[1]

An *Avatar* was expected about every six hundred years.[2]   At the
time of Jesus of Nazareth an Avatar was expected not by some of
the Jews alone, but by most every eastern nation.[3]   Many persons
were thought at that time to be, and undoubtedly thought themselves to be, *the* Christ, and the only reason why the name of Jesus
of Nazareth succeeded above all others, is because the *Essenes* —
who were expecting an Angel-Messiah — espoused it.   Had it not
been for this almost indisputable fact, the name of Jesus of Nazareth would undoubtedly not be known at the present day.

Epiphanius, a Christian bishop and writer of the fourth century,
says, in speaking of the Essenes :

"They who believed on Christ were called JESSÆI (or Essenes), *before they
were called Christians.*   These derived their constitution from the signification of
the name Jesus, which in Hebrew signifies the same as *Therapeutes*, that is, a
saviour or physician."

Thus we see that, according to Christian authority, the Essenes
and Therapeutes are one, and that the Essenes espoused the cause
of Jesus of Nazareth, accepted him as an Angel-Messiah, and be-

---

[1] Rhys Davids' Buddhism, p. 179.

[2] This is clearly shown by Mr. Higgins in
his Anacalypsis.   It should be remembered that
Gautama Buddha, the "Angel-Messiah," and
Cyrus, the "Anointed" of the Lord, are placed
about six hundred years before Jesus, the
"Anointed."   This cycle of six hundred years
was called the "*great year.*" Josephus, the Jewish historian, alludes to it when speaking of the
patriarchs that lived to a great age.   "God afforded them a longer time of life," says he, "on
account of their virtue, and the good use they
made of it in astronomical and geometrical
discoveries, which would not have afforded the
time for foretelling (the periods of the stars),
unless they had lived *six hundred years ;* for the
great year is completed in that interval." (Josephus, Antiq., bk. i. c. iii.)   " From this cycle of
six hundred," says Col. Vallancey, "came the
name of the bird Phœnix, called by the Egyptians Phenn, with the well-known story of its
going to Egypt to burn itself on the altar of the
Sun (at Heliopolis) and rise again from its
ashes, at the end of a certain period."

[3] " Philo's writings prove the probability,
almost rising to a certainty, that already in his
time the Essenes did expect an Angel-Messiah
as one of a series of divine incarnations.
Within about fifty years after Philo's death,
Elkesai the Essene probably applied this doctrine to Jesus, and it was promulgated in Rome
about the same time, if not earlier, by the
Pseudo-Clementines." (Bunsen : The Angel-
Messiah, p. 118.)

"There was, at this time (i. e., at the time
of the birth of Jesus), a prevalent expectation
that some remarkable personage was about to
appear in Judea.   The Jews were anxiously
looking for the coming of the *Messiah.*   By
computing the time mentioned by Daniel (ch.
ix. 25–27), they knew that the period was approaching when the Messiah should appear.
This personage, *they supposed,* would be a
temporal prince, and they were expecting that
he would deliver them from Roman bondage.
*It was natural that this expectation should
spread into other countries.*" (Barnes' Notes,
vol. i. p. 27.)

came known to history as *Christians*, or believers in the Anointed Angel.

This ascetic *Buddhist* sect called Essenes were therefore expecting an Angel-Messiah, for had not Gautama announced to his disciples that another Buddha, and therefore another angel in human form, another organ or advocate of the wisdom from above, would descend from heaven to earth, and would be called the "Son of Love."

The learned Thomas Maurice says :

"From the earliest post-diluvian age, to that in which the Messiah appeared, together with the traditions which so expressly recorded the fall of the human race from a state of original rectitude and felicity, there appears, from an infinite variety of hieroglyphic monuments and of written documents, to have prevailed, from generation to generation, *throughout all the regions of the higher Asia*, an uniform belief that, in the course of revolving ages, *there should arise a sacred personage, a mighty deliverer of mankind from the thraldom of sin and of death*. In fact, the memory of the grand original promise, that the seed of the woman should eventually crush the serpent, was carefully preserved in the breasts of the *Asiatics* ; it entered deeply into their symbolic superstitions, and was engraved aloft amidst their mythologic sculptures."[1]

That an Angel-Messiah was generally expected at this time may be inferred from the following facts : Some of the Gnostic sects of Christians, who believed that Jesus was an emanation from God, likewise supposed that there were several *Æons*, or emanations from the Eternal Father. Among those who taught this doctrine was *Basilides* and his followers.[2]

SIMON MAGUS was believed to be "He who should come." Simon was worshiped in Samaria and other countries, as the expected Angel-Messiah, as a God.

Justin Martyr says :

"After the ascension of our Lord into heaven, certain *men* were suborned by demons as their agents, who said that they were gods (*i.e., the* Angel Messiah). Among these was *Simon*, a certain Samaritan, whom nearly all the Samaritans and a few also of other nations, worshiped, confessing him as a Supreme God."[3]

His miracles were notorious, and admitted by all. His followers became so numerous that they were to be found in all countries. In Rome, in the reign of Claudius, a statue was erected in his honor. Clement of Rome, speaking of Simon Magus, says that :

"He wishes to be considered an exalted person, and to be considered 'the Christ.' He claims that he can never be dissolved, asserting that he will endure to eternity."

---

[1] Hist. Hindostan, vol. ii. p. 273.   [2] Apol. 1, ch. xxvi.
[3] See Lardner's Works, vol. viii. p. 353.

Montanus was another person who evidently believed himself to be an Angel-Messiah. He was called by himself and his followers the "Paraclete," or "Holy Spirit."[1]

Socrates, in his Ecclesiastical History, tells us of one *Buddhas* (who lived after Jesus):

> "Who afore that time was called Terebynthus, which went to the coasts of Babylon, inhabited by Persians, and there published of himself many false wonders : that he was born of a virgin, that he was bred and brought up in the mountains, etc."[2]

He was evidently one of the many fanatics who believed themselves to be the Paraclete or Comforter, the "Expected One."

Another one of these *Christs* was *Apollonius*. This remarkable man was born a few years before the commencement of the Christian era, and during his career, sustained the role of a philosopher, religious teacher and reformer, and a worker of miracles. He is said to have lived to be a hundred years old. From the history of his life, written by the learned sophist and scholar, Philostratus, we glean the following :

Before his birth a god appeared to his mother and informed her that he himself should be born of her. At the time of her delivery, the most wonderful things happened. All the people of the country acknowledged that he was the "Son of God." As he grew in stature, his wonderful powers, greatness of memory, and marvelous beauty attracted the attention of all. A great part of his time was spent, when a youth, among the learned doctors; the disciples of Plato, Chrysippus and Aristotle. When he came to man's estate, he became an enthusiastic admirer and devoted follower of Pythagoras. His fame soon spread far and near, and wherever he went he reformed the religious worship of the day. He went to Ephesus, like Christ Jesus to Jerusalem, where the people flocked about him. While at Athens, in Greece, he cast out an evil spirit from a youth. As soon as Apollonius fixed his eyes upon him, the demon broke out into the most angry and horrid expressions, and then swore he would depart out of the youth. He put an end to a plague which was raging at Ephesus, and at Corinth he raised a dead maiden to life, by simply taking her by the hand and bidding her arise. The miracles of Apollonius were extensively believed, *by Christians as well as others*, for centuries after his time. In the fourth century Hierocles drew a parallel between the two Christs — Apollonius and Jesus — which was answered by Eusebius, the great champion

---

[1] See Lardner's Works, vol. viii. p. 593.   [2] Socrates : Eccl. Hist., lib. i. ch. xvii.

of the Christian church. In it he admits the miracles of Apollonius, but attributes them to sorcery.

Apollonius was worshiped as a god, in different countries, as late as the fourth century. A beautiful temple was built in honor of him, and he was held in high esteem by many of the Pagan emperors. Eunapius, who wrote concerning him in the fifth century, says that his history should have been entitled "*The Descent of a God* upon Earth." It is as Albert Reville says:

" The universal respect in which Apollonius was held by the whole pagan world, testified to the deep impression which the life of this *Supernatural Being* had left indelibly fixed in their minds ; an expression which caused one of his contemporaries to exclaim, ' *We have a God living among us.*' "

A Samaritan, by name Menander, who was contemporary with the apostles of Jesus, was another of these fanatics who believed himself to be the Christ. He went about performing miracles, claiming that he was a SAVIOUR, "sent down from above from the invisible worlds, *for the salvation of mankind.*"[1] He baptized his followers in his own name. His influence was great, and continued for several centuries. Justin Martyr and other Christian Fathers wrote against him.

Manes evidently believed himself to be "the Christ," or "he who was to come." His followers also believed the same concerning him. Eusebius, speaking of him, says:

' He presumed to represent the person of Christ ; he proclaimed himself to be the Comforter and the Holy Ghost, and being puffed up with this frantic pride, chose, as if he were Christ, *twelve* partners of his new-found doctrine, patching into one heap false and detestable doctrines of old, rotten, and rooted out heresies, *the which he brought out of Persia.*"[2]

The word Manes, says Usher in his Annals, has the meaning of Paraclete or Comforter or Saviour. This at once lets us into the secret — a new incarnation, an Angel-Messiah, a Christ — born from the side of his mother, and put to a violent death — flayed alive, and hung up, or crucified, by a king of Persia.[3] This is the teacher with his twelve apostles on the rock of Gualior.

Du Perron, in his life of Zoroaster, gives an account of certain prophecies to be found in the sacred books of the *Persians*. One of these is to the effect that, at successive periods of time, there will appear on earth certain "Sons of Zoroaster," who are to be the

[1] Eusebius: Eccl. Hist., lib. 3, ch. xxiii.
[2] Ibid. lib. 7, ch. xxx.
[3] The death of Manes, according to Socrates, was as follows: The King of Persia, hearing that he was in Mesopotamia, "made him to be apprehended, flayed him alive, took his skin, filled it full of chaff, and hanged it at the gates of the city." (Eccl. Hist., lib. 1, ch. xv.)

result of *immaculate conceptions.* These virgin-born gods will
come upon earth for the purpose of establishing the law of God. It
is also asserted that Zoroaster, when on earth, declared that in the
"latter days" a pure virgin would conceive, and bear a son, and
that as soon as the child was born a *star* would appear, blazing even
at noonday, with undiminished splendor. This Christ is to be
called *Sosiosh.* He will redeem mankind, and subdue the .Devs,
who have been tempting and leading men astray ever since the fall
of our first parents.

Among the Greeks the same prophecy was found. The Oracle
of Delphi was the depository, according to Plato, of an ancient
and *secret* prophecy of the birth of a "Son of Apollo," who was to
restore the reign of justice aud virtue on the earth.[1]

Those who believed in successive emanations of Æons from the
Throne of Light, pointed to the passage in the Gospels where Jesus
is made to say that he will be succeeded by the Paraclete or Comforter. Mahommed was believed by many to be this Paraclete, and
it is said that he too told his disciples that *another* Paraclete would
succeed him. From present appearances, however, there is some
reason for believing that the Mohammedans are to have their ancient prophecy set at naught by the multiplicity of those who pretend to 'be divinely appointed to fulfill it. The present year was
designated as the period at which this great reformer was to arise,
who should be almost, if not quite, the equal of Mahommed. His
mission was to be to purify the religion from its corruptions; to
overthrow those who had usurped its control, and to rule, as a great
spiritual caliph, over the faithful. According to accepted tradition,
the prophet himself designated the line of descent in which his most
important successor would be found, and even indicated his personal
appearance. The time having arrived, it is not strange that the
man is forthcoming, only in this instance there is more than one
claimant. There is a "holy man" in Morocco who has allowed it
to be announced that he is the designated reformer, while cable reports show that a rival pretender has appeared in Yemen, in southern Arabia, and his supporters, sword in hand, are now advancing
upon Mecca, for the purpose of proclaiming their leader as caliph
within the sacred city itself.

History then relates to us the indisputable fact that at the time
of Jesus of Nazareth an Angel-Messiah was expected, that many
persons claimed, and were believed to be, *the* "Expected One," and

[1] Plato in Apolog. Anac., ii. p. 189.

that the reason why *Jesus* was accepted above all others was because the Essenes — a very numerous sect — believed him to be the true Messiah, and came over to his followers in a body. It was because there were so many of these *Christs* in existence that some follower of Jesus — but no one knows *who* — wrote as follows :

"If any man shall say to you, Lo, *here is Christ*, or, lo, he is *there;* believe him not; for *false Christs* and false prophets shall rise, *and shall show signs and wonders* to seduce, if it were possible, even the elect."[1]

The reasons why Jesus was not accepted as the Messiah by the *majority* of the Jews was because the majority expected a daring and irresistible warrior and conqueror, who, armed with greater power than Cæsar, was to come upon earth to rend the fetters in which their hapless nation had so long groaned, to avenge them upon their haughty oppressors, and to re-establish the kingdom of Judah ; and this Jesus — although he evidently claimed to be the Messiah — did not do.

Tacitus, the Roman historian, says :

"The generality had a strong persuasion that it was contained in the ancient writings of the priests, that at that very time the east should prevail : and that some one, who should come out of Judea, *should obtain the empire of the world ;* which ambiguities foretold Vespasian and Titus. But the common people (of the Jews), according to the influence of human wishes, appropriated to themselves, by their interpretation, this vast grandeur foretold by the fates, nor could be brought to change their opinion for the true, by all their adversities."

Suetonius, another Roman historian, says :

"There had been for a long time all over the east a constant persuasion that it was recorded in the fates (books of the fates, or foretellings), that at that time some one who should come out of Judea *should obtain universal dominion.* It appears by the event, that this prediction referred to the Roman emperor ; but the Jews, referring it to themselves, rebelled."

This is corroborated by Josephus, the Jewish historian, who says :

"That which chiefly excited them (the Jews) to war, was an *ambiguous prophecy*, which was also found in the sacred books, that at that time some one, within their country, should arise, that should obtain *the empire of the whole world..* For this they had received by tradition, that it was spoken of one of their nation ; and many wise men were deceived with the interpretation. But, in truth, Vespasian's empire was designed in this prophecy, who was created emperor (of Rome) *in Judea.*"

As the Rev. Dr. Geikie remarks, the central and dominant characteristic of the teaching of the rabbis, was the certain advent of a great national *Deliverer* — the Messiah — but not a God from heaven.

For a time *Cyrus* appeared to realize the promised Deliverer, or, at least, to be the chosen instrument to prepare the way for him, and, in his turn, *Zerubabel* became the centre of Messianic hopes. In fact, the national mind had become so inflammable, by constant brooding on this one theme, that any bold spirit, rising in revolt against the Roman power, could find an army of fierce disciples who trusted that it should be he who would redeem Israel.[1]

The "*taxing*" which took place under Cyrenius, Governor of Syria (A. D. 7), excited the wildest uproar against the Roman power. The Hebrew spirit was stung into exasperation ; the puritans of the nation, the enthusiasts, fanatics, the zealots of the law, the literal constructionists of prophecy, appealed to the national temper, revived the national faith, and fanned into flame the combustible elements that smoldered in the bosom of the race. The Messianic hope was strong in these people; all the stronger on account of their political degradation. Born in sorrow, the anticipation grew keen in bitter hours. That Jehovah would abandon them could not be believed. The thought would be atheism. The hope kept the eastern Jews in a perpetual state of insurrection. The cry "Lo here, lo there!" was incessant. Claimant after claimant of the dangerous supremacy of the *Messiah* appeared, pitched a camp in the wilderness, raised the banner, gathered a force, was attacked, defeated, banished, or crucified; but the frenzy did not abate.

The last insurrection among the Jews, that of Bar-Cochba — "Son of the Star" — revealed an astonishing frenzy of zeal. It was purely a *Messianic* uprising. Judaism had excited the fears of the Emperor Hadrian, and induced him to inflict unusual severities on the people. The effect of the violence was to stimulate that conviction to fury. The night of their despair was once more illumined by the star of the east. The banner of the Messiah was raised. Potents, as of old, were seen in the sky ; the clouds were watched for the glory that should appear. *Bar-Cochba* seemed to fill out the popular idea of the deliverer. Miracles were ascribed to him ; flames issued from his mouth. The vulgar imagination made haste to transform the audacious fanatic into a child of David. Multitudes flocked to his standard. The whole Jewish race throughout the world was in commotion. The insurrection gained head. The heights about Jerusalem were seized and occupied, and fortifi-

[1] Geikie: Life of Christ, vol. i. p. 79.

cations were erected; nothing but the "host of angels" was needed to insure victory. The angels did not appear; the Roman legions did. The "Messiah," not proving himself a conqueror, was held to have proved himself an impostor, the "son of a lie."[1]

The impetuous zeal with which the Jews rushed to the standard of this Messianic impostor, in the 130th year of the Christian era, demonstrates the true Jewish character, and shows how readily any one who made the claim, was believed to be "He who should come." Even the celebrated Rabbi Akiba sanctioned this daring fraud. Akiba declared that the so-called prophecy of Balaam,—"*a star shall rise out of Jacob*,"—was accomplished. Hence the impostor took his title of *Bar-Cochabas*, or *Son of the Star;* and Akiba not only publicly anointed him "KING OF THE JEWS," and placed an imperial diadem upon his head, but followed him to the field at the head of four-and-twenty thousand of his disciples, and acted in the capacity of master of his horse.

Those who believed on the meek and benevolent Jesus — and whose number was very small — were of that class who believed in the doctrine of the *Angel-Messiah*,[2] first heard of among them when taken captives to Babylon. These believed that just as Buddha appeared at different intervals, and as Vishnu appeared at different intervals, the avatars appeared among the Jews. Adam, and Enoch, and Noah, and Elijah or Elias, might in outward appearance be different men, but they were really the self-same divine person successively animating various human bodies.[3] Christ *Jesus* was the *avatar* of the ninth age, Christ *Cyrus* was the *avatar* of the eighth. Of the hero of the eighth age it is said : "Thus said the Lord to his Anointed (*i. e.*, his *Christ*), his Messiah, to Cyrus,

---

[1] Frothingham's Cradle of the Christ.

[2] "The prevailing opinion of the Rabbis and the people alike, in Christ's day, was, that the Messiah would be simply a great prince, who should found a kingdom of matchless splendor." "With a few, however, the conception of the Messiah's kingdom was pure and lofty. . . . Daniel, and all who wrote after him, painted the 'Expected One' as a *heavenly being*. He was the 'messenger,' the 'Elect of God,' appointed from eternity, to appear in due time, and *redeem* his people." (Geikie's Life of Christ, vol. i. pp, 80, 81.)

In the book of *Daniel*, by some supposed to have been written during the captivity, by others as late as Antiochus Epiphanes (B. C. 175), the restoration of the Jews is described in tremendous language, and the Messiah is portrayed as a supernatural personage, in close relation with Jehovah himself. In the book of

Enoch, supposed to have been written at various intervals between 144 and 120 (B. C.) and to have been completed in its present form in the first half of the second century that preceded the advent of Jesus, the figure of the Messiah is invested with superhuman attributes. He is called "The Son of God," "whose name was spoken before the Sun was made ;" "who existed from the beginning in the presence of God," that is, was pre-existent. At the same time his human characteristics are insisted on. He is called "Son of Man," even "Son of Woman," "The Anointed" or "The Christ," "The Righteous One," &c. (Frothingham : The Cradle of the Christ, p. 20.)

[3] This is clearly seen from the statement made by the Matthew narrator (xvii. 9–13) that the disciples of Christ Jesus supposed John the Baptist was Elias.

23

whose right hand I have holden to subdue nations."[1]   The eighth
period began about the Babylonish captivity, about six hundred years
before Christ *Jesus*.   The ninth began with Christ Jesus, making
in all eight cycles before Jesus.

"What was known in Judea more than a century before the
birth of Jesus Christ cannot have been introduced among Buddhists by Christian missionaries.   It will become equally certain that
the bishop and church-historian, Eusebius, was right when he wrote,
that he considered it highly probable that the writings of the Essenic Therapeuts in Egypt had been incorporated into our Gospels,
and into some Pauline epistles."[2]

For further information on the subject of the connection be-
tween Essenism and Christianity, the reader is referred to Taylor's
Diegesis, Bunsen's Angel-Messiah, and the works of S. F. Dunlap.
We shall now speak of another powerful lever which was brought
to bear upon the promulgation of Christianity; namely, that of
FRAUD.

It was a common thing among the early Christian Fathers and
saints to lie and deceive, if their lies and deceits helped the cause
of their Christ.   Lactantius, an eminent Christian author who
flourished in the fourth century, has well said:

"Among those who seek power and gain from their religion, there will never
be wanting an inclination to forge and lie for it."[3]

Gregory of Nazianzus, writing to St. Jerome, says:

"A little jargon is all that is necessary to impose on the people.   The less
they comprehend, the more they admire.   Our forefathers and doctors have
often said, not what they thought, but what circumstances and necessity dictated."[4]

The celebrated *Eusebius*, Bishop of CÆSAREA, and friend of
Constantine the Great, who is our chief guide for the early history
of the Church, *confesses that he was by no means scrupulous to record the whole truth concerning the early Christians in the various
works which he has left behind him.*[5]   Edward Gibbon, speaking
of him, says:

'The gravest of the ecclesiastical historians, Eusebius himself, indirectly
confesses that he has related what might redound to the glory, and that he has
suppressed all that could tend to the disgrace of religion.   Such an acknowledg-
ment will naturally excite a suspicion that a writer who has so openly violated
one of the fundamental laws of history, has not paid a very strict regard to the

---

[1] Isaiah, xlv. 1.
[2] Bunsen: The Angel-Messiah, p. 17.
[3] Quoted in Middleton's Letters from Rome,
p. 51.
[4] Hieron ad Nep.   Quoted Volney's Ruins,
p. 177, *note*.
[5] See his Eccl. Hist., viii. 21.

observance of the other ; and the suspicion will derive additional credit from the character of Eusebius, which was less tinctured with credulity, and more practiced in the arts of courts, than that of almost any of his contemporaries."[1]

The great theologian, Beausobre, in his "Histoire de Manichee," says:

" We see in the history which I have related, a sort of hypocrisy, that has been perhaps, but too common at all times ; that churchmen not only do not say what they think, but they do say the direct contrary of what they think. Philosophers in their cabinets ; out of them they are content with fables, though they well know they are fables. Nay, more ; they deliver honest men to the executioner, for having uttered what they themselves know to be true. How many atheists and pagans have burned holy men under the pretext of heresy? Every day do hypocrites consecrate, and make people adore the host, though as well convinced as I am, that it is nothing but a bit of bread."[2]

M. Daille says:

" This opinion has always been in the world, that to settle a certain and assured estimation upon that which is good and true, it is necessary to remove out of the way, whatsoever may be an hinderance to it. *Neither ought we to wonder that even those of the honest, innocent, primitive times made use of these deceits, seeing for a good end they made no scruple to forge whole books.*"[3]

Reeves, in his " Apologies of the Fathers," says :

" It was a Catholic opinion among the philosophers, that pious frauds were good things, and that the people ought to be imposed on in matters of religion."[4]

Mosheim, the ecclesiastical historian, says:

" It was held as a maxim that it was not only lawful but praiseworthy to *deceive*, and even to use the expedient of a *lie*, in order to advance the cause of truth and piety."[5]

Isaac de Casaubon, the great ecclesiastical scholar, says :

" It mightily affects me, to see how many there were in the earliest times of the church, who considered it as a capital exploit, to lend to heavenly truth the help of their own inventions, in order that the new doctrine might be more readily allowed by the wise among the Gentiles. *These officious lies, they were wont to say, were devised for a good end.*"[6]

---

[1] Gibbon's Rome, vol. ii. pp. 79, 80.

[2] " On voit dans l'histoire que j'ai rapportée. une sorte d'hypocrisie, qui n'a peut-être été que trop commune dans tous les tems. C'est que des ecclésiastiques, non-seulement ne disent pas ce qu'ils pensent, mais desent tout le contraire de ce qu'ils pensent. Philosophes dans leur cabinet, hors delà, ils content des fables, quoiqu'ils sachent bien que ce sont des fables. Ils font plus ; ils livrent au bourreau des gens de biens, pour l'avoir dit. Combiens d'athées et de profanes ont fait bruler de saints personnages, sous prétexte d'hérésie ? Tous les jours des hypocrites, consacrent et font adorer l'hostie, bein qu'ils soient aussi convaincus que moi, que cen'est qu'un morceau de pain.' (Tom. 2, p. 568.)

[3] On the Use of the Fathers, pp. 36, 37.

[4] Quoted in Taylor's Syntagma, p. 170.

[5] Mosheim : vol. 1, p. 198.

[6] " Postremo illud quoque me vehementer movet, quod videam primis ecclesiæ temporibus, quam plurimos extitisse, qui facinus palmarium judicabant, cælestem veritatem, figmentis suis ire adjutum, quo facilius nova doctrina a gentium sapientibus admitteretur Officiosa hæc mendacia vocabant bono fine exeogitata." (Quoted in Taylor's Diegesis, p. 44, and Giles' Hebrew and Christian Records vol ii. p. 19.)

The Apostolic Father, Hermas, who was the fellow-laborer of St. Paul in the work of the ministry; who is greeted as such in the New Testament; and whose writings are expressly quoted as of divine inspiration, by the early Fathers, ingenuously confesses that lying was the easily-besetting sin of a Christian. His words are:

"O Lord, I never spake a true word in my life, but I have always lived in dissimulation, and affirmed a lie for truth to all men, and no man contradicted me, but all gave credit to my words."

To which the holy angel, whom he addresses, condescendingly admonishes him, that as the lie was up, now, he had better keep it up, and as in time it would come to be believed, it would answer as well as truth.[1]

Dr. Mosheim admits, that the Platonists and Pythagoreans held it as a maxim, that it was not only lawful, but praiseworthy, to deceive, and even to use the expedient of a lie, in order to advance the cause of truth and piety. The Jews who lived in Egypt, had learned and received this maxim from them, before the coming of Christ Jesus, as appears incontestably from a multitude of ancient records, *and the Christians were infected from both these sources, with the same pernicious error.*[2]

Of the fifteen letters ascribed to Ignatius (Bishop of Antioch after 69 A. D.), *eight have been rejected by Christian writers as being forgeries*, having no authority whatever. " *The remaining seven* epistles were accounted genuine by most critics, although disputed by some, previous to the discoveries of Mr. Cureton, *which have shaken, and indeed almost wholly destroyed the credit and authenticity of all alike.*"[3]

Paul of Tarsus, who was preaching a doctrine which had already been preached to every nation on earth,[4] inculcates and avows the principle of deceiving the common people, talks of his having been upbraided by his own converts with being crafty and catching them with guile,[5] and of his known and willful lies, abounding to the glory of God.[6]

Even the orthodox Doctor Burnet, an eminent English author, in his treatise " *De Statu Mortuorum,*" purposely written in Latin,

---

[1] See the Vision of Hermas, b. 2, c. iii.

[2] Mosheim, vol. i. p. 197. Quoted in Taylor's Diegesis, p. 47.

[3] Dr. Giles : Hebrew and Christian Records, vol. ii. p. 99.

[4] "Continue in the faith grounded and settled, and be not moved away from the hope of the gospel, which ye have heard, and which was preached to every creature which is under heaven ; whereof I Paul am made a minister." (Colossians, i. 23.)

[5] "Being crafty, I caught you with guile." (II. Cor. xii. 16.)

[6] "For if the truth of God had more abounded *through my lie* unto his glory, why yet am I also judged as a sinner." (Romans, iii 7.)

that it might serve for the instruction of the clergy only, and not come to the knowledge of the laity, because, as he said, "*too much light is hurtful for weak eyes*," not only justified but recommended the practice of the most consummate hypocrisy, and would have his clergy seriously preach and maintain the reality and eternity of hell torments, even though they should believe nothing of the sort themselves.[1]

The incredible and very ridiculous stories related by Christian Fathers and ecclesiastical historians, *on whom we are obliged to rely for information on the most important of subjects*, show us how untrustworthy these men were. We have, for instance, the story related by St. Augustine, who is styled "the greatest of the Latin Fathers," of his preaching the Gospel to people *without heads*. In his 33d Sermon he says:

'I was already Bishop of Hippo, when I went into Ethiopia with some servants of Christ there to preach the Gospel. In this country we saw many men and women without heads, who had two great eyes in their breasts; and in countries still more southly, we saw people who had but one eye in their foreheads."[2]

This same holy Father bears an equally unquestionable testimony to several resurrections of the dead, of *which he himself had been an eye-witness.*

In a book written "towards the close of the second century, by some zealous believer," and fathered upon one Nicodemus, who is said to have been a disciple of Christ Jesus, we find the following:

"We all know the blessed Simeon, the high priest, who took Jesus when an infant into his arms in the temple. This same Simeon had two sons of his own, *and we were all present at their death and funeral.* Go therefore and see their

[1] "Si me tamen audire velis, mallem te pænas has dicere indefinitas quam infinitas. Sed veniet dies, cum non minus absurda, habebitur et odiosa hæc opinio quam transubstantiatio hodie." (De Statu Mort., p. 304. Quoted in Taylor's Diegesis, p. 43.)

[2] Quoted in Taylor's Syntagma, p. 52.
Among the ancients, there were many stories current of countries, the inhabitants of which were of peculiar size, form or features. Our Christian saint evidently believed these tales, and thinking thus, sought to make others believe them. We find the following examples related by *Herodotus:* "Aristeas, son of Caystrobius, a native of Proconesus, says in his epic verses that, inspired by Apollo, he came to the Issedones; that beyond the Issedones dwell the Arimaspians, *a people that have only one eye.*" (Herodotus, book iv. ch. 13.) "When one has passed through a considerable extent of the rugged country (of the Scythians), a people are found living at the foot of lofty mountains, *who are said to be all bald from their birth*, both men and women alike, and they are flat-nosed, and have large chins." (Ibid. ch. 23.) "These bald men say, what to me is incredible, that *men with goat's feet* inhabit these mountains; and when one has passed beyond them, other men are found, *who sleep six months at a time*, but this I do not at all admit." (Ibid. ch. 24.) In the country westward of Libya, "there are enormous serpents, and lions, elephants, bears, asps, and asses with horns, and monsters with dog's heads and without heads, *who have eyes in their breasts*, at least, as the Libyans say, and wild men and wild women, and many other wild beasts which are not fabulous." (Ibid. ch. 192.)

tombs, for these are open, and they are risen ; and behold, *they are in the city of Arimathæa, spending their time together in offices of devotion.*"[1]

Eusebius, " the Father of ecclesiastical history," Bishop of Cæsarea, and one of the most prominent personages at the Council of Nice, relates as truth, the ridiculous story of King Agbarus writing a letter to Christ Jesus, and of Jesus' answer to the same.[2] And Socrates relates how the Empress Helen, mother of the Emperor Constantine, went to Jerusalem for the purpose of finding, if possible, "the cross of Christ." This she succeeded in doing, also the nails with which he was nailed to the cross.[3]

Beside forging, lying, and deceiving for the cause of Christ, the Christian Fathers destroyed all evidence against themselves and their religion, which they came across. Christian divines seem to have always been afraid of too much light. In the very infancy of printing, Cardinal Wolsey foresaw its effect on Christianity, and in a speech to the clergy, publicly forewarned them, that, *if they did not destroy the Press, the Press would destroy them.*[4] There can be no doubt, that had the objections of Porphyry,[5] Hierocles,[6] Celsus,[7] and other opponents of the Christian faith, been permitted to come down to us, the plagiarism in the Christian Scriptures from previously existing Pagan documents, is the specific charge they would have presented us. But these were ordered to be burned, by the prudent piety of the Christian emperors.

In Alexandria, in Egypt, there was an immense library, founded by the Ptolemies. This library was situated in the Alexandrian Museum ; the apartments which were allotted for it were beautifully sculptured, and crowded with the choicest statues and pictures ; the building was built of marble. This library eventually comprised

---

[1] Nicodemus, Apoc., ch. xii.

[2] See Eusebius : Eccl. Hist., lib. 1, ch. xiv.

[3] Socrates : Eccl. Hist., lib. 1, ch. xiii.

[4] In the year 1444, Caxton published the first book ever printed in England. In 1474, the then Bishop of London, in a convocation of his clergy, said : "*If we do not destroy this dangerous invention, it will one day destroy us.*" (See Middleton's Letters from Rome, p. 4.) The reader should compare this with Pope Leo X.'s avowal that, "*it is well known how profitable this fable of Christ has been to us ;*" and Archdeacon Paley's declaration that "*he could ill afford to have a conscience.*"

[5] *Porphyry,* who flourished about the year 270 A.D., a man of great abilities, published a large work of fifteen books against the Christians. " His objections against Christianity," says Dr. Lardner, " were in esteem with Gentile

people for a long while ; and the Christians were not insensible of the importance of his work ; as may be concluded from the several answers made to it by Eusebius, and others in great repute for learning." (Vol. viii. p. 158.) There are but fragments of these *fifteen* books remaining, *Christian magistrates* having ordered them to be destroyed. (Ibid.)

[6] *Hierocles* was a Neo-Platonist, who lived at Alexandria about the middle of the fifth century, and enjoyed a great reputation. He was the author of a great number of works, a few extracts of which alone remain.

[7] *Celsus* was an Epicurean philosopher, who lived in the second century A.D. He wrote a work called " The True Word," against Christianity, but as it has been destroyed we know nothing about it. Origen claims to give quotations from it.

four hundred thousand volumes. In the course of time, probably on account of inadequate accommodation for so many books, an additional library was established, and placed in the temple of Serapis. The number of volumes in this library, which was called the daughter of that in the museum, was eventually three hundred thousand. There were, therefore, *seven hundred thousand volumes in these royal collections.*

In the establishment of the museum, Ptolemy Soter, and his son Philadelphus, had three objects in view: 1. The perpetuation of such knowledge as was then in the world; 2. Its increase; 3. Its diffusion.

1. *For the perpetuation of knowledge.* Orders were given to the chief librarian to buy, at the king's expense, whatever books he could. A body of transcribers was maintained in the museum, whose duty it was to make correct copies of such works as their owners were not disposed to sell. *Any books brought by foreigners into Egypt* were taken at once to the museum, and when correct copies had been made, the transcript was given to the owner, and the original placed in the library. Often a very large pecuniary indemnity was paid.

2. *For the increase of knowledge.* One of the chief objects of the museum was that of serving as the home of a body of men who devoted themselves to study, and were lodged and maintained at the king's expense. In the original organization of the museum the residents were divided into four faculties,—Literature, Mathematics, Astronomy, and Medicine. An officer of very great distinction presided over the establishment, and had general charge of its interests. Demetius Phalareus, perhaps the most learned man of his age, who had been Governor of Athens for many years, was the first so appointed. Under him was the librarian, an office sometimes held by men whose names have descended to our times, as Eratosthenes and Apollonius Rhodius. In connection with the museum was a botanical and a zoological garden. These gardens, as their names imply, were for the purpose of facilitating the study of plants and animals. There was also an astronomical observatory, containing armillary spheres, globes, solstitial and equatorial armils, astrolabes, parallactic rules, and other apparatus then in use, the graduation on the divided instruments being into degrees and sixths.

3. *For the diffusion of knowledge.* In the museum was given, by lectures, conversation, or other appropriate methods, instruction in all the various departments of human knowledge.

There flocked to this great intellectual centre, students from all countries. It is said that at one time not fewer than fourteen thousand were in attendance. Subsequently even the Christian church received from it some of the most eminent of its Fathers, as Clemens Alexandrinus, Origen, Athanasius, &c.

The library in the museum was burned during the siege of Alexandria by Julius Cæsar. To make amends for this great loss, the library collected by Eumenes, King of Pergamus, was presented by Mark Antony to Queen Cleopatra. Originally it was founded as a rival to that of the Ptolemies. It was added to the collection in the Serapion, or the temple of Serapis.[1]

It was not destined, however, to remain there many centuries, as this very valuable library was willfully destroyed by the Christian Theophilus, and on the spot where this beautiful temple of Serapis stood, in fact, on its very foundation, was erected a church in honor of the " noble army of martyrs," who had never existed.

This we learn from the historian Gibbon, who says that, after this library was destroyed, "the appearance of the empty shelves excited the regret and indignation of every spectator, whose mind was not totally darkened by religious prejudice."[2]

The destruction of this library was almost the death-blow to free-thought — wherever Christianity ruled — for more than a thousand years.

The death-blow was soon to be struck, however, which was done by *Saint Cyril*, who succeeded *Theophilus* as Bishop of Alexandria.

Hypatia, the daughter of Theon, the mathematician, endeavored to continue the old-time instructions. Each day before her academy stood a long train of chariots; her lecture-room was crowded with the wealth and fashion of *Alexandria*. They came to listen to her discourses on those questions which man in all ages has asked, but which have never yet been answered : " What am I? Where am I? What can I know?"

Hypatia and Cyril; philosophy and bigotry; they cannot exist together. As Hypatia repaired to her academy, she was assaulted by (Saint) Cyril's mob — *a mob of many monks*. Stripped naked in the street, she was dragged into a *church,* and there killed *by the club of Peter the Reader.* The corpse was cut to pieces, the flesh was scraped from the bones with shells, and the remnants cast into a fire. *For this frightful crime Cyril was never called to account.*

[1] Draper : Religion and Science, pp. 18–21.   [2] Gibbon s Rome, vol. lii. p. 146.

It seemed to be admitted that the end sanctified the means. So ended Greek philosophy in Alexandria, so came to an untimely close the learning that the Ptolemies had done so much to promote.

The fate of Hypatia was a warning to all who would cultivate profane knowledge. *Henceforth there was to be no freedom for human thought. Every one must think as ecclesiastical authority ordered him ;* A.D. 414. In Athens itself philosophy awaited its doom. Justinian at length prohibited its teaching and caused all its schools in that city to be closed.'

After this followed the long and dreary *dark ages,* but the *sun of science,* that bright and glorious luminary, was destined to rise again.

The history of this great Alexandrian library is one of the keys which unlock the door, and exposes to our view the manner in which the Hindoo incarnate god *Crishna,* and the meek and benevolent *Buddha,* came to be worshiped under the name of *Christ Jesus.* For instance, we have just seen :

1. That, " orders were given to the chief librarian to buy at the king's expense *whatever books he could.*"

2. That, " one of the chief objects of the museum was that of serving as the home of a *body of men* who devoted themselves to study."

3. That, " any books brought by foreigners into Egypt were taken at once to the museum and correct copies made."

4. That, " there flocked to this great intellectual centre students from all countries."

5. That, " the Christian church received from it some of the most eminent of its Fathers."

And also :

6. That, the chief doctrines of the Gnostic Christians " had been held for centuries before their time in many of the cities in Asia Minor. There, it is probable, they first came into existence as ' Mystæ,' *upon the establishment of a direct intercourse with India* under the Seleucidæ and the Ptolemies."

7. That, " the College of ESSENES at Ephesus, the Orphies of Thrace, the Curetes of Crete, *are all merely branches of one* antique and common religion, *and that originally Asiatic.*"

8. That, " *the introduction of Buddhism into Egypt and Pales-*

---

¹ Draper : Religion and Science, pp. 55, 56. See also, Socrates' Eccl. Hist., lib. 7, ch. xv.

tine affords the only true solution of innumerable difficulties in the history of religion."

9. That, " *Buddhism* had actually been planted in the dominions of the Seleucidæ and Ptolemies (Palestine belonging to the former) *before the beginning of the third century* B. C., and is proved to demonstration by a passage in the edicts of Asoka."

10. That, "it is very likely that the commentaries (Scriptures) which were among them (the *Essenes*) were the Gospels."

11. That, " the principal doctrines and rites of the *Essenes* can be connected with the East, with Parsism, and especially with *Buddhism.*"

12. That, "among the doctrines which the *Essenes* and *Buddhists* had in common was that of the *Angel-Messiah.*"

13. That, " they (the *Essenes*) had a flourishing university or corporate body, established at *Alexandria, in Egypt*, long before the period assigned for the birth of Christ."

14. That, "the *very ancient* and Eastern doctrine of the *Angel-Messiah* had been applied to Gautama Buddha, *and so it was applied to Jesus Christ by the Essenes of Egypt and Palestine*, who introduced this new Messianic doctrine into Essenic Judaism and Essenic Christianity."

15. That, " we hear very little of them (the *Essenes*) after A.D. 40; and there can hardly be any doubt that the *Essenes* as a body must have embraced Christianity."

Here is the solution of the problem. The sacred books of Hindoos and Buddhists were among the *Essenes*, and in the library at Alexandria. The *Essenes*, who were afterwards called *Christians*, applied the legend of the *Angel-Messiah*—" the very ancient Eastern doctrine," which we have shown throughout this work—to Christ Jesus. It was simply a transformation of names, *a transformation which had previously occurred in many cases.*[1] After this came *additions* to the legend from other sources. Portions of the legends related of the Persian, Greek and Roman Saviours and Redeemers of mankind, were, from time to time, added to the already legendary history of the Christian Saviour. Thus his-

---

[1] We have seen this particularly in the cases of Crishna and Buddha. Mr. Cox, speaking of the former, says: " If it be urged that the attribution to Crishna of qualities or powers belonging to the other deities is a mere device by which *his* devotees sought to supersede the more ancient gods, *the answer must be that nothing has been done in his case which has not* been done in *the case of almost every other member of the great company of the gods.*" (Aryan Mythology, vol. ii. p. 130.) These words apply to the case we have before us. Jesus was simply attributed with the qualities or powers which *had been previously attributed to other deities.* This we hope to be able to fully demonstrate in our chapter on " *Explanation.*"

tory was repeating itself. Thus the virgin-born God and Saviour, worshiped by all nations of the earth, though called by different names, was but one and the same.

In a subsequent chapter we shall see *who* this One God was, and *how* the myth originated.

Albert Revillé says :

"*Alexandria*, the home of Philonism, and Neo-Platonism (and we might add *Essenism*), was naturally the centre *whence spread the dogma of the deity of Jesus Christ.* In that city, through the third century, flourished a school of transcendental theology, afterwards looked upon with suspicion by the conservators of ecclesiastical doctrine, but not the less the real cradle of orthodoxy. It was still the Platonic tendency which influenced the speculations of Clement, Origen and Dionysius, and the theory of the Logos was at the foundation of their theology."[1]

Among the numerous gospels in circulation among the Christians of the first three centuries, there was one entitled " The Gospel of the *Egyptians*." Epiphanius (A. D. 385), speaking of it, says :

" Many things are proposed (in this Gospel of the Egyptians) in a hidden, *mysterious manner*, as by our Saviour, as though he had said to his disciples, that the Father was the same person, the Son the same person, and the Holy Ghost the same person."

That this was one of the "*Scriptures* " of the Essenes, becomes very evident when we find it admitted by the most learned of Christian theologians that it was in existence "*before either of the canonical Gospels*," and that it contained the doctrine of the *Trinity*, a doctrine not established in the Christian church until A. D. 327, but which was taught by this Buddhist sect in Alexandria, in Egypt, which has been well called, " Egypt, the land of Trinities."

The learned Dr. Grabe thought it was composed by *some Christians in Egypt*, and that it was published *before either of the canonical Gospels*. Dr. Mill also believed that it was composed *before either of the canonical Gospels*, and, what is more important than all, *that the authors of it were Essenes*.

These " Scriptures " of the Essenes were undoubtedly amalgamated with the " Gospels " of the Christians, the result being the canonical Gospels as we now have them. The " Gospel of the Hebrews," and such like, on the one hand, and the " Gospel of the Egyptians," or Essenes, and such like, on the other. That the " Gospel of the Hebrews " spoke of Jesus of Nazareth as the son of Joseph and Mary, *according to the flesh*, and that it taught *nothing* about his miracles, his resurrection from the dead, and other such

---

[1] " Dogma of the Deity of Jesus Christ," p. 41.

prodigies, is admitted on all hands. That the " Scriptures " of the Essenes contained the whole legend of the Angel-Messiah, which was afterwards added to the history of Jesus, *making him a* CHRIST, *or an Anointed Angel,* is a probability almost to a certainty. Do we now understand how all the traditions and legends, originally *Indian,* escaping from the great focus through *Egypt,* were able to reach Judea, Greece and Rome ?

To continue with our subject, "why Christianity prospered," we must now speak of another great support to the cause, *i. e., Persecution.* Ernest de Bunsen, speaking of Buddha, says :

" His religion has never been propagated by the sword. It has been effected entirely by the influence of peaceable and persevering devotees." .

Can we say as much for what is termed " the religion of Christ?" No! this religion has had the aid of the sword and firebrand, the rack and the thumb-screw. *"Persecution"* is to be seen written on the pages of ecclesiastical history, from the time of Constantine even to the present day.[1] This Christian emperor and saint was the first to check free-thought.

" We search in vain," (says M. Renan), " in the collection of Roman laws *before Constantine,* for any enactment aimed at free thought, or in the history of the emperors, for a persecution of abstract doctrine. Not a single *savant* was disturbed. Men whom the Middle Ages would have burned—such as Galen, Lucian, Plotinus—lived in peace, protected by the law."[2]

Born and educated a pagan, Constantine embraced the Christian faith from the following motives. Having committed horrid crimes, in fact, having committed murders,[3] and,

" When he would have had his (Pagan) priests purge him by sacrifice, of these horrible murders, and could not have his purpose (for they answered plainly, it lay not in their power to cleanse him)[4] he lighted at last upon an *Egyptian* who came out of Iberia, and being persuaded by him that the Christian faith was of force to wipe away every sin, were it ever so heinous, he embraced willingly at whatever the Egyptian told him."[5]

---

[1] Adherents of the old religion of Russia have been persecuted in that country within the past year, and even in enlightened England, a gentleman has been persecuted by government officials because he believes in neither a personal God or a personal Devil.

[2] Renan, Hibbert Lectures, p. 22.

[3] The following are the names of his victims :

Maximin,	His wife's father,	A.D. 310
Bassianus,	His sister's husband,	A.D. 314
Licinius,	His nephew,	A.D. 319
Fausta,	His wife,	A.D. 320
Sopater,	His former friend,	A.D. 321
Licinius,	His sister's husband,	A.D. 325
Crispus,	His own son,	A.D. 326

Dr. Lardner, in speaking of the murders committed by this Christian saint, is constrained to say that : " The death of Crispus is altogether without any *good* excuse, so likewise is the death of the young Licinianus, who could not have been more than a little above eleven years of age, and appears not to have been charged with any fault, and could hardly be suspected of any."

[4] The Emperor Nero could not be *baptized* and be initiated into Pagan Mysteries—as Constantine was initiated into those of the Christians—on account of the murder of his mother. And he did not dare to *compel*—which he certainly could have done—the priests to initiate him.

[5] Zosimus, in Socrates, lib. iii. ch. xl.

Mons. Dupuis, speaking of this conversion, says :

"Constantine, soiled with all sorts of crimes, and stained with the blood of his wife, after repeated perjuries and assassinations, presented himself before the heathen priests in order to be absolved of so many outrages he had committed. He was answered, that amongst the various kinds of expiations, there was none which could expiate so many crimes, and that no religion whatever could offer efficient protection against the justice of the gods ; and Constantine was emperor. One of the courtiers of the palace, who witnessed the trouble and agitation of his mind, torn by remorse, which nothing could appease, informed him, that the evil he was suffering was not without a remedy ; that there existed in the religion of the Christians certain purifications, which expiated every kind of misdeeds, of whatever nature, and in whatsoever number they were : that one of the promises of the religion was, that whoever was converted to it, as impious and as great a villain as he might be, could hope that his crimes were immediately forgotten.[1] From that moment, Constantine declared himself the protector of a sect which treats great criminals with so much lenity.[2] He was a great villain, who tried to lull himself with illusions to smother his remorse."[3]

By the delay of baptism, a person who had accepted the *true* faith could venture freely to indulge their passions in the enjoyment of this world, while they still retained in their own hands the means of salvation ; therefore, we find that Constantine, although he accepted the faith, did not get baptized until he was on his death-bed, as he wished to continue, as long as possible, the wicked life he was leading. Mr. Gibbon, speaking of him, says :

"The example and reputation of Constantine seemed to countenance the delay of baptism. Future tyrants were encouraged to believe, that the innocent blood which they might shed in a long reign would instantly be washed away in the waters of regeneration ; and the abuse of religion dangerously undermined the foundations of moral virtue."[4]

---

[1] "The sacrament of baptism was supposed to contain a full and absolute expiation of sin ; and the soul was instantly restored to its original purity and entitled to the promise of eternal salvation. Among the proselytes of Christianity, there were many who judged it imprudent to precipitate a salutary rite, which could not be repeated. By the delay of their baptism, they could venture freely to indulge their passions in the enjoyments of this world, while they still retained in their own hands the means of a sure and speedy absolution." (Gibbon : ii. pp. 272, 273.)

[2] "Constantine, as he was praying about noon-tide, God showed him a vision in the sky, which was the sign of the cross lively figured in the air, with this inscription on it : 'In hoc vince ;' that is, 'By this overcome.'" This is the story as related by Eusebius (Life of Constantine, lib. 1, ch. xxii.), but it must be remembered that Eusebius acknowledged that he told falsehoods. That night Christ appeared unto Constantine in his dream, and commanded him to make the figure of the cross which he had seen, and to wear it in his *banner* when he went to battle with his enemies. (See Eusebius' Life of Constantine. lib. 1, ch. xxiii. See also, Socrates : Eccl. Hist., lib. 1, ch. ii.)

[3] Dupuis, p. 405.

[4] Gibbon's Rome, vol. ii. p. 373. The Fathers, who censured this criminal delay, could not deny the certain and victorious efficacy even of a death-bed baptism. The ingenious rhetoric of Chrysostom (A.D. 347-407) could find only three arguments against these prudent Christians. 1. "That we should love and pursue virtue for her own sake, and not merely for the reward. 2. That we may be surprised by death without an opportunity of baptism. 3. That although we shall be placed in heaven, we shall only twinkle like little stars, when compared to the suns of righteousness who have run their appointed course with labor, with success, and with glory." (Chrysostom in Epist. ad Hebræos. Homil. xiii. Quoted in Gibbon's "Rome," ii. 272.)

Eusebius, in his "Life of Constantine," tells us that ·

"*When he thought that he was near his death*, he confessed his sins, desiring pardon for them of God, and was baptized.

"Before doing so, he assembled the bishops of Nicomedia together, and spake thus unto them:

"'Brethren, the salvation which I have earnestly desired of God these many years, I do now this day expect. It is time therefore that we should be sealed and signed with the badge of immortality. And though I proposed to receive it in the river Jordan, in which our Saviour for our example was baptized, yet God, knowing what is fittest for me, hath appointed that I shall receive it in this place, *therefore let me not be delayed.*'"

"And so, after the service of baptism was read, they baptized him with all the ceremonies belonging to this mysterious sacrament. So that Constantine was the first of all the emperors who was regenerated by the new birth of baptism, and that was signed with the sign of the cross."[1]

When Constantine had heard the good news from the Christian monk from Egypt, he commenced by conferring many dignities on the Christians, and those only who were addicted to Christianity, he made governors of his provinces, &c.[2] He then issued edicts against heretics,—*i. e.*, those who, like Arius, did not believe that Christ was "*of one substance with the Father*," and others — calling them "enemies of truth and eternal life," "authors and councillors of death," &c.[3] He "*commanded by law*" that none should dare "to meet at conventicles," and that "all places where they were wont to keep their meetings should be *demolished*," or "confiscated to the Catholic church;"[4] *and Constantine was emperor.* "By this means," says Eusebius, "*such as maintained doctrines and opinions contrary to the church, were suppressed.*"[5]

This Constantine, says Eusebius:

"Caused his image to be engraven on his gold coins, in the form of prayer, with his hands joined together, and looking up towards Heaven." "And over divers gates of his palace, he was drawn praying, and lifting up his hands and eyes to heaven."[6]

After his death, "effigies of this blessed man" were engraved on the Roman coins, "sitting in and driving a chariot, and a hand reached down from heaven to receive and take him up."[7]

The hopes of wealth and honors, the example of an emperor, his exhortations, his irresistible smiles, diffused conviction among

---

[1] Lib. 4, chs. lxi. and lxii., and Socrates: Eccl. Hist., lib. 2, ch. xxvi.

[2] Eusebius: Life of Constantine, lib. 2, ch. xliii.

[3] Ibid. lib. 3, ch. lxii.

[4] Ibid. lib. 3, ch. lxiii.

[5] Ibid. lib. 3, ch. lxiv.

[6] Ibid. lib. 4, ch. xv.

[7] Ibid. ch. lxiii.

Plato places the ferocious tyrants in the Tartarus, such as Ardiacus of Pamphylia, who had slain his own father, a venerable old man, also an elder brother, and was stained with a great many other crimes. Constantine, covered with similar crimes, was better treated by the Christians, who have sent him to heaven, **and** *sainted* him besides.

the venal and obsequious crowds which unsually fill the apartments of a palace, and as the lower ranks of society are governed by example, the conversion of those who possessed any eminence of birth, of power, or of riches, *was soon followed by dependent multitudes.* Constantine passed a law which gave freedom to all the slaves who should embrace Christianity, and to those who were not slaves, he gave a white garment and twenty pieces of gold, upon their embracing the Christian faith. The common people were thus *purchased* at such an easy rate that, in one year, *twelve thousand men were baptized at Rome,* besides a proportionable number of women and children.[1]

To suppress the opinions of philosophers, which were contrary to Christianity, the Christian emperors published edicts. The respective decrees of the emperors Constantine and Theodosius,[2] generally ran in the words, " that all writings adverse to the claims of the Christian religion, in the possession of whomsoever they should be found, should be committed to the fire," as the pious emperors would not that those things tending to provoke God to wrath, should be allowed to offend the minds of the piously disposed.

The following is a decree of the Emperor Theodosius of this purport :

"We decree, therefore, that all writings, whatever, which Porphyry or any one else hath written against the Christian religion, in the possession of whomsoever they shall be found should be committed to the fire ; for we would not suffer any of those things so much as to come to men's ears, which tend to provoke God to wrath and offend the minds of the *pious.*"[3]

A similar decree of the emperor for establishing the doctrine of the Trinity, concludes with an admonition to all who shall object to it, that,

" Besides the condemnation of divine justice, they must expect to suffer the severe penalties, which *our* authority, guided by heavenly wisdom, may think proper to inflict upon them."[4]

This orthodox emperor (Theodosius) considered every heretic (as he called those who did not believe as he and his ecclesiastics *professed*) a rebel against the supreme powers of heaven and of

---

[1] Gibbon's Rome, vol. ii. p. 274.

[2] " Theodosius, though a professor of the orthodox Christian faith, was not baptized till 380, and his behavior after that period stamps him as one of the most cruel and vindictive persecutors who ever wore the purple. His arbitrary establishment of the Nicene faith over the whole empire, the deprivation of civil rites of all apostates from Christianity and of the Eunomians, the sentence of death on the Manicheans, and Quarto-decimans, all prove this." (Chambers's Encyclo., art. Theodosius.)

[3] Quoted in Taylor's Syntagma, p. 54.

[4] Gibbon's Rome, vol. iii. p. 81.

earth (he being one of the supreme powers of earth), *and each of the powers* might exercise their peculiar jurisdiction *over the soul and body of the guilty.*

The decrees of the Council of Constantinople had ascertained the *true* standard of the faith, *and the ecclesiastics, who governed the conscience of Theodosius, suggested the most effectual methods of persecution.* In the space of fifteen years he promulgated at least fifteen severe edicts against the heretics, *more especially against those who rejected the doctrine of the Trinity.*[1]

Arius (the presbyter of whom we have spoken in Chapter **XXXV.**, as declaring that, in the nature of things, *a father must be older than his son*) was *excommunicated* for his so-called *heretical* notions concerning the Trinity. His followers, who were very numerous, were called Arians. Their writings, *if they had been permitted to exist,*[2] would undoubtedly contain the lamentable story of the persecution which affected the church under the reign of the impious Emperor *Theodosius.*

In Asia Minor the people were persecuted by orders of Constantius, and these orders were more than obeyed by Macedonius. The civil and military powers were ordered to obey his commands; the consequence was, he disgraced the reign of Constantius. "The rites of baptism were conferred on women and children, who, for that purpose, had been torn from the arms of their friends and parents; the mouths of the communicants were held open by a wooden engine, while the consecrated bread was forced down their throats; the breasts of tender virgins were either burned with red-hot egg-shells, or inhumanly compressed between sharp and heavy boards."[3] The principal assistants of Macedonius — the tool of Constantius — in the work of persecution, were the two bishops of Nicomedia and Cyzicus, who were esteemed for their virtues, and especially for their charity.[4]

Julian, the successor of Constantius, has described some of the theological calamities which afflicted the empire, and more especially in the East, in the reign of a prince who was the slave of his own passions, and of those of his eunuchs: " Many were imprisoned, and persecuted, and driven into exile. Whole troops of those who are styled *heretics* were massacred, particularly at Cyzicus, and at Samosata. In Paphlagonia, Bithynia, Gallatia, and in many

---

[1] Gibbon's Rome, vol. iii. pp. 91, 92.
[2] All their writings were ordered to be destroyed.
[3] Gibbon's Rome, vol. ii. p. 359.
[4] Ibid. note 154.

other provinces, towns and villages were laid waste, and utterly destroyed."[1]

Persecutions in the name of Christ Jesus were inflicted on the heathen in most every part of the then known world. Even among the Norwegians, the Christian sword was unsheathed. They clung tenaciously to the worship of their forefathers, and numbers of them died real martyrs for their faith, after suffering the most cruel torments from their persecutors. It was by sheer compulsion that the Norwegians embraced Christianity. The reign of Olaf Tryggvason, a Christian king of Norway, was in fact entirely devoted to the propagation of the new faith, by means the most revolting to humanity. His general practice was to enter a district at the head of a formidable force, summon a *Thing*,[2] and give the people the alternative of fighting with him, or of being baptized. Most of them, of course, preferred baptism to the risk of a battle with an adversary so well prepared for combat; and the recusants were tortured to death with fiend-like ferocity, and their estates confiscated.[3]

These are some of the reasons "why Christianity prospered."

---

[1] Julian: Epistol. lii. p. 436. Quoted in Gibbon's Rome, vol. ii. p. 360.

[2] "*Thing*"—a general assembly of the freemen, who gave their assent to a measure by striking their shields with their drawn swords.

[3] See Mallet's Northern Antiquities, pp. 180, 351, and 470.

NOTE.—The learned Christian historian Pagi endeavors to smoothe over the crimes of Constantine. He says: "As for those few murders (which Eusebius says nothing about), had he thought it worth his while to refer to them, he would perhaps, with Baronius himself have said, that the young Licinius (his infant nephew), although the fact might not generally have been known, had most likely been an accomplice in the treason of his father. That as to the murder of his son, the Emperor is rather to be considered as unfortunate than as criminal. And with respect to his putting his wife to death, he ought to be pronounced rather a just and righteous judge. As for his numerous friends, whom Eutropius informs us he put to death one after another, we are bound to believe that most of them deserved it, and they were found out to have abused the Emperor's too great credulity, for the gratification of their own inordinate wickedness, and insatiable avarice ; and such no doubt was that SOPATER the philospher, who was at last put to death upon the accusation of Adlabius, and that by the righteous dispensation of God, for his having attempted to alienate the mind of Constantine from the true religion." (*Pagi Ann.* 324, quoted in Latin by Dr. Lardner, vol. iv. p. 371, in his notes for the benefit of the *learned* reader, but gives no rendering into English.)

29

CHAPTER XXXVIII.

WE shall now compare the great antiquity of the sacred books and religions of Paganism with those of the Christian, so that there may be no doubt as to which is the original, and which the copy. Allusions to this subject have already been made throughout this work, we shall therefore devote as little space to it here as possible.

In speaking of the sacred literature of India, Prof. Monier Williams says :

"' Sanskrit literature, embracing as it does nearly every branch of knowledge is entirely deficient in one department. It is wholly destitute of trustworthy historical records. Hence, little or nothing is known of the lives of ancient Indian authors, and the dates of their most celebrated works cannot be fixed with certainty. A fair conjecture, however, may be arrived at by comparing the most ancient with the more modern compositions, and estimating the period of time required to effect the changes of structure and idiom observable in the language. In this manner we may be justified in assuming that the hymns of the Veda were probably composed by a succession of poets at different dates between 1500 and 1000 years B. C."[1]

Prof. Wm. D. Whitney shows the great antiquity of the Vedic hymns from the fact that,

"The language of the Vedas is an *older* dialect, varying very considerably, both in its grammatical and lexical character, from the classical Sanscrit."

And M. de Coulanges, in his "Ancient City," says :

"We learn from the hymns of the *Vedas,* which are certainly very ancient, and from the laws of Manu," "what the Aryans of the east thought nearly thirty-five centuries ago."[2]

That the *Vedas* are of very high antiquity is unquestionable; but however remote we may place the period when they were written, we must necessarily presuppose that the Hindostanic race had

---

[1] Williams' Hinduism, p. 19. See also, Prof. Max Müller's Lectures on the Origin of Religion, pp. 145-158, and p. 67, where he speaks of "the Hindus, who, thousands of years ago, had reached in Upanishads the loftiest heights of philosophy."

[2] The Ancient City, p. 18.

already attained to a comparatively high degree of civilization, otherwise men capable of framing such doctrines could not have been found. Now this state of civilization must necessarily have been preceded by several centuries of barbarism, during which we cannot possibly admit a more refined faith than the popular belief in elementary deities.

We shall see in our next chapter that these very ancient Vedic hymns contain the *origin* of the legend of the Virgin-born God and Saviour, the great benefactor of mankind, who is finally put to death, and rises again to life and immortality on the third day.

The *Geetas* and *Puranas*, although of a comparatively modern date, are, as we have already seen, nevertheless composed of matter to be found in the two great epic poems, the *Ramayana* and the *Mahabharata*, which were written many centuries before the time assigned as that of the birth of Christ Jesus.[1]

The Pali sacred books, which contain the legend of the virgin-born God and Saviour — Sommona Cadom — are known to have been in existence 316 B. C.[2]

We have already seen that the religion known as Buddhism, and which corresponds in such a striking manner with Christianity, has now existed for upwards of twenty-four hundred years.[3]

Prof. Rhys Davids says :

"There is every reason to believe that the *Pitakas* (the sacred books which contain the legend of 'The Buddha'), now extant in Ceylon, are substantially identical with the books of the Southern Canon, as settled at the Council of Patna about the year 250 B. C.[4] As no works would have been received into the Canon which were not *then* believed to be very old, the *Pitakas* may be approximately placed in the *fourth century* B. C., and parts of them possibly reach back very nearly, if not quite, to the time of Gautama himself."[5]

The religion of the ancient *Persians*, which corresponds in so very many respects with that of the Christians, was established by Zoroaster—who was undoubtedly a Brahman[6]—and is contained

---

[1] See Monier Williams' Hinduism, pp. 109, 110, and Indian Wisdom, p. 493.

[2] See Isis Unveiled, vol. ii. p. 576, for the authority of Prof. Max Müller.

[3] "The religion known as Buddhism—from the title of 'The Buddha,' meaning 'The Wise.' 'The Enlightened'—has now existed for 2460 years, and may be said to be the prevailing religion of the world." (Chambers's Encyclo.)

[4] This Council was assembled by Asoka in the eighteenth year of his reign. The name of this king is honored wherever the teachings of Buddha have spread, and is reverenced from the Volga to Japan, from Ceylon and

Siam to the borders of Mongolia and Siberia. Like his Christian prototype Constantine, he was converted by a miracle. After his conversion, which took place in the tenth year of his reign, he became a very zealous supporter of the new religion. He himself built many monasteries and dagabas, and provided many *monks* with the necessaries of life ; and he encouraged those about his court to do the same. He published edicts throughout his empire, enjoining on all his subjects morality and justice.

[5] Rhys Davids' Buddhism, p. 10.

[6] See Chapter VII.

in the *Zend-Avesta,* their sacred book or Bible. This book is very ancient. Prof. Max Müller speaks of "the sacred book of the Zoroastrians" as being "older in its language than the cuneiform inscriptions of Cyrus (B. C. 560), Darius (B. C. 520), and Xerxes (B. C. 485) those ancient Kings of Persia, who knew that they were kings by the grace of *Auramazda,* and who placed his sacred image high on the mountain-records of Behistun."[1] That ancient book, or its fragments, at least, have survived many dynasties and kingdoms, and is still believed in by a small remnant of the Persian race, now settled at Bombay, and known all over the world by the name of Parsees.[2]

"The Babylonian and Phenician sacred books date back to a fabulous antiquity;"[3] and so do the sacred books and religion of Egypt.

Prof. Mahaffy, in his "Prolegomena to Ancient History," says:

"There is indeed hardly a great and fruitful idea in the Jewish or Christian systems which has not its analogy in the Egyptian faith, and *all these theological conceptions pervade the oldest religion of Egypt.*"[4]

The worship of Osiris, the Lord and Saviour, must have been of extremely ancient date, for he is represented as "Judge of the Dead," in sculptures contemporary with the building of the Pyramids, centuries before Abraham is said to have been born. Among the many hieroglyphic titles which accompany his figure in those sculptures, and in many other places on the walls of temples and tombs, are, "Lord of Life," "The Eternal Ruler," "Manifester of Good," "Revealer of Truth," "Full of Goodness and Truth," etc.

In speaking of the "Myth of Osiris," Mr. Bonwick says:

"This great mystery of the Egyptians demands serious consideration. Its antiquity—its universal hold upon the people for over five thousand years—its identification with the very life of the nation—*and its marvellous likeness to the creed of modern date,* unite in exciting the greatest interest."[5]

---

[1] Müller: Lectures on the Science of Religion, p. 235.

[2] This small tribe of Persians were driven from their native land by the Mohammedan conquerors under the Khalif Omar, in the seventh century of our era. Adhering to the ancient religion of Persia, which resembles that of the *Veda,* and bringing with them the records of their faith, the *Zend-Avesta* of their prophet Zoroaster, they settled down in the neighborhood of Surat, about one thousand one hundred years ago, and became great merchants and shipbuilders. For two or three centuries we know little of their history.

Their religion prevented them from making proselytes, and they never multiplied within themselves to any extent, nor did they amalgamate with the Hindoo population, so that even now their number only amounts to about seventy thousand. Nevertheless, from their busy, enterprising habits, in which they emulate Europeans, they form an important section of the population of Bombay and Western India.

[3] Movers: Quoted in Dunlap's Spirit Hist., p. 261.

[4] Prolegomena, p. 417.

[5] Bonwick's Egyptian Belief, p. 162.

This myth, and that of Isis and Horus, were known before the Pyramid time.[1]

The worship of the Virgin Mother in Egypt—from which country it was imported into Europe[2]—dates back thousands of years B. C. Mr. Bonwick says:

"In all probability she was worshiped three thousand years before Moses wrote. 'Isis nursing her child Horus, was represented,' says Mariette Bey, 'at least six thousand years ago.' We read the name of Isis on monuments of the fourth dynasty, and she lost none of her popularity to the close of the empire."

"The Egyptian Bible is by far the most ancient of all holy books." "Plato was told that Egypt possessed hymns dating back ten thousand years before his time."[3]

Bunsen says :

"The origin of the ancient prayers and hymns of the 'Book of the Dead,' is anterior to Menes; it implies that the system of Osirian worship and mythology was already formed."[4]

And, says Mr. Bonwick:

"Besides opinions, we have facts as a basis for arriving at a conclusion, and justifying the assertion of Dr. Birch, that the work dated from a period long anterior to the rise of Ammon worship at Thebes."[5]

Now, "this most ancient of all holy books," establishes the fact that a virgin-born and resurrected Saviour was worshiped in Egypt thousands of year before the time of Christ Jesus.

P. Le Page Renouf says:

"The *earliest monuments* which have been discovered present to us the *very same* fully-developed civilization and the *same religion* as the later monuments. . . . The gods whose names appear in the *oldest tombs* were worshiped down to the Christian times. The same kind of priesthoods which are mentioned in the tablets of Canopus and Rosetta in the Ptolemaic period are as ancient as the pyramids, and more ancient than any pyramid of which we know the date."[6]

In regard to the doctrine of the *Trinity*. We have just seen that "the development of the One God into a Trinity" pervades the oldest religion of Egypt, and the same may be said of India. Prof. Monier Williams, speaking on this subject, says:

"It should be observed that the native commentaries on the Veda often allude to thirty-three gods, which number is also mentioned in the Rig-Veda. This is a multiple of *three*, which is a sacred number constantly appearing in the Hindu religious system. It is probable, indeed, that although the Tri-murti is

---

[1] Bonwick's Egyptian Belief, p. 163.
[2] Ibid. p. 142, and King's Gnostics, p. 71.
[3] Bonwick's Egyptian Belief, pp. 185, 140, and 143.
[4] Quoted in Ibid. p. 186.
[5] Ibid.
[6] Renouf : Religion of Ancient Egypt, p. 81

not named in the Vedic hymns,[1] yet the Veda is the real source of this Triad of personifications, afterwards so conspicuous in Hindu mythology. This much, at least, is clear, that the Vedic poets exhibited a tendency to group all the forces and energies of nature under three heads, and the assertion that the number of the gods was thirty-three, amounted to saying that each of the three leading personifications was capable of eleven modifications."[2]

The great antiquity of the legends referred to in this work is demonstrated in the fact that they were found in a great measure on the continent of America, by the first Europeans who set foot on its soil. Now, how did they get there? Mr. Lundy, in his "Monumental Christianity," speaking on this subject, says:

"So great was the resemblance between the two sacraments of the Christian Church (viz., that of Baptism and the Eucharist) and those of the ancient Mexicans; so many other points of similarity, also, in *doctrine* existed, as to the unity of God, the Triad, the Creation, the Incarnation and Sacrifice, the Resurrection, etc., that Herman Witsius, no mean scholar and thinker, was induced to believe that Christianity had been preached on this continent by some one of the apostles, perhaps St. Thomas, from the fact that he is reported to have carried the Gospel to India and Tartary, whence he came to America."[3]

Some writers, who do not think that St. Thomas could have gotten to America, believe that St. Patrick, or some other saint, must have, in some unaccountable manner, reached the shores of the Western continent, and preached their doctrine there.[4] Others have advocated the devil theory, which is, that the devil, being jealous of the worship of Christ Jesus, set up a religion of his own, and imitated, nearly as possible, the religion of Christ. All of these theories being untenable, we must, in the words of Burnouf, the eminent French Orientalist, "learn one day that all ancient traditions disfigured by emigration and legend, *belong to the history of India.*"

That America was inhabited by Asiatic emigrants, and that the American legends are of *Asiatic origin*, we believe to be indisputable. There is an abundance of proof to this effect.[5]

In contrast to the great antiquity of the sacred books and religions of Paganism, we have the facts that the Gospels were not written by the persons whose names they bear, that they were written many years after the time these men are said to have lived, and that they are full of interpolations and errors. The first that

---

[1] That is, the Tri-murti Brahmā, Vishnu and Siva, for he tells us that the three gods, Indra, Agni, and Surya. constitute the *Vedic* chief triad of Gods. (Hinduism, p. 24.) Again he tells us that the idea of a Tri-murti was *first* dimly shadowed forth in the Rig-Veda, where a triad of principal gods—Agni, Indra and Surya—is recognized. (Ibid. p. 83.) The worship of the three members of the Tri-murti, Brahmā, Vishnu and Siva, is to be found in the period of the epic poems, from 500 to 300 B. C. (Ibid. pp. 109, 110, 115.)

[2] Williams' Hinduism, p. 25.

[3] Monumental Christianity, p. 390.

[4] See Mexican Antiquities, vol. vi.

[5] See Appendix A.

we know of the four gospels is at the time of Irenæus, who, in the second century, intimates that he had received four gospels, as authentic scriptures. This pious forger was probably the author of the *fourth*, as we shall presently see.

Besides these gospels there were many more which were subsequently deemed apocryphal; the narratives related in them of Christ Jesus and his apostles were stamped as forgeries.

"The Gospel according to Matthew" is believed by the majority of biblical scholars of the present day to be the oldest of the four, and to be made up principally of a pre-existing one, called "The Gospel of the Hebrews." The principal difference in these two gospels being that "*The Gospel of the Hebrews*" commenced with giving the genealogy of Jesus from David, through Joseph "*according to the flesh*." The story of Jesus being born of a virgin *was not to be found there*, it being an afterpiece, originating either with the writer of "*The Gospel according to Matthew*," or some one after him, and was evidently taken from "The Gospel of the Egyptians." "*The Gospel of the Hebrews*" — from which, we have said, the *Matthew* narrator copied — *was an intensely Jewish gospel*, and was to be found — in one of its forms — among the Ebionites, who were the narrowest Jewish Christians of the second century. "*The Gospel according to Matthew*" is, therefore, the most Jewish gospel of the four; in fact, the most Jewish book in the New Testament, excepting, perhaps, the *Apocalypse* and the *Epistle of James.*

Some of the more conspicuous Jewish traits, to be found in this gospel, are as follows:

Jesus is sent *only* to the lost sheep of the house of *Israel*. The twelve are forbidden to go among the *Gentiles* or the *Samaritans*. They are to sit on twelve thrones, *judging the twelve tribes of Israel*. The genealogy of Jesus is traced back to *Abraham*, and there stops.[1] The works of the *law* are frequently insisted on. There is a superstitious regard for the *Sabbath*, &c.

There is no evidence of the existence of the Gospel of Matthew, — *in its present form* — until the year 173, A. D. It is at this time, also, that it is first ascribed to Matthew, by Apollinaris, Bishop of Hierapolis. The original oracles of the Gospel of the Hebrews, however,—which were made use of by the author of our present

---

[1] The genealogy which traces him back to *Adam* (Luke iii.) makes his religion not only a Jewish, but a *Gentile* one. According to this Gospel he is not only a Messiah sent to the Jews, but to all nations, sons of Adam.

Gospel of Matthew,—were written, likely enough, not long before the destruction of Jerusalem, but the Gospel itself dates from about A. D. 100.[1]

"*The Gospel according to Luke*" is believed to come next — in chronological order — to that of Matthew, and to have been written some fifteen or twenty years after it. The author was a *foreigner*, as his writings plainly show that he was far removed from the events which he records.

In writing his Gospel, the author made use of that of Matthew, the Gospel of the Hebrews, and Marcion's Gospel. He must have had, also, still other sources, as there are parables peculiar to it, which are not found in them. Among these may be mentioned that of the "*Prodigal Son*," and the "*Good Samaritan*." Other parables peculiar to it are that of the two debtors; the friend borrowing bread at night; the rich man's barns; Dives and Lazarus; the lost piece of silver; the unjust steward; the Pharisee and the Publican.

Several miracles are also peculiar to the Luke narrator's Gospel, the raising of the widow of Nain's son being the most remarkable. Perhaps these stories were delivered to him *orally*, and perhaps *he is the author of them*, — we shall never know. The foundation of the legends, however, undoubtedly came from the "*certain scriptures*" of the Essenes in Egypt. The principal *object* which the writer of this gospel had in view was to reconcile *Paulinism* and the *more Jewish* forms of Christianity.[2]

The next in chronological order, according to the same school of critics, is "The Gospel according to Mark." This gospel is supposed to have been written within ten years of the former, and its author, as of the other two gospels, is unknown. It was probably written at *Rome*, as the Latinisms of the author's style, and the apparent motive of his work, strongly suggest that he was a Jewish citizen of the Eternal City. He made use of the Gospel of Matthew as his principal authority, and probably referred to that of Luke, as he has things in common with Luke only.

The object which the writer had in view, was to have a neutral go-between, a compromise between Matthew as too Petrine (Jewish), and Luke as too Pauline (Gentile). The different aspects of Matthew and Luke were found to be confusing to believers, and provocative of hostile criticism from without; hence the idea of writing a shorter gospel, that should combine the most essential elements of both. Luke was itself a compromise between the op-

---

[1] See The Bible of To-Day, under "*Matthew.*"   [2] See Ibid. under "*Luke.*"

posing Jewish and universal tendencies of early Christianity, but Mark endeavors by avoidance and omission to effect what Luke did more by addition and contrast. Luke proposed to himself to open a door for the admission of Pauline ideas without offending Gentile Christianity; Mark, on the contrary, in a negative spirit, to publish a Gospel which should not hurt the feelings of either party. Hence his avoidance of all those disputed questions which disturbed the church during the first quarter of the second century. The genealogy of Jesus is omitted; this being offensive to Gentile Christians, and even to some of the more liberal Judaizers. The supernatural birth of Jesus is omitted, this being offensive to the Ebonitish (extreme Jewish) and some of the Gnostic Christians. For every Judaizing feature that is sacrificed, a universal one is also sacrificed. Hard words against the Jews are left out, but with equal care, hard words about the Gentiles.[1]

We now come to the fourth, and last gospel, that "*according to John*," which was not written until many years after that "according to Matthew."

"It is impossible to pass from the Synoptic[2] Gospels," says Canon Westcott, "to the fourth, without feeling that the transition involves the passage from one world of thought to another. No familiarity with the general teachings of the Gospels, no wide conception of the character of the Saviour, is sufficient to destroy the contrast which exists in form and spirit between the earlier and later narratives."

The discrepancies between the fourth and the Synoptic Gospels are numerous. If Jesus was the *man* of Matthew's Gospel, he was not the *mysterious being* of the fourth. If his ministry was only *one* year long, it was not *three*. If he made but *one* journey to Jerusalem, he did not make *many*. If his method of teaching was that of the Synoptics, it was not that of the fourth Gospel. If he was the *Jew* of Matthew, he was not the *Anti-Jew* of John.[3]

---

[1] See the Bible of To-Day, under "*Mark*."

[2] "*Synoptics;*" the Gospels which contain accounts of the same events—"parallel passages," as they are called—which can be written side by side, so as to enable us to make a general view or *synopsis* of all the three, and at the same time compare them with each other. Bishop Marsh says: "The most eminent critics are at present decidedly of opinion that one of the two suppositions must necessarily be adopted, either that the three Evangelists copied from each other, or that all the three drew from a common source, and that the notion of an absolute independence, in respect

to the composition of the three first Gospels, is no longer tenable."

[3] "On opening the New Testament and comparing the impression produced by the Gospel of Matthew or Mark with that by the Gospel of John, the observant eye is at once struck with as salient a contrast as that already indicated on turning from the *Macbeth* or *Othello* of Shakespeare to the *Comus* of Milton or to Spenser's *Faerie Queene*." (Francis Tiffany.)

"To learn how far we may trust them (the Gospels) we must in the first place compare them with each other. The moment we do so

Everywhere in John we come upon a more developed stage of Christianity than in the Synoptics. The scene, the atmosphere, is different. In the Synoptics Judaism, the Temple, the Law and the Messianic Kingdom are omnipresent. In John they are remote and vague. In Matthew Jesus is always yearning for *his own* nation. In John he has no other sentiment for it than *hate and scorn.* In Matthew the sanction of the Prophets is his great credential. In John his dignity can tolerate no previous approximation.

"Do we ask," says Francis Tiffany, "who wrote this wondrous Gospel? Mysterious its origin, as that wind of which its author speaks, which bloweth where it listeth, and thou hearest the sound thereof and canst not tell whence it cometh or whither it goeth. As with the Great Unknown of the book of Job, the Great Unknown of the later Isaiah, the ages keep his secret. *The first absolutely indisputable evidence of the existence of the book dates from the latter half of the second century.*"

The first that we know of the *fourth* Gospel, for certainty, is at the time of Irenæus (A. D. 179).[1] We look in vain for an express recognition of the *four* canonical Gospels, or for a *distinct mention* of any one of them, in the writings of St. Clement (A. D. 96), St. Ignatius (A. D. 107), St. Justin (A. D. 140), or St. Polycarp (A. D. 108). All we can find is incidents from the life of Jesus, sayings, etc.

That Irenæus is the author of it is very evident. This learned and pious forger says:

"John, the disciple of the Lord, wrote his Gospel to confute the doctrine *lately* taught by Cerinthus, and a great while before by those called Nicolaitans, a branch of the Gnostics; and to show that there is one God who made all things by his WORD: and not, as they say, that there is one the Creator, and another the Father of our Lord: and one the Son of the Creator, and another, even the Christ, who descended from above upon the Son of the Creator, and continued impassible, and at length returned to his pleroma or fulness."[2]

The idea of God having inspired *four* different men to write a history of the *same transactions*—or rather, of many dif-

---

we notice that the *fourth* stands quite alone, while the *first three form a single group*, not only following the same general course, but sometimes even showing a verbal agreement which cannot possibly be accidental." (The Bible for Learners, vol. ii. p. 27.)

[1] "Irenæus is the first person who mentions the four Gospels by name." (Bunsen : Keys of St. Peter, p. 328.)

"Irenæus, in the second century, is the first of the fathers who, though he has nowhere given us a professed catalogue of the books of the New

Testament, intimates that he had received four Gospels, as authentic Scriptures, the authors of which he describes." (Rev. R. Taylor : Syntagma, p. 109.)

"The authorship of the *fourth* Gospel has been the subject of much learned and anxious controversy among theologians. *The earliest, and only very important external testimony we have is that of* IRENÆUS (A.D. 179.)" (W. R. Grey : *The Creed of Christendom*, p. 159.)

[2] Against Heresies, bk. i i. ch. xi. sec. 1.

ferent men having undertaken to write such a history, of whom God inspired *four only* to write correctly, leaving the others to their own unaided resources, and giving us no test by which to distinguish the inspired from the uninspired—certainly appears self-confuting, and anything but natural.

The reasons assigned by Irenæus for their being *four* Gospels are as follows:

"It is impossible that there could be more or less than *four*. For there are *four* climates, and *four* cardinal winds ; but the Gospel is the pillar and foundation of the church, and its breath of life. *The church therefore was to have four pillars, blowing immortality from every quarter, and giving life to man.*"[1]

It was by this Irenæus, with the assistance of Clement of Alexandria, and Tertullian, one of the Latin Fathers, that the four Gospels were introduced into *general* use among the Christians.

In these four spurious Gospels, and in some which are considered *Apocryphal*—because the bishops at the Council of Laodicea (A. D. 365) rejected them—we have the only history of Jesus of Nazareth. Now, if all accounts or narratives of Christ Jesus and his Apostles were forgeries, as it is admitted that all the *Apocryphal* ones were, what can the superior character of the received Gospels prove for them, but that they are merely superiorly executed forgeries? The existence of Jesus is implied in the New Testament outside of the Gospels, *but hardly an incident of his life is mentioned, hardly a sentence that he spoke has been preserved.* Paul, writing from twenty to thirty years after his death, has but a single reference to anything he ever said or did.

Beside these four Gospels there were, as we said above, many others, for, in the words of Mosheim, the ecclesiastical historian :

"Not long after Christ's ascension into heaven, several histories of his life and doctrines, full of *pious frauds* and *fabulous wonders*, were composed by persons whose intentions, perhaps, were not bad, but whose writings discovered the greatest superstition and ignorance. Nor was this all ; *productions appeared, which were imposed upon the world by fraudulent men, as the writings of the holy apostles.*"[2]

Dr. Conyers Middleton, speaking on this subject, says:

"There never was any period of time in all ecclesiastical history, in which so many rank heresies were publicly professed, *nor in which so many spurious books were forged* and published by the Christians, under the names of Christ, and the Apostles, and the Apostolic writers, as in those primitive ages. *Several of these forged books are frequently cited and applied to the defense of Christianity, by the most eminent fathers of the same ages, as true and genuine pieces.*"[3]

---

[1] Against Heresies, bk. iii. ch. xi. sec. 8.   [3] Middleton's Works, vol. i. p. 59.
[2] Mosheim: vol. i. p. 109.

Archbishop Wake also admits that:

"It would be useless to insist on all the spurious pieces which were attribu ted to St. Paul alone, in the primitive ages of Christianity."[1]

Some of the "spurious pieces which were attributed to St. Paul," may be found to day in our canonical New Testament, and are believed by many to be the word of God.[2]

The learned Bishop Faustus, in speaking of the authenticity of the *New Testament*, says:

"It is certain that the New Testament was not written by Christ himself, nor by his apostles, but a long while after them, *by some unknown persons*, who, lest they should not be credited when they wrote of affairs they were little acquainted with, affixed to their works the names of the apostles, or of such as were supposed to have been their companions, asserting that what they had written themselves, was written according to these persons to whom they ascribed it."[3]

Again he says:

"Many things have been inserted by our ancestors in the speeches of our Lord, which, though put forth under his name, agree not with his faith; especially since—*as already it has been often proved*—these things were not written by Christ, nor his apostles, but a long while after their assumption, by I know not what sort of half Jews, not even agreeing with themselves, who made up their tale out of reports and opinions merely, and yet, fathering the whole upon the names of the apostles of the Lord, or on those who were supposed to follow the apostles, they mendaciously pretended that they had written their lies and conceits according to them."[4]

What had been said to have been done in *India*, was said by these "half-Jews" to have been done in *Palestine;* the change of names and places, with the mixing up of various sketches of the Egyptian, Persian, Phenician, Greek and Roman mythology, was all that was necessary. They had an abundance of material, and with it they built. The foundation upon which they built was undoubtedly the "*Scriptures*," or Diegesis, of the Essenes in Alexandria in Egypt, which fact led Eusebius, the ecclesiastical historian—"without whom," says Tillemont, "we should scarce have had any knowledge of the history of the first ages of Christianity, or of the authors who wrote in that time"—to say that the sacred writings used by this sect were none other than "*Our Gospels*."

[1] Genuine Epist. Apost. Fathers, p. 98.
[2] See Chadwick's Bible of To-Day, pp. 191, 192.
[3] "Nec ab ipso scriptum constat, nec ab ejus apostolis sed longo post tempore a quibusdam incerti nominis viris, qui ne sibi non haberetur fides scribentibus quæ nescirent, partim apostolorum, partim eorum qui apostolos secuti viderentur nomina scriptorum suorum frontibus indiderunt, asseverantes secundum eos, se scripsisse quæ scripserunt." (Faust. lib. 2. Quoted by Rev. R. Taylor: Diegesis, p. 114.)
[4] "Multa enim a majoribus vestris, eloquiis

We offer below a few of the many proofs showing the Gospels to have been written a long time after the events narrated are said to have occurred, and by persons unacquainted with the country of which they wrote.

"He (Jesus) came unto the sea of Galilee, through the midst of the coasts of Decapolis," is an assertion made by the Mark narrator (vii. 31), when there were no coasts of Decapolis, nor was the name so much as known before the reign of the emperor Nero.

Again, "He (Jesus) departed from Galilee, and came into the coasts of Judea, beyond Jordan," is an assertion made by the Matthew narrator (xix. 1), when the Jordan itself was the eastern boundary of Judea, and there were no coasts of Judea beyond it.

Again, "But when he (Joseph) heard that Archelaus did reign in Judea, in the room of his father Herod, he was afraid to go thither, notwithstanding, being warned of God in a dream, he turned aside into the parts of Galilee, and he came and dwelt in a city called Nazareth; that it might be fulfilled, which was spoken by the prophets, he shall be called a Nazarene," is another assertion made by the Matthew narrator (ii. 22, 23), when—1. It was a son of Herod who reigned in Galilee as well as Judea, so that he could not be more secure in one province than in the other; and when —2. It was impossible for him to have gone from Egypt to Nazareth, without traveling through the whole extent of Archelaus's kingdom, or making a peregrination through the deserts on the north and east of the Lake Asphaltites, and the country of Moab; and then, either crossing the Jordan into Samaria or the Lake of Gennesareth into Galilee, and from thence going to the city of Nazareth, which is no better geography, than if one should describe a person as *turning aside* from Cheapside into the parts of Yorkshire; and when—3. There were no prophets whatever who had prophesied that Jesus "*should be called a Nazarene.*"

The Matthew narrator (iv. 13) states that "He departed into Galilee, and leaving Nazareth, came and dwelt in Capernaum," as if he imagined that the city of Nazareth was not as properly in Galilee as Capernaum was; which is much such geographical accuracy, as if one should relate the travels of a hero, who departed into Middlesex, and leaving London, came and dwelt in Lombard street.[1]

Domini nostri inserta verba sunt; quæ nomine signata ipsius, cum ejus fide non congruant, præsertim, quia, ut jam sæpe probatum a nobis est, nec ab ipso hæc sunt, nec ab ejus apostolis scripta, sed multo post eorum assumptionem, a nescio quibus, et ipsis inter se non concordantibus SEMI-JUDÆIS, per famas opin-ionesque comperta sunt; qui tamen omnia eadem in apostolorum Domini conferentes nomina vel eorum qui seccuti apostolos viderentur, errores ac mendacia sua secundum eos se scripsisse mentiti sunt." (Faust.: lib. 33. Quoted in Ibid. p. 66.)

[1] Taylor's Diegesis.

There are many other falsehoods in gospel geography beside these, which, it is needless to mention, plainly show that the writers were not the persons they are generally supposed to be.

Of gospel statistics there are many falsehoods; among them may be mentioned the following:

" Annas and Caiaphas being the high priests, the word of God came unto John the son of Zacharias in the wilderness," is an assertion made by the Luke narrator (Luke iii. 2); when all Jews, or persons living among them, must have known that there never was but *one* high priest at a time, as with ourselves there is but one mayor of a city.

Again we read (John vii. 52), " Search (the Scriptures) and look, for out of Galilee ariseth no prophet," when the most distinguished of the Jewish prophets—Nahum and Jonah—were both Galileans.

See reference in the Epistles to " *Saints*,".a religious order, owing its origin to the popes. Also, references to the distinct orders of " *Bishops*," " *Priests*," and " *Deacons*," and calls to a monastic life; to fasting, etc., when, the titles of " Bishop," " Priest," and " Deacon " were given to the Essenes—whom Eusebius calls Christians—and, as is well known, *monasteries* were the abode of the Essenes or Therapeuts.

See the words for " *legion*," " *aprons*," " *handkerchiefs*," " *centurion*," etc., in the original, not being Greek, but Latin, written in Greek characters, a practice first to be found in the historian Herodian, in the third century.

In Matt. xvi. 18, and Matt. xviii. 17, the word " *Church* " is used, and its *papistical* and infallible authority referred to as then existing, which is known not to have existed till ages after. And the passage in Matt. xi. 12:—" From the days of John the Baptist until *now*, the kingdom of heaven suffereth violence," etc., could not have been written till a very late period.

Luke ii. 1, shows that the writer (whoever he may have been) lived long after the events related. His dates, about the fifteenth year of Tiberius, and the government of Cyrenius (the only indications of time in the New Testament), are manifestly false. The general ignorance of the four Evangelists, not merely of the geography and statistics of Judea, but even of its language,—their egregious blunders, which no writers who had lived in that age could be conceived of as making,—prove that they were not only no such persons as those who have been willing to be deceived have taken them to be, but that they were not Jews, had never been in Palestine, and neither lived at, or at anywhere near the times to which their narratives seem to refer. The ablest divines at the present day, of all denominations, have yielded as much as this.[1]

The Scriptures were in the hands of the clergy only, and they had every opportunity to insert whatsoever they pleased; thus we find them full of *interpolations.* Johann Solomo Semler, one of the most influential theologians of the eighteenth century, speaking of this, says:

"The Christian doctors never brought their sacred books before the common people ; although people in general have been wont to think otherwise ; during the first ages, they were in the hands of the clergy only."[2]

Concerning the *time* when the canon of the New Testament was settled, Mosheim says:

"The opinions, or rather the *conjectures*, of the learned concerning the *time* when the books of the New Testament were collected into one volume ; as also about the authors of that collection, are extremely different. This important question is attended with great and almost insuperable difficulties to us in these later times."[3]

The Rev. B. F. Westcott says:

"It is impossible to point to any period as marking the date at which our present canon was determined. When it first appears, it is presented not as a novelty, but as an ancient tradition."[4]

Dr. Lardner says:

"Even so late as the middle of the *sixth century*, the canon of the New Testament had not been settled by any authority that was decisive and universally

---

[1] Says Prof. Smith upon this point : " All the earliest external evidence points to the conclusion that *the synoptic gospels are non-apostolic digests of spoken and written* apostolic tradition, and that the arrangement of the earlier material in orderly form took place only gradually and by many essays."

Dr. Hooykaas, speaking of the four " Gospels," and " Acts," says of them : " Not one of these five books was really written by the person whose name it bears, and they are all of more recent date than the heading would lead us to suppose."

" We cannot say that the " Gospels " and book of " Acts " are *unauthentic*, for not one of them professes to give the name of its author. *They appeared anonymously.* The titles placed above them in our Bibles owe their origin to a later ecclesiastical tradition which deserves no confidence whatever." (Bible for Learners, vol. iii. pp. 24, 25.)

These Gospels " can hardly be said to have had authors at all. *They had only editors or compilers.* What I mean is, that those who enriched the old Christian literature with these

Gospels did not go to work as independent writers and compose their own narratives out of the accounts they had collected, but simply took up the different stories or sets of stories which they found current in the *oral* tradition or already reduced to writing, *adding here* and *expanding there*, and so sent out into the world a very artless kind of composition. These works were then, from time to time, somewhat enriched by *introductory matter or interpolations* from the hands of later Christians, and perhaps were modified a little here and there. Our first two Gospels appear to have passed through more than one such revision. The third, whose writer says in his preface, that 'many had undertaken to put together a narrative (Gospel),' before him, appears to proceed from a single collecting, arranging, and modifying hand." (Ibid. p. 29.)

[2] " Christiani doctores non in vulgus prodebant libros sacros, licet soleant plerique aliter opinari, erant tantum in manibus clericorum, priora per sæcula." (Quoted in Taylor's Diegesis, p. 48.)

[3] Mosheim: vol i. pt. 2, ch. ii.

[4] General Survey of the Canon, p. 469.

acknowledged, but Christian people were at liberty to judge for themselves concerning the genuiness of writings proposed to them as apostolical, and to determine according to evidence."[1]

The learned Michaelis says:

"No manuscript of the New Testament now extant is prior to the *sixth century*, and what is to be lamented, various readings which, as appears from the quotations of the Fathers, were in the text of the Greek Testament, are to be found in none of the manuscripts which are at present remaining."[2]

And Bishop Marsh says:

"It is a certain fact, that several readings in our common printed text are nothing more than *alterations* made by Origen, whose authority was so great in the Christian Church (A. D. 230) that emendations which he proposed, though, as he himself acknowledged, they were supported by the evidence of no manuscript, were very generally received."[3]

In his Ecclesiastical History, Eusebius gives us a list of what books at that time (A. D. 315) were considered canonical. They are as follows:

"The four-fold writings of the Evangelists," "The Acts of the Apostles," "The Epistles of Peter," "after these the *first* of John, and that of Peter," "*All these are received for undoubted.*" "The Revelation of St. John, *some disavow.*"

"The books which are *gainsaid*, though well known unto many, are these: the Epistle of James, the Epistle of Jude, the *latter* of Peter, the *second* and *third* of John, *whether they were John the Evangelist, or some other of the same name.*"[4]

Though Irenæus, in the second century, is the first who mentions the evangelists, and Origen, in the third century, is the first who gives us a catalogue of the books contained in the New Testament, Mosheim's admission still stands before us. We have no grounds of assurance that the mere mention of the *names* of the evangelists by Irenæus, or the arbitrary drawing up of a particular catalogue by Origen, were of any authority. It is still unknown *by whom*, or *where*, or *when*, the canon of the New Testament was settled. But in this absence of positive evidence we have abundance of negative proof. We know when it was *not* settled. We know it was not settled in the time of the Emperor Justinian, nor in the time of Cassiodorus; that is, not at any time *before the middle of the sixth century*, "by any authority that was decisive and universally acknowledged; but Christian people were at liberty to judge for themselves concerning the genuineness of writings proposed to them as apostolical."

---

[1] Credibility of the Gospels.
[2] Marsh's Michaelis, vol. ii. p. 160. The Sinaitic MS. is believed by Tischendorf to belong to the fourth century.
[3] Ibid. p. 368.
[4] Eusebius: Ecclesiastical Hist. lib. 8, ch. xxii.

We cannot do better than close this chapter with the words of Prof. Max Müller, who, in speaking of Buddhism, says :

"We have in the history of Buddhism an excellent opportunity for watching the process by which a canon of sacred books is called into existence. We see here, *as elsewhere*, that during the life-time of the teacher, no record of events, no sacred code containing the sayings of the Master, was wanted. His presence was enough, and thoughts of the future, and more particularly, of future greatness, seldom entered the minds of those who followed him. It was only after Buddha had left the world to enter into *Nirvána*, that his disciples attempted to recall the sayings and doings of their departed friend and master. At that time, everything that seemed to redound to the glory of Buddha, however extraordinary and incredible, was eagerly welcomed, while witnesses who would have ventured to criticise or reject unsupported statements, or to detract in any way from the holy character of Buddha, had no chance of ever being listened to. And when, in spite of all this, differences of opinion arose, they were not brought to the test by a careful weighing of evidence, but the names of 'unbeliever' and 'heretic' were quickly invented in India *as elsewhere*, and bandied backwards and forwards between contending parties, till at last, when the doctors disagreed, the help of the secular power had to be invoked, and kings and emperors assembled councils for the suppression of schism, for the settlement of an orthodox creed, and for the completion of a *sacred canon*."[1]

That which Prof. Müller describes as taking place in the religion of Christ Buddha, is exactly what took place in the religion of Christ Jesus. That the miraculous, and many of the non-miraculous, events related in the Gospels never happened, is demonstrable from the facts which we have seen in this work, that nearly all of these events, had been previously related of the gods and goddesses of heathen nations of antiquity, more especially of the Hindoo Saviour *Crishna*, and the Buddhist Saviour *Buddha*, whose religion, with less alterations than time and translations have made in the Jewish Scriptures, may be traced in nearly every dogma and every ceremony of the evangelical mythology.

---

[1] The Science of Religion, pp. 30, 31.

NOTE.—The *Codex Sinaiticus*, referred to on the preceding page, (*note* 2,) was found at the Convent of St. Catherine on Mt. Sinai, by Tischendorf, in 1859· He *supposes* that it belongs to the 4th cent. ; but Dr. Davidson (in Kitto's Bib. Ency., Art. MSS.) thinks different. He says : "*Probably* it is of the 6th *cent.*," while he states that the *Codex Vaticanus* "is *believed* to belong to the 4th cent.," and the *Codex* Alexandrinus to the 5th cent. McClintock & Strong's Ency. (Art. MSS.,) relying probably on Tischerdorf's conjecture, places the *Codex Sinaiticus* first. "It is *probably* the oldest of the MSS. of the N. T., and of the 4th cent.," say they. The *Codex Vaticanus* is considered the next oldest, and the *Codex Alexandrinus* is placed third in order, and "was *probably* written in the first half of the 5th cent." The writer of the art. N. T. in Smith's *Bib. Dic.* says : "The *Codex Sinaiticus* is probably the oldest of the MSS. of the N. T., and of the 4th cent.;" and that the *Codex Alexandrinus* "was *probably* written in the first half of the 5th cent." Thus we see that in determining the dates of the MSS. of the N. T., Christian divines are obliged to resort to *conjecture ;* there being no certainty whatever in the matter. But with all their "suppositions," "probabilities," "beliefs" and "conjectures," we have the words of the learned Michaelis still before us, that : "No MSS. of the N. T. now extant are prior to the *sixth cent.*" This remark, however, does not cover the *Codex Sinaiticus*, which was discovered since Michaelis wrote his work on the N. T. ; but, as we saw above, Dr. Davidson does not agree with Tischendorf in regard to its antiquity, and places it in the 6th cent.

CHAPTER XXXIX.

AFTER what we have seen concerning the numerous virgin-born, crucified and resurrected Saviours, believed on in the Pagan world for so many centuries before the time assigned for the birth of the Christian Saviour, the questions naturally arise : were they real personages ? did they ever exist in the flesh ? whence came these stories concerning them ? have they a foundation in truth, or are they simply creations of the imagination ?

The *historical* theory—according to which *all* the persons mentioned in mythology were once real human beings, and the legends and fabulous traditions relating to them were merely the additions and embellishments of later times—which was so popular with scholars of the last century, has been altogether abandoned.

Under the historical point of view the gods are mere deified mortals, either heroes who have been deified after their death, or Pontiff-chieftains who have passed themselves off for gods, and who, it is gratuitously supposed, found people stupid enough to believe in their pretended divinity. This was the manner in which, formerly, writers explained the mythology of nations of antiquity ; but a method that pre-supposed an historical Crishna, an historical Osiris, an historical Mithra, an historical Hercules, an historical Apollo, or an historical Thor, was found untenable, and therefore, does not, at the present day, stand in need of a refutation. As a writer of the early part of the present century said :

"We shall never have an ancient history worthy of the perusal of men of common sense, till we cease treating poems as history, and send back such personages as Hercules, Theseus, Bacchus, etc., to the heavens, whence their history is taken, and whence they never descended to the earth."

The historical theory was succeeded by the *allegorical* thory, which supposes that all the myths of the ancients were *allegorical* and *symbolical*, and contain some moral, religious, or philosophical

[466]

truth or historical fact under the form of an allegory, which came in process of time to be understood literally.

In the preceding pages we have spoken of the several virgin-born, crucified and resurrected Saviours, as real personages. We have attributed to these individuals words and acts, and have regarded the words and acts recorded in the several sacred books from which we have quoted, as said and done by them. But in doing this, we have simply used the language of others. These gods and heroes were not real personages; *they are merely personifications of the* SUN. As Prof. Max Müller observes in his Lectures on the Science of Religion :

" One of the earliest objects that would strike and stir the mind of man, and for which a *sign* or a *name* would soon be wanted, is surely the *Sun*.[1] It is very hard for us to realize the feelings with which the first dwellers on the earth looked upon the Sun, or to understand fully what they meant by a morning prayer or a morning sacrifice. Perhaps there are few people who have watched a sunrise more than once or twice in their life ; few people who have ever known the meaning of a morning prayer, or a morning sacrifice. But think of man at the very dawn of time. . . . think of the Sun. awakening the eyes of man from sleep, and his mind from slumber ! Was not the sunrise to him the first wonder, the first beginning of all reflection, all thought, all philosophy ? Was it not to him the first revelation, the first beginning of all trust, of all religion? . . . .

" Few nations only have preserved in their ancient poetry some remnants of the natural awe with which the earlier dwellers on the earth saw that brilliant being slowly rising from out of the darkness of the night, raising itself by its own might higher and higher, till it stood triumphant on the arch of heaven, and then descended and sank down in its fiery glory into the dark abyss of the heaving and hissing sea. In the hymns of the *Veda*, the poet still wonders whether the Sun will rise again ; he asks how he can climb the vault of heaven ? why he does not fall back ? why there is no dust on his path ? And when the rays of the morning rouse him from sleep and call him back to new life, when he sees the Sun, as he says, stretching out his golden arms to bless the world and rescue it from the terror of darkness, he exclaims, ' Arise, our life, our spirit has come back ! the darkness is gone, the light approaches."

Many years ago, the learned Sir William Jones said:

" We must not be surprised at finding, on a close examination, that the characters of all the Pagan deities, male and female, melt into each other, and at last into one or two ; for it seems as well founded opinion, that the whole crowd of gods and goddesses of ancient Rome, and modern Varānes, mean only the powers of nature, and principally those of the SUN, expressed in a variety of ways, and by a multitude of fanciful names."[2]

---

[1] " In the *Vedas*, the *Sun* has twenty different names, not pure equivalents, but each term descriptive of the Sun in one of its aspects. It is brilliant (Sûrya),the friend (Mitra), generous (Aryaman), beneficent (Bhaga), that which nourishes (Pûshna), the Creator (Tvashtar), the master of the sky (Divaspati), and so on." (Rev. S. Baring-Gould : Orig. Relig. Belief, vol. i. p. 150.)

[2] Asiatic Researches, vol. i. p. 267.

Since the first learned president of the Royal Asiatic Society paved the way for the science of *comparative mythology*, much has been learned on this subject, so that, as the Rev. George W. Cox remarks, "recent discussions on the subject seem to justify the conviction that the foundations of the science of *comparative mythology* have been firmly laid, and that its method is unassailable."[1]

If we wish to find the gods and goddesses of the ancestors of our race, we must look to the sun, the moon, the stars, the sky, the earth, the sea, the dawn, the clouds, the wind, &c., *which they personified and worshiped*. That these have been the gods and goddesses of all nations of antiquity, is an established fact.[2]

The words which had denoted the sun and moon would denote not merely living things but living persons. From personification to deification the steps would be but few; and the process of disintegration would at once furnish the materials for a vast fabric of mythology. All the expressions which had attached a living force to natural objects would remain as the description of personal and anthropomorphous gods. Every word would become an attribute, and all ideas, once grouped around a simple object, would branch off into distinct personifications. The sun had been the lord of light, the driver of the chariot of the day; he had toiled and labored for the sons of men, and sunk down to rest, after a hard battle, in the evening. But now the lord of light would be Phoibos Apollon, while Helios would remain enthroned in his fiery chariot, and his toils and labors and death-struggles would be transferred to Hercules. The violet clouds which greet his rising and his setting would now be represented by herds of cows which feed in earthly pastures. There would be other expressions which would still remain as floating phrases, not attached to any definite deities. These would gradually be converted into incidents in the life of heroes, and be woven at length into systematic narratives. Finally, these gods or heroes, and the incidents of their mythical career, would receive each "a local habitation and a name." *These would remain as genuine history, when the origin and meaning of the words had been either wholly or in part forgotten.*

For the proofs of these assertions, the Vedic poems furnish indisputable evidence, that such as this was the origin and growth of Greek and Teutonic mythology. In these poems, the names of many, perhaps of most, of the Greek gods, indicate natural objects which, if endued with life, have not been reduced to human per-

---

[1] Preface to "Tales of Anct. Greece."   [2] See Appendix B.

sonality. In them Daphne is still simply the morning twilight
ushering in the splendor of the new-born sun ; the cattle of Helios
there are still the light-colored clouds which the dawn leads out into
the fields of the sky. There the idea of Hercules has not been
separated from the image of the toiling and struggling sun, and the
glory of the life-giving Helios has not been transferred to the god
of Delos and Pytho. In the Vedas the myths of Endymion, of
Kephalos and Prokris, Orpheus and Eurydike, are exhibited in the
form of detached mythical phrases, which furnished for each their
germ. The analysis may be extended indefinitely: but the conclusion can only be, that in the Vedic language we have the foundation,
not only of the glowing legends of Hellas, but of the dark and
sombre mythology of the Scandinavian and the Teuton. Both alike
have grown up chiefly from names which have been grouped around
the sun ; but the former has been grounded on those expressions
which describe the recurrence of day and night, the latter on the
great tragedy of nature, in the alternation of summer and winter.

Of this vast mass of solar myths, some have emerged into independent legends, others have furnished the groundwork of whole
epics, others have remained simply as floating tales whose intrinsic
beauty no poet has wedded to his verse.[1]

" The results obtained from the examination of language in its
several forms leaves no room for doubt that the general system of
mythology has been traced to its fountain head. We can no longer
shut our eyes to the fact that there was a stage in the history of
human speech, during which all the abstract words in constant use
among ourselves were utterly unknown, when men had formed no
notions of virtue or prudence, of thought and intellect, of slavery
or freedom, but spoke only of the man who was strong, who could
point the way to others and choose one thing out of many, of the
man who was not bound to any other and able to do as he pleased.

" That even this stage was not the earliest in the history of language is now a growing opinion among philologists; but for the
comparison of legends current in different countries it is not necessary to carry the search further back. Language without words
denoting abstract qualities implies a condition of thought in which
men were only awakening to a sense of the objects which surrounded them, and points to a time when the world was to them
full of strange sights and sounds, some beautiful, some bewildering,
some terrific, when, in short, they knew little of themselves beyond

---

[1] Aryan Mytho., vol ii. pp. 51-53.

the vague consciousness of their existence, and nothing of the phenomena of the world without. *In such a state they could but
attribute to all that they saw or touched or heard, a life which was
like their own in its consciousness, its joys, and its sufferings.*
That power of sympathizing with nature which we are apt to regard
as the peculiar gift of the poet was then shared alike by all.   This
sympathy was not the result of any effort, it was inseparably bound
up with the words which rose to their lips.   It implied no special
purity of heart or mind; it pointed to no Arcadian paradise where
shepherds knew not how to wrong or oppress or torment each other.
We say that the morning light rests on the mountains; they said
that the sun was greeting his bride, as naturally as our own poet
would speak of the sunlight clasping the earth, or the moonbeams
as kissing the sea.

   " We have then before us a stage of language corresponding to a
stage in the history of the human mind *in which all sensible objects
were regarded as instinct with a conscious life.* The varying
phases of that life were therefore described as truthfully as they
described their own feelings or sufferings; and hence every phase
became a picture.   But so long as the conditions of their life remained unchanged, they knew perfectly what the picture meant,
and ran no risk of confusing one with another.   Thus they had but
to describe the things which they saw, felt, or heard, in order to
keep up an inexhaustible store of phrases faithfully describing the
facts of the world from their point of view.   This language was
indeed the result of an observation not less keen than that by which
the inductive philosopher extorts the secrets of the natural world.
Nor was its range much narrower.   Each object received its own
measure of attention, and no one phenomenon was so treated as to
leave no room for others in their turn.   They could not fail to
note the changes of days and years, of growth and decay, of calm
and storm; *but the objects which so changed were to them living
things, and the rising and setting of the sun, the return of winter and summer, became a drama in which the actors were their
enemies or their friends.*

   " That this is a strict statement of facts in the history of the human mind, philology alone would abundantly prove; but not a few
of these phrases have come down to us in their earliest form, and
point to the long-buried stratum of language of which they are the
fragments. *These relics exhibit in their germs the myths which
afterwards became the legends of gods and heroes with human*

forms, and furnished the groundwork of the epic poems, whether of the eastern or the western world.

"The mythical or mythmaking language of mankind had no partialities; and if the career of the *Sun* occupies a large extent of the horizon, we cannot fairly simulate ignorance of the cause. Men so placed would not fail to put into words the thoughts or emotions roused in them by the varying phases of that mighty world on which we, not less than they, feel that our life depends, although we may know something more of its nature.

"Thus grew up a multitude of expressions which described the sun as the child of the night, as the destroyer of the darkness, as the lover of the dawn and the dew—of phrases which would go on to speak of him as killing the dew with his spears, and of forsaking the dawn as he rose in the heaven. The feeling that the fruits of the earth were called forth by his warmth would find utterance in words which spoke of him as the friend and the benefactor of man; while the constant recurrence of his work would lead them to describe him as a being constrained to toil for others, as doomed to travel over many lands, and as finding everywhere things on which he could bestow his love or which he might destroy by his power. His journey, again, might be across cloudless skies, or amid alternations of storm and calm; his light might break fitfully through the clouds, or be hidden for many a weary hour, to burst forth at last with dazzling splendor as he sank down in the western sky. He would thus be described as facing many dangers and many enemies, none of whom, however, may arrest his course; as sullen, or capricious, or resentful; as grieving for the loss of the dawn whom he had loved, or as nursing his great wrath and vowing a pitiless vengeance. Then as the veil was rent at eventide, they would speak of the chief, who had long remained still, girding on his armor; or of the wanderer throwing off his disguise, and seizing his bow or spear to smite his enemies; of the invincible warrior whose face gleams with the flush of victory when the fight is over, as he greets the fair-haired Dawn who closes, as she had begun, the day. To the wealth of images thus lavished on the daily life and death of the Sun there would be no limit. He was the child of the morning, or her husband, or her destroyer; he forsook her and he returned to her, either in calm serenity or only to sink presently in deeper gloom.

"So with other sights and sounds. The darkness of night brought with it a feeling of vague horror and dread; the return of daylight cheered them with a sense of unspeakable gladness; and thus the

Sun who scattered the black shade of night would be the mighty
champion doing battle with the biting snake which lurked in its
dreary hiding-place. But as the Sun accomplishes his journey day
by day through the heaven, the character of the seasons is changed..
The buds and blossoms of spring-time expand in the flowers and
fruits of summer, and the leaves fall and wither on the approach
of winter. Thus the daughter of the earth would be spoken of as
dying or as dead, as severed from her mother for five or six weary
months, not to be restored to her again until the time for her return from the dark land should once more arrive. But as no other
power than that of the Sun can recall vegetation to life, this child
of the earth would be represented as buried in a sleep from which
the touch of the Sun alone could arouse her, when he slays the
frost and cold which lie like snakes around her motionless form..

"*That these phrases would furnish the germs of myths or legends·
teeming with human feeling, as soon as the meaning of the phrases·
were in part or wholly forgotten, was as inevitable as that in the·
infancy of our race men should attribute to all sensible objects the·
same kind of life which they were conscious of possessing themselves.*"

Let us compare the history of the *Saviour* which we have al--
ready seen, with that of the *Sun*, as it is found in the *Vedas*.

We can follow in the *Vedic* hymns, step by step, the development which changes the *Sun* from a mere luminary into a "*Creator*," "*Preserver*," "*Ruler*," and "*Rewarder of the World*"—in
fact, into a *Divine or Supreme Being*.

The first step leads us from the mere light of the Sun to that
light which in the morning wakes man from sleep, and seems to-
give new life, not only to man, but to the whole of nature. He
who wakes us in the morning, who recalls all nature to new life, is·
soon called "*The Giver of Daily Life.*"

Secondly, by another and bolder step, the Giver of Daily Light:
and Life becomes the giver of light and life in general. *He who·
brings light and life to-day, is the same who brought light and life
on the first of days.* As light is the beginning of the day, so light
was the beginning of creation, and the Sun, from being a mere light-
bringer or life-giver, becomes a Creator, and, if a Creator, then soon
also a Ruler of the World.

Thirdly, as driving away the dreaded darkness of the night,
and likewise as fertilizing the earth, the Sun is conceived as a " Defender " and kind " Protector " of all living things.

Fourthly, the Sun sees everything, both that which is good and that which is evil; and how natural therefore that the evil-doer should be told that the sun sees what no human eye may have seen, and that the innocent, when all other help fails him, should appeal to the sun to attest his guiltlessness!

Let us examine now, says Prof. Müller, from whose work we have quoted the above, a few passages (from the *Rig-Veda*) illustrating every one of these perfectly natural transitions.

"In hymn vii. we find the Sun invoked as '*The Protector of everything that moves or stands, of all that exists.*'"

"Frequent allusion is made to the Sun's power of seeing everything. The stars flee before the all-seeing Sun, like thieves (R. V. vii.). He sees the right and the wrong among men (Ibid.). He who looks upon the world, knows also all the thoughts in men (Ibid.)."

"As the Sun sees everything and knows everything, he is asked to forget and forgive what he alone has seen and knows (R. V. iv.)."

"The Sun is asked to drive away illness and bad dreams (R. V. x.)."

"Having once, and more than once, been invoked as the life-bringer, the Sun is also called the breath or life of all that moves and rests (R. V. i.); and lastly, he becomes *the maker of all things*, by whom all the worlds have been brought together (R. V. x.), and . . . Lord of man and of all living creatures."

"He is the God among gods (R. V. i.); he is the divine leader of all the gods (R. V. viii.)."

"He alone rules the whole world (R. V. v.). "The laws which he has established are firm (R. V. iv.), and the other gods not only praise him (R. V. vii.), but have to follow him as their leader (R. V. v.)."[1]

That the history of *Christ* Jesus, the Christian Saviour,— "the true *Light*, which lighteth every man that cometh into the world,"[2] — is simply the history of the *Sun* — the real Saviour of mankind — is demonstrated beyond a doubt from the following indisputable facts:

1. *The birth of Christ Jesus* is said to have taken place at *early dawn*[3] on the 25th day of December. Now, this is the *Sun's birthday*. At the commencement of the sun's apparent annual revolution round the earth, he was said to have been born, and, on the first moment after midnight of the 24th of December, all the heathen nations of the earth, as if by common consent, celebrated the accouchement of the "*Queen of Heaven*," of the "*Celestial Virgin of the Sphere*," and the birth of the god *Sol*. On that day the sun having fully entered the winter solstice, the *Sign of the Virgin* was rising on the eastern horizon. The woman's symbol of this stellar sign was represented first by ears of corn, then with a new-born male child in her arms. Such was the picture of the *Persian* sphere cited by Aben-Ezra:

---

[1] Müller: Origin of Religions, pp. 264-268.
[2] John, i. 9.
[3] The Christian ceremonies of the Nativity are celebrated in Bethlehem and Rome, even at the present time, *very early in the morning*.

"The division of the first decan of the Virgin represents a beautiful virgin with flowing hair, sitting in a chair, with two ears of corn in her hand, and suckling an infant called IESUS by some nations, and *Christ* in Greek."[1]

This denotes the *Sun*, which, at the moment of the winter solstice, precisely when the Persian magi drew the horoscope of the new year, was placed on the bosom of the Virgin, rising heliacally in the eastern horizon. On this account he was figured in their astronomical pictures under the form of a child suckled by a chaste virgin.[2]

Thus we see that Christ Jesus was born on the same day as Buddha, Mithras, Osiris, Horus, Hercules, Bacchus, Adonis and other *personifications of the* SUN.[3]

2. *Christ Jesus was born of a Virgin.* In this respect he is also the *Sun*, for 'tis the sun alone who can be born of an immaculate virgin, who conceived him without carnal intercourse, and who is still, after the birth of her child, a virgin.

This Virgin, of whom the Sun, the true "Saviour of Mankind," is born, is either the bright and beautiful *Dawn*,[4] or the dark *Earth*,[5] or *Night*.[6] Hence we have, as we have already seen, the *Virgin*, or *Virgo*, as one of the signs of the zodiac.[7]

This Celestial Virgin was feigned to be a mother. She is represented in the Indian Zodiac of Sir William Jones, with ears of corn in one hand, and the lotus in the other. In Kircher's Zodiac of Hermes, she has corn in both hands. In other planispheres of the Egyptian priests she carries ears of corn in one hand, and the infant Saviour *Horus* in the other. In Roman Catholic countries, she is

---

[1] Quoted by Volney, Ruins, p. 166, and *note.*

[2] See Ibid. and Dupuis : Origin of Religious Belief, p. 236.

[3] See Chap. XXXIV.

[4] The *Dawn* was *personified* by the ancients as a *virgin mother*, who bore the *Sun*. (See Max Müller's Chips, vol. ii. p. 137. Fiske's Myths and Mythmakers, p. 156, and Cox : Tales of Ancient Greece, and Aryan Mytho.)

[5] In Sanscrit "Idâ" is the *Earth*, the wife of Dyaus (the Sky), and so we have before us the mythical phrase, "the *Sun* at its birth rests on the earth." In other words, "the Sun at birth is nursed in the lap of its mother."

[6] "The moment we understand the *nature* of a myth, all impossibilities, contradictions and immoralities disappear. If a mythical personage be nothing more than a name of the *Sun*, his birth may be derived from ever so many different mothers. He may be the son of the *Sky* or of the *Dawn* or of the *Sea* or of the *Night*." (Renouf's Hibbert Lectures, p. 108.)

[7] "The sign of the *Celestial Virgin* rises above the horizon at the moment in which we fix the birth of the Lord Jesus Christ." (Higgins : Anacalypsis, vol. i. p. 314, and Bonwick : Egyptian Belief, p. 147.)

"We have in the first decade the *Sign of the Virgin*, following the most ancient tradition of the Persians, the Chaldeans, the Egyptians, Hermes and Æsculapius, a young woman called in the Persian language, *Seclinidos de Darzama* ; in the Arabic, *Aderenedesa*—that is to say, a chaste, pure, immaculate virgin, suckling an infant, which some nations call *Jesus* (i. e., Saviour), but which in Greek call *Christ.*" (Abulmazer.)

"In the first decade of the Virgin, rises a maid, called in Arabic, 'Aderenedesa,' that is : 'pure immaculate virgin,' graceful in person, charming in countenance, modest in habit, with loosened hair, holding in her hands two ears of wheat, sitting upon an embroidered throne, nursing a BOY, and rightly feeding him in the place called *Hebraea.* A boy, I say, names IESSUS by certain nations, which signifies Issa, whom they also call *Christ* in Greek." (Kircher, Œdipus Ægypticus.)

generally represented with the child in one hand, and the lotus or lily in the other. In Vol. II. of Montfaucon's work, she is represented as a female nursing a child, with ears of corn in her hand, and the legend IAO. She is seated on clouds, a star is at her head. The reading of the Greek letters, from right to left, show this to be very ancient.

In the Vedic hymns Aditi, *the Dawn*, is called the "*Mother of the Gods.*" "She is the mother with powerful, terrible, with *royal sons.*" She is said to have given birth to the *Sun.*[1] "As the *Sun* and all the *solar deities* rise from the *east*," says Prof. Max Muller, " we can well understand how Aditi (the Dawn) came to be called the 'Mother of the Bright Gods.'"[2]

The poets of the Veda indulged freely in theogonic speculations without being frightened by any contradictions. They knew of Indra as the greatest of gods, they knew of Agni as the god of gods, they knew of Varuna as the ruler of all; but they were by no means startled at the idea that their Indra had a mother, or that Varuna was nursed in the lap of Aditi. All this was true to nature; for their god was the *Sun*, and the mother who bore and nursed him was the *Dawn.*[3]

We find in the *Vishnu Purana*, that Devaki (the virgin mother of the Hindoo Saviour Crishna, whose history, as we have seen, corresponds in most every particular with that of Christ Jesus) *is called Aditi*,[4] which, in the *Rig-Veda*, is the name for the *Dawn*. Thus we see the legend is complete. Devaki is Aditi, Aditi is the Dawn, and the Dawn is the Virgin Mother. "The Saviour of Mankind" who is born of her is the Sun, the Sun is Crishna, and Crishna is Christ.

In the *Mahabharata*, Crishna is also represented as the "Son of Aditi."[5] As the hour of his birth grew near, the mother became more beautiful, and her form more brilliant.[6]

Indra, the sun, who was worshiped in some parts of India as a *Crucified God*, is also represented in the Vedic hymns as the *Son of the Dawn*. He is said to have been born of Dahana, who is Daphne, a personification of the Dawn.[7]

The *humanity* of this SOLAR GOD-MAN, this demiurge, is strongly

[1] Max Müller : Origin of Religions, p. 261.
[2] Ibid. p. 230.
[3] "With scarcely an exception, all the names by which the *Virgin goddess* of the Akropolis was known point to this mythology of the Dawn." (Cox: Aryan Myths, vol. i. p. 228.)
[4] We also read in the Vishnu Purana that: "The Sun of Achyuta (God, the Imperishable) rose in the dawn of Devaki, to cause the lotus petal of the universe (*Crishna*) to expand. On the day of his birth the quarters of the horizon were irradiate with joy," &c.
[5] Cox: Aryan Myths, vol. iii. pp. 105, and 130, vol. ii.
[6] Ibid. p. 133. See Legends in Chap. XVI.
[7] Fiske : Myths and Mythmakers, p. 113.

insisted on in the *Rig-Veda*. He is the son of God, but also the
son of Aditi. He is Purusha, the man, the male. Agni is frequently called the " Son of man." It is expressly explained that
the titles Agni, Indra, Mitra, &c., all refer to *one Sun-god* under
" many names." And when we find the name of a mortal, *Yama*,
who once lived upon earth, included among these names, the humanity of the demiurge becomes still more accentuated, and we get
at the root idea.

Horus, the Egyptian Saviour, was the son of the virgin *Isis*.
Now, this Isis, in Egyptian mythology, is the same as the virgin
Devaki in Hindoo mythology. She is the *Dawn*.[1] *Isis*, as we
have already seen, is represented suckling the infant Horus, and,
in the words of Prof. Renouf, we may say, " in whose lap can the
Sun be nursed more fitly than in that of the *Dawn ?*"[2]

Among the goddesses of Egypt, the highest was Neith, who
reigned inseparably with Amun in the upper sphere. She was
called " Mother of the gods," " Mother of the sun." She was the
feminine origin of all things, as Amun was the male origin. She
held the same rank at Sais as Amun did at Thebes. Her temples
there are said to have exceeded in colossal grandeur anything ever
seen before. On one of these was the celebrated inscription thus
deciphered by Champollion :

" I am all that has been, all that is, all that will be. No mortal has ever
raised the veil that conceals me. *My offspring is the Sun.*"

She was mother of the *Sun*-god *Ra*, and, says Prof. Renouf, "is
commonly supposed to represent *Heaven ;* but some expressions
which are hardly applicable to heaven, render it more probable that
she is one of the many names of the *Dawn.*"[3]

If we turn from Indian and Egyptian, to Grecian mythology,
we shall also find that their *Sun-gods* and *solar heroes* are born of
the same virgin mother. Theseus was said to have been born of
Aithra, " *the pure air*," and Œdipus of Iokaste, " *the violet light
of morning.*" Perseus was born of the virgin Danae, and was
called the " *Son of the bright morning.*"[4] In Io, the mother of the
" sacred bull,"[5] the mother also of Hercules, we see the *violet-tinted
morning* from which the sun is born ; all these gods and heroes
being, like *Christ* Jesus, *personifications of the Sun.*[6]

---

[1] Renouf : Hibbert Lectures, p. 111 and 161.
[2] Ibid. p. 161 and 179.
[3] Ibid. pp. 179.
[4] See Tales of Ancient Greece, pp. xxxi. and
82.
[5] The *Bull* symbolized the productive force

in nature, and hence it was associated with
the SUN-gods. This animal was venerated by
nearly all the peoples of antiquity. (Wake :
Phallism in Anct. Religs., p. 45.)
[6] See Aryan Myths, vol. i. p 229.

"The Saviour of Mankind" was also represented as being born of the "*dusky mother*," which accounts for many Pagan, and so-called Christian, goddesses being represented *black*.[1] This is the *dark night*, who for many weary hours travails with the birth of her child. The Sun, which scatters the darkness, is also the child of the darkness, and so the phrase naturally went *that he was born of her*. Of the two legends related in the poems afterwards combined in the "Hymn to Apollo," the former relates the birth of Apollo, the *Sun*, from Leto, the *Darkness*, which is called his mother.[2] In this case, Leto would be *personified* as a "black virgin," either with or without the child in her arms.

The *dark earth* was also represented as being the mother of the god Sun, who apparently came out of, or was born of her, in the East,[3] as Minos (the sun) was represented to have been born of Ida (the earth).[4]

In Hindoo mythology, the *Earth*, under the name of *Prithivi*, receives a certain share of honors as one of the primitive goddesses of the Veda, being thought of as the "*kind mother*." Moreover, various *deities* were regarded as the progeny resulting from the fancied union of the Earth with Dyaus (*Heaven*).[5]

Our Aryan forefathers looked up to the *heavens* and they gave it the name of *Dyaus*, from a root-word which means "*to shine*." And when, out of the forces and forms of nature, they afterwards fashioned other gods, this name of Dyaus became *Dyaus pitar*, the *Heaven-father*, or Lord of All; and in far later times, when the western Aryans had found their home in Europe, the *Dyaus pitar* of the central Asian land became the *Zeupater* of the Greeks, and the *Jupiter* of the Romans, and the first part of his name gave *us* the word *Deity*.

According to Egyptian mythology, Isis was also the Earth.[6] Again, from the union of Seb and Nut sprung the mild Osiris. Seb is the *Earth*, Nut is *Heaven*, and Osiris is the *Sun*.[7]

Tacitus, the Roman historian, speaking of the Germans in A. D. 98, says:

"There is nothing in these several tribes that merit attention, except that they all agree in worshiping the goddess *Earth*, or as they call her, *Herth*, whom they consider as the common mother of all."[8]

---

[1] See Chap. XXXII.
[2] See Tales of Ancient Greece, p. xviii.
[3] "The idea entertained by the ancients that these god-begotten heroes were engendered without any carnal intercourse, and that they were the sons of Jupiter, is, in plain language, the result of the ethereal spirit, *i. e.*, the Holy Spirit, operating on the virgin mother

Earth." (Knight: Ancient Art and Mythology, p. 156.)
[4] Cox: Aryan Myths, p. 87.
[5] See Williams' Hinduism, p. 24, and Müller's Chips, vol. ii. pp. 277 and 290.
[6] See Bulfinch, p. 389.
[7] See Renouf's Hibbert Lectures, pp. 110–111.
[8] Manners of the Germans, p. xi.

These virgin mothers, and virgin goddesses of antiquity, were also, at times, personifications of the *Moon*, or of Nature.[1]

Who is "God the *Father*," who overshadows the maiden? The overshadowing of the maiden by "God the Father," whether he be called Zeus, Jupiter or Jehovah, is simply the *Heaven*, the *Sky*, the "*All-father*,"[2] looking down upon with love, and overshadowing the maiden, the broad flushing light of *Dawn*, or the *Earth*. From this union the *Sun* is born without any carnal intercourse. The *mother* is yet a *virgin*. This is illustrated in Hindoo mythology by the union of Pritrivi, "*Mother Earth*," with Dyaus, "Heaven." Various deities were regarded as their progeny.[3] In the Vedic hymns the *Sun*—the Lord and Saviour, the Redeemer and Preserver of Mankind—is frequently called the "*Son of the Sky*."[4]

According to Egyptian mythology, Seb (the *Earth*) is overshadowed by Nut (*Heaven*), the result of this union being the beneficent Lord and Saviour, Osiris.[5] The same thing is to be found in ancient Grecian mythology. Zeus or Jupiter is the *Sky*,[6] and Danae, Leto, Iokaste, Io and others, are the *Dawn*, or *the violet light of morning*.[7]

---

[1] See Knight : Ancient Art and Mythology, pp. 81, 99, and 166.

The Moon was called by the ancients, "The Queen;" "The Highest Princess;" "The Queen of Heaven;" "The Princess and Queen of Heaven;" &c. She was Istar, Ashera, Diana, Artemis, Isis, Juno, Lucina, Astarté. (Goldzhier, pp, 158, 158. Knight, pp. 99, 100.)

In the beginning of the eleventh book of Apuleius' Metamorphosis, Isis is represented as addressing him thus: "I am present ; I who am *Nature*, the parent of things, queen of all the elements, &c., &c. The primitive Phrygians called me *Pressinuntica, the mother of the gods;* the native Athenians, Ceropian Minerva ; the floating Cyprians, Paphian Venus ; the arrow-bearing Cretans, Dictymian Diana ; the three-tongued Sicilians, Stygian Proserpine ; and the inhabitants of Eleusis, the ancient goddess Ceres. Some again have invoked me as *Juno*, others as *Bellona*, others as Hecate, and others as Rhamnusia : and those who are enlightened by the emerging rays of the rising *Sun*, the Ethiopians, Ariians and Egyptians, powerful in ancient learning, who reverence my divinity with ceremonies perfectly proper, call me by a true appellation, 'Queen *Isis*.'" (Taylor's Mysteries, p. 76.)

[2] The "God the Father" of all nations of antiquity was nothing more than a personification of the *Sky* or the *Heavens*. "The term *Heaven* (pronounced *Thien*) is used everywhere in the Chinese classics for the *Supreme Power*, ruling and governing all the affairs of men with an omnipotent and omniscient righteousness and goodness." (James Legge.)

In one of the Chinese sacred books—the Shu-king—*Heaven* and *Earth* are called "Father and Mother of all things." Heaven being the Father, and Earth the Mother. (Taylor : Primitive Culture, pp. 294-296.)

The "God the Father" of the Indians is *Dyaus*, that is, the *Sky*. (Williams' Hinduism, p. 24.)

Ormuzd, the god of the ancient Persians, was a personification of the sky. Herodotus, speaking of the Persians, says : "They are accustomed to ascend the highest part of the mountains, and offer sacrifice to Jupiter (Ormuzd), *and they call the whole circle of the heavens by the name of Jupiter*." (Herodotus, book 1, ch. 131.)

In Greek iconography Zeus is the *Heaven*. As Cicero says : "The refulgent Heaven above is that which all men call, unanimously, Jove."

The Christian God supreme of the nineteenth century is still *Dyaus* Pitar, the "Heavenly Father."

[3] Williams' Hinduism, p. 24.

[4] Müller : Origin of Religions, pp. 261, 290.

[5] Renouf : Hibbert Lectures, pp. 110, 111.

[6] See Note 2.

[7] See Cox : Tales of Ancient Greece, pp. xxxi. and 82, and Aryan Mythology, vol. i. p. 229.

' The *Sky* appeared to men (says Plutarch), to perform the functions of a *Father*, as the *Earth* those of a *Mother*. The sky was the father, for it cast seed into the bosom of the earth, which in receiving them became fruitful, and brought forth, and was the mother."[1]

This union has been sung in the following verses by Virgil:

> " Tum pater omnipotens fecundis imbribis æther
> Conjugis in grenium lætæ descendit." (Geor. ii.)

The *Phenician* theogony is founded on the same principles. *Heaven* and *Earth* (called Ouranos and Ghè) are at the head of a genealogy of æons, whose adventures are conceived in the mytho-logical style of these physical allegorists.[2]

In the Samothracian mysteries, which seem to have been the most anciently established ceremonies of the kind in Europe, the *Heaven* and the *Earth* were worshiped as a male and female *divinity*, and as the *parents of all things*.[3]

The Supreme God (the *Al-fader*), of the ancient *Scandinavians* was *Odin*, a personification of the *Heavens*. The principal god-dess among them was *Frigga*, a personification of the *Earth*. It was the opinion among these people that this Supreme Being or Celestial God had united with the Earth (Frigga) to produce " Bal-dur the Good" (the Sun), who corresponds to the Apollo of the Greeks and Romans, and the Osiris of the Egyptians.[4]

Xiuletl, in the Mexican language, signifies *Blue*, and hence was a name which the Mexican gave to *Heaven*, from which *Xiuleti-cutli* is derived, an epithet signifying " *the God of Heaven*," which they bestowed upon *Tezcatlipoca*, who was the " Lord of All," the " Supreme God." He it was who overshadowed the Virgin of Tula, Chimelman, who begat the Saviour Quetzalcoatle (the Sun).

3. *His birth was foretold by a star.* This is the bright *morn-ing star*—

> " Fairest of stars, last in the train of Night,
> If better, thou belongst not to the Dawn,
> Sure pledge of day, that crown'st the smiling morn
> With thy bright circlet " —

which heralds the birth of the god *Sol*, the benificent Saviour.

A glance at a geography of the heavens will show the " chaste, pure, immaculate Virgin, suckling an infant," preceded by a

---

[1] Quoted by Westropp : Phallic Worship, p. 24.

[2] Squire : Serpent Symbol, p. 66. "In Phenician Mythology Ouranos (Heaven) weds Ghe (the Earth) and by her becomes father of

Oceanus, Hyperon, Iapetus, Cronos, and other gods." (Phallic Worship, p. 26.)

[3] Squire : Serpent Symbol, p. 64.

[4] See Mallet's Northern Antiquities, pp. 80, 93, 94, 406, 510, 511.

Star, which rises immediately preceding the Virgin and her child. This can truly be called "*his Star*," which informed the "Wise Men," the "Magi"—*Astrologers and Sun-worshipers*—and "the shepherds who watched their flocks by night" that the Saviour of Mankind was about to be born.

4. *The Heavenly Host sang praises.* All nature smiles at the birth of the Heavenly Being. "To him all angels cry aloud, the heavens, and all the powers therein." "Glory to God in the highest, and on earth peace, good will towards men." "The quarters of the horizon are irradiate with joy, as if moonlight was diffused over the whole earth." "The spirits and nymphs of heaven dance and sing." "Caressing breezes blow, and a marvelous light is produced." For the Lord and Saviour is born, "to give joy and peace to men and Devas, *to shed light in the dark places*, and to give sight to the blind."[1]

5. *He was visited by the Magi.* This is very natural, for the Magi were *Sun-worshipers*, and at early dawn on the 25th of December, the astrologers of the Arabs, Chaldeans, and other Oriental nations, greeted the infant Saviour with gold, frankincense and myrrh. They started to salute their God long before the rising of the Sun, and having ascended a high mountain, they waited anxiously for his birth, facing the East, and there hailed his first rays with incense and prayer.[2] The shepherds also, who remained in the open air watching their flocks by night, were in the habit of prostrating themselves, and paying homage to their god, the Sun. And, like the poet of the Veda, they said:

" Will the powers of darkness be conquered by the *god of light?* "

And when the Sun rose, they wondered how, just born, he was so mighty. They greeted him:

"Hail, Orient Conqueror of Gloomy Night."

And the human eye felt that it could not bear the brilliant majesty of him whom they called, "The Life, the Breath, the Brilliant Lord and Father." And they said:

"Let us worship again the *Child of Heaven*, the Son of Strength, Arusha, the Bright Light of the Sacrifice." "He rises as a mighty flame, he stretches out his wide arms, he is even like the wind." "His light is powerful, and his (virgin) mother, the Dawn, gives him the best share, the first worship among men."[3]

6. *He was born in a Cave.* In this respect also, the history of

---

[1] See Chap. XIV.
[2] See Dupuis: Orig. Relig. Belief, p. 234. Higgins' Anacalypsis, vol. ii. pp. 96, 97, and

Prog. Relig. Ideas, vol. i. p. 272.
[3] Extracts from the Vedas. Müller's Chips, vol. ii. pp. 96 and 137.

Christ Jesus corresponds with that of other Sun-gods and Saviours, for they are nearly all represented as being born in a cave or dungeon. This is the dark abode from which the wandering *Sun* starts in the morning.[1] As the Dawn springs fully armed from the forehead of the cloven Sky, so the eye first discerns the blue of heaven, as the first faint arch of light is seen in the East. This arch is the cave in which the infant is nourished until he reaches his full strength—in other words, until the day is fully come.

As the hour of his birth drew near, the mother became more beautiful, her form more brilliant, while the dungeon was filled with a heavenly light as when Zeus came to Danae in a golden shower.[2]

At length the child is born, and a halo of serene light encircles his cradle, just as the Sun appears at early dawn in the East, in all its splendor. His presence reveals itself there, in the dark cave, by his first rays, which brightens the countenances of his mother and others who are present at his birth.[3]

6. *He was ordered to be put to death.* All the Sun-gods are fated to bring ruin upon their parents or the *reigning monarch.*[4] For this reason, they attempt to prevent his birth, and failing in this, seek to destroy him when born. Who is the dark and wicked Kansa, or his counterpart Herod? He is *Night*, who reigns supreme, but who must lose his power when the young prince of glory, the Invincible, is born.

The *Sun* scatters the *Darkness;* and so the phrase went that the child was to be the destroyer of the reigning monarch, or his parent, *Night;* and oracles, and magi, it was said, warned the latter of the doom which would overtake him. The newly-born babe is therefore ordered to be put to death by the sword, or exposed on the bare hillside, as the Sun seems to rest on the Earth (Ida) at its rising.[5]

---

[1] Cox: Aryan Mythology, vol. i. p. 153.

[2] Aryan Mythology, vol. ii. p. 133.

[3] When Christ Jesus was born, on a sudden there was a great light in the cave, so that their eyes could not bear it. (Protevangelion, Apoc. ch. xiv.)

[4] "Perseus, Oidipous, Romulus and Cyrus are doomed to bring ruin on their parents. They are exposed in their infancy on the hill-side, and rescued by a shepherd. *All the solar heroes begin life in this way.* Whether, like Apollo, born of the dark night (Leto), or like Oidipous, of the violet dawn (Iokaste), they are alike destined to bring destruction on their parents, as the Night and the Dawn are both destroyed by the Sun." (Fiske: p. 198.)

[5] "The exposure of the child in infancy represents the long rays of the morning sun resting on the hill-side." (Fiske: Myths and Mythmakers, p. 198.)

The Sun-hero Paris is exposed on the slopes of Ida, Oidipous on the slopes of Kithairon, and Æsculapius on that of the mountain of Myrtles. This is the rays of the newly-born sun resting on the mountain-side. (Cox: Aryan Myths, vol. i. pp. 64 and 80.)

In Sanscrit *Ida* is the Earth, and so we have the mythical phrase, the Sun at its birth is exposed on Ida—the hill-side. The light of the sun must rest on the hill-side long before it reaches the dells beneath. (See Cox: vol. i. p. 221, and Fiske: p. 114.)

In oriental mythology, the destroying principle is generally represented as a serpent or dragon.[1] Now, the position of the sphere on Christmas-day, the birthday of the Sun, shows the Serpent all but touching, and certainly aiming at the woman — that is, the figure of the constellation *Virgo* — who suckles the child Iessus in her arms. Thus we have it illustrated in the story of the snake who was sent to kill Hercules, when an infant in his cradle;[2] also in the story of Typhon, who sought the life of the infant Saviour Horus. Again, it is illustrated in the story of the virgin mother Astrea, with her babe beset by Orion, and of Latona, the mother of Apollo, when pursued by the monster.[3] And last, that of the virgin mother Mary, with her babe beset by Herod. But like Hercules, Horus, Apollo, Theseus, Romulus, Cyrus and other *solar heroes, Christ Jesus* has yet a long course before him. Like them, he grows up both wise and strong, and the "old Serpent" is discomfited by him, just as the sphynx and the dragon are put to flight by others.

7. *He was tempted by the devil.* The temptation by, and victory over the evil one, whether Mara or Satan, is the victory of the *Sun* over the clouds of storm and darkness.[4] Growing up in obscurity, the day comes when he makes himself known, tries himself in his

[1] Even as late as the seventeenth century, a German writer would illustrate a thunderstorm destroying a crop of corn, by a picture of a dragon devouring the produce of the field with his flaming tongue and iron teeth. (See Fiske: Myths and Mythmakers, p. 17, and Cox: Aryan Mythology, vol. ii.)

[2] The history of the Saviour Hercules is so similar to that of the Saviour Christ Jesus, that the learned Dr. Parkhurst was forced to say, "The labors of Hercules seem to have been originally designed as emblematic memorials of what the REAL Son of God, the Saviour of the world, was to do and suffer for our sakes, *bringing a cure for all our ills,* as the Orphic hymn speaks of Hercules."

[3] Bonwick's Egyptian Belief, pp. 158, 166, and 168.

[4] In ancient mythology, all heroes of light were opposed by the "Old Serpent," the Devil, symbolized by Serpents, Dragons, Sphinxes and other monsters. The Serpent was, among the ancient Eastern nations, the symbol of *Evil,* of *Winter,* of *Darkness* and of *Death.* It also symbolized the *dark cloud,* which, by harboring the *rays of the Sun,* preventing its shining, and therefore, is apparently *attempting to destroy it.* The Serpent is one of the chief mystic personifications of the *Rig-Veda,* under the names of *Ahi, Suchna,* and others. They represent the *Cloud,* the enemy of the *Sun,* keeping back the fructifying rays. Indra struggles victoriously against him, and spreads life on the earth, with the shining

warmth of the Father of Life, the Creator, *the Sun.*

Buddha, the Lord and Saviour, was described as a superhuman organ of light, to whom a superhuman organ of darkness, Mara, the Evil Serpent, was opposed. He, like *Christ* Jesus, resisted the temptations of this evil one, and is represented sitting on a serpent, as if its conqueror. (See Bunsen's Angel-Messiah, p. 39.)

Crishna also overcame the evil one, and is represented "bruising the head of the serpent," and standing upon it. (See vol. i. of Asiatic Researches, and vol. ii. of Higgins' Anacalypsis.)

In Egyptian Mythology, one of the names of the god-*Sun* was *Râ.* He had an adversary who was called *Apap,* represented in the form of a serpent. (See Renouf's Hibbert Lectures, p. 109.)

Horus, the Egyptian incarnate god, the Mediator, Redeemer and Saviour, is represented in Egyptian art as overcoming the Evil Serpent, and standing triumphantly upon him. (See Bonwick's Egyptian Belief, p. 158, and Monumental Christianity, p. 402.)

Osiris, Ormuzd, Mithras, Apollo, Bacchus, Hercules, Indra, Œdipus, Quetzalcoatle, and many other *Sun-gods,* overcame the Evil One, and are represented in the above described manner. (See Cox's Tales of Ancient Greece, p. xxvii. and Aryan Mythology, vol. ii. p. 129. Baring-Gould's Curious Myths, p. 256. Bulfinch's Age of Fable, p. 34. Bunsen's Angel-Messiah, p. x., and Kingsborough's Mexican Antiquities, vol. vi. p. 176.)

first battles with his gloomy foes, and *shines* without a rival. He is rife for his destined mission, but is met by the demon of storm, who runs to dispute with him in the duel of the storm. In this struggle against darkness the beneficent hero remains the conqueror, the gloomy army of Mara, or Satan, broken and rent, is scattered ; the Apsaras, daughters of the demon, the last light vapors which float in the heaven, try in vain to clasp and retain the vanquisher ; he disengages himself from their embraces, repulses them ; they writhe, lose their form, and vanish.

Free from every obstacle, and from every adversary, he sets in motion across space his disk with a thousand rays, having avenged the attempts of his eternal foe. He appears then in all his glory, and in his sovereign splendor ; the god has attained the summit of his course, it is the moment of triumph.

8. *He was put to death on the cross.* The Sun has now reached his extreme Southern limit, his career is ended, and he is at last overcome by his enemies. The powers of *darkness*, and of *winter*, which had sought in vain to wound him, have at length won the victory. The bright Sun of summer is finally slain, *crucified in the heavens*, and pierced by the arrow, spear or thorn of winter.[1] Before he dies, however, he sees all his disciples — his retinue of light, and the *twelve* hours of the day, or the twelve months of the year — disappear in the sanguinary mêlée of the clouds of the evening

Throughout the tale, the *Sun-god* was but fulfilling his doom. These things must be. The suffering of a violent death was a necessary part of the mythos ; and, when his hour had come, he must meet his doom, as surely as the Sun, once risen, must go across the sky, and then sink down into his bed beneath the earth or sea. It was an iron fate from which there was no escaping.

Crishna, the crucified Saviour of the Hindoos, is a personification of the Sun crucified in the heavens. One of the names of the Sun in the Vedic hymns is *Vishnu*,[2] and Crishna is Vishnu in human form.[3]

---

[1] The crucifixion of the Sun-gods is simply the power of Darkness triumphing over the "Lord of Light," and Winter overpowering the Summer. It was at the *Winter* solstice that the ancients wept for Tammuz, the fair Adonis, and other Sun-gods, who were put to death by the boar, slain by the thorn of winter. (See Cox : Aryan Mythology, vol. ii. p. 113.)

Other versions of the same myth tell us of Eurydike stung to death by the hidden serpent, of Sifrit smitten by Hagene (the Thorn), of Isfendiyar slain by the thorn or arrow of Rustem, of Achilleus vulnerable only in the heel, of Brynhild enfolded within the dragon's coils,

of Meleagros dying as the torch of doom is burnt out, of Baldur, the brave and pure, smitten by the fatal mistletoe, and of Crishna and others being crucified.

In Egyptian mythology, Set, the destroyer, triumphs in the *West*. He is the personification of *Darkness* and *Winter*, and the Sun-god whom he puts to death, is Horus the Saviour. (See Renouf's Hibbert Lectures, pp. 112–115.)

[2] "In the *Rig-Veda* the god *Vishnu* is often named as a manifestation of the *Solar* energy, or rather as a form of the Sun." (Indian Wisdom, p. 322.)

[3] Crishna says : "I am Vishnu, Brahma,

In the hymns of the *Rig-Veda* the *Sun* is spoken of as " *stretching out his arms,*" in the heavens, " to bless the world, *and to rescue it from the terror of darkness.*"

Indra, the crucified Saviour worshiped in Nepal and Tibet,[1] is identical with Crishna, the Sun.[2]

The principal Phenician deity, El, which, says Parkhurst, in his Hebrew Lexicon, " was the very name the heathens gave to their god SOL, their Lord or Ruler of the Hosts of Heaven," was called " *The Preserver* (or *Saviour*) of *the World,*" for the benefit of which *he offered a mystical sacrifice.*[3]

The crucified *Iao* (" Divine Love " personified) is the crucified Adonis, the Sun. The Lord and Saviour Adonis was called *Iao.*[4]

Osiris, the Egyptian Saviour, was crucified in the heavens. To the Egyptian the cross was the symbol of immortality, an emblem of the *Sun,* and the god himself was crucified to the tree, which denoted his fructifying power.[5]

Horus was also crucified in the heavens. He was represented, like Crishna and Christ Jesus, with *outstretched arms in the vault of heaven.*[6]

The story of the crucifixion of *Prometheus* was allegorical, for Prometheus was only a title of the SUN, expressing *providence* or *foresight,* wherefore his being *crucified* in the extremities of the earth, signified originally no more than the restriction of the power of the SUN during the winter months.[7]

Who was *Ixion,* bound on the wheel? He was none other than the god *Sol,* crucified in the heavens.[8] Whatever be the origin of the name, *Ixion* is the "*Sun of noonday,*" crucified in the heavens, whose four-spoked wheel, in the words of Pindar, is seen whirling in the highest heaven.[9]

Indra, and the source as well as the destruction of things, the creator and the annihilator of the whole aggregate of existences. (Cox : Aryan Mythology, vol. ii. p. 131.)

[1] See Chap. XX.

[2] *Indra,* who was represented as a crucified god, is also the *Sun.* No sooner is he born than he speaks to his mother. Like Apollo and all other Sun-gods he has *golden locks,* and like them he is possessed of an inscrutable wisdom. He is also born of a virgin—the Dawn. Crishna and Indra are one. (See Cox : Aryan Mythology, vol. i. pp. 88 and 341 ; vol. ii. p. 131.)

[3] Wake : Phallism, &c., p. 55.

[4] See Cox : Aryan Mythology, vol. ii. p. 113.

[5] Ibid. pp. 115 and 125.

[6] See Bonwick's Egyptian Belief, p. 157.

[7] Knight : Ancient Art and Mythology, p. 88.

A great number of the Solar heroes or Sun-gods are forced to endure being bound, which indicates the tied-up power of the sun in winter. (Goldzhier : Hebrew Mythology, p. 406.)

[8] The Sun, as climbing the heights of heaven, is an arrogant being, given to making exorbitant claims, who must be bound to the fiery cross. " The phrases which described the Sun as revolving daily on his four-spoked *cross,* or as doomed to sink in the sky when his orb had reached the zenith, would give rise to the stories of *Ixion* on his flaming wheel." (Cox : Aryan Mythology, vol. ii. p. 27.)

[9] " So was Ixion bound on the fiery wheel, and the sons of men see the flaming spokes day by day as it whirls in the high heaven.''

The *wheel* upon which Ixion and criminals were said to have been extended *was a cross*, although the name of the thing was dissembled among Christians; it was a St. Andrew's cross, of which two spokes confined the arms, and two the legs. (See Fig. No. 35.)

The allegorical tales of the triumphs and misfortunes of the *Sun*-gods of the ancient Greeks and Romans, signify the alternate exertion of the generative and destructive attributes.

Hercules is torn limb from limb; and in this catastrophe we see the *blood-red sunset* which closes the career of Hercules.[1] The Sun-god cannot rise to the life of the blessed gods until he has been slain. The morning cannot come until the Eôs who closed the previous day has faded away and died in the black abyss of night.

FIG. 35

Achilleus and *Meleagros* represent alike the *short-lived Sun*, whose course is one of toil for others, ending in an early death, after a series of wonderful victories alternating with periods of darkness and gloom.[2]

In the tales of the Trojan war, it is related of Achilleus that he expires at the Skaian, or *western gates of the evening.* He is slain by Paris, who here appears as the Pani, or dark power, who blots out the light of the Sun from the heaven.[3]

We have also the story of *Adonis*, born of a virgin, and known in the countries where he was worshiped as "The Saviour of Mankind," killed by the wild *boar*, afterwards "rose from the dead, and ascended into heaven." This Adonis, Adonai—in Hebrew "My Lord"—is simply the *Sun.* He is crucified in the heavens, put to death by the wild boar, *i.e., Winter.* "Babylon called Typhon or Winter *the boar;* they said he killed Adonis or the fertile *Sun.*"[4]

The *Crucified Dove* worshiped by the ancients, was none other than the crucified Sun. Adonis was called the *Dove.* At the ceremonies in honor of his resurrection from the dead, the devotees said, "Hail to the Dove! the Restorer of Light."[5] Fig. No. 35 is the "Crucified Dove" as described by Pindar, the great lyric poet of Greece, born about 522 B. C.

---

[1] Cox: Tales of Ancient Greece, p. xxxii.
[2] Ibid. p. xxxiii.
[3] "That the story of the Trojan war is almost wholly mythical, has been conceded even by the stoutest champions of Homeric unity." (Rev. G. W. Cox.)
[4] See Müller's Science of Religion, p. 186.
[5] See Calmet's Fragments, vol. ii. pp. 21, 22.

"We read in Pindar, (says the author of a learned work entitled "Nimrod,") of the venerable bird Iynx bound to the wheel, and of the pretended punishment of Ixion. But this rotation was really no punishment, being, as Pindar saith, *voluntary*, and prepared *by himself* and *for himself;* or if it was, it was appointed in derision of his false pretensions, whereby he gave himself out as *the crucified spirit of the world."* "The four spokes represent St. Andrew's cross, adapted to the four limbs extended, and furnish perhaps the oldest *profane* allusion to the crucifixion. The same cross of St. Andrew was the *Tau*, which Ezekiel commands them to mark upon the foreheads of the faithful, as appears from all Israelitish coins whereon that letter is engraved. The same idea was familiar to Lucian, who calls T *the letter of crucifixion.* Certainly, the veneration for the cross is very ancient. Iynx, the bird of Mautic inspiration, bound to the four-legged wheel, gives the notion of *Divine Love crucified.* The wheel denotes the world, of which she is the spirit, and the cross *the sacrifice made for that world."*[1]

This "*Divine Love,*" of whom Nimrod speaks, was "*The First-begotten Son* " of the Platonists. The crucifixion of "*Divine Love* " is often found among the Greeks. Iönah or Juno, according to the *Iliad,* was bound with fetters, and *suspended in space,* between heaven and earth. Ixion, Prometheus, Apollo of Miletus, (anciently the greatest and most flourishing city of Ionia, in Asia Minor), were all crucified.[2]

Semi-Ramis was both a queen of unrivaled celebrity, and also a goddess, worshiped under the form of a Dove. Her name signifies the *Supreme Dove.* She is said to have been slain by the last survivor of her sons, while others say, she flew away as a bird—a Dove. In both Grecian and Hindoo histories this mystical queen Semiramis is said to have fought a battle on the banks of the Indus, with a king called Staurobates, in which she was defeated, and from which she flew away in the form of a Dove. Of this Nimrod says:

"The name Staurobates, the king by whom Semiramis was finally overpowered, *alluded to the cross on which she perished,"* and that, " *the crucifixion was made into a glorious mystery by her infatuated adorers."*[3]

Here again we have the crucified Dove, the *Sun,* for it is well known that the ancients personified the Sun *female* as well as male.

We have also the fable of the Crucified Rose, illustrated in the jewel of the *Rosicrucians.* The jewel of the Rosicrucians is formed

---

[1] Nimrod : vol. i. p. 278, in Anac., i. p. 503.
[2] At Miletus was the crucified Apollo—Apollo, who overcome the Serpent or evil principle. Thus Callimachus, celebrating this achievement, in his hymn to Apollo, has these remarkable words :
"Thee thy blest *mother* bore, and pleased assign'd
The willing SAVIOUR of distressed mankind."

[3] These words apply to *Christ* Jesus, as well as Semiramis, according to the Christian Father Ignatius. In his Epistle to the Church at Ephesus, he says : " Now the virginity of Mary, and he who was born of her, was kept in secret from the prince of this world, as was also the death of our Lord : *three o the mysteries the most spoken of throughout the world, yet done in secret by God."*

of a transparent red stone, with a red *cross* on one side, and a red *rose* on the other—thus it is a *crucified rose.* "The Rossi, oi Rosy-crucians' idea concerning this emblematic red cross," says Hargrave Jennings, in his *History of the Rosicrucians,* "probably came from the fable of *Adonis—who was the Sun whom we have so often seen crucified*—being changed into a red rose by Venus."[1]

The emblem of the *Templars* is a red rose on a cross. "When it can be done, it is surrounded with a glory, and placed on a calvary (Fig. No. 36). This is the Naurutz, Natsir, or Rose of Isuren, of Tamul, or Sharon, or the Water Rose, the Lily Padma, Pena, Lotus, *crucified in the heavens for the salvation of man.*[2]

Fig. 36.

Christ Jesus was called the Rose—the Rose of Sharon—of Isuren. He was the renewed incarnation of *Divine Wisdom.* He was the son of Maia or Maria. He was the Rose of Sharon and the Lily of the Valley, which bloweth in the month of his mother Maia. Thus, when the angel Gabriel gives the salutation to the Virgin, he presents her with the lotus or lily; as may be seen in hundreds of old pictures in Italy. We see therefore that Adonis, "the Lord," "the Virgin-born," "the Crucified," "the Resurrected Dove," "the Restorer of Light," is one and the same with the "Rose of Sharon," the crucified Christ Jesus.

Plato (429 B. C.) in his *Pimœus,* philosophizing about the Son of God, says :

"The *next power* to the Supreme God was decussated or figured *in the shape of a cross on the universe.*"

This brings to recollection the doctrine of certain so-called Christian *heretics,* who maintained that Christ Jesus was crucified in the heavens.

The *Chrèstos* was the Logos, the *Sun* was the manifestation of the Logos or Wisdom to men ; or, as it was held by some, it was his peculiar habitation. The Sun being crucified at the time of the winter solstice was represented by the young man slaying the *Bull* (*an emblem of the Sun*) in the Mithraic ceremonies, and the slain *lamb* at the foot of the cross in the Christian ceremonies. The Chrèst was the Logos, or Divine Wisdom, or a portion of divine

---

wisdom incarnate; in this sense he is really the Sun or the solar power incarnate, and to him everything applicable to the Sun will apply.

Fig. No. 37, taken from Mr. Lundy's "Monumental Christianity," is evidently a representation of the Christian Saviour *crucified in the heavens*. Mr. Lundy calls it "Crucifixion in Space," and believes that it was intended for the Hindoo Saviour Crishna, who is also represented crucified in space (See Fig. No. 8, Ch. XX.). This

FIG. 37.

(Fig. 37) is exactly in the form of a Romish crucifix, *but not fixed to a piece of wood*, though the legs and feet are put together in the usual way. There is a glory over it, *coming from above*, not shining *from the figure*, as is generally seen in a Roman crucifix. It has a pointed *Parthian coronet* instead of a crown of thorns. All the avatars, or incarnations of Vishnu, are painted with Ethiopian or Parthian coronets. For these reasons the Christian author will not own that it is a representation of the "True Son of Justice," for he *was not* crucified in space; but whether it was intended to represent Crishna, Wittoba, or Jesus,[1] it tells a secret: it shows that some one was represented *crucified in the heavens*, and undoubtedly has something to do with "The next power to the Supreme God," who, according to Plato, "was decussated or figured *in the shape of a cross on the universe.*"

Who was the crucified god whom the ancient Romans worshiped, and whom they, according to Justin Martyr, represented as *a man on a cross?* Can we doubt, after what we have seen, that he was this same *crucified Sol*, whose birthday they annually celebrated on the 25th of December?

In the poetical tales of the ancient *Scandinavians*, the same legend is found. Frey, *the Deity of the Sun*, was fabled to have been killed, at the time of the winter solstice, by the same boar who put the god Adonis to death, therefore a boar was annually offered

---

[1] The Sun-gods Apollo, Indra, Wittoba or Crishna, and Christ Jesus, are represented as having their feet pierced with nails (See Cox: Aryan Mytho., vol. ii. p. 23, and Moor's Hindu Pantheon.)

to him at the great feast of Yule.[1] "Baldur the Good," son of the supreme god Odin, and the virgin-goddess Frigga, was also put to death by the sharp thorn of winter.

The ancient *Mexican* crucified Saviour, Quetzalcoatle, another personification of the Sun, was sometimes represented as crucified in space, *in the heavens*, in a circle of nineteen figures, the number of the metonic cycle. A *serpent* (the emblem of evil, darkness, and winter) is depriving him of the organs of generation.[2]

We have seen in Chapter XXXIII. that Christ Jesus, and many of the heathen saviours, healers, and preserving gods, were represented in the form of a Serpent. This is owing to the fact that, *in one of its attributes*, the Serpent was an emblem of the *Sun*. It may, at first, appear strange that the Serpent should be an emblem of evil, and yet also an emblem of the beneficent divinity; but, as Prof. Renouf remarks, in his *Hibbert Lectures*, "The moment we understand the nature of a myth, all impossibilities, contradictions, and immoralities disappear." The serpent is an emblem of evil when represented with his *deadly sting;* he is the emblem of eternity when represented *casting off his skin;*[3] and an emblem of the Sun when represented *with his tail in his mouth*, thus forming a circle.[4] Thus there came to be, not only good, but also bad, serpents, both of which are referred to in the narrative of the Hebrew exodus, but still more clearly in the struggle between the good and the bad serpents of Persian mythology, which symbolized Ormuzd, or Mithra, and the evil spirit Ahriman.[5]

As the Dove and the Rose, emblems of the Sun, were represented on the cross, so was the Serpent.[6] The famous "Brazen Serpent," said to have been "set up" by Moses in the wilderness, is called in the Targum (the general term for the Aramaic versions of the Old

[1] Knight: Anct. Art and Mytho., pp. 87, 88.
[2] Anacalypsis, vol. ii. p. 32.
[3] "This notion is quite consistent with the ideas entertained by the Phenicians as to the Serpent, which they supposed to have the quality of putting off its old age, and assuming a second youth." Sanchoniathon: Quoted by Wake: Phallism, &c., p. 43.)
[4] Une serpent qui tient sa queue dans sa gueule et dans le circle qu'il decrit, ces trois lettres Grecques ΓΞΕ, qui sont le nombre 365. Le Serpent, qui est d'ordinaire un emblème de l'eternetè est ici celui de *Soleil* et des ses revolutions. (Beausobre: Hist. de Manich. tom. ii. p. 55. Quoted by Lardner, vol. viii. p. 379.)
"This idea existed even in *America*. The great century of the Aztecs was encircled by *a serpent grasping its own tail*, and the great *calendar stone* is entwined by serpents bearing human heads in their distended jaws."
"The annual passage of the Sun, through the signs of the zodiac, being in an oblique path, resembles, or at least the ancients thought so, the tortuous movements of the Serpent, and the facility possessed by this reptile of casting off his skin and producing out of itself a new covering every year, bore some analogy to the termination of the old year and the commencement of the new one. Accordingly, all the ancient spheres—the Persian, Indian, Egyptian, Barbaric, and Mexican—were surrounded by the figure of a serpent *holding its tail in its mouth*." (Squire: Serpent Symbol, p. 249.)
[5] Wake: Phallism, p. 42.
[6] See Cox: Aryan Mytho., vol. ii. p. 128.

Testament) the SAVIOUR. It was probably a serpentine crucifix, as it is called a *cross* by Justin Martyr. The crucified serpent (Fig. No. 38) denoted the *quiescent Phallos*, or the Sun after it had lost its power. It is the Sun in winter, crucified on the tree, which denoted its fructifying power.[1] As Mr. Wake remarks, "There can be no doubt that both the Pillar (Phallus) and the Serpent were associated with many of the *Sun-gods* of antiquity."[2]

This is seen in Fig. No. 39, taken from an ancient medal, which represents the serpent with rays of glory surrounding his head.

The Ophites, who venerated the serpent as an emblem of Christ

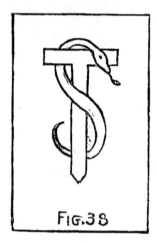

FIG. 38

FIG. 39

Jesus, are said to have maintained that the serpent of Genesis—who brought *wisdom* into the world — was Christ Jesus. The brazen serpent was called the WORD by the Chaldee paraphrast. The Word, or Logos, was *Divine Wisdom*, which was crucified; thus we have the cross, or Linga, or Phallus, with the serpent upon it. Besides considering the serpent as the emblem of Christ Jesus, or of the Logos, the Ophites are said to have revered it as the cause of all the arts of civilized life. In Chapter XII. we saw that several illustrious females were believed to have been selected and impregnated by the Holy Ghost. In some cases, a serpent was supposed to be the form which it assumed. This was the incarnation of the Logos.

[1] Being the most intimately connected with the reproduction of life on earth, the *Linga* became the symbol under which the *Sun*, invoked with a thousand names, has been worshiped throughout the world as the restorer of the powers of nature after the long sleep or death of Winter. In the brazen *Serpent* of the Pentateuch, the two emblems of the *Cross* and *Serpent*, the quiescent and energizing *Phallos*, are united. (Cox: Aryan Mytho., vo . ii. pp. 113–118.)

[2] Wake : Phallism, &c., p. 60.

The serpent was held in great veneration by the ancients, who, as we have seen, considered it as the symbol of the beneficent Deity, and an emblem of eternity. As such it has been variously expressed on ancient sculptures and medals in various parts of the globe.

Although generally, it did not always, symbolize the god *Sun*, or the power of which the Sun is an emblem ; but, invested with various meanings, it entered widely into the primitive mythologies. As Mr. Squire observes:

"It typified wisdom, power, duration, the *good* and *evil* principles, life, reproduction — in short, in Egypt, Syria, Greece, India, China, Scandinavia, America, everywhere on the globe, it has been a prominent emblem."[1]

The serpent was the symbol of Vishnu, the preserving god, the Saviour, the *Sun*.[2] It was an emblem of the *Sun*-god Buddha, the Angel-Messiah.[3] The Egyptian *Sun*-god Osiris, the Saviour, is associated with the snake.[4] The Persian Mithra, the Mediator, Redeemer, and Saviour, was symbolized by the serpent.[5] The Phenicians represented their beneficent *Sun*-god, Agathodemon, by a serpent.[6] The serpent was, among the Greeks and Romans, the emblem of a *beneficent genius*. Antipator of Sidon, calls the god Ammon, the "Renowned Serpent."[7] The Grecian Hercules—the Sun-god—was symbolized as a serpent; and so was Æsculapius and Apollo. The Hebrews, who, as we have seen in Chapter XI., worshiped the god Sol, represented him in the form of a serpent. This is the *seraph* — spoken of above — as set up by Moses (Num. xxi. 3) and worshiped by the children of Israel. SE RA PH is the singular of seraphim, meaning *Semilicè—splendor, fire, light —* emblematic of the fiery disk of the Sun, and which, under the name of *Nehush-tan*, "Serpent-dragon," was broken up by the reforming Hezekiah.

The principal god of the *Aztecs* was *Tonac*-atlcoatl, which means the *Serpent Sun*.[8]

The Mexican virgin-born Lord and Saviour, Quetzalcoatle, was represented in the form of a serpent. In fact, his name signifies "*Feathered Serpent*." Quetzalcoatle was a personification of the *Sun*.[9]

Under the aspect of the *active principle*, we may rationally

[1] Squire : Serpent Symbol, p. 155.
[2] Wake : Phallism in Anct. Religs., p. 72.
[3] Ibid. p. 73. Squire : Serpent Symbol, p. 195.
[4] Faber : Orig. Pagan Idol., in Squire, p. 158.
[5] Ibid.
[6] Kenrick's Egypt, vol. i. p. 375.
[7] Ibid.
[8] Squire : p. 161.
[9] Ibid. p. 185.

connect the *Serpent* and the *Sun*, as corresponding symbols of the *reproductive* or *creative power*. Figure No. 40 is a symbolical sign, representing the disk of the *Sun* encircled by the serpent *Uraeus*, meaning the " KING SUN," or " ROYAL SUN," as it often surmounts the persons of Egyptian monarchs, confirmed by the *emblem of* LIFE depending from the serpent's neck.[1]

The mysteries of Osiris, Isis, and Horus, in *Egypt ;* Atys and Cybele, in *Phrygia;* Ceres and Proserpine, at *Eleusis;* of Venus and Adonis, in *Phenicia;* of Bona Dea and Priapus, in *Rome*, are all susceptible of one explanation. They all set forth and illustrated,

FIG No. 40

by solemn and impressive rites, and *mystical symbols*, the grand phenomenon of *nature*, especially as connected with the creation of things and the perpetuation of life. In all, it is worthy of remark, the SERPENT was more or less conspicuously introduced, and always as symbolical of the invigorating or active energy of nature, the SUN.

We have seen (in Chapter XX.) that in early Christian art Christ Jesus also was represented as a *crucified Lamb*. This crucified lamb is " the Lamb of God taking away the sins of the world, and slain from the foundation of the world."[2] In other words, the crucified lamb typifies the *crucified Sun*, for the lamb was another symbol of the Sun, as we shall presently see.

We find, then, that the stories of the crucifixions of the different so-called SAVIOURS of mankind *all melt into* ONE, and that they are *allegorical*, for " *Saviour* " was only a title of the *Sun*,[3] and his being put to death on the cross, signifies no more than the restriction of the power of the Sun in the winter quarter. With Justin Martyr, then, we can say :

" There exists not a people, whether Greek or barbarian, or any other race of men, by whatsoever appellation or manners they may be distinguished, how- ever ignorant of arts or agriculture, whether they dwell under the tents, or wan-

---

[1] Squire : p. 169.

[2] Lundy : Monumental Christianity, p. 185.

[3] " SAVIOUR was a common title of the Sun- gods of antiquity." (Wake : Phallism in Anct. Religs., p. 55.)

The ancient Greek writers speak of the Sun, as the " Generator and Nourisher of all Things ;" the " Ruler of the World ;" the " First of the Gods," and the " Supreme Lord of all Beings." (Knight : Ancient Art and Mytho., p. 37.)

Pausanias (500 B. C.) speaks of " The Sun

having the surname of SAVIOUR." (Ibid. p. 98, *note*.)

" There is a very remarkable figure copied in Payne Knight's Work, in which we see on a man's shoulders a *cock's* head, whilst on the pediment are placed the words : " THE SAVIOUR OF THE WORLD." (Inman : Anct. Faiths, vol. i. p. 537.) This refers to the SUN. The cock being the natural herald of the day, he was therefore sacred, among the ancients, to the Sun." (See Knight : Anct. Art and Mytho., p. 70, and Lardner : vol. viii. p. 377.)

der about in crowded wagons, among whom prayers are not offered up in the name of A Crucified Saviour[1] to the Father and creator of all things."[2]

9. *"And many women were there beholding afar off."*[3] The tender mother who had watched over him at his birth, and the fair maidens whom he has loved, will never forsake him. They yet remain with him, and while their tears drop on his feet, which they kiss, their voices cheer him in his last hour. In these we have the *Dawn*, who bore him, and the fair and beautiful lights which flush the Eastern sky as the Sun sinks or dies in the West.[4] Their tears are the tears of dew, such as Eôs weeps at the death of her child.

All the Sun-gods forsake their homes and virgin mothers, and wander through different countries doing marvellous things. Finally, at the end of their career, the mother, from whom they were parted long ago, is by their side to cheer them in their last hours.[5]

The ever-faithful women were to be found at the last scene in the life of *Buddha.* Kasyapa having found the departed master's feet soiled and wet, asked Nanda the cause of it. "He was told that a weeping woman had embraced Gautama's feet shortly before his death, and that her tears had fallen on his feet and left the marks on them."[6]

In his last hours, *Œdipous* (the Sun) has been cheered by the presence of Antigone.[7]

At the death of *Hercules*, Iole (*the fair-haired Dawn*) stands by his side, cheering him to the last. With her gentle hands she sought to soothe his pain, and with pitying words to cheer him in his woe. Then once more the face of Hercules flushed with a deep joy, and he said:

"Ah, Iole, brightest of maidens, thy voice shall cheer me as I sink down in the sleep of death. I saw and loved thee in the bright *morning time*, and now again thou hast come, *in the evening*, fair as the soft clouds which gather around the *dying Sun.*"

The *black mists* were spreading over the sky, but still Hercules sought to gaze on the fair face of Iole, and to comfort her in her sorrow.

"Weep not, Iole," he said, "my toil is done, and now is the time for rest. I shall see thee again in the bright land which is never trodden by the feet of night."

---

[1] The name *Jesus* is the same as *Joshua,* and signifies *Saviour.*
[2] Justin Martyr: Dialog. Cum Typho. Quoted in Gibbon's Rome, vol. i. p. 582.
[3] Matt. xxvii. 55.
[4] The ever-faithful woman who is always near at the death of the Sun-god is "the fair and tender light which sheds its soft hue over the Eastern heaven as the Sun sinks in death beneath the Western waters." (Cox: Aryan Myths, vol. i. p. 223.)
[5] See Ibid. vol. i. p. 80.
[6] Bunsen: The Angel-Messiah, p. 49.
[7] Cox: Aryan Mythology, vol. i. p. 223.

The same story is related in the legend of *Apollo*. The Dawn, from whom he parted in the early part of his career, comes to his side at *eventide*, and again meets him when his journey on earth has well nigh come to an end.[1]

When the Lord *Prometheus* was crucified on Mt. Caucasus, his especially professed friend, Oceanus, the fisherman, as his name, Petræus, indicates,[2] being unable to prevail on him to make his peace with Jupiter, by throwing the cause of human redemption out of his hands,[3] " forsook him and fled." None remained to be witnesses of his dying agonies, but the chorus of ever-amiable and ever-faithful women, which also bewailed and lamented him, but were unable to subdue his inflexible philanthropy.[4]

10. " *There was darkness all over the land.*"[5] In the same manner ends the tale of the long toil and sorrows of other Sun-gods. The last scene exhibits a manifest return to the spirit of the solar myth. He must not die the common death of all men, for no disease or corruption can touch the body of the brilliant Sun. After a long struggle against the dark clouds who are arrayed against him, he is finally overcome, and dies. Blacker and blacker grow the evening shades, and finally " there is darkness on the face of the earth," and the din of its thunder clashes through the air.[6]

It is the picture of a sunset in wild confusion, of a sunset more awful, yet not more sad, than that which is seen in the last hours of many other *Sun*-gods.[7] It is the picture of the loneliness of the *Sun*, who sinks slowly down, with the ghastly hues of death upon his face, while none is nigh to cheer him save the ever-faithful women.

11. "*He descended into hell.*"[8] This is the *Sun's* descent into the *lower regions*. It enters the sign Capricornus, or the Goat, and

---

[1] See Tales of Ancient Greece, p. xxxi.

[2] PETRÆUS was an interchangeable synonym of the name Oceanus.

[3] " Then Peter took him, and began to rebuke him, saying, Be it far from thee, Lord, this shall not be unto thee." (Matt. xvi. 22.)

[4] See Potter's Æschylus.

[5] Matt. xxvii. 45.

[6] As the Sun dies, or sinks in the West, blacker and blacker grows the evening shades, till there is darkness on the face of the earth. Then from the high heavens comes down the thick clouds, and the din of its thunder crashes through the air. (Description of the death of Hercules, Tales of Ancient Greece, pp. 61, 62.)

[7] It is the battle of the clouds over the dead or dying Sun, which is to be seen in the legendary history of many Sun-gods. (Cox: Aryan Mythology, vol. ii. p. 91.)

[8] This was one of the latest additions of the Sun-myth to the history of *Christ* Jesus. This has been proved not only to have been an invention after the Apostles' time, but even after the time of Eusebius (A.D. 325). The doctrine of the descent into hell was not in the ancient creeds or rules of faith. It is not to be found in the rules of faith delivered by Irenæus (A.D. 190), by Origen (A.D. 230), or by Tertullian (A.D. 200–210). It is not expressed in those creeds which were made by the Councils as larger explications of the Apostles' Creed ; not in the Nicene, or Constantinopolitan ; not in those of Ephesus, or Chalcedon ; not in those confessions made at Sardica, Antioch, Selencia, Sirmium, &c.

the astronomical winter begins. The days have reached their short-est span, and the *Sun* has reached his extreme southern limit. The winter solstice reigns, and the Sun seems to stand still in his southern course. For three days and three nights he remains in hell — the lower regions.[1] In this respect *Christ* Jesus is like other Sun-gods.[2]

In the ancient sagas of Iceland, the hero who is the Sun person-ified, descends into a tomb, where he fights a vampire. After a desperate struggle, the hero overcomes, and rises to the surface of the earth. "This, too, represents the Sun in the northern realms, descending into the tomb of winter, and there overcoming the power of darkness."[3]

12. *He rose again from the dead, and ascended into heaven.* Resurrections from the dead, and ascensions into heaven, are gen-erally acknowledged to be *solar* features, as the history of many solar heroes agree in this particular.

At the *winter solstice* the ancients wept and mourned for *Tam-muz*, the fair Adonis, and other Sun-gods, done to death by the boar, or crucified — slain by the thorn of winter — and on the *third day* they rejoiced at the resurrection of their "Lord of Light."[4]

With her usual policy, the Church endeavored to give a Christian significance to the rites which they borrowed from heathenism, and in this case, the mourning for Tammuz, the fair Adonis, became the mourning for Christ Jesus, and joy at the rising of the natural Sun became joy at the rising of the "Sun of Righteousness"— at the resurrection of Christ Jesus from the grave.

This festival of the Resurrection was generally held by the an-cients on the 25th of March, when the awakening of *Spring* may be said to be the result of the return of the Sun from the lower or far-off regions to which he had departed. At the equinox — say, the

---

[1] At the end of his career, the Sun enters the *lowest regions*, the bowels of the earth, therefore nearly all Sun-gods are made to "descend into hell," and remain there for three days and three nights, for the reason that from the 22d to the 25th of December, the Sun apparently remains in the same place. Thus Jonah, a personification of the Sun (see Chap. IX.), who remains three days and three nights in the bowels of the earth—typified by a fish—is made to say : "Out of the belly of hell cried I, and thou heardst my voice."

[2] See Chapter XXII.

[3] Baring-Gould : Curious Myths, p. 260.

"The mighty Lord appeared in the form of a man, and enlightened those places which had ever before been in darkness ; and broke asun-der the fetters which before could not be broken; and with his *invincible power* visited those who sat in the deep darkness by iniquity, and the shadow of death by sin. Then the King of Glory trampled upon Death, seized the Prince of Hell, and deprived him of all his power." (Description of *Christ's* Descent into Hell. Nicodemus : Apoc.)

[4] "The women weeping for Tammuz was no more than expressive of the Sun's loss of power in the winter quarter." (King's Gnos-tics, p. 102. See also, Cox : Aryan Mytho., vol. ii. p. 113.)

After remaining for three days and three nights in the lowest regions, the Sun begins to ascend, thus he "rises from the dead," as it were, and "ascends into heaven."

vernal—at *Easter*, the Sun has been below the equator, and suddenly rises above it. It has been, as it were, dead to us, but now it exhibits a resurrection.[1] The Saviour rises triumphant over the powers of darkness, to life and immortality, on the 25th of March, when the Sun rises in Aries.

Throughout all the ancient world, *the resurrection of the god Sol*, under different names, was celebrated on March 25th, with great rejoicings.[2]

In the words of the Rev. Geo. W. Cox:

"The wailing of the Hebrew women at the death of Tammuz, the crucifixion and resurrection of Osiris, the adoration of the Babylonian Mylitta, the Sacti ministers of Hindu temples, the cross and crescent of Isis, the rites of the Jewish altar of Baal-Peor, wholly preclude all doubt of the real nature of the great *festivals* and *mysteries* of Phenicians, Jews, Assyrians, Egyptians, and Hindus."[3]

All this was *Sun* and Nature worship, symbolized by the *Linga* and *Yoni*. As Mr. Bonwick says:

"The philosophic theist who reflects upon the story, known from the walls of China, across Asia and Europe, to the plateau of Mexico, cannot resist the impression that no *materialistic* theory of it can be satisfactory."[4]

Allegory alone explains it.

"The Church, at an early date, selected the heathen festivals of *Sun worship* for its own, ordering the *birth at Christmas*, a fixed time, and the *resurrection at Easter*, a varying time, as in all Pagan religions; since, though the Sun rose directly after the vernal equinox, the festival, to be correct in a *heathen* point of view, had to be associated with the new moon."[5]

The Christian, then, may well say:

"When thou hadst overcome the sharpness of winter, thou didst open the kingdom of heaven (*i. e,* bring on the reign of summer), to all believers."

13. *Christ Jesus is Creator of all things.* We have seen (in Chapter XXVI.) that it was not God the Father, who was supposed by the ancients to have been the *Creator* of the world, but God the Son, the Redeemer and Saviour of Mankind. Now, this Redeemer and Saviour was, as we have seen, the Sun, and Prof. Max Müller tells us that in the *Vedic* mythology, the Sun is not the bright Deva only, "who performs his daily task in the sky, but he is supposed to perform much greater work. He is looked upon, in fact, as the *Ruler*, as the *Establisher*, as the *Creator of the world*."[6]

Having been invoked as the "Life-bringer," the Sun is also

---

[1] Bonwick: Egyptian Belief, p. 174.
[2] Anacalypsis, vol. ii. p. 100.
[3] Aryan Mythology, vol. ii. p. 125.

[4] Egyptian Belief, p. 182.
[5] Ibid.
[6] Origin of Religions, p. 264.

called — in the Rig-Veda — "the Breath or Life of all that move and rest;" and lastly he becomes " *The Maker of all things*," by whom all the worlds have been brought together.[1]

There is a prayer in the *Vedas*, called *Gayatree*, which consists of three measured lines, and is considered the holiest and most efficacious of all their religious forms. Sir William Jones translates it thus :

" Let us adore the supremacy of that spiritual Sun, the godhead, who illuminates all. who re-creates all, from whom all proceed, to whom all must return ; whom we invoke to direct our undertakings aright in our progress toward his holy seat."

With Seneca (a Roman philosopher, born at Cordova, Spain, 61 B. C.) then, we can say :

" You may call the Creator of all things by different names (Bacchus, Hercules, Mercury, etc.), but they are only different names of the same divine being, the *Sun*."

14. *He is to be Judge of the quick and the dead.* Who is better able than the Sun to be the judge of man's deeds, seeing, as he does, from his throne in heaven, all that is done on earth ? The Vedas speak of Sûrya—the pervading, irresistible luminary—as seeing all things and hearing all things, *noting the good and evil deeds of men.*[2]

According to Hindoo mythology, says Prof. Max Müller :

" The Sun sees everything, both what is good and what is evil ; and how natural therefore that (in the Indian Veda) both the evil-doer should be told that the sun sees what no human eye may have seen, and that the innocent, when all other help fails him, should appeal to the sun to attest his guiltlessness."

" Frequent allusion is made (in the Rig-Veda), to the sun's power of seeing everything. The stars flee before the all-seeing sun, like thieves. He sees the right and the wrong among men. He who looks upon the world knows also the thoughts in all men. As the sun sees everything and knows everything, he is asked to forget and forgive what he alone has seen and knows."[3]

On the most ancient Egyptian monuments, Osiris, the Sun personified, is represented as Judge of the dead. The Egyptian " Book of the Dead," the oldest Bible in the world, speaks of Osiris as " seeing all things, and hearing all things, noting the good and evil deeds of men."

15. *He will come again sitting on a white horse.*

The " second coming " of Vishnu (Crishna), *Christ* Jesus, and other Sun-gods, are also *astronomical allegories*. The *white horse*,

---

[1] Origin of Religions, p. 268.   [2] Aryan Mythology, vol. i. p. 384.
[3] Origin of Religion, pp. 264-268.

which figures so conspicuously in the legend, was the universal symbol of the Sun among Oriental nations.

Throughout the whole legend, *Christ* Jesus is the toiling Sun,
laboring for the benefit of others, not his own, and doing hard service for a mean and cruel generation. Watch his sun-like career
of brilliant conquest, checked with intervals of storm, and declining
to a death clouded with sorrow and derision. He is in constant
company with his *twelve* apostles, the *twelve signs of the zodiac.*[1]
During the course of his life's journey he is called "The God of
Earthly Blessing," "The Saviour through whom a new life springs,"
"The Preserver," "The Redeemer," &c. Almost at his birth the
Serpent of darkness attempts to destroy him. Temptations to sloth
and luxury are offered him in vain. He has his work to do, and
nothing can stay him from doing it, as nothing can arrest the Sun
in his journey through the heavens. Like all other solar heroes, he
has his faithful women who love him, and the Marys and Martha
here play the part. Of his toils it is scarcely necessary to speak in
detail. They are but a thousand variations on the story of the great
conflict which all the Sun-gods wage against the demon of darkness.
He astonishes his tutor when sent to school. This we might expect
to be the case, when an incomparable and incommunicable wisdom
is the heritage of the Sun. He also represents the wisdom and be-
neficence of the bright Being who brings life and light to men. As
the Sun wakens the earth to life when the winter is done, so Crishna, Buddha, Horus, Æsculapius, and *Christ* Jesus were raisers of
the dead. When the leaves fell and withered on the approach of
winter, the "daughter of the earth" would be spoken of as dying
or dead, and, as no other power than that of the Sun can recall vegetation to life, this child of the earth would be represented as
buried in a sleep from which the touch of the Sun alone could
rouse her.

Christ Jesus, then, is the Sun, in his short career and early
death. He is the child of the Dawn, whose soft, violet hues tint

---

[1] The number twelve appears in many of
the Sun-myths. It refers to the twelve hours
of the day or night, or the twelve moons of the
lunar year. (Cox : Aryan Mythology, vol. i.
p. 165. Bonwick : Egyptian Belief, p. 175.)

Osiris, the Egyptian Saviour, had twelve
apostles. (Bonwick, p. 175.)

In all religions of antiquity the number
twelve, which applies to the twelve signs of the
zodiac, are reproduced in all kinds and sorts
of forms. For instance : such are the *twelve*
great gods ; the *twelve* apostles of Osiris ; the
twelve apostles of Jesus ; the *twelve* sons of

Jacob, or the *twelve* tribes ; the *twelve* altars
of James ; the *twelve* labors of Hercules ; the
twelve shields of Mars ; the *twelve* brothers
Arvaux ; the *twelve* gods Consents ; the *twelve*
governors in the Manichean System ; the
adectyas of the East Indies ; the *twelve* asses
of the Scandinavians ; the city of the *twelve*
gates in the Apocalypse ; the *twelve* wards of
the city ; the *twelve* sacred cushions, on which
the Creator sits in the cosmogony of the Japanese ; the *twelve* precious stones of the *rational*,
or the ornament worn by the high priest of the
Jews, &c., &c. (See Dupuis, pp. 39, 40.)

the clouds of early morn; his father being the Sky, the "Heavenly Father," who has looked down with love upon the Dawn, and over-shadowed her. When his career on earth is ended, and he expires, the loving mother, who parted from him in the morning of his life, is at his side, looking on the death of the Son whom she cannot save from the doom which is on him, while her tears fall on his body like rain at sundown. From her he is parted at the beginning of his course; to her he is united at its close. But *Christ Jesus*, like Crishna, Buddha, Osiris, Horus, Mithras, Apollo, Atys and others, *rises again*, and thus the myth takes us a step beyond the legend of Serpedon and others, which stop at the end of the æastward journey, when the night is done.

According to the Christian calendar, the birthday of John the Baptist is on the day of the summer solstice, when the sun begins to decrease. How true to nature then are the words attributed to him in the fourth Gospel, when he says that he must *decrease*, and Jesus *increase*.

Among the ancient Teutonic nations, fires were lighted, on the tops of hills, on the 24th of June, in honor of the WENDING SUN. This custom is still kept up in Southern Germany and the Scotch highlands, and it is the day selected by the Roman Catholic church to celebrate the nativity of John the Baptist.[1]

Mosheim, the ecclesiastical historian, speaking of the uncertainty of the time when *Christ* Jesus was born, says: "The uncertainty of this point is of no great consequence. We know that the *Sun of Righteousness* has shone upon the world; and although we cannot fix the precise period in which he arose, this will not preclude us from enjoying the direction and influence of his vital and salutary beams."

These sacred legends abound with such expressions as can have no possible or conceivable application to any other than to the " God of day." He is " a light to lighten the Gentiles, and to be the glory (or brightness) of his people."[2] He is come " a light into the world, that whosoever believeth in him should not abide in darkness."[3] He is " the light of the world."[4] He " is light, and in him no darkness is."[5]

" Lighten our darkness, we beseech thee, Adonai, and by thy great mercy defend us from all perils and dangers of this night."—*Collect, in Evening Service.*
" God of God, light of light, very God of very God."—*Nicene Creed.*

---

[1] See Mallet's Northern Antiquities, p. 505.
[2] Luke, ii. 32.
[3] John, xii. 46.
[4] John, ix. v.
[5] I. John, i. 5.

"Merciful Adonai, we beseech thee to cast thy bright beams of light upon thy Church."—*Collect of St. John.*

"To thee all angels cry aloud, the heavens, and all the powers therein."

"Heaven and earth are full of the majesty of thy glory" (or brightness).

"The glorious company of the (*twelve months,* or) apostles praise thee."

"Thou art the King of Glory, O Christ !"

"When thou tookest upon thee to deliver man, thou passest through the constellation, or zodiacal sign—the Virgin."

"When thou hadst overcome the sharpness of winter, thou didst open the kingdom of heaven (*i. e.,* bring on the reign of the summer months) to all believers."

"All are agreed," says Cicero, "that Apollo is none other than the Sun, because the attributes which are commonly ascribed to Apollo do so wonderfully agree thereto."

Just so surely as Apollo is the Sun, so is the Lord *Christ* Jesus the Sun. That which is so conclusive respecting the Pagan deities, applies also to the God of the Christians; but, like the Psalmist of old, they cry, "Touch not MY Christ, and do my prophets no harm."

Many Christian writers have seen that the history of their Lord and Saviour is simply the history of the Sun, but they either say nothing, or, like Dr. Parkhurst and the Rev. J. P. Lundy, claim that the Sun is a type of the true Sun of Righteousness. Mr. Lundy, in his "Monumental Christianity," says :

"Is there no bright Sun of Righteousness — no *personal* and loving Son of God, *of whom the material Sun has been the type or symbol, in all ages and among all nations?* What power is it that comes from the Sun to give light and heat to all created things ? If the symbolical Sun leads such a great earthly and heavenly flock, what must be said to the *true* and only begotten Son of God ? If Apollo was adopted by early Christian art as a *type* of the Good Shepherd of the New Testament, *then this interpretation of the Sun-god among all nations must be the solution of the universal mythos, or what other solution can it have ?* To what other *historical* personage but Christ can it apply ? *If this mythos has no spiritual meaning, then all religion becomes mere idolatry, or the worship of material things.*"[1]

Mr. Lundy, who seems to adhere to this once-upon-a-time favorite theory, illustrates it as follows:

"The young *Isaac* is his (Christ's) Hebrew type, bending under the wood, as Christ fainted under the cross ; *Daniel* is his type, stripped of all earthly fame and greatness, and cast naked into the deepest danger, shame and humiliation." "*Noah* is his type, in saving men from utter destruction, and bringing them across the sea of death to a new world and a new life." "*Orpheus* is a type of Christ. *Agni* and *Crishna* of India ; *Mithra* of Persia ; *Horus* and *Apollo* of Egypt, are all types of Christ." "*Samson* carrying off the gates of Gaza and defeating the Philistines by his own death, was considered as a type of Christ bursting open and carrying away the gates of Hades, and conquering His and our enemies by his death and resurrection."[1]

According to this theory, the whole Pagan religion was typical of Christ and Christianity. Why then were not the Pagans the Lord's *chosen* people instead of the children of Israel?

The early Christians were charged with being a sect of *Sun worshipers.*[2] The ancient Egyptians worshiped the god *Serapis*, and Serapis was the *Sun*. Fig. No. 11, page 194, shows the manner in which Serapis was personified. It might easily pass for a representation of the Sun-god of the Christians. Mr. King says, in his "Gnostics, and their Remains":

"There can be no doubt that the head of Serapis, marked as the face is by a grave and pensive majesty, *supplied the first idea for the conventional portraits of the Saviour.*"[3]

The Imperial Russian Collection *boasts* of a head of Christ Jesus which is said to be very ancient. It is a fine intaglio on emerald. Mr. King says of it:

"It is in reality a head of *Serapis*, seen in front and crowned with Persia boughs, easily mistaken for thorns, though the bushel on the head leaves no doubt as to the real personage intended."[4]

It must not be forgotten, in connection with this, that the worshipers of Serapis, or the Sun, were called *Christians.*[5]

Mrs. Jameson, speaking on this subject, says:

"We search in vain for the lightest evidence of his (Christ's) human, individual semblance, in the writing of those disciples who knew him so well. In this instance the instincts of earthly affection seem to have been mysteriously overruled. He whom all races of men were to call brother, was not to be too closely associated with the particular lineaments of any one. St. John, the beloved disciple, could lie on the breast of Jesus with all the freedom of fellowship, but not even he has left a word to indicate what manner of man was the Divine Master after the flesh. . . . Legend has, in various form, supplied this natural craving, but it is hardly necessary to add, that all accounts of pictures of our Lord taken from Himself are without historical foundation. *We are therefore left to imagine the expression* most befitting the character of him who took upon himself our likeness, and looked at the woes and sins of mankind through the eyes of our mortality."[6]

The Rev. Mr. Geikie says, in his "Life of Christ":

"No hint is given in the New Testament of Christ's *appearance*; and the early Church, in the absence of all guiding facts, had to fall back on imagination."

[1] See Monumental Christianity, pp. 186, 191, 192, 238, and 296.
[2] See Bonwick's Egyptian Belief, p. 283.
[3] King's Gnostics, p. 68.
[4] Ibid. p. 187.
[5] See Chapter XX.
[6] Hist. of Our Lord in Art, vol. 1. p. 81.

"In its *first* years, the Christian church fancied its Lord's visage and form *marred more than those of other men ;* and that he must have had no attractions of personal beauty.   Justin Martyr (A. D. 150–160) speaks of him as *without beauty or attractiveness,* and of *mean appearance.*   Clement of Alexandria (A. D. 200), describes him as of an *uninviting appearance,* and *almost repulsive.*   Tertullian (A. D. 200–210) says he had not even *ordinary human beauty,* far less heavenly. Origen (A. D. 230) went so far as to say that he was '*small in body and deformed,*' as well as low-born, and that, '*his only beauty was in his soul and life.*'"[1]

One of the favorite ways finally, of depicting him, was, as Mr. Lundy remarks :

"Under the figure of a beautiful and adorable youth, of about fifteen or eighteen years of age, beardless, with a sweet expression of countenance, *and long and abundant hair flowing in curls over his shoulders.*   His brow is sometimes encircled by a diadem or bandeau, *like a young priest of the Pagan gods ;* that is, in fact, the favorite figure.   On sculptured sarcophagi, in fresco paintings and Mosaics, Christ is thus represented as a graceful youth, *just as Apollo was figured by the Pagans,* and as angels are represented by Christians."[2]

Thus we see that the Christians took the paintings and statues of the Sun-gods Serapis and Apollo *as models*, when they wished to represent *their* Saviour.   That the former is the favorite at the present day need not be doubted when we glance at Fig. No. 11, page 194.

Mr. King, speaking of this god, and his worshipers, says :

"There is very good reason to believe that in the *East* the worship of *Serapis* was at first combined with *Christianity,* and gradually merged into it with an entire change of name, *not substance,* carrying with it many of its ancient notions and rites."[3]

Again he says :

"In the second century the syncretistic sects that had sprung up in *Alexandria,* the very hotbed of Gnosticism, found out in *Serapis* a prophetic *type* of Christ, or the Lord and Creator of all."[4]

The early *Christians*, or worshipers of the Sun, under the name of "*Christ*," had, as all Sun-worshipers, *a peculiar regard to the East*—the quarter in which their god rose—*to which point they ordinarily directed their prayers.*[5]

The followers of Mithra always turned towards the East, when they worshiped ; the same was done by the Brahmans of the East, and the Christians of the West.   In the ceremony of baptism, the catechumen was placed with his face to the West, the symbolical representation of the prince of darkness, in opposition to the East, and made to spit towards it at the evil one, and renounce his works.

---

[1] Geikie : Life of Christ. vol. i. p. 151.   [4] Ibid. p. 68.
[2] Monumental Christianity, p. 231.   [5] See Bell's Pantheon, vol. i. p. 13.
[3] King's Gnostics, p. 48.

Tertullian says, that Christians were taken for worshipers of the Sun because they prayed towards the East, after the manner of those who adored the Sun. The Essenes — whom Eusebius calls Christians — always turned to the east to pray. The Essenes met once a week, and spent the night in singing hymns, &c., which lasted till sun-rising. As soon as dawn appeared, they retired to their cells, after saluting one another. Pliny says the Christians of Bithynia met before it was light, and sang hymns to Christ, as to a God. After their service they saluted one another. Surely the circumstances of the two classes of people meeting before daylight, is a very remarkable coincidence. It is just what the Persian Magi, who were Sun worshipers, were in the habit of doing.

When a Manichæan Christian came over to the orthodox Christians, he was required to curse his former friends in the following terms :

"I curse Zarades (Zoroaster ?) who, Manes said, had appeared as a god before his time among the Indians and Persians, *and whom he calls the Sun.* I curse those who say *Christ is the Sun*, and who make prayers to the *Sun*, and who do not pray to the true God, only towards the East, but who turn themselves round, following the motions of the Sun with their innumerable supplications. *I curse those person who say that Zarades and Budas and Christ and the Sun are all one and the same.*"

There are not many circumstances more striking than that of Christ Jesus being originally worshiped under the form of a Lamb — the actual "Lamb of God, which taketh away the sins of the world." As we have already seen (in Chap. XX.), it was not till the Council of Constantinople, called *In Trullo*, held so late as the year 707, that pictures of Christ Jesus were ordered to be drawn in the form of a man. It was ordained that, in the place of the figure of a Lamb, the symbol used to that time, the figure of a man nailed to a cross, should in future be used.[1] From this decree, the identity of the worship of the *Celestial Lamb* and the Christian Saviour is certified beyond the possibility of doubt, and the mode by which the ancient superstitions were propagated is satisfactorily shown. Nothing can more clearly prove the general practice than the order of a council to regulate it.

The worship of the constellation of *Aries* was the worship of the Sun in his passage through that sign. "This constellation was

---

[1] Following are the words of the decree now in the Vatican library : "In quibusdam sanctorum imaginum picturis agnus exprimitur, &c. Nos igitur veteres figuras atque umbras, et veritatis notas, et signa ecclesiæ tradita, complectentes, gratiam, et veritatem anteponi- mus, quam ut plenitudinem legis acceptimus. Itaque id quod perfectum est, in picturis etiam omnium oculis subjiciamus, agnum illum qui mundi peccatum tollit, Christam Deum nostrum, loco veteris Ayni, humanâ formâ posthæ exprimendum decrevimus," &c.

called by the ancients the *Lamb of God*. He was also called the *Saviour*, and was said to save mankind from their sins. He was always honored with the appellation of *Dominus* or *Lord*. He was called *The Lamb of God which taketh away the sins of the world*. The devotees addressed him in their litany, constantly repeating the words, '*O Lamb of God, that taketh away the sins of the world, have mercy upon us. Grant us thy peace.*'"

On an ancient medal of the *Phenicians*, brought by Dr. Clark from Citium (and described in his "Travels," vol. ii. ch. xi.) this *Lamb of God* is described with the Cross and the Rosary, which shows that they were both used in his worship.

Yearly the Sun-god, as the zodiacal horse (Aries) was supposed by the Vedic Aryans *to die to save all flesh*. Hence the practice of sacrificing horses. The "guardian spirits" of the prince Sakya Buddha sing the following hymn:

> " Once when thou wast the *white horse*,[1]
> In pity for the suffering of man,
> Thou didst fly across heaven to the region of the evil demons,
> *To secure the happiness of mankind.*
> Persecutions without end,
> Revilings and many prisons,
> *Death and murder ;*
> These hast thou suffered with love and patience,
> *Forgiving thine executioners.*"[2]

We have seen, in Chapter XXXIII., that Christ Jesus was also symbolized as a *Fish*, and that it is to be seen on all the ancient Christian monuments. But what has the Christian Saviour to do with a *Fish?* Why was he called a *Fish?* The answer is, *because the fish was another emblem of the* Sun. Abarbanel says:

"The sign of his (Christ's) coming is the junction of Saturn and Jupiter, *in the Sign Pisces.*"[3]

Applying the astronomical emblem of *Pisces* to Jesus, does not seem more absurd than applying the astronomical emblem of the Lamb. They applied to him the monogram of the Sun, IHS, the astronomical and alchemical sign of Aries, or the ram, or Lamb ♈ ; and, in short, what was there that was *Heathenish* that they have not applied to him ?

The preserving god Vishnu, the Sun, was represented as a fish, and so was the Syrian Sun-god Dagon, who was also a Preserver or Saviour. The Fish was sacred among many nations of antiquity,

---

[1] " The *solar horse*, with two serpents upon his head (the Buddhist Aries) is Buddha's symbol, and Aries is the symbol of Christ." (Arthur Lillie : Buddha and Early Buddhism,

p. 110.)

[2] Quoted by Lillie : Buddha and Early Buddhism, p. 93.

[3] Quoted by King : The Gnostics &c., p. 138.

and is to be seen on their monuments. Thus we see that everything at last centres in the Sun.

Constantine, the first Christian emperor, had on his *coins* the figure of the Sun, with the legend: "To the Invincible Sun, my companion and guardian," as being a representation, says Mr. King, "either of the ancient Phœbus, *or the* new *Sun of Righteousness*, equally acceptable to both Christian and Gentile, from the double interpretation of which the type was susceptible."[1]

The worship of the Sun, under the name of Mithra, "long survived in Rome, *under the Christian emperors*, and, doubtless, much longer in the remoter districts of the semi-independent provinces."[2]

FIG. 41

Christ Jesus is represented with a halo of glory surrounding his head, a florid complexion, long golden locks of hair, and a flowing robe. Now, all *Sun*-gods, from Crishna of India (Fig. No. 41) to Baldur of Scandinavia, are represented with a halo of glory surrounding their heads, and the flowing locks of golden hair, and the flowing robe, are not wanting.[3] By a process of metaphor, the rays

[1] Quoted by King : The Gnostics, &c.,p. 49.
[2] Ibid. p. 45.
[3] *Indra,* the crucified Sun-god of the Hindoos, was represented with golden locks. (Cox : Aryan Myths. vol, i. p. 341.)
Mithras, the Persian Saviour, was represented with long flowing locks.
Izdubar, the god and hero of the Chaldeans, was represented with long flowing locks of hair (Smith : Chaldean Account of Genesis, p. 193), and so was his counterpart, the Hebrew Samson.
"The Sâkya-prince (Buddha) is described as an Aryan by Buddhistic tradition ; his face was reddish, his hair of light color and curly, his general appearance of great beauty." (Bunsen : The Angel-Messiah, p. 15.)
"Serapis has, in some instances, long hair formally turned back, and disposed in ringlets hanging down upon his breast and shoulders like that of a woman. His whole person, too, is always enveloped in drapery reaching to his feet." (Knight : Ancient Art and Mythology, p. 104.)
"As for *yellow hair,* there is no evidence that Greeks have ever commonly possessed it ; but no other color would do for a solar hero, and it accordingly characterizes the entire company of them, wherever found." (Fiske : Myths and Mythmakers, p. 202.)
Helios (the Sun) is called by the Greeks the "yellow-haired." (Goldzhier : Hebrew Mytho., p. 137.)
The Sun's rays is signified by the flowing

golden locks which stream from the head of Kephalos, and fall over the shoulders of Bellerphon. (Cox : Aryan Mytho., vol. i. p. 107.)
Perseus, son of the virgin Danae, was called the "Golden Child." (Ibid. vol. ii. p. 58.) "The light of early morning is not more pure than was the color on his fair cheeks, and the golden locks streamed bright over his shoulders, like the rays of the sun when they rest on the hills at midday." (Tales of Ancient Greece, p. 83.)
The Saviour Dionysus wore a long flowing robe, and had long golden hair, which streamed from his head over his shoulders. (Aryan Mythology, vol. ii. p. 293.)
Ixion was the "Beautiful and Mighty," with golden hair flashing a glory from his head, dazzling as the rays which stream from Helios, when he drives his chariot up the heights of heaven ; and his flowing robe glistened as he moved, like the vesture which the Sun-god gave to the wise maiden Medeia, who dwelt in Kolchis. (Tales of Ancient Greece, p. 47.)
Theseus enters the city of Athens, as Christ Jesus is said to have entered Jerusalem, with a long flowing robe, and with his *golden hair* tied gracefully behind his head. His "soft beauty" excites the mockery of the populace, who pause in their work to jest with him. (Cox : Aryan Mythology, vol. ii. p. 63.)
Thus we see that long locks of golden hair, and a flowing robe, are mythological attributes of the Sun.

of the Sun were changed into golden hair, into spears and lances, and robes of light. From the shoulders of Phoibus Lykêgenes, the light-born, flow the sacred locks over which no razor might pass. On the head of Nisos, as on that of Samson, they became a palladium invested with a mysterious power. From Helios, the Sun, who can scorch as well as warm, comes the robe of Medeia, which appears in the poisoned garments of Deianeira.[1]

We see, then, that *Christ* Jesus, like *Christ* Buddha,[2] Crishna, Mithra, Osiris, Horus, Apollo, Hercules and others, is none other than a personification of the Sun, and that the Christians, like their predecessors the Pagans, are really Sun worshipers. It must not be inferred, however, that we advocate the theory that no such person as *Jesus of Nazareth* ever lived in the flesh. The *man* Jesus is evidently an historical personage, just as the Sakaya prince Buddha, Cyrus, King of Persia, and Alexander, King of Macedonia, are historical personages; but the *Christ* Jesus, the *Christ* Buddha, the mythical Cyrus, and the mythical Alexander, *never lived in the flesh.* The *Sun-myth* has been added to the histories of these personages, in a greater or less degree, just as it has been added to the history of many other real personages. If it be urged that the attribution to Christ Jesus of qualities or powers belonging to the Pagan deities would hardly seem reasonable, the answer must be that nothing is done in his case which has not been done in the case of almost every other member of the great company of the gods. The tendency of myths to *reproduce themselves*, with differences only of *names* and *local coloring*, becomes especially manifest after perusing the legendary histories of the gods of antiquity. It is a fact demonstrated by history, that when one nation of antiquity came in contact with another, *they adopted each other's myths without hesitation.* After the Jews had been taken captives to Babylon, around the history of *their King Solomon* accumulated the fables which were related of *Persian heroes.* When the fame of Cyrus and Alexander became known over the then known world, the popular *Sun-myth* was interwoven with their true history. The mythical history of Perseus is, in all its essential features, the history of the Attic hero Theseus, and of the Theban Œdipus, and they all reappear with heightened colors in the myths of Hercules. We have the same thing again in the mythical and religious history of Crishna; it is, in nearly all its essential features, the history of

---

[1] Cox: Aryan Mythology, vol. i. p. 40.
[2] We have already seen (in Chapter XX.) that the word "*Christ*" signifies the "Anointed," or the "Messiah," and that many other personages beside Jesus of Nazareth had this *title* affixed to their names.

Buddha, and reappears again, with heightened colors, in the history of *Christ* Jesus. The myths of Buddha and Jesus differ from the legends of the other virgin-born Saviours only in the fact that in their cases it has gathered round unquestionably historical personages. In other words, an old myth has been added to names undoubtedly historical. But it cannot be too often repeated that from the *myth* we learn nothing of their history. How much we really know of the man Jesus will be considered in our next, and last, chapter.[1] That his biography, as recorded in the books of the New Testament, contains some few grains of actual history, is all that the historian or philosopher can rationally venture to urge. But the very process which has stripped these legends of all value as a chronicle of actual events has invested them with a new interest. Less than ever are they worthless fictions which the historian or philosopher may afford to despise. These legends of the birth, life, and death of the Sun, present to us a form of society and a condition of thought through which all mankind had to pass before the dawn of history. Yet that state of things was as real as the time in which we live. They who spoke the language of these early tales were men and women with joys and sorrows not unlike our own. In the following verses of Martianus Capella, the universal veneration for the Sun is clearly shown :

"Latium invokes thee, *Sol*, because thou alone art in honor, *after the Father*, the centre of light ; and they affirm that thy sacred head bears a golden brightness in twelve rays, because thou formest that number of months and that number of hours. They say that thou guidest four winged steeds, because thou alone rulest the chariot of the elements. For, dispelling the darkness, thou revealest the shining heavens. Hence they esteem thee, Phœbus, the discoverer of the secrets of the future ; or, because thou preventest nocturnal crimes. Egypt worships thee as Serapis, and Memphis as Osiris. Thou art worshiped by different rites as Mithra, Dis, and the cruel Typhon. Thou art alone the beautiful Atys, and the fostering son of the bent plough. Thou art the Ammon of arid Libya, and the Adonis of Byblos. *Thus under a varied appelation the whole world worship thee.* Hail ! thou true image of the gods, and of thy father's face ! thou whose sacred name, surname, and omen, three letters make to agree with the number 608.[2] Grant us, oh Father, to reach the eternal intercourse of mind, and to know the starry heaven under this sacred name. May the great and universally adorable Father increase these his favors."

---

[1] The theory which has been set forth in this chapter, is also more fully illustrated in Appendix C.

[2] These three letters, *the monogram of the Sun*, are the celebrated I. S. H., which are to be seen in Roman Catholic churches at the present day, and which are now the monogram of the Sun-god *Christ* Jesus. (See Chapter XXXVI.)

CHAPTER XL.

WE now come to the last, but certainly not least, question to be answered; which is, what do we really know of the man Jesus of Nazareth? How much of the Gospel narratives can we rely upon as fact?

Jesus of Nazareth is so enveloped in the mists of the past, and his history so obscured by legend, that it may be compared to footprints in the sand. We know *some one* has been there, but as to what manner of man he may have been, we certainly know little as fact. The Gospels, *the only records we have of him*,[1] have been proven, over and over again, unhistorical and legendary; to state *anything as positive* about the man is nothing more nor less than *assumption;* we can therefore *conjecture* only. Liberal writers philosophize and wax eloquent to little purpose, when, after demolishing the historical accuracy of the New Testament, they end their task by eulogizing the man Jesus, claiming for him the *highest* praise, and asserting that he was the *best* and *grandest* of our race;[2] but this manner of reasoning (undoubtedly consoling to many) *facts* do not warrant. We may consistently revere his name, and place it in the long list of the great and noble, the reformers and religious teachers of the past, all of whom have done their part in bringing about the freedom we now enjoy, but to go beyond this, is, to our thinking, unwarranted.

If the life of Jesus of Nazareth, as related in the books of the New Testament, be in part the story of a man who really lived and suffered, that story has been so interwoven with images borrowed

---

[1] "For knowledge of the man Jesus, of his idea and his aims, and of the outward form of his career, the *New Testament* is our only hope. If this hope fails, the pillared firmament of his starry fame is rottenness; the base of Christianity, so far as it was personal and individual, is built on stubble." (John W. Chadwick.)

[2] M. Renan, after declaring Jesus to be a "*fanatic*," and admitting that, "his friends thought him, at moments, beside himself;" and that, "his enemies declared him possessed by a devil," says : "The man here delineated merits a place at the summit of human grandeur." "This is the Supreme man, a sublime personage;" "to call him divine is no exaggeration." Other liberal writers have written in the same strain.

from myths of a bygone age, as to conceal forever any fragments of history which may lie beneath them. Gautama Buddha was undoubtedly an historical personage, yet the Sun-god myth has been added to his history to such an extent that we really know nothing positive about him. Alexander the Great was an historical personage, yet his history is one mass of legends. So it is with Julius Cesar, Cyrus, King of Persia, and scores of others. " The story of Cyrus' perils in infancy belongs to *solar* mythology as much as the stories of the magic slipper, of Charlemagne and Barbarossa. His grandfather, Astyages, is purely a mythical creation, his name being identical with that of the night demon, Azidahaka, who appears in the Shah-Nameh as the biting serpent."

The actual Jesus is inaccessible to scientific research. His image cannot be recovered. He left no memorial in writing of himself; his followers were illiterate; the mind of his age was confused. Paul received only traditions of him, how definite we have no means of knowing, apparently not significant enough to be treasured, nor consistent enough to oppose a barrier to his own speculations. As M. Renan says: " The Christ who communicates private revelations to him *is a phantom of his own making ;*" " it is *himself* he listens to, *while fancying that he hears Jesus.*"[1]

In studying the writings of the early advocates of Christianity, and Fathers of the Christian Church, where we would naturally look for the language that would indicate the real occurrence of the facts of the Gospel — if real occurrences they had ever been — we not only find no such language, but everywhere find every sort of sophistical ambages, ramblings from the subject, and evasions of the very business before them, as if on purpose to balk our research, and insult our skepticism. If we travel to the very sepulchre of Christ Jesus, it is only to discover that he was never there : *history* seeks evidence of his existence as a man, but finds no more trace of it than of the shadow that flits across the wall. " The Star of Bethlehem " shone not upon *her* path, and the order of the universe was suspended without *her* observation.

She asks, with the Magi of the East, " Where is he that is born King of the Jews?" and, like them, finds no solution of her inquiry, but the guidance that guides as well to one place as another ; descriptions that apply to Æsculapius, Buddha and Crishna, as well

---

[1] " The Christ of Paul was not a person, but an *idea;* he took no pains to learn the facts about the individual Jesus. He actually boasted that the Apostles had taught him nothing. *His* Christ was an ideal conception, evolved from his own feeling and imagination, and taking on new powers and attributes from year to year to suit each new emergency." (John W. Chadwick.)

as to Jesus; prophecies, without evidence that they were ever
prophesied; miracles, which those who are said to have seen, are
said also to have denied seeing; narratives without authorities, facts
without dates, and records without names.   In vain do the so-called
disciples of Jesus point to the passages in Josephus and Tacitus;[1]
in vain do they point to the spot on which he was crucified; to the
fragments of the true cross, or the nails with which he was pierced,
and to the *tomb* in which he was laid.   Others have done as much
for scores of *mythological personages* who never lived in the flesh.
Did not Damis, the beloved disciple of Apollonius of Tyana, while
on his way to India, see, on Mt. Caucasus, the identical chains with
which Prometheus had been bound to the rocks?   Did not the
Scythians[2] say that Hercules had visited their country? and did
they not show the print of his foot upon a rock to substantiate their
story?[3]   Was not his *tomb* to be seen at Cadiz, where his *bones* were
shown?[4]   Was not the *tomb* of Bacchus to be seen in Greece?[5]
Was not the *tomb* of Apollo to be seen at Delphi?[6]   Was not the
tomb of Achilles to be seen at Dodona, where Alexander the Great
honored it by placing a crown upon it?[7]   Was not the *tomb* of Æsculapius to be seen in Arcadia, in a grove consecrated to him, near
the river Lusius?[8]   Was not the *tomb* of Deucalion—he who was
saved from the Deluge—long pointed out near the sanctuary of
Olympian Jove, in Athens?[9]   Was not the *tomb* of Osiris to be
seen in Egypt, where, at stated seasons, the priests went in solemn
procession, and covered it with flowers?[10]   Was not the tomb of
Jonah—he who was "swallowed up by a big fish"—to be seen at
Nebi-Yunus, near Mosul?[11]   Are not the *tombs* of Adam, Eve, Cain,
Abel, Seth, Abraham, and other Old Testament characters, to be
seen even at the present day?[12]   And did not the Emperor Constantine dedicate a beautiful church over the *tomb* of St. George, the
warrior saint?[13]   Of what value, then, is such evidence of the existence of such an individual as Jesus of Nazareth?   The fact is, "the
records of his life are so very scanty, and these have been so shaped
and colored and modified by the hands of ignorance and superstition

---

[1] This subject is considered in Appendix D.
[2] *Scythia* was a name employed in ancient
times, to denote a vast, indefinite, and almost
unknown territory north and east of the Black
Sea, the Caspian, and the Sea of Aral.
[3] See Herodotus, book 4, ch. 82.
[4] See Dupuis, p. 264.
[5] See Knight's Anct. Art and Mythology, p.
96, and Mysteries of Adoni, p. 90.

[6] See Dupuis, p. 264.
[7] See Bell's Pantheon, vol. i. p. 7.
[8] See Ibid. vol. i. p. 27.
[9] Ibid.
[10] Ibid. vol. i. p. 2, and Bonwick, p. 155.
[11] See Chambers, art. "Jonah."
[12] See Bible for Learners, vol. i. p. 152, and
Goldzhier, p. 280.
[13] See Curious Myths, p. 264.

and party prejudice and ecclesiastical purpose, that it is hard to be sure of the original outlines."

In the first two centuries the professors of Christianity were divided into many sects, but these might be all resolved into two divisions—one consisting of Nazarenes, Ebionites, and orthodox; the other of *Gnostics*, under which all the remaining sects arranged themselves. The former are supposed to have believed in Jesus crucified, in the common, literal acceptation of the term; the latter —believers in the *Christ* as an *Æon*—though they admitted the crucifixion, considered it to have been in some *mystic* way—perhaps what might be called *spiritualiter*, as it is called in the Revelation: but notwithstanding the different opinions they held, they all denied that *the Christ* did really die, in the literal acceptation of the term, on the cross.[1] The Gnostic, or Oriental, Christians undoubtedly took their doctrine from the *Indian crucifixion*[2] (of which we have treated in Chapters XX. and XXXIX.), as well as many other tenets with which we have found the Christian Church deeply tainted. They held that:

"To deliver the soul, a captive in darkness, the 'Prince of Light,' the 'Genius of the Sun,' charged with the redemption of the intellectual world, of which the Sun is the type, manifested itself among men; that the light appeared in the darkness, but the darkness comprehended it not; that, in fact, light could not unite with darkness; it put on only the appearance of the human body; that at the crucifixion Christ Jesus only *appeared* to suffer. His person having disappeared, the bystanders saw in his place a cross of light, over which a celestial voice proclaimed these words; 'The Cross of Light is called Logos, Christos, the Gate, the Joy.'"

Several of the texts of the Gospel histories were quoted with great plausibility by the Gnostics in support of their doctrine. The story of Jesus passing through the midst of the Jews when they were about to cast him headlong from the brow of a hill (Luke iv. 29, 30), and when they were going to stone him (John iii. 59; x. 31, 39), were examples not easily refuted.

The Manichean Christian Bishop Faustus expresses himself in the following manner:

"Do you receive the gospel? (ask ye). Undoubtedly I do! Why then,

---

[1] "Whilst, in one part of the Christian world, the chief objects of interest were the *human* nature and *human* life of Jesus, in another part of the Christian world the views taken of his person because so *idealistic*, that his humanity *was reduced to a phantom without reality*. The various *Gnostic* systems generally agreed in saying that the Christ was an *Æon*, the redeemer of the *spirits* of men, and that he had little or no contact with their corporeal nature." (A. Réville: Hist. of the Dogma of the Deity of Jesus.)

[2] Epiphanius says that there were TWENTY heresies BEFORE CHRIST, and there can be no doubt that there is much truth in the observation, for most of the rites and doctrines of the Christians of all sects existed before the time of Jesus of Nazareth.

you also admit that Christ was born ? Not so ; for it by no means follows that in believing the gospel, I should therefore believe that Christ was born ! Do you then think that he was of the Virgin Mary ? Manes hath said, ' Far be it that I should ever own that Our Lord Jesus Christ . . . . ' " etc. [1]

Tertullian's manner of reasoning on the evidences of Christianity is also in the same vein, as we saw in our last chapter.[2]

Mr. King, speaking of the Gnostic Christians, says :

" Their chief doctrines had been held for centuries before (their time) in many of the cities in *Asia Minor*.   There, it is probable, they first came into existence as *Mystæ*, upon the establishment of direct intercourse with *India*, under the Seleucidæ and Ptolemies.   The college of *Essenes* and *Megabyzæ* at Ephesus, the *Orphics* of Thrace, the *Curets* of Crete, *are all merely branches of one antique and common religion, and that originally Asiatic.*"[3]

These early Christian Mystics are alluded to in several instances in the New Testament.   For example :

" Every spirit that confesseth that Jesus Christ is come *in the flesh* is of God ; and every spirit that confesseth not that Jesus Christ is come in the flesh is not of God."[4]   For many deceivers are entered into the world, who confess not that Jesus Christ is come in the flesh."[5]

This is language that could not have been used, if the reality of Christ Jesus' existence as a man could not have been denied, or, it would certainly seem, if the apostle himself had been able to give any evidence whatever of the claim.

The quarrels on this subject lasted for a long time among the early Christians.   *Hermas*, speaking of this, says to the brethren :

" Take heed, my children, that your dissensions deprive you not of your lives. How will ye instruct the elect of God, when ye yourselves want correction ? Wherefore admonish one another, and be at peace among yourselves ; that I, standing before your father, may give an account of you unto the Lord."[6]

Ignatius, in his Epistle to the Smyrnæans, says :[7]

" Only in the name of Jesus Christ, I undergo all, to suffer together with him ; he who was made a perfect man strengthening me.   *Whom some, not knowing, do deny* ; or rather have been denied by him, being the advocates of death, rather than of the truth.   Whom neither the prophecies, nor the law of Moses, have persuaded ; *nor the Gospel itself even to this day*, nor the sufferings

---

[1] " Accipis avengelium ? et maxime. Proinde ergo et natum accipis Christum. Non ita est.   Neque enim sequitur ut si evangelium accipio, idcirco et natum accipiam Christum. Ergo non putas eum ex Maria Virgine esse ? Manes dixit, Absit ut Dominum nostrum Jesum Christum per naturalia pudenda mulieris descendisse confitear." (Lardner's Works, vol. iv. p. 20.)

[2] " I maintain," says he, " that the Son of God was *born* ; why am I not ashamed of maintaining such a thing ? Why ? because it is

itself a shameful thing—I maintain that the Son of God *died* : well, *that* is wholly credible because it is monstrously absurd.   I maintain that after having been buried, *he rose again* : and *that* I take to be absolutely true, *because it was manifestly impossible.*"

[3] King's Gnostics, p. 1.
[4] I. John, iv. 2, 3.
[5] II. John, 7.
[6] 1st Book Hermas : Apoc , ch. iii.
[7] Chapter II.

of any one of us. *For they think also the same thing of us ;* for what does a man profit me, if he shall praise me, and blaspheme my Lord ; *not confessing that he was truly made man !* "

In his Epistle to the Philadelphians he says :[1]

"I have heard of some who say, *unless I find it written in the originals,* I will not believe it to be written in the Gospel. And when I said, It is written, they answered what lay before them in their corrupted copies."

Polycarp, in his Epistle to the Philippians, says :[2]

"Whosoever does not confess that Jesus Christ is come in the flesh, he is Antichrist : *and whosoever does not confess his sufferings upon the cross,* is from the devil. And whosoever perverts the oracles of the Lord to his own lusts ; and says that there shall neither be any resurrection, nor judgment, he is the first-born of Satan."

Ignatius says to the Magnesians :[3]

"Be not deceived with strange doctrines ; nor with old fables which are un-profitable. For if we still continue to live according to the Jewish law, we do confess ourselves *not* to have received grace. For even the most holy prophets lived according to Jesus Christ. . . . Wherefore if they who were brought up in these ancient laws came nevertheless to the newness of hope ; no longer ob-serving Sabbaths, but keeping the Lord's Day, in which also our life is sprung up by him, and through his death, *whom yet some deny.* By which *mystery* we have been brought to believe, and therefore wait that we may be found the disciples of Jesus Christ, our only master. . . . . These things, my beloved, I write unto you, not that I know of any among you *that be under this error ;* but as one of the least among you, I am desirous to forewarn you that ye fall not into the snares of vain doctrine."

After reading this we can say with the writer of Timothy,[4] "Without controversy, great is the MYSTERY of godliness."

Beside those who denied that Christ Jesus had ever been mani-fest *in the flesh,* there were others who denied that *he* had been crucified.[5] This is seen from the words of Justin Martyr, in his *Apology* for the Christian Religion, written A. D. 141, where he says :

"As to the *objection* to *our* Jesus's being crucified, I say, suffering was com-mon to all the Sons of Jove."[6]

This is as much as to say : "*You* Pagans claim that *your* incar-nate gods and *Saviours* suffered and died, then why should not *we* claim the same for *our* Saviour ?"

---

[1] Chapter II.
[2] Chapter III.
[3] Chapter III.
[4] I. Timothy, iii. 16.
[5] Irenæus, speaking of them, says : "They hold that men ought not to confess him who *was crucified,* but him who came in the form of man, *and was supposed to be crucified,* and was called Jesus." (See Lardner : vol. viii. p. 353.) They could not conceive of "the first-begotten Son of God" being put to death on a cross, and suffering like an ordinary being, so they thought Simon of Cyrene must have been substituted for him, as the ram was substituted in the place of Isaac. (See Ibid. p. 357.)
[6] Apol. 1, ch. xxi.

The *Koran*, referring to the *Jews*, says :

"They have not believed in Jesus, and have spoken against Mary a grievous calumny, and have said: ' Verily we have slain Christ Jesus, the son of Mary ' (the apostle of God). *Yet they slew him not, neither crucified him, but he was represented by one in his likeness. And verily they who disagreed concerning him were in a doubt as to this matter, and had no sure knowledge thereof, but followed only an uncertain opinion."*[1]

This passage alone, from the Mohammedan Bible, is sufficient to show, if other evidence were wanting, that the early Christians "disagreed concerning him," and that "they had no sure knowledge thereof, but followed only an uncertain opinion."

In the books which are *now* called *Apocryphal,* but which *were* the most quoted, and of equal authority with the others, and which were *voted not* the word of God—for obvious reasons—and were therefore cast out of the canon, we find many allusions to the strife among the early Christians. For instance ; in the " First Epistle of Clement to the Corinthians,"[2] we read as follows :

" Wherefore are there ·strifes, and anger, and divisions, and schisms, and wars, among us ? . . . Why do we rend and tear in pieces the members of Christ, and raise seditions against our own body ? and are come to such a height of madness, as to forget that we are members one of another."

In his Epistle to the Trallians, Ignatius says :[3]

" I exhort you, or rather not I, but the love of Jesus Christ, that ye use none but Christian nourishment ; abstaining from pasture which is of another kind. I mean *Heresy.* For they that are heretics, confound together the doctrine of Jesus Christ with their own poison ; whilst they seem worthy of belief. . . . Stop your ears, therefore, as often as any one shall speak contrary to Jesus Christ, who was of the race of David, of the Virgin Mary. Who was *truly* born, and did eat and drink; was *truly* persecuted under Pontius Pilate; was *truly* crucified and dead; both those in heaven and on earth, and under the earth, being spectators of it. . . . But if, as some who are atheists, that is to say, infidels, pretend, *that he only seemed to suffer,* why then am I bound ? Why do I desire to fight with beasts ? Therefore do I die in vain."

We find St. Paul, the very first Apostle of the Gentiles, expressly avowing that *he was made a minister of the gospel, which had already been preached to every creature under heaven,*[4] and preaching *a God manifest in the flesh,* who had been *believed on in the world,*[5] therefore, *before the commencement of his ministry;* and who could not have been the man of Nazareth, who had certainly not been preached, *at that time,* nor generally believed on in the world, till ages after that time.[6] We find also that :

---

[1] Koran, ch. iv.
[2] Chapter XX.
[3] Chapter II.

[4] Col. i. 23.
[5] I. Timothy, iii. 16.
[6] The authenticity of these Epistles has

1. This Paul owns himself a *deacon*, the lowest ecclesiastical grade of the *Therapeutan* church.

2. The Gospel of which these Epistles speak, had been extensively preached and fully established before the time of Jesus, by the Therapeuts or Essenes, who believed in the doctrine of the Angel-Messiah, the Æon from heaven.[1]

Leo the Great, so-called (A. D. 440–461), writes thus:

"Let those who with impious murmurings find fault with the Divine dispensations, and who complain about the *lateness* of our Lord's nativity, cease from their grievances, as if what was *carried out* in later ages of the world, had not been impending *in time past*. . . .

"What the Apostles preached, the prophets (in Israel) had announced before, and what has *always been (universally) believed*, cannot be said to have been *fulfilled* too late. By this delay of his work of salvation, the wisdom and love of God have only made us more fitted for his call ; so that, *what had been announced before by many Signs and Words and Mysteries during so many centuries*, should not be doubtful or uncertain in the days of the gospel. . . God has not provided for the interests of men by a *new council* or by a *late compassion ;* but he had instituted from the beginning for all men, *one and the same path of salvation*."[2]

This is equivalent to saying that, "God, in his '*late compassion*,' has sent his Son, Christ Jesus, to save *us*, therefore do not complain or 'murmur.' about 'the lateness of his coming,' for the Lord has already provided for those who *preceded us;* he has given them '*the same path of salvation*.' by sending to *them*, as he has sent to *us*, a *Redeemer* and a *Saviour*."

Justin Martyr, in his dialogue with Typho,[3] makes a similar confession (as we have already seen in our last chapter), wherein he says that there exists not a people, civilized or semi-civilized, who have not offered up prayers in the name of a *crucified Saviour* to the Father and Creator of all things.

Add to this medley the fact that St. Irenæus (A. D. 192), one of the most celebrated, most respected, and most quoted of the early Christian Fathers, tells us on the authority of his master, Polycarp, who had it from St. John himself, and from all the old people of Asia, that Jesus was not crucified at the time stated in the Gospels, but that he lived to be nearly *fifty* years old. The passage which, most fortunately, has escaped the destroyers of all such evidence, is to be found in Irenæus' second book against heresies,[4] of which the following is a portion:

---

been freely questioned, even by the most conservative critics.

[1] See Bunsen's Angel-Messiah, and Chapter XXXVII, this work.

[2] Quoted by Max Müller : The Science of Relig., p. 228.

[3] Ch. cxvii.

[4] Ch. xxii.

"As the chief part of thirty years belongs to youth, and every one will confess him to be such till the fortieth year: but from the fortieth year to the fiftieth he declines into old age, *which our Lord (Jesus) having attained he taught us the Gospel, and all the elders who, in Asia, assembled with John, the disciple of the Lord, testify; and as John himself had taught them.* And he (John ?) remained with them till the time of Trajan. And some of them saw not only John but other Apostles, *and heard the same thing from them, and bear the same testimony to this revelation.*"

The escape of this passage from the destroyers can be accounted for only in the same way as the passage of Minucius Felix (quoted in Chapter XX.) concerning the Pagans worshiping a crucifix. These two passages escaped from among, probably, hundreds destroyed, of which we know nothing, under the decrees of the emperors, yet remaining, by which they were ordered to be destroyed.

In John viii. 56, Jesus is made to say to the Jews: "Your father Abraham rejoiced to see my day: and he saw it and was glad." Then said the Jews unto him: "Thou art not yet *fifty* years old, and hast thou seen Abraham ?"

If Jesus was then but about *thirty* years of age, the Jews would evidently have said: "thou art not yet *forty* years old," and would not have been likely to say: "thou art not yet *fifty* years old," unless he was past forty.

There was a tradition current among the early Christians, that *Annas* was high-priest when Jesus was crucified. This is evident from the *Acts.*[1] Now, Annas, or Ananias, *was not high-priest until about the year* 48 A. D.;[2] therefore, if Jesus was crucified at that time he must have been about *fifty* years of age;[3] but, as we remarked elsewhere, there exists, outside of the New Testament, no evidence whatever, in book, inscription, or monument, that Jesus of Nazareth was either scourged or crucified under Pontius Pilate. Josephus, Tacitus, Plinius, Philo, nor any of their contemporaries, ever refer to the fact of this crucifixion, or express any belief thereon.[4] In the Talmud—the book containing Jewish traditions —Jesus is not referred to as the "crucified one," but as the "hanged one,"[5] while elsewhere it is narrated he was *stoned* to death ; so that it is evident they were ignorant of the manner of death which he suffered.[6]

---

[1] Ch. iv. 5.

[2] Josephus : Antiq., b. xx. ch. v. 2.

[3] It is true there was another Annas high-priest at Jerusalem, but this was when *Gratus* was procurator of Judea, some twelve or fifteen years before Pontius Pilate held the same office. (See Josephus : Antiq., book xviii. ch. ii. 3.)

[4] See Appendix D.

[5] See the Martyrdom of Jesus, p. 100.

[6] According to Dio Cassius, Plutarch, Strabo and others, there existed, in the time of Herod, among the Roman Syrian heathens, a widespread and deep sympathy for a "*Crucified King of the Jews.*" This was the youngest son of Aristobul, the heroic Maccabee. In the year 43 B. C., we find this young man—*Antigonus*—in Palestine claiming the crown, his cause having been declared just by Julius Cæsar. Allied with the Parthians, he main-

In *Sanhedr.* 43 *a*, Jesus is said to have had five disciples, among whom were Mattheaus and Thaddeus. He is called "That Man," "The Nazarine," "The Fool," and "The Hung." Thus Aben Ezra says that Constantine put on his *labarum* "a figure of the hung;" and, according to R. Bechai, the Christians were called "Worshipers of the Hung."

Little is said about Jesus in the *Talmud*, except that he was a scholar of Joshua Ben Perachiah (who lived a century before the time assigned by the Christians for the birth of Jesus), accompanied him into Egypt, there learned magic, and was a seducer of the people, and was finally put to death by being stoned, and then hung as a blasphemer.

"The conclusion is, that no clearly defined traces of the personal Jesus remain on the surface, or beneath the surface, of Christendom. The silence of Josephus and other secular historians may be accounted for without falling back on a theory of hostility or contempt.' The *Christ*-idea cannot be spared from Christian development, but the personal Jesus, in some measure, can be."

"The person of Jesus, though it may have been immense, is indistinct. That a great character was there may be conceded; but precisely wherein the character was great, is left to our *conjecture.* Of the eminent persons who have swayed the spiritual destinies of mankind, none has more completely disappeared from the critical view. The ideal image which Christians have, for nearly two thousand years, worshiped under the name of Jesus, has no authentic, distinctly visible, counterpart in history."

"His followers have gone on with the process of idealization, placing him higher and higher; making his personal existence more and more essential; insisting more and more urgently on the necessity of private intercourse with him; letting the Father subside into the background, as an 'effluence,' and the Holy Ghost lapse from individual identity into impersonal influence, in order that he

---

tained himself in his royal position for six years against Herod and Mark Antony. At last, after a heroic life and reign, he fell in the hands of this Roman. "*Antony now gave the kingdom to a certain Herod, and, having stretched Antigonus on a cross and scourged him, a thing never done before to any other king by the Romans, he put him to death.*" (Dio Cassius, book xlix. p. 405.) The fact that all prominent historians of those days mention this extraordinary occurrence, and the manner they did it, show that 't was considered one of Mark Antony's worst

crimes: and that the sympathy with the "Crucified King" was wide-spread and profound. (See The Martyrdom of Jesus of Nazareth, p. 106.)

Some writers think that there is a connection between this and the Gospel story; that they, in a certain measure, put Jesus in the place of Antigonus, just as they put Herod in the place of Kansa. (See Chapter XVIII.)

' Canon Farrar thinks that Josephus silence on the subject of Jesus and Christianity, was as deliberate as it was dishonest. (See his Life of Christ, vol. i. p. 63.)

might be all in all as Regenerator and Saviour. From age to age the personal Jesus has been made the object of an extreme adoration, till now *faith* in the living Christ is the heart of the Gospel; philosophy, science, culture, humanity are thrust resolutely aside, and the great teachers of the age are extinguished in order that *his* light may shine." But, as Mr. Frothingham remarks, in "The Cradle of the Christ": "In the order of experience, historical and biographical truth is discovered by stripping off layer after layer of exaggeration, and going back to the statements of contemporaries. As a rule, figures are *reduced*, not enlarged, by criticism. The influence of admiration is recognized as distorting and falsifying, while exalting. The process of legend-making begins immediately, goes on rapidly and with accelerating speed, and must be liberally allowed for by the seeker after truth. In scores of instances the historical individual turns out to be very much smaller than he was painted by his terrified or loving worshipers. In no single case has it been established that he was greater, or as great. It is, no doubt, conceivable that such a case should occur, but it never has occurred, in known instances, and cannot be presumed to have occurred in any particular instance. The presumptions are against the correctness of the glorified image. The disposition to exaggerate is so much stronger than the disposition to underrate, that even really great men are placed higher than they belong oftener than lower. The historical method works backwards. Knowledge shrinks the man."[1]

---

[1] Many examples might be cited to confirm this view, but the case of *Joseph Smith*, in our own time and country, will suffice.

The Mormons regard him very much as Christians regard Jesus; as the Mohammedans do Mohammed; or as the Buddhists do Buddha. A coarse sort of religious feeling and fervor appears to have been in Smith's nature. He seems, from all accounts, to have been cracked on theology, as so many zealots have been, and cracked to such an extent that his early acquaintances regarded him as a downright fanatic.

The common view that he was an impostor is not sustained by what is known of him. He was, in all probability, of unbalanced mind, a monomaniac, as most prophets have been; but there is no reason to think that he did not believe in himself, and substantially in what he taught. He has declared that, when he was about fifteen, he began to reflect on the importance of being prepared for a future state. He went from one church to another without finding anything to satisfy the hunger of his soul, consequently, he retired into himself; he

sought solitude; he spent hours and days in meditation and prayer, after the true manner of all accredited saints, and was soon repaid by the visits of angels. One of these came to him when he was but eighteen years old, and the house in which he was seemed filled with consuming fire. The presence—he styles it a personage—had a pace like lightning, and pro claimed himself to be an angel of the Lord. He vouchsafed to Smith a vast deal of highly important information of a celestial order. He told him that his (Smith's) prayers had been heard, and his sins forgiven; that the covenant which the Almighty had made with the old Jews was to be fulfilled; that the introductory work for the second coming of Christ was now to begin; that the hour for the preaching of the gospel in its purity to all peoples was at hand, and that Smith was to be an instrument in the hands of God, to further the divine purpose in the new dispensation. The celestial stranger also furnished him with a sketch of the origin, progress, laws and civilization of the American aboriginals, and declared that the blessing of heaven had finally been with-

As we are allowed to *conjecture* as to what is true in the Gospel history, we shall now do so.

The death of Herod, which occurred a few years before the time assigned for the birth of Jesus, was followed by frightful social and political convulsions in Judea. For two or three years all the elements of disorder were abroad. Between pretenders to the vacant throne of Herod, *and aspirants to the Messianic throne of David*, Judea was torn and devastated. Revolt assumed the wildest form, the higher enthusiasm of faith yielded to the lower fury of *fanaticism;* the celestial visions of a kingdom of heaven were completely banished by the smoke and flame of political hate. *Claimant after claimant of the dangerous supremacy of the Messiah appeared, pitched a camp in the wilderness, raised the banner, gathered a*

drawn from them. To Smith was communicated the momentous circumstance that certain plates containing an abridgment of the records of the aboriginals and ancient prophets, who had lived on this continent, were hidden in a hill near Palmyra. The prophet was counseled to go there and look at them, and did so. Not being holy enough to possess them as yet, he passed some months in spiritual probation, after which the records were put into his keeping. These had been prepared, it is claimed, by a prophet called Mormon, who had been ordained by God for the purpose, and to conceal them until he should produce them for the benefit of the faithful, and unite them with the Bible for the achievement of his will. They form the celebrated Book of Mormon—whence the name Mormon—and are esteemed by the Latter-Day Saints as of equal authority with the Old and New Testaments, and as an indispensable supplement thereto, because they include God's disclosures to the Mormon world. These precious records were sealed up and deposited A.D. 420 in the place where Smith had viewed them by the direction of the angel.

The records were, it is held, in the reformed Egyptian tongue, and Smith translated them through the inspiration of the angel, and one Oliver Cowdrey wrote down the translation as reported by the God-possessed Joseph. This translation was published in 1830, and its divine origin was attested by a dozen persons—all relatives and friends of Smith. Only these have ever pretended to see the original plates, which have already become traditional. The plates have been frequently called for by skeptics, but all in vain. Naturally, warm controversy arose concerning the authenticity of the Book of Mormon, and disbelievers have asserted that they have indubitable evidence that it is, with the exception of various unlettered interpolations, principally borrowed from a queer,

rhapsodical romance written by an eccentric ex-clergyman named Solomon Spalding.

Smith and his disciples were ridiculed and socially persecuted; but they seemed to be ardently earnest, and continued to preach their creed, which was to the effect that the millennium was at hand; that our aboriginals were to be converted, and that the New Jerusalem—the last residence and home of the saints—was to be near the centre of this continent. The Vermont prophet, later on, was repeatedly mobbed, even shot at. His narrow escapes were construed as interpositions of divine providence, but he displayed perfect coolness and intrepidity through all his trials. The Church of Jesus Christ of the Latter-Day Saints was first established in the spring of 1830 at Manchester, N. Y.; but it awoke such fierce opposition, particularly from the orthodox, many of them preachers, that Smith and his associates deemed it prudent to move farther west. They established themselves at Kirtland, O., and won there many converts. Hostility to them still continued, and grew so fierce that the body transferred itself to Missouri, and next to Illinois, settling in the latter state near the village of Commerce, which was renamed Nauvoo.

The Governor and Legislature of Illinois favored the Mormons, but the anti-Mormons made war on them in every way, and the custom of "sealing wives," which is yet mysterious to the Gentiles, caused serious outbreaks, and resulted in the incarceration of the prophet and his brother Hiram at Carthage. Fearing that the two might be released by the authorities, a band of ruffians broke into the jail, in the summer of 1844, and murdered them in cold blood. This was most fortunate for the memory of Smith and for his doctrines. It placed him in the light of a holy martyr, and lent to them a dignity and vitality they had never before enjoyed.

force, was attacked, defeated, banished or crucified; but *the frenzy did not abate.*

The popular aspect of the Messianic hope was *political,* not re-ligious or moral. The name *Messiah* was synonymous with *King of the Jews;* it suggested *political designs and aspirations.* The assumption of that character by any individual drew on him the vigilance of the police.

That Jesus of Nazareth assumed the character of *"Messiah,"* as did many before and after him, and that his crucifixion[1] was simply an act of the law on *political grounds,* just as it was in the case of other so-called *Messiahs,* we believe to be the truth of the matter.[2]

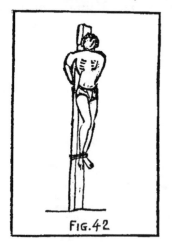

FIG. 42

FIG. 43

"He is represented as being a native of *Galilee,* the *insurgent dis-trict of the country;* nurtured, if not born, in Nazareth, one of its chief cities; reared as a youth amid traditions of patriotic devotion, and amid scenes associated with heroic dreams and endeavors. The Galileans were restless, excitable people, beyond the reach of con-ventionalities, remote from the centre of power, ecclesiastical and secular, simple in their lives, bold of speech, independent in thought,

[1] When we speak of Jesus being *crucified,* we do not intend to convey the idea that he was put to death on a cross of the *form* adopted by Christians. This cross was the symbol of *life and immortality* among our heathen an-cestors (see Chapter XXXIII.), and in adopting *Pagan religious symbols,* and baptizing them anew, the Christians took this along with others. The crucifixion was not a symbol of the *earliest* church; no trace of it can be found in the Catacombs. Some of the earliest that did appear, however, are similar to figures No. 42 and No. 43, above, which represent two of the

modes in which the Romans crucified their slaves and criminals. (See Chapter XX., on the Crucifixion of Jesus.)

[2] According to the Matthew and Mark nar-rators, Jesus' head was *anointed* while sitting at table in the house of Simon the leper. Now, this practice was common among the kings of Israel. It was the sign and symbol of royalty. The word "*Messiah*" signifies the "Anointed One," and none of the kings of Israel were styled the Messiah unless anointed. (See **The Martyrdom of Jesus of Nazareth, p. 42.**)

thoroughgoing in the sort of radicalism that is common among people who live 'out of the world,' who have leisure to discuss the exciting topics of the day, but too little knowledge, culture, or sense of social responsibility to discuss them soundly. Their mental discontent and moral intractability were proverbial. They were belligerents. The Romans had more trouble with them than with the natives of any other province. *The Messiahs all started out from Galilee, and never failed to collect followers round their standard.* The Galileans, more than others, lived in the anticipation of the Deliverer. The reference of the Messiah to Galilee is therefore already an indication of the character he is to assume."

To show the state the country must have been in at that time, we will quote an incident or two from Josephus.

A religious enthusiast called the Samaritans together upon Mount Gerizim, and assured them that he would work a miracle. "So they came thither *armed*, and thought the discourse of the man probable; and as they abode at a certain village, which was called Tirathaba, they got the rest together of them, and desired to go up the mountain in a great multitude together: but Pilate prevented their going up, by seizing upon the roads by a great band of horsemen and footmen, who fell upon those who were gotten together in the village; and when it came to an action, some of them they slew, and others of them they put to flight, and took a great many alive, the principal of whom, and also the most potent of those that fled away, Pilate ordered to be slain."[1]

Not long before this Pilate pillaged the temple treasury, and used the "sacred money" to bring a current of water to Jerusalem. The *Jews* were displeased with this, "and many ten thousands of the people got together and made a clamor against him. Some of them used reproaches, and abused the man, as crowds of such people usually do. So he habited a great number of his soldiers in their habits, who carried daggers under their garments, and sent them to a place where they might surround them. So he bade the Jews himself go away; but they boldly casting reproaches upon him, he gave the soldiers that signal which had been beforehand agreed on; who laid upon them with much greater blows than Pilate had commanded them, and equally punished those that were tumultuous, and those that were not; nor did they spare them in the least: and since the people were unarmed, and were caught by men prepared for what they were about, there were a great number

---

[1] Josephus: Antiquities, book xviii. ch. iv. 1.

of them slain by this means, and others ran away wounded. And thus an end was put to this sedition."[1]

It was such deeds as these, inflicted upon the Jews by their oppressors, that made them think of the promised Messiah who was to deliver them from bondage, and which made many zealous fanatics imagine themselves to be "He who should come."[2]

There is reason to believe, as we have said, that Jesus of Nazareth assumed the title of "*Messiah.*" His age was throbbing and bursting with suppressed energy. The pressure of the Roman Empire was required to keep it down. "The Messianic hope had such vitality that it condensed into moments the moral result of ages. The common people were watching to see the heavens open, interpreted peals of thunder as angel voices, and saw divine potents in the flight of birds. Mothers dreamed their boys would be Messiah. The wildest preacher drew a crowd. The heart of the nation swelled big with the conviction that the hour of destiny was about to strike, that the kingdom of heaven was at hand. *The crown was ready for any kingly head that might assume it.*"[3]

The actions of this man, throughout his public career, we believe to be those of a zealot whose zeal overrode considerations of wisdom; in fact, a Galilean fanatic. Pilate condemns him reluctantly, feeling that he is a harmless visionary, but is obliged to condemn him as one of the many who persistently claimed to be the "*Messiah,*" or "*King of the Jews,*" an enemy of Cæsar, an instrument against the empire, a pretender to the throne, a bold inciter to rebellion. The death he undergoes is the death of the traitor and mutineer,[4] the death that was inflicted on many such claimants, the death that would have been decreed to Judas the Galilean,[5] had he been captured, and that was inflicted on thousands of his deluded followers. *It was the Romans, then, who crucified the man Jesus, and not the Jews.*

[1] Josephus : Antiquities, book xviii. chap. iii. 2.

[2] "From the death of Herod, 4 B. C., to the death of Bar-Cochba, 132 A.D., no less than *fifty* different enthusiasts set up as the Messiah, and obtained more or less following." (John W. Chadwick.)

[3] "There was, at *this time,* a prevalent expectation that some remarkable personage was about to appear in Judea. The Jews were anxiously looking for the coming of the MESSIAH. This personage, they supposed, would be a *temporal prince,* and they were expecting that he would deliver them from Roman bondage." (Albert Barnes : Notes, vol. i. p. 7.)

"The central and dominant characteristic of the teaching of the Rabbis, was the certain advent of a great national Deliverer—the MESSIAH. . . . The national mind had become so inflammable, by constant brooding on this one theme, *that any bold spirit rising in revolt against the Roman power, could find an army of fierce disciples who trusted that it should be he who would redeem Israel.*" (Geikie : The Life of Christ, vol. i. p. 79.)

[4] "The penalty of *crucifixion,* according to Roman law and custom, was inflicted on slaves, and in the provinces *on rebels only.*" (The Martyrdom of Jesus, p. 96.)

[5] Judas, the *Gaulonite* or *Galilean,* as Josephus calls him, declared, when Cyrenius came to tax the Jewish people, that "this taxation was no better than an introduction to

"In the Roman law the *State* is the main object, for which the individual must live and die, with or against his will. In Jewish law, the *person* is made the main object, for which the State must live and die ; because the fundamental idea of the Roman law is power, and the fundamental idea of Jewish law is justice."[1] *Therefore Caiaphas and his conspirators did not act from the Jewish standpoint.* They represented *Rome*, her principles, interest, and barbarous caprices.[2] Not one point in the whole trial agrees with Jewish laws and custom.[3] It is impossible to save it ; it must be given up as a transparent and unskilled invention of a *Gentile Christian*, who knew nothing of Jewish law and custom, and was ignorant of the state of civilization in Palestine, in the time of Jesus.

Jesus had been proclaimed the "*Messiah*," the "*Ruler of the Jews*," and the restorer of the kingdom of heaven. No Roman ear could understand these pretensions, otherwise than in their rebellious sense. That Pontius Pilate certainly understood under the title, "*Messiah*," the king (the political chief of the nation), is evident from the subscription of the cross, "Jesus of Nazareth, King of the Jews," which he did not remove in spite of all protestations of the Jews. There is only one point in which the *four* Gospels agree, and that is, that early in the morning Jesus was delivered over to the *Roman governor*, Pilate ; that he was accused of high-treason against *Rome*—having been proclaimed King of the Jews —and that in consequence thereof he was condemned first to be

---

slavery," and exhorted the nation to assert their liberty. He therefore prevailed upon his countrymen to revolt. (See Josephus : Antiq., b. xviii. ch. i. 1, and Wars of the Jews, b. ii. ch. viii. 1.)

[1] The Martyrdom of Jesus of Nazareth, p. 30.

[2] "That the High Council did accuse Jesus, I suppose no one will doubt ; and since they could neither wish or expect the Roman Governor to make himself judge of *their sacred law*, it becomes certain that their accusation was *purely political*, and took such a form as this : ' He has accepted tumultuous shouts that he is the legitimate and predicted *King of Israel*, and in this character has ridden into Jerusalem with the forms of state understood to be *royal* and *sacred ;* with what purpose, we ask, if not to overturn *our* institutions, and *your* dominion ?' If Jesus spoke, at the crisis which Matthew represents, the virulent speech attributed to him (Matt. xxiii.), we may well believe that this gave a new incentive to the rulers ; for it is such as ne government in Europe would over-

look or forgive ; *but they are not likely to have expected Pilate to care for any conduct which might be called an ecclesiastical broil.* The assumption of *royalty* was clearly the point of their attack. Even the mildest man among them may have thought his conduct dangerous and needing repression." (Francis W. Newman, "What is Christianity without Christ ?")

According to the Synoptic Gospels, Jesus was completely innocent of the charge which has sometimes been brought against him, *that he wished to be considered as a God come down to earth.* His enemies certainly would not have failed to make such a pretension the basis and the continual theme of their accusations, if it had been possible to do so. *The two grounds upon which he was brought before the Sanhedrim were, first, the bold words he was supposed to have spoken about the temple ; and, secondly and chiefly, the fact that he claimed to be the Messiah*, i. e., "*The King of the Jews.*" (Albert Réville : "The Doctrine of the Dogma of the Deity of Jesus," p. 7.)

[3] See The Martyrdom of Jesus, p. 30.

scourged, and then to be crucified; all of which was done in hot haste. *In all other points the narratives of the Evangelists differ widely*, and so essentially that one story cannot be made of the four accounts; nor can any particular points stand the test of historical criticism, and vindicate its substantiality as a fact.

The Jews could not have crucified Jesus, *according to their laws*, if they had inflicted on him the highest penalty of the law, since crucifixion was *exclusively Roman.*[1] If the priests, elders, Pharisees, Jews, or all of them wanted Jesus out of the way so badly, why did they not have him quietly put to death while he was in their power, and done at once. The writer of the fourth Gospel seems to have understood this difficulty, and informs us that they could not kill him, *because he had prophesied what death he should die;* so he could die no other. It was dire necessity, that the heathen symbol of life and immortality—the cross[2]—should be brought to honor among the early Christians, and Jesus had to die on the cross (the Roman Gibbet), *according to John*[3] simply because it was so *prophesied.* The fact is, the crucifixion story, like the symbol of the crucifix itself, *came from abroad.*[4] It was told with the avowed intention of exonerating the Romans, and criminating the Jews, so they make the Roman governor take water, "and wash his hands before the multitude, saying, *I* am innocent of the blood of this *just person:* see *ye* to it." To be sure of their case, they make the Jews say: "*His blood be on us, and on our children.*"[5]

"Another fact is this. Just at the period of time when misfortune and ruination befell the Jews most severely, in the first post-apostolic generation, the Christians were most active in making proselytes among Gentiles. To have then preached that *a crucified Jewish Rabbi of Galilee* was their Saviour, would have sounded supremely ridiculous to those heathens. To have added thereto, that the said Rabbi was crucified by command of a Roman Governor, because he had been proclaimed 'King of the Jews,' would have been fatal to the whole scheme. In the opinion of the vulgar heathen, where the Roman Governor and Jewish Rabbi came in conflict, the former must unquestionably be right, and the latter decidedly wrong. To have preached a Saviour who was justly condemned to die the death of a slave and villain, would certainly have proved fatal to the whole enterprise. Therefore it was neces-

---

[1] See *note* 4, p. 522.
[2] See Matt. xx. 19.
[3] John xviii. 31, 32.

[4] That is, the crucifixion story *as related in the Gospels.* See *note* 1. p. 520.
[5] Matthew xxvii. 24, 25.

sary to exonerate Pilate and the Romans, and to throw the whole burden upon the Jews, in order to establish the innocence and mar-tyrdom of Jesus in the heathen mind."

That the crucifixion story, as related in the synoptic Gospels, was written *abroad*, and *not* in the Hebrew, or in the dialect spoken by the Hebrews of Palestine, is evident from the following particular points, noticed by Dr. Isaac M. Wise, a learned · Hebrew scholar :

The *Mark* and *Matthew* narrators call the place of crucifixion "*Golgotha*," to which the Mark narrator adds, "which is, being interpreted, *the place of skulls.*" The Matthew narrator adds the same interpretation, which the John narrator copies without the word "*Golgotha*," and adds, *it was a place near Jerusalem.* The Luke narrator calls the place of crucifixion "*Calvary*," which is the LATIN *Calvaria*, viz., "*the place of bare skulls.*" Therefore the name does not refer to the form of the hill, *but to the bare skulls upon it.*[1] Now "*there is no such word as* GOLGOTHA *anywhere in Jewish literature, and there is no such place mentioned anywhere near Jerusalem or in Palestine by any writer;* and, in fact, there was no such place; there could have been none near Jerusalem. The Jews buried their dead carefully. Also the executed convict had to be buried before night. No bare skulls, bleaching in the sun, could be found in Palestine, especially not near Jerusalem. *It was law, that a bare skull, the bare spinal column, and also the imperfect skeleton of any human being, make man unclean by contact, and also by having either in the house.* Man, thus made unclean, could not eat of any sacrificial meal, or of the sacred tithe, before he had gone through the ceremonies of purification ; and whatever he touched was also unclean (Maimonides, Hil. Tumath Meth., iii. 1). Any impartial reader can see that the object of this law was to prevent the barbarous practice of heathens of having human skulls and skeletons lie about exposed to the decomposing influences of the atmosphere, as the Romans did in Palestine after the fall of Bethar, when for a long time they would give no permission to bury the dead patriots. This law was certainly enforced most rigidly in the vicinity of Jerusalem, of which they maintained " Jerusalem is more holy than all other cities surrounded with walls," so that it was not permitted to keep a dead body over night in the city, or to

---

[1] Commentators, in endeavoring to get over this difficulty, say that, "it *may* come from the look or form of the spot itself, bald, round, and skull-like, and therefore a mound or hillock," but, if it means "*the place of bare skulls*," no such construction as the above can be put to the word.

transport through it human bones. Jerusalem was the place of the sacrificial meals and the consumption of the sacred tithe, which was considered very holy (Maimonides, Hil. Beth Habchirah, vii. 14); there,
and in the surroundings, skulls and skeletons were certainly never
seen on the surface of the earth, and consequently there was no place
called "*Golgotha*," and there was no such word in the Hebrew dialect. It is a word coined by the Mark narrator to translate the
Latin term "*Calvaria*," which, together with the crucifixion story,
came from Rome. But after the Syrian word was made, nobody
understood it, and the Mark narrator was obliged to expound it."[1]

In the face of the arguments produced, the crucifixion story, as
related in the Gospels, cannot be upheld as an historical fact. There
exists, certainly, no rational ground whatever for the belief that the
affair took place *in the manner the Evangelists describe it*. All that
can be saved of the whole story is, that after Jesus had answered
the first question before Pilate, viz., "Art thou the King of the
Jews?" which it is natural to suppose he was asked, and also this
can be supposed only, he was given over to the Roman soldiers to
be disposed of as soon as possible, before his admirers and followers
could come to his rescue, or any demonstration in his favor be made.
He was captured in the night, as quietly as possible, and guarded
in some place, probably in the high-priest's court, completely secluded from the eyes of the populace; and early in the morning he
was brought before Pilate as cautiously and quietly as it could be
done, and at *his* command, disposed of by the soldiers as quickly
as practicable, and in a manner not known to the mass of the people. All this was done, most likely, while the multitude worshiped
on Mount Moriah, and nobody had an intimation of the tragical end
of the Man of Nazareth.

The bitter cry of Jesus, as he hung on the tree, "My God, my
God, why hast thou forsaken me?" disclosed the hope of deliverance that till the last moment sustained his heart, and betrayed the
anguish felt when the hope was blighted; the sneers and hooting
of the Roman soldiers expressed their conviction that he had pretended to be what he was not.

The miracles ascribed to him, and the moral precepts put into
his mouth, in after years, are what might be expected; history was
simply repeating itself; the same thing had been done for others.
"The preacher of the Mount, the prophet of the Beatitudes, does

---

[1] The Martyrdom of Jesus of Nazareth, pp. 109–111.

but repeat, with persuasive lips, what the law-givers of his race pro-claimed in mighty tones of command."[1]

The martyrdom of Jesus of Nazareth has been gratefully acknowledged by his disciples, whose lives he saved by the sacrifice of his own, and by their friends, who would have fallen by the score had he not prevented the rebellion ripe at Jerusalem.[2] Posterity, infatuated with Pagan apotheoses, made of that simple martyrdom an interesting legend, colored with the myths of resurrection and ascension to that very heaven which the telescope has put out of man's way. It is a novel myth, made to suit the gross conceptions of ex-heathens. Modern theology, understanding well enough that the myth cannot be saved, seeks refuge in the greatness and self-denial of the man who died for an idea, as though Jesus had been the only man who had died for an idea. Thousands, tens of thousands of Jews, Christians, Mohammedans and Heathens, have died for ideas, and some of them were very foolish. But Jesus did not die for an idea. He never advanced anything new, that we know of, to die for. He was not accused of saying or teaching anything *original*. Nobody has ever been able to discover anything new and original in the Gospels. He evidently died to save the lives of his friends, and this is much more meritorious than if he had died for a ques-tionable idea. But then the whole fabric of vicarious atonement is demolished, and modern theology cannot get over the absurdity that the Almighty Lord of the Universe, the infinite and eternal cause of all causes, had to kill some innocent person in order to be reconciled to the human race. However abstractly they speculate and subtilize, there is always an undigested bone of man-god, god-man, and vicarious atonement in the theological stomach. There-fore theology appears so ridiculous in the eyes of modern philoso-phy. The theological speculation cannot go far enough to hold pace with modern astronomy. However nicely the idea may be dressed, the great God of the immense universe looks too small upon the cross of Calvary; and the human family is too large, has too numerous virtues and vices, to be perfectly represented by, and dependent on, one Rabbi of Galilee. Speculate as they may, one way or another, they must connect the Eternal and the fate of the human family with the person and fate of Jesus. That is the very thing which deprives Jesus of his crown of martyrdom, and brings

---

[1] O. B. Frothingham: The Cradle of the Christ, p. 11.

The reader is referred to "Judaism: Its Doctrines and Precepts," by Dr. Isaac M. Wise. Printed at the office of the "American Israel-ite," Cincinnati, Ohio.

[2] If Jesus, instead of giving himself up quietly, had *resisted* against being arrested, there certainly would have been bloodshed, as there was on many other similar occasions.

religion in perpetual conflict with philosophy. It was not the religious idea which was crucified in Jesus and resurrected with him,
as with all its martyrs; although his belief in immortality may
have strengthened him in the agony of death. It was the idea of
duty to his disciples and friends which led him to the realms of
death. This deserves admiration, but no more. It demonstrates
the nobility of human nature, but proves nothing in regard to providence, or the providential scheme of government.

The Christian story, *as the Gospels narrate it*, cannot stand the
test of criticism. You approach it critically and it falls. *Dogmatic
Christology* built upon it, has, therefore, a very frail foundation.
Most so-called lives of Christ, or biographies of Jesus, are works of
fiction, erected by imagination on the shifting foundation of mea-
gre and unreliable records. There are very few passages in the
Gospels which can stand the rigid application of honest criticism.
In modern science and philosophy, orthodox *Christology* is out of
the question.

"This 'sacred tradition' has in itself a glorious vitality, which
Christians may unblameably entitle immortal. But it certainly will
not lose in beauty, grandeur, or truth, if all the details concerning
Jesus which are current in the Gospels, and all the mythology of
his person, be forgotten or discredited. Christianity will remain
without Christ.

"This formula has in it nothing paradoxical. Rightly interpreted, it simply means: *All that is best in Judæo-Christian sentiment, moral or spiritual, will survive, without Rabbinical fancies, cultured by perverse logic; without huge piles of fable built
upon them: without the Oriental Satan, a formidable rival to
the throne of God; without the Pagan invention of Hell and
Devils.*"

In modern criticism, the Gospel sources become so utterly worthless and unreliable, that it takes more than ordinary faith to believe
a large portion thereof to be true. The *Eucharist* was not established by Jesus, and cannot be called a sacrament. The trials of
Jesus are positively not true: they are pure inventions.[1] The crucifixion story, *as narrated*, is certainly not true, and it is extremely
difficult to save the bare fact that Jesus was crucified. What can
the critic do with books in which a few facts must be ingeniously
guessed from under the mountain of ghost stories,[2] childish mira-

---

[1] It what is recorded in the Gospels on the   could fail to have noticed it, but instead of this
subject was true, no historian of that day   there is *nothing*.
[2] See Matthew, xxvii. 51–53.

·cles,[1] and dogmatic tendencies ?' It is absurd to expect of him to regard them as sources of religious instruction, in preference to any ·other mythologies and legends. That is the point at which modern ·critics have arrived, therefore, the Gospels have become books for the museum and archæologist, for students of mythology and an. ·cient literature. The spirit of dogmatic Christology hovers still over a portion of civilized society, in antic organizations, disciplines, and hereditary forms of faith and worship; in science and philosophy, in the realm ·of criticism, its day is past. The universal, religious, and ethical ·element of Christianity has no connection whatever with Jesus or his apostles, with the Gospel, or the Gospel story; *it exists independent of any person or story*. Therefore it needs neither the ·Gospel story nor its heroes. If we profit by the example, by the teachings, or the discoveries of men of past ages, to these men we ·are indebted, and are in duty bound to acknowledge our indebtedness; but why should we give to *one* individual, Jesus of Nazareth, the credit of it *all ?* It is true, that by selecting from the Gospels whatever portions one may choose, a *common practice among Christian writers*, a noble and grand character may be depicted, *but who was the original of this character?* We may find the same individual outside of the Gospels, and before the time of Jesus. The moral precepts of the Gospels, also, were in existence before the ·Gospels themselves were in existence.' Why, then, extol the hero ·of the Gospels, and forget all others?

---

[1] See Matt. xiv. 15–22 : Mark, iv. 1–3, and xi. 14 ; and Luke. vii. 26–37

[2] See Mark, xvi. 16.

[3] This fact has at last been admitted by the most orthodox among the Christians. The Rev. ·George Matheson, D.D., Minister of the Parish ·of Innellan, and a member of the Scotch Kirk, speaking of the precept uttered by Confucius, five hundred years before the time assigned for the birth of Jesus of Nazareth ("Whatsoever ye would not that others should do unto you, do ·not ye unto them")-says : "That Confucius is the *author* of this precept is undisputed, *and therefore it is indisputable that Christianity has incorporated an article of Chinese morality*. It has appeared to some as if this were to the disparagement of Christianity—as if the originality of its Divine Founder were impaired by consenting to borrow a precept from a heathen source. *But in what sense does Christianity set up the claim of moral originality?* When we speak of the religion of Christ as having introduced into the world a purer life and a ·surer guide to conduct, what do we mean ?

Do we mean to suggest that Christianity has, *for the first time*, revealed to the world the existence of a set of self-sacrificing precepts—that here, *for the first time*, man has learned that he ought to be meek, merciful, humble, forgiving, sorrowful for sin, peaceable, and pure in heart ? The proof of such a statement would destroy Christianity itself, for an *absolute original code of precepts* would be equivalent to a foreign language. *The glory of Christian morality is that it is* NOT ORIGINAL–that its words appeal to something which *already exists within the human heart*, and on that account have a meaning to the human ear : *no new revelation can be made except through the medium of an old one.* When we attribute originality to the ethics of the Gospel, we do so on the ground, *not that it has given new precepts*, but that it has given us a new impulse to obey the moral instincts of the soul. Christianity itself claims on the field of morals this originality, *and this alone*—' A new commandment give I unto you, that you love one another.' " (St. Giles

34

As it was at the end of Roman Paganism, so is it now: the masses are deceived and fooled, or do it for themselves, and persons of vivacious fantasies prefer the masquerade of delusion, to the simple sublimity of naked but majestic truth. The decline of the church as a political power proves beyond a doubt the decline of Christian faith. The conflicts of Church and State all over the European continent, and the hostility between intelligence and *dogmatic Christianity*, demonstrates the death of *Christology* in the consciousness of modern culture. It is useless to shut our eyes to these facts. Like rabbinical Judaism, dogmatic Christianity was the product of ages without typography, telescopes, microscopes, telegraphs, and power of steam. "These right arms of intelligence have fought the titanic battles, conquered and demolished the ancient castles, and remove now the débris, preparing the ground upon which there shall be the gorgeous temple of humanity, one universal republic, one universal religion of intelligence, and one great universal brotherhood. This is the new covenant, the gospel of humanity and reason."

> "—— Hoaryheaded selfishness has felt
> Its death-blow, and is tottering to the grave:
> A brighter morn awaits the human day;
> War with its million horrors, and fierce hell,
> Shall live but in the memory of time,
> Who, like a penitent libertine, shall start,
> Look back, and shudder at his younger years."

Lectures, Second Series: The Faiths of the World. Religion of China, by the Rev. George Matheson. D. D., Minister of the Parish of Innellan. Wm. Blackwood & Sons: Edinburgh, 1882.)

APPENDIX.

APPENDIX A.

AMONG the ancient Mexicans, Peruvians, and some of the Indian tribes of North and South America, were found fragments of the *Eden Myth*. The Mexicans said that the primeval mother was made out of a *man's bone*, and that she was the mother of *twins*.[1]

The Cherokees supposed that heavenly beings *came down* and made the world, after which they made a man and woman of *clay*.[2] The intention of the creators was that men should live always. But the Sun, when he passed over, told them that there was not land enough, and that people had better die. At length, *the daughter of the Sun* was bitten by a *Snake*, and died. The Sun, however— whom they worshiped as a god—consented that human beings might live always. He intrusted to their care a *box*, charging them that they should not open it. However, impelled by curiosity, they opened it, contrary to the injunction of the Sun, and the *spirit* it contained escaped, *and then the fate of all men was decided, that they must die.*[3]

The inhabitants of the New World had a legend of a *Deluge*, which destroyed the human race, excepting a few who were saved in a boat, which landed on a *mountain*.[4] They also related that *birds* were sent out of the ark, for the purpose of ascertaining if the flood was abating.[5]

The ancient Mexicans had the legend of the *confusion of tongues*, and related the whole story as to how the gods destroyed the tower which mankind was building so as to reach unto heaven.[6]

The Mexicans, and several of the Indian tribes of North America, believe in the doctrine of *Metempsychosis*, or the transmigration of souls from one body into another.[7] This, as we have already seen,[8] was universally believed in the Old World.

The legend of *the man being swallowed by a fish*, and, after a

---

[1] Baring-Gould's Legends of the Patriarchs, p. 46.

[2] Squire's Serpent Symbol, p. 67.

[3] Ibid. Here we see the parallel to the *Grecian* fable of Epimetheus and Pandora.

[4] Brinton : Myths of the New World, p. 203.

[5] Ibid.

[6] Brinton : Myths of the New World, p. 204.

[7] See Chapter V.

[8] See Ibid. and Chambers's Encyclo., art. "*Transmigration*."

three days' sojourn in his belly, coming out safe and sound, was found among the Mexicans and Peruvians.[1]

The ancient Mexicans, and some Indian tribes, practiced *Circumcision*, which was common among all Eastern nations of the Old World.[2]

They also had a legend to the effect that one of their holy persons commanded *the sun to stand still*.[3] This, as we have already seen,[4] was a familiar legend among the inhabitants of the Old World.

The ancient Mexicans were *fire-worshipers ;* so were the ancient Peruvians. They kept a fire continually burning on an altar, just as the fire-worshipers of the Old World were in the habit of doing.[5] They were also *Sun-worshipers*, and had "temples of the Sun."[6]

The *Tortoise-myth* was found in the New World.[7] Now, in the Old World, the Tortoise-myth belongs especially to *India*, and the idea is developed there in a variety of forms. The tortoise that holds the world is called in Sanscrit Kura-mraja, "King of the Tortoises," and many Hindoos believe to this day that the world rests on its back. "The striking analogy between the Tortoise-myth of North America and India," says Mr. Tyler, "is by no means a matter of new observation ; it was indeed remarked upon by Father Lafitau nearly a century and a half ago. Three great features of the Asiatic stories are found among the North American Indians, in the fullest and clearest development. The earth is supported on the back of a huge floating tortoise, the tortoise sinks under the water and causes a deluge, and the tortoise is conceived as being itself the earth, floating upon the face of the deep."[8]

We have also found among them the belief in an Incarnate God born of a virgin ;[9] the One God worshiped in the form of a Trinity ;[10] the crucified *Black* god ;[11] the descent into hell ;[12] the resurrection and ascension into heaven,[13] all of which is to be found in the oldest Asiatic religions. We also found monastic habits—friars and nuns.[14]

---

[1] See Chapter XI.

[2] See Chapter X.

[3] See Chapter XI.

[4] Ibid.

[5] See Early Hist. Mankind, p. 252; Squire's Serpent Symbol; and Prescott: Con. Peru.

[6] See Ibid., and the Andes and the Amazon, p. 454.

[7] See Early Hist. Mankind, p. 342.

[8] Ibid.

[9] See Chapter XII.

[10] See Chapter XXV.

[11] See Chapter XX.

Mr. Prescott, speaking of the Pyramid of Cholula, in his Mexican History, says : "On

the summit stood a sumptuous temple, in which was the image of the mystic deity (*Quetzalcoatle*), with *ebon* features, unlike the fair complexion which he bore upon earth." And Kenneth R. H. Mackenzie says (in Cities of the Ancient World, p. 180) : "From the woolly texture of the hair, I am inclined to assign to the Buddha of India, the Fuhi of China, the Sommonacom of the Siamese, the Xaba of the Japanese, and the Quetzalcoatle of the Mexicans, the same, and indeed an African, or rather Nubian, origin."

[12] See Chapter XXII.

[13] See Chapter XXIII.

[14] See Chapter XXVI.

The Mexicans denominated their high-places, sacred houses, or "*Houses of God.*" The corresponding sacred structures of the Hindoos are called " *God's House.*"[1]

Many nations of the *East* entertained the notion that there were *nine heavens,* and so did the ancient Mexicans.[2]

There are few things connected with the ancient mythology of *America* more certain than that there existed in that country before its discovery by Columbus, extreme veneration for the *Serpent.*[3] Now, the Serpent was venerated and worshiped throughout the East.[4]

The ancient Mexicans and Peruvians, and many of the Indian tribes, believed the Sun and Moon not only to be brother and sister, but man and wife ; so, likewise, among many nations of the Old World was this belief prevalent.[5] The belief in were-wolves, or man-wolves, man-tigers, man-hyenas, and the like, which was almost universal among the nations of Europe, Asia and Africa, was also found to be the case among South American tribes.[6] The idea of calling the earth " mother," was common among the inhabitants of both the Old and New Worlds.[7] " In the mythology of Finns, Lapps, and Esths, Earth-Mother is a divinely honored personage. It appears in China, where *Heaven* and *Earth* are called in the *Shuking*—one of their sacred books—"Father and Mother of all things." .

Among the native races of *America* the Earth-Mother is one of the great personages of mythology. The Peruvians worshiped her as *Mama-Phacha,* or Earth-Mother. The Caribs, when there was an earthquake, said it was their mother-earth dancing, and signifying to them to dance and make merry likewise, which they accordingly did.[8]

It is well-known that the natives of Africa, when there is an eclipse of the sun or moon, believe that it is being devoured by some great monster, and that they, in order to frighten and drive it away, beat drums and make noises in other ways. So, too, the rude Moguls make a clamor of rough music to drive the attacking Arachs (Râhu) from Sun or Moon.[9]

The Chinese, when there is an eclipse of the Sun or Moon, proceed to encounter the ominous monster with gongs and bells.[10]

The ancient Romans flung firebrands into the air, and blew trumpets, and clanged brazen pots and pans.[11] Even as late as the

---

[1] Squire : Serpent Symbol, p. 77.
[2] Ibid. p. 109.
[3] See Ferguson's Tree and Serpent Worship, and Squire's Serpent Symbol.
[4] See Ibid.
[5] See Tylor, Primitive Culture, vol. i. p. 261, and Squire's Serpent Symbol.
[6] Primitive Culture, vol. i. p. 280, and Squire's Serpent Symbol.
[7] Primitive Culture, vol. i. p. 294, and Squire's Serpent Symbol.
[8] Tylor : Primitive Culture, vol. i. pp. 295, 296.
[9] Ibid. p. 300. [10] Ibid. [11] Ibid. p. 301.

seventeenth century, the Irish or Welsh, during eclipses, ran about beating kettles and pans.[1] Among the native races of America was to be found the same superstition. The Indians would raise a frightful howl, and shoot arrows into the sky to drive the monsters off.[2] The Caribs, thinking that the demon Maboya, hater of all light, was seeking to devour the Sun and Moon, would dance and howl in concert all night long to scare him away. The Peruvians, imagining such an evil spirit in the shape of a monstrous beast, raised the like frightful din when the Moon was eclipsed, shouting, sounding musical instruments, and beating the dogs to join their howl to the hideous chorus.[3]

The starry band that lies like a road across the sky, known as the *milky way*, is called by the Basutos (a South African tribe of savages), "The Way of the Gods;" the Ojis (another African tribe of savages), say it is the "Way of Spirits," which souls go up to heaven by. North American tribes know it as "the Path of the Master of Life," the "Path of Spirits," "the Road of Souls," where they travel to the land beyond the grave.[4]

It is almost a general belief among the inhabitants of Africa, and was so among the inhabitants of Europe and Asia, that monkeys were once men and women, and that they can even now really speak, but judiciously hold their tongues, lest they should be made to work. This idea was found as a serious matter of belief, in Central and South America.[5] "The Bridge of the Dead," which is one of the marked myths of the Old World, was found in the New.[6]

It is well known that the natives of South America told the Spaniards that inland there was to be found a fountain, the waters of which turned old men back into youths, and how Juan Ponce de Leon fitted out two caravels, and went to seek for this "Fountain of Youth." Now, the "Fountain of Youth" is known to the mythology of India.[7]

The myth of foot-prints stamped into the rocks by gods or mighty men, is to be found among the inhabitants of Europe, Asia, and Africa. Egyptians, Greeks, Brahmans, Buddhists, Moslems, and Christians, have adopted it as relics each from their own point of view, and *Mexican* eyes could discern in the solid rock at Tlanepantla the mark of hand and foot left by the mighty Quetzalcoatle.[8]

---

[1] Tylor; Primitive Culture, vol. i. p. 301.
[2] Ibid. p. 296.
[3] Ibid.
[4] Ibid. p. 294.
[5] Ibid. p. 239 and 343.

[6] Early Hist. Mankind, pp. 357 and 361.
[7] Ibid. p. 361.
The legend of the "Elixir of Life" of the Western World, was well-known in *China.* (Buckley : Cities of the Ancient World, p. 167.)
[8] Ibid. p. 118, and Squire's Serpent Symbol.

The Incas, in order to preserve purity of race, married their own sisters, as did the Kings of Persia, and other Oriental nations.[1] The Peruvian embalming of the royal dead takes us back to *Egypt;* the burning of the wives of the deceased Incas reveals *India;* the singularly patriarchical character of the whole Peruvian policy is like that of *China* in the olden time; while the system of espionage, of tranquillity, of physical well-being, and the iron-like immovability in which their whole social frame was cast, bring before us *Japan*—as it was a very few years ago. In fact, there is something strangely Japanese in the entire cultus of Peru as described by all writers.[2]

The dress and costume of the Mexicans, and their sandals, resemble the apparel and sandals worn in early ages in the East.[3]

Mexican priests were represented with a Serpent twined around their heads, so were Oriental kings.[4] The Mexicans had the head of a rhinoceros among their paintings,[5] and also the head of an elephant on the body of a man.[6] Now, these animals were unknown in America, but well known in Asia; and what is more striking still is the fact that the man with the elephant's head is none other than the Ganesa of India; the God of Wisdom. Humboldt, who copied a Mexican painting of a man with an elephant's head, remarks that "it presents some remarkable and apparently *not accidental* resemblances with the Hindoo Ganesa."

The horse and the ass, although natives of America,[7] became extinct on the Western Continent in an early period of the earth's history, yet the Mexicans had, among their hieroglyphics, representations of both these animals, which show that it must have been seen in the old world by the author of the hieroglyph. When the Mexicans saw the horses which the Spaniards brought over, they were greatly astonished, and when they saw the Spaniards on horseback, they imagined man and horse to be *one.*

Certain of the temples of *India* abound with sculptural representations of the symbols of *Phallic Worship.* Turning now to the temples of *Central America,* which in many respects exhibit a strict correspondence with those in India, *we find precisely the same symbols, separate and in combination.*[8]

We have seen that many of the religious conceptions of *America* are identical with those of the *Old World,* and that they are em-

[1] Fusang, p. 56.
[2] Ibid. p. 55.
[3] Mexican Antiquities, vol. vi. p. 181.
[4] Ibid., and Squire's Serpent Symbol.
[5] Mexican Antiq., vol. vi. p. 180.
[6] Early Hist. Mankind, p. 311.
[7] The traveler, James Orton, found fossil bones of an extinct species of the horse, the mas-

todon, and other animals, near Punin, in South America, all of which had passed away before the arrival of the human species. This native American horse was succeeded, in after ages, by the countless herds descended from a few introduced with the Spanish colonists. (See the Andes and the Amazon, pp. 154, 155.)
[8] Serpent Symbol, p. 47.

bodied or symbolized under the same or cognate forms; and it is confidently asserted that a comparison and analysis of her primitive systems, in connection with those of other parts of the globe, philosophically conducted, would establish the grand fact, that in ALL their leading elements, and in many of their details, they are essentially the same.[1]

The *architecture* of many of the most ancient buildings in South America resembles the Asiatic. Around Lake Titicaca are massive monuments, which speak of a very ancient and civilized nation.[2]

R. Spence Hardy, says:

"The ancient edifices of Chi Chen, in Central America, bear a striking resemblance to the topes of India. The shape of one of the domes, its apparent size, the small tower on the summit, the trees growing on the sides, the appearance of masonry here and there, the style of the ornaments, and the small doorway at the base, are so exactly similar to what I had seen at Anurádhapura, *that when my eye first fell upon the engravings of these remarkable ruins, I supposed that they were presented in illustration of the dágobas of Ceylon.*"[3]

E. G. Squire, speaking of this, says:

"The Bud'hist temples of Southern India, and of the islands of the Indian Archipelago, as described to us by the learned members of the Asiatic Society, and the numerous writers on the religion and antiquities of the Hindoos, correspond, with great exactness, in all their essential and in many of their minor features, with those of *Central America.*"[4]

Structures of a *pyramidal* style, which are common in India, were also discovered in Mexico. The pyramid tower of Cholula was one of these.[5]

Sir R. Kir Porter writes as follows:

"What striking analogies exist between the monuments of the old continents and those of the Toltecs, who, arriving on Mexican soil, built several of these colossal structures, truncated pyramids, divided by layers, like the temple of Belus at Babylon. *Whence did they take the model of these edifices? Were they of the Mongolian race? Did they descend from a common stock with the Chinese, the Hiong-nu, and the Japanese?*"[6]

The similarity in *features* of the Asiatic and the American race is very striking. Alexander de Humboldt, speaking of this, says:

"There are striking contrasts between the Mongol and American races."[7] "Over a million and a half of square leagues, from the Terra del Fuego islands to the River St. Lawrence and Behring's Straits, we are struck at the first glance with the general resemblance in the features of the inhabitants. *We think we perceive that they all descended from the same stock*, notwithstanding the enormous diversity of language which separates them from one another."[8]

---

[1] Serpent Symbol, p. 193.
[2] The Andes and the Amazon, p. 454.
[3] Eastern Monachism, p. 222.
[4] Serpent Symbol, p. 43.
[5] See Ibid.
[6] Travels in Persia, vol. ii. p. 280.
[7] New Spain, vol. i. p. 136.
[8] Ibid. p. 141.

" This analogy is particularly evident in the color of the skin and hair, in the defective beard, high cheek-bones, and in the direction of the eyes."[1]

Dr. Morton says :

" In reflecting on the aboriginal races of America, we are at once met by the striking fact, that their physical characters are wholly independent of all climatic or known physical influences. Notwithstanding their immense geographical distribution, embracing every variety of climate, it is acknowledged by all travellers, that there is among this people a prevailing type, around which all the tribes—north, south, east and west—cluster, though varying within prescribed limits. With trifling exceptions, all our American Indians bear to each other some degree of family resemblance, quite as strong, for example, as that seen at the present day among full-blooded Jews."[2]

James Orton, the traveler, was also struck with the likeness of the American Indians to the Chinese, including the flatted nose. Speaking of the Zaparos of the Napo River, he says :

" The Zaparos in physiognomy somewhat resemble the Chinese, having a middle stature, round face, small eyes set angularly, and a broad, flat nose."[3]

Oscar Paschel says :

" The obliquely-set eyes and prominent cheek-bones of the inhabitants of Veragua were noticed by Monitz Wagner, and according to his description, out of four Bayano Indians from Darien, three had thoroughly Mongolian features, including the flatted nose."

In 1866, an officer of the Sharpshooter, the first English man-of-war which entered the Paraná River in Brazil, remarks in almost the same words of the Indians of that district, that their features vividly reminded him of the Chinese. Burton describes the Brazilian natives at the falls of Cachauby as having thick, round Kalmuck heads, flat Mongol faces, wide, very prominent cheek bones, oblique and sometimes narrow-slit Chinese eyes, and slight mustaches.

Another traveler, J. J. Von Tschudi, declares in so many words that he has seen Chinese whom at the first glance he mistook for Botocudos, and that since then he has been convinced that the American race ought not to be separated from the Mongolian. His predecessor, St. Hilaire, noticed narrow, obliquely-set eyes and broad noses among the Malali of Brazil. Reinhold Hensel says of the Coroados, that their features are of Mongoloid type, due especially to the prominence of the cheek-bones, but that the oblique position of the eyes is not perceptible. Yet the oblique opening of the eye, which forms a good though not an essential characteristic of the Mongolian nations, is said to be characteristic of all the Guarani tribes in Brazil. Even in the extreme south, among the

---

[1] New Spain, vol. i. p. 153.   [2] Types of Mankind, p. 273.
[3] The Andes and the Amazon, p. 170.

Hiullitches of Patagonia, King saw a great many with obliquely set eyes. Those writers who separate the Americans as a peculiar race fail to give distinctive characters, common to them all, which distinguish them from the Asiatic Mongols. All the tribes have stiff, long hair, cylindrical in section. The beard and hair of the body is always scanty or totally absent. The color of the skin varies considerably, as might be expected in a district of 110° of latitude; it ranges from a light South European darkness of complexion among the Botocudos, of the deepest dye among the Aymara, or to copper red in the Sonor tribes. But no one has tried to draw limits between races on account of these shades of color, especially as they are of every conceivable gradation.[1]

Charles G. Leland says :

The Tunguse, Mongolians, and a great part of the Turkish race formed originally, according to all external organic tokens, as well as the elements of their language, but one people, closely allied with the Esquimaux, the *Skräling*, or dwarf of the Norseman, and the races of the New World. This is the irrefutable result to which all the more recent inquiries in anatomy and physiology, as well as comparative philology and history, have conduced. All the aboriginal Americans have those distinctive tokens which forcibly recall their neighbors dwelling on the other side of Behring's Straits. They have the four-cornered head, high cheek-bones, heavy jaws, large angular eye-cavities, and a retreating forehead. The skulls of the oldest Peruvian graves exhibit the same tokens as the heads of the nomadic tribes of Oregon and California."[2] It is very certain that thousands of American Indians, especially those of small stature or of dwarfish tribes, bear a most extraordinary likeness to Mongols."[3]

John D. Baldwin, in his "*Ancient America*," says :

" I find myself more and more inclined to believe that the wild Indians of the North came originally from *Asia*, where the race to which they belong seems still represented by the *Koraks* and *Cookchees*, found in that part of Asia which extends to Behring's Straits."[4]

Hon. Charles D. Poston, late commissioner of the United States of America in Asia, in a work entitled, "*The Parsees*," speaking of an incident which took place "beyond the Great Wall," says :

" A Mongolian came riding up on a little black pony, followed by a servant on a camel, rocking like a windmill. He stopped a moment to exchange pantomimic salutations. He was full of electricity, and alive with motion; the blood was warm in his veins, and the fire was bright in his eye. I could have sworn that he was an *Apache ;* every action, motion and look reminded me of my old enemies and neighbors in *Arizona*. They are the true descendants of the nomadic Tartars of Asia and preserve every instinct of the race. He shook hands friendlily but timidly, keeping all the time in motion like an Apache."[5]

[1] Paschel : Races of Man, pp. 402–404.
[2] Fusang, p. 7.
[3] Ibid. 118.
[4] Quoted in Ibid.
[5] Quoted in Ibid. p. 94.

That the continents of Asia and America were at one time joined together by an isthmus, at the place where the channel of Behring's straits is now found, is a well known fact. That the severance of Asia from America was, geologically speaking, very recent, is shown by the fact that not only the straits, but the sea which bears the name of Behring, is extraordinarily shallow, so much so, indeed, that whalers lie at anchor in the middle of it.[1] This is evidently the manner in which America was peopled.[2]

During the *Champlain* period in the earth's history the climate of the northern portion of the American continent, instead of being frigid, and the country covered with sheets of ice, was more like the climate of the Middle States of the present day. Tropical animals went North, and during the Terrace period—which followed the Champlain—the climate changed to frigid, and many of these tropical animals were frozen in the ice, and some of their remains were discovered centuries after.

It was probably during the time when the climate in those northern regions was warm, that the aborigines crossed over, and even if they did not do so at that time, we must not be startled at the idea that Asiatic tribes crossed over from Asia to America, when the country was covered with ice. There have been nations who lived in a state of nudity among ice-fields, and, even at the present day, a naked nation of fishermen still exist in Terra del Fuego, where the glaciers stretch down to the sea, and even into it.[3]

Chas. Darwin, during his voyage round the world in H. M. S. Beagle, was particularly struck with the hardiness of the Fuegians, who go in a state of nudity, or almost entirely so. He says:

"Among these central tribes the men generally have an otter-skin, or some small scrap, about as large as a pocket-handkerchief, to cover their nakedness, which is barely sufficient to cover their backs as low down as their loins."[4]

One day while going on shore near Wollaston Island, Mr. Darwin's party pulled alongside a canoe which contained six Fuegians, who were, he says, "quite naked, and even one full-grown woman was absolutely so. It was raining heavily, and the fresh water, together with the spray, trickled down her body. In another harbor not far distant, a woman, who was suckling a recently-born child, came one

---

[1] Paschel: Races of Man, pp. 400, 401.
[2] To those who may think that the Old World might have been peopled from the new, we refer to Oscar Paschel's "Races of Man," p. 32. The author, in speaking on this subject, says: "There at one time existed a great continent, to which belonged Madagascar and perhaps portions of Eastern Africa, the Maldives and Laccadives, and also the Island of Ceylon, which was never attached to India, perhaps even the island of Celebes in the far East, which possesses a perplexing fauna, with semi-African features." On this continent, which was situated in the now Indian Ocean, must we look for the *cradle of humanity*.
[3] Paschel: Races of Man, p. 31.
[4] Darwin's Journal, p. 213.

day alongside the vessel, and remained there out of mere curiosity, whilst the sleet fell and thawed on her naked bosom, and on the skin of her naked baby !"[1]

This was during the winter season.

A few pages farther on Mr. Darwin says that on the night of the 22d December, a small family of Fuegians—who were living in a cove near the quarters—" soon joined our party round a blazing fire. We were well clothed, and though sitting close to the fire were far from too warm ; yet these naked savages, though further off, were observed, to our great surprise, to be streaming with perspiration at undergoing such a scorching. They seemed, however, very well pleased, and all joined in the chorus of the seamen's songs ; but the manner in which they were invariably a little behind was quite ludicrous."[2]

The Asiatics who first crossed over to the American continent were evidently in a very barbarous stage, although they may have known how to produce fire, and use bows and arrows.[3] The tribe who inhabited Mexico at the time it was discovered by the Spaniards was not the first to settle there ; they had driven out a people, and had taken the country from them.[4]

That Mexico was visited by Orientals, who brought and planted their religion there, in a comparatively recent period, is very probable. Mr. Chas. G. Leland, who has made this subject a special study, says :

"While the proofs of the existence or residence of Orientals in America are extremely vague and uncertain, and while they are supported only by coincidences, the antecedent probability of their having come hither, or having been able to come, is stronger than the Norse discovery of the New World, or even than that of Columbus himself would appear to be. Let the reader take a map of the Northern Pacific; let him ascertain for himself the fact that from Kamtschatka, which was well known to the old Chinese, to Alaska the journey is far less arduous than from China proper, and it will be seen that there was in all probability intercourse of some kind between the continents. In early times the Chinese were bold and skillful navigators, to whom the chain of the Aleutian Islands would have been simply like stepping-stones over a shallow brook to a child. For it is a well ascertained fact, that a sailor in an open boat might cross from Asia to America by the Aleutian Islands in summer-time, and hardly ever

[1] Darwin's Journal, p. 213.
[2] Ibid. pp. 220, 221.
[3] This is seen from the fact that they did not know the use of iron. Had they known the use of this metal, they would surely have gone to work and dug into their mountains, which are abundantly filled with ore, and made use of it.
[4] The Aztecs were preceded by the Toltecs, Chichimecks, and the Nahualtecs. (Humboldt's New Spain, p. 133, vol. i.)
"The races of barbarians which successively followed each other from the north to the south always murdered, hunted down, and subdued the previous inhabitants, and formed in course of time a new social and political life upon the ruins of the old system, to be again destroyed and renewed in a few centuries, by a new invasion of barbarians. The later native conquerors in the New World can, of course, no more be considered in the light of original inhabitants than the present races of men in the Old World."

be out of sight of land, and this in a part of the sea generally abounding in fish, as is proved by the fishermen who inhabit many of these islands, on which fresh water is always to be found."[1]

Colonel Barclay Kennon, formerly of the U. S. North Pacific surveying expedition, says:

"From the result of the most accurate scientific observation, it is evident that the voyage from China to America can be made without being out of sight of land more than a few hours at any one time. To a landsman, unfamiliar with long voyages, the mere idea of being 'alone on the wide, wide sea,' with nothing but water visible, even for an hour, conveys a strange sense of desolation, of daring, and of adventure. But in truth it is regarded as a mere trifle, not only by regular seafaring men, but even by the rudest races in all parts of the world; and I have no doubt that from the remotest ages, and on all shores, fishermen in open boats, canoes, or even coracles, guided simply by the stars and currents, have not hesitated to go far out of sight of land. At the present day, natives of many of the South Pacific Islands undertake, without a compass, and successfully, long voyages which astonish even a regular Jack-tar, who is not often astonished at anything. If. this can be done by savages, it hardly seems possible that the Asiatic-American voyage was not successfully performed by people of advanced scientific culture, who had, it is generally believed, the compass, and who from an early age were proficient in astronomy."[2]

Prof. Max Müller, it would seem, entertains similar ideas to our own, expressed as follows:

"In their (the American Indians') languages, as well as in their religions, traces may possibly still be found, before it is too late, *of pre-historic migrations of men from the primitive Asiatic to the American Continent, either across the stepping-stones of the Aleutic bridge in the North, or lower South, by drifting with favorable winds from island to island, till the hardy canoe was landed or wrecked on the American coast, never to return again to the Asiatic home from which it had started.*"[3]

It is very evident then, that the religion and mythology of the Old and New Worlds, have, in part, at least, a common origin. Lord Kingsborough informs us that the Spanish historians of the 16th century were not disposed to admit that America had ever been colonized from the West, "chiefly on account of the state in which religion was found in the new continent."[4]

And Mr. Tylor says:

"Among the mass of Central American traditions . . . there occur certain passages in the story of an early emigration of the Quiché race, which have much the appearance of vague and broken stories derived in some way from high Northern latitudes."[5]

Mr. McCulloh, in his "Researches," observes that:

[1] Fusang, p. 56.
[2] Quoted in Fusang, p. 71.
[3] Science of Religion, p. 121.
[4] Mexican Antiq., vol. vi. p. 181.
[5] Early Hist. Mankind, p. 307.

"In analyzing many parts of their (the ancient Americans') institutions, especially those belonging to their cosmogonal history, their religious superstitions, and astronomical computations, we have, in these abstract matters, found abundant proof to assert that there has been formerly a connection between the people of the two continents. Their communications, however, have taken place at a very remote period of time; for those matters in which they more decidedly coincide, are undoubtedly those which belong to the earliest history of mankind."

It is unquestionably from *India* that we have derived, partly through the Persians and other nations, most of our metaphysical and theological doctrines, as well as our nursery tales. Who then can deny that these same doctrines and legends have been handed down by oral tradition to the chief of the Indian tribes, and in this way have been preserved, although perhaps in an obscure and imperfect manner, in some instances at least, until the present day? The facts which we have before us, with many others like them which are to be had, point with the greatest likelihood to a common fatherland, the cradle of all nations, from which they came, taking these traditions with them.

APPENDIX B.

COMMENCING at the farthest East we shall find the ancient religion of *China* the same as that which was universal in all quarters of the globe, viz., an adoration of the Sun, Moon, Stars and elements.[1] That the Chinese religion was in one respect the same as that of India, is seen from the fact that they named successive days for the same seven planets that the Hindoos did.[2] The ancient books of the Chinese show that astronomy was not only understood by them at a very early period but that it formed an important branch of state policy, and the basis of public ceremonies. Eclipses are accurately recorded which occurred twenty centuries before Jesus; and the Confucian books refer continually to observations of the heavenly bodies and the rectification of the calendar. The ancient Chinese astronomers seem to have known precisely the excess of the solar year beyond 365 days. The *religion* of China,

---

[1] "All Paganism is at bottom *a worship of nature* in some form or other, and in all Pagan religions the deepest and most awe-inspiring attribute of *nature* was its power of reproduction." (Encyclo. Brit., art. "Christianity.")

[2] In Montfaucon's L'Antiquité Expliquée (vol. i.), may be seen a representation of the seven planets *personified*. It was by such personifications that the real objects worshiped became unknown. At first the real Sun, Moon, Stars, &c., would be worshiped, but as soon as man personified them, other terms would be introduced, and peculiar rites appropriated to each, so that in time they came to be considered as so many different deities.

under the emperors who preceded the first dynasty, is an enigma. The notices in the only authentic works, the *King*, are on this point scanty, vague, and obscure. It is difficult to separate what is spoken with reference to the science of *astronomy* from that which may relate to *religion*, properly so called. The terms of reverence and respect, with which the *heavenly bodies* are spoken of in the *Shoo-King*, seem to warrant the inference that those terms have more than a mere astronomical meaning, *and that the ancient religion* of *China partook of star-worship, one of the oldest heresies in the world.*[1]

In *India* the Sun, Moon, Stars and the powers of Nature were worshiped and personified, and each quality, mental and physical, had its emblem, which the Brahmans taught the ignorant to regard as realities, till the Pantheon became crowded.

"Our Aryan ancestors learned to look up to the sky, the Sun, and the dawn, and there to see the presence of a living power, half-revealed, and half-hidden from their senses, those senses which were always postulating something beyond what they could grasp. They went further still. In the bright sky they perceived an *Illuminator*, in the all-encircling firmament an *Embracer*, in the roar of the thunder or in the voice of the storm they felt the presence of a *Shouter* and of furious *Strikers*, and out of the rain they created an *Indra*, or giver of rain."[2]

Prof. Monier Williams, speaking of "the hymns of the *Veda*," says :

"To what deities, it will be asked, were the prayers and hymns of these collections addressed ? The answer is: They worshiped *those physical forces* before which *all nations*, if guided solely by the light of nature, have in the early period of their life, instinctively bowed down, and before which even the most civilized and enlightened have always been compelled to bend in awe and reverence, if not in adoration."[3]

The following sublime description of *Night* is an extract from the *Vedas*, made by Sir William Jones :

"Night approaches, illumined with stars and planets, and, looking on all sides with numberless eyes, overpowers all meaner lights. The immortal goddess pervades the firmament, covering the low valleys and shrubs, the lofty mountains and trees, but soon she disturbs the gloom with celestial effulgence. Advancing with brightness, at length she recalls her sister *Morning;* and the nightly shade gradually melts away. May she at this time be propitious! She, in whose early watch we may calmly recline in our mansions, as birds repose upon the trees. Mankind now sleep in their towns; now herds and flocks peacefully slumber, and the winged creatures, swift falcons, and vultures. O Night!

---

[1] Thornton : Hist. China, vol. i. pp. 14, 49 and 50.   [2] Max Müller : The Science of Religion, p. 298.
[3] Indian Wisdom, p. 10.

avert from us the she-wolf and the wolf; and, oh! suffer us to pass thee in soothing rest! Oh, morn! remove in due time this black, yet visible overwhelming darkness, which at present enfolds me, as thou enablest me to remove the cloud of their dells. *Daughter of Heaven,* I approach thee with praise, as the cow approaches her milker; accept, O Night! not the hymn only, but the oblation of thy suppliant, who prays that his foes may be subdued."

Some of the principal gods of the Hindoo Pantheon are, Dyaus (the Sky), Indra (the Rain-giver), Sûrya (the Sun), the Maruts (Winds), Aditi, (the Dawn), Parvati (the Earth,)[1] and Siva, her consort. The worship of the SUN is expressed in a variety of ways, and by a multitude of fanciful names. One of the principal of these is *Crishna.* The following is a prayer addressed to him :

"Be auspicious to my lay, O Chrishna, thou only God of the seven heavens, who swayest the universe through the immensity of space and matter. O universal and resplendent Sun! Thou mighty governor of the heavens ; thou sovereign regulator of the connected whole; thou sole and universal deity of mankind; thou gracious and Supreme Spirit; my noblest and most happy inspiration is thy praise and glory. Thy power I will praise, for thou art my sovereign Lord, whose bright image continually forces itself on my attention, eager imagination. Thou art the Being to whom heroes pray in perils of war; nor are their supplications vain, when thus they pray; whether it be when thou illuminest the eastern region with thy orient light, when in thy meridian splendor, or when thou majestically descendest in the West."

Crishna is made to say :

"I am the light in the Sun and Moon, far, far beyond the darkness. I am the brilliancy in flame, the radiance in all that's radiant, and the light of lights."[2]

In the *Maha-bharata,* Crishna, who having become the son of Aditi (the Dawn), is called *Vishnu,* another name for the Sun.[3] The demon *Putana* assaults the child Crishna, which identifies him with Hercules, the Sun-god of the Greeks.[4] In his Solar character he must again be the slayer of the Dragon or Black-snake *Kulnika,* the "Old Serpent" with the thousand heads.[5] Crishna's amours with the maidens makes him like Indra, Phoibus, Hercules, Samson, Alpheios, Paris and other Sun-gods. This is the hot and fiery Sun greeting the moon and the dew, or the Sun with his brides the *Stars.*[6]

Moore, in his Hindu Pantheon, observes :

"Although all the Hindu deities partake more or less remotely of the nature and character of Surya, or the SUN, and all more or less directly radiate from, or merge in, him, yet no one is, I think, so intimately identified with him as Vishnu; whether considered in his own person, or *in the character of his most glorious Avatara of* CRISHNA."

---

[1] The emblem of Parvati, the "Mother Goddess," was the YONI, and that of her consort Siva, the LINGHAM.

[2] Williams Hinduism, p. 213.

[3] See Cox : Aryan Mytho., vol. ii. pp. 105 and 130.

[4] Ibid. p. 135.

[5] Ibid. p. 137.

[6] See Ibid. p. 88, and Moor's Hindu Pantheon, p. 63.

The ancient religion of EGYPT, like that of Hindostan, was founded on astronomy, and eminently metaphysical in its character. The Egyptian priests were far advanced in the science of astronomy. They made astronomy their peculiar study. They knew the figure of the earth, and how to calculate solar and lunar eclipses. From very ancient time, they had observed the order and movement of the stars, and recorded them with the utmost care. Ramses the Great, generally called Sesostris, is supposed to have reigned one thousand five hundred years before the Christian era, about coeval with Moses, or a century later. In the tomb of this monarch was found a large massive circle of wrought gold, divided into three hundred and sixty-five degrees, and each division marked the rising and setting of the stars for each day.[1] This fact proves how early they were advanced in astronomy. In their great theories of mutual dependence between all things in the universe was included a belief in some mysterious relation between the Spirits of the Stars and human souls, so that the destiny of mortals was regulated by the motions of the heavenly bodies. This was the origin of the famous system of Astrology. From the conjunction of planets at the hour of birth, they prophesied what would be the temperament of an infant, what life he would live, and what death he would die. Diodorus, who wrote in the century preceding Christ Jesus, says :

"They frequently foretell with the greatest accuracy what is about to happen to mankind; showing the failure or abundance of crops, and the epidemic diseases about to befall men or cattle. Earthquakes, deluges, rising of comets, and all those phenomena, the knowledge of which appears impossible to common comprehensions, they foresee by means of their long continued observation."

P. Le Page Renouf, who is probably the best authority on the religion of ancient Egypt which can be produced, says, in his Hibbert Lectures :[2]

"The Lectures on the Science of Language, delivered nearly twenty years ago by Prof. Max Müller, have, I trust, made us fully understand how, among the *Indo-European* races, the names of the *Sun*, of *Sunrise* and *Sunset*, and of other such phenomena, come to be talked of and considered as *personages*, of whom wondrous legends have been told. *Egyptian* mythology not merely admits, but imperatively *demands, the same explanation.* And this becomes the more evident when we consider the question how these mythical personages came to be invested with the attributes of divinity by men who, like the Egyptians, had so lively a sense of the divine."

Kenrick, in his "History of Egypt," says :

[1] "According to Champollion, the tomb of Ramses V. at Thebes, contains tables of the constellations and of their influence (on human beings) for every hour of every month of the year." (Kenrick's Egypt, vol. i. p. 456.)
[2] p. 118.

"We have abundant evidence that the Egyptian theology had its origin in the personification of the powers of nature, under male and female attributes, and that this conception took a sensible form, such as the mental state of the people required, by the identification of these powers with the elements and the heavenly bodies, fire, earth, water, the sun and moon, and the Nile. Such appears *everywhere* to be the origin of the objective form of polytheism; and it is equally evident among the nations most closely allied to the Egyptians by position and general character—the Phenicians, the Babylonians, and in remote connection, the Indians on the one side and the Greeks on the other."

The gods and goddesses of the ancient PERSIANS were also personifications of the Sun, Moon, Stars, the elements, &c.

Ormuzd, "The King of Light," was god of the *Firmament,* and the "Principle of Goodness" and of Truth. He was called "The Eternal Source of Sunshine and Light," "The Centre of all that exists," "The First-born of the Eternal One," "The Creator," "The Sovereign Intelligence," "The All-seeing," "The Just Judge." He was described as "sitting on the throne of the good and the perfect, in regions of pure light," crowned with rays, and with a ring on his finger—a circle being an emblem of infinity; sometimes as a venerable, majestic man, seated on a Bull, their emblem of creation.

"*Mithras the Mediator*" was the god-Sun. Their most splendid ceremonials were in honor of Mithras. They kept his birth-day, with many rejoicings, on the twenty-fifth of December, when the Sun perceptibly begins to return northward, after his long winter journey; and they had another festival in his honor, at the vernal equinox. Perhaps no religious festival was ever more splendid than the "*Annual Salutation of Mithras,*" during which *forty days* were set apart for thanksgiving and sacrifice. The procession to salute the god was formed long before the rising of the Sun. The High Priest was followed by a long train of the Magi, in spotless white robes, chanting hymns, and carrying the sacred fire on silver censers. Then came three hundred and sixty-five youths in scarlet, to represent the days of the year and the color of fire. These were followed by the Chariot of the Sun, empty, decorated with garlands, and drawn by superb *white horses* harnessed with pure gold. Then came a white horse of magnificent size, his forehead blazing with gems, in honor of Mithras. Close behind him rode the king, in a chariot of ivory inlaid with gold, followed by his royal kindred in embroidered garments, and a long train of nobles riding on camels richly caparisoned. This gorgeous retinue, facing the East, slowly ascended Mount Orontes. Arrived at the summit, the High Priest assumed his tiara wreathed with myrtle, and hailed the first rays of the rising Sun with incense and prayer. The other Magi gradually joined him in singing hymns to Ormuzd, the source of all blessing, by whom the radiant Mithras had been sent to gladden the earth and preserve the principle of life. Finally, they all joined in one universal chorus of praise, while king, princes and nobles, prostrated themselves before the orb of day.

The HEBREWS worshiped the Sun, Moon, Stars, and "all the host of heaven."[1] *El-Shaddai* was one of the names given to the god Sun. Parkhurst, in his "Hebrew Lexicon," says, "*El* was the very name the heathens gave to their god *Sol*, their Lord or Ruler of the hosts of heaven." *El,* which means "the strong one in heaven"—the Sun, was invoked by the ancestors of all the Semitic nations, before there were Babylonians in Babylon, Phenicians in Sydon and Tyrus, before there were Jews in Mesopotamia or Jerusalem.[2]

The Sun was worshiped by the Hebrews under the names of Baal, Moloch, Chemosh, &c.; the Moon was Ashtoreth, the "Queen of Heaven."[3]

The gods of the ancient GREEKS and ROMANS were the same as the gods of the Indian epic poems. We have, for example : Zeupiter (Jupiter), corresponding to Dyaus-pitar (the Heaven-father), Juno, corresponding to Parvati (the Mother Goddess), and Apollo, corresponding to Crishna (the Sun, the Saviour).[4] Another name for the Sun among those people was *Bacchus.* An Orphic verse, referring to the Sun, says, " he is called Dionysos (a name of Bacchus) because he is carried with a circular motion through the immensely extended heavens."[5]

Dr. Prichard, in his "Analysis of Egyptian Mythology,"[6] speaking of the ancient Greeks and Romans, says :

"That the worship of the *powers of nature,* mitigated, indeed, and embellished, constituted the foundation of the Greek and Roman religion, will not be disputed by any person who surveys the fables of the Olympian Gods with a more penetrating eye than that of a mere antiquarian."

M. De Coulanges, speaking of them, says :

"The *Sun,* which gives fecundity; the *Earth,* which nourishes; the *Clouds,* by turns beneficent and destructive,—*such were the different powers of which they could make gods.* But from each one of these elements thousands of gods were created; because the same physical agent, *viewed under different aspects,* received from men different names. The Sun, for example. was called in one place *Hercules* (the glorious); in another, *Phœbus* (the shining); and still again, *Apollo* (he who drives away night or evil); one called him *Hyperion* (the elevated being); another, *Alexicacos* (the beneficent); and in the course of time groups of men, who had given these various names to the brilliant luminary, *no longer saw that they had the same god.*"[7]

---

[1] See Chapter XI.
[2] Müller : The Science of Relig., p. 190.
[3] See Chapter XI.
[4] See Indian Wisdom, p. 426.
[5] Taylor's Mysteries, p. 163.
[6] Page 239.
[7] The Ancient City, p. 162.

Richard Payne Knight says :

"The primitive religion of the *Greeks*, like that of all other nations not enlightened by *Revelation*, appears to have been *elementary*, and to have consisted
in an indistinct worship of the Sun, the Moon, the Stars, the Earth, and
the Waters, or rather, the spirits supposed to preside over these bodies, and
to direct their motions, and regulate their modes of existence. Every river,
spring or mountain had its local genius, or peculiar deity; and as men naturally endeavored to obtain the favor of their gods by such means as they feel
best adapted to win their own, the first worship consisted in offering to them
certain portions of whatever they held to be most valuable. At the same time,
the regular motions of the heavenly bodies, the stated returns of summer and
winter, of day and night, with all the admirable order of the universe, taught
them to believe in the existence and agency of such superior powers; the irregu-
lar and destructive efforts of nature, such as lightnings and tempests, inunda-
tions and earthquakes, persuaded them that these mighty beings had passions
and affections similar to their own, and only differed in possessing greater
strength, power, and intelligence."[1]

When the Grecian astronomers first declared that the Sun was
not a person, but a huge hot ball, instantly an outcry arose against
them. They were called *"blaspheming atheists,"* and from that
time to the present, when any new discovery is made which seems to
take away from man his god, the cry of "*Atheist*" is instantly raised.

If we turn from the ancient Greeks and Romans, and take a look
still farther West and North, we shall find that the gods of all the
Teutonic nations were the same as we have seen elsewhere. They
had Odin or Woden—from whom we have our *Wednesday*—the Al-
fader (the Sky), Frigga, the Mother Goddess (the Earth), "Baldur
the Good," and Thor—from whom we have our Thursday (personifications of the Sun), besides innumerable other *genii*, among
them Freyja—from whom we have our Friday—and as she was the
"Goddess of Love," we eat *fish* on that day.[2]

The gods of the ancient inhabitants of what are now called the
"British Islands" were identically the same. The *Sun*-god wor-
shiped by the Ancient Druids was called *Hu, Beli, Budd* and
Buddu-gre.[3]

The same worship which we have found in the Old World, from
the farthest East to the remotest West, may also be traced in
America, from its simplest or least clearly defined form, among the
roving hunters and squalid Esquimaux of the North, through every
intermediate stage of development, to the imposing systems of
Mexico and Peru, where it took a form nearly corresponding that
which it at one time sustained on the banks of the Ganges, and on
the plains of Assyria.[4]

---

[1] Ancient Art and Mythology, p. 1.
[2] See Mallet's Northern Antiquities. Though
spoken of in Northern mythology as distinct,
Frigga and Freyja are *originally* one.
[3] See Myths of the British Druids, p. 116.
[4] See Squire's Serpent Symbol.

Father Acosta, speaking of the Mexicans, says :

"Next to Viracocha, or their Supreme God, that which most commonly they have, and do adore, is the *Sun ;* and after, those things which are most remarkable in the celestial or elementary nature, as the Moon, Stars, Sea, and Land.

"Whoso shall merely look into it, shall find this manner which the Devil hath used to deceive the Indians, to be the same wherewith he hath deceived the Greeks and Romans, and other ancient Gentiles, giving them to understand that these notable creatures, the Sun, Moon, Stars, and elements, had power or authority to do good or harm to men."[1]

We see, then, that the gods and heroes of antiquity were originally personifications of certain elements of Nature, and that the legends of adventures ascribed to them are merely mythical forms of describing the phenomena of these elements.

These legends relating to the elements of Nature, whether they had reference to the Sun, the Moon, the Stars, or a certain natural phenomenon, became, in the course of time, to be regarded as accounts of men of a high order, who had once inhabited the earth. Sanctuaries and temples were erected to these heroes, their bones were searched for, and when found—which was always the case— were regarded as a great source of strength to the town that possessed them ; all relics of their stay on earth were hallowed, and a form of worship was specially adapted to them.

The idea that heavenly luminaries were inhabited by spirits, of a nature intermediate between God and men, first led mortals to address prayers to the orbs over which they were supposed to preside. In order to supplicate these deities, when Sun, Moon, and Stars were not visible, *they made images of them,* which the priests consecrated with many ceremonies. Then they pronounced solemn invocations to draw down the spirits into the statues provided for their reception. By this process it was supposed that a mysterious connection was established between the spirit and the image, so that prayers addressed to one were thenceforth heard by the other. This was probably the origin of image worship everywhere.

The *motive* of this worship was the same among all nations of antiquity, *i. e.,* fear. They supposed that these deities were irritated by the sins of men, but, at the same time, were merciful, and capable of being appeased by prayer and repentance ; for this reason men offered to these deities sacrifices and prayers. How natural that such should have been the case, for, as Abbé Dubois observes : "To the rude, untutored eye, the 'Host of Heaven,' clothed in that calm beauty which distinguishes an Oriental night, might well appear to be instinct with some divine principle, endowed with consciousness, and the power to influence, from its throne of unchanging splendor on high, the fortunes of transitory mortals."

---

[1] Acosta : vol. ii. pp. 303–305.

APPENDIX C.

All the chief stories that we know so well are to be found in all times, and in almost all countries. *Cinderella*, for one, is told in the language of every country in Europe, and the same legend is found in the fanciful tales related by the Greek poets ; and still further back, it appears in very ancient Hindoo legends. So, again, does *Beauty and the Beast ;* so does our familiar tale of *Jack, the Giant-Killer ;* so also do a great number of other fairy stories, each being told in different countries and in different periods, with so much likeness as to show that all the versions came from the same source, and yet with enough difference to show that none of the versions are directly copied from each other. "Indeed, when we compare the myths and legends of one country with another, and of one period with another, we find out how they have come to be so much alike, and yet in some things so different. We see that there must have been *one origin* for all these stories, that they must have been invented by *one people*, that this people must have been afterwards divided, and that each part or division of it must have brought into its new home the legends once common to them all, and must have shaped and altered these according to the kind of place in which they came to live ; those of the North being sterner and more terrible, those of the South softer and fuller of light and color, and adorned with touches of more delicate fancy." And this, indeed, is really the case. All the chief stories and legends are alike, because they were first made by *one people ;* and all the nations in which they are now told in one form or another tell them because they are all descended from this one common stock, the *Aryan*.

From researches made by Prof. Max Müller, The Rev. George W. Cox, and others, in England and Germany, in the science of *Comparative Mythology*, we begin to see something of these ancient forefathers of ours ; to understand what kind of people they were, and to find that our *fairy stories* are really made out of *their religion*.

The mind of the Aryan peoples in their ancient home was full of imagination. They never ceased to wonder at what they saw and heard in the sky and upon the earth. Their language was highly figurative, and so the things which struck them with wonder, and which they could not explain, were described under forms and names which were familiar to them. "Thus, the thunder was to them the bellowing of a mighty beast, or the rolling of a great chariot. In the lightning they saw a brilliant serpent, or a spear shot across the sky, or a great fish darting swiftly through the sea of cloud. The clouds were heavenly cows, who shed milk upon the earth and refreshed it ; or they were webs woven by heavenly women who drew water from the fountains on high and poured it down as rain." Analogies which are but fancy to us, were realities to these men of past ages. They could see in the water-spout a huge serpent who elevated himself out of the ocean and reached his head to the skies. They could feel, in the pangs of hunger, a live creature gnawing within their bodies, and they heard the voices of the hill-dwarfs answering in the echo. The *Sun*, the first object which struck them with wonder, was, to them, the child of Night; the Dawn came before he was born, and died as he rose in the heavens. He strangled the serpents of the night; he went forth like a bridegroom out of his chamber, and like a giant to run his course.[1] He had to do battle with clouds and storms.[2] Sometimes his light grew dim under their gloomy veil, and the children of men shuddered at the wrath of the hidden Sun.[3] Sometimes his ray broke forth, only, after brief splendor, to sink beneath a deeper darkness; sometimes he burst forth at the end of his course, trampling on the clouds which had dimmed his brilliancy, and bathing his pathway with blood.[4] Sometimes, beneath moun-tains of clouds and vapors, he plunged into the leaden sea.[5] Some-times he looked benignly on the face of his mother or his bride who came to greet him at his journey's end.[6] Sometimes he was the lord of heaven and of light, irresistible in his divine strength; sometimes he toiled for others, not for himself, in a hard, unwill-ing servitude.[7] His light and heat might give light and destroy it.[8] His chariot might scorch the regions over which it passed, his flam-ing fire might burn up all who dared to look with prying eyes into his dazzling treasure-house.[9] He might be the child destined to slay his parents, or to be united at the last in an unspeakable peace, to the bright Dawn who for a brief space had gladdened his path in the morning.[10] He might be the friend of the children of men, and the remorseless foe of those powers of darkness who had stolen away his bride.[11] He might be a warrior whose eye strikes terror

---

[1] This picture would give us the story of Hercules, who strangled the serpent in his cradle, and who, in after years, in the form of a giant, ran his course.

[2] This would give us St. George killing the Dragon.

[3] This would give us the story of the mon-ster who attempted to devour the Sun, and whom the "untutored savage" tried to frighten away by making loud cries.

[4] This would give us the story of Samson, whose strength was renewed at the end of his career, and who slew the Philistines—who had dimmed his brilliance—and bathed his path with blood.

[5] This would give us the story of Oannes or Dagon, who, beneath the clouds of the evening sky, plunged into the sea.

[6] This would give us the story of Hercules and his bride Iôle, or that of Christ Jesus and his mother Mary, who were at their side at the end of their career.

[7] This would give us the story of the labors of Hercules.

[8] This is the Sun as *Seva*.

[9] Here again we have the Sun as Siva the *Destroyer*.

[10] Here we have Apollo, Achilleus, Bellero-phon and Odysseus.

[11] This would give us the story of Samson, who was "the friend of the children of men, and the remorseless foe of those powers of darkness" (the Philistines), who had stolen away his bride. (See Judges, ch. xv.)

into his enemies, or a wise chieftain skilled in deep and hidden knowledge.[1] Sometimes he might appear as a glorious being doomed to an early death, which no power could avert or delay.[2] Sometimes grievous hardships and desperate conflicts might be followed by a long season of serene repose.[3] Wherever he went, men might welcome him in love, or shrink from him in fear and anguish.[4] He would have many brides in many lands, and his offspring would assume aspects beautiful, strange or horrible.[5] His course might be brilliant and beneficent; or gloomy, sullen, and capricious.[6] As compelled to toil for others, he would be said to fight in quarrels not his own; or he might for a time withhold the aid of an arm which no enemy could withstand.[7] He might be the destroyer of all whom he loved, he might slay the Dawn with his kindling rays, he might scorch the Fruits, who were his children; he might woo the deep blue sky, the bride of heaven itself, and an inevitable doom might bind his limbs on the blazing wheel for ever and ever.[8] Nor in this crowd of phrases, all of which have borne their part in the formation of mythology, is there one which could not be used naturally by ourselves to describe the phenomena of the outward world, and there is scarcely one, perhaps, which has not been used by our own poets. There is a beauty in them, which can never grow old or lose its charm. Poets of all ages recur to them instinctively in times of the deepest grief or the greatest joy; but, in the words of Professor Max Müller, "it is impossible to enter fully into the thoughts and feelings which passed through the minds of the early poets when they formed names for that far East from whence even the early Dawn, the Sun, the Day, their own life seemed to spring. A new life flashed up every morning before their eyes, and the fresh breezes of the Dawn reached them like greetings wafted across the golden threshold of the sky from the distant lands beyond the mountains, beyond the clouds, beyond the dawn, beyond the immortal sea which brought us hither! The Dawn seemed to them to open golden gates for the Sun to pass in triumph; and while those gates were open, their eyes and their minds strove, in their childish way, to pierce beyond the limits of this finite world. That silent aspect wakened in the human mind the conception of the Infinite, the Immortal, the Divine; and the names of the Dawn became naturally the names of higher powers.[9]

---

[1] This would give us the stories of *Thor*, the mighty warrior, the terror of his enemies, and those of Cadmus, Romulus or Odin, the wise chieftains, who founded nations, and taught their people knowledge.

[2] This would give us the story of Christ Jesus, and other Angel-Messiahs; Saviours of men.

[3] This would give us the stories of spellbound maidens, who sleep for years.

[4] This is Hercules and his counterparts.

[5] This again is Hercules.

[6] This would depend upon whether his light was obscured by clouds, or not.

[7] This again *is* Hercules.

[8] This is Apollo, Siva and Ixion.

[9] Rev. G. W. Cox.

" This imagery of the Aryans was applied by them to all they saw in the sky. Sometimes, as we have said, the clouds were cows ; they were also dragons, which sought to slay the Sun ; or great ships floating across the sky, and casting anchor upon earth ; or rocks, or mountains, or deep caverns, in which evil deities hid the golden light. Then, also, they were shaped by fancy into animals of various kinds—the bear, the wolf, the dog, the ox ; and into giant birds, and into monsters which were both bird and beast.

" The winds, again, in their fancy, were the companions or ministers of India, the sky-god. The spirits of the winds gathered into their host the souls of the dead—thus giving birth to the Scandinavian and Teutonic legend of the Wild Horseman, who rides at midnight through the stormy sky, with his long train of dead behind him, and his weird hounds before.[1] The Ribhus, or Arbhus, again, were the sunbeams or the lightning, who forged the armor of the gods, and made their thunderbolts, and turned old people young, and restored out of the hides alone the slaughtered cow on which the gods had feasted."[2]

Aryan myths, then, were no more than poetic fancies about light and darkness, cloud and rain, night and day, storm and wind ; and when they moved westward and southward, *the Aryan race brought these legends with it;* and out of these were shaped by degrees innumerable gods and demons of the Hindoos, the devs and jinns of the Persians ; the great gods, the minor deities, and nymphs, and fauns, and satyrs of Greek mythology and poetry ; the stormy divinities, the giants, and trolls of the cold and rugged North ; the dwarfs of the German forests ; the elves who dance merrily in the moonlight of an English summer ; and the " good people " who play mischievous tricks upon stray peasants among the Irish hills. *Almost all, indeed, that we have of a legendary kind comes to us from our Aryan forefathers*—sometimes scarcely changed, sometimes so altered that we have to puzzle out the links between the old and the new ; but all these myths and traditions, and old-world stories, when we come to know the meaning of them, take us back to the time when the Aryan race dwelt together in the high lands of central Asia, and they all mean the same things—that is, the relation between the Sun and the earth, the succession of night and day, of winter and summer, of storm and calm, of cloud and tempest, and golden sunshine, and bright blue sky. And this is the source from which we get our fairy stories, and tales of gods and heroes ; for underneath all of them there are the same fanciful meanings, only changed and altered in the way of putting them by the lapse of ages

---

[1] Who has not heard it said that the howling or whining of a dog forebodes death ?
[2] Bunce : Fairy Tales, Origin and Meaning.

of time, by the circumstances of different countries, and by the fancy of those who kept the wonderful tales alive without knowing what they meant.

Thousands of years ago, the Aryan people began their march out of their old country in mid-Asia. From the remains of their language, and the likeness of their legends to those among other nations, we know that ages and ages ago their country grew too small for them, so they were obliged to move away from it. Some of them turned southward into India and Persia, and some of them went westward into Europe—the time, perhaps, when the land of Europe stretched from the borders of Asia to the islands of Great Britain, and when there was no sea between them and the main land. How they made their long and toilsome march we know not. But, as Kingsley writes of such a movement of an ancient tribe, so we may fancy these old Aryans marching westward—"the tall, bare-limbed men, with stone axes on their shoulders and horn bows at their backs, with herds of gray cattle, guarded by huge lap-eared mastiffs, with shaggy white horses, heavy-horned sheep, and silky goats, moving always westward through the boundless steppes, whither or why we know not, but that the Al-Father had sent them forth. And behind us (he makes them say) the rosy snow-peaks died into ghastly gray, lower and lower, as every evening came; and before us the plains spread infinite, with gleaming salt-lakes, and ever fresh tribes of gaudy flowers. Behind us, dark lines of living beings streamed down the mountain slopes; around us, dark lines crawled along the plains—all westward, westward ever. Who could stand against us? We met the wild asses on the steppe, and tamed them, and made them our slaves. We slew the bison herds, and swam broad rivers on their skins. The python snake lay across our path; the wolves and wild dogs snarled at us out of their coverts; we slew them and went on. Strange giant tribes met us, and eagle visaged hordes, fierce and foolish; we smote them, hip and thigh, and went on, westward ever."[1] And so they went on, straight toward the West, or, as they turned North and South, and thus overspread new lands, *they brought with them their old ways of thought and forms of belief*, and the stories in which these had taken form; *and on these were built up the gods and heroes*, and all wonder-working creatures and things, and the poetical fables and fancies which have come down to us, and which still linger in our customs and our fairy tales; bright and sunny and many-colored in the warm regions of the South, sterner and wilder and rougher in the North, more home-like in the middle and western countries; but always alike in their

---

[1] Quoted by Bunce: Fairy Tales.

main features, and always having the same meaning when we come to dig it out, and these forms and their meaning being the same in the lands of the West Aryans as in those still peopled by the Aryans of the East.

The story of *Cinderella* is one of the many fairy tales which help us to find out their meaning, and take us straight back to the far-off land where fairy legends began, and to the people who made them. This well-known fairy tale has been found among the myths of our Aryan ancestors, and from this we know that it is the story of the *Sun* and the *Dawn*. Cinderella, gray and dark and dull, is all neglected when she is away from the Sun, obscured by the envious clouds, her sisters, and by her step-mother, the Night. So she is Aurora, the Dawn, and the Fairy Prince is the Morning Sun, ever pursuing her, to claim her for his bride. This is the legend as it is found in the ancient Hindoo books ; and this explains at once the *source* and the *meaning* of the fairy tale.[1]

Another tale which helps us in our task is that of *Jack the Giant-Killer*, who is really one of the very oldest and most widely known, characters in wonder-land. Now, who is this wonderful little fellow ? He is none other than the hero who, in all countries and ages, fights with monsters and overcomes them ; like Indra, the ancient Hindoo Sun-god, whose thunderbolts slew the demons of drought in the far East ; or Perseus, who, in Greek story, delivers the maiden from the sea-monster ; or Odysseus, who tricks the giant Polyphemus, and causes him to throw himself into the sea ; or Thor, whose hammer beats down the frost giants of the North. "The gifts bestowed upon Jack are found in Tartar stories, Hindoo tales, in German legends, and in the fables of Scandinavia."

Still another is that of *Little Red Riding-Hood*. The story of Little Red Riding Hood, as we call her, or Little Red-Cap, as she is called in the German tales, also comes from the same source, and (as we have seen in Chapter IX.), refers to the *Sun* and *Night*.

" One of the fancies in the most ancient Aryan or Hindoo stories was that there was a great dragon that was trying to devour the Sun, to prevent him from shining upon the earth, and filling it with brightness and life and beauty, and that Indra, the Sun-god, killed the dragon. Now, this is the meaning of Little Red Riding-Hood, as it is told in our nursery tales. Little Red Riding-Hood is the Evening *Sun*, which is always described as red or golden ; the old grandmother is the *Earth*, to whom the rays of the Sun bring warmth and comfort. The wolf—which is a well-known figure for

---

[1] See Bunce : Fairy Tales, p. 34.

the *Clouds* and blackness of *Night* (in Teutonic mythology)[1]—is the dragon in another form. First, he devours the grandmother; that is, he wraps the earth in thick clouds, which the Evening Sun is not strong enough to pierce through. Then, with the darkness of Night, he swallows up the Evening Sun itself, and all is dark and desolate. Then, as in the German tale, the night-thunder and the storm.winds are represented by the loud snoring of the wolf; and then the huntsman, the *Morning Sun,* comes in all his strength and majesty, and chases away the night clouds and kills the wolf, and revives old grandmother Earth and Little Red Riding Hood to life again."

Nor is it in these stories alone that we can trace the ancient Hindoo legends, and the Sun-myth. There is, as Mr. Bunce observes in his "Fairy Tales, their Origin and Meaning," scarcely a tale of Greek or Roman mythology, no legend of Teutonic or Celtic or Scandinavian growth, no great romance of what we call the middle ages, no fairy story taken down from the lips of ancient folk, and dressed for us in modern shape and tongue, that we do not find, in some form or another, in these Eastern poems, *which are composed of allegorical tales of gods and heroes.*

When, in the Vedic hymns, Kephalos, Prokris, Hermes, Daphne, Zeus, Ouranos, stand forth as simple names for the Sun, the Dew, the Wind, the Dawn, the Heaven and the Sky, each recognized as such, yet each endowed with the most perfect consciousness, we feel that the great riddle of mythology is solved, and that we no longer lack the key which shall disclose its most hidden treasures. When we hear the people saying, "Our friend the Sun is dead. Will he rise? Will the Dawn come back again?" we see the death of Hercules, and the weary waiting while Leto struggles with the birth of Phoibos. When on the return of day we hear the cry—

"Rise! our life, our spirit has come back, the darkness is gone, the light draws near!"

—we are carried at once to the Homeric hymn, and we hear the joyous shout of all the gods when Phoibos springs to life and light on Delos.[2]

That the peasant folk-lore of modern Europe still displays

---

[1] "The *Sun,*" said *Gaugler,* "speeds at such a rate as if *she* feared that some one was pursuing her for her destruction." "And well she may," replied *Har,* "for he that seeks her is not far behind, and she has no way to escape but to run before him." "And who is he," asked *Gaugler,* "that causes her this anxiety?" "It is the *Wolf* Sköll," answered *Har,* "who pursues the Sun, and it is he that she fears,

for he shall one day overtake and devour her." (Scandinavian *Prose Edda.* See Mallet's Northern Antiquities, p. 407). This Wolf is, as we have said, a personification of *Night* and *Clouds,* we therefore have the almost universal practice among savage nations of making noises at the time of eclipses, to frighten away the monsters who would otherwise devour the Sun.

[2] Aryan Mythology, vol. i. p. 108.

episodes of nature-myth, may be seen in the following story of *Vassalissa, the Beautiful.*

Vassalissa's stepmother and two sisters, plotting against her life, send her to get a light at the house of *Bàba Yagà,* the witch, and her journey contains the following history of the *Day,* told, as Mr. Tylor says, in truest mythic fashion :

"Vassalissa goes and wanders, wanders in the forest. She goes, and she shudders. Suddenly before her bounds a rider, he himself white, and clad in white, and the trappings white. *And Day began to dawn.* She goes farther, when a second rider bounds forth, himself red, clad in red, and on a red horse. *The Sun began to rise.* She goes on all day, and towards evening arrives at the witch's house. Suddenly there comes again a rider, himself black, clad in all black, and on a black horse; he bounded to the gates of the *Bàba Yagà,* and disappeared *as if he had sunk through the earth. Night fell.* After this, when Vassalissa asks the witch, 'Who was the white rider ?' she answered, 'That is my clear *Day;'* 'Who was the red rider ?' 'That is my red *Sun;'* 'Who was the black rider ?' 'That is my black *Night.* They are all my trusty friends.'"[1]

We have another illustration of allegorical mythology in the Grecian story of Hephæstos splitting open with his axe the head of Zeus, and Athene springing from it, full armed ; for we perceive behind this savage imagery Zeus as the bright *Sky,* his forehead the *East,* Hesphæstos as the young, not yet risen *Sun,* and Athene as the *Dawn,* the daughter of the Sky, stepping forth from the fountain-head of light,—with eyes like an owl, pure as a virgin ; the golden ; lighting up the tops of the mountains, and her own glorious Parthenon in her own favorite town of Athens ; whirling the shafts of light ; the genial warmth of the morning ; the foremost champion in the battle between night and day ; in full armor, in her panoply of light, driving away the darkness of night, and awakening men to a bright life, to bright thoughts, to bright endeavors.[2]

Another story of the same sort is that of Kronos. Every one is familiar with the story of Kronos, who devoured his own children. Now, Kronos is a mere creation from the older and misunderstood epithet Kronides or Kronion, the ancient of days. When these days or time had come to be regarded as a person the myth would certainly follow that he devoured his own children, as Time is the devourer of the Dawns.[3] Saturn, who devours his own children, is the same power whom the Greeks called Kronos (Time), which may truly be said to destroy whatever it has brought into existence.

The idea of a *Heaven,* the "Elysian fields," is also born of the sky.

The *"Elysian plain"* is far away in the *West,* where the sun

[1] Tylor: Primitive Culture, vol. i. p. 308.   [2] Müller : The Science of Religion, p. 65.
[3] Cox : Aryan Mythology, vol. ii. p. 1.

goes down beyond the bonds of the earth, when Eos gladdens the
close of day as she sheds her violet tints over the sky. The
"Abodes of the Blessed" are golden islands sailing in a sea of blue,
—*the burnished clouds floating in the pure ether.* Grief and sorrow
cannot approach them; plague and sickness cannot touch them.
The blissful company gathered together in that far *Western land* in-
herits a tearless eternity.

Of the other details in the picture the greater number would be
suggested directly by these images drawn from the phenomena of
sunset and twilight. What spot or stain can be seen on the deep
blue ocean in which the "Islands of the Blessed" repose forever?
What unseemly forms can mar the beauty of that golden home,
lighted by the radiance of a *Sun* which can never set? Who then
but the pure in heart, the truthful and the generous, can be suffered
to tread the violet fields? And how shall they be tested save by
judges who can weigh the thoughts and the interests of the heart?
Thus every soul, as it drew near that joyous land, was brought before the august tribunal of Minos, Rhadamanthys, and Aiakos; and
they whose faith was in truth a quickening power, might draw from
the ordeals those golden lessons which Plato has put into the mouth
of Socrates, and some unknown persons into the mouths of Buddha
and Jesus. The belief of earlier ages pictured to itself the meetings
in that blissful land, the forgiveness of old wrongs, and the reconciliation of deadly feuds,[1] just as the belief of the present day
pictures these things to itself.

The story of a *War in Heaven,* which was known to all nations
of antiquity, is allegorical, and refers to the battle between light
and darkness, sunshine and storm cloud.[2]

As examples of the prevalence of the legend relating to the
struggle between the co-ordinate powers of good and evil, light and
darkness, the Sun and the clouds, we have that of Phoibos and
Python, Indra and Vritra, Sigurd and Fafnir, Achilleus and Paris,
Oidipous and the Sphinx, Ormuzd and Ahriman, and from the
character of the struggle between Indra and Vritra, and again be-

---

[1] As the hand of Hector is clasped in the
hand of the hero who slew him. There, as the
story ran, the lovely Helen "pardoned and
purified," became the bride of the short-lived,
yet long-suffering Achilleus, even as Iole comforted the dying Hercules on earth, and Hebe
became his solace in Olympus. But what is
the meeting of Helen and Achilleus, of Iole
and Hebe and Hercules, but the return of the
violet tints to greet the Sun in the *West,* which
had greeted him in the East in the morning?
The idea was purely physical, yet it suggested
the thoughts of trial, atonement, and purifica-

tion; and it is unnecessary to say that the
human mind, having advanced thus far, must
make its way still farther. (Cox: Aryan Mythology, vol. ii. p. 322.)

[2] The black storm-cloud, with the flames of
lightning issuing from it, was the original of
the dragon with tongues of fire. Even as late as
A.D. 1600, a German writer would illustrate a
thunder-storm destroying a crop of corn by a
picture of a dragon devouring the produce of
the field with his flaming tongue and iron teeth
(Baring-Gould: Curious Myths, p. 342.)

tween Ormuzd and Ahriman, we infer that a myth, purely *physical*, in the land of the Five Streams, assumed a moral and spiritual meaning in Persia, and the fight between the co-ordinate powers of good and evil, *gave birth to the dualism which 'from that time to the present has exercised so mighty an influence through the East and West.*

The Apocalypse exhibits Satan with the physical attributes of Ahriman ; he is called the "dragon," the "old serpent," who fights against God and his angels. The *Vedic myth*, transformed and exaggerated in the Iranian books, *finds its way through this channel* into Christianity. The idea thus introduced was that of the struggle between Satan and Michael, which ended in the overthrow of the former, and the casting forth of all his hosts out of heaven, but it coincides too nearly with a myth spread in countries held by all the Aryan nations to avoid further modification. Local tradition substituted St. George or St. Theodore for Jupiter, Apollo, Hercules, or Perseus. It is under this disguise that the Vedic myth has come down to our own times, and has still its festivals and its monuments. Art has consecrated it in a thousand ways. St. Michael, lance in hand, treading on the dragon, is an image as familiar now as, *thirty centuries ago*, that of Indra treading under foot the demon Vritra could possibly have been to the Hindoo.[1]

The very ancient doctrine of a TRINITY, three gods in one, can be explained, rationally, by allegory only. We have seen that the Sun, in early times, was believed to be the *Creator*, and became the first object of adoration. After some time it would be observed that this powerful and beneficent agent, the solar fire, was the most potent *Destroyer*, and hence would arise the first idea of a Creator and Destroyer united in the same person. But much time would not elapse before it must have been observed, that the destruction caused by this powerful being was destruction only in appearance, that destruction was only reproduction in another form—*regeneration;* that if he appeared sometimes to destroy, he constantly repaired the injury which he seemed to occasion—and that, without his light and heat, everything would dwindle away into a cold, inert, unprolific mass. Thus, at once, in the same being, became concentrated, the creating, the preserving, and the destroying powers—the latter of the three being at the same time both the *Destroyer* and *Regenerator.* Hence, by a very natural and obvious train of reasoning, arose the *Creator*, the *Preserver*, and the *Destroyer* —in India *Brahmā, Vishnu*, and *Siva;* in Persia *Oromasdes, Mithra*, and *Arimanius ;* in Egypt *Osiris, Horus*, and *Typhon :* in each case THREE PERSONS AND ONE GOD. And thus undoubtedly arose the TRIMURTI, or the celebrated Trinity.

[1] M. Bréal, and G. W. Cox.

Traces of a similar refinement may be found in the Greek mythology, in the Orphic *Phanes, Ericapeus* and *Metis,* who were all identified with the *Sun,* and yet embraced in the first person, *Phanes,* or *Protogones,* the Creator and Generator.[1] The invocation to the Sun, in the Mysteries, according to Macrobius, was as follows: "O all-ruling *Sun! Spirit* of the world! *Power* of the world! *Light* of the world!"[2]

We have seen in Chap. XXXV, that the *Peruvian* Triad was represented by three statues, called, respectively, "Apuinti, Churiinti, and Intihoaoque," which is, "Lord and Father *Sun;* Son *Sun;* and Air or Spirit, Brother *Sun.*"[3]

Mr. Faber, in his "Origin of Pagan Idolatry," says:

"The peculiar mode in which the Hindoos identify their *three great gods* with the *solar orb,* is a curious specimen of the physical refinements of ancient mythology. At night, in the west, the Sun is *Vishnu;* he is *Brahmā* in the east and in the morning; and from noon to evening he is *Siva.*"[4]

Mr. Moor, in his "Hindu Pantheon," says:

"Most, if not all, of the gods of the Hindoo Pantheon will, on close investigation, resolve themselves into the *three powers* (Brahmā, Vishnu, and Siva), and those powers into *one Deity,* Brahm, *typified by the Sun.*"[5]

Mr. Squire, in his "Serpent Symbol," observes:

"It is highly probable that the triple divinity of the Hindoos was originally no more than a personification of the *Sun,* whom they called *Three-bodied,* in the triple capacity of *producing* forms by his general *heat, preserving* them by his *light,* or *destroying* them by the counteracting force of his *igneous* matter. *Brahmā,* the *Creator,* was indicated by the *heat of the Sun;* Vishnu, the *Preserver,* by the *light of the Sun,* and *Siva,* the *Reproducer,* by the *orb of the Sun.* In the morning the Sun was *Brahmā,* at noon *Vishnu,* at evening *Siva.*"[6]

"He is at once," says Mr. Cox, in speaking of the Sun, "the 'Comforter' and 'Healer,' the 'Saviour' and 'Destroyer,' who can slay and make alive at will, and from whose piercing glance no secret can be kept hid."[7]

Sir William Jones was also of the opinion that the whole Triad of the Hindoos were identical with the Sun, expressed under the mythical term O. M.

The idea of a *Tri-murti,* or triple personification, was developed gradually, and as it grew, received numerous accretions. It was first dimly shadowed forth and vaguely expressed in the *Rig-Veda,* where a triad of principal gods, *Agni, Indra,* and *Surya* is recognized. And these three gods are *One,* the SUN.[8]

---

[1] Squire: Serpent Symbol, p. 59.
[2] Ibid.
[3] Ibid. p. 181.
[4] Book iv ch. i. In Anac,. vol. i. p. 137.
[5] p. 6.
[6] Squire: Serpent Symbol, p. 88.
[7] Aryan Mytho., vol. ii. p. 83.
[8] Williams' Hinduism, p. 68.

We see then that the religious myths of antiquity and the fireside legends of ancient and modern times, have a common root in the mental habits of primeval humanity, and that they are the earliest recorded utterances of men concerning the visible phenomena of the world into which they were born. At first, thoroughly understood, the *meaning* in time became unknown. How stories originally told of the Sun, the Moon, the Stars, &c., became believed in as facts, is plainly illustrated in the following story told by Mrs. Jameson in her "History of Our Lord in Art :" "I once tried to explain," says she, "to a good old woman, the meaning of the word *parable,* and that the story of the *Prodigal Son* was not a fact ; she was scandalized—she was quite sure that Jesus would never have told anything to his disciples that was not true. Thus she settled the matter in her own mind, and I thought it best to leave it there undisturbed."

Prof. Max Müller, in speaking of "the comparison of the different forms of Aryan religion and mythology in India, Persia, Greece, Italy and Germany," clearly illustrates how such legends are transformed from intelligible into unintelligible myths. He says :

"In each of these nations there was a tendency to change the original conception of divine powers, to misunderstand the many names given to these powers, and to misinterpret the praises addressed to them. In this manner some of the divine names were changed into half-divine, half-human heroes, and at last the myths which were true and intelligible as told originally of the *Sun,* or the *Dawn,* or the *Storms,* were turned into legends or fables too marvelons to be believed of common mortals. This process can be watched in India, in Greece, and in Germany. The same story, or nearly the same, is told of gods, of heroes, and of men. The divine myth became an heroic legend, and the heroic legend fades away into a nursery tale. Our nursery tales have well been called the modern *patois* of the ancient mythology of the Aryan race."[1]

In the words of this learned author, "we never lose, we always gain, when we discover the most ancient intention of sacred traditions, instead of being satisfied with their later aspect, and their modern misinterpretations."

---

[1] Müller's Chips, vol. ii. p. 260.

APPENDIX D.

WE maintain that not so much as one single passage purporting to be written, *as history*, within the first hundred years of the Christian era, can be produced to show the existence *at* or before that time of such a person as Jesus of Nazareth, called the Christ, or of such a set of men as could be accounted his disciples or followers. Those who would be likely to refer to Jesus or his disciples, but who have not done so, wrote about :

A. D. 40 Philo.[1]
40 Josephus.
79 C. Plinius Second, the Elder.[2] ⎫
69 L. Ann. Seneca.   ⎬ Philosophers.
79 Diogenes Laertius.   ⎭
79 Pausanias.   ⎫
79 Pompon Mela. ⎬ Geographers.
79 Q. Curtius Ruf. ⎫
79 Luc. Flor.   ⎪
110 Cornel Tacitus. ⎬ Historians.
123 Appianus.   ⎪
140 Justinus.   ⎪
141 Ælianus.   ⎭

Out of this number it has been claimed that one (Josephus) spoke of Jesus, and another (Tacitus) of the Christians. Of the former it is almost needless to speak, as that has been given up by Christian divines many years ago. However, for the sake of those who still cling to it we shall state the following :

Dr. Lardner, who wrote about A.D. 1760, says :

1. It was never quoted by any of our Christian ancestors before *Esuebius*.

2. Josephus has nowhere else mentioned the name or word *Christ*, in any of his works, except the testimony above mentioned,[3] and the passage concerning James, the Lord's brother.[4]

3. It interrupts the narrative.

4. The language is quite Christian.

5. It is *not* quoted by Chrysostom,[5] though he often refers to Josephus, and could not have omitted quoting it, had it been *then*, in the text.

---

[1] The Rev. Dr. Giles says : "Great is our disappointment at finding nothing in the works of Philo about the Christians, their doctrines, or their sacred books. About the *books* indeed we need not expect any notice of these works, but about the Christians and their doctrines his silence is more remarkable, seeing that he was about sixty years old at the time of the crucifixion, and living mostly in Alexandria, so closely connected with Judea, and the Jews, could hardly have failed to know something of the *wonderful events* that had taken place in the city of Jerusalem." (Hebrew and Christian Records, vol. ii. p. 61.)

The Rev. Dr. assumes that these "wonderful events" really took place, but, if they did not take place, of course Philo's silence on the subject is accounted for.

[2] Both these philosophers were living, and must have experienced the immediate effects, or received the earliest information of the existence of Christ Jesus, had such a person as the Gospels make him out to be ever existed. Their ignorance or their willful silence on the the subject, is not less than *improbable*.

[3] Antiquities, bk. xviii. ch. iii. 3.

[4] Ibid. bk. xx. ch. ix. 1.

[5] John, Bishop of Constantinople, who died

APPENDIX.   565

6. It is *not* quoted by Photius, though he has thiee articles concerning Josephus.

7. Under the article *Justus of Tiberius*, this author (Photius) expressly states that this historian (Josephus), being a Jew, *has not taken the least notice of Christ*.

8. Neither Justin, in his dialogue with Typho the Jew, nor Clemens Alexandrinus, who made so many extracts from ancient authors, nor Origen against Celsus, *have even mentioned this testimony*.

9. But, on the contrary, Origen openly affirms (ch. xxxv., bk. i., against Celsus), that Josephus, who had mentioned John the Baptist, *did not acknowledge Christ*.[1]

In the "Bible for Learners," we read as follows :

"Flavius Josephus, the well-known historian of the Jewish people, was born in A. D. 37, only two years after the death of Jesus; but though his work is of inestimable value as our chief authority for the circumstances of the times in which Jesus and his Apostles came forward, yet he does not seem to have ever mentioned Jesus himself. At any rate, the passage in his '*Jewish Antiquities*' that refers to him is certainly spurious, and was inserted by a later and a *Christian hand*. The *Talmud* compresses the history of Jesus into a single sentence, and later Jewish writers concoct mere slanderous anecdotes. The ecclesiastical fathers mention a few sayings or events, the knowledge of which they drew from oral tradition or from writings that have since been lost. The Latin and Greek historians just mention his name. This meager harvest is all we reap from sources outside the Gospels."[2]

Canon Farrar, who finds himself *compelled* to admit that this passage in Josephus is an interpolation, consoles himself by saying :

"The single passage in which he (Josephus) alludes to Him (Christ) is interpolated, if not wholly spurious, and no one can doubt that his silence on the subject of Christianity was as deliberate as it was dishonest."[3]

The Rev. Dr. Giles, after commenting on this subject, concludes by saying :

"*Eusebius* is the first who quotes the passage, and our reliance on the judgment, *or even the honesty*, of this writer *is not so great as to allow of our considering everything found in his works as undoubtedly genuine*."[4]

Eusebius, then, is the first person who refers to these passages.[5] Eusebius, "*whose honesty is not so great as to allow of our considering everything found in his works as undoubtedly genuine*." Eusebius, who says that *it is lawful to lie and cheat for the cause of Christ*.[6] This Eusebius is the sheet-anchor of reliance for most we know of the first three centuries of the Christian history. What then must we think of the *history* of the first three centuries of the Christian era ?

---

1 Lardner : vol. vi. ch. iii.
2 Bible for Learners, vol. iii. p. 27.
3 Life of Christ, vol. I. p. 63.
4 Hebrew and Christ. Rec. vol. ii. p. 62.
5 In his Eccl. Hist. lib. 2. ch. xii.
6 Ch. 31, bk. xii. of Eusebius *Præ paratio Evangelica* is entitled : "How far it may be proper to use falsehood as a medium for the benefit of those who require to be deceived ;" and he closes his work with these words : "I have repeated whatever may rebound to the glory, and suppressed all that could tend to the disgrace of our religion."

The celebrated passage in Tacitus which Christian divines—and even some liberal writers—attempt to support, is to be found in his *Annals.* In this work he is made to speak of *Christians,* who "had their denomination from *Christus,* who, in the reign of Tiberius, was put to death as a criminal by the procurator Pontius Pilate."

In answer to this we have the following :

1. This passage, which would have served the purpose of Christian quotation better than any other in all the writings of Tacitus, or of any Pagan writer whatever, *is not quoted by any of the Christian Fathers.*

2. It is not quoted by Tertullian, though he had read and largely quotes the works of Tacitus.

3. And though his argument immediately called for the use of this quotation with so loud a voice (Apol. ch. v.), that his omission of it, if it had really existed, amounts to a *violent improbability.*.

4. This Father has spoken of Tacitus in a way that it is absolutely impossible that he should have spoken of him, had his writings contained such a passage.

5. It is not quoted by Clemens Alexandrinus, *who set himself entirely to the work of adducing and bringing together all the admissions and recognitions which Pagan authors had made of the existence of Christ Jesus or Christians before his time.*

6. It has been nowhere stumbled upon by the laborious and all-seeking Eusebius, who could by no possibility have overlooked it, and whom it would have saved from the labor of forging the passage in Josephus ; of adducing the correspondence of Christ Jesus and Abgarus, and the Sibylline verses ; of forging a divine revelation from the god Apollo, in attestation of Christ Jesus' ascension into heaven ; and innumerable other of his pious and holy cheats.

7. Tacitus has in no other part of his writings made the least allusion to " *Christ* " or " *Christians.*"

8. The use of this passage as part of the evidences of the Christian religion, is absolutely modern.

9. There is no vestige nor trace of its existence anywhere in the world before the 15th century.[1]

---

[1] The original MSS. containing the "Annals of Tacitus" were "discovered" in the fifteenth century. Their existence cannot be traced back further than that time. And as it was an age of imposture, some persons are disposed to believe that not only portions of the *Annals,* but the whole work, was forged at that time. Mr. J. W. Ross, in an elaborate work published in London some years ago, contended that the *Annals* were forged by Poggio Bracciolini, their professed discoverer. At the time of Bracciolini the temptation was great to palm off literary forgeries, especially of the chief writers of antiquity, on acount of the Popes, in their efforts to revive learning, giving money rewards and indulgences to those who should procure MS. copies of any of the ancient Greek or Roman authors. Manuscripts turned up as if by magic, in every direction ; from libraries of monasteries, obscure as well as famous ; the most out-of-the-way places,—the bottom of exhausted wells, besmeared by snails, as the History of Velleius Paterculus, or from garrets, where they had been contending with cobwebs and dust, as the poems of Catullus.

10. No reference whatever is made to this passage by any writer or historian, monkish or otherwise, before that time,[1] which, to say the least, is very singular, considering that after that time it is quoted, or referred to, in an endless list of works, which by itself is all but conclusive that it was not in existence till the fifteenth century; which was an age of imposture and of credulity so immoderate that people were easily imposed upon, believing, as they did, without sufficient evidence, whatever was foisted upon them.

11. The interpolator of the passage makes Tacitus speak of "*Christ*," not of Jesus *the* Christ, showing that—like the passage in Josephus—it is, comparatively, a modern interpolation, for

12. The word "*Christ*" is *not a name*, but a TITLE;[2] it being simply the Greek for the Hebrew word "*Messiah.*" Therefore,

13. When Tacitus is made to speak of Jesus as "Christ," it is equivalent to my speaking of Tacitus as "Historian," of George Washington as "General," or of any individual as "Mister," without adding a *name* by which either could be distinguished. And therefore,

14. It has no sense or meaning as he is said to have used it.

15. Tacitus is also made to say that the *Christians* had their denomination from *Christ*, which would apply to any other of the so-called *Christs* who were put to death in Judea, as well as to Christ Jesus. And

16. "The disciples were *called* Christians first at Antioch" (Acts xi. 26), not because they were followers of a certain Jesus who claimed to be the Christ, but because "Christian" or "Chrēstian," was a name applied, at that time, to any good man.[3] And,

---

[1] A portion of the passage—that relating to the manner in which the Christians were put to death—is found in the *Historia Sacra* of Sulpicius Severus, a Christian Father, who died A. D. 420; but it is evident that this writer did not take it from the *Annals*. On the contrary, the passage was taken—as Mr. Ross shows—from the *Historia Sacra*, and bears traces of having been so appropriated. (See Tacitus & Bracciolini, the Annals forged in the XVth century, by J. W. Ross.)

[2] "*Christ* is a name having no spiritual signification, *and importing nothing more than an ordinary surname.*" (Dr. Giles: Hebrew and Christian Records, vol. ii. p. 64.)

"The name of *Jesus* and *Christ* was both known and honored among the ancients." (Eusebius : Eccl. Hist., lib. 1, ch. iv.)

"The name *Jesus* is of Hebrew origin, and signifies *Deliverer*, and *Savior*. It is the same as that translated in the Old Testament *Joshua*. The word *Christ*, of Greek origin, is properly *not a name* but *a title* signifying *The Anointed*. The whole name is therefore, *Jesus the Anointed* or *Jesus the Messiah.*"

(Abbott and Conant; Dic. of Relig. Knowledge, art. "*Jesus Christ.*")

In the oldest Gospel extant, that attributed to Matthew, we read that Jesus said unto his disciples, "Whom say ye that I am?" whereupon Simon Peter answers and says : "Thou art THE CHRIST, the Son of the living God. . . . Then charged he his disciples that they should tell no man that he was Jesus THE Christ." (Matt. xvi. 15-20.)

This clearly shows that "*the Christ*" was simply a *title* applied to the man Jesus, therefore, if a *title*, it cannot be a *name*. All passages in the New Testament which speak of *Christ* as a *name*, betray their modern date.

[3] "This name (Christian) occurs but three times in the New Testament, and is never used by Christians of themselves,only as spoken by or coming from those without the Church. The general names by which the early Christians called themselves were 'brethren,' 'disciples,' 'believers,' and 'saints.' The presumption is that the name *Christian* was originated by the *Heathen.*" (Abbott and Conant : Dic. of Relig. Knowledge, art. "Christian.")

17. The worshipers of the Sun-god, *Serapis*, were also called "Christians," and his disciples "Bishops of Christ."[1]
So much, then, for the celebrated passage in Tacitus.

"We are called Christians (*not*, we call ourselves Christians). So, then, *we are the best of men* (Chrēstians), and it can never be just to hate what is (Chrēst) *good and kind ;*" [or, "therefore to hate what is *Chrestian* is unjust."] (Justin Martyr : *Apol.* 1. c. iv.)

"Some of the ancient writers of the Church have not scrupled expressly to call the Athenian *Socrates*, and some others of the *best* of the heathen moralists, by the name of *Christians*." (Clark : Evidences of Revealed Relig., p. 284. Quoted in Ibid. p. 41.)

"Those who lived according to the Logos, (*i. e.*, the *Platonists*), were really *Christians*." (Clemens Alexandrinus, in *Ibid*.)

"Undoubtedly we are called *Christians*, for this reason, *and none other*, than because *we are anointed with the oil of God*." (Theophilus of Antioch, in Ibid. p. 399.)

"Christ is the Sovereign Reason of whom the whole human race participates. *All those who have lived conformably to a right reason, have been Christians,* notwithstanding that they have always been looked upon as Atheists." (Justin Martyr : *Apol.* 1. c. xlvi.)

Lucian makes a person called Triepbon answer the question, whether the affairs of the *Christians* were recorded in heaven. "All nations are there recorded, since Chrēstus exists even among the Gentiles."

[1] "Egypt, which you commended to me, my dearest Servianus, I have found to be wholly fickle and inconsistent, and continually wafted about by every breath of fame. The worshipers of SERAPIS (here) are called *Christians*, and those who are *devoted* to the god Serapis (I find), call themselves *Bishops of Christ*." (The Emperor *Adrian* to Servianus, written A.D. 134. Quoted by Dr. Giles, vol. ii. p. 86.)

NOTE.—Tacitus says—according to the passage attributed to him—that "those who confessed [to be Christians] were first seized, and then on their evidence *a huge multitude* (*Ingens Multitudo*) were convicted, not so much on the charge of incendiarism as for *their hatred to mankind*." Although M. Renan may say (*Hibbert Lectures*, p. 70) that the authenticity of this passage "cannot be disputed," yet the absurdity of "a huge multitude" of Christians being in Rome, in the days of Nero, A. D. 64—about thirty years after the time assigned for the crucifixion of Jesus—has not escaped the eye of thoughtful scholars. Gibbon—who saw how ridiculous the statement is—attempts to reconcile it with common sense by supposing that Tacitus knew so little about the Christians that he confounded them with the Jews, and that the hatred universally felt for the latter fell upon the former. In this way he believes Tacitus gets his "huge multitude," as the Jews established themselves in Rome as early as 60 years B. C., where they multiplied rapidly, living together in the Traslevere—the most abject portion of the city, where all kinds of rubbish was put to rot—where they became "old clothes" men, the porters and hucksters, bartering tapers for broken glass, hated by the mass and pitied by the few. Other scholars, among whom may be mentioned Schwegler (*Nachap Zeit.*, ii. 239); Köstlin (*Johann-Lehrbegr.*, 472); and Baur (*First Three Centuries*, i. 183); also being struck with the absurdity of the statement made by some of the early Christian writers concerning the wholesale prosecution of Christians, said to have happened at that time, suppose it must have taken place during the persecution of Trajan, A. D. 101. It is strange we hear of no Jewish martyrdoms or Jewish persecutions till we come to the times of the Jewish war, and then chiefly in Palestine ! But fables must be made realities, so we have the ridiculous story of a "huge multitude" of Christians being put to death in Rome, in A. D. 64, evidently for the purpose of bringing Peter there, making him the first Pope, and having him crucified head downwards. This absurd story is made more evident when we find that it was not until about A. D. 50—only 14 years before the alleged persecution—that the first Christians—a mere handful—entered the capitol of the Empire. (See Renan's *Hibbert Lectures*, p. 55.) They were a poor dirty set, without manners, clad in filthy gaberdines, and smelling strong of garlic. From these, then, with others who came from Syria, we get our "huge multitude" in the space of 14 years. The statement attributed to Tacitus is, however, outdone by Orosius, who asserts that the persecution extended "through all the provinces." (Orosius, ii. 11.) That it was a very easy matter for some Christian writer to interpolate or alter a passage in the *Annals* of Tacitus may be seen from the fact that the MS. was not known to the world before the 15th century, and from information which is to be derived from reading Daillé *On the Right Use of the Fathers*, who shows that they were accustomed to doing such business, and that these writings are, to a large extent, unreliable.

INDEX.

A

Abraham, story of, 38; Hindoo parallel, 39; other parallels, 39, 40; the foundation of, 103; his birth announced by a star, 144; supposed to have had the same soul as Adam, David, and the Messiah, 504.

Absolution from sin by sacrifice of ancient origin, 181; by baptism, 316; refused to Constantine by Pagan priests, 444.

Abury, the temple at, 180.

Achilleus, a personification of the Sun, 485.

Adam, was reproduced in Noah, Elijah, and other Bible celebrities, 44 ; no trace of the story of the fall of, in the Hebrew Canon, after the Genesis account, 99.

Aditi, "Mother of the Gods," 475; a personification of the Dawn, 475; is identified with Devaki, 475.

Adonis, is born of a Virgin, 191; has title of "Saviour," 191, 217; is slain, 191; rises from the dead, 218; is creator of the world, 249; his temple at Bethlehem, 220; his birth on December 25th, 364; a personification of the Sun, 484; in Hebrew "My Lord," 485.

Æolis, son of Jupiter, 125.

Æon, Christ Jesus an, 427; there have been several, 427; the Gnostics believed Christ Jesus to have been an, 511; the Essenes believed in the doctrine of an, 515.

Æschylus' Prometheus Bound, 192.

Æsculapius, a son of Jove, 128; worshiped as a God, 128; is called the "Saviour," 194; the "Logos," 374; Death and Resurrection of, 217.

Agni, represented with seven arms, 32; a Hindoo God, 32; the Cross a symbol of, 340.

Agnus Dei, the, succeeded the Bulla, 405; worn by children, 405.

Agony, the, on Good Friday, is the weeping for Tammuz, the fair Adonis, 226.

Akiba, Rabbi, believed Bar-Cochaba to be the Messiah, 433.

Alcmena, mother of Hercules, 124.

Alexander, divides the Pamphylian Sea, 61; believed to be a divine incarnation, 127; visits the temple of Jupiter Ammon, 127; and styles himself "Son of Jupiter Ammon," 127.

Alexandria, the library of, 438; the great intellectual centre, 440; and the cradle of Christianity, 219, 442.

Allegorical, the, interpretation of the Scriptures practiced by Rabbis, 100; the historical theory succeeded by, 466, 552, 563.

Allegory, the story of the "Fall of Man" an, 100.

All-father, the, of all nations, a personification of the Sky, 478.

Alpha and Omega, Jesus believed to be, 250; Crishna, 250; Buddha, 250; Lao-Kiun, 250; Ormuzd, 251; Zeus, 251; Bacchus, 251.

Ambrose, St., affirms that the Apostles made a creed, 385.

Atys, the Crucified, 190; is called the
' Only-begotten Son," and "Saviour," 190; rose from the dead, 223.
Augustine, St., saw men and women
without heads, 437.
Aurora placida, made into St. Aura
and St. Placida, 399.
Avatar, Jesus considered an, 111: a star
at birth of every, 143, 479: an "Angel-
Messiah," a "Christ," 196; an, expected about every 600 years, 426.

B.

Baal, and Moloch, worshiped by the
children of Israel, 108.
Baal-peor, the Priapos of the Jews, 47.
Babel, the tower of, 33; literally "the
Gate of God," 34; built at Babylon,
34; a parallel to in other countries, 35;
built for astronomical purposes, 35.
Babylonian Captivity, the, put an end
to Israel's idolatry, 108.
Bacab, the Son, in the Mexican Trinity,
378.
Bacchus, performed miracles, 50; passed through the Red Sea dry-shod, 51:
divided the waters of the rivers
Orontes and Hydaspus, 51; drew
water from a rock, 51; was a law-
giver, 52; the son of Jupiter, 124;
was born in a cave, 156; torn to
pieces, 193, 209; was called the "Saviour," 193; "Only-begotten Son,"
193; "Redeemer," 193; the sun darkened at his death, 208; ascended into
heaven, 208; rose from the dead, 228;
a personification of the sun, 492.
Baga, the, of the cuneiform inscriptions a name of the Supreme Being,
391; is in English associated with an
ugly fiend, 391.
Balaam, his ass speaks, 91; parallels to
in Egypt, Chaldea and Greece, 91.
Bala-rama, the brother of Crishna, 74;
the Indian Hercules, 74.
Baldur, called "The Good," 129; "The
Beneficent Saviour," 129; Son of the
Supreme God Odin, 129; is put to
death and rises again, 224; a personification of the sun, 479.
Bambino, the, at Rome is black, 336.
Baptism, a heathen rite adopted by the
Christians, 317; practiced in Mongo-

lia and Thibet, 317; by the Brah-
mins, 317; by the followers of Zoro-
aster, 318; administered in the Mith-
raic mysteries, 319 ; performed by
the ancient Egyptians, 319.
Baptismal fonts, used by the Pagans,
406.
Bar-Cochba, the "Son of a Star," 144;
believed to be the Messiah, 432.
Beads (see Rosary).
Beatitudes, the, the prophet of, 527.
Belief, or faith, salvation by, existed in
the earliest times, 184.
Bellerophon, a mighty Grecian hero, 75.
Belus, the tower of, 34.
Benares, the Hindoo Jerusalem, 296.
Berosus, on the flood, 22.
Bible, the Egyptian, the oldest in the
world, 24.
Birth, the Miraculous, of Jesus, 111;
Crishna, 113; Buddha, 115; Codom,
118; Fuh-he, 119; Lao-Kiun, 120;
Yu, Hau-Ki, 120; Confucius, 121;
Horus, 122 ; Zoroaster, 123 ; and
others, 123–131.
Birth-day, the, of the gods, on Decem-
ber 25th, 364.
Birth-place, the, of Christ Jesus, in a
cave, 154; the, of other saviours, in
a cave, 155–158.
Black God, the, crucified, 201,
Black Mother, the, and child, 336.
Bochia, of the Persians, performed mir-
acles, 256.
Bochica, a god of the Muyscas, 130.
Bodhisatva, a name of Buddha, 115.
Books, sacred, among heathen nations,
61.
Brahma, the first person in Hindoo
Trinity, 369.
Brahmins, the, perform the rite of baptism, 317.
Bread and Wine, a sacrifice with, celebrated by the Grand Lama of Thibet,
306; by the Essenes, 306; by Melchizedek, 307; by those who were
initiated into the mysteries of Mithras, 307.
Blind Man, cured by Jesus, 268; by
the Emperor Vespasian at Alexandria, 268.
Brechin, the fire tower of, 199; a crucifix cut upon, 198.

Buddha, born of the Virgin Maya, 115; his birth announced by a star, 143; demonstrations of delight at his birth, 147; is visited by Asita, 151; was of royal descent, 168; a dangerous child, 168; tempted by the devil, 176; fasted, 176; died and rose again to life, 216; ascended into heaven, 216; compared with Jesus, 289.

Buddhism, the established religion of Burmah, Siam, Laos, Pegu, Cambodia, Thibet, Japan, Tartary, Ceylon, and Loo-Choo, 297.

Buddhist religion, the, compared with Christianity, 302.

Buddhists, the monastic system among, 401.

Bull, the, an emblem of the sun, 476.

Bulla, the, worn by Roman children, 405; and now a lamb, the Agnus Dei, 405.

C

Cabala, the, had its Trinity, 376.

Cadiz, the gates of, 70.

Cæsar (Augustus), was believed to be divine, 126.

Cæsar (Julius), was likened to the divine, 126.

Calabrian Shepherds, the, a few weeks before Winter solstice, came into Rome to play on the pipes, 365.

Cam-Deo, the God of Love, 216.

Capricorn, when the planets met in, the world was deluged with water, 102.

Cardinals, the, of Rome, wear the robes once worn by Roman senators, 400.

Carmelites, the, and Essenes the same, 422.

Canon, the, of the New Testament, when settled, 463.

Carne-vale, a farewell to animal food, 227.

Carnutes, the, of Gaul, 198, the Lamb of, 199.

Castles, Lord, a ring found on his estate, 199.

Catholic rites and ceremonies are imitations of those of the Pagans, 384.

Catholic theory, the, of the fall of the angels, 386.

Cave, Jesus born in a, 154; Crishna born in a, 156; Abraham born in a,

156; Apollo born in a, 156; Mithras born in a, 156; Hermes born in a, 156.

Caves, all the oldest temples were in, 286.

Celibacy, among Pagan priests, 400–404.

Celts, the, Legend of the Deluge found among, 27.

Cerinthus, denied the divinity of Jesus, 136.

Ceylon, never believed to have been the Paradise, 13.

Chaldean, the, account of the Deluge, 22.

Chaldeans, the, Legend of the Deluge borrowed from, 101; worshiped the Sun, 480.

Champlain period, the, 28.

Chandragupta, a dangerous child, 171.

Chastity, among Mexican priests, 404.

Charlemagne, the Messiah of medieval Teutondom, 239.

Cherokees, the, had a priest and lawgiver called Wasi, 130.

Cherubim, the, of Genesis, a dragon, 14.

Child, the dangerous, 165.

Chiliasm, the thousand years when Satan is bound, 242.

Chimalman, the Mexican virgin, 334.

Chinese, the, have their Age of Virtue, 14; have a legend of a deluge, 25; worship a Virgin-born God, 119; worship a "Queen of Heaven," 327; worship a Trinity, 371; have "Festivals of gratitude to Tien," 392; have monasteries for priests, friars and nuns, 401; identified with the American race, 539.

Cholula, the tower of, 36.

Chrēst, the, 568.

Christ (Buddha), compared with Jesus, 289.

Christ (Crishna), compared with Jesus, 278.

Christ (Jesus), born of a Virgin, 111; a star heralds his birth, 140; is visited by shepherds and wise men, 150; is born in a cave, 154; is of royal descent, 160; is tempted by the devil, 175; fasts for forty days, 175; is put to death, 181; no early representations of, on the cross, 201; descends into hell, 211; rises from the dead, 215;

in India, 340; adored by the Buddhists of Thibet, 340; found on Egyptian monuments, 342; found under the temple of Serapis, 342; universally adored before the Christian era, 339–347.

Crucifixes, the earliest Christian, described, 203–205.

Crucifixion, the, of Jesus, 180; of "Saviours" before the Christian era, 181–193; of all the gods, explained, 484, 485.

Crux Ansata, the, of Egypt, 341.

Cuneiform Inscriptions, the, of Babylonians, relate the legends of creation and fall of man, 9, 98.

Cybele, the goddess, called "Mother of God," 333.

Cyril, St., caused the death of Hypatia, 440.

Cyrus, king of Persia, 127; considered divine, 127; called the "Christ," 127, 196; believed to be the Messiah, 433; sun myth added to the history of, 506.

D.

Dag, a, Hercules swallowed up by, 78.

Dagon, a fish-god of the Philistines, 82; identical with the Indian fish Avatar of Vishnu, 82.

Danae, a "Virgin Mother," 124.

Dangerous Child, the, myth of, 165.

Daphne, a personification of the morning, 469.

Darkness, at crucifixion of Jesus, 206; parallels to, 206–210; the, explained, 494.

David, killed Goliath, 90; compared with Thor, 91.

Dawn, the, personified, and called Aditi, the "Mother of the Gods," 475.

Day, the, swallowed up by night, 79.

December 25th, birth-day of the gods, 359.

Delphi, Apollo's tomb at, 510.

Deluge, the, Hebrew legend of, 19; parallels to, 20–30.

Demi-gods, the, of antiquity not real personages, 467.

Demons, cast out, by Jews and Gentiles, 269.

Denis, St., is Dionysus, 399.

Deo Soli, pictures of the Virgin inscribed with the words, 338.

Derceto, the goddess, represented as a mermaid, 83.

Deucalion, the legend of, 26; derived from Chaldean sources, 101.

Devaki, a virgin mother, 326.

Devil, the, counterfeits the religion of Christ, 124; formerly a name of the Supreme Being, 391.

Diana, called "Mother," yet famed for her virginity, 333.

Dionysus, a name of Bacchus, 51.

Divine incarnation, the idea of redemption by a, was general and popular among the Heathen, 183.

Divine incarnations, common before the time of Jesus, 112.

Divine Love, crucified, 484; the sun, 487.

Divus, the title of, given to Roman emperors, 125.

Docetes, Asiatic Christians who invented the phantastic system, 136.

Dove, the, a symbol of the Holy Ghost among all nations of antiquity, 357; the, crucified, 485.

Dragon, a, protected the garden of the Hesperides, 11; the cherub of Genesis, 14.

Drama of Life, the, 29.

Druids, the, of Gaul, worshiped the Virgo-Paritura as the Mother of God, 333.

Durga, a fish deity among the Hindoos, 82.

Dyaus, the Heavenly Father, 478; a personification of the sky, 478.

E

East, turning to in worship, practiced by Christians, 503.

Easter, origin of, 226; observed in China, 227; controversies about, 227; dyed eggs on, of Pagan origin, 228; the primitive was celebrated on March 25th, 335.

Eating, the forbidden fruit, the story of, figurative, 101.

Ebionites, the first Christians called, 134.

Ecclesiastics, the Essenes called, 424.

Eclectics, the Essenes called, 424.

Eclipse, an, of the Sun. occurred at the death of Jesus, 206; of Romulus, 207; of Julius Cæsar 207; of Æsculapius, 208; of Hercules, 208 ; of Quirinius, 208.

Edda, the, of the Scandinavians speaks of the " Golden " Age, 15; describes the deluge, 27.

Egypt, legend of the Deluge not known in, 23; the Exodus from, 48; circumcision practiced in, 85; virginborn gods worshiped in, 122; kings of considered gods, 123; Virgin Mother worshiped in, 329, 330; the cross adored in, 341.

Egyptian faith, hardly an idea in the Christian system which has not its analogy in the, 414.

Egyptian kings considered gods, 123.

Egyptians, the, had a legend of the " Tree of Life," 12; received their laws direct from God, 60; practiced circumcision at an early period, 85; were great astrologers, 142; were familiar with the war in heaven, 387.

El, the Phenician deity, 484; called the "Saviour," 484.

Elephant, the, a symbol of power and wisdom, 117; cut on the fire tower at Brechin, in Scotland, 198; in America, 537.

Eleusinian, the, Mysteries, 310.

Eleusis, the ceremonies at, 310.

Elijah ascends to heaven, 90; its parallel, 90.

Elohistic, the, narrative of the Creation and Deluge differs from the Jehovistic, 93.

Elysium, the, of the Greeks, 11; meaning of, 101·

Emperors, the, of Rome considered divine, 126.

Eocene period, the, 29.

Eostre, or *Oster*, the Saxon Goddess, 226, 227.

Epimetheus, the first man, brother of Prometheus, 10.

Equinox, at the Spring, most nations set apart a day to implore the blessings of their gods, 492.

Esdras, the apocryphal book of, 95.

Essenes, the, and the Therapeute the same, 419; the origin of not known, 419; compared with the primitive Christians, 420; their principal rites connected with the East, 423 : the "Scriptures" of, 443.

Etruscan, baptism, 320; Goddess, 330.

Etruscans, the, had a legend of creation similar to Hebrew, 75 ; performed the rite of baptism, 320; worshiped a "Virgin Mother," 330.

Eucharist, the, or Lord's Supper, 305; instituted before the Christian era, 305; performed by various ancient nations, 305–312.

Eudes, the, of California, worshiped a mediating deity, 131.

Eusebius, speaks of the Ebionites, 134; of Easter, 226; of Simon Magus, 265; of Menander the "Wonder Worker," 266; of an "ancient custom" among the Christians, 316; the birth of Jesus, 361; calls the Essenes Christians, 422.

Eve, the first woman, 3.

Evil, origin of, 4.

Exorcism, practiced by the Jews before the time of Jesus, 268.

Explanation, the, of the Universal Mythos, 466.

Ezra, added to the Pentateuch, 94.

F.

Faith, salvation by, taught before the Christian era, 184.

Fall of Man, the, Hebrew account of, 4; parallels to, 7–16; hardly alluded to outside of Genesis, 99; allegorical meaning of, 101.

Fall of the Angels, the, 386.

Fasting, for forty days, a common occurrence, 179 ; at certain periods, practiced by the ancients, 177, 392.

Father, Son and Holy Ghost, the, of Pagan origin, 369.

Females, the, of the Orinoco tribes, fasted forty days before marriage, 179;

Festivals, held by the Hindoos, the Chinese, the Egyptians, and others, 392.

Fifty, Jesus said to have lived to the age of, 515.

Pole, or Pillar, a, worshiped by the ancients, 46, 47.

Polynesian Mythology, in, a fish is emblematic of the earth, 80.

Pontius Pilate (see Pilate).

Poo-ta-la, the name of a Buddhist monastery found in China, 401.

Pope, the, thrusts out his foot to be kissed as the Roman Emperors were in the habit of doing, 400.

Portuguese, the, call the mountain in Ceylon, Peco d' Adama, 13.

Porus, the troops of, carried on their standards the figure of a man, 198.

Prayers, for the dead, made by Buddhist priests, 401.

Priests, the Buddhist, have fasting, prayers for the dead, holy water, rosaries of beads, the worship of relics, and a monastic habit resembling the Franciscans, 401.

Priestesses, among the ancients, similar to the modern nuns, 403, 404.

Primeval male, the, offered himself a sacrifice for the gods, 181.

Prithivi, the Earth worshiped under the name of, by the Hindoos, 477.

Prometheus, a deity who united the divine and human nature in one person, 124; a crucified Saviour, 192; an earthquake happened at the time of the death of, 207; the story of the crucifixion of, allegorical, 484; a title of the Sun, 484.

Prophet, the, of the Beatitudes, does but repeat the words of others, 526.

Protogenia, mother of Æthlius, 125.

Ptolemy (Soter), believed to have been of divine origin, 127.

Puranas, the, 451.

Purgatory, the doctrine of, of pre-Christian origin, 389.

Purim, the feast of, 44; the book of Esther written for the purpose of describing, 44.

Pyrrha, the wife of Deucalion, 26; was saved from the Deluge by entering an ark with her husband, 26.

Pythagoras, taught that souls dwelt in the Galaxy, 45; had divine honors paid to him, 128; his mother impregnated through a spectre, 128.

Q.

Quetzalcoatle, the Virgin-born Saviour, 129; was tempted and fasted, 178; was crucified, 199; rose from the dead, 225; will come again, 239; is a personification of the Sun, 489.

Queen of Heaven, the, was worshiped by all nations of antiquity before the Christian era, 326–336.

Quirinius, a name of Romulus, 126; educated among shepherds, 208; torn to pieces at his death, 208; ascended into heaven, 208; the Sun darkened at his death, 208.

R.

Râ, the Egyptian God, born from the side of his mothe., 122.

Raam-sees, king of Egypt, 123; means "Son of the Sun," 123.

Rabbis, the, taught the allegorical interpretation of Scripture, 100; performed miracles, 267; taught the mystery of the Trinity, 376.

Rakshasas, the, of our Aryan ancestors, the originals of all giants, ogres or demons, 19; are personifications of the dark clouds, 19; fought desperate battles with Indrea, and his spirits of light, 387.

Ram or Lamb, the, used as a symbol of Christ Jesus, 202; a symbol of the Sun, 503, 504.

Rama, an incarnation of Vishnu, 143; a star at his birth, 143; is hailed by aged saints, 152.

Rayme, a Mexican festival held in the month of, answering to our Christmas celebration, 366.

Rays of glory, surround the heads of all the Gods, 505.

Real Presence, the, in the Eucharist, borrowed from Paganism, 305–312.

Red-Riding-Hood, the story of, explained, 80.

Red Sea, the, divided by Moses, 50; divided by Bacchus, 51.

Religion, the, of Paganism, compared with Christianity, 384.

Religions, the, of all nations, formerly a worship of the sun, moon, stars and elements, 544.

worshiped by the Christians, 355;
symbolized the Sun, 490; called the
Word, or Divine Wisdom, 490.
Seven, the number, sacred among all
nations of antiquity, 31.
Seventh-day, the, kept sacred by the
ancients, 392, 393.
Seventy-two, Confucius had, disciples,
121.
"*Shams-on*," the Sun in Arabic, 73.
Sharon, the Rose of, Jesus called, 486.
Shepherds, the infant Jesus worshiped
by, 150.
Shoo-king, the, a sacred book of the
Chinese, 25; speaks of the deluge, 25.
Siamese, the, had a virgin-born god,
118.
Simon Magus, believed to be a god, 129;
his picture placed among the gods
in Rome, 129; professed to be the
"Word of God;" the "Paraclete,"
or "Comforter," 164; performed
great miracles, 125.
Sin-Bearer, the, Bacchus called, 193.
Sin, Original, the doctrine of, believed
in by Heathen nations, 181, 184.
Siva, the third god in the Hindoo Trin-
ity, 369; the Hindoos held a festival
in honor of, 392.
Skylla delivers Nisos into the power of
his enemies, 72; a Solar Myth, 72.
Slaughter, the, of the innocents at the
time of Jesus, 165; parallels to, 166–
172.
Sochiquetzal, mother of Quetzalcoatle,
129; a Virgin Mother, 129; called the
"Queen of Heaven," 129.
Socrates, visited at his birth by Wise
Men, and presented with gifts, 152.
Sol, crucified in the heavens, 484.
Soma, a god of the Hindoos, 306; gave
his body and blood to man, 306.
Sommona Codom (see Codom).
Son of a Star (see Bar-Cochba).
Son of God, the Heathen worshiped a
mediating deity who had the title of,
111–129.
Son of the Sun, the name Raam-ses
means, 123.
"*Sons of Heaven*," the virgin-born men
of China called, 122.
Song, the, of the Heavenly Host, 147;
parallels to, 148–150.

Soul, the, immortality of, believed in
by nations of antiquity, 385.
Sosiosh, the virgin-born Messiah, 146;
yet to come, 146.
Space, crucifixion in, 488.
Spanish monks, the first, who went to
Mexico were surprised to find the
crucifix there, 199.
Spirit, the Hebrew word for, of femi-
nine gender, 134.
Standards, the, of the ancient Romans,
were crosses gilt and beautiful, 345.
Star, the, of Bethlehem, 140; parallels
to, 142–145.
Staurobates, the King by whom Semiramis was overpowered, 486.
Stone pillars, set up by the Hebrews
were emblems of the Phallus, 46.
"*Strong Rama*," the, of the Hindoos, a
counterpart of Samson, 73.
Suddho-dana, the dreams of, compared
with Pharaoh's two dreams, 88.
Sun, the, nearly all the Pagan deities
were personifications of, 467; Christ
Jesus said to have been born on the
birth-day of, 473; Christ Jesus a per-
sonification of, 500; universally worshiped, 507.
Sun-day, a pagan holiday adopted by
the Christians, 394–396.
Sun-gods, Samson and Hercules are,
71–73.
Sun-myth, the, added to the histories of
Jesus of Nazareth, Buddha, Cyrus,
Alexandria and others, 506.
Sweden, the famous temple at Upsal in,
dedicated to a triune deity, 377.
Symbolical, the history of the gods, 466.
Synoptic Gospels, the discrepancies be-
tween the fourth and the, numerous,
457.

T.

Tacitus, the allusion to Jesus in, a forgery.
Tables of Stone, the, of Moses, 58; of
Bacchus, 59.
Talmud, the books containing Jewish
tradition, 95; in the, Jesus is called
the "hanged one," 516.
Tammuz, the Saviour, after being put
to death, rose from the dead, 217;

V.

Valentine, St., formerly the Scandinavian god Vila, 399.

Valhalla, the Scandinavian Paradise, 390.

Vasudeva, a name of Crishna, 114.

Vedas, the, antiquity of, 450.

Vedic Poems, the, show the origin and growth of Greek and Teutonic mythology, 468.

Venus, the Dove was sacred to the goddess, 357.

Vernal equinox, the, festivals held at the time of, by the nations of antiquity, 392.

Vespasian, the Miracles of, 268, 269.

Vestal Virgins, the, were bound by a solemn vow to preserve their chastity for a space of thirty years, 403.

Vicar of God on Earth, the Grand Lama of the Tartars considered to be the, 118.

Vila, the god, of the Scandinavians, changed to St. Valentine, 399.

Virgin, the worship of a, before the Christian era, 326.

Virgo, the, of the Zodiac personified as a Virgin Mother.

Vishnu, appeared as a fish, at the time of the Deluge, 25; the mediating or preserving God in the Hindoo Trinity, 369.

Votan, of Guatemala, 130.

Votive offerings, given by the Heathen to their gods, and now practiced by the Christians, 258, 259.

Vows of Chastity, taken by the males and females who entered Pagan monasteries, 402, 403.

W.

War in Heaven, the, believed in by the principal nations of antiquity, 368.

Wasi, the priest and law-giver of the Cherokees, 130.

Water, purification from sin by, a Pagan ceremony, 317–323.

Wednesday, Woden's or Odin's day, 393.

Welsh, the, as late as the seventeenth century, during eclipses, ran about beating kettles and pans, 536.

West, the sun-gods die in the, 493.

Wisdom, Ganesa the god of, 117.

Wise Men, worshiped the infant Jesus, 150; worshiped the infant Crishna, 151; worshiped the infant Buddha, 151; and others, 151, 152.

Wittoba, the god, crucified, 185.

Wodin, or Odin, the supreme god of the Scandinavians, 393.

Wolf, the, an emblem of the Destroying power, 80.

Word, or Logos, the, of John's Gospel, of Pagan origin, 374.

World, the, destroy by a deluge, whenever all the planets met in the sign of Capricorn, 103.

X.

Xaca, born of a Virgin, 119.

Xelhua, one of the seven giants rescued from the flood, 37.

Xerxes, the god of, is the *devil* of today, 391; the Zend-avesta older than the inscriptions of, 452.

Xisuthrus, the deluge happened in the days of, 22; was the tenth King of the Chaldeans, 23; had three sons, 23; was translated to heaven, 90.

X-P, the, was formerly a monogram of the Egyptian Saviour Osiris, but now the monogram of Christ Jesus, 350.

Y.

Yadu, Vishnu became incarnate in the House of, 113.

Yao, or Jao, a sacred name, 49.

Yan-hwuy, the favorite disciples of Confucius, 121.

Yar, the angel, borrowed from Chaldean sources, 109.

Yen-she, the mother of Confucius, 121.

Y-ha-ho, a name esteemed sacred among the Egyptians, 48; the same as Jehovah, 48.

Yezua, the name Jesus is pronounced in Hebrew, 196.

Yoni, the, attached to the head of the crucified Crishna, 185; symbolized nature, 496.

Yôsêr, the term (Creator) first brought into use by the prophets of the Captivity, 99.

SUPERNATURAL RELIGION.

Complete in 1 vol , from the latest London edition.
8vo, 1,115pp., Cloth, $4 ; Leather, 5. [Former price, $12.50]

CONTENTS OF VOL. I.

CONTENTS OF VOL. II.

THE ORDER OF CREATION.

THE CONFLICT BETWEEN GENESIS AND GEOLOGY.

CONTENTS:

12mo, 178 pp. Paper, 50 cents; cloth, 75 cents.

THE TRUTH SEEKER COMPANY,

28 Lafayette Place, New York.

HEBREW MYTHOLOGY,

—OR THE—

RATIONALE OF THE BIBLE.

WHEREIN

IT IS SHOWN

THAT THE

HOLY

SCRIPTURES

TREAT OF

NATURAL

PHENOMENA

ONLY.

—BY—

Milton Woolley.

—

Illustrated.

—

1 vol., 8vo.,

Cloth, 613 pp.

Price, $2.50.

SPECIMEN ILLUSTRATION.

THE TRUTH SEEKER COMPANY,

28 Lafayette Place, New York.

THE CHRIST OF PAUL;

Or, the Enigmas of Christianity. A Critical Study of the Origins of Christian Doctrines and Canonical Scriptures.

BY GEORGE REBER.

Extra cloth, 12mo, 400pp., $2.

An endeavor to find, by careful analysis of the writings themselves, by researches into the history of the periods to which they are ascribed, and by examinations of the patristic writers, the solution of a problem which has perplexed many wise heads during many centuries. The hypothesis which he builds upon the result of his labors has the merit of plausibility, consistence, synchronism with the facts of history, and substantiation by internal evidences.—[Sacramento Daily Union.

There is a general sentiment that we want Christ's Christianity more than Paul's or the churchmen's or the whole succession of theologians. Let us have it. If this book lights the way to it, let us follow it. If there is a truer way, show it. Men prefer to walk where there is most light.—[St. Louis Republican.

It is written in a terse, colloquial, attractive style, and will have thoughtful readers.—[Phrenological Journal.

PERSONAL IMMORTALITY,
AND OTHER PAPERS.
By Josie Opp nheim.
Extra cloth, 12mo, 98pp., 75cts.

The spirit of the author is unexceptionable, and she states with the utmost candor the arguments for and against the doctrine of immortality. There is evidence of much reading and careful thinking. The book may be taken as a very fair index of the state of mind of a great many moral, intelligent, and fair-minded people who have begun to " trust their intellects."—[Critical Review.

ANCIENT SEX WORSHIP.
A Curious and Remarkable Work—
Traces of Ancient Myths in the Religions of To-Day.
Extra cloth, gold side stamp, 26 illustrations. 12mo., $1.

Containing much mythological lore and a chapter on the Phalli of California. A work of interest to scholars.—[New Bedford Standard.

Much curious information is presented, and the hint imparted that much of what is deemed sacred has a very inferior origin.—[Boston Commonwealth.

To the investigator of early religious history, who can view all evidence without prejudice . . . entertainment undeniably fresh.—[Literary World.

A curious, learned, and painfully suggestive book. Especial pains is taken to deal delicately with the subject.—[Chicago Journal.

The attempt is to show that the cross, as a religious emblem, is much older than Jesus Christ, and to trace in the religions of to-day the relics of ancient passional worship. Much research and deep scholarship are displayed, and the work is high-toned, but it is not designed for immature minds.—[Portland Transcript.

ROME OR REASON.

A Memoir of Christian and Extra-Christian Experience.

By NATHANIEL RAMSAY WATERS.

Extra cloth, 12mo, 352pp. - - - $1.75.

We have found it interesting above works of its class, and its intelligent comment upon the literature of the several religious bodies is a valuable feature.—[Boston Congregationalist.

A very critical analysis of Protestantism and Catholicism, from the vantage ground of an intimate personal experience with both systems. His analysis of the Protestant principle will be new to some Protestants, as will his philosophy of Catholicism to many Catholics. The work is strikingly original, deeply earnest, and its manifest sincerity will commend it to readers of various shades of opinions. It is very argumentative, with touches of liveliness, serving to relieve its general gravity. It deals the most trenchant blows which pure logic is capable of inflicting.—[Critical Review.

FAITH AND REASON.

A Concise Account of the Christian Religion, and all the Prominent Religions Before and Since Christianity.

By HALSEY R. STEVENS.

(With elaborate Index—17pp)   Extra cloth, 12mo, 441pp , $1.50.

Among the contents are: Aryan Religions, Myths, and Legends; Ethnic and Catholic Religions; Religion of China—Confucianism; Brahmanism and Hinduism; Buddhism; Ancient Religion of Persia and Zoroaster; Religion and Sacred Books of Egypt; The Gods and Religions of Greece; The Gods and the Religion of Rome; Teutonic and Scandinavian Religions; Mohammedanism, and other systems.

A popularized account of Oriental religions, illustrated with many apt quotations from the Sacred Books of the East, which give the gist of their ideas. Nowhere else, we venture to say, can so much knowledge of what is generally unknown in Europe and America be obtained in such compact form.—[Literary Review.

The Ethics of Positivism

A Critical Study and Survey of the Moral Philosophy of the Present Century. By GIACOMO BARZELLOTTI, Professor of Philosophy at the Liceo Dante, Florence.

Extra cloth, 12mo, 327pp., $2.

This work defends the principles of morality against the pretensions of utilitarianism, or the theory of absolute moral obligation against the claims of empirical expediency; exhibiting the results of modern psychology, as presented in the latest investigations of the facts of the moral world. It must be regarded as an important, as well as a novel, contribution to the history of modern speculative thought, and will be welcomed by philosophical students. —[New York Tribune.

The Martyrdom of Man. A Compendium of Universal History. By WINWOOD READE. Second edition. Large clear type, toned paper, broad margins, extra cloth, 12mo, 543pp., $3.

AUTHORITIES.—On *Egypt*, Wilkinson, Rawlinson's Herodotus, Bunsen; *Ethiopia or Abyssinia*, Bruce, Baker, Lepsius; *Carthage*, Heeren's African Nations, Niebuhr, Mommsen; *East Africa*, Vincent's Periplus, Guillain, Hakluyt Society's Publications; *Moslem Africa (Central)*, Park, Caille, Denham and Clapperton, Lander, Barth, Ibn Batuta, Leo Africanus; *Guinea and South Africa*, Azurara, Barros, Major, Hakluyt, Purchas, Livingstone.

Assyria, Sir H. Rawlinson, Layard; *India*, Max Mueller, Weber; *Persia*, Heeren's Asiatic Nations; *Central Asia*, Burnes, Wolff, Vambery; *Arabia*, Niebuhr, Caussin de Perceval, Sprenger, Deutsch, Muir, Burckhardt, Burton, Palgrave; *Palestine*, Dean Stanley, Renan, Döllinger, Spinoza, Robinson, Neander.

Greece, Grote, O. Mueller, Curtius, Heeren, Lewes, Taine, About, Becker's Charicles; *Rome*, Gibbon, Macaulay, Becker's Gallus; *Dark Ages*, Hallam, Guizot, Robertson, Prescott, Irving; *Philosophy of History*, Herder, Buckle, Comte, Lecky, Mill, Draper; *Science*, Darwin, Lyell, Herbert Spencer, Huxley, Tyndall, Vestiges of Creation, Wallace, Tylor, Lubbock.

It is really a remarkable book, in which universal history is "boiled down" with surprising skill.—*Literary World.*

You turn over his pages with a fascination similar to that experienced in reading Washington Irving.—*Inter-Ocean.*

His history has a continuity, a rush, a carrying power, which reminds us strikingly of Gibbon.—*New Haven Palladium.*

The sketch of early Egyptian history, in the first chapter, is a masterpiece of historical writing. He has a style that reminds us of Macaulay. —*Penn Monthly.*

We could scarcely have supposed it possible for any writer, however gifted, to put into one volume, reasonable in size and price, so much reliable information, sound logic and inspiring thought.—*Literary Review.*

Mr. Reade's historical survey of the world of nature and man, marvelous as it is, in its multitude of details, in its comprehensive sweep, in its terse, splendid paragraphs, in its evidence of wide and careful reading, and its general accuracy, gives the impression of a reading as immense as that of Hume, Gibbon, or of Buckle.—*Christian Register.*

Theology and Mythology. An Inquiry into the Claims of Biblical Inspiration and the Supernatural Element in Religion. By ALFRED H. O'DONOGHUE, Counselor at Law, formerly of Trinity College, Dublin. Extra cloth, 12mo, 194pp., $1.

An able and thorough treatment of the subject, remarkable for its candor, earnestness, and freedom from partisan bias. The author presents all the important arguments for and against the idea of inspiration, and states his conclusions in a fair and independent manner. The book will be widely read, and will create a new train of thought in the minds of many.—*Critical Review.*

The Anonymous Hypothesis of Creation. By JAMES J. FURNISS. Extra flexible cloth, 12mo, 55pp., 50 cts.

The object has been to present the subject as concisely as practicable, for the benefit of those who have not the time or the inclination to peruse the more voluminous works.—*Introduction*

THE

REIGN OF THE STOICS.

Their History, Religion, Philosophy,

And Maxims of Self-Control, Self-Culture, Benevolence, and Justice.

With Citations of Authors Quoted from on Each Page;
Full List of Authorities and Copious Index.

By FREDERIC MAY HOLLAND.

———

Read the philosophers, and learn how to make life happy, seeking useful precepts and brave and noble words which may become deeds.—SENECA.

———

The " Reign of the Stoics" is a thoroughly accurate, well classified, and valuable compend of the Stoic teachings in philosophy, ethics, and religion, together with a fine summary of their history as a system. No better book on the subject can be found.— Prof. F. E. ABBOT (Boston, Mass.)

———